NATURAL LAW AND THE
THEORY OF SOCIETY

NATURAL LAW AND THE THEORY OF SOCIETY
1500 TO 1800

BY
OTTO GIERKE

With a Lecture on
The Ideas of Natural Law and Humanity
by ERNST TROELTSCH

TRANSLATED WITH AN INTRODUCTION
BY
ERNEST BARKER

CAMBRIDGE
AT THE UNIVERSITY PRESS
1958

PUBLISHED BY
THE SYNDICS OF THE CAMBRIDGE UNIVERSITY PRESS
Bentley House, 200 Euston Road, London, N.W. 1
American Branch: 32 East 57th Street, New York 22, N.Y.

First Edition 1934 (in two vols.)
Reprinted 1950 (in one vol.)
Reprinted 1958 (in one vol.)

First printed in Great Britain at the University Press, Cambridge
Reprinted by offset-litho by De IJsel Press Ltd., Deventer, Holland

CONTENTS

PART I

I

TRANSLATOR'S INTRODUCTION

1. The Texts translated — *page* ix
2. Law and political theory — xviii
3. The Law of Nature — xxxiv
4. The School of Historical Law — l
5. The Personality of Groups — lvii
6. The Translation — lxxxviii

II

ANALYTICAL SUMMARY — *page* 1

III

GIERKE'S TEXT — 33

CHAPTER I. The Period down to the Middle of the Seventeenth Century — 33

SECTION V. The Influence of the Natural-Law Theory of Society — 35

§ 14. **The Natural-Law Conception of the State** — 35

  I. *General view of Natural Law* — 35
  II. *General view of Sovereignty in natural-law theory* — 40
  III. *People and Ruler as separate personalities* — 44
  IV. *Attempts to eliminate the dualism of People and Ruler. The idea of a single State-personality* — 50

§ 15. **The Natural-Law Theory of Associations (*Die engeren Verbände*)**   62

    I. GROUPS WITHIN THE STATE   62

        (1) *The unitary or centralist interpretation*   62

        (2) *The federalist interpretation, especially in Althusius and Grotius*   70

        (3) *The interpretation of Hobbes*   79

    II. GROUPS ABOVE THE STATE   85

    III. GROUPS PARALLEL WITH THE STATE   87

        The Church   87

CHAPTER II. **The Period from the Middle of the Seventeenth to the Beginning of the Nineteenth Century**   93

SECTION I. **The Natural-Law Theory of Society during the Period of its Ascendancy**   93

§ 16. **The General Theory of the Group (*Verbandstheorie*) in Natural Law**   95

    I. *The vogue of Natural Law and its individualistic basis*   95

    II. *The priority of the individual to the community, and the consequent views of law and property*   96

    III. *The natural-law view of the source of group-authority*   105

    IV. *Natural Law and the idea of contract as explaining the origin of Groups*   107

    V. *The natural-law view of the purposes of Society and its various Groups*   111

Contents

VI. *The natural-law view of the Being of Groups*   114
   The views of Pufendorf: the persona moralis—
   The atomistic conception of the nature of Associations in eighteenth-century Germany—English and French theory in the eighteenth century: Locke and Rousseau—Fichte and Kant

   General Retrospect   135

§ 17. The Natural-Law Theory of the State   137
I. *General view*   137
II. *The theory of the Sovereignty of the Ruler*   141
III. *The theory of Popular Sovereignty*   149
IV. *The theory of the Mixed Constitution*   154
V. *The contributions made by the natural-law theory of the State to the development of public law*   159

§ 18. The Natural-Law Theory of Corporations   162
I. ASSOCIATIONS CONTAINED IN THE STATE   162
  (1) *Divergence of centralist and federalist views*   163
  (2) *The relation of the Corporation to the State*   165
    (a) *Views inimical to Corporations*—
    (b) *Views favourable to Corporations: especially that of Nettelbladt*
  (3) *The natural-law conception of the internal nature of Corporations, as affected by the fact of their inclusion in the State*   180
    (a) *The Corporation as an Institution* (Anstalt)—(b) *The Corporation as a Fellowship* (Genossenschaft), *especially in the theory of Nettelbladt*
II. GROUPS ABOVE THE STATE   195
III. GROUPS WITHIN THE STATE   198
   The Church   198

IV
APPENDICES

 I. Ernst Troeltsch. The Ideas of Natural Law and Humanity in World Politics   201

 II. Gierke's Conception of Law   223

PART II
V
GIERKE'S NOTES

§ 14. The Natural-Law Conception of the State   229
§ 15. The Natural-Law Theory of Associations   269
§ 16. The General Theory of the Group in Natural Law   288
§ 17. The Natural-Law Theory of the State   333
§ 18. The Natural-Law Theory of Corporations   367

VI
LISTS OF AUTHORITIES

 A. 1500–1650   401
 B. 1650–1800   409

VII
INDEX   418

INTRODUCTION

§ 1

THE TEXTS TRANSLATED

In 1900 Professor Maitland published, under the title of *Political Theories of the Middle Age*, a translation of one of the sections in the third volume of Dr Gierke's work on 'The German Law of Associations' (*Das deutsche Genossenschaftsrecht*), which had appeared, nearly twenty years before, in 1881. The present work, which deals with the political theories of the modern age, from 1500 to 1800, is a translation of five subsections in Gierke's fourth volume, which was published just twenty years ago, in 1913. In a chronological sense, it is a complement to Professor Maitland's work. In all other respects, it is a separate and independent book. It must be judged on its own account; and it cannot claim, in any way, to inherit the prestige or carry the authority which the weight of Professor Maitland's learning, and the arresting power of his style, have justly won for the *Political Theories of the Middle Age*, and especially for its Introduction.

The theme of the present volume is the natural-law theory of Society and the State. In other words, it deals with the views of the State, and of other groups (whether contained in the State, or parallel to it, or transcending it), which were professed in the School of Natural Law, or influenced by the ideas of that school, during the three centuries which lie between the Reformation and the French Revolution. But to elucidate fully the nature of the volume, some words must be said about its place in the history of Gierke's publications. In 1880 he published a work entitled *Johannes Althusius and the Development of Natural-Law Theories of the State*. This was, in a sense, a 'chip from his workshop' and a by-product of his prolific pen; but it was also a harbinger of the third and fourth volumes of his *Genossenschaftsrecht*.* Primarily intended to resuscitate a forgotten German thinker, it also made him a peg on which were hung both a history of the medieval theories which preceded his system of thought, and a survey of the modern theories which followed upon it.† In the next year, 1881, Gierke published

* The first volume had appeared in 1868, and the second in 1873.

† Gierke himself, in the preface to the second edition of his *Althusius* in 1902 (p. 323), speaks of having 'appended a history of the evolution of natural-law theories of the State to an account of the life and teaching of Althusius'.

the third volume of the *Genossenschaftsrecht*, which dealt generally with 'the theory of State and Corporation in classical and medieval times', and in which a special section (the section translated by Maitland) was devoted to a more systematic account of medieval political theory than that already given in the book on Althusius. Finally, in 1913, he published the fourth and last volume of his great work, dealing generally with 'the theory of State and Corporation in modern times', and largely devoted (the part here translated is nearly one half of the whole) to a revised and comprehensive exposition of the modern natural-law theories of Society and the State which he had already sketched in his work of 1880.*

Though it was only published in 1913, the last volume of the *Genossenschaftsrecht* had been written some twenty years before. The occasion of its publication was a reprint of the first three volumes, which decided Gierke to give to the world the manuscript of his fourth as it stood, in spite of the years which had accumulated upon it and the gaps which it contained. 'I do not believe', he pleaded, 'that any other writer will soon tread again the paths I have taken. They lead, in part at any rate, through utterly desert regions.' As it finally appeared, the new volume fell into two parts. The first described the history of modern social and political theory down to 1650: the second carried it forward from 1650 to 1800. What is here translated is the two concluding subsections of the first part, and the first three of the second. The concluding subsections of the first part treat of the influence of the growing natural-law theory of human society, as it developed during the century and a half of the period of the Reformation, from the Diet of Worms in 1521 to the Treaty of Westphalia in 1648. The first three subsections of the second part deal with the development of natural-law theory during the period of its ascendancy, from the accession of Louis XIV to the French Revolution, or (in other words) from Hobbes and Pufendorf to Kant and Fichte. The five subsections taken together, as Gierke says in his preface, 'form a whole'; and it is that whole which is presented here. There is one gap, for which Gierke expressed his sorrow, and for which the translator would venture to express his own regret. The natural-law theory of the relation of Church and State, which had been treated briefly but suggestively in its first phase, during the period of the Reformation, is not treated at all in its later phase, during

* An English translation of Gierke's book on Althusius is being undertaken by an American scholar, Dr Bernard Freyd.

the period between 1650 and 1800. The niche is there, as the reader will notice if he surveys the plan of the work; but it remains an empty niche. Otherwise the whole of which Gierke speaks is a rounded and finished whole, with a central theme developed in its various ramifications.

It is the value of this whole that it gives a connected and critical account of the general theory of human society—the theory of politics, of constitutional law, and of the law of associations—which was developed by the great school of Natural Law. That theory was a theory of the ideal or natural Law of human society, and of the ideal or natural Rights of man. It was a theory which culminated in the American Declaration of Independence in 1776 and the French Revolution of 1789. It was a theory adorned by many illustrious names—Hooker and Suarez; Althusius, Grotius and Pufendorf; Milton and Sidney; Hobbes, Locke and Rousseau; Spinoza and Leibniz; Thomasius and Wolff (less known in England, but none the less names of fame and power in the eighteenth century); Vico and Beccaria; Fichte and Kant. This is the theory which Gierke expounds, and these are the names with which he conjures. There are omissions in his work. The name of Hooker (though it recurs in the pages of Locke) is never mentioned by Gierke. He never refers to the name of Vattel, though his *Droit des Gens, ou Principes de la Loi naturelle*, of the year 1758, is still a text-book recommended for study in English Universities. He never touches on the efflorescence of natural-law ideas (partly promoted by the study of Vattel's book among the lawyers of Boston), which is so marked a feature of the American Revolution. Paine's *Rights of Man* is absent from his pages; and he never refers to the theory of Burke, or the criticism of Natural Law in the early writings of Bentham. As there are omissions, so there are also slips. The account which Gierke gives of the views of some of the many writers with whom he deals—Suarez, for example, or Spinoza, or even (on some points) Locke—occasionally stands in need of supplement or correction. On a journey of exploration so prolonged and so extensive it could hardly be otherwise.

But there are two things to be said on the other side, which make any slips or omissions fly up in the balance until they disappear from view. In the first place, Gierke has studied the original texts of a multitudinous literature—Catholic and Protestant, legal and political, German, French, English, Italian and Spanish; and the rich apparatus of his notes, with their abundant quotations of crucial passages from his authorities, enables the reader to follow his sources and test his conclusions. In the second place, he has not sought simply to analyse and describe his material. Always concerned with the conception of the Group, and especially with that form of Group which he calls the Fellowship (*Genossenschaft*), and always anxious to discover the essence of group-life, the source and nature of group-authority, and the significance of group-personality, he has brought his own categories and problems to the study of his material; he has attempted to elicit its meaning in terms of these categories and in answer to these problems; and he has thus imprinted the form of his own scheme and system of thought upon the matter of his study. The danger of such a method is that it tends to make the theories of the past square with the demands of a particular system of the present. The criticism in which it issues is external rather than immanent; and every writer, placed in a Procrustean frame, is adjusted to its plan and sized by its dimensions. But every age is apt to measure previous ages by its own ideas. Few of us apply 'the leaden standard of Lesbian architecture', which bends to its material,

> And alters when it alteration finds.

We generally use fixed canons of judgment—be they those of Hegelianism, or Darwinism, or Marxism —according to our particular philosophy and our own *parti pris*. Gierke was in the tradition of Romanticism; of the Hegelian movement which fed on Romanticism; of the Historical School of Law (and particularly of the Germanist variety of that school) which drew upon both. He had also the foot-rules and set-squares of the German lawyer; he brought to his work conceptions of 'State-personality', of its *Träger* or bearer, of its 'organs', and of its (and their) capacity for being a 'Subject' or owner of rights. We have to remember, as we read his pages, the tradition he follows and the tools he uses. But the very fact that his tradition and his tools are different from our own adds a stimulus and a zest to the study of his writings. To see the development of western Europe during three centuries as Gierke saw it is to gain new angles of vision and new hooks of apprehension.

Many of the writers cited in these pages have long been buried in oblivion, at any rate for English readers. The dust is heavy on their forgotten tomes; and why (it may be asked) should it be disturbed? What are Bortius and Busius to us, or even Hertius and

Heineccius; and what are we to them? Perhaps we may answer the question, as John Morley once answered a similar question, by pleading that it is not only the great writers who have fertilised human thought; the multitudinous little leaves, which have seemed to flutter unregarded to the ground, have also played their part. But there is also a further answer. These writers were the exponents, in their day, of the great idea of Natural Law; and it was their exposition which, directly or indirectly, fed the thought of Locke and Rousseau, and again of Fichte and Kant. We can hardly even understand Rousseau, the great populariser (as we may call him without offence) of natural-law speculation, until we get back to his sources. He was not the inventor of the *personne morale*, or its *volonté générale*. They were as old as Pufendorf, and even older. 'Style is the man', and style is fame; but the scholar must go behind the stylist to those who dug the quarry, and hewed the stone, upon which the stylist drew. Even Kant and Fichte, who were thinkers rather than stylists, drew generously upon the great quarry of Natural Law for their ideas.

Many of these forgotten thinkers were in their day professors of law. Some of them professed law in the Dutch Universities of Franeker, Leiden and Utrecht; but most of them taught in the Universities of Germany. Althusius lectured at Herborn: Pufendorf at Heidelberg; and lawyers less famous lectured at Göttingen, Jena, Marburg and Tübingen. But conspicuous among all other Universities, in the study of law and politics, was the University of Halle, in Prussia, near the borders of Saxony. Founded in 1694, and rapidly becoming a centre of legal studies, it included among its teachers Thomasius and Heineccius, and (later in the eighteenth century) Wolff and Nettelbladt. The German writers whom Gierke cites are mostly professors of law, and many of them professors of law at Halle. They are worth remembering, if only because we may learn from them the contribution of German thought to political speculation in the seventeenth and eighteenth centuries —a contribution which was mainly made by the professors of the German Universities. But the matter goes deeper than that. These German professors not only contributed to the general development of European political thought: they also played a great and active part in the development of law, and we may almost say of the State, in Germany itself. There were no Inns of Court in Germany to control the teaching of law and the development of the legal system. The Universities had a free course. In England the teaching of law, in the Universities of Oxford and Cambridge (the only Universities down to 1832), was mainly confined to the lectures of the Regius Professors of Civil Law, who had been instituted by Henry VIII; and the Roman Law which they taught, however valuable it might be in itself, had little bearing on English life. It was far otherwise in Germany. Here there were chairs of every sort of law—Roman Law in its *usus modernus*, as it had developed since the 'Reception' at the beginning of the sixteenth century; Natural Law; International Law; Public Law. The professors covered a wide field, which ranged from the niceties of private law to the mysteries of public law and practical politics. They were springs of water in a thirsty land. On the one hand, they could help to build a practical scheme of law. There was no common law in Germany, or in any of its States, analogous to the Common Law of England; and not until 1791 did even Prussia acquire its *Allgemeines Preussisches Landrecht*. On the other hand they could furnish from their own ranks, or train among the ranks of their pupils, the judges, the statesmen, the officials and the ambassadors who were urgently needed by the German States. The legal faculties of the Universities were the reservoirs of the German *Beamtentum* (one of the greatest creations of the German genius), in its highest and its widest sense. We shall not do justice to some of the names which are mentioned in this volume unless we remember that they had this background. Unknown to us in England, and perhaps lapsing into oblivion even in their own country, they yet laboured in the practical life of their day, and helped to determine its structure.* But, being professors, and therefore (according to the nature of that tribe) 'naturally speculative animals', they also laboured in the more austere fields of the pure theory of law and politics; and they have left abiding if musty monuments of their labours in those fields. They did the spade-work for the political theorist; and by their work on the theory of Natural Law, in particular, they released ideas which were to have a far greater practical effect, over a far greater area, than all their practical labours in their own immediate surroundings. For those ideas were

* Even to-day, in the conditions of contemporary life, the professor of law plays a far greater part in the general life of continental countries than he is ever expected to do in England. We need only reflect on the labours of German professors in connection with the Civil Code or the Constitution of Weimar: on the work of French professors in elucidating the Code of Napoleon; or on the position of the Italian professor of law in Italian jurisprudence and politics.

Translator's Introduction

to prove a dynamite which helped to explode the connection between Great Britain and her American colonies, and to shatter the ancient monarchy of France.

Of the connection of law with political theory, and of the special connection of Natural Law both with political theory and political practice, more must be said, in a more appropriate place, in a later section of this introduction. For the present it remains to explain the inclusion in this volume, by way of an appendix, of the translation of a lecture by Professor Troeltsch, delivered before the Hochschule für Politik in Berlin, in 1922, on 'The Ideas of Natural Law and Humanity'. Like Gierke, but from the angle of the theologian and in terms of Christian thought, Troeltsch had worked his way through the centuries, exploring the historic systems of group-life, and the controlling ideas by which they were permeated, from the days of the early Church to the days of medieval Catholicism, and thence to the days of Protestantism and the various Protestant 'sects'. The result of his explorations appeared in a great work on *Die Soziallehren der christlichen Kirchen*, which was published in 1912, the year before the publication of the last volume of Gierke's *Genossenschaftsrecht*. The philosophies of human history and of human society which we find in Gierke and Troeltsch are in some respects parallel, and in some ways even complementary, to one another. But Troeltsch was a younger man than Gierke (who was nearly 80 at the end of the War), and his thought was less fixed in worn and habitual channels. In 1922, at the age of 57, he set himself to reflect, under the impulse of German defeat, on the lines of German thought which had been current since the days of the Romantic Movement; to set them over against the natural-law lines of thought current in the more western countries of Europe; and to appreciate both lines of thought in terms of a general and catholic European outlook, inspired and deepened by a wide view of the history of European thought. The lecture in which he recorded his reflections is valuable in itself, and well worthy of translation for its own intrinsic contents. But that would not explain, or excuse, the inclusion of a translation of the lecture in this volume. It is included here because it contains a fundamental appreciation of the conception of Natural Law, with which Gierke was dealing: it is included because it contains a similar appreciation of the Romantic and 'Germanist' conceptions, in terms of which Gierke was thinking. It will help the reader in understanding both the subject which Gierke approached, and the lines of his approach; and perhaps, if the reader will pardon a word of advice, the appendix may be worthy of his consultation before he turns to a study of the main contents of this volume.

The contrast drawn by Troeltsch between German thought and the thought of western Europe is a contrast which, as he himself remarks, can only be accepted with modifications and qualifications. Perhaps it needs still further qualifications than those which he has himself suggested. On the one hand the theory of Natural Law, during the period of its elaboration in the seventeenth and eighteenth centuries, was far from being confined to the countries of western Europe, or even from being particularly cultivated there: it was peculiarly developed, and peculiarly taught, in the Universities of Germany. On the other hand the deification of super-personal Groups, and particularly of the State, which has been current in Germany since the Romantic Movement, is far from being confined to Germany: it has its analogies, if not its affiliations, in the doctrines of a school of French nationalism (the *action Française*), and in the philosophy of Fascist Italy, with its cult of the nation as 'an organism superior to the individuals, separate or grouped, of whom it is composed'.* But there is none the less a distinction between the thought of western Europe (and particularly of France) and the thought of Germany. Many of us have long been fascinated, and are fascinated still, by the profundity of German thought. But its solemn and high-piled clouds, great and gigantic, are not our natural sky. (Even the language in which it speaks is a language essentially different from ours. The vocabulary of the German thinker has a great and distant sonority: it speaks, as it were, with a sound of thunder; but what does the thunder actually say?...It is a question which a translator must often ask himself in perturbation of mind.) When we turn to the thought of France—formal as it may sometimes be, or even superficial—we turn to a clearer air; we converse with simple and classical ideas; we move among limpidity. German thought—like

* Carta di Lavoro of 1927, §1. The French traditionalists and nationalists have equally repudiated the old French Republican creed of Natural Law and the rights of Humanity. 'Laissez ces grands mots de toujours et d'universel, et puisque vous êtes français préoccupez-vous d'agir selon l'intérêt français à cette date' (Barrès). 'Le pouvoir politique en France est contraint, sous les plus effroyables pénalités, de tenir pour étranger à l'humanité tout intérêt étranger à sa nation propre' (Maurras). Cited in R. Soltau, *French Political Thought in the Nineteenth Century*, c. xii.

the German nation itself, in the long travail of its development—is a heaving and tumultuous thing. When it becomes a thought about Groups and 'super-personal realities', it becomes (at any rate to the realist) a matter of billowy cloud and rolling nebulosities. We begin to see Groups as great Brocken-spectres, confronting us as we walk. Now we may admire the nation moving and heaving: we may admire the surge of its thought: we may admire the philosophy of super-personal Group-persons—the Folk: the Fellowship: the *Verband* in all its forms. It is, indeed, a philosophy which can ennoble the individual, and lift him above self-centred concern in his own immediate life. But it may also be a philosophy which engulfs his life, and absorbs his individuality; and it may end, in practice, in little more than the brute and instinctive automatism of the hive. We have to admit, after all, the justice of Troeltsch's saying, that the end of the idealisation of Groups may be 'to brutalise romance, and to romanticise cynicism'. We have to confess that the cult of super-personal Beings has had some tragic results. It began with Herder's Folk-poetry and Folk-music; it grew into Hegel's Folk-mind and Savigny's Folk-right (the right or law which is just a particular people's sense of justice in its own particular phase of development): it culminated in Scharnhorst's Folk-army. While it has grandeur and flame, it has also a cloud of smoke. Individualism is often used as a word of reproach; but it is good to see simple shapes of 'men as trees, walking', and to think in simple terms of human persons. Persons—individual persons—have a finitude or limit which can satisfy our intelligence, and an infinity or extension which can satisfy our faith. They have finitude or limit in the sense that, in any and every scheme of social order, each of them occupies a definite position, with its definite sphere of rights and duties, under the system of law which necessarily regulates their external relations with one another. They have infinity or extension in the sense that, *sub specie aeternitatis*, each of them is 'a living soul' (as nothing but the individual person is or can be), with an inner spring of spiritual life which rises beyond our knowledge and ends beyond our ken. If we look at Groups from this angle, we shall not call them persons. We shall call them organisations of persons, or schemes of personal relations, in all their successive phases, from the village or club to the State or the League of Nations. And because they are organisations or schemes, made by the mind of man, we shall regard them as constructed by the thought of persons, consisting in the thought of persons, sustained by the thought of persons, and revised (or even destroyed) by the thought of persons—but never as persons themselves, in the sense in which individuals are persons.

§2

LAW AND POLITICAL THEORY

We have already spoken, incidentally, of the connection between the study of law and the study of social and political theory. The method, and the substance, of Gierke's writings must naturally impel us to some further consideration of the nature of that connection. He was himself a lawyer, and a lawyer in a double sense. Not only was he a lawyer of the chair, immersed in the study and exposition of legal history and legal principles; he was also a lawyer of the battle-field, who plunged into the busy war of ideas which attended the construction of the German Civil Code in the latter years of the nineteenth century. The two sides of his activity were closely connected. He explains himself, in the preface to the last volume of his *Genossenschaftsrecht*, that if he had turned aside from history into contemporary struggles, it was in the same faith, and with the same object, that he had written history—'to penetrate the new code with a Germanistic spirit; to develop its Germanic content upon an historical basis; to foster the growth of its Germanism in the future'. We must remember, as we read his writings, that he is bringing a view of the German State and of German society, derived from his long studies, not only to interpret their development in the past, but also to shape their development in the present, during the great years of political and legal construction that lie between the new constitution of 1871 and the new Civil Code of 1898. It is in this spirit that he approaches the theory of State and Society in the period from 1500 to 1800, when the idea of a universal Natural Law was in the air. What was there of truth in those three centuries, which accorded with the long historic trend of German life and thought and could be incorporated into the German present? What was there of error, which must be banished? Some truth there was; and the passage from Gierke's work on Althusius, translated in Appendix II, will show how strongly he felt the value of the fundamental idea of Natural Law—the idea that there is a natural justice, based on the reason of man, which lies behind all positive law. But there was also something of error; and the reader of this volume will see, from Gierke's criticism of the individualistic basis of Natural Law, how strongly he felt that error, and how deeply concerned he was to urge his own philosophy, that the world is a world of 'real Group-beings' as well as of individuals.

The connection between law and political science is far closer on the Continent than it is in England. With us, the subjects have generally tended towards a divorce; and there has been little study of political science in terms of law. Hobbes was not ignorant of English law; but he used the language of physics and behaviouristic psychology rather than the language of law. Locke employed the conception of 'trust'; but he was a physician, a philosopher and a politician rather than a lawyer. Few of our lawyers have turned their attention to the fundamental questions of politics. We may count the names of Blackstone and Bentham, Austin and Maine, Dicey and Maitland; but they are scattered lights rather than a constellation, and the light of Blackstone is somewhat dim. On the whole our law has been a close and empirical preserve of the legal profession; and our political science has proceeded not from lawyers or professors of law, but from politicians with a philosophic gift or philosophers with a practical interest. We have gained something from our defect—if indeed it is a defect. The politician with a philosophic gift—be it Sidney or Burke, Morley or Bryce—can bring a bracing sense of reality to his speculations. The philosopher with a practical interest—Adam Smith and Paley in the eighteenth century; Sidgwick, T. H. Green and Bosanquet in the nineteenth—can carry practical questions into the high and ultimate regions of ethical principle. The English system of political science, so far as we can speak of such a thing, has combined an instinct for actual fact with some sense of the moral foundations on which the action of States, like all human action, must necessarily be based. The tradition of humanism in our Universities—the tradition which carried back teacher and taught to the writings of Plato and Aristotle, and imbued not only the master, but also the pupil destined for political affairs, with the ethico-political ideas of the *Republic* and the *Politics*—corroborated a native sense of the moral foundations of politics. Our political science acquired what a German scholar might call a 'normative' character. A study of politics which is primarily legal may become a desiccated study of *Staatsrecht*, and revolve about questions of legal metaphysics such as the nature of 'State-personality' or the essence of 'State-sovereignty'. Our English political philosophy has been sporadic; it has hardly developed any 'school', unless we can call Benthamism a school; but it has generally been occupied in discussing the moral norms or standards by which the State and its activities should be controlled. Perhaps we shall not be over-kind to it if we see it in our mind's eye, as Aristotle saw Socrates, περὶ τὰ ἠθικὰ πραγματευόμενος.

On the Continent—if we may draw a rough and crude contrast, which needs many qualifications—political education and political speculation have generally gone along the lines of law. Law has been the preparation for the service of the State, in its administrative as well as its judicial activities; and law has been the basis of the theory of the State. On the one hand, it has provided the training of the *Staatsbeamtentum*: on the other hand it has provided the concepts and the line of approach for *Staatswissenschaft*. '*Summa legalitas*', we may almost say; 'the lawyer is ubiquitous'. Certainly, the political theory of France and Germany bears his mark. To study modern French political theory is to study the lawyers—Esmein, Hauriou, Barthélemy, Duguit: it is to study works which generally go by the style of *Traité du Droit constitutionnel*. To study modern German political theory is equally to study the lawyers—Jellinek, Kelsen and Schmitt; and if treatises are written on the theory of the State (*allgemeine Staatslehre*), as well as on *Staatsrecht* proper, we find they are written by professors of law. We are face to face with a great and general trend; and we are bound to examine its significance, and to see whether it may not have lessons to teach us. Our English political science has hitherto had no great method; and we may, at the very least, learn some lessons in that respect.

Now it may be true that the legal approach to political science tends to lead us into apparently arid regions of legal metaphysics. It may also be true that such an approach tends to convert the State into a legal institution, rather than 'a fellowship in the good life'. But there are other things which are also true. In the first place the State is so much identified with law, in all its daily operations (which are operations of declaring and sanctioning law, and thereby declaring and sanctioning the rights of all its members), that we are bound to study law if we wish to study the State. In the second place, the study of the State in terms of law makes political science a genuine discipline, and demands from the student a genuine grasp of legal conceptions and the general legal point of view. Political science which is not rooted and grounded in some such discipline becomes a loose congeries of facile *aperçus*. In the third place, the whole vocabulary of political science is steeped in terms of law; and this etymological fact is the reflection and the expression of a long historical process. Throughout the centuries political science has been borrowing the conceptions of law; and it is in the language of law that it has learned to speak and to utter articulate words.

It has been said that 'the world which derives its civilisation from western Europe may be divided into the lands of the English law, and lands where in outward form at least the law is Roman'.* Political science, for reasons to which we have already referred, is no great debtor to the vocabulary of English law. But it stands deeply indebted to the law of Rome. When men tried to interpret the State as a 'society', they were borrowing the term *societas* from Roman private law. When they tried to interpret government as the exercise of an authority which had been delegated by the 'society', they were borrowing the conception of *mandatum* from the same source. These were matters of the borrowing of private-law terms and conceptions and their application to the sphere of public law. In other words, what was involved was the use of the rules of law relating to private groups and private activities in the State to explain the character and the activity of the State itself. Difficulties naturally arose, as Gierke sufficiently indicates, from this transference of the ideas of one sphere to explain the life of another. But Roman law could supply the political theorist with something more than private-law notions. It had conceptions of the nature of *jus* and *lex*, and of the part played by the People in the making of *leges*: it had conceptions of *imperium* and *majestas*: it had the conception of the *Lex regia*, by which the People transferred *imperium* and *potestas* to the Prince. All these conceptions became the stuff of political theory; and they were developed in the steady and continuous work of the commentators on Roman law during the Middle Ages. We study the ideas of Dante and Marsilio of Padua; but we have to remember that by their side stood their contemporary, the great legist Bartolus of Sassoferrato, and that the ideas of Bartolus, themselves derived from the old Roman heritage, became in turn the heritage of the sixteenth century, and are quoted and used by most of its writers on politics.

* Professor Geldart, in *The Unity of Western Civilisation* (edited by F. S. Marvin), p. 133.

There were other heritages besides the legal heritage of Rome which lay at the disposal of the political theorist. There was the heritage of Aristotle, received in the thirteenth century; there was the heritage of the Christian Fathers, and not least of St Augustine, which had been continuously cherished by the Church. But Roman law had a special volume and importance. It was more than a heritage; it was a living body of actual law, practised in courts and developed by jurists. It was a consistent body of vital ideas, which could not only be used by the theorist, but was also affecting political life and development. Its history during the Middle Ages, as Vinogradoff writes at the end of his *Roman Law in Medieval Europe*, 'testifies to the latent vigour and organising power of *ideas*, in the midst of shifting surroundings'. It is little wonder that the political theory of modern Europe, when it emerges in the sixteenth century, is largely expounded by lawyers, and expounded in terms of Roman law. Bodin, Althusius, Grotius, Pufendorf are the typical figures; and they are all lawyers. True, there are the clergy, concerned to find a theory of the Church and its relations to the State; but even the clergy largely follow the fashion of law (have they not their own Canon Law?), and the great work of Suarez is entitled *Tractatus de legibus ac Deo legislatore*. True, there are the philosophers, concerned to find the eternal principles of politics; but they too generally betake themselves to law. Fichte writes a *Grundlage des Naturrechts* and a *System der Rechtslehre*; Hegel himself writes a work entitled *Philosophy of Law and Outlines of the State*.

Political science has thus for many centuries largely spoken the language of law, and mainly of Roman law. (Natural Law, as we shall presently see, is the term which theorists often used to grace their measure; but Natural Law, as we shall also see, is itself a conception of the Roman lawyers.) But what, we may ask, is the conception which we may properly form to-day, in our present state of experience and opinion, about the relation between political science and law? We may begin our enquiry by drawing a distinction between Society and the State. Society, or community, which in our modern life takes the form of national society or community, is a naturally given fact of historical experience. Each national society is a unity; and each expresses its unity in a common way of looking at life in the light of a common tradition, and in the development of a common culture, or way of life, in all its various forms. But each society is also a plurality. It is a rich web of contained groups—religious and educational; professional and occupational; some for pleasure and some for profit; some based on neighbourhood and some on some other affinity; all dyed by the national colour, and yet all (or most of them) with the capacity, and the instinct, for associating themselves with similar groups in other national societies, and thus entering into some form of international connection. Such is society, at once one and many, but always, in itself, the play of a voluntary life and the operation of the voluntary activity of man. This is the material on which there is stamped the form of the State. The State, we may say, is a national society which has turned itself into a legal association, or a juridical organisation, by virtue of a legal act and deed called a constitution, which is henceforth the norm and standard (and therefore the 'Sovereign') of such association or organisation. This constitution need not be a single document: it may be a set of historical documents; and over and above that it may also be a set of unwritten constitutional conventions, backing and reinforcing whatever documents there be. Constituted by and under this constitution, and thus created by a legal act (or series of acts), the State exists to perform the legal or juridical purpose for which it was constituted. It declares and enforces, subject to the primary rule of the constitution, a body of secondary rules, or system of ordinary law, which regulates the relations of its members as 'legal persons' (a term to which we must recur in a later section), and assigns these 'persons' the rights and duties which form their 'legal personality'. It creates a scheme of working relations, in such areas of life as are susceptible of uniform and compulsory regulation, and it calls this scheme by the name of law: it creates a position for each member under the scheme, and it calls that position by the name of rights and duties. Law is the method of its operation: the rights and duties of 'persons' (which, as we shall see later, may be individuals or groups) are the objects of its operation. But though the State, and with it law, and with law the compulsory regulation of human relations in certain areas, has supervened, as it were, upon Society, Society still remains. If Society has turned itself into a legal association, it has not turned the whole of itself into that form; nor has it perished in producing the State. It still remains, with its common way of looking at life, engaged in the development of its common culture: it still includes its rich web of groups, which may still pursue their voluntary activities in the social area not regulated by law. Behind the organised legal State there runs the life of national society; and there is thus a rich country stretching outside the four walls of State-regulated life.

Before we seek to study the relation between law and political theory on the basis of these ideas, we may pause to enquire, for a moment, into Gierke's own conception of the relation between Society and the State. *Gesellschaft*, in his vocabulary, is the sum total of human groupings, and the general and comprehensive expression of human associations. It ranges from the universal society of all humanity down to the village and the family in the village. From this point of view the State is one of the forms of *Gesellschaft*; and you may thus have a general theory of *Gesellschaft* which colours and determines your view of the State. So far as this goes, the State is just a circle in a series of concentric circles. But Gierke seems also to have another point of view; and this point of view appears to be dominant. From this point of view, the State shifts into the centre. All other groups are arranged according to the relation in which they stand to it. There are some groups which are *in* the State; there are others which are *side by side* with it (the Church being the only example): there are others (such as federations and the general international society of States) which are *above* it—though it is not made very clear whether this means simply that they are larger, or whether it means that they are superior. So far as this goes, the State seems to hold the interior lines. But there is still another point of view which also has to be taken into account. We have to remember Gierke's fundamental belief in the reality of the Group-person.* On this basis the State becomes a real person; but so also do those groups in the State which are more than mere partnerships or simple collections of individual persons; and so, again, does the Church, as a group which stands side by side with the State. One real Group-person may somehow be greater and more authoritative than another; but so far as they are all 'real', they all seem to be on a level. It is hardly clear how Gierke really conceives the relation of State and Society. But on the whole he seems to regard the State as a force controlling and regulating society and its various groups; and he is anxious that it should do its shaping liberally, recognising, in its regulation of groups, that it is regulating 'real persons'.

Returning from this digression, and adopting, for the purposes of our argument, the distinction between State and Society which

* *Der Zentralgedanke der realen Gesammtpersönlichkeit*; preface to vol. IV, p. xi.

was suggested before we digressed, we may now examine the proper scope of political theory, and the nature of its relation to law. Political theory, we may begin by observing, is not concerned with the State alone. It is also concerned with Society, because it is impossible to understand the State unless we see it in connection with the Society from which it proceeds, upon which it reacts, and which reacts upon it. The word 'political', if by it we only mean the adjective of the noun 'State', is not broad enough for our purposes; and from this point of view we might more properly, if also more cumbrously, prefer to speak of 'social and political theory'. But we need not quarrel about adjectives; and we may content ourselves with the traditional term 'political theory' (or 'political science', though the word 'science' seems to make a large claim for any study of things human), provided it be understood that we are not obliged to study the State alone, or to study it in isolation. So conceived, political theory will deal with three main matters. It will deal with the nature of Society and the process of its activity. It will deal with the nature of the State, as a legal association, and with the whole process and intention of its legal activity. It will deal with the relation of Society to the State, and of the State to Society.

In dealing with the second of these matters, political theory will largely be using legal material, and it will make itself largely the debtor of law. It will study public or constitutional law, seeking to understand and to interpret the 'frame of government' which the constitution prescribes, and also (if there be any 'declaration of rights') the general system of rights, and the general system of duties, which it declares. It will also study what may be called social law, or the law of associations, seeking to understand and to interpret the principles on which the State deals with groups. It will even study the private law which deals with individuals; for the action of the legal association will not be clear unless we know something of the concrete rights and duties which express and fix the position of its members and determine the nature of their relations with one another. But in dealing with this legal material, the political theorist will often be forced to transcend its purely legal aspect. In dealing with the public institutions of the State, for example, he has not only to see them as they legally are: he has also to see them as they actually work. A scheme of representative institutions prescribed in a constitution is one thing: the actual working of such a system, under the influence of party organisations and other factors, may be quite another. Society and social forces are always making their impact on the legal State and its legal factors and instruments. The influence of party organisations (which strictly speaking are social formations in the area of Society, rather than legal institutions in the area of the State) is an example of such impact. Political theory, even in the act of studying the State, is bound to turn its attention outside the State to the Society which lies behind it and is always acting upon it. It cannot long study the second of the three main matters mentioned above before it finds itself driven back to the first, and forward into the third.

Here, in some measure, the political theorist finds himself compelled to go beyond the lawyer—though the lawyer who seeks to expound a 'philosophy of law' (Professor Pound, for example)* will not readily be outdistanced, and will march by his side with equal steps. (After all, there is little difference between a 'philosophy of law' and a 'philosophical theory of the State'.) But there is also another way in which the political theorist has to go beyond the lawyer—unless, again, the lawyer be also a legal philosopher. It is not enough for him to consider the actual form and operation of State and Society. He has to consider the ends or purposes by which they should ideally be controlled. He is not only concerned with what legally is and what actually works: he is also concerned with what should ideally be. Here he has to move into the kingdom of ultimate ends. If, like Aristotle, we believe that ethics is the study *par excellence* of the purposive activities of man and the ends by which they are guided, and if we accordingly hold that ethics has an 'architectonic' quality, we shall say that the political theorist must betake himself ultimately to the moralist. He must find the touchstone of social life and political activity in some ultimate ethical principle. To many that ultimate principle has always seemed to be the intrinsic value of the human personality; and men have been fain to believe that the State and its law were instruments for serving the conditions of the free emergence and free development of that ultimate and intrinsic value. *Autres temps, autres mœurs.* Ethics seems to be dethroned; and the emergence of the free human personality, described as being merely 'the maximum of free individual self-assertion', has been rejected as an idea appropriate to 'the age of expansion' from the sixteenth to the nineteenth century, but inappropriate to our own. Economics reigns, having driven out ethics; and notions of 'solidarity' or

* *Introduction to the Philosophy of Law.*

'social utility' have expelled, or are seeking to expel, the old notion of the intrinsic value of the human personality. To Duguit, the ultimate source of *la règle du droit* is the economic fact of solidarity, which is so ultimate, and so overwhelming, that the standard of social and political life may be expressed in the one principle, 'Do nothing contrary to social solidarity, and co-operate, as far as possible, in its realisation'. To Professor Pound, the ultimate end of law (and therefore of the State, as a legal association) is to be found in social utility. Law exists to provide 'a maximum satisfaction of wants'—these wants being understood in the sense of 'social wants' which are felt by different social sections and interests. It seeks to strike some sort of balance between their conflicting claims and demands; it serves as a sort of social engineering, 'giving effect to as much as we may with the least sacrifice', so far as such effect can be given 'by an ordering of human conduct through politically organised society'.*

It is not necessary for us to seek to appreciate, or to criticise, these different conceptions of the ultimate end of social life and political organisation. Gierke himself, in the general remarks on law which are translated in Appendix II, has said some words on the matter which are well worthy of consideration. It is sufficient for our purposes if we recognise that political theory must necessarily culminate in a study of ultimate ends, in whatever way it may seek to conceive the nature of those ends. We may now resume, in two propositions, the conclusions to which we have been led by our argument in regard to the relations between law and political theory. In the first place political theory, while it is concerned with Society as well as the State, and while it has to study the interaction between the two, is specifically concerned with the State; and here—just because the State, as such, is a legal association—it must borrow its material largely from law (public, social and private), though it is bound to study the actual working as well as the legal forms of such material. (Political theory which is concentrated exclusively on legal form becomes merely a matter of *droit constitutionnel*: political theory which is concentrated entirely on the actual working of institutions becomes merely descriptive politics, and the description given, if it loses hold of the firm ground of legal rule, may also become tendencious and partisan.) In the second place, political theory must ultimately rise into a philo-

* Op. cit. c. 2, on 'The End of Law', especially the conclusion of the chapter.

sophy of political values and a doctrine of the ultimate ends of organised society. It must, in a word, assume a normative character, whether it finds its norms in pure ethics, or in some more or less economic theory of social solidarity or social utility. Here the philosophy of law may join hands with political philosophy; and though the legal philosopher will talk of the ends of law, and the political philosopher will speak of the ends of the State, there will be little difference between them. For the State is essentially law, and law is the essence of the State. The State is essentially law in the sense that it exists in order to secure a right order of relations between its members, expressed in the form of declared and enforced rules. Law, as a system of declared and enforced rules, is the essence of the State in the same sort of sense as his words and acts are the essence of a man.

When we come to consider Natural Law, we shall see how much a philosophy of law (for Natural Law, in a sense, is simply a philosophy of law) can contribute to political theory—how much, indeed, it *is* a political theory. For the present it only remains, in conclusion of the present argument, to consider briefly some other ways of approach to political theory, besides the way of law. There are two such ways to which Gierke alludes in the course of his writings. One we may call the biological, and the other the psychological. It is the biological way of approach which seems particularly to have attracted Gierke, as it has also attracted many other writers since the middle of the nineteenth century.

We may consider the biological approach to social and political theory from two different points of view. From one point of view we may say that Society and the State, whatever they are in themselves, have a biological basis. This is obviously true. Every national Society, and every State, has the biological basis both of the physical breed or stock of its members, and also of the physical characteristics and influences of its territory. This basis will necessarily react upon that which is built upon it; and to understand fully any particular State or Society we must therefore study this basis. But there is also another point of view, which is very different. From this point of view it may be contended, and it has often been contended, that Society and the State are themselves of the nature of biological structures, or organisms, in the sense that they are so analogous to such structures that they must be interpreted in the same terms and by the same language. This is a point of view which is not so obviously true. But it recurs in the writings of Gierke, and it is particularly developed and pressed in a rectorial address which he delivered in 1902 on 'The Nature of Human Groups' (*Das Wesen der menschlichen Verbände*). It is a point of view which would make both law and political science indebted to biology for the conceptions which they use to interpret their material, and the language which they employ to express their conceptions.

How far can we accept such a point of view? We may admit that the analogy between the physical body and the body politic is one which has long been employed. We may also admit that it was natural, and indeed inevitable, that the new growth of biological science in the nineteenth century, which threw a flood of light on the development and the nature of the physical organism, should have resulted in a vastly extended use of the old analogy. Finally, we may admit that Gierke was under a particular temptation to press the analogy. He was arguing that groups were real persons—real 'unitary' persons, existing over and above the multiple individual persons of which they were composed. It seemed a corroboration of the argument to add that they were also real bodies or organisms—or rather, that they were so analogous to real bodies or organisms that they must necessarily be described in terms drawn from such bodies. But what seems to be a corroboration may really be a confusion; and Gierke, like other thinkers who have pressed the organic analogy, has not entirely escaped this risk. It is one thing to predicate of a group that it possesses personality. This is to say that it is a spiritual existence, and possesses a spiritual attribute. It is another thing to predicate of a group that it is an organism, and possesses an organic character. This is to say that it is a physical existence, and possesses physical attributes. Gierke is really aware of the difference between these two things. He is convinced that the group really and truly *is* a person. He is *not* convinced that it is an organism, but only that it is like an organism—like, and yet (he confesses) unlike.* But while he can make

* 'Properly understood, the analogy only suggests that we find in the social body a unity of life, belonging to a whole composed of different parts, such as otherwise we can only perceive in natural organisms. We do not forget that the inner structure of a Whole whose parts are men must be of a character for which the natural Whole affords no analogy; that here there is a spiritual connection, which is created and developed, actuated and dissolved, by action that proceeds from psychological motives: that here the realm of natural science ends, and the realm of the science of mind begins.' *Das Wesen der menschlichen Verbände*, pp. 15, 16.

this distinction, he can also let it disappear; and sometimes he lets it disappear altogether. When he writes that there is a 'scientific justification for the assumption of a real *corporeal* and spiritual unity in human groups',* he has let the group-personality take to itself the flesh of a group-organism; and he has forgotten his own warning. An analogy which is consistent with differences has dropped the differences; and ceasing to be an analogy, it has become an identity. It is well to insist that biology only furnishes law and political science with an analogy. So does engineering; so does chemistry; and so may any science. The biological analogy may be the best of the various analogies; and indeed we may frankly confess that it is. But we may also confess that 'organism' is itself an analogy drawn from mechanism; for 'organ' means a tool or instrument, and when we speak of 'organs' of the body we are using an engineering analogy. The 'social organism' is an analogy which is based upon an analogy; and if biology can supply political science with a good metaphor for the understanding of the nature of Society and the State, it has itself been supplied already with a good metaphor in advance.

The psychological approach to political theory is more direct, and issues in a closer contact, than the biological. Psychology is a science of the mind; and it has a natural relation to studies such as political theory which deal with the social products and creations of the mind. The psychologist who seeks to elucidate 'human nature in politics' (or, more exactly, to explain the processes and operation of the human mind in its political activities) can bring a point of view which supplements, and may correct, the findings of the older style of political theory. Such theory has tended to speak, in intellectual terms, of the rational apprehension and conscious volition of purposes. Psychology can take us into the dim country which lies behind the conscious intellect—the country of emotions and instincts in which there rise so many of the springs that run through social life. This is a contribution of clear and definite value. But there is also another contribution which psychology has sought to make to political theory. Not only has it emphasised the subconscious factors of the individual mind which play their part in politics: it has also sought to discover the existence, and to explain the nature, of a supposed group-mind, with group-emotions, group-instincts, and even a group-intellect. We

* Ibid. p. 23.

might have expected that this form of psychological theory would have attracted Gierke. His own language is language of the group-person and the group-will; and this, at first sight, seems cognate to the psychological theory of the group-mind. Why should he not have used that theory, and used it in preference to the biological analogy of the organism on which he lays so much emphasis?

In one or two passages of his lecture on 'The Nature of Human Groups', Gierke refers to psychological theory. He speaks of a *Volksseele*: he mentions, as parallel to his own 'organic' theory of the group, the speculations of Wundt and the development of *Völkerpsychologie*. But on the whole he makes little use of the material or the theories of the psychologist. Two reasons may be suggested. In the first place, the group which he has in mind, with its group-personality and its group-will, is not a psychological tissue, connecting the threads of individual minds: it is a sort of higher reality, of a transcendental order, which stands out as something distinct from, and something superior to, the separate reality of the individual. Gierke borrows from Hegelian philosophy rather than from group-psychology; and when he writes that 'human group-life is a life of a higher order, in which the individual life is incorporated',* he is in a different world of ideas from the psychologist—a Hegelian world of graded manifestations of the eternal mind: a world of values, higher and lower, which does not come within the ken of the psychologist, who simply deals with the actuality (or the supposed actuality) of mental units and processes. In the second place, the psychological theory of the group-mind was largely elaborated after Gierke had formed his theory, and it is mainly a French theory. It is the theory of M. Durkheim and M. Le Bon, but especially of the former, with his view of the social mind as the one real mind, which thinks in and through the physical brains of individuals, but only uses them as its tools. This later theory, cultivated in France and exported to England and America in the beginning of the twentieth century, lay outside Gierke's range of interest and knowledge. But even if it had come within his range, it could hardly have affected his thought. The 'group-beings' among which he moves are very different from the 'minds of groups' (or crowds, or even herds) which appear in some of the later forms of psychological theory.

---

* *Das Wesen der menschlichen Verbände*, p. 10.

We may now summarise, in the light of the general considerations which we have assembled, the nature of the contribution which Gierke makes to political theory. He is a lawyer, and he examines as a lawyer the legal nature of groups which have a legal character—the State, with its legal character defined in public law: the associations contained in the State, with their legal character defined in a 'social' law or law of associations. So far, he provides a body of legal material which political science is bound to accept and use. But Gierke is more than a lawyer; he goes beyond law—and that in two ways. In the first place, he is a philosopher, or rather he makes certain philosophical assumptions. He assumes that groups in general—both those which have a legal character, as belonging to the area of the State, and those which have not, since they simply belong to the area of Society—have the capacity of being real persons. Not all groups are actually such persons: a mere partnership between individual partners simply remains a sum of individual persons, and never becomes a real person itself. But groups which are more than partnerships—which are not mere combinations of individuals for greater ease in securing their own private benefits, but have a genuine unity of purpose uniting their members, as members of one body, in the pursuit of a common good—are always real persons; and so far as law is connected with such groups, it must recognise the fact of their real personality, and give that fact true legal expression. In the second place, we may say that Gierke is a sociologist as well as a lawyer, if by 'sociologist' we mean that he is a student of Society as well as of the State. He does not entirely confine his exposition of groups to groups which have a legal character. He deals, incidentally, in the chapters translated in this volume, with the group which he calls international society, which for him stands outside and above the State, and again with the group which we call religious society, or the Church, which in his view stands outside and beside the State. He admits, and indeed he insists, that law, as law, is concerned only with groups 'whose unity is expressed in a legal organisation'—groups 'which act in the area of law'.* But the groups which lie beyond the immediate scope of law are not entirely excluded from the lawyer's ken. The folk, or national society, is a powerful factor affecting law, and it has to be considered in the study of law: international community issues in law, if it is not in itself a legal entity; and religious society has a similar

* Ibid. pp. 23, 30.

quality.* Law proper—law in its strict and limited sense—is necessarily one-sided. In a passage of his lecture on 'The Nature of Human Groups', Gierke seeks to delimit the exact nature of its sphere, and to explain how the lawyer must recognise both the limits to which he is confined and the factors which lie beyond them. 'The life of law is only one side, and by no means the most important side, of community life. The science of law must never forget this one-sidedness. It must always bear in mind that the living forces of the various social organisms express themselves outside the area of law (*Recht*), in all the movements of might (*Macht*) and of culture in the general community life, and achieve their greatest triumphs independently of law—and even in opposition to law. Legal science must leave it to other sciences to discover the cohesions that exist, and to trace the unities that act, in all this extra-legal sphere. But while the science of law must thus receive from other branches of science the confirmatory evidence which they can give of the reality of community, it can also make a claim upon them. It can ask that its own account of the legal expression of this reality should be duly considered in any thorough and genuine investigation of social data other than legal.'†

Such is Gierke's own view of the relation of legal science to social and political theory. Legal science primarily studies legally organised groups as such—the State, as legally organised under public law: the legally organised groups inside the State, as organised under the law of associations. It may also study, secondarily, such groups as are not legally organised, but none the less affect law—groups such as national society, international community, and religious bodies. On the whole, however, it leaves to other sciences (the social and political sciences) the general study of these social groups, and it accepts from those sciences the evidence which they provide. *Per contra*, it may fairly claim that they shall accept *its* evidence, and shall take into account *its* theory of legally organised groups.

In its general features, and in its broad lines, this view must command our allegiance. On the other hand it does not follow that Gierke's particular theory of the real personality of groups must necessarily be accepted. It is something more than a legal

* Ibid. p. 24. In reading what Gierke says of international community we must remember that he was writing before the days of a legally organised League of Nations.

† Ibid. p. 31.

theory. It is a legal theory which starts from philosophical assumptions which we may question, and presses a biological analogy to a length which may raise our doubts. Nor is it easy to accept an ethical corollary which Gierke seeks to draw from his legal theory. Ethical theories may lead to legal corollaries; but it is difficult to see why a legal theory should issue in a moral rule. Yet at the end of his address on 'The Nature of Human Groups', Gierke seems to take this line. 'One thing', he says, 'may be permitted to a jurist: he may suggest the moral significance which belongs to the idea of the real unity of the community.' He proceeds to argue that it is only this idea of a 'real unity' which can produce the belief that a group is of value in itself; and only the belief that a Whole has a higher value, as compared with its parts, can justify, in turn, the moral duty of man to live and die for the Whole.* We may fairly rejoin, to such an argument, that a theory is not proved to be true by being proved to be necessary to the ethical rule of 'living and dying for the Whole' unless that rule is true in itself. We may also rejoin that the rule of living and dying for the Whole, even if it be accepted as true, does not necessarily require as its basis any idea that the Whole is 'real' in the sense of being an entity or a person. Even if a group is only 'ideal', in the sense of being a common idea or set of ideas entertained by its members, we have to recognise that thousands of our kind have died for the sake of an idea. Even if a group is only individuals, one man may die for the sake of others, if he believes that he best serves their happiness thereby and that he ought to serve their happiness.

§ 3

THE LAW OF NATURE

The conception of a Law of Nature goes back, like so many of our conceptions, to the Greeks. Aristotle, in the *Rhetoric*, distinguishes between law which is 'particular', or positive, and law which is 'common', or 'according to nature'.† This implies the idea of a common law which is natural to all humanity. Similarly, in the *Ethics*, in speaking of 'civic justice', which regulates the relations between citizen and citizen, he distinguishes between the 'natural'

* Ibid. p. 31. There seems to be a leap from the idea that a group has value in itself to the idea that it has a *higher* value.
† *Rhetoric*, 1373 b 4.

element, which has the same validity everywhere and does not depend on enactment, and the 'conventional' element which is purely positive.* In Aristotle's general terminology the word 'natural', as applied to man and human things, has three senses. It is something which is immanent in the primordial constitution of man, as a potentiality of development. Again it is something which has developed with his development—something which is a growth of his potentiality, but a growth in which his 'art', or creative mind (which is part of his constitution), has co-operated with the promptings of what we may roughly call his instinct, or immanent impulse. Finally, it is something which is inherent in the final development of man, and part of his final cause or purpose. All three senses are interconnected, and interconnected in virtue of the idea of development. If we take them all into consideration, we shall see that a 'natural law' will not merely mean a law which is co-extensive with man, or universal: it will also mean a law which has grown concurrently with man, and is, in a sense, evolutionary—yet not so evolutionary but that man's 'art' has co-operated in its growth. The antithesis between natural and conventional, which is only a *prima facie* antithesis, will disappear; and we shall have a vision of an historically developed law which has both a positive quality and a root in the nature of man.

If Athens had possessed a more highly developed body of law, and if Aristotle had applied his general conception of 'nature' to it, legal speculation might have run a different course, and the world might have escaped a long conflict between the natural and the positive schools of law. As it was, the little that he said on this topic of natural and positive law bore little fruit; and it was another school of philosophy—the Stoic—which was destined to influence the history of jurisprudence. To the Stoics Nature was synonymous with Reason, and Reason was synonymous with God. They believed that the true city or polity of mankind was a single 'city of God', or cosmopolis (transcending the old historical and positive cities), and that all men were united, as reasonable creatures, in this city of God, which was also a city of Reason and of Nature. They believed that true law was the law of this city—the law of Reason; the Law of Nature. According to the teaching of Zeno, the founder of Stoicism, men should not live in different cities, divided by separate rules of justice: they should consider

* *Ethics*, 1134 b 18–21.

all men fellow-citizens, and there should be one life and order, as of a flock on a common pasture feeding together under a common law.* This common law (κοινὸς νόμος), which is the law universal and natural, may remind us of the κοινή or *lingua franca* of the Hellenistic period. It is the legal corollary to the linguistic fact of a universally diffused speech, which in turn was the corollary to Alexander's world-State. But the κοινή was actual fact: the κοινὸς νόμος remained an aspiration. It was an ideal law which could only become actual if men were purely rational. Its principles were ideal principles. Among these ideal principles was that of equality. By nature, and as reasonable creatures, all human beings were equal. By nature the woman was equal to the man, and the slave to the master. This was the teaching of Zeno; and it was a teaching which had its effects, in later days, in Rome.

In Rome we find a highly developed body of law such as Athens never attained. Indeed we find, by the time of Cicero, three different bodies or conceptions of law. The first is the *jus civile*, which is the law applicable only to Roman citizens. The second is the *jus gentium*. From a practical point of view we may regard *jus gentium* as a body of commercial law, enforced by the Roman courts in all commercial cases, whether the parties to such cases were citizens or foreigners. From this point of view its essential content is the law of contract, including the contract of *societas* and that of *mandatum*. From a theoretical point of view *jus gentium* was defined by the Roman jurists as 'the universal element, in antithesis to the national peculiarities (*jus civile*), to be found in the positive law of every State'.† Here we recur to something very like the 'common law' or 'natural justice' of which Aristotle speaks. Hence, too, it is easy to move forward to the third conception of law which we find in the Roman lawyers—that of *jus naturale*. We may define *jus naturale* as 'the law imposed on mankind by common human nature, that is, by reason in response to human needs and instincts'.‡ It is difficult to distinguish between *jus gentium*, as defined from the theoretical point of view, and *jus naturale*; and indeed the Roman jurists were never agreed that there was any distinction between the two. But we may at any rate say that while *jus gentium* can be regarded from a practical point of view, and when so regarded is

---

* Plutarch, *de Alex. Fort.*, I, 6. The Greek word for law is the same as that for pasture, except for a difference of accent (νόμος and νομός).

† Professor de Zulueta, in the *Legacy of Rome*, p. 201.

‡ Ibid. p. 204.

mainly a body of commercial law concerned with contracts, *jus naturale* is always a general legal ideal. It is, in its essence, the Stoic ideal of a common law of all humanity, which is a law of Reason and Nature. It is permeated by the Stoic principle of equality: *omnes homines natura aequales sunt*—they are equal persons in the great court of Nature. It is not a body of actual law, which can be enforced in actual courts. It is a way of looking at things—a spirit of 'humane interpretation' in the mind of the judge and the jurist—which may, and does, affect the law which is actually enforced, but does so without being actual law itself. No Roman jurist ever asserted that Natural Law overrode concrete and positive law, as was asserted in the Middle Ages and afterwards; all that they did was to allow their idea of Natural Law to affect the actual law when it came to be applied in the courts. Nor did any Roman jurist ever associate Natural Law with a particular date or epoch, or assign it to the days of a state of nature, 'when man came from the hand of his Maker'. Natural Law was timeless; but if there was any time at which it attained its zenith, that time was in the fullness of the days, and not in their beginning.

Stoicism had passed into the *jus naturale* of Rome. The *jus naturale* of Rome passed in turn into the tradition of the Christian Church. But the early Christian Fathers, holding that man's pure nature had been vitiated by the Fall, drew a distinction between what we may call (following the interpretation of Troeltsch) the 'absolute' Law of Nature, and 'relative' Natural Law. The absolute Law of Nature, in man's uncorrupted state of primitive grace, is a law which knows no *dominium*. There is no *dominium* of government over subjects, or of owners over property, or of masters over slaves: 'by nature' men are free from the State, they own all things in common, and they are equal to one another. But there is also a relative Natural Law, adjusted to the change of man's nature after the Fall, and relative to that change. The State, and property, and even slavery, can all find their place in the scheme of this law; but they must all have something of an ideal character, and rise above sin to the dignity of remedies for sin, if they are to be really entitled to that place. The relative Law of Nature is a sort of half-way house between an absolute ideal, vanished beyond recall, and the mere actuality of positive law. It was not easy to occupy a half-way house without being exposed to attacks from either side. Sometimes the absolute ideal might rise in insurrection against property and political authority and human inequality; more often the positive fact asserted its absolute right. But the tradition of a Law of Nature, which generally took the form of relative Natural Law, continued to survive in the Catholic Church, not only during the Middle Ages, but also in modern history. St Thomas Aquinas found room in his philosophy for four species of law, all hung by golden chains to God. There was the positive law enacted for mankind by God Himself, in His revelation of His will through the Scriptures (*lex divina*); there was the positive law enacted for its members by a human community, through a representative prince, in virtue of an authority of which the *principium* came from God (*lex humana*). Behind the positive law enacted by God—and indeed, we may add, behind all other law whatsoever—there was the law of all creation resident in the supreme and unchanging purpose of God for all His creatures (*lex aeterna*); and behind the positive law enacted by a human community there was the Natural Law discovered by man's divine faculty of reason, as it sought to apprehend the purpose of God's Will and the rule of His Reason (*lex naturalis*).* This was the scheme on which the thought of the Church continued to move; and in that scheme the idea of Natural Law continued to play a conspicuous part, even after the end of the Middle Ages. The great moral theologians of the sixteenth century (or, as Gierke calls them, 'the ecclesiastical writers on Natural Law'), who were occupied with the study of moral and political philosophy in its relations to theology, discussed political philosophy in terms of Natural Law. Conspicuous among them is the great Spanish Jesuit, Suarez, who regarded the Sovereign as 'the disciple of the law natural'; but there were many others of his Order (among them Lessius, Lugo and Molina) who wrote works *de justitia et jure* expounding a natural-law philosophy of Society and the State; and members of other Orders (such as the Dominican Soto) followed the same example.

But to understand the full bearing of the tradition of Natural Law even during the Middle Ages themselves, we must return from the Church to the Roman lawyers; for without the substance and content of Roman law—not merely its conception of *jus naturale*, but its whole general body and sum of conceptions—Natural Law

---

* It became a question among ecclesiastical thinkers whether Natural Law was a command of Divine Will or a rule of Divine Reason: see below, p. 98. On St Thomas's general view of law, see G. de Lagarde, *Esprit politique de la Réforme*, Introduction.

would always have been a tenuous and shadowy thing.* Here we must go back to the great Renaissance of the study of Roman law which began with the Bolognese jurists at the end of the eleventh century. The *Corpus Juris* of Justinian—the Code, or body of statute-law, and the Digest, or body of case-law—now became a subject of study (primarily in Italy and southern France, but eventually in all the Universities of Europe) on which legal and political thought was nourished. Nor was it only a subject of study. A *caput mortuum* might have been that. But Roman law was a *lex animata*, which moved and inspired the living world. On the ecclesiastical side it passed into the active body of Canon Law, which was not only taught by the canonists, but also practised in the ecclesiastical courts. On the temporal side it began to be adapted to the needs of secular life and the requirements of secular courts. If the early commentators of the twelfth and thirteenth centuries (the Glossators) had confined themselves to the study of Roman law as it stood in the actual text of Justinian, the commentators of the fourteenth and subsequent centuries (the post-Glossators or Bartolists) sought to bring their studies to a practical point, and attempted to adapt Roman-law principles to the needs of actual life. Their labours produced two different and contradictory results. Immediately, by adjusting Roman law to the needs of general contemporary life, they helped to secure its general diffusion as a European body of practical law which could claim, as a whole, to be universal and 'natural'. Ultimately, by giving it a practical and positive character as a body of practical and positive rules, they helped to produce a reaction (though this reaction does not become evident till the sixteenth and seventeenth centuries), which ran in favour of a new view of Natural Law as something distinct from Roman law—a 'pure' law which transcended the merely 'applied' law of the civilians.†

* In other words, the Natural Law which was a *part* of Roman Law, and one of its conceptions, is a conception which was adopted and developed by the Church. But when the question came to be asked, 'What does this conception of Natural Law actually contain or include?', the answer tends to be, during the Middle Ages generally and down to the rise of a new School of Natural Law after 1500, 'It contains or includes the *whole* of Roman Law, which is, *as a whole*, both supremely reasonable and universally diffused, and is therefore natural.'

† Roman law in general came in the Middle Ages to be called by the name of *Jus civile*, which is thus used in a far wider sense than the *jus civile* of the Roman lawyers themselves. The teacher and student of 'Civil Law' is the *civilista*, or civilian. The teacher and student of Canon Law is the *canonista* or *decretista*.

The immediate result is that which meets us in the later Middle Ages, and is still to be found in the sixteenth century. During this period, there are still bodies of old customary law in the various countries of Europe; in England, indeed, there is a consolidated body of common law which will resist any Romanist trend. But on the Continent, at any rate, Roman legists are busy in most States; and even in England, Roman law is entering into branches of law other than the common law proper. In all the Universities, the English included, it is a great subject of general and international study. Practised in some degree almost everywhere, and taught everywhere, 'it was the law of an international civilisation, and relatively universal'. Because it was thus universal, it could already be called natural; and for this reason alone we may say that 'its veneration in the Middle Ages as Natural Law was not entirely unjustified'.* But it could be regarded as natural not only because it was universal, but also because it seemed to be supremely reasonable. It was the expression of human reason in a great body of scripture (*ratio scripta*), which might seem to be parallel, in things earthly, to the heavenly Scripture committed to the Church. And indeed 'the artificial perfection of reason', which the classical Roman jurisprudents had 'gotten by long study', and which the civilians had sought to assimilate by their conning and adaptation of the *Corpus Juris*, was a very high reach of reason.

But the very triumph of Roman law was, in one sense, its undoing. Just because it tended so much to become an actual law—just because it was not a 'good old bed-ridden law', but a very lively law which walked the streets and entered the courts—it left room for a new idea of Natural Law, as something distinct from actual Roman Law, which might be professed and studied in Universities as a separate branch of enquiry. When the reception of Roman law began to be achieved in Germany about 1500, and the civil law of Rome became a current law in the Empire and its principalities, the German interest in the *Corpus Juris* became very largely practical. The old Bartolist tradition of adapting Roman law to the needs of actual contemporary life (which had been contradicted but not checked by the humanists of the sixteenth century, such as Cujas, who wished to understand Roman law as an historical fact of the past in terms of historical scholarship) assumed a new and vigorous life; and a *usus modernus*—a modernisation of the *Digest* or *Pandects* of Justinian, which its votaries called *Pandekten-*

* Professor de Zulueta, op. cit. p. 181.

recht, but which a modern scholar has called 'Wardour Street Roman Law'—occupied the attention of scholars. But free speculative thought still survived, triumphant over particular and immediate exigencies; and the great general problems of the sixteenth and seventeenth centuries afforded a large material for general speculation. There was the problem of the new system of national States; of the principles on which their relations should be based; of the source and the nature of the body of law by which their relations should be adjusted. There was the problem of the new system of national Churches; of their relation to the State; of the nature of both Church and State, and the character of the common framework into which they could both be fitted. Problems such as these demanded a new wealth of conceptions. A new School of Natural Law arose and attempted to open a new mine of thought which should provide that new wealth.

The great age of this School of Natural Law is the seventeenth and eighteenth centuries. It runs from Grotius and Pufendorf to Fichte and Kant. But its work was already begun in the sixteenth century; and indeed the great problems with which it sought to deal were problems which had been posed by the development of the sixteenth century. In the sections which are translated in this volume, Gierke accordingly seeks to study the 'natural-law' speculation of the three centuries from 1500 to 1800. We may observe two general features in such speculation. In the first place, the Natural Law which is in question is a secular Natural Law. True the Catholic writers on Natural Law, in the later sixteenth century, continue to speak in terms which go back to St Thomas, and indeed beyond St Thomas—terms of divine dispensation: terms which make Natural Law appear as an objective scheme of divinely constituted realities and rules (the reality of the family, for example, and the rules of marriage and the general family system), to which man has to adjust his life if he is to be true to his own divine essence.* But the general view of the thinkers of the School of Natural Law refers that law, and all that depends upon it, to the play of the natural light of human reason. The School is thus a rationalistic school, emancipated from the Church; its tendency, we may say, is to subject the Church to Natural Law rather than Natural Law to the Church; and its thinkers seek to determine the nature of the Church, and the proper scheme of its relations to the

* Cf. infra, in the translator's notes to §14, note 60 and note 62.

State, by principles which are themselves independent of the Church. In the second place, the school of Natural Law is not only emancipated from the Scriptures of the Church: it is also emancipated from the *ratio scripta* of Roman law. Its Natural Law is based on pure *ratio*, without any adjective or qualification: it is the product of the free lucubration of the legal philosopher, researching *in scrinio pectoris sui*. But the accumulations of the past cannot be easily shed; and researches 'in the desk of one's breast' may only result in the discovery of an absence of material. In actual fact, the School of Natural Law continued to be in the debt of the *Corpus Juris*. When it sought to elaborate the natural rules of international law, it used materials which were mainly drawn from Roman law. When it sought to construct a natural system of constitutional law for the State, and natural rules of 'social' law for groups and associations, it equally used the tools provided by Roman law. It started from Roman-law conceptions of contract and 'partnership' and 'mandate'; it adopted and adapted Roman-law ideas of the *universitas* or corporation. We have spoken of the School of Natural Law as working a new mine of thought. More justly and accurately we might say that it took the minted coin of the Roman lawyers, in the form which it had attained after centuries of circulation and revaluation among the canonists and civilians, and sought to melt the metal down and stamp it with a new die.

This process of rationalising and (if we may use that word) 'naturalising' old legal conceptions is a process parallel to a phase which we have already had reason to notice in the development of classical Roman law. The theorists and teachers of the new Natural Law (which became a subject of professorial chairs in many Universities), were once more attempting to bring a spirit of 'humane interpretation' into the exegesis of law, as the old Roman jurists who thought in terms of *jus naturale* had attempted to do long before. But if we note an analogy, we must also note a great difference. The Roman *jurisconsulti* who applied the conception of *jus naturale* were closely connected with the actual profession and administration of law. They belonged to the aristocratic *élite* of Rome, and occupied a high position in the hierarchy of the Roman State. The theorists of the new Natural Law might often pass into the service of the State, and hold judicial or administrative or diplomatic posts; but in itself Natural Law was a speculation of theorists and professors. It had (in no derogatory sense of the word) an academic quality. Its immediate life was the life of lectures and text-books; and it moved more in the world of thought than in the world of action.

But the world of thought is an important world, and the School of Natural Law was deeply entrenched in its recesses. Its very academic quality brought it into close contact with the philosophies and the philosophers of the seventeenth and eighteenth centuries. Grotius and Pufendorf must count among the great thinkers of their day. Burlamaqui brought the principles of Cartesianism to the elucidation of Natural Law in his *Principes du droit naturel*, published at Geneva in 1747.* Wolff put the philosophy of Leibniz to a similar use in his *Jus naturae*, published at Frankfort from 1740 to 1748; and Vattel, another follower of Leibniz, followed much the same line in his *Droits des Gens, ou Principes de la loi naturelle* (1758), which is largely based on the work of Wolff. Just as the writers on Natural Law go to the philosophers for their principles, so the philosophers have recourse to Natural Law for their political terminology and many of their political ideas. Hobbes and Spinoza write in these terms—though the *jus naturae* of Spinoza, coloured by his pantheism, is rather a universal force, flowing from the power of God, than the dictate of man's natural reason and the human sense of right. Locke and Rousseau (if we may count Rousseau among the philosophers) have frequented the writers of the School of Natural Law; and we might even be tempted to say that Rousseau simply stylised their material, were it not that such a saying would be unjust to the intuitions of genius, and the insight of imagination, which Rousseau was able to add to the charm of his style and the clarity of his exposition. Kant and Fichte have an even larger background of natural-law theory and material; and we can hardly study their legal and political philosophy with a just appreciation, unless we remember the preparatory foundations laid by the great German writers on Natural Law during the eighteenth century—Heineccius, Thomasius, Wolff and Nettelbladt.

From one point of view, the School of Natural Law was engaged in the general study of all forms and phases of human society which were capable of developing a law or of being regulated by law. It

* It was from this work, translated into English in 1748, that Blackstone drew the observations on Natural Law which curiously diversify the introduction to his *Commentaries*, and which stirred Bentham to indignation and the publication of his *Fragment on Government*. Bentham did not realise that in attacking Blackstone (who had never acknowledged his source) he was really attacking Burlamaqui. Cf. the article on Blackstone in the *Dictionary of National Biography*.

dealt with the State: it dealt with the relations of State to State, in peace and in war; it dealt with groups other than the State, from churches to commercial companies, and it dealt with the relations of the State to such groups. From this point of view we may say that the study of Natural Law issues in some four different branches of theory—a theory of Society at large: a theory of the State; a theory of the relations of States—or, in other words, of international law; and a theory of associations and their relation to the State. From another point of view, however, the Law of Nature might seem to find its specific and particular application in the one subject of international law. The relation of States, it might be argued, stood in special need of the illumination of Natural Law, because there was so little law of any other sort by which they could be explained or regulated. From this point of view a treatise on the Law of Nations (*droit des gens*) might bear the title, or at any rate the alternative title, of a treatise on the Law of Nature (*droit naturel*). In the general conception, however, the study of the Law of Nature continued to be a general study of the State, in the whole of its range and extent, not only on its external side and in regard to the proper rules of its international relations, but also on its internal side and in regard to the proper system of its constitutional and civil law. Vattel, if he devoted three of the four books of his treatise to 'the nation considered in its relations to others', assigned the whole of the first to 'the nation considered in itself'. Rousseau, if he dealt with the State only on its internal side in his *Contrat Social*, and if he thus limited his interpretation of Natural Law to the scope of Vattel's first book, intended to pursue his interpretation further, into the field of the State's external relations. 'Après avoir posé les vrais principes du droit politique', he writes in his final chapter, 'et taché de fonder l' État sur sa base, il resterait à l'appuyer par ses relations externes, ce qui comprendrait le droit des gens.' His publisher pressed him to complete his design, and he seems actually to have begun work; but the *Contrat Social* remained the only completed half of the intended whole.*

Rousseau is a Janus-like figure in the history of the School of Natural Law. He turns to it, and belongs to it: he turns away from it, and belongs elsewhere. He is not, by profession, a master of Natural Law; he is a man of letters who makes a brilliant incursion

* Professor A. de Lapradelle, preface to the edition of Vattel in Classics of International Law, vol. I, p. xxxi.

into its field, and returns in triumph with *opima spolia*.* But there is a deeper and a more philosophic sense in which he may be said both to belong and not to belong to the School of Natural Law. On the one hand he has the individualism of that school; and he has also its universalism. He believes in the free individual, who is everywhere born free: he believes in a universal system of *droit politique*, which rests on a ubiquitous basis of individual liberty. If he had followed this line of belief to its ultimate conclusion, he would have been a votary of the natural rights of man, and an apostle of undiluted liberalism. But there is another side to his teaching—a side which is at once very different, and, in its ultimate influence, far more important. The final sovereign of Rousseau is not an individual or a body of individuals. The final norm of social life is not a body of Natural Law, issuing in a system of natural rights, which proceeds from the reason of the individual, and is everywhere the same because that reason is everywhere identical. The sovereign of which he speaks is a 'moral person'; and the final norm is the 'general will' of that person. Now it is true that *persona moralis* was a term of art in the School of Natural Law, by which it was used to signify the nature of a corporate group, as a 'person' which was something other than a physical person; and it is also true that the idea of the will of *omnes ut universi*, as distinct from the will of *omnes ut singuli*, was an idea also current in that school. But it is equally true that the 'moral person' and 'general will' of Rousseau are ideas which transcend the limits of natural-law thought. Rousseau was a romantic before Romanticism; and he prepared the way for the new style of German thought which was to divinise the Folk-person, and to historicise law as the expression in time of the general will or consciousness of right which proceeds from that person. Hegelianism and the Historical School of Law can find their nutriment in him, if he himself found his nutriment in the School of Natural Law; and while the springs of the past flow into his teaching, the springs of the future also issue from it. It is in this sense above all that he is a Janus-like figure. It is from this point of view that we may also say that he is a bridge across the gulf which, in the theory of Troeltsch, divides the *Naturrecht und Humanität* of western Europe from the Historical Law and the Folk-cult of Germany. Rousseau touches at one end the internationalism, and the sense of an all-

* On the relations of Rousseau to the School of Natural Law, and his use of its conceptions and terms, see the translator's remark in note 197 to § 16.

pervading impersonal Right, which were among the merits of the old School of Natural Law; but he also touches at the other the nationalism, and what we may call the personalism, which were to be the marks of a new dispensation of thought.

But this is to anticipate; and we must return from Rousseau (who is both the consummation and the end of *Naturrecht*) to the School of Natural Law as it stood in itself, apart from the new ingredients which he introduced. There was dynamite in Rousseau; but there was also dynamite in the pure School of Natural Law. To begin with, there was the current conception that Natural Law somehow overbore law positive, so that enactments and acts of State which ran contrary to its prescriptions were strictly null and void, even if in actual practice, owing to the absence of any machinery for their disallowance, these acts and enactments retained their validity. Such a conception—applied in various forms, sometimes with a greater and sometimes with a less degree of reverence for actual law—was a ready solvent of political obligation. The rebel against constituted authority could easily plead obedience to the higher law, and could readily allege that he was only exerting, or defending, the natural rights which he enjoyed under that law. The idea of a natural system of public, or constitutional, law was particularly explosive. According to that idea there was a natural 'law of the constitution' common to every State. Historic constitutions were threatened in any case by such an idea; but if the idea were made to issue in a natural 'frame of government' based upon general popular assent, and a 'declaration of natural rights' proceeding from the general popular voice, the threat became obvious and definite.

The American Revolution, as it ran its course from 1764 to 1776 —from the first beginnings of resistance down to the Declaration of Independence and the creation of new colonial constitutions— was inspired by the doctrines of Natural Law. An English judge had uttered the *obiter dictum*, in 1614, that 'even an Act of Parliament made against natural equity...is void in itself; for *jura naturae sunt immutabilia*, and they are *leges legum*'. In England the dictum had carried no weight;* but it lived and grew to a great

---

* Blackstone, in the introduction to his *Commentaries*, § II, where he is borrowing from Burlamaqui, remarks, 'This law of nature...is of course superior in obligation to any other...no human laws are of any validity if contrary to this, and such of them as are valid derive all their force...from this original'. But later in the same introduction, when he is writing independently, at the end of

power in the North American colonies. James Otis, one of the Boston lawyers, is already declaring, in 1764, 'should an Act of Parliament be against any of His natural laws...the declaration would be contrary to eternal truth, equity and justice, and consequently void'.* The very phrase of 1614, 'the immutable laws of nature', becomes a battle-cry: it is often used by the great Boston agitator, Samuel Adams; and perhaps at his instigation it is inserted in the Declaration of the first Continental Congress, in 1774, when the deputies declare that the colonies, by the immutable laws of nature, have certain rights, and that certain Acts of Parliament are violations and infringements of these rights.† In the Puritan atmosphere of North America the secular Law of Nature recovers its theological basis: Samuel Adams claims for his countrymen the indefeasible rights with which 'God and Nature have invested' them;‡ and the Declaration of Independence claims for the people of America the station to which they are entitled by 'the Laws of Nature and of Nature's God'.§ It was the Law of Nature which, more than any other force, exploded the authority of the British Parliament and the British connection; and it is curious to reflect that Vattel's work on the principles of Natural Law was currently used in the *sodalitas* of the Boston lawyers (a sort of political science club) during the crucial years of the Revolution.‖ Nor was it only in the work of destruction that the theory of Natural Law was employed. It also served the cause of construction. The Virginian 'Declaration of Rights' and the Virginian 'Constitution or Form of Government' of 1776, and the Pennsylvania Constitution of the same year, which contains both a declaration of rights and 'a plan or frame of government', are both founded on the theory of Natural Law. If we seek to find the general ideas by which these documents were inspired, we shall find them in the first book of Vattel's treatise, and particularly in its second and third chapters. Whether or no the framers of the documents had Vattel actually before them, they were using the common stock of ideas on which he had drawn, and which he had presented in lucid French.¶

§III, he observes, 'If the parliament will positively enact a thing to be done which is unreasonable, I know of no power that can control it'.
* S. E. Morison, *Sources and documents illustrating the American Revolution*, p. 7.
† Ibid. pp. 119, 121.
‡ Ibid. p. 94. § Ibid. p. 157.
‖ Van Tyne, *Causes of the War of American Independence*, vol. 1.
¶ Cf. A. de Lapradelle, *op. cit.* p. xxx (and especially note 1), where an account is given of the vogue of Vattel in North America, especially after 1775.

Nothing need here be said about the effects of the theory of Natural Law on the course of the French Revolution. It is a theme on which Gierke himself dwells.* Nor need any words be said about the elements of natural-law theory which appear in Kant and Fichte. Of that also Gierke himself has spoken. But there are two things which ought to be mentioned before we leave the School of Natural Law. One is that its views were not always explosive and anarchical, or even liberal and democratic. If there were some writers who made positive law a mere earthen vessel as compared with the solid iron of the law natural, there were others who gave the victory to positive law, and others again who, in a spirit of happy optimism, believed that the framers of positive law would be sure to follow the dictates of Nature and to avoid the possibility of quarrel. Nor was it always the case that, in treating of the principles of natural public law (or, as Rousseau calls them, *les principes du droit politique*), the natural-law thinkers committed themselves to the proposition that the people should properly frame its own constitution, or elect its own governors, or bind them in the iron fetters of its own declaration of rights. On the contrary, as Gierke shows, there were always two lines of opinion on these matters in the School of Natural Law; and while in the eighteenth century, from Locke to Vattel and Rousseau, and from Vattel and Rousseau to Fichte himself (in the earlier stage of his thought), opinion inclined to what we may call 'popularism', the thinkers of the seventeenth century mainly inclined to the absolutist cause. Grotius and Pufendorf were too near to the problems of the nascent modern State to desert the cause of authority; and Nature could be used to consecrate the monarch as well as the people. All through the history of the School of Natural Law we can find advocates of the Sovereignty of the Ruler as well as of the Sove-

---

* As we have already mentioned, in an earlier passage of this introduction, Gierke did not extend his researches into the American Revolution. He is silent about Vattel, and he has not comprehended in his scope Paine's 'Rights of Man', a *naturrechtlich* pamphlet based on American experience. He also omits some other English writers of the later eighteenth century who were influenced by the American and French Revolutions, and whose thought had natural-law elements, such as Dr Price, Dr Priestley and William Godwin. In a word, he has dealt generally with the great European thinkers, and he has devoted particular attention to the thought of Germany; but he has not been able to find time or space for lesser lights in other countries. (He deals, for example, with Bodin in the sixteenth century, but not with Loyseau in the seventeenth; he considers the Huguenot writers of 1570 and afterwards, but not the Huguenot writers (such as Jurieu) of 1680 and afterwards.)

reignty of the People—not to mention the champions of the 'double sovereignty' of both, or the exponents of the 'mixed constitution', who sought to achieve an eirenicon between the two causes.

In the second place, we must not too readily dismiss the School of Natural Law as unhistorical, or as crudely individualistic, or as vitiated by a fundamental error of rationalism. There would, of course, be a measure of truth in all these accusations. Natural-law thinkers were apt to talk of an unhistorical 'state of nature', and of an unhistorical act of contract by which men issued from it. They played with individuals as counters, and they often forgot the deeper unities of social life. They thought of men as acting by rational calculation: they neglected the areas that lie below reason, or by the side of reason; and they did not sufficiently recognise that reason itself is a 'bank and capital of the ages' which grows by a gradual process of social accumulation and transmission. On the other hand, historical criticism of the School of Natural Law which makes merry with its state of nature and its contract may very well miss the mark. The natural-law thinkers were not really dealing with the historical antecedents of the State: they were concerned with its logical presuppositions; and there is still a case to be made for the view that the State, as distinct from Society, is a legal association which fundamentally rests on the presupposition of contract. In the same way, the individualism of natural-law thought may be readily exaggerated; and in any case, if we hold that individual personality is the one intrinsic value of human life, we shall have no very great reason to fling stones at a theory which rested on a similar basis. It is what we may call the short-time rationalism of the natural-law school which is open to a juster criticism. It is not the νόησις μονόχρονος of the philosophic jurist which can discover the deep foundations of social life. There is a long-time process of social thought, revolving and ruminating the problem of a right order of human relations (or, in other words, the problem of justice), which lays the foundations on which the State is built, and on which it builds. Social thought about justice, issuing in the constitution of a State, and then translated by the government of that State into a declared and enforced law—this is the basis on which we must build our philosophy of law and the State. Here the historical argument enters again, in a deeper sense than when it is used to refute the historical existence of states of nature and social contracts. The long-time process of social thought is a great historic fact; and we must reckon with that fact. This is the fundamental justification of the School of Historical Law which arose in Germany at the end of the eighteenth and in the beginning of the nineteenth century. And yet it is not enough to hold that law is simply an historical product, evolved in this or that direction, under this or that set of contingencies, by this or that peculiar people. To hold such a view is to be content with a law which is merely an empirical fact, and has no anchor in the flux of history. Social thought, as it operates in time, is indeed a basis of justice; but the mind of man will always demand that the core of justice shall be beyond time and space—*quod semper, quod ubique*. The School of Natural Law had some sense of that timeless and spaceless core. That is why, as Gierke writes in a noble passage of his work on Althusius, the undying spirit of Natural Law can never be extinguished. That is why we must somehow incorporate that undying spirit in our modern conception of Historical Law. For then 'the sovereign independence of the idea of Justice, secured before by the old conception of Natural Law, will still continue to be firmly secured by our new conception of Law as something thoroughly positive—no matter whether the idea which opposes that conception be the idea of social utility, or the idea of collective power'.*

§4

THE SCHOOL OF HISTORICAL LAW

The beginnings of the School of Historical Law in Germany are rooted, in their immediate origins, in a reaction against Natural Law—a reaction against its rationalism, against its universalism, and against its individualism. Instead of pure *ratio*, covering the world and time with its system of rational rules, and proceeding from and returning upon the individual, there was to be substituted the *Volksgeist*, immersed in the historical flood of its own particular development, and immersing the individual in the movement of its own collective life. Law, on this view, is essentially *Volksrecht*: it is the product, in each nation, of the national genius. A new movement of thought thus recurred to the idea of national law, which Rome had slowly transcended in the millennium of legal development which lay between the Twelve Tables of 450 B.C. and the issue of the Digest in A.D. 533. It rejected, as an incubus

* See Appendix II, p. 224.

upon the growing life of nations, the conception of a supernational rule of right, whether that conception took the form of adhesion to Roman law as a *ratio scripta* for all humanity, or issued in the proclamation of a new Natural Law based on pure *ratio naturalis*. The Nation revolted against *Natura*. This was the essence of the revolution in German thought which began a century and a half ago.

It was a revolution which was contemporary with, and largely influenced by, the French Revolution. The French Revolution, it is true, was in some respects fundamentally different. It was a revolution not against 'Nature', but in the name of 'Nature'; it proclaimed the natural and imprescriptible rights of men and citizens, as recited in the Declaration of 1789, against an outmoded absolutism and an outworn social system. But the Revolution also proclaimed the rights of the Nation and the principle of *souveraineté nationale*; and its future course—whether, by edicts of fraternity, it sought to elicit national movements in its own support, or whether, by the oppression of its tutelage and its exactions, it involuntarily produced national movements directed against itself —was destined to encourage the philosophy of the *Volk*. It was amid the storm and thunder of the Revolution and the Empire, and, in particular, amid the passionate fervours of the movement of Liberation which followed on the battle of Jena, that the theory of the *Volksgeist* and of *Volksrecht* attained its strength and its splendour.

But the Romantic movement, from which the revolution in German thought takes its beginnings, is even earlier than the French Revolution. It is a movement which we may trace as early as 1770. It is a movement back to the Middle Ages; back again, behind them, to the primaeval sources of Teutonic antiquity; back, in a word, to the homely and indigenous core of the life of the German people. It is a literary movement; but it is a literary movement with an immanent philosophy of its own. That philosophy is a philosophy of the Folk, as a Being which creates language for its utterance; which utters itself through its language in folk-songs and folk-tales; and which sets the folk-songs it has written to the folk-tunes it has composed. Herder first expressed this general philosophy, from 1784 onwards, in his *Ideen zur Geschichte der Philosophie der Menschheit*—a work which Gierke repeatedly cites in his footnotes, and to which, in a lecture delivered before the University of Berlin in 1903, he ascribes a large creative influence in producing the School of Historical Law.* Whether it was the creator, or whether it was only the harbinger, Herder's work was certainly followed by a rich Romantic harvest. The general nature of that harvest is set out in the lecture by Professor Troeltsch which is translated as an appendix to this volume. All that need here be said is some few words about three particular fields —the field of language and literature; the field of Hegelian philosophy; and the field of law. In all of them we shall find the idea of the folk-soul winning its conquests, and vindicating its magic as a universal key of interpretation.

To understand the folk-soul it was necessary, first of all, to collect and appreciate the monuments of its speech, its songs, its tales. Between 1806 and 1808 Arnim and Brentano published *Des Knaben Wunderhorn*—a golden treasury of *Volkslieder* which inspired, and has continued to inspire, German poets and musicians. In 1812 the brothers Jacob and William Grimm published the first volume of their *Märchen*—fairy-tales, as we now say, but the word 'folk-tale' would be nearer to the purpose of the compilers. Jacob Grimm, whose long life only ended in 1863, was to carry his researches into folk-literature and language through many realms of study. He studied language in the four volumes of his *German Grammar*, seeking to relate its growth to the development of the people's voice and the evolution of the people's thought. He traced folk-poetry in law; and he sought to recover the legal antiquities and to collect the ancient 'dooms' of primitive Germany. In his *German Mythology* he recreated the ancient gods, and revealed the old figures of Folk-religion and popular superstition. In his hands the Folk became no longer an abstraction, or a postulate of theory, but a storied and documented being, expressed in language and ballad and saga, in legal *Weistümer* and religious myths.

The conception of the folk-soul not only inspired the philologist and student of literature. It also inspired the historian; and we may trace its efforts in Niebuhr's *Roman History* and his method of using conjectured ballads of the Roman People to discover the early history of Rome. Above all, it also inspired the philosopher. We may say of Hegel and the Hegelians that they took the Folk and lifted it into the heavens of metaphysics. In their philosophy the Folk becomes a Mind—and not only a Mind, but also an incarnation of the Eternal Mind. In its eternal process, the Eternal Mind

* See the address on 'The Historical School of Law and the Germanists', p. 5 and note 7.

incorporates itself in folk-minds, which are the incarnations of God in time and space, and indeed *are* God, as He operates within the limits of Here and Now. They are therefore divine; and because they are divine they cover every range of life, and they are also final and right, within their space and time, for all that they cover. Organised in the State, which is the highest power of its life, the Folk attains the highest synthesis of all its faculties. The State reconciles the private 'Morality' of its individual members with the formal system of 'Law' which has been developed on the plane, and to meet the needs, of a common 'economic society' (*die bürgerliche Gesellschaft*); and it reconciles them both in the higher unity of a system of social ethics, or *Sittlichkeit*, which is the final reach of the mind of the Folk, strung tense by the power of the State —a reach that carries it back 'into the life of the universal substance'.

The great tide of Romantic thought (which has flowed in Germany ever since, now deep and now diminished, and has risen to a *fluctus decumanus* in this year of grace 1933) flowed also over the field of law. Indeed it appeared in law even earlier than in philosophy. Hegel's *Philosophy of Law and Outlines of the State* was published in 1821; but the foundations of the School of Historical Law, which regarded law as the historic product of the folk-mind (with the jurist in some way collaborating in the process of production) go back to the eighteenth century. Mention has already been made of the influence of Herder's *Ideen* of the years 1784–5; and Justus Möser, lawyer and statesman in the bishopric of Osnabrück, who published his *Patriotic Phantasies* between 1774 and 1776, may also be counted among the forerunners. Hugo, Professor of Law at Göttingen, was already teaching, about 1789, that 'the law of a people could only be understood through the national life itself, since it was itself a part and expression of that life'.* But the definite appearance of the School of Historical Law may be dated from the foundation of the University of Berlin in 1809. The foundation of the University was itself the expression of a national movement: it had been preceded by Fichte's *Reden an die deutsche Nation*: it counted among its earliest professors Fichte himself, the historian Niebuhr, and two great jurists—Eichhorn the Germanist, and Savigny the Romanist. It was these two (both young men, of about the age of thirty, when they began to lecture in Berlin) who wedded law to history, under the common auspices of the Folk which lives

* G. P. Gooch, *History and Historians in the Nineteenth Century*, pp. 42–3.

in time and speaks in law. They founded in collaboration a journal of historical jurisprudence; and they devoted long and laborious lives (both lived on into the latter half of the nineteenth century) to the historical study of law.

Savigny was the greater of the two; and it was Savigny's genius which impressed its influence on the new School of Historical Law. The programme of the school was enunciated in his work of 1814, 'On the Vocation of our Time for Legislation and Jurisprudence'. Its motto may be expressed in Savigny's dictum, *Das Gesetz ist das Organ des Volksrechts*. 'For law, as for language', Savigny argued, 'there is no movement of cessation. It is subject to the same movement and development as every other expression of the life of the people.... All law was originally formed by custom and popular feeling, next by jurisprudence—that is by silently operating forces.'* In the strength of this view he protested against codification, which would imprison the development of law in an iron cage; he protested against *Naturrecht* and all its works; he sought to secure free course for the flood of a people's thought, flowing 'with pomp of waters unwithstood'. It is in this succession that Gierke, though he does far more justice than Savigny to the idea of Natural Law, essentially and fundamentally stands. Has he not said, *ex cathedra*, that 'in any scheme of thought which proceeds on the premiss that the social life of man is the life of super-individual entities, the introduction of the *Volksgeist* into the theory of law will always continue to be regarded as the starting-point of a deeper and profounder theory of society'?†

But we shall not fully understand Gierke's own position until we have considered a further development in the School of Historical Law. At first the Germanists and the Romanists—those who delved in the history of German law proper, like Eichhorn in his *History of German Law and Institutions*, and those who researched into the history of Roman law, like Savigny in his *History of Roman Law in the Middle Ages*—worked amicably together. After all, the law of Germany, at any rate since the Reception, contained both elements; and why should not the history of both elements be studied in scholarly amity? But there was an inherent difficulty in this position; and it was not long in manifesting itself. If law was the expression of a *Volksgeist*, German law must be the ex-

* Quoted from Savigny's *Vom Beruf unserer Zeit* in Gooch, *op. cit.* p. 49.
† Lecture on 'The Historical School of Law', p. 8.

pression of a German *Volksgeist*; and in that case what was to be said of Roman law in Germany? Was it not a foreign body? And should it not be purged away in favour of native and national law, until the German people had recovered its inheritance? When such questions were asked, a rift began to emerge between Germanist and Romanist views. The Romanists, in adopting a national-historical view of law, had put themselves into a position which was logically somewhat untenable; and the more they clung to pure Roman law, uncontaminated by the accretions of the medieval post-glossators and the more recent additions of the German *usus modernus*, the more untenable they made their position. Pure Roman law might be the expression of the soul of the dead and gone people of Rome: it could hardly be the expression of the soul of the German people. Savigny might plead that the German people was destined by its nature to assimilate and appropriate Roman law: his followers might contend that the law of Rome, at any rate in the sphere of *Privatrecht*, was meant for mankind and transcended national limits; but the plea of Savigny was perilously like special pleading, and the contention of his followers contradicted the basic principle of the Historical School to which they professed to belong. Still, Roman law—deeply entrenched both in actual law and in the teaching of the Universities—held its ground; and an opinionated battle inevitably came to be joined between Romanists and Germanists. Twice the Germanist lawyers rallied to the attack. In the troubled times about 1848, backed by philologists like Grimm and historians like Ranke, the Germanist lawyers demanded a body of German law based on German history and the German nation. The demand died down in the reaction after 1848: it was renewed, with less ardour but in a more practical form, when a definite scheme for a new civil code for the German Empire was published in 1888.

The scheme, in its first draft, contained (or was held to contain) too large an element of Roman law. The effort of the Germanists, which lasted from 1888 until the enactment of the new civil code in 1896, was directed to redressing the balance in favour of Germanism. Gierke, trained by the Germanist Beseler, and himself a foremost figure among the Germanists, threw himself vigorously into the effort. He had recently been appointed Professor at Berlin, in 1887: he had published three great volumes on German *Genossenschaftsrecht*; in the strength of his chair and his publications he contended for a Germanist treatment of associations in the new code. Something was won by Gierke and the Germanists, if not all that they could have desired; and the struggle ended with both parties resting honourably on their weapons. German law was embedded in the new code—but Roman law had not disappeared. German law was taught in the Universities—but so also, *pari passu*, was Roman. Germany retained the double past of her legal development; and the two contending parties in the School of Historical Law remained true to their contentions. Both were necessary, Gierke confessed in a lecture of 1903, and both would continue to be necessary, if the historical roots of the double past were to be properly traced and interpreted. 'The Romanists will still continue to apply to current law, wherever they can, the great model which is to be found in Roman jurisprudence. The Germanists will never be weary of seeking to champion the independent character of their own country's legal ideas, and to develop further the genuinely German content of our law, along lines of expansion which will bring it into closer accordance with the national genius.'*

There is a calm of reconciliation about these words. But we have to remember, as we read all Gierke's writings, that he was from first to last a soldier in the Germanist section of the School of Historical Law. He was arming it by his historical researches before 1888; he was fighting in its ranks between 1888 and 1896; and even after the new civil code came finally into force (as it did at the beginning of 1900), he was still deeply concerned to secure, as we have already had reason to note, that 'the new law should be penetrated by a Germanist spirit...and that the growth of its Germanism in the future should be fostered and encouraged'.† He had, as we have already seen, a just view of the inner core of truth in the School of Natural Law. He could also, as we have just noticed, make a due acknowledgment of the part which Roman law must still continue to play in German legal thought. But he is a Germanist of the Germanists, nurtured in the tradition of the Folk, and instinct with the philosophy of *Volksgeist* and *Volksrecht*. Born in 1841, he was carried along on the wave of the general movement of Romantic thought. His theory of the Group and of Group-personality, to which it is now time to turn, is a part of that general movement.

* Lecture on 'The Historical School of Law,' p. 33.
† Preface to vol. IV of the *Genossenschaftsrecht*, p. xii; cf. supra, § 2, ad initium.

§ 5

THE PERSONALITY OF GROUPS

Gierke, as we have seen, speaks of all his researches, in all the four volumes of his *Genossenschaftsrecht*, as illuminated by 'the central idea of real group-personality'. We must seek to understand the duality, or rather the mixture, of elements in the legal past of Germany, if we are to grasp the inspiration and the significance of this idea.

We may begin by a contrast between the fortunes of England and those of Germany in the two spheres of law and language. In England law has developed, in the limits of an island State, as a single and native system—a 'common law' cast in one mould and resting on one general basis of legal ideas. In Germany, on the other hand, subject by virtue of its central position to the infiltration and 'reception' of Roman influences, law has developed on a double basis; it has been cast in two different moulds; it has rested on two different foundations of Latin and Teutonic legal ideas. Curiously enough, in the sphere of language, the opposite has been the case. In England our language, at any rate in its vocabulary, if not in its grammar, is dual: it is a mixture of Latin and Teutonic words; and the mixture has enriched our vocabulary and enlarged the expression of our thought. In Germany, on the other hand, language is pure and unmixed: the Latin words are few, and the old 'folk-speech' is almost undiluted. So far as there is any analogy in these matters between England and Germany, it is a sort of cross analogy. German law is different from English law, and the German language from the English; but there is some sort of analogy between German law and the English language. Even here, however, there is a difference. The Latin and the Teutonic words in the English vocabulary have settled down easily together, and except for some few 'Saxon' purists we all accept contentedly the happy amalgam with which we have been presented by history. The Latin and the Teutonic elements in German law did not fuse so happily; and a struggle for the recovery of a native *Volksrecht*, in harmony with the native *Volkssprache*, was the result of their imperfect fusion.

In the matter of groups or associations, the tradition and teaching of Roman law presented Germany with the conception of the

Universitas and the *Societas*—the strict legal corporation and the strict business partnership of business partners. But were there not also Teutonic conceptions still surviving, relics of a richer past, which might be rediscovered by study, and even recreated by an act of will and a policy of restoration? There was the *Gemeinde*, or local community, with a history running back to Teutonic antiquity, and with survivals of co-ownership, or something even higher than co-ownership, in its possession of forest and waste. There was the *Genossenschaft*—the company of brothers, linked by the right hand of fellowship, and knit together by a spirit of fraternity, who pursued the common interest of their group (whether based on profession, or occupation, or the simple foundation of voluntary association), and vindicated its common honour with a common ardour. The further you went back, the deeper seemed the idea and the closer the cohesion of this *Genossenschaft*, or (as we may call it, in a word which carries the same medieval flavour) this system of Fellowship. It runs back to early tribalism; it has the very savour and warm intimacy of the tribe. 'Guilds, fraternities, comminalities, companies or brotherheads'*—such things are indigenous in the Hercynian forest. There is the *comitatus* described by Tacitus, whose members were so linked to their chief, and to one another, that they will die round him as one body in the stern hour of defeat. There is the *trustis dominica* of the Frankish kings, which is the *comitatus* in a courtly guise—the group of *scholares* and *convivae regis*, who have sworn common trust and fealty to their sovereign. But the common folk too have their fellowships; and 'brotherheads' run through all grades of society. There is the kin-group or *maegth* of common blood; there is the religious guild of common faith and charity; there is the workaday guild or 'craft' of co-workers. A brotherly clannishness breathes in the early German air, and still survives in the atmosphere of the German Middle Ages; and may not we English also say, remembering our own medieval guilds and communities, that there was a time when we too breathed a similar inspiration? Certainly it is an English writer who loved to go back to the Middle Ages, William Morris, who has celebrated 'fellowship' most highly, in words that have often been quoted. 'Fellowship is heaven, and the lack of fellowship is hell; fellowship is life, and the lack of fellowship is death; and the deeds that ye do upon the earth, it is for fellow-

* Words from a statute of Henry VIII, quoted by Maitland in the introduction to *Political Theories of the Middle Ages*, p. xxix.

ship's sake that ye do them, and the life that is in it shall live on for ever, and each one of you part of it.'

It is tempting to contrast this Teutonic passion for fellowship with the unassociative habit of the Latin. Maitland, paraphrasing Gierke, has spoken of Roman law as 'the law of an unassociative people'—absolutistic in its conception of the State; individualistic in its treatment of the members of the State. Yet there is nothing which is more closely knit than the Latin family group: few peoples have shown a tougher cohesive fibre (especially in moments of crisis) than the Romans of the Republic, or have exhibited a definite national genius more clearly and consciously; and if guilds or colleges of merchants and artisans were regulated, and transformed into administrative agencies, by the Roman Emperors, they had flourished before with tolerable freedom under the Roman Republic. It was the genius of Latin imperialism, rather than the Latin genius *per se*, which was hostile to the free fellowship. But we have to admit that the genius of Latin imperialism had coloured and controlled the content of the *Corpus Juris*; and we must also confess that survivals of old Teutonic comradeship, in the *Gemeinde* or the *Genossenschaft*, could never move easily under the scheme of Roman law which Germany had so largely received about 1500 A.D., when, by an apparent paradox, the German princes were simultaneously ejecting the Roman papacy by a movement of Reformation, and introducing Roman law by a movement of Reception. (Princely self-interest, which profited by both movements, is a sufficient explanation of the seeming paradox.) Already, in the popular revolts which simmered in Germany after 1520, we find protests against the courts where Romanist lawyers adjudicated (the *rotwelschen Gerichte*), and demands for the abolition of their 'impious law', which bore hardly on townsman and peasant.* Then, for nearly three centuries, there was a long sleep. The sleep was ended, and fellowship awoke again, in town and country, when the Romantic revolution began. The Romantic philosophy of the *Volksgeist* could be extended by analogy to cover the local community and the fellowship of good comrades. If the Folk had a being and a reality, why should not the local community, which was a microcosm of the Folk, have also being and reality? The fellowship too—was it not also a microcosm and a member of the people, and did it not deserve a legal recognition of its true nature, which might be found by a return to the past and

* Lagarde, *L'Esprit politique de la Réforme*, p. 103.

a study of old Teutonic law? To lift the disguising veil of imperial Rome, and to find, in an inner shrine, the figures of truth—old German truth, and comradeship, and attendant honour—this became a sacred duty of the new philosophy. In the cause of liberty of association, there must be a return to the past; ancient realities must again be revealed: the being, the mind, the person of the group—the local community, the fellowship—must be awakened from their long slumber.

Here we must pause to draw a distinction. It is one thing to plead the cause of liberty of associations: it is another thing—or at any rate it is a further thing, and an added consideration—to plead that associations are beings or minds or real persons. If we confine ourselves to the simple ground of liberty of association, there is much that we shall admit, or rather claim, even on that simple ground. We can argue that liberty of association was impeded in Germany by the law of imperialist Rome, especially in the expanded (or should we say tightened?) form in which it had come to be interpreted by the Romanist lawyers, who turned the scattered dicta to be found in Roman law into a body of doctrine that might sometimes have amazed Justinian's advisers. We can argue that the modern State should lay a cool and easy hand on the formation and action of associations—not limiting their formation by making a specific concession necessary in each case, and not tying their action down within the limits of such concession. We can admit that our English State, in a casual and haphazard way, and largely owing to the growth of our 'equitable' law of trusts, which has enabled associations to form themselves and to act behind the screen of trustees, has been generally easy-handed, though it has sometimes taken away with the right hand of the common law much of what it had conceded with the left hand of equity.* We can equally admit that the various States of Germany afforded no such shelter; that associations here had to face the inquisitive eye of government unsheltered by any screen; and that a general theory which would protect liberty of association was a more urgent necessity in Germany than it has ever been in England.

What was that general theory to be? Was it possible to find a theoretical basis for liberty of association, without recourse to a

* The common law of conspiracy has long restrained 'combinations' of workers, while at equity they might be holding funds, through their trustees, for the free promotion of their purposes.

doctrine of the real personality of groups? In imagination we may frame for ourselves an answer to the first of these questions, which will enable us also to answer the second, and to answer it in the affirmative. We may say that the modern State, which is based on the consent of the governed and respects the liberty of individuals, is bound by its very nature to acknowledge the liberty of individuals to associate with one another, provided that the purpose of such association is compatible with its own purpose and well-being as the general and comprehensive association of all individuals. We may go further, and we may say that the acknowledgment of liberty of association should be expressed in a general law of associations, which translates the principle into detail and formulates its consequences. The historical State, as it has grown in time, has scattered its rules about associations under different heads, according to the accidents of its growth: it may even have deposited discrepant rules in different branches of its law—Germanist rules which conflict with Romanist; rules of equity which diverge from the rules of common law. The modern State, as it stands to-day, may well unify these rules, and unify them in view of its own developed character as a free association of free individuals.*

Such an answer to the problem of associations may be accused of doctrinaire and individualistic liberalism. Associations, it may be said, are something more than a liberty of individuals to associate: they are entities in themselves, or at any rate they become such entities in the course of their development. To explain their freedom by the freedom of individuals to associate with one another is to leave them without either body or animating soul: it is to dissolve their life into a lifeless nexus of contractual relations between the associated members, and to forget the pulsation of a common purpose which surges, as it were from above, into the mind and behaviour of the members of any true group. Whether or no we pin our own faith to such a view, we may recognise that it was natural to a German thinker in the latter half of the nineteenth century. 'You who live to the west of the Rhine', he might say, 'with your democratic States which themselves seem to rest

---

* 'Can we continue to leave our law of associations (to use a neutral word) disjointed and scattered as it now is, so that for parts of it we must look under the law of agency, for parts under the law of trusts, for part under contract, for part under corporations?' Professor Geldart, *Inaugural Lecture on Legal Personality*, p. 7.

on a basis of contract, may talk of groups in general—not only your State, but also your churches and colleges and all sorts of unions—as the products of freedom of contract. We live to the east of the Rhine, and we live in our own German world. Our State is interpreted to us as a mind and a personality; and if we do not ascribe to our groups some mind and personality, where will they be, in the face of this great spiritual Leviathan? We have no protecting screen of trustees to shelter our groups; and the heat of the State is a fiery heat. Unless we make them real in the same sort of way as our State is interpreted as being real, they will hardly survive at all. Our German form of liberalism must be the vindication of the reality of the group: that is our one way of saving some sort of liberty, other than the liberty of the State to be what it likes and to do what it will. For this reason we can claim the sympathy, and expect the support, of you who are western Liberals. Surely you will recognise that our groups must have real personality if they are to have any real liberty—any power of owning funds and pursuing policies and moving at large as free agents in the general world of action?'

The problem of liberty of association thus carries us forward, after all, into the problem of the real personality of associations. Is an association, then, a 'reality', an 'organism', a 'personality'? Reality, we may reply, is a term of high metaphysics; and it lies beyond our scope. Organism is a term of biology, or, at the most, of biological metaphor; but our business is with human society, and before we seek to walk by the uncertain and lunar light of biological metaphor, we must study the essential language which is proper to such society. Personality is a term which belongs to that essential language. It is a term of psychology, of ethics, and of law; and since political science is vitally connected with those studies, it is also a term of political science. We may therefore address ourselves to that term: we may seek to define its exact connotation; and in the light of such definition we may then be able to suggest in what sense a Group—a State, a Church, a Trade Union, a college, a club—may properly be described as a person.

There are three main senses in which we use the term 'personality'; and they correspond to the three studies of psychology, ethics and law. In the first place, there is psychological personality. By this we mean, primarily, the power or capacity of self-consciousness which belongs to a sentient being aware of its own sensations. We also mean, secondarily, a power or capacity of self-determination, by considerations of pleasure and pain, which arises from such self-consciousness, and turns it into a higher activity than its primary activity of awareness. Psychological personality, by its nature, is resident in an individual being who is a focus and centre of sentiency. In the second place, there is moral personality. Here we come upon a term which has had two historic usages, and by which we are therefore apt to be perplexed. In its first and intrinsic usage, it signifies the power or capacity of a self-conscious and rational being to determine himself, not by temporary and particular considerations of pleasure and pain, but by permanent and universal considerations of a right way of conducting life which is common to all such beings. Moral personality, in this sense, is built upon psychological personality; but it transcends that upon which it is built. Like psychological personality, it is resident in the individual being; but it is only resident in him in so far as he recognises that he is not unique, but shares with his fellows a common life and common rules of life. But besides this first and intrinsic usage, there has been another usage of the term 'moral personality'. It has been used, by many legal writers, as a term of law. It has been used, without any ethical implication, to signify the legal power or capacity of a group, which, without being a 'natural' or 'physical' person, acts in the same sort of way as such a person in the sphere of legal action. Here the word moral is used in much the same sense as when we speak of a moral certainty or a moral victory. We need not quarrel with the usage, provided that we are clear that it is peculiar,* and that it belongs exclusively to the sphere of law; but in our own argument the term moral personality will be confined to what we have called its first and intrinsic usage. It will be a term of ethics, and of ethics only. It will denote the power or capacity of moral action.

There is a third use of the term personality, which belongs to the sphere of law. Legal personality, as distinct from psychological and ethical personality, is a power or capacity for legal action—a capacity recognised by law (and only existing when recognised by law) for originating such action as belongs to the scheme of law. From this point of view the existence of legal personality not only presupposes, as that of moral personality does, the presence of human society: it also presupposes the presence of an organised

* Moral personality, in the intrinsic ethical sense, is essentially individual. Moral personality, in this legal sense, is essentially non-individual.

legal association. It is a thing bound up with rights; in fact it is a capacity for rights; and rights, in the full sense of the word, are only possible in such an association. Now rights may belong, and obviously do belong, to groups as well as to individuals. In the field of the organised legal association we must therefore assign legal personality to groups as well as to individuals, and here we have to admit that there are Group-persons as well as individual persons. Legal personality differs from psychological and moral personality: it is not only resident in individual beings: it is also resident in any group of such beings which serves, in the legal sphere, as a single entity. To discover the exact nature, or being, or essence, of this entity may be difficult; but the fact of its existence is obvious. The organised legal association itself—in other words, the State—is an entity which possesses and exercises rights, and to which we must therefore ascribe a legal personality. In brief, the State is a legal person, or, as the Germans say, a 'Subject'. Similarly many of the groups contained in the State are legal persons. They have a capacity for rights; and a capacity for rights means a legal personality.

In the area of the organised legal association, and under the category of legal personality which belongs to that area, we have thus to reckon with the fact that there are Group-persons as well as individual persons. The association itself, as the great and inclusive group, is a Group-person: contained groups, in so far as they own and exercise rights, are group-persons; and both these 'clusters' or constellations of personality, the one great and the many lesser, exist by the side of the innumerable 'points' of individual personality. How are we to conceive the being and the essence of these Group-persons? The individual himself, as a 'point' of personality, is simple. He is essentially one—a single psychological and moral person who also acts as a single legal person. But the 'cluster' or group is complex, or at any rate twofold. It is both 'itself' (whatever that may be) and all the individuals of which it is composed. How can it be both, at one and the same time? How does its unity stand related to its multiplicity?

We may note some three different answers to this question which recur, like different and dissonant notes, in the pages of Gierke's argument. The first answer takes the form of the Fiction theory. According to this theory, the real fact behind the existence of a legal group is the fact of the many individuals of which it is composed, and the unity of such a group is only a pretence or fiction. When the group acts as one, and enjoys rights as a single person, that person is only a *persona ficta*; and if it be asked who it is that pretends or feigns this person into its fictitious existence, the answer will be that the State, or, more exactly, the sovereign of the State, is the great and magnificent maker of fictions. The Fiction theory may also be termed the Concession theory; or at any rate we may say that it leads, by a natural descent, to the idea that the unity of a legal group is due to an act of concession by the authority of the State. We may also note a further variant of the Fiction theory. This is the theory of the 'Moral' person, which has already been mentioned incidentally. According to this theory a group which acts as one, and enjoys rights as a single person, should properly be described as a *persona moralis*. But it is far from clear that the change of adjective, from *ficta* to *moralis*, imports any change of sense, or gives us any new light. The adjective 'moral' is only used in a negative sense, as the antithesis of 'natural' or 'physical'. It only suggests that a legal group is something which is somehow different from the natural and physical fact of a corporeal human being. And the danger of the adjective is twofold. On the one hand it blurs the old (though possibly erroneous) distinction between real and fictitious persons by the suggestion of a dim interlunar person which is neither. On the other hand it encourages a confusion of thought which turns the 'moral person' into something ethical and good; and Rousseau, in his theory of the *personne morale* whose general will is always right, seems to fall into this confusion.

A second answer to our problem is provided by the Collective theory. According to this theory we need not concern ourselves to discover the unity of a Group-person, whether in the pretence of a *persona ficta* or in the semi-pretence of a *persona moralis*. Such a thing as a single Group-person does not exist at all, even in a fictitious or semi-fictitious form. The one fact is a number of persons; and this number of persons (let us say, *exempli gratia*, 100) are not united in any genuine unity when they act as a group—they are simply collected in an aggregate, as when we collect arithmetical figures in a sum, or algebraical symbols in a bracket. A group of 100 is $1 + 1 + 1$, until we reach the sum 100. The legal instrument of manipulation, for the purpose of collecting a number of individuals in a single aggregate, is contract. It is contract which unites the first individual to the second, the second to the third, and so on to the hundredth individual. We may therefore call this theory a theory of the Collective contract, or again we may call it, as Maitland has done, in the language of mathematical metaphor, the Bracket theory. There is a variant of this theory which at first sight seems not merely a variant, but something totally different, and yet, in reality, rests on the same fundamental basis. This is what Gierke calls the Representative theory. According to this theory a group of 100 persons is something more than 100 persons collected together by contract. It is really 99 represented persons plus a hundredth person who is their representative, and who has been appointed to his position by the act and deed of each of the 99. This representative person carries in himself the persons of the 99: in his person they become one person; and unity thus supervenes, or seems to supervene, on multiplicity. In reality, however, the Representative theory is simply the Collective theory taken at two bites. Contract, and addition of units achieved by process of contract, is still its basis. The 99 first contract, by one sort of contract, with one another; and they then contract, by another sort, with a hundredth person. The whole group of 100 persons remains a contractual group; and although Hobbes, the great apostle of this Representative theory, may argue that his Leviathan is a creative essence of unity, transcending the sphere of contract, Leviathan is himself, after all, included in a contractual bracket, and it is this including bracket of contract which really creates such unity as Leviathan himself appears, but only appears, to provide.

We come to the third of the theories which seek to explain the inner core of legal Group-persons. This is Gierke's own theory—the theory of the reality of the Group-person. When we seek to discover what lies behind the legal Group-person, and constitutes its inner core, we must not talk of 'fictions' which hover in a shadowy and unreal existence above a number of real individuals; we must not talk of 'collections' or 'brackets' or contractual nets, flung over so many individuals to bind them one to another in the bonds of an impersonal nexus. We must purge our eyes to see something which is real and not fictitious—something which has living personality, and is not an impersonal nexus. We must believe that there really exists, in the nature of things itself, such a thing as a real Group-person, with a real being or essence which is the same in kind as that of the individuals who are its members. 'Itself can will, itself can act', in the same way that they will and act. When 100 persons unite to form a group which wills and acts as one, we must say that there is a real new person present—the hundred and first person, the super-person—in which these 100 individuals live and have their being, at the same time that they also continue to live and have their being as so many separate persons. Behind the legal Group-person there is therefore a real Group-being, just as there is a real individual human being behind the individual legal person. Legal group-personality is the shadow cast by real group-personality: it is the reflection of reality in the mirror of law. The law does not write fiction, and it does not do sums in addition, when it introduces its legal Group-persons; it simply paints, to the best of its power, a legal portrait of a real being. This was the view which Gierke sought to express in his rectorial address of 1902 on the 'Nature of Human Groups'. It is best expressed in his own words; and we may therefore quote some essential paragraphs from that address.*

'Do social life-unities actually exist? No direct proof of their existence can be given; but it is equally impossible to prove directly the existence of any individual life-unity. We can furnish, however, an indirect argument for the existence of such unities by pointing to their effects. The cogency of such a method of argument will not be the same for all. Its weight will depend in part on our general attitude to life. But even the foundations of scientific investigation which seem to be fixed most firmly are only, in the last resort, well-grounded hypotheses.

'Primarily, it is our external experience which impels us to assume the existence of active and effective group-unities. We find from our observation of the social processes among which our life is spent—and, above all, from any profound study of the history of humanity—that nations and other communities determine by their activities the balance of forces in our world, and produce our material and spiritual civilisation. Now just because communities are composed of individuals, we must admit that it is in individuals, and through individuals, that these results are produced. But since the contributions of individuals are involved in the social nexus in which they live and move, we must equally acknowledge that individuals are affected by bodily and mental influences which arise from the fact of their connection. We observe, it is true, that certain outstanding individuals intervene creatively, and modify society by something unique which is derived from them and them only. But an achievement of this

* *Op. cit.* pp. 19–22.

nature is only possible when the community, at the very least, co-operates receptively, by appropriating as its own the individual element which has been imported into it. It is possible to hold very different opinions about the extent to which the active force, which has been operative in great transformations of the common life, proceeds from groups or from individuals. But whether we prostrate ourselves in a one-sided worship of "Heroes", or abandon ourselves to an equally one-sided "collective" view of history, we can never be blind to the fact that there is a constant interaction between the two factors. In any case, therefore, the community is something active and effective. Now the effects which we are obliged to ascribe to the community are so constituted, that they cannot be explained as the result of a mere aggregation of individual elements. They cannot be produced separately by separate human beings, in such a way that the total contribution can be regarded as a sum which is similar in kind to the partial contributions, and only greater in degree: they are *sui generis*. We have only to consider phenomena such as the organisation of power, or law, or the social code (*Sitte*), or national economy (*Volkswirthschaft*), or language, in order to realise this fact at once. If this is true of the effects, then it follows that the community which produces them must also be something different from the sum of the individuals who constitute it. It must be a Whole, with a life-unity which is itself super-individual. We do not, therefore, transcend in any way the limits of our external experience, if we argue from the facts of the history of civilisation to the existence of real group-unities. The abstract conception of real group-unity, which we attain by emphasising the efficient cause we have thus discovered, is a conception which we are justified in applying, as an axiomatic scientific conception, in the whole range of the social sciences.

'Our internal experience corroborates the truth which we learn from external experience. We discover the reality of the community in our own inner consciousness, as well as in the world of external fact. The incorporation of our Ego in a social Being of a higher order is a matter of our own inner life. We are conscious of our self as a being enclosed in itself; but we are also conscious of our self as a part of a living whole which is operative in us. If we abstract our membership of our particular nation and State, our religious community and Church, our family and a variety of other groups and associations, we cannot recognise ourselves in the pitiable residue. But if we reflect on all these factors, we see that there is here no question of merely external bonds and fetters by which we are chained. It is a matter of psychical connections which extend down into our inmost being, and constitute integral parts of our spiritual existence. We feel that a part of the impulses which determine our activity proceeds from the communities by which we are permeated. We are conscious that we share in a life of community. If we derive from our internal experience a certainty of the reality of our Ego, this certainty is not limited to the fact of our being an individual life-unity: it also extends to the fact of our being a part-unity within the higher life-unities. It is true that we cannot discover these higher life-unities themselves within our consciousness. The Whole cannot be within us, because we are only parts of the Whole. We can only learn directly from our internal experience the simple fact that group-unities exist: we cannot learn from it directly anything about their character. Indirectly, however, we can deduce, from the effects of communities upon us, the conclusion that social Wholes are of a corporeal-spiritual nature. We can do so because these effects consist of spiritual processes which are corporeally mediated. This is the reason why we speak, not only of social "bodies" and their "members", but also of the folk-soul, folk-feeling, folk-opinion and folk-will—of class-spirit (*Standesgeist*), *esprit de corps*, family-feeling and the like. We use these terms to denote psychical forces with an active life and a reality which are not least present to our consciousness in the very moment when, calling our individuality into play, we rise in revolt against them. In our ordinary daily life any effort of attentive introspection will suffice to convince us of the existence of these spiritual forces. But there are times when the spirit of the community reveals itself to us with an elemental power, in an almost visible shape, filling and mastering our inward being to such an extent that we are hardly any longer conscious of our individual existence, as such. Here, in Berlin, in the Unter den Linden, I lived through such an hour of consecration on the 15th of July, in the year 1870.'*

* On July 13th, William I of Prussia had interviewed the French envoy, Benedetti, at Ems. He sent a telegram describing the events of the 13th to Bismarck. Bismarck published the telegram, in a condensed form which he had prepared for the press. The effect of the publication on German opinion was instantaneous, and produced a profound emotion. It is this emotion which Gierke describes. It is also this emotion which serves for him as evidence of the existence of a spiritual reality, or personality, which transcends the individual.

We have now traversed three territories in our study of the different theories of the Group-person—the territory of the Fiction; the territory of the contractual Collection; the territory of Real Group-personality. Shall we settle down in any of the three, or may we explore still further? Gierke has spoken, in a passage of some irony, of 'the eye resolved upon "reality" which refuses to recognise, in the living and permanent unity of the existence of a People, anything more than an unsubstantial shadow'.* But perhaps the eye which is resolved upon reality—which seeks, in other words, to face the really perceived facts of actual life, and to square its theories with these facts—may discover something which is more than an unsubstantial shadow, and yet less than real Group-personality; something above a fiction or a collection, and yet less than a super-person. If we seek to explore new territory in this spirit, we may begin our argument from a distinction which has already been assumed in a previous passage—the distinction between Society and the State. A Society is a *community* of human beings who seek to fulfil the general purposes of human life in all its aspects. A State is an *association* of the same beings, in legal form, for the specific purpose of regulating human life, in the sphere of external action, by rules designed to secure the minimum of friction between its members and the maximum of their development. The State is a sphere of legal action: we may even call it the scene of a legal drama (a δρᾶμα, involving a common and concerted performance of parts). It is a place of legal actors, all of whom play a rôle, and each of whom may be called a *dramatis persona*. There is a sense in which we may say that all the State is a stage, and all the agents within it are actors. In this sense it may be called artificial, like the stage itself (and yet, like the stage, it holds a mirror up to nature); and in the same sense those who walk across its boards may be called artificial persons.

In order to understand this sense, we must examine the term *persona*. In its original meaning, the word was a term of the theatre. It signified a mask, appropriate to the part performed by him, which was worn by an actor in a play. The usage of the theatre was carried into the law. The agents who played an active part under its scheme, or possessed a capacity for playing such a part, were regarded as having *personae*, and came, by a natural transference, to be called *personae* themselves. Now just as the parts in a play are created and assigned by the dramatist and the pro-

* Cf. *infra*, p. 47.

ducer, so we may hold that *personae* in law are created and assigned by similar agencies—let us say, for the moment, by the legislator and the judge. And just as there is an element of feigning, or even of artificiality, about the parts of a play, so there is also an element of feigning, or even of artificiality, about *personae* in law. They are, in a sense, juridical creations, or artifices, or fictions. The term *persona ficta* is not altogether wrong (though, as we shall see, it is far from being the whole of the truth), if we apply it to *all* forms of legal personality—not only to the legal person of the group, but also to the legal person of the individual. Pufendorf held this doctrine, as we may see from the account which Gierke gives of his views.* One of his disciples, Titius, puts the matter simply, when he says that jurisprudence deals almost exclusively with 'moral persons' (that is to say, artificial persons), whether they are singular or compound—in other words, whether they are individuals or groups. It is not the natural Ego which enters a court of law. It is a right-and-duty-bearing person, created by the law, which appears before the law.

Legal personality, therefore, is a mask, or as Pufendorf says a *modus*, which is created by an agency, and attached by that agency to an object. Two questions thus arise. What is the creating and attaching agency, and by what processes does it act? What are the objects to which the mask is attached?

In general terms, the creating agency which attaches *personae* to objects (or, as a German writer would say, to 'Subjects') is the whole legal association. Every person who is a person in the eye of the law is made such, in the last resort, by that general body. In actual detail, the process of recognition will proceed along various channels. Normally, the regular process will be that of legislation, accompanied and applied by judicial interpretation. But the judge will not necessarily stop at an exact interpretation of the mere letter of existing law. He may recognise legal personality (at any rate when he is dealing with the matter of group-personality) on the ground of analogy, assigning *personae* to bodies which are in an analogous position to those already recognised under existing law. He may give recognition, again, on the ground of custom and usage, arguing, like Julianus in the *Digest*, that *inveterata consuetudo pro lege non immerito custoditur*, and acting on the principle that where a group has been allowed by custom to act as a legal person, it may properly be treated as such by law. One

* *Infra*, pp. 118–119.

State will differ from another in the degree of liberality with which the gift of legal personality is made. States will also differ (when the question is one of Group-personality) in the number of masks or *personae* which they keep, as it were, in stock. One State may only be able to provide the mask of full corporate personality. It may only keep in stock the *persona* of the *universitas*; and since that mask is hard to fit, and not suited for all, such a State may be chary in giving it. Another State may be in the position of a Clarkson's shop: it may be a general repertory of masks; and here Group-persons may abound because there are different forms which they are able to assume. The English State, we may say, has been a State of this latter character. It has not only supplied the mask of the Corporation: it has also furnished the mask (we may even call it, with Maitland, the 'screen', because it conceals a group so thoroughly) of the Trust and its body of trustees. In Germany, when Gierke began to write, the State was less richly equipped: it was thus more chary in giving; and it was also more rigorous in superintending what it had given.

We have dealt with the giving of masks: we have now to deal with the objects to which they are given. So far, we may seem to have simply adopted the Concession theory, which explains Group-personality as the grant of the State, and to have made it even worse by making it cover individual persons as well as the persons of groups. But just as we have argued that there is some truth, though by no means all, in the Fiction theory, so we may also argue that there is some truth (though again it is not the whole of the truth) in the cognate theory of Concession. There is a sense in which all legal personality is a concession made by the State. But having said this we must instantly ask ourselves whether the State is free to choose, at its own discretion, the objects to which it concedes that personality; or whether it is not rather bound, by its own very nature, to concede such personality to certain objects, in virtue of their nature. After all, if masks are to fit and be worn and used, there must be appropriate objects behind them. What is the nature of these objects? And which of them are entitled, in virtue of their proper nature, to claim the award of legal personality?

Historically the State, in dealing with this problem, would seem to have acted with no little arbitrariness. It has been chary of giving legal personality to individuals, as well as to groups. For many centuries slaves had no legal personality. For many centuries

individual, and when it is ascribed, as it is in other cases, to the purpose in pursuing which a number of individuals are joined. We cannot say that legal personality in the one sort of case is an artifice, and in the other not. There is no difference of kind between them—though there may be a difference of degree, and one sort of case may present more of artifice than the other. But we must not unduly labour the notion of artifice. Legal personality is a mental construction; but it is not therefore a fiction. It is a juristic creation—a legally created capacity of sustaining rights and duties, which are also legal creations themselves; but it does not follow that it is not something real. In one sense it is artificial, as all things thought into being by us are artificial. In another and deeper sense it is real, as all things thought into permanent being by us are real. If we ascribe reality to the general body of law, which itself has been thought and willed into permanent being by the mind of man, we must equally ascribe it to the essential elements of law, which have been similarly thought and willed into permanent being by the same agency.

Legal personality is thus a mental construction—but a mental construction which is a fact in our human world, and a real part of our human experience. Being a mental construction, and not an immediate datum of perception or consciousness, it can be imputed by the mind not only to the visible being of an individual, but also to the invisible being of a purpose in the pursuit of which a body of individuals are permanently united. Such a purpose may have property attached to it, and own that property: it may have duties attached to it, and owe those duties; it may be a party to legal action in order to vindicate its property or to suffer vindication of its duties. In all these ways it acts as a *persona juris*; and for all these reasons we may call it a *persona juris*. The essence of the unity of a group is its expressed purpose; and legal personality belongs to that essence. With the individual it is different. The essence of his life-unity is a continuing spring or power of purpose; and that is the essence to which his legal personality belongs.

It may be objected that paradox is running to an extreme when an impersonal purpose is vested with personality. But the purpose is not impersonal. When we say that a purpose may be a legal person, a 'Subject' or owner of rights, we are not saying that the impersonal may put on personality. We are only saying that a purpose which is continuously entertained by many individual persons may enter the legal sphere as a bearer of legal rights and

kinds'; we may even speak of 'national sin'.* Do not our awards of praise and blame imply that we attach moral responsibility to groups, and that we treat them as responsible persons in the usual sense of the word? It is difficult to give any brief answer to such searching questions; but this may be said. Responsibility is a word which is used both in a legal and a moral sense. We have to distinguish carefully between the two senses. Legal responsibility may be fully and absolutely incurred by all groups which act as legal persons—as fully and as absolutely as it is incurred by an individual legal person. It is true that it is not always fully incurred by all such groups under our English system of law. The State itself, when it acts as a legal person, incurs only a modified responsibility if it breaks its contracts, and little if any responsibility if it inflicts a tort or injury. But apart from such exceptions, which it is difficult to defend, we may lay it down that all groups, when acting as legal persons, incur full legal responsibility. It is a very different matter to say that a group incurs, or ever can incur, a moral responsibility. There is no moral being of the group which can be visited with our praise or blame. There is no moral personality of the group which does good, or is responsible for evil. But this is not to say that there is no moral responsibility anywhere. On the contrary, when the action of a group runs contrary to a recognised moral rule, there will be a large area of such responsibility. Those who advised and promoted the action will be morally responsible. Those who supported the action will be morally responsible. Even those who accepted the action, as consenting parties, will also be morally responsible.† Moral responsibility falls only on the individual moral agent. But it falls on him in full measure, alike when he is acting with others and when he is acting alone. It is a dangerous doctrine which would avert it from him, and make it fall on any transcendent being.

From the personality which is psychological, and the personality which is moral, we now turn to that which is legal. This is a personality of a different order. Psychological personality is a datum of immediate perception. Moral personality is a datum of moral consciousness. Legal personality is something which is not a datum. It is a mental construction, or juristic creation. It has, as we have seen, a certain character of artificiality; and it has this character both when it is ascribed, as it is in the vast majority of cases, to an

* Introduction to *Political Theories of the Middle Ages*, pp. xl–xli.
† Cf. Bosanquet, *Philosophical Theory of the State*, pp. 332 ff.

constitutes the legal person. The 'person' which owns the property of an Oxford or Cambridge college is neither the founder, now gone, nor the body of his living successors. It is the purpose which animated the founder and which continues (it may be, as we shall see, in a new and modified form) to animate his successors.

In order to develop and explain this view, it will be well to go back to what has already been said about the different kinds of personality (psychological, moral and legal), and to show the bearing of that distinction upon our present argument. Psychological personality, we have said, is a spring of self-consciousness and a fountain of self-determination by immediate considerations of sense. In the words of Leibniz, which really apply to this species of personality, '*Persona est cujus aliqua voluntas est, seu cujus datur cogitatio, affectus, voluptas, dolor*'.* Such personality is resident only in an individual. He alone is a spring of self-consciousness and a fountain of self-determination. No group has personality in this sense; and if it is this personality which is 'real' personality, no group is a 'real' person.

But there is also moral personality. This is the personality of a moral agent, who acts under a self-imposed moral rule, and who is morally responsible for any offence against that rule. This personality, again, is resident only in an individual. A group is not a moral being in the moral sphere. It is a number of individual moral beings, all acting together for a purpose. That purpose may well be a factor, and a factor of profound influence, in the moral sphere; but the group itself is not a moral person, acting as such in the moral sphere. From the moral point of view we may again say what we said from the psychological—'no group has personality in *this* sense, and if it be *this* personality which is "real" personality, no group is a "real" person'.

This may seem a hard saying, and a saying which contradicts the life and speech of mankind. We speak of the munificence of groups: we find one group recording its gratitude for the munificence of another; and are not munificence, and its sister gratitude, moral attributes, which presuppose the presence of a moral personality?† Again, as we award praise, so we also award blame: we award it, as Maitland has said, 'to group-units of all sorts and

---

* Quoted in W. Wallace, *Lectures and Essays*, p. 273.
† W. M. Geldart, *Legal Personality*, p. 8.

women had an inferior grade of personality. Even to-day the State seems to pick and choose, within certain limits, the persons whom it consents to vest with full legal personality. In France the penalty of 'civil death' may deprive an offender of civil rights, and prevent him from being a person at all in the eye of the law. In other countries the members of a racial minority may be visited with partial deprivation of rights and the partial loss of legal personality. If individuals have thus been treated with some latitude of discretion, we can hardly be astonished if the State has claimed an even greater latitude in the award of legal personality to groups. Far from granting such personality to *all* groups, it has often been tempted to limit it to a few. It has judged the issue of giving or withholding the grant not by the inherent nature or the just claims of the group, but by the prospect of advantage or menace to itself which would follow on the giving or the withholding.

But if history seems to show that the State has exercised a power of selection in the award of legal personality, we need not conclude that the power of selection has been guided by mere discretion, or by mere calculations of self-interest. There has been a principle of selection, determined by the very nature of the State; and this principle has been progressively clarified and extended. The State, we have said, is by its nature an association designed to secure the minimum of friction, and the maximum of development, among all the moral personalities which are members of that association. From this point of view, it will necessarily be guided by a definite principle in selecting the recipients of the guaranteed capacity of action within the scheme of its life which constitutes legal personality. Primarily, it will award legal personality to every individual who possesses moral personality, in the primary and intrinsic sense of that word. Secondly, it will award legal personality to every organising idea, every common purpose, which permanently unites a number of individuals as the common content of their minds and the common intention of their wills, provided that such idea and purpose are compatible, or to the extent that they are compatible, with the free action and development of all members of the State. In the first case, the recipient of legal personality is the individual moral person. In the second, it is not a moral person who is vested with a guaranteed capacity of legal action. Neither is it, strictly speaking, a number of such persons. It is a common and continuing purpose, continuously entertained by a continuing body of persons, which owns the capacity and duties in the same way, and on the same sort of ground, as individuals do. But the purpose must always be entertained by living minds. Otherwise it will be a dead purpose; and a dead purpose is incapable of bearing anything, or of doing anything whatsoever. The Fellows of a College must always continue to entertain the purpose of a college if that purpose is to be a bearer of rights and duties according to the intention of the founder. Of course it is tempting to say that the Fellows themselves, as a body, are the real bearer. But not to speak of the ambiguity of the word 'body' (does it mean a collection of individuals, or something which is somehow more than a collection of individuals?), we should have to qualify this saying at once by adding that the Fellows only constitute a single person, and act as a single bearer of rights and duties, with a part of themselves—that is to say, with the part which entertains and serves the purpose of the College. A person so constituted would be a somewhat abstract person; for it would have to be constituted by abstracting part of the personality of each Fellow and then adding the parts together in some way which was more than simple addition or mere collection. It is really simpler, and it expresses the truth more exactly, to say that the essence of the College consists, and the legal personality of the College resides, in its purpose. The purpose is something total, and something permanent; the Fellows who entertain the purpose only entertain it partially, as one among other guests which are present in their minds, and they only entertain it temporarily, during the days of their fellowship.

Upon this view the life-unity of a group, which may continue from century to century, will involve no idea of an unaging real person which lives that continuous life: it will simply involve the idea of a real purpose, or rather a common purpose, which continuously moves and animates the members of a group, because it is continuously entertained by their minds. Upon such a view, again, we shall not speak of organisms; we shall speak of organisations of men, created and sustained by organising ideas, and continuing to survive so long as these ideas survive.* But ideas, if they are to live, must also change, since change is part of life. Here we encounter a new difficulty, and enter upon a new stage of our

* Gierke often confronts the reader with the dilemma, 'Organism or mechanism—which will you take?' But is there not a *tertium quid*—the organisation of men created and sustained by a common human purpose?

argument. Not only must the organising idea, or common purpose, which constitutes the unity of a group, be entertained by living minds in order that it may live at all: it must also be capable of being modified and developed by those minds, in order that it may live and grow. The purpose, in the process of time, will necessarily enter into new conjunctures of circumstance; and unless there is room and space for its being varied to meet such conjunctures, it may lie like a heavy encumbrance on the general life of the present, and it may even strain to breaking-point the allegiance of many of its own particular votaries. The Scottish Church case, finally decided by the House of Lords in 1904, has often been cited in illustration of this danger. Here a purpose of the Free Church of Scotland, formulated some sixty years before, was decided to be fundamental and unalterable under the constitution of that Church; and this decision, so long as it stood, not only encumbered the general movement of the time towards the union of the Free Church with another of the churches of Scotland on the basis of a developing purpose, but it also split the members of the Free Church into opposing camps—the camp of the few who clung to the original purpose formulated in 1843, and the camp of the many who were anxious to see a development of that purpose. Much was said, in this connection, against 'impersonal immutable purpose'; much was said in favour of the 'personal living group', competent by its nature, as a real personality with a real power of purpose, to develop freely according to the needs of its life. But there is another and simpler moral which we may draw from the case. The real danger is not the conception of purpose: it is the conception of original purpose as fundamental and invariable. The danger partly proceeds from courts of law, which are naturally prone, and indeed are bound, to attach great weight to any original formulation of purpose; but it proceeds far more from the original founders and formulators, who wish to make the purpose, *as they see it*, permanently valid. There is a passion of men, in making wills, to tie up the future. There is a similar passion of founders, in formulating purposes, to do the like.* Wise founders, desiring that the purpose

---

* 'A voluntary society may so fix its articles of faith and conditions of government as to deprive itself of any power of development or change. This has been done by the Free Church of Scotland.... It has also been done more precisely by the Primitive Wesleyan Methodist Society of Ireland, which has put its doctrine, discipline and rules into an Act of Parliament, with a provision that the discipline and rules may be altered in a manner prescribed by the Act, but that the doctrine is not to be altered' (Anson, *Law and Custom of the Constitution*,

they formulate shall live, and recognising that change is part of life, will leave latitude of variation to their successors, who continue to entertain and serve the purpose. Similarly the Courts, in interpreting purpose, may well allow some latitude of development, even if it be not expressly warranted in the original deed. We can hardly expect the State to prohibit the rigid definition of purpose *ab initio*. But the State always stands in reserve to provide a remedy for rigidity, after the event, by its power of legislation. This was the way in which Parliament acted, in its final solution of the Scottish Church case, by the Churches (Scotland) Act of 1905.

We are thus brought to consider, once more, the general relation of the State to the purposes which constitute the being and the unity of groups, and serve as legal persons owning rights and owing duties. We have argued that purposes must necessarily be entertained by individual minds which accept and serve them. We have argued that they must necessarily be variable, in order to suit new conjunctures of circumstance, by the minds which are pledged to their support and think they can support them best by adapting them to new needs. We have now to add that the minds of all the members of the general community, represented in and by the operative criticism of the State, are always playing upon the purposes of groups and the working of these purposes. No common purpose is accepted, and awarded a legal position and a legal personality, simply because it is a common purpose. A common purpose must be weighed and measured, and found to possess some degree of quality. There are some common purposes, such as that of the Mafia, which no State will tolerate. Each common purpose must be compared with other common purposes, and all must be capable of adjustment to one another and of living amicably side by side. All partial common purposes must be set alongside the general common purpose of the State, and must be compatible with the attainment of that sovereign common purpose. This is not to say that the State should, or can, exercise a ubiquitous supervision of groups. It is only to say that it can never abrogate a duty of constructive criticism and sympathetic adjustment. We may well pray

---

Vol. II, c. II, §v). On this basis we may say that the Scottish Church case does not demonstrate the need for a conception of the real personality of the group. It rather demonstrates the weakness of a group which tries to prevent the purpose by which it is constituted from being capable of growth with the growth of the minds of its members.

that groups should abound, each dedicated to its own specific common purpose. The life of man is manifold; and the specific group, dedicated to specific purpose, is an essential element in the development of man's variety. The one State which is also one race, one Church, one party, one economic organisation, is a lonely wilderness. But a State which was a home of real Group-persons, if such a State could be, would also have its defects. It would be far from being a wilderness; but it might well be a chaos. If we desire to escape both wilderness and chaos, we must leave room both for the free clustering of groups round freely formed purposes, and for the criticism and adjustment of such purposes by the State.

The view which has thus been suggested in regard to the inner core of the legal personality of groups is based neither on the ideas of Fiction and Concession, nor on the idea of a Collection or Bracket of individuals, nor on the idea of the Real Personality of the Group. On the other hand it contains elements of all these ideas, and it may help to explain how all these ideas have come to be held. We have allowed some element of fiction, and some element of concession by the State, in the legal personality ascribed to the purpose of a group; but we have also allowed the same elements in the legal personality ascribed to the individual. We have admitted that a sum or collection of individuals must entertain the common purpose, and must also have the power of developing that purpose; but we have also admitted that the common purpose is a permanent unity which transcends the collection of individuals who are united in its service. We have denied that there is a real Group-person, in any way parallel to a real individual person, behind the legal personality of a group; but we have argued that a real purpose, analogous to the individual's real power of purpose, must underlie such personality—and in that sense we too may claim to be 'Realists'. At the end of our argument we are left with a legal world in which there move two sorts of legal persons—the individual legal person, with a legal personality based on the power of purpose which constitutes the essence of an individual; and the group legal person, with a legal personality based on the permanent purpose which constitutes the essence of a group. The two sorts of person differ, in as far as the basis of the one is a power of indeterminate purpose, and the basis of the other is a declared and determinate purpose. But it is not an absolute difference, and both sorts of persons can move easily in the same world. The power of indeterminate purpose in the individual is limited by his previous declarations of purpose; and the determinate purpose of the group must always, as we have seen, be compatible with its further growth and development.

All this might seem mere logomachy, a contention about words and a tilting at windmills, if it were not the case that the theory of the real personality of groups ran outside the domain of doctrine, and spilled into the general life and thought of the world outside. So far as Gierke's own theory stands, considered in itself, it is as if he had said to the world of scholars, 'Eureka: I have found the hidden reality which lies behind this puzzling Group-person of the law; and the reality is that of a real person, who is real in the same sort of way as you and I are real'. That saying, in itself, is a matter of high doctrine: it is a philosophical explanation of a legal fact, intended for those who study the philosophy of law. But the world outside, hearing the reverberations of legal philosophy, adopts the term 'real Group-personality' into its own language; it gives it a new and positive sense; and it proceeds to draw practical conclusions from the positive sense which it gives to the term. Adapting to our purposes a saying of Luther, we may say that 'the doctrine comes to the ordinary man ghostly' (and we may also add, for reasons which we shall presently see, that it comes to him qualified), 'and he makes it fleshly'. In other words, men apply the conception of real Group-personality to their own particular group —their Church, their profession, Trade Union, whatever the society be that engages their immediate ardour; and then, feeling that real persons must enjoy rights, but forgetting (or tending to forget) that they must also owe obligations, they become the prophets of the rights, and not only of the rights, but also of the autonomy, and even, in the last resort, of the sovereignty, of their own particular group. This is the way of syndicalism; and Gierke's doctrine—at any rate in our own country, and since Maitland first gave it vogue in 1900—has been drawn into that way. We must not be pragmatical, nor judge the truth of a doctrine by the uses to which it is subsequently put. But at any rate we may examine the company which it keeps, and if we are already inclined to question its truth on fundamental and essential grounds, we may perhaps find that the results of such examination serve to corroborate our doubts.

Syndicalism is a theory of French parentage. In its more extreme form, it is a theory which would eliminate the State in favour of groups—economic groups—on the ground that economic groups are anterior, and should be superior, to political organisation, and that *droit économique* is similarly anterior, and should be similarly superior, to *droit politique*. In its more moderate form, it is a theory of *condominium* between the State and groups, on the basis of some system of 'plural' sovereignty which will divide its attributes between both. Neither in its more extreme nor in its more moderate form has it found acceptance in England. But there has been some approximation to it; and we find such an approximation in the writings of Dr Figgis, and particularly perhaps in his *Churches in the Modern State*, published in 1913. Here the authority of Gierke is invoked to support a line of theory which runs counter to the idea of the unitary State and the unity of its sovereignty. Starting from a deep conviction of the spiritual independence of the Church, Dr Figgis proceeds to a general doctrine of the 'inherent, self-developing life' of all societies. He regards the general community as 'a vast hierarchy of interrelated societies, each alive, each personal'; and he seeks to vindicate for each of these societies 'the necessary independence of a self-developing personality'. The Church is foremost in his thought; but he seeks to link the cause of the Church with the cause of groups in general—groups economic and national as well as ecclesiastical. He rejects what he calls 'the old conception of the position of corporate groups in the State', because in his view it is false to the general facts of the world. 'It makes the world consist of a mass of self-existing individuals on the one hand and an absolute State on the other; whereas it is perfectly plain to anybody who truly sees the world that the real world is composed of several communities, large and small, and that a community is something more than the sum of persons composing it—in other words, it has a real personality, not a fictitious one. This is the essence of what is true in modern nationalism, and in the claims for the rights of Churches and of Trade Unions.'*

Now it is only just to Gierke to begin by admitting that such an interpretation of his views (which, by the way, is by no means peculiar to Dr Figgis) is really alien to the logic of his general theory. He was a good German and a thorough Germanist, whose thought had already been fixed in all its main lines by 1880. Syndicalism in any form, whether moderate or extreme, was a thing beyond his ken. He accepted the German system of territorial churches, as it stood in his day; he accepted the economic organisation of contemporary German society. He was anxious,

* *Op. cit.* p. 250, in an essay containing a study of Maitland.

Translator's Introduction

as a lawyer, that corporate bodies in Germany should be based on the Germanist tradition of law, and not on the Romanist; but the bodies of which he thought belonged to a traditional past, and not to a revolutionary future. They were *Gemeinde* and *Genossenschaften*, steeped in the national history of the German people, and therefore belonging by right of descent to the national law of the German State. The affinities of Gierke are not with Duguit, the legal philosopher of French syndicalism: they are with Herder, the harbinger of German Romanticism. The figure of the *Volk* remains in the background of his thought; and the majority of the *Volk* is incarnate in a State which remains sovereign, even if it recognises that there are other group-realities besides itself. Are not these other beings parts of the Folk-whole; and must they not find their life in the higher life in which they are necessarily included? The State, to Gierke, is 'elevated above all groups by its sovereign plenitude of power' (*seine souveräne Machtvollkommenheit*).* The authority of the State is 'the highest right upon earth'.† The law of the State exerts a far greater control over the legal group than over the individual. 'The legal scheme, in dealing with groups, does not stop, as it does in dealing with individuals, at rules of external conduct. It also controls and penetrates their inner life....The group, in contrast to the individual, must necessarily be a form of life in which the relation of the unity of the whole to the multiplicity of the parts is amenable to regulation by external norms for human wills.'‡

It is easy to realise, from passages such as these, that Gierke's doctrine of the real personality of groups is, as we have already observed, a rarified and a qualified doctrine. But it is also easy to see how the rarity and the qualifications may be forgotten. Men sometimes think and write to other consequences than those which they have themselves intended. A fate of this order seems to have befallen the theory and writings of Gierke. He himself insisted on the need for the articulation of contained groups in the containing State; he regarded the life of the lower groups as necessarily integrated in that of the higher. Yet if he thus believed in the necessity of a higher Whole, which included all lesser wholes as its parts and members, he taught after all a doctrine of the real and inherent personality of groups in general. Now if we concentrate

---

* *Das Wesen der menschlichen Verbände*, p. 29.
† *Ibid*. p. 28.
‡ *Ibid*. pp. 5, 12; cf. also p. 25.

our attention on that doctrine in itself, and if, in addition, we proceed to confine its benefits to groups other than the State, we can easily glide into a form of syndicalism. It will not be true to the mind of the master; but it will have a sort of rough verisimilitude. We can then say that we have quitted an abstract and unreal world of self-existing individuals and the absolute State; we can then proclaim our entry into a concrete and real world of real groups, with a real State conditioned by their inherent rights; and we can then plead that Gierke's writings provide an historico-philosophical justification of this new world.

But this is not the whole of the matter. The theory of the real personality of groups may not only trend towards syndicalism. It may also keep other company; and it may trend towards that very doctrine of the absolute State from which it is supposed to be our rescue. We can only make the theory a defence and buttress against the State if we suppose that it does not apply to the State, and if we say that there is no real person standing behind the State, as there is behind other groups. But are we justified in making that supposition? We can hardly say that we are. On the contrary, if we once accept the theory of the real personality of groups, we are bound to see behind the State the figure of the greatest and the most real of all groups—the figure of the nation and Folk itself. The theory presents us, after all, with two sorts of real Group-persons. One of these is the real person of the *Volk*, with its own *Volksseele* and its own *Volksleben*. The other is the real person of the contained group.* Gierke himself may seek to comprehend both sorts of real persons in a synthesis which does justice to both. But the two sorts will always tend to break apart, and each of them will then seek to claim a separate and sovereign existence. If the claim of groups other than the State is heard and accepted, the result will be some form of syndicalist philosophy. If the claim of the great national group, incarnate in the national State, calls aloud with a greater and more resonant voice, the result will be some form of absolutist or dictatorial politics. And of the two results it is the latter which is the more to be apprehended.

It often seems as if the theory of the real personality of groups

* It will be noticed that Dr Figgis, in the passage quoted above, speaks of the theory of real Group-personality as 'the essence of what is true in modern nationalism, and in the claims for the rights of Churches and of Trade Unions'. Perhaps he was thinking of the claims of national minorities when he used the phrase 'modern nationalism'. But the phrase may equally apply to the claims of a national majority to control the whole of life.

were advocated with a sort of tacit exception—as though it did not apply to the State; as though it were something external to it, which served to limit and tame it. But if the theory be true at all, must it not be true of the State—and true of the State above all? Is it not the peculiar danger of the theory that it may tend, in the last resort, to attach itself to the figure of the State with a particular fascination? The Nation, at any rate when it is organised and expressed in a national State, is a great and obvious group. If we make groups real persons, we shall make the national State a real person. If we make the State a real person, with a real will, we make it indeed a Leviathan—a Leviathan which is not an automaton, like the Leviathan of Hobbes, but a living reality. When its will collides with other wills, it may claim that, being the greatest, it must and shall carry the day; and its supreme will may thus become a supreme force. If and when that happens, not only may the State become the one real person and the one true group, which eliminates or assimilates others: it may also become a mere personal power which eliminates its own true nature as a specific purpose directed to Law or Right. If personal power should thus shed purpose, an old saying of Luther may be repeated, with a new application, '*Die Person wird euch nichts helfen, wenn euch das Recht verdampt*'.*

The experience of our own day goes to corroborate such hypothetical fears. Italy has embraced the theory of real Group-personality, 'the organism superior to the individuals of whom it is composed'. The Corporative State is a structure of many elements. It is not always clear which of them are intended to act, and which are intended to be the simulacrum of action. But there seems to be little personality, and no autonomy, in the corporate groups contained in the Italian State; and if we read *La Dottrina del Fascismo* we can hardly doubt that the one Group-person which is really intended to act is the Italian nation as 'integrally realised' in the Fascist State of Italy. 'The higher personality (*personalità superiore*) is that of the Nation...The Fascist State, synthesis and unity of all values, interprets, develops and actuates the whole of the life of the People....For Fascism the State is an absolute, in whose presence individuals and groups are the relative....It is *anima dell' anima...realtà etica...voluntà etica universale*.'†

---

* Quoted in W. Wallace, *Lectures and Essays*, p. 269.

† Benito Mussolini, *La Dottrina del Fascismo*, 1932 (reprinted from the article in the *Enciclopedia Italiana*). The quotations are mainly taken from the more philosophic Part I.

Of the new Germany which came into existence in 1933 it is perhaps premature to write. *Incedimus per ignes*. But this may be said. The home of groups and *Genossenschaften* is going through a great process of *Gleichschaltung*—a process by which they are all being 'assimilated' to the new character now assumed by the person of the *Volk*, as organised and incarnate to-day in the National Socialist State. The assimilation of groups to this person has touched and transformed churches and trade unions: it has swept like a deluge over the old territorial communities and the political parties of Germany; it has modified, where it has not abolished, the whole of what Gierke would call the corporate articulation of the State. It would be wrong to draw permanent conclusions from what may be only a temporary phase of revolutionary ardour. But so far as the evidence goes, it suggests a simple reflection. When the idea of the real person of the Nation, organised in a national State, obtains the victory, in an hour of revolution, the groups in the State are abolished or altered with the alteration of the times. The ideas on which they rest, and the purposes which are their essence, are swept away or refashioned. We may deprecate the victorious idea of the State: we may say that it means a sacrifice of *Recht* on the altar of *Volkstum* and the personal *Volk*: we may urge that it means a surrender of fixed purpose to oscillating personality; but we have to admit, in one respect, the vigour and sweep of its action. Germany herself, the ancient mother of groups, has demonstrated to the world—at any rate for the time being—that the groups contained in the State are simply purposes, and not real persons, and that these purposes can be re-fashioned, or even abrogated, when the hour of revolution strikes, by the State in which they are contained. All revolutions have something of a similar character. They shake and test men's common purposes. Some, like leaves, come fluttering to the ground; some remain, but change their colour and their nature. It is not that real Group-persons have died, or changed the nature of their personality. It is simply that common purposes have been shaken in the minds of those who held them; and some have changed, and some—because they have ceased to be held with the tenacity which alone will suffice to preserve their existence—have disappeared.

But do we then leave the State surviving as the one omnipotent real person, which shakes all the trees but stands itself unmoved? The whole of our argument forbids. The State, on our general theory of purpose, is not an ultimate or absolute person, which can do or omit to do what it chooses at its will. It is a group or association; and it stands on the same footing as other groups or associations. Its essence or being consists in its purpose, just as the essence or being of all other groups consists in their purpose. Not only is purpose the essence of the groups contained in the State: it is also the essence of the State itself. When we are speaking of the relation of the State to groups, we are speaking of the relation of one common purpose to a number of other such purposes. The characteristic of the purpose of the State is that it is a specific purpose of Law. Other purposes, so far as they concern or affect this purpose, must necessarily be squared with it. This is the same as to say that other groups, so far as they hold or assume a legal position, must necessarily be adjusted to the legal group which we call the State. They are not thereby adjusted to its will: they are adjusted to its purpose, which is Law. The State would be failing to attain its purpose, and thereby to discharge its duty, if it failed to secure such adjustment. But the adjustment is not a matter of discretion, and it is not absolute: it is controlled by the purpose of the State, and it is relative to that purpose. To reject the theory of the real personality of groups is not to fall into any worship of the omnicompetent or absolute State. It is to find the essence of the State in its purpose of Law, and to subject it to its purpose, just as we find the essence of other groups also in their particular purpose, and just as we make them too the servants and ministers of their purpose. Only if we make the State, like every other group, a common purpose, and not a real Group-person, shall we escape the tyranny of mere will. Purpose is something specific; and if we are face to face with a State which is specific purpose, we are face to face with the finite. In a word, we see and accept the sovereignty of Law—both the law of the Constitution, which expresses the fundamental purpose on which the State is based, and the ordinary law of the courts, duly made in accordance with the Constitution, which expresses that purpose in detail, through the various ranges of human life, in all the area of external conduct amenable to its control.

§ 6

THE TRANSLATION

It remains in conclusion to say some technical words (which must also be, in large measure, words of apology) in regard to the nature of the translation which is offered to the reader. It has proved difficult, and indeed impossible, to put Gierke's thought into an English style which would seem natural and easy to English readers. I have taken the liberty of breaking up many of the long paragraphs of the original; but I have been careful, in doing so, only to make a break where some transition of thought, or some new phase in the development of the argument, permitted it to be made. I have also added headings and sub-headings, both in the text and the analytical summary, in order to make reference easier; and I have appended, by the side of the more important notes, a brief marginal indication of their contents. Occasionally, where a technical point seemed to need elucidation, or some comment or paraphrase seemed likely to be of service, a footnote has been added, or some few words, enclosed in square brackets, have been included in the actual text. In some few cases, too, I have added some remarks, similarly enclosed in square brackets, to Gierke's footnotes, partly in order to give references to new works which have appeared since he wrote, and partly with the object of suggesting some different view of the evidence which he quotes, or some different interpretation of a theory which he describes. If such additions seem to the reader, or to the student of Gierke's original German, more numerous than they need have been, the translator would apologise for his excess of zeal.

Two main additions have been made which it is hoped may prove of service. One is an index of some of the main subjects, and some of the main writers, treated in the volume. It might well have been fuller than it is; but while an author may index his own volume on his own scheme, a translator is bound to walk warily. The other addition is that of a new bibliography. Gierke had prepared and printed a list of the main writers whose works he had used in writing the sections which deal with the period from 1650 to 1800. There was no similar list of the main writers whose works he had used in writing the sections which deal with the period from 1500 to 1650. I have therefore selected what seemed to me the main writers of this period (sometimes including, for some particular reason, a less considerable writer); and I have thus added a second bibliography, on the same lines as that which is given by Gierke himself. In addition, as many of the names to which Gierke refers in his own bibliography are little known, if known at all, to most English students, I have occasionally added to his text some brief account, in two or three lines, of the *curriculum vitae* of an author. I have marked by square brackets the passages of this nature which have been added.*

I may end by making two confessions. I am the more bold to make them, because they have already been made by Maitland, at the end of his Introduction. In the first place, I have not attempted to check or verify Gierke's quotations. As Maitland wrote, 'I have thought it best to repeat Dr Gierke's references as I found them and not to attempt the perilous task of substituting others'. I confess that I began to make the attempt. I checked Gierke's references to the *Vindiciae contra Tyrannos* by my own copy, which is the original edition of 1579. But I found that he had used another edition (that of 1631): I soon realised that, though some of his references seemed to me dubious, I could not readily set them right; I said to myself, *Periculosae plenum opus aleae*; and I desisted from a work which I saw stretching out indefinitely before me, with little or nothing gained at the end, since the very few changes that I might have been able to make would hardly have made an iota of difference.

In the second place I would confess once more at the end of this introduction, as I have already done at the beginning, that I cannot be sure that I have rendered faithfully the exact sense of many of the German terms. Here, once more, I may quote some words of Maitland: 'The task of translating into English the work of a German lawyer can never be perfectly straightforward. To take the most obvious instance, his *Recht* is never quite our *Right* or quite our *Law*'. I confess that I found *Recht* even more difficult

---

* The translator is also bound to mention that he has changed the order in which the writers appear in Gierke's own bibliography. There they are printed in chronological order. The translator, finding from his own experience the difficulty of referring to a list of names so printed, has substituted an alphabetical order for the convenience of the reader.

than Maitland suggests. Not only does it mean something which is neither exactly our Right nor exactly our Law: it also means something which is like our 'rights', and yet not exactly the same. *Recht*, to the German writer, is not only something 'objective', in the sense of a body of rules (either natural or positive) which is in one way or another obligatory: it is also something 'subjective', in the sense of a body of rights belonging to a person or 'Subject' as his share in (or perhaps we should rather say his position under) the system of 'objective' Right. If *Recht* was thus troublesome, *Naturrecht*, and its adjective *naturrechtlich*, were even more so. Maitland was so much troubled by the adjective that he invented the English term *nature-rightly*. I found myself shy of that term, and I have translated Gierke's *die naturrechtliche Gesellschaftslehre* as 'the natural-law theory of Society'. But I know that I have not exactly hit the mark. As Maitland says, 'a doctrine may be *naturrechtlich* though it is not a doctrine of Natural Law nor even a doctrine about Natural Law'.

To meet such difficulties, I have put the German equivalent in the text, by the side of the English word, wherever I thought that the reader would like to know what it was, and I have added an explanatory footnote wherever I thought that it was necessary. But that is far from solving all difficulties. A word in one language has a variety of connotations, which it may not have in another. *Gesellschaft*, for instance, means both Society at large, and the sort of particular society which is a partnership or company or *societas*. Our English 'society' will not do the same work; and I have had to translate *Gesellschaft* differently in different places. *Verein* is more like our English 'society', and I have translated it accordingly. *Verband* I have generally translated by the term 'group'; but for *die engeren Verbände* I have used the term 'associations', which seems to correspond best to Gierke's meaning. But there is a plethora of 'group' terms in Gierke's vocabulary, as we should naturally expect in the writer of a *Genossenschaftsrecht*; and to distinguish their shades of meaning, and to find their English equivalents, is as delicate a matter as the matching of fine colours. I have left *Genossenschaft* as 'fellowship', following good authority. *Anstalt* and *Stiftung*, Maitland has said, find their best correspondent in the English term 'charity'; but I have been driven to translate the one as 'institution', and the other as 'foundation'. Let me conclude by begging the reader to remember that in Gierke's sense 'collective' and 'individual' are the same thing, or rather, two different aspects of the same thing. For 'collective' is not connected for him with the notion of Collectivism, but with that of a mere collection of individuals; and any 'collective' view is thus an individualistic view, which stands in diametrical opposition to his own central principle of real Group-personality.

E. B.

September 1933

THE THEORY OF
STATE & CORPORATION IN MODERN TIMES
DOWN TO 1650 IN GENERAL AND
DOWN TO 1800 IN REGARD TO NATURAL LAW

ANALYTICAL SUMMARY

ANALYTICAL SUMMARY

CHAPTER I

THE PERIOD DOWN TO THE MIDDLE OF THE SEVENTEENTH CENTURY

[The first four sections of this chapter, with their subsections, have dealt with (I) the later history of the medieval theory of the Corporation, (II) the theory of the Corporation in legal practice, (III) the influence of 'elegant' jurisprudence, and (IV) the influence of the study of German public law. Then follows the final section (V) of the chapter, with its two subsections, §14 and §15.]

SECTION V

THE INFLUENCE OF THE NATURAL-LAW THEORY OF SOCIETY

§§ 14 and 15

CHAPTER I: SECTION V, § 14

THE NATURAL-LAW CONCEPTION OF THE STATE

[The divisions of this subsection are not Gierke's own: they are due to the translator.]

I. *General view of Natural Law*

1. Natural Law as an independent system, distinct from the civilian and canonist body of doctrine, 35. The profound importance of the natural-law theory of the State, 35. Its connection with historical events, 35. Its radical tendency, 35; and its practical objects, 35.

2. The influence of the connection between legal philosophy and political theory in determining the external form of the natural-law theory of the State, 36. The system of political theory based on the law of Reason in the ecclesiastical writers on Natural Law, 36. The culmination of that system in Suarez, 36. The construction by Grotius of a general secular philosophy of law covering the whole area of political life, 36. The 'political' literature proper, 36. The connection between political theory and general public law (*Staatsrecht*), 36. Political treatises independent of Natural Law, 36. The victory of the natural-law theory of the State in Bodin's theory of sovereignty, 37. The controversy between the writers who advocate popular sovereignty and those who advocate the sovereignty of the Ruler on the basis of Natural Law, 37. The *Politica* of Althusius, 37. His successors, 37. Besold's peculiar combination of a natural-law view of the State with an historico-legal view, 37. The crucial importance of Hobbes, 37.

3. The reasons for the increasing influence of Natural Law on public law, 37. The development of a clearer conception of the relation between natural and positive law in the jurisprudence of the civilians, 38. The division of law in general into *jus naturale, jus gentium* and *jus civile*, and the subdivision of these, in connection with previous medieval theories, 38. The relation of *jus publicum* to these divisions, 38. The severance of *jus gentium* from *jus publicum*, and the dichotomy of law into natural and positive, 38. The development of a pure theory of Natural Law, 38. New conception of *jus gentium* as international law, 39. Natural Law as the pre-political source and indestructible basis of civil society and political authority, 39. The superiority of Natural Law to positive law which is entailed thereby, 39. The extent and the bearing of such superiority in the field of public law, 39. The irrefragable rule of Reason as the canon of all existing institutions, 39. The finding of a rational ideal for the efforts of all reformers, 39.

4. The theories of the nature of the State developed upon this basis, if opposed to one another, have one thing in common—they all depart from the medieval theocratic conception of the State, 40. The exploration of the State in the light of its own nature, 40.

II. *General view of Sovereignty in natural-law theory*

1. The resultant characteristics of the prevalent conception of the State—(1) human community and (2) sovereign authority, 40. After Bodin the characteristic of sovereignty is primarily emphasised, 40. The conception of sovereignty in natural-law theory, 40. The transformation of an originally negative to a positive conception, 41. Differences of opinion in regard to the extent and the content of sovereignty, 41. They are the result of different conceptions of the end of the State, more especially as between ecclesiastical and secular theories, 41. Different ideas in regard to the [legal] limits of sovereignty, 41; and in regard to its division, its multiplication and its limitations, 41. General agreement, notwithstanding, that sovereignty is an inherent and indestructible original right of the State, which includes all rights of authority whatsoever, 41.

2. The controversy about the 'Subject' or owner of sovereignty under Natural Law, 42. The problem separated from the question of the different forms of the State, 42. The question of the position of the People and the Ruler, 43. The transference to the Republic of ideas originally developed in reference to Monarchy, both among the advocates and among the opponents of monarchical absolutism, 43. The division of the natural-law theory of the State into theories (*a*) of Popular Sovereignty and (*b*) of the Sovereignty of the Ruler, 43. Intermediate theory (*c*) of 'double majesty', 43. In addition, various refinements of these main theories, as determined by the attitude adopted towards the problem of the limits of sovereignty, 43. Only in the third place [i.e. after the questions have been treated (1) whether the 'Subject' of sovereignty is People or Ruler or both, and (2) whether refine-

Analytical Summary

ments of these notions of the 'Subject' are necessitated by a theory of the limits of sovereignty] do the further questions arise (a) of the relation of positive law to the more exact determination of the 'Subject' of Ruling authority, and (b) of the divisibility of ruling authority either in its substance or (short of that) in its exercise, 43.

III. *People and Ruler as separate personalities*

1. General recognition of the People as a personality until the time of Hobbes, 44. A basis found for such recognition in the theory of Contract, 44. The People as a merely 'collective' personality [i.e. a 'bracket' including a sum of individuals, but not an 'organic' unity], 45. This [collective conception] also appears in the systems of thought which seek to apply the ideas and rules of the [Roman-law] theory of Corporations to the question, 45. The People regarded as a *societas civilis*, 45. The attempts made—particularly by the ecclesiastical exponents of the philosophy of law, Molina and Suarez—to attain the conception of a self-subsistent popular community, notwithstanding this individualist point of view, 46. The conclusions drawn from the 'social' [i.e. partnership] nature of the State, 46. The combination [of the idea of the State as a 'society' or partnership of individuals] with a corporate point of view, in Althusius and Grotius, 46. None the less, the 'collective' point of view triumphs, 46. The relation of the Ruler to the ruled considered as a result of the antithesis of *omnes ut universi* and *omnes ut singuli*, 47. The common will and the agreed will of all individuals, 47. Requirement in principle of unanimity [i.e. the agreed will of all individuals], 47. Identification of majority-will with the group-will by means of a fiction, 47. The possibility of Representation of the group based upon similar foundations [i.e. upon an agreement of all, fictitiously assumed to be present], 47. Reservation of the rights of the popular community itself as against its representatives, 48.

2. A separate personality is generally recognised as also belonging to the Ruler, 48. It is recognised even by the theory of popular sovereignty, 48. The different nature of the personality of the Ruler under different constitutions, 48. (a) When a number of persons are vested with the right of Ruling by a given constitution, the conception of 'collective' personality is again applied [i.e. the People *qua* Ruler, just as much as the People *qua* People, is regarded as a collection of individuals], 49. The unity of the personality of the Ruler even when there is such a system of the Rule of Many, 49. The relation of the ruled to the Ruling body in aristocracy and in democracy, 49. The identification of the majority with the whole body, 49. (b) A single person as the 'Subject' or owner of Ruling authority, 49. Interpretation of the right of the Ruler as being of the nature of an independent right of the monarch, regarded as a natural person, 49. The right of the Ruler only distinguished from the sphere of his private rights 'objectively' [i.e. by the difference of the 'objects' to which it relates], 49. Occasional appli-

cation of the idea of a double personality of the monarch, 50. The point of view of the private law of inheritance applied to the succession to the throne, 50. Grotius, 50.

IV. *Attempts to eliminate the dualism of People and Ruler*
The idea of a single State-personality

1. The tendency of the theory of Natural Law to work out the idea of a single State-personality in place of the dualism of the two personalities of People and Ruler, 50. As a result of its individualistic point of view, however, all that it achieves is an exaggeration of one or other side of the dualism—i.e. an exaggeration either of the personality of the People, or of that of the Ruler, 50.

The relics of the organic conception of the State [surviving from classical and medieval times] still to be found in Natural Law, 50. The comparison with the human body, 51.

The juristic result of this comparison, 51. The idea of the social organism, even among the advocates of the theory of Contract, 51. This idea particularly present in Molina and Suarez, 51. The *corpus symbioticum* of Althusius, 51. The organic unity of the State in Grotius, 51. None of these systems of thought achieves recognition of a ruling State-personality as the true 'Subject' or owner of political rights, 52. The supposed organism proves in the last resort to be only a mechanism, 52. The conscious development of a mechanical conception in Hobbes, 52. The conception of the unity of the State-personality could thus be only attained by an exclusive attribution of it to one or the other element of the body politic [Ruler or People], 52.

2. The theory of popular sovereignty is marked by an attempt to elevate the personality of the People to the position of the one and only 'Subject' of political rights, 53. Identification of People and State in the writings of the *Monarchomachi*, 53. To maintain the complete identity of the personality of the People and that of the State proves, however, impossible, in view of the fact that the Ruler is simultaneously acknowledged to be an independent bearer of authority, 53. The dualism of 'persons' cannot be transcended so long as the theory of a contract of government is the basis of argument, 53. It is only when this theory has been entirely eliminated that (1) the idea of the Ruler's personality can be dropped, and (2) the personality of the State can be confined altogether within the limits of the community of individuals, 53. No thinker previous to Rousseau goes to this extreme of Radicalism, 54.

3. The advocates of a 'double sovereignty' also really identify the State and the People, 54. Their distinction between *majestas realis* and *majestas personalis* equally fails, therefore, to produce any recognition of a single State-personality, 54. The relation of these two sovereignties to one another, on the basis of the theory of Contract, 54. Superiority accorded to the *majestas realis* of the People, 54. The results of according that superiority, 54. At the same time the Ruler is regarded as having an independent right to the exercise of *majestas personalis*, 55. Different views in regard to the delimitation of the rights of the Ruler, 55.

Analytical Summary

4. Grotius' theory of the double 'Subject' of sovereignty, 55. The State regarded as the *subjectum commune*, and the Ruler as the *subjectum proprium*, 55. None the less, in spite of this apparently unambiguous formulation of the sovereignty of the State, Grotius also fails, as the result of his individualistic point of view, to attain any recognition of a single State-personality, 55. His 'collective' view of *populus* and *universitas* [as mere aggregates of individuals], 56. The consequent defects of his interpretation of State-sovereignty, 56. At bottom, Grotius only regards the sovereignty of the State as a sort of continuation, and that merely in idea, of the [original] sovereignty of the People, 56. The conclusions which follow, as regards the continuity of the State when the form of its constitution changes, 56. The distinction between the political and the juristic view of the State [note 124]. The *subjecta propria*, 56. In a given State, the People may be, at one and the same time, both *commune* and *proprium subjectum*, 57. Conversely, the Ruler may have acquired full and complete sovereignty, and possess such sovereignty as his *patrimonium*, 57. As a rule, however, there continue to exist reserved rights of the popular community to participate in the control of the State, 57. The Ruler regarded as the usufructuary, and the People as the owner, of political authority and the territory and property of the State, 57. Further limitations upon the Ruler, in virtue of particular rules of the constitution, 57. The possibility of a *forma mixta*, with complete division of sovereignty as between the Ruler and the People, 58. The failure of Grotius' theory of sovereignty to achieve a permanent hold, 58.

5. The theory of the advocates of the Sovereignty of the Ruler, which makes his personality the one and only active 'Subject' in political life, 58. But so long as they acknowledge the existence of a personality of the People, the upholders of this view also fail to attain the idea of a single State-personality, 58. All modifications of the Ruler's sovereignty simply issue in the doctrine that the People as a personality has a share in the activity of the State, 58. (1) When the doctrine is held—as it is, more especially, by the ecclesiastical writers on Natural Law—that there are inalienable popular rights derived from the very essence of the State, the body of the ruled assumes to a larger extent the character of a definite State-personality, 59. (2) The theory of a conditional contract of government [i.e. a contract in which there is not an absolute surrender to the Ruler] produces similar results, 59. (3) Among the advocates of a mixed constitution the personality of the Ruler itself is bifurcated [i.e. not merely is there a dualism between it and the personality of the People outside it, but there is also a dualism inside it], and political authority is actually divided, or at any rate shared in common, 59. In opposition to such tendencies, the strictly absolutist systems of political thought are directed to a concentration of State-personality in a single person, either individual or collective, 59. The views of Bodin, 59. Even in Bodin, however, and also in other absolutist thinkers, there is a recognition of the personality of the People as existing side by side with that of the Ruler, 59. The terms *respublica* and *civitas* in the writings of Arnisaeus, 60.

6. Hobbes is the first thinker to transcend this dualism completely, 60. His view of the one original contract, 60. He acknowledges no rights of the People, 60; and no contract between the Ruler and the People, 60. His belief in the total sovereignty of the Ruler in all forms of State, 60. His rejection of a mixed form of State, 60. The visible manifestation of the Ruler's personality, in a single man or in an assembly, 60. The concentration of the personality of the State in this personality of the Ruler, as based on a political contract according to Natural Law, 60. The People without a Ruler is in no way a *universitas*, but only a 'multitude', 61. The Ruler as the only mind of the State, 61. The personality of the State (*persona civitatis*) is thus made the core of public law, 61. Theories which are similar, if not so logically developed to their conclusions, in Graszwinkel and Salmasius [note 159].

The relation of the theory of Hobbes to natural-law individualism, 61. The importance of his theory of the unitary personality of the State in the further development of the natural-law theory of the State, 61.

CHAPTER I: SECTION V, §15

THE NATURAL-LAW THEORY OF ASSOCIATIONS
(*DIE ENGEREN VERBÄNDE*)

The influence of the natural-law conception of the State on the theory of other groups (1) through its theory of Sovereignty, and (2) through its theory of Contract, 62.

I. GROUPS WITHIN THE STATE

(1) *The unitary or centralist interpretation*

The local communities and corporate bodies contained in the State differ generally from it in not possessing any sovereignty, 62. But the development of the theory of sovereignty none the less determined the extent to which a community-life of their own could be preserved for these bodies, 62.

In general [a centralist view prevails, that is] we find a refusal to allow that local communities and corporate bodies have a social existence of their own, 62. Reluctance to admit the natural-law origin of these groups, 63. Thus, the theory of the organic [or natural] origin of the State recognises an ascending series of groups [culminating in the State], but regards the Family as the only one of these groups which is a naturally given unit, 63. The division of the Family into the three domestic societies—husband and wife; parents and children; master and servants, 63. The Family as the immediate basis of the State, 63. Communities and corporate bodies, on the other hand, are regarded as formations within the State which are not a necessity of nature, but a creation of positive law, 63. The theory of a Social Contract is even more definitely adverse [than the theory of the natural origin of the

Analytical Summary

State] to any recognition of the State as a Whole which is organised in corporate bodies on the basis of Natural Law, 64. The result is that groups have no clearly defined sphere of rights as against either the State or the Individual, 64.

[a] As concerns the relation of groups to the State, the absolutist theory of sovereignty refused to admit the existence of any independent social authority other than that of the State in the domain of public law, 64. Bodin on the corporate structure of the State, 64. His distinction between *corpus, collegium* and *universitas*, 64. He assigns the origin of these forms of association to a period prior to the foundation of the State, 65. Their significance for the State, 65. The advantage of corporate Estates and their meetings, 65. None the less, limitations [of their powers] are necessary in certain circumstances, 66. Moreover, all corporate institutions are always unconditionally dependent on the Sovereign, 66. Their existence, their right of meeting and their corporate authority are based on the State's concession, 66. The different degrees of powers assigned [by Bodin] to different forms of corporate authority, as a result of his view of all corporations as State-institutions, 66. His classification of *collegia*, 66. The capacity for owning property not an essential attribute of corporations, 67. Delicts of corporations, and their punishment, 67.

A similar view is to be found in other absolutist writers on politics, 67. Gregorius Tholosanus, Bornitius, Arnisaeus, 67. Even the more moderate absolutists adopt the view that corporations are State-institutions, 67. Besold, 67. The denial of any inherent corporate authority by the writers on Natural Law proper, 67. Particularly by the ecclesiastical writers, 68. The rejection of any idea of the autonomy of corporations by Suarez, 68. The application of these ideas to the interpretation of customary law, 68. The State's exclusive right of taxation, 68. The transference of this centralist point of view to the sovereign Church, 68.

[b] As concerns the relation of groups to the Individual, there is similarly no recognition of an independent existence of associations [apart from the individuals of whom they are composed], 68. The classification of the Corporation and the Family as forms of private 'society' [i.e. as 'partnerships' of individuals], 68. The old [Roman-law] theory of the Corporation only applied formally and externally, in connection with deviations from the usual form of the contract of 'society' or partnership, 68. The question whether a corporate body has a personality of its own, 68. In general, a merely 'collective' view of that personality [as an aggregate or sum of individuals] holds the field, 69. This view is apparent in the explanations given of the majority-principle, and in the theories about the delicts of corporations, 69. The application of the idea of *societas*, by the ecclesiastical writers on Natural Law, for the purpose of preserving the 'Fellowship' principle in regard to commons, 69. The rights of the [mere] community and those of the corporation in the theory of Suarez, 69. *Communitates perfectae* and *imperfectae*, and further subdivisions of *communitas* [note 30].

(2) *The federalist interpretation, especially in Althusius and Grotius*

On the other hand, a federalist trend of thought is also to be found in the theory of Natural Law, which applies the general idea of a 'social contract' to associations also, as well as to the State, and thus preserves for them a common sphere of their own [as defined and secured by the terms of their particular contract of association], 70.

The way for this federalist theory is prepared by doctrines about a right of resistance as belonging to the different parts of a country when the authority of the State is tyrannically employed, 70. The doctrine of Languet [i.e. of the author of the *Vindiciae contra Tyrannos* of 1579] about the right of provinces and towns to secede when the Ruler breaks the contract, 70. The support given to this doctrine by historical events, 70. The relations of this federalist theory (1) to the constitution of the Protestant churches, and (2) to the political institutions of Holland, Switzerland and Germany, 70.

The systematisation of federal ideas by Althusius, 70. Although he holds to the idea that sovereignty is the essential attribute of the State, he recognises associations as possessing a sphere of rights of their own, 71. The difference between his theory and the theory of medieval federalism, 71. He regards the social contract as the basis of the whole system of public law, 71. Five stages of groups (the Family, the Fellowship, the local community, the Province and the State), each with its own independent authority, 71. The higher groups composed of the lower, 71. The inherent and inviolable sphere of power belonging to each of the constituent bodies, 72. The rights of resistance and secession, 72. In accordance with his general theory, Althusius constructs his system of politics 'from below upwards', 72. (1) The Family (the Household and the Kin-group), 72. (2) The 'Fellowship' in its various forms, 72. The higher groups [i.e. the three which follow], as 'mixed political associations', brought under the general conception of *universitas*, 73. (3) The local community in its various forms, 73. (4) The *universitas provinciae*, 73. (5) The State, 73. *Majestas* as the one essential distinction between the State and other associations, 73. The creative force of the social contract, in regard to all the five stages of groups, 74. All through the series, the group has authority over its constituent members, though with different limits in each case, 74. Rule and obedience, 74. The general body of the ruled regarded as the true 'Subject' or owner of the community-authority, 74. The assembly representing the group is therefore treated as superior to its executive, 75. The application of the traditional [Roman-law] theory of corporations, within the framework of this theory, 75. The agreement between Althusius' system of politics and his juristic theory of groups, 75. The results of his doctrine, as regards the rights of corporations, 76.

The influence of the theory of a social contract upon other writers on Natural Law, 76. Their recognition of associations as possessing an independent common life of their own, 76. Their use of the federal scheme of Althusius, 76.

Analytical Summary

The federalist theory [of groups] in the writings of Grotius, 77. His system, 77. The contract of association and the contract of government, and the other *raisons d'être* of ruling authority, 77. Grotius attains on this basis a general natural-law theory of Society at large, 77. The relation of associations to the State, 77. The basing of all groups on the idea that they are systems of relations between rights of individuals, 78. Accordingly, Grotius draws no clear line of distinction between partnership (*Sozietät*) and corporation, 78. The majority-principle regarded as the result of an agreement, 78. The rights of the members of a group *ut universi* and *ut singuli*, 78. The relation of *singuli* to the debts and delicts of the general body, 79.

(3) *The interpretation of Hobbes*

The theory of associations in Hobbes, 79. The contractual basis of all social formations, 79. The generic idea of the *Systema*, 79. A. *Systemata regularia*. These are divided into (*a*) *absoluta*, i.e. States, and (*b*) *subordinata*, which are subject to the authority of the State, 79. The latter are divided in turn into (1) *corpora politica* and (2) *corpora privata*, 80. Another division based on the object or purpose of the 'System', 80. B. *Systemata irregularia*. Licit and illicit unions and assemblies, 80. In any case, however, it is only the mere *existence* of associations which can be based upon the principle of liberty of association, 80. No group-*authority*, of any kind whatsoever, can be made to issue from that principle, 81. All corporate authority is delegated State-authority, 81. The identification of the group and its members in relation to the State, 81. The application of these ideas to Parliaments, 81.

This point of view makes it possible for Hobbes to erect a general theory of Society, which embraces both the State and associations, without incurring any risk to his absolutist tendencies, 81. His conception of the unitary personality of the group, 81. His general theory of 'persons', 82. Representative and represented 'persons', 82. Representation of a multitude of men by a 'person', individual or collective, authorised thereto, 82. The subordinate group-personalities regarded, like the State, as *personae repraesentativae*, 82. The contrast between the monarchical and the republican constitution, as it appears in associations [as well as in the State], 83. The different effects of the unauthorised actions of a *persona repraesentativa*, according as that *persona* is *unus homo* or *unus coetus*, 83. The corresponding distinction between the delict of a single representative officer and that of a representative assembly, 83. The application of this distinction to questions of debt, 84.

The historical importance of this individualistic system of thought, in its bearing on the development of a natural-law conception of the Group-person, 84.

II. GROUPS ABOVE THE STATE

Rejection of the idea of a world-monarchy, 85. Its place is taken by the idea of a community based on international law, 85. The controversy about the *societas gentium*, 85. International law as binding in the form of Natural Law, 85–86.

Particular unions of States [i.e. federations], 86. The incompatibility of a federal State with the natural-law doctrine of sovereignty, 86. None the less, corporate elements are imported into the idea of the *foedus*, 86. Grotius' distinction between contracts of confederation and organised unions, and again between unions which are 'personal' and those which have a 'real' character, 86.

III. GROUPS PARALLEL WITH THE STATE

The Church

The idea of such groups is incompatible in principle with the natural-law theory of sovereignty, 87. The Church, 87. The doctrine of the independent sovereign authority of the Church, as expounded by Catholic writers on Natural Law who apply the theory of the Two Swords, 87. Other views with regard to the relations of Church and State, 88.

The Protestant doctrine. (*a*) According to the Lutheran view, State and Church are separate sovereign groups, of unlike origin, but under a common head, 88. The episcopal system and the theory of the three Estates, 88. (*b*) The community-principle in the 'Reformed Church' [i.e. the Calvinist], 89. The people as both secular and ecclesiastical sovereign, 89.

With the development of Natural Law, it became necessary for its exponents to bring the Church into the scheme of their theory of the State, 89. [Hence we find] (*c*) the purely 'territorial' doctrine, 89. The Church, in its external legal manifestation, is regarded as a State-institution, 90. The different attempts to delimit the power of the State over religious life in the 'territorial' system of thought, 90. (*d*) Contrasted with the 'territorial' is the 'collegial' system, 90. According to this, the Church is regarded as an association within the State, based on an ecclesiastical social contract, 90. The relation of this theory to the 'territorial' system, 90. At first there is hardly an antithesis, 90. Grotius' theory of Church government, 91. His view of ecclesiastical group-authority as a *regimen constitutivum ex consensu*, distinct from the *regimen imperativum* which belongs to the State, 91. The sovereignty of the State in the ecclesiastical sphere, 91. Other representatives of the 'collegial' system, 91. Conring, 92. The rise of an antithesis between this system and the 'territorial' system, when it comes to be held [by the advocates of the former] that associations have a group-authority of their own, 92. The theory of Voetius, 92. His view that each congregation is based on a contract between the professing members, and the larger Church-group on a union of congregations, 92. The idea of a natural group-authority developed on this basis, in regard to doctrine, ritual and discipline, 92. Preservation of ecclesiastical independence as against the State, 92. The attacks on Voetius by the advocates of the 'territorial' system, 92.

CHAPTER II

THE PERIOD FROM THE MIDDLE OF THE SEVENTEENTH TO THE BEGINNING OF THE NINETEENTH CENTURY

SECTION I

THE NATURAL-LAW THEORY OF SOCIETY DURING THE PERIOD OF ITS ASCENDANCY

§§ 16 to 18

CHAPTER II: SECTION I, §16

THE GENERAL THEORY OF THE GROUP (*VERBANDSTHEORIE*) IN NATURAL LAW

I. *The vogue of Natural Law and its individualistic basis*

Supremacy of Natural Law in this period, 95. Development of a general natural-law theory of associations, 95. Individualism its guiding star, 96.

II. *The priority of the individual to the community, and the consequent views of law and property*

The priority of the individual to the group, 96. The problem of discovering a system of legal relations among sovereign individuals in the state of nature, 96. The importance of the solution of this problem in its bearing on international law and [internal] public law, 97.

As against the pure conception of Power in Hobbes and Spinoza, the dominant theory holds fast to the conception that Natural Law has the character of Right, 97. Thomasius' view of the merely 'internal' obligation of Natural Law, 98. But there is a prevalent recognition of its being externally obligatory, 98. The compatibility of such obligation with natural liberty, 98. Derivation of Natural Law from the Divine Will, or the nature of the Divine Being, 98. The sanction of Natural Law by the threat of Divine punishment, 99. Such theories, however, have no practical importance, 99. The basing of the obligation of Natural Law on the mutual claim of individuals to its observance, 99. The right of self-help, 99. Application of these ideas to international law and [internal] public law, 99.

The contradiction between recognition of a natural legal obligation and denial of the existence of any community anterior to law, 100. Grotius' principle of 'sociability' is an attempt to reconcile this contradiction, 100. Civil society as the development of a sociable state of nature, 100. The consequent theory of the natural-law content of positive law, 100. The attempts to construct a later system of 'social natural law', over and above the original system of 'pure natural law', 100.

In opposition to this line of thought there is the view, developed under the influence of Hobbes, which regards the state of nature as altogether unsocial, 101. Locke, 101. Rousseau's doctrine of the perfect liberty of the state of nature, 101. Similar doctrines in Germany, 101. The zenith attained in Fichte's earlier system of thought, 101. His derivation of Law (or Right) from the voluntary limitation of the sovereign Ego, 102. Right, it is true, can be realised only by the State, 102. But the Right which is enacted by the State is based on Reason, 102. Kant, 102. He bases Right on the categorical imperative, 102. The priority of the individual to the community, 102. The State obliged by the law of Reason as an *a priori* principle, 103. Theories of the origin of property, 103. The assumption of an original community in all things, but only in the form of a *communio negativa*, 103. The importance of this view in its bearing on private property, 103. Locke bases property in the state of nature on labour or occupation, 103. Diffusion of the doctrine of the pre-social origin of property, 103. Rousseau, 104. Justus Möser, 104. Kant, 104. Side by side with this doctrine, however, there continued to exist a theory which based property on the authority of the State, partly as a survival of older theories, and partly by developing the new idea of a contract of property, 104. Fichte's theory almost socialistic, 104.

These theories of the priority of the individual were confronted by a theory which assumed the existence of primitive society, 104. The theological basis of this theory, 104. It never attained a proper logical development, 104. Leibniz, 104. The beginnings of an historical view of social evolution, 104. Montesquieu, 104. Möser's attack on the law of Reason, 104. Other representatives of this trend of thought, 105. Herder, 105. The importance of the survival of these theories side by side with individualism, 105.

III. *The natural-law view of the source of Group-authority*

Derivation of the community [and of community-authority] from the individual in the prevalent form of natural-law doctrine, 105.

There are, it is true, some views which diverge from this prevalent form, 105. For example, among the advocates of an unsocial state of nature, we find one divergent view which is based on the assumption of the divine origin of social authority, 105. Horn, 105. Again, among the advocates of the idea of original community, we find another divergent view which is based on the assumption of a naturally given social authority, 106.

But apart from these divergent views, the original sovereignty of the individual was universally held to be the only source of group-authority, 106. In this matter, the absolutist doctrine, the doctrine of popular sovereignty, and the intermediate doctrine [of a 'double majesty'], were all agreed, 106. Rousseau in particular adopts this view, 106. It is used by Beccaria in order to attack the practice of capital punishment, 106.

By the end of the eighteenth century, it is almost an unchallenged axiom that all social authority is derived from the devolution of individual rights, 107. The comparison in Möser and Sièyes between the original formation of Society and the foundation of a company, 107. Fichte, 107. Kant, 107.

IV. *Natural Law and the idea of contract as explaining the origin of Groups*

The free act of the individual will as the only legal mode of forming a community, 107. The original social contract as a natural-law dogma, 107. Different views with regard to the transition to the social state, 107. According to the prevalent form of doctrine, both a contract of society and a contract of government served to produce that transition, 107. Modifications, 108. The theories of a single original contract [either a contract of government, or a contract of society], 108. The importance of the act of the individual will as regards the single contract of government, 108; and as regards the single contract of society, 108.

Discrepant views, among those who agreed in holding a theory of contract, with regard to the motives for concluding the social contract, 108. Social instinct, or external needs, 108. But all thinkers alike attempt to find the legal basis of society in the will of individuals, 108. This is true even of Kant, 108. The universal tendency to emphasise the free act of will as the basis of the social condition, 109.

Different views with regard to the actual existence of the original contracts, 109. The original contracts as historical facts, 109. Various modifications of this view, 109. In opposition [to this historical view] we find Kant working out a purely idealistic interpretation of the political contract [i.e. he holds that it is an *a priori* assumption, rather than an historical fact], 109.

The individualistic point of view with regard to the continuing force of the original contracts, 110. Doubts concerning the bindingness of majority-decisions, 110. The fiction of new contracts to explain the obligation of later generations, 110. Entry into the State and exit from it, and the formation of separate autonomous bodies, 110. The extremest development of these ideas in Fichte [note 88].

The theory of a social contract, developed first in connection with the State, is applied to all human groups, 110. The difficulty of applying the theory to the Family, 111. Marriage as a contract of partnership (*Sozietät*), 111.

Revolts against the theory of contract in this period, 111. Ineffectual attacks against it, based on theocratic ideas, 111. In particular, Horn's attack, 111. The survival of the old view of the natural origin of the State, 111. The precursors of the historical and organic conception of the State, 111. Revolts based on a more realistic treatment of the State, 111. Hume, 111.

V. *The natural-law view of the purposes of Society and its various Groups*

The purposes of a common life based upon such foundations could only be individual purposes, 111.

The purpose of the State, in particular, 112. General agreement that the sphere of power of any community is limited by its purpose, and therefore that the sphere of the authority of the State is limited by *its* purpose, 112. None the less, there were fundamental differences of view in regard to the way in which the relation between society and the individual ought to be defined, 112. Theories which make the attainment of the community-purpose depend on the complete self-surrender of the individual, 112. Their extreme development in Hobbes, 112. Spinoza's proviso in favour of intellectual and moral liberty, 112. The apparent security provided by Rousseau for the inviolable rights of man, 112. The prevalent form of theory, which makes the individual pool only a part of his original rights, 113. Protection against the abuse of social authority, 113. Recognition of only *limited* social purposes, 113. Limitation of the State's object to the provision of external and internal security and the realisation of a system of legal relations, 113. Particularly in Locke, W. von Humboldt and Kant [note 110]. The growth of the theory of the Rights of Man, 113. Innate and acquired rights, 113. The theory used to defend freedom of conscience, especially by Thomasius, 113. It is also used, at the same time, in the cause of economic liberty, especially by Locke, 113. Doctrinaire elaboration of the theory in Wolff, 113. It develops into a fixed system, and takes the shape of constitutional 'declarations', 114.

But opposite consequences could also be drawn from the basic tenet of individualism, 114. Such opposite consequences especially drawn in the writings of Fichte, 114. Socialistic and communistic movements based on the individualistic point of view, 114.

Occasional and sporadic efforts to recognise that Society, like the individual, has its own life-purpose, 114.

VI. *The natural-law view of the Being of Groups*

The natural-law conception of the *Being* or essential nature of groups [as distinct from their *origin* and *purpose*, which have been treated in IV and V], 114. The conclusions drawn from individualism, 114. All groups regarded as mere systems of legal relations between individuals, on the analogy of the partnership which is based on individual rights, 115. None the less, there is a clinging to the conception of group-personality, 115. General adhesion to the views of Hobbes, 115.

Horn alone rejects *in toto* the conception of Group-personality, 115. His views in detail, more particularly as regards the 'Subject' of State-authority, 115. The difference between his theory of monarchies and his theory of republics, 116. In opposition to this theory of Horn, thinkers in general recognise the community as a 'Subject' of rights, 116. They only differ in their interpretations [some regarding the community

Analytical Summary

as only being a 'Subject' when it has a Representative, and others regarding it as being itself 'collectively' a 'Subject'], 116.

The principle of Representation in the absolutist systems, 116. The principle of Collectivity used to supplement this principle, 116. Particularly in non-monarchical corporate bodies, the idea of a collective unity of persons is made the basis of the position of groups as 'Subjects' of rights, 117. The majority of the writers on Natural Law, however, start from the 'Fellowship' idea of a collective unity of persons, 117. But they use the principle of Representation to supplement this idea [just as, conversely, the absolutist writers use the principle of Collectivity to supplement their principle of Representation], 117.

The views of Pufendorf: the persona moralis

Pufendorf combines 'collective' and 'representative' unity in his conception of the *persona moralis composita*, 118. The effect of the contract of association in constituting such a *persona*, but the need of its being supplemented by a further contract of government, 118. Pufendorf's philosophical explanation of the general idea of *persona moralis*, as embracing both group-persons and individual persons, 118. *Entia moralia* as the units in a system of law, 118. *Personae morales* regarded as *entia moralia ad analogiam substantiarum concepta*, 119. The *persona moralis simplex*, 119. The *persona moralis composita*, 119. This formal unity [of the composite moral person] has no real social Whole corresponding to it, 120. Pufendorf thus reverts [in spite of his attempt to combine them] to a separate treatment of 'representative' and 'collective' unity, 120.

How Pufendorf's new idea is treated in the writings of his successors, 121. The conception of *persona moralis* is narrowed down, 121. It becomes merely a technical term in Natural Law to designate a Group-person, 121. The conception of *persona composita* disappears, 121. The relation between 'collective' and 'representative' unity among Pufendorf's disciples, 121. The theory of Hert, 122. Generally, he ascribes any living Group-personality to the presence of a representative authority derived from the State, 122. For the rest, [he holds that] there is a variety of cases in which the conception of 'person' and that of 'man' are not co-extensive, 122. Here he introduces the ideas (1) *de uno homine plures sustinente personas*, and (2) *de pluribus hominibus personam unam sustinentibus*, 122. He also distinguishes cases of a unity of many men in one person according as they are based (1) on legal fiction, or (2) on contract, 123. But he has no effective conception of a corporate body, 123. In Gundling and other writers, we find the personality of the State identified with the representative personality of the Ruler; but otherwise they interpret the *universitas* in strict terms of 'collective' unity [without reference to any 'representation'], 123.

This contrast [between the State, which becomes a single 'person' through its 'representative' Ruler, and the ordinary *universitas*, which remains merely a 'collective' person] is accentuated by being interpreted as an example of the general contrast between 'unequal' and 'equal' *societates*, 123. 'Collective' unity in the *societas aequalis*, and 'representative' unity in the *societas inaequalis*, as expounded, more particularly, in the writings of J. H. Boehmer, 123. The more perfect unity of the 'unequal Society', 123. The exaltation of the State, and the idea of a fundamental distinction between it and the corporate body, based on this contrast [of the 'unequal' and the 'equal' Society], 124.

The atomistic conception of the nature of associations in eighteenth-century Germany

Disintegration of the natural-law conception of Group-personality, 124. The conception of the 'moral person' ceases to be used, except in interpreting 'Fellowship' systems of connection, 124. Even in this limited sphere, the conception is only used in regard to the external relations of a society, while its internal rights and duties are dissolved into mere relations of individuals to one another, 124. Thus even the State itself is treated as being a *persona moralis* only at international law [i.e. in regard to its external relations], 125. Disappearance of any distinction between the corporate body [Körperschaft] and the mere society [Gesellschaft], 125. Isolated tendencies in an opposite direction, 125. On the whole, however, the thought of the eighteenth century strictly adheres to an 'atomistic' view, 125. Wolff, 125. Daries, 125. Nettelbladt and his detailed theory of *societas*, 126. Achenwall and his essentially similar view, 126. Scheidemantel's approach to the idea of the 'composite person', 126. Controversy in regard to the majority-principle, 127. The gradual victory of the view that unanimity is essentially necessary, 127. This means the final dissolution of any idea of group-unity [because it lays the real emphasis on each unit of the group], 127. A. L. von Schlözer flatly reduces 'collective' unity to a mere sum of individuals, 127. His theory of sovereignty [note 186]. The common will as the sum of individual wills, 127. C. von Schlözer takes the same view of the common will and the majority-principle, 127. Hoffbauer, 127. W. von Humboldt even demands legal recognition and enforcement of this [atomistic] point of view, 127.

English and French theory in the eighteenth century: Locke and Rousseau

The conception of the collective person as it appears in the English and French theory of popular sovereignty, 128. Here there is no distinction between 'equal' and 'unequal society', 128. The search for a 'Subject' of group-rights [not in a 'Representative person', but] in the associated community itself, 128. The system of Locke, 128. His derivation of the majority-principle from Natural Law, though he also maintains that the principle has a foundation in contract, 128. The theory of Rousseau, 128. He elevates the collective unit into a living Group-person, 128. This real Group-being, regarded as a *personne morale* is placed by Rousseau on the same footing as an individual externally, and given the position of 'Subject' of State-authority internally, 129. But Rousseau remains in the trammels of an individualistic conception

Analytical Summary

of the Group-person, 129. While he distinguishes *volonté générale* from *volonté de tous*, he does not recognise any real common will, 129. He bases the majority-principle on a previous unanimous agreement, 129. The double rôle of the individual, as both partner in Sovereignty and subject to it, 129. The sovereign moral person co-extensive with the assembly of all, 130. Rousseau excludes representation altogether, 130. He has no conception of an 'organ' [through which the people acts], 130. His artificial interpretation of the governing body as a secondary 'person' created by the primary sovereign 'person', 130. But the governing body [though thus regarded by him as a 'person'] is also [like the People itself] merely a collective unit, 130.

The influence of Rousseau's view on the natural-law theory of Group-personality, 130. Its transformation into a popular form in France, more especially by Sieyès, 131. Re-introduction of the idea of Representation, 131.

Fichte and Kant

The reception of Rousseau's theory in Germany, 131. The advocates of the sovereignty of the Ruler adopt only some of its elements, 131. Fichte, on the other hand, accepts it as a whole, 131. But he shows a still sterner individualism, 131. He regards men as being partners in sovereignty and free individuals, 131. The State as a single body, 131. The assumption of a real Whole, as a contracting party already present at the time of the contract of association, 132. Justification of this assumption, 132. The comparison of the State to a tree, 132. The life of the Whole as the aggregate of the lives of the parts, 132. Fichte's juridical person is thus no real personality, 133. He does not apply the conception of person to the State at all, 133. He bases international law on the relations between individual citizens [of different States, and not on the relations between States themselves], 133. Fichte's attempt to discover a common will operative in the internal life of the State, 133. His rejection of the majority-principle, 133. He regards the common will as realised by the assembly of all, but he gives some limited recognition to the principle of representation, 133. He does not attain the conception of a corporate 'organ', 133. In his later writings, he approaches an organic view of society, 133. Kant, 134. Fundamentally, he limits the conception of personality to the individual, 134. At the same time, he uses the expression 'moral person', 134. He applies it, for example, to States, in the sphere of international law, 134. And also to the various holders of authority, in the sphere of internal public law, 134. His conception of the three powers [legislative, executive and judicial] as moral persons, 134; and of the State and the People as similar persons, 134. His view of the common will as the sum of individual wills, 134. He bases the majority-principle, and the theory of representation, on contract, 134. But his individualism is modified by his introduction of the conception of the *homo noumenon*, as contrasted with the *homo phaenomenon*, 134–135.

GENERAL RETROSPECT

General view, in retrospect, of the disintegration of the civilian and canonical doctrine of corporations by the theory of Natural Law, 135. The introduction of the 'moral' person in lieu of the 'fictitious' person, 135. But, in spite of this advance, individualism prevents any recognition of groups as possessing a living unity of their own, 135. In spite of the use of organic analogies, there is a purely mechanical conception of society, 136. The analogy of the machine gains ground, 136.

The opponents of the individualistic interpretation of society start from the conception of a social Whole, but they fail to attain the conception of a personality immanent in that Whole, 136. Justi [note 251]. Mevius and S. de Cocceji [note 252]. Leibniz [note 253]. Frederick the Great [note 254]. Herder [note 254].

CHAPTER II: Section I, §17

THE NATURAL-LAW THEORY OF THE STATE

I. *General view*

The natural-law theory of the State which is based on the general natural-law theory of Society at large can be divided into (*a*) the theory of natural public law (*jus publicum universale*), and (*b*) political theory (*Politik*), 137.

It includes (1) the application to the State of the general idea of *societas*, as already described in the previous subsection, and (2) the various problems arising from the attempt to combine that idea with the idea of sovereignty, 137. The fundamental antinomy between the traditional theory of sovereignty and the conception of the Law-State which is immanent in the theory of Natural Law, 138. To solve the antinomy, thinkers (1) assume a reserved sovereignty of the individual, 138; (2) recognise that groups have their own systems of group-rights, 138; and (3) divide the personality of the State into a number of 'persons', 138. The natural-law conception of the personality of the State is prevented by its individualistic basis from contributing to the solution of the antinomy, 139. The result is a continuance of the controversy about the 'Subject' of sovereignty, 139. The value and defects of the formal natural-law conception of State-sovereignty, 140. Rejection of the theory of 'double majesty', 140. Transformation of [Grotius'] theory of the *subjectum commune* of 'majesty', 140. The controversy thus confined to a dispute between the two extremes of the pure sovereignty of the Ruler and the pure sovereignty of the People, 140.

II. *The theory of the Sovereignty of the Ruler*

Immediately, the victory lies with the theory of the sovereignty of the Ruler, 141.

Analytical Summary

The State, as the 'Subject' of supreme authority, is identified with the 'representative' personality of the Ruler, 141. The application of this idea to different forms of State, 141. The interpretation of 'the Ruler' in a democracy, 141.

The possibility of a collective personality of the People, as distinct from the Ruler, 141.

The rejection of this possibility by the absolutist writers on Natural Law, 141. The stricter school of thought regards it as inconceivable that there can be any system of public or constitutional law which juridically obliges the sovereign, 141. The adherents of this school of thought, 142. In Germany a more moderate school holds the field, 142. Horn recognises certain limitations on absolute monarchy, 142. So, especially, does Pufendorf, 142. True, he attacks the idea that the community of the ruled can have rights as against the Ruler, 142. But his theory allows limitations on the Ruler arising from differences in the *modus habendi* of majesty: thus he draws a distinction between the patrimonial State and the normal monarchy in which the Ruler for the time being only enjoys the usufruct of authority, 143. The compatibility of an *imperium limitatum* with the full Sovereignty of the Ruler, 143. The nature of the assent of the People, or the Estates, which is involved in such a case, 143. That assent is only a *conditio sine qua non* of the volition of the monarch, which is the real expression of the will of the State, 143. The actual object of such volition can never be imposed on the Ruler by a will alien to his own, 144. The great success of this theory of Pufendorf, 144. The followers of his theory, 144. The extremer form which it assumes in Boehmer, 144. Its modification by other writers, in the direction of an extension of constitutional limits, 144.

The recognition, in the writers on Natural Law who incline to constitutionalist views, of a collective personality of the People as continuing to exist over against the Sovereign, 144. They base this view on the theory of Contract, 145. They measure the rights of this collective personality of the People (1) by the standard of the original contracts, and (2) by that of express constitutional provisos, 145. Huber on the constitutional State, 145. He believes in the unity of majesty, in spite of any limitation by the rights of the People, under *all* forms of constitution, 145. The *leges fundamentales* regarded as contracts, 146. The People regarded as a *universitas*, which confronts the personality of the State embodied in the Ruler, 146. Huber's use of this system of ideas to combat popular as well as monarchical absolutism, 146. His self-contradictory application of the system to democracy, 146. A similar theory used by other writers to justify the rights of the territorial Estates in Germany, 146. Leibniz introduces the idea of sovereignty as being only 'relative', 146. The idea of a collective personality of the People in the followers of Pufendorf, 147. The gradual recognition of popular rights even among the advocates of the sovereignty of the Ruler, 147. The approach to a theory of popular sovereignty in Wolff, 147. And similarly in Nettelbladt, 148. The idea of a separate 'moral personality' as belonging to the People, and also to the assembly which represents the People, 148. The personality of People and Estates as conceived by Hoffbauer, 148. Even among those thinkers who lay a greater emphasis on the sovereignty of the Ruler we find the view propounded of a constitutional State, in which Ruler and People are related to one another as contracting parties, 148. Daries, Achenwall, Scheidemantel, Schlözer, 148. The revolutionary results which follow in the event of a breach of contract, 148.

The controversy about the relation between People and Ruler is connected with the controversy about the various possible forms which the ruling 'Subject' may assume, 148. The problem arises of the possibility and value of a mixed form of State, 148.

III. *The theory of Popular Sovereignty*

The theory of popular sovereignty, 149. It continues to survive in England, and the theory of a contract of government continues to be held in connection with it, 149. The superior position of the People in this contractual relationship [between People and Government], 149. Sidney, 149. Locke, 149.

Rousseau breaks away from the idea of a contractual relationship between People and Ruler, 149. He bases an unlimited and illimitable popular sovereignty on the one foundation of a contract of association, 149. He regards the appointment of a governing authority as nothing more than a commission which is always revocable at will, 150. He banishes entirely the idea of a State based on law and a constitution, 150. None the less, he fails to escape from dualism in his conception of the 'Subject' of political rights, 150. His attitude to existing law, 150.

The development of the revolutionary theory of the State in the framework of Rousseau's system of ideas, 150. The doctrine of popular sovereignty modified as a result of greater attention to actual facts, 150. Approach to the idea of the constitutional State, through accepting a system of popular representation or the fact of an independent governing authority, 150. Thus Fichte limits the sovereignty of the People by an obligatory system of constitutional law, 151. He believes in the necessity of transferring 'absolute positive right' to a magistrate, 151. He regards the People as bound to reconstitute itself into a 'community' if it seeks to exercise its reserved rights of sovereignty, 151. The fixing of periodical assemblies for this purpose, in smaller States, 151. In larger States, the election of 'Ephors', with 'absolute negative power', who can bring the whole system of a government to a standstill, and then summon the people to meet as a 'community' for the purposes of sovereign decision, 151. The right of resistance in certain cases, 152. The unity of the 'Subject' of political rights on this theory, 152. The reasons for the disappearance of his earlier idea of the personality of the State in Fichte's later theory, 152.

Popular sovereignty in the theory of constitutionalism, 152. Montesquieu's adhesion to English theory, 152. Popular sovereignty, however, recedes into the background, 152. In fact, the whole conception of sovereignty (like the conception of the personality of the State) disappears altogether in the course of Montesquieu's development of the idea of the constitutional State, 153. Frederick the Great's attitude to popular sovereignty [note 94]. Justi's attempt to unite the theory of constitutionalism with the idea (which is required by the conception of the 'body politic') of a unity of power and will, 153. Popular sovereignty in Kant, as an 'idea of Reason', 153. His recognition of a sovereignty of the Ruler based on historical grounds, 153. His ideal sketch of a constitutional State, 153.

The approximation [of constitutional theories which start from the idea of the sovereignty of the People] to the theory of the constitutional State which proceeds on the assumption of the sovereignty of the Ruler, 153. Here, again, the question is raised of the possibility of a mixed form of State, 153.

IV. *The theory of the Mixed Constitution*

The question inherited from the Middle Ages, 154.

Thinkers who adopted the theory of the sovereignty of the Ruler rejected the mixed form of State, as a result of their strict insistence on the conception of sovereignty, 154. This negative attitude, however, caused difficulties when these writers had to deal with actual constitutions based on historical development, 154. Attempts to find a solution, 154. The triumph of Pufendorf's doctrine of the irregularity of all mixed forms, 154. His successors, 155. Modifications of the conception of irregularity, 155. Otto, 155. Titius, 155.

The idea of an undivided co-partnership among a number of 'Subjects' of majesty, 155. The way for this idea prepared by Besold, 155. Its application to the German constitution, 155. Huber's serious attempt to interpret the constitutional State along these lines without abandoning the idea of the unity of State-authority, 155. His theory of the possession of majesty on a system of joint ownership [*zu gesamter Hand*], 156. The different forms assumed by such joint ownership of governing authority, 156. Similar views propounded by other writers, 156. The defects of their theories, 156. The recurrent tendency to slip back into the idea of a division of rights of majesty, 156. Achenwall, 157.

The survival of the theory of divided sovereignty, 157. This theory does not permit any fruitful recognition of that unitary sovereignty of the State which lies behind all division, 157. Leibniz's distinction between the 'substance' and the 'exercise' of sovereignty, 157.

The combination of the theory of the mixed form of State with the demand for a *qualitative* division of powers in the doctrine of constitutionalism, 157. The importance of division of powers in judging the form of a State, 157. Locke, 157. Montesquieu, 158. The mixed form of State as a constitutional ideal, 158.

The idea of division of powers as applied in the theory of popular sovereignty, 158. The contradiction between popular sovereignty and the constitutionalist system, 158. Rousseau accordingly attacks division of powers, 158. His theory, however, by separating the legislative and the executive powers, still preserves the principle of a division of powers,

158. But a closer approach to the idea of separation of powers may be found among the later radical advocates of the doctrine of popular sovereignty, 159.

As the theory of constitutionalism wins ground, the doctrine of Montesquieu triumphs, with its combination of the conception of the mixed constitution and the principle of division of powers, 159. After the middle of the eighteenth century, we find thinkers recognising the mixed form of State, with a division of sovereignty, even when they still adhere to the idea of the sovereignty of the Ruler, 159. The diffusion of this theory in Germany, 159. Kant's explanation of the principle of division of powers as a rule of logic, 159.

V. *The contributions made by the natural-law theory of the State to the development of public law*

The dissolution of the conception of sovereignty, and the disintegration of the personality of the State, as the ultimate results of the natural-law theory of public law, 159. But this theory, thanks to its formal conception of personality, also leads to progress, 160.

(a) The idea of the continuity of political rights and duties, in spite of changes in personnel and territory, and even of alterations in the form of the State, 160. Continuity in spite of the division of a State, or of a union of States, 160.

(b) The representative position of the Ruler as a 'Subject' of rights distinguished from his private position, 160. The application of the principles of the law of corporations to the volition and action of a representative collective-person [i.e. a representative assembly], and thus to the volition and action of the State, 160. The two 'persons' of the one Ruler, 161. Separation of his public-law from his private-law sphere, 161. His 'government' acts and his 'private' acts, 161. The treatment of the official acts of public officials as State-acts, 161. The successor in title obliged by the acts of his predecessor, 161. This idea, however, is often combined with ideas which are simply drawn from the law of private inheritance, 161. Representation of the personality of the State by the 'illegitimate' ruler during an interregnum, 161.

(c) A clear line of division is drawn between State-property and the private property of the Ruler, 161. The ownership [of the former] vested in the State, 161. The Ruler limited in its use, 161. Controversies in regard to the distinction of the different species of State-property, 161. The position of the demesne [*Kammergut*] in territorial principalities, 161. Differentiation between the private property of the State and its public-law authority over the State's territory, 162. The intermediate idea of the State's *dominium eminens*, 162.

CHAPTER II: Section I, §18

THE THEORY OF CORPORATIONS IN NATURAL LAW*

I. ASSOCIATIONS CONTAINED IN THE STATE

The general basis of the natural-law theory of associations, as contrasted with the traditional theory of corporations [in the civilians and canonists], 162. The different conclusions attained [in natural-law theory], according as unitary or federal tendencies predominate, 162.

(1) *Divergence of centralist and federalist views*

The natural-law grading of associations, 163. The inclusion of all groups under the rubric of *societas*, 163. The question whether intermediate groups have a natural existence or depend on artificial creation, 163.

(*a*) Predominance of the centralist tendency, 163. The Family and the State as the only groups existing by Natural Law, 163. The local community regarded as a stage preliminary to the State, but as becoming merely a part of it when once the State is constituted, 163. The 'Fellowship' as a *societas arbitraria*, 163. The rights and duties of corporations treated in connection with the theory of the position of subjects (*subditi*), 164. Accentuation of the centralist tendency in theories based on the teaching of Hobbes, 164.

(*b*) On the other hand, we find a federalist view in Germany, 164. The natural-law character of associations, 164. The theory of a natural articulation of human society into groups, especially in Leibniz, 164. Recognition of the Corporation and the State as co-equal, 164. The fullest development of this theory to be found in Nettelbladt, 164. Systems similar to his, 165.

(2) *The relation of the Corporation to the State*

(*a*) *Views inimical to Corporations.*

Refusal to recognise associations as having a basis in Natural Law results in their not being allowed any sanction in Natural Law, 165. The result of that, in turn, is that they are not allowed any sphere of rights exempt from the State, 165. In connection with the unhistorical outlook of the period of Enlightenment, we find the very existence of the Corporation called in question, 165. This negative view is used by

* This subsection is closely analogous to §15 above. That subsection dealt with the natural-law theory of Associations from 1500 to 1650: this subsection deals with the natural-law theory of Corporations from 1650 to 1800. Like §15, the present subsection is arranged on a scheme by which separate consideration is given (1) to groups within the State, (2) groups above the State, (3) groups parallel to the State.

the State to attack the existing social system of Corporations and Estates, 165.

At first, the absolutists only demand a limitation of corporations, 166. The exaltation of the State's suzerainty over corporations, 166. The demand that the formation and meeting of groups should receive the assent of government, 166. The right of the State to supervise groups and to co-operate in their action, 166. The right of the State to abolish or transform groups, on grounds of public well-being, 166. Schemes for ideal States, with a mechanical and rationalistic articulation of the body politic [Spinoza and Hume], 166 and n. 14.

The struggle to annihilate corporations, after the middle of the eighteenth century, especially in France, 166. Turgot's extreme theory, 166. Rousseau's refusal to admit any idea of the corporative organisation of society, 166. The abolition of all particular societies regarded as the aim to be attained, 166. The influence of this theory on the Revolution, 166. Its application in the confiscation of ecclesiastical property, 167. The development of new self-contradictions in revolutionary theory, as the result of its recognising the necessity of intervening groups, 167. Along with this recognition, however, there is still a steady rejection of the old conception of the corporation, 167. Sieyès, 167.

Rousseau's ideas in Germany, 167. Modified application, 167. The Church regarded by Justi as the only corporate element [n. 26]. Scheidemantel's conception of public and private societies as State-institutions, 168. Fichte substitutes the conception of the State-institution altogether for that of the Corporation, 168. The factor of the State-institution in the theory of Kant, 168. His confusion of 'corporation' and 'foundation', 168. His theory of the unlimited power of the State in regard to corporations, 168. The dissolution of 'moral bodies' regarded by him as a postulate of the law of Reason, 169.

(*b*) *Views favourable to Corporations: especially in the theory of Nettelbladt.*

But ideas still continue to survive in the natural-law theory of Society, which prepare a renascence of the liberty of corporations in a rejuvenated form, 169. The natural right of associations to exist, regarded as a consequence of the theory of the Social Contract, 169.

A natural liberty of association is recognised in principle even by the opponents of the independence of corporations, following the lines already suggested by Hobbes, 169. Pufendorf's doctrine of associations, 169. All groups other than the Family are posterior to the State, 170. *Corpora privata* and *publica*, 170. The latter only become *corpora legitima* by permission of the State, 170. The group-authority which they exercise derived from the State, 170. The results of this dependence, 170. The State a body composed of other bodies which are its 'members', 170. The use of the conceptions of *societas aequalis* and *inaequalis* to attain similar results, 170. Hert explains the relation of the corporate body to the State by basing it on the distinction between the *societas aequatoria* and the *societas rectoria*, 170. J. H. Boehmer's formulation of this new theory of corporations, 171. He limits the natural principle of liberty of association (1) by holding that associations have no separate group-authority of their own, and (2) by subjecting them [in a special degree] to the authority of the State, 171. Boehmer's theory of the State's suzerainty over corporations, and of the various rights to control their liberty which it involves, 171. The State's right to prohibit associations, and to require them to apply for its consent, 171. Erection of *collegia publica* by the State, 171. Its supervision of *collegia privata*, 172. No corporate right of self-legislation, self-jurisdiction, or self-administration, 172. Customary rights, municipal autonomy, by-laws [note 47]. Rights of taxation [note 49]. Boehmer rejects the conception of corporate office, 172. He leaves corporate privileges in a defenceless condition, 172. He delivers corporate property into the hands of the State, 172.

The rights of corporations assigned to the sphere of private law, on the ground of the distinction between *societas aequalis* and *inaequalis*, 172. Boehmer's elaboration of this point of view, 173. Its adoption by Titius, 173.

The natural-law theory of the contract of society is brought into line with the civilian theory of corporations, 173. The antithesis of *societas aequalis* and *inaequalis* thus comes to be connected with the antithesis of *societas* and *universitas*, 173. Huber's theory of *universitates*, 173. *Certum regimen* considered as the attribute of the *universitas* in contradistinction to the *societas*, 173. This leads to the view that confirmation by the State is the logical differentia of the *universitas*, 174. Huber's view of organised group-authority as exercised in the name of the Sovereign, 174. Similar theories in other writers, 174. On the whole, however, the natural-law doctrine seeks to attain a homogeneous theory of all 'societies', by eliminating the distinction between *societas* and *universitas*, 174.

The result of this attempt is often to produce a favourable attitude to the independence of corporate bodies, 175. Leibniz assumes the existence of an inherent social authority in such bodies, 175. Wolff takes a similar view, 175. Autonomy and jurisdiction regarded as the essential rights of a society, 175. The State's suzerainty over corporations held to be merely a part of its general sovereign suzerainty, 175. Other exponents of this point of view, 175.

The freedom of the corporate body in Nettelbladt's system of jurisprudence, 175. His recognition of the inherent natural rights of societies, 175. His view of the origin of societies, 175. He allows acquired as well as inherent rights, 176. *Potestas* and *regimen societatis*, 176. The different 'Subjects' of group-authority, according as societies differ, 176. The transference of group-authority to others, 176. *Imperium* as a part of all group-authority, 176. The content of group-authority, 176. Nettelbladt explains the distinction between *societas aequalis* and *inaequalis* by differences in the 'Subject' of group-authority [and not by the presence or absence of group-authority, which he regards as always present], 176. The internal rights of corporations, considered as *jura socialia societatis*, 177. Nettelbladt's application of these principles to the problem of the relation of corporate bodies to the State, 177. Various modes and forms of this relation, 177. The five main species of 'societies', 177. Particularly the fifth and last species—that of *societates privatae in republica*, 177. Their creation, 178. Their social authority, 178. The rights of the sovereign in respect of them, 178. The possibility of their being exempt, or privileged, 178. But it is also possible, conversely, for the political sovereign to possess not only political, but also social authority over such societies, 178. In such a case, there is need for a clear distinction between his political and his social authority, 178.

Achenwall has fundamentally similar views, though he does not attain the same logical development of the theory of *societas*, 178. Hoffbauer, 178. His views on the right of citizens to form unions, 179. We also find liberty of association vindicated against the State as a fundamental right even by the sternest of individualists, 179. A. L. von Schlözer, 179. W. von Humboldt, 179.

Simultaneously, there is also a reaction, based on historical grounds, against State-absolutism and its enmity to corporations, 179. The recognition of the necessity of independent associations in the State, 179. Mevius [note 90]. Montesquieu's doctrine of the importance of privileged corporations as a defence against despotism, 179. Justus Möser's fight on behalf of the liberty of corporations, 179. His historical disquisitions on towns, guilds and leagues (the Hansa); on fraternities and crafts; on the territorial constitution [in the German principalities] and the growth of territorial Estates [note 92]. The political lessons which he draws from these data, 180. His defence of autonomy, 180. His proposals for new social formations on the 'Fellowship' model, 180.

(3) *The natural-law conception of the internal nature of Corporations, as affected by the fact of their inclusion in the State*

The natural-law conception of the internal nature of the corporation is a theme which can only be treated here from one particular angle: we shall only enquire how far the general conception of the nature of groups was affected or modified when the fact of their inclusion in the State came to be taken into account, 180. Two opposing tendencies, 180.

(a) *The Corporation as an Institution* (Anstalt).

The 'institution' view, which is connected with the basing of a society's corporate rights on the existence of a Ruling authority imposed upon it *ab extra* and *de supra*, 180.

The view prepared by a line of theory developed in connection with Hobbes' doctrine, 181. The importance of the 'institution' element as the determining factor in the theory of Pufendorf, 181. But a 'Fellowship' view still remains concurrently active in his theory, 181. The clearer emergence of a 'partnership' [or *societas*] point of view in Pufendorf's successors—Thomasius, Treuer and Titius, 181 and note 99. And, particularly, the obliteration of any distinction between partnership and corporation in Gundling and Hert, 182.

Huber's clear-cut conception of the corporation, following the lines of the traditional [Roman-law] theory of corporations, 182. His differentiation of the corporation from the State and the Family; from the

Analytical Summary

ordinary society or community; from 'institutions' without a constitution of their own, and from collegiate magistracies with no specific purpose, 182. His combination of the principle of a collective Group-personality with that of the State-'institution' to produce the conception of the *universitas*, 182. His distinction of *societas* and *collegium*, particularly with reference to the majority-principle [note 108]. Similar views in Schmier and in other writers, 183 and note 110. The upshot of such views is that the corporation is treated as being a 'Fellowship' from the point of view of private law, and a State-'institution' from the point of view of public law, 183.

A similar result is attained, on an exclusively natural-law basis [and without any reference to the traditional civilian and canonist law of corporations] by J. H. Boehmer and his successors, 183. Development of the rights of corporations from the conception of the *societas aequalis*, regarded as a society without any social authority, 183. This is supplemented by the idea of the State-'institution', 183.

The 'Fellowship' principle could be applied when it was assumed that an 'equal society' might possess social authority, or, again, when it was admitted that an 'unequal society' could be created by contract alone [without State-intervention], 183. But even on this basis we find *public* bodies, e.g. local communities, treated as merely State-'institutions', 183.

The State-'institution' point of view pressed to its conclusion in the theories inimical to corporations which originate in France, 183. Here there is no distinction between corporations and simple 'foundations' [*Stiftungen*], 184. Turgot [note 116]. Scheidemantel [note 116]. Kant, 184. W. von Humboldt, 184 and note 118.

(*b*) *The Corporation as a Fellowship* (Genossenschaft), *especially in the theory of Nettelbladt*.

The 'Fellowship' point of view, as it appears in the form of natural-law theory which explains the legal position of corporations as arising from a voluntary contract of society, 184.

To some extent, this is the inevitable result of the general natural-law theory of society, 184. The recognition of the 'Fellowship' group as being a 'Subject' of rights which, though it may be imperfect, is none the less, so far as it goes, independent [i.e. is inherently a 'Subject', and does not owe that position to the State], 184. The *societas* as a moral person in the theory of Huber, 184. In Pufendorf's type of theory, purely 'collective' persons are also recognised, 184. The *societas aequalis* as a moral person in the theories of Hert and Boehmer, 185. The imperfection of the 'collective' person constituted on this sort of basis, 185. It is, at bottom, only a case of the 'joint hand', 185.

The 'Fellowship' as possessing the full rights of a corporate body on the basis of a contract of society, 185. It is presupposed, on such a view, that the contract can produce a social authority, 185. The attempts to justify this view in Germany, and especially that of Wolff, 185. The development of this doctrine by Nettelbladt, and his application of it to positive law, 185. He bases the internal rights of corporations upon a foundation of contract, 186. He explains social authority as a sum of rights of individuals, 186. The exercise of this authority by all the individual members, except in so far as it has been transferred by contract into other hands, 186. Majority-decisions and the acts of representatives, 186. Alterations in personnel through the reception of new members by means of a new contract, 186. The exclusion of members by the same means, 186. The appointment of officers of a society, 186. The *persona moralis* thus constituted, 187. The elaboration of these ideas in connection with both natural and positive law in Nettelbladt's scheme of *Jurisprudentia socialis*, 187. The matters dealt with in this scheme, 187. (1) The theory of corporate acts or decisions, 187. The majority-principle and *jura singulorum* in other writers on Natural Law (Wolff, Daries, Achenwall, Hoffbauer, C. von Schlözer) [note 139]. (2) Nettelbladt's account of the things which may be the objects of corporate ownership, 188. The *dominium solitarium* of the *societas*, 188. *Res societatum patrimoniales* and *res societatum in specie sic dictae*, 188. The application of these categories in the field of positive law, 188. (3) *Leges societatum*, either as *leges conventionales*, or as *leges proprie sic dictae*, 189. *Statuta universitatis* and 'observances' in the field of positive law, 189. (4) The legal proceedings of corporate bodies, considered as *negotia publica*, or as *privata*, 189. (5) *Obligationes societatum*: *obligationes singulorum* and *obligationes societatis*, 189. Obligations *ex delicto* on the part of a *universitas* exist, according to Nettelbladt, only at positive law, since a corporate body is naturally and inherently incapable of a delict, 189. But a capacity for delict is recognised by most of the writers on Natural Law, 190. (6) Nettelbladt's theory of the *jura singulorum*, 190. The classification of these *jura*, 190. Application of the theory of such *jura* in the field of positive law, 191. (7) Possession and quasi-possession by societies, 191. The acquisition and loss of possession as against a *universitas*, 191. (8) *Remedia juris in applicatione ad societates*, 191.

This natural-law theory [of Nettelbladt] may be considered as a reaction of the German conception of 'Fellowship' against the foreign conception of the corporation, 191. But he has no conception of the existence of a substantive Group-being, 192.

The restoration of the German conception of the 'joint hand' by the school of Natural Law, 192. The fusion of individual spheres in a common sphere, 192. The application of the conception of the *persona moralis* even to mere cases of the 'joint hand', 192. Its use in reference to the position of the family-community, 192. Its extension by Nettelbladt to broader family-groups—the aristocratic 'House' and the House-property belonging to 'the line', 193. The organs and parts of a group regarded as distinct moral persons, 193. The union of different 'Subjects' in a [supposed] moral person in the cases of partnership for profit, co-ownership and other legal relations involving common rights and duties, 193. When, however, the gap between what is 'joint' and what is 'common' is thus closed, the conception of a real Group-personality is lost, 193. The dropping of the idea of a Group-person which is distinct from all individual persons, 194. The attenuation of corporate unity, 194. The introduction of a *persona repraesentativa* in order to produce an independent group-unity, 194.

The dissolution of all group-existence is the ultimate result of these theories, 194. The conception of the moral person reduced to a technical figure of speech, 194. The extremest formulation of the final results of this tendency is that of W. von Humboldt, 194–195.

II. GROUPS ABOVE THE STATE

International society and federations

Conflicting views in the natural-law theory of corporations reflected in the treatment of super-State groups, 195.

International Society, 195. The absolute rejection of the idea of such a society, on the assumption that a non-social state of nature still continues to exist in the relation of States, 195. Pufendorf, 195. Justi [note 172]. In opposition to this view, there is the assumption of a natural society of States, 196. The recognition of positive international law, 196. Mevius, 196. Leibniz, 196. Thomasius, 196. Wolff and his successors, 196. The nature of the society of States, as a *societas aequalis*, 196. Side by side with this view, we also find the idea of a *civitas maxima*, 196. Kant's world-State [note 177]. Fichte [note 177].

Recognition of particular societies of States [i.e. federations], 196. Rejection of the idea of the 'composite' State, under the influence of Pufendorf, 196. Federal relations, 196. The peculiar theory of Thomasius [note 179]. *Foedera simplicia* and *systemata civitatum*, 196. The classification of 'Systems of States', 197. Real Unions, 197. *Corpora confoederatorum* not real States, 197. In contradistinction to Pufendorf, we find some writers making an approach to the idea of a truly federal form of State, by assuming the possibility of a federal authority, 197. Recognition of intervening forms, with reference to the German constitution, 197. The re-introduction of the conception of the federal State into Natural Law, 197. Leibniz, 197. Montesquieu, 197. Nettelbladt, 197. His *respublica composita*, 198. Its harmony with the positive law of the German constitution, 198.

III. GROUPS WITHIN THE STATE: THE CHURCH

The Church and its relation to the State, as interpreted under the influence of the natural-law theory of society, 198.

CHAPTER I

THE PERIOD DOWN TO THE MIDDLE OF THE SEVENTEENTH CENTURY

SECTION V

The Influence of the Natural-law Theory of Society

§§ 14 and 15

CHAPTER I: SECTION V, §14

THE NATURAL-LAW CONCEPTION OF THE STATE

I. *General view of Natural Law*

1. The intellectual force which finally dissolved the medieval view of the nature of human Groups was the Law of Nature. Quickening, during this epoch,* the germs of thought which had already developed in the course of the Middle Ages, and combining them, in a growing independence of their own, into an organic unity, the theory of Natural Law now confronted the doctrinal edifice of the civilists and the canonists as a definite system, which not only claimed universal theoretical validity, but also demanded practical application.

The Law of Nature issued in a natural-law theory of the State; and it was by developing such a theory that it affected the movement of history most powerfully(1). The natural-law theory of the State was a guide to all the political efforts and struggles from which the modern State proceeds. It is true that speculation was also affected by action, and that every development of the world of thought in this period was an echo and reverberation of historical events. But the relation of the natural-law theory of the State to the actual process of history was never purely passive. On the contrary, it served as a pioneer in preparing the transformation of human life; it forged the intellectual arms for the struggle of new social forces; it disseminated ideas which, long before they even approached realisation, found admittance into the thought of influential circles, and became, in that way, the objects of practical effort. In opposition to positive jurisprudence, which still continued to show a Conservative trend, the natural-law theory of the State was Radical to the very core of its being. Unhistorical in the foundations on which it was built, it was also directed, in its efforts and its results, not to the purpose of scientific explanation of the

---

* The theories discussed, and the works cited, in this and the following subsection (§ 15) belong to the period 1500–1650.

(All notes marked thus * † ‡ are by the translator. Notes marked by a number are by Gierke himself, and are printed separately in the latter part of the volume.)

past, but to that of the exposition and justification of a new future which was to be called into existence.

2. The form of expression which the natural-law theory of the State assumed, and which was destined to control the course of future thought, was due to the intimate connection established, from 1570 onwards, between legal philosophy and political theory. It is true that, at first, the State was only incidentally mentioned in the works which dealt with the Law of Nature(2). But the ecclesiastical writers on Natural Law, who generally belong to the Jesuit or the Dominican Order, are already [in the sixteenth century] constructing a system of political theory which is based entirely on the law of Reason(3). Such a system may be found, in its most developed form, in the writings of Suarez(4). It was a definite epoch in the history of thought when Grotius proceeded to elaborate a purely secular philosophy of law which embraced the whole of the life of the State, external as well as internal(5). Long before his time, however, the theory of the State had been placed upon a basis of Natural Law by the writers who dealt with politics proper. It is true that there always continued to exist a political literature which sought exclusively, or at any rate mainly, to handle practical questions of pure utility, and only referred incidentally, at the most, to the legal bases of public life(6). We may even say that the treatises which dealt with *raison d'état* were expressly directed against any exaggeration of the value of juristic interpretation(7). But it was generally regarded as the duty of political theory to include the legal nature of the State in the sphere of its investigations, and to propound accordingly a theory of 'general public law' (*allgemeines Staatsrecht*);* and this method of procedure increasingly strengthened the tendency to think in terms of Natural Law. We must admit, indeed, that the thinkers who still persisted in making the *Politics* of Aristotle their basis, or followed other classical models, were far from adopting all the elements of the new mode of speculation. The *De Republica* of Gregorius Tholosanus, for example(8), the writings of Arnisaeus(9), the numerous political disquisitions of Conring(10), and many other works on political theory, both of an earlier and a later date(11), can none of them be ascribed to the authentic current of natural-law speculation. But, on the whole, the natural-law theory

---

* Public Law (*Staatsrecht* or *öffentliches Recht*) is what we should call Constitutional Law—the law concerned with the rights and duties of the State. It is contrasted with private law, which deals with the rights and duties of subjects *inter se*.

§ 14. *The natural-law conception of the State*

of the State finally won the day when Bodin, in his *De Republica*, emancipated the theory of public law from the classical tradition, and made the modern conception of sovereignty the pivot of his argument(12).

In particular, the literary controversies on the political and religious issues of the day increasingly tended, after his time, to broaden out into fundamental differences about the nature of sovereignty; and throughout the course of these controversies the champions of popular sovereignty(13), like the defenders of the sovereignty of the Ruler(14), availed themselves of the weapons of Natural Law. Espousing the cause of popular sovereignty, Althusius then proceeded, early in the seventeenth century, to erect the first complete system of political theory which was wholly based on Natural Law(15). After his time we find numerous text-books of political theory which, however widely they may diverge in their fundamental tendencies, are nearly always agreed in attempting to find the justification of their contentions in a natural-law theory of the State(16). Besold stood alone in combining an interpretation of the State in terms of Natural Law (an interpretation which, as we have already had reason to notice,* now begins to pervade the scientific treatment even of *positive* public law) with an historico-legal justification of the *status quo*(17). Finally, at the end of this period [i.e. about 1650], the political theory based upon Natural Law received from the Radical audacity of Hobbes a form which was at once the culmination of its past and the foundation of its future development(18). Overreaching itself in the very rigour of its logic, his theory threatened the utter extinction of any genuine public law.

3.. The natural-law point of view affected public law at an earlier date, and with greater force, than it affected private law; and this in spite of the fact (or perhaps because of the fact) that opinions about the relation between natural and positive law continued to be more fluid, and more uncertain, in the sphere of public than they were in that of private law. The reason was that public law lacked the solid basis which the jurisprudence of the civilians,†

---

* The reference is to an earlier subsection (§ 2) which is not here translated.

† The civilians are the lawyers of Roman law, which had been studied and developed during the whole of the Middle Ages, in western Europe at large, and continued to be studied and developed in Germany, as a *usus modernus*, during the period from 1500 to 1800, of which Gierke treats. On the whole, as Gierke implies, the civilians were mainly concerned with questions of private law.

interminably though it was occupied in spinning a web of controversies about the nature and the extent of Natural Law, was always able to find in its reliance upon texts of Roman law. The jurists generally started from a division (at bottom only appropriate to the sphere of private law), according to which law fell into the three branches of *jus naturale*, *jus gentium*, and *jus civile*. They often proceeded, following the lines of the theories of the Middle Ages, to distinguish between the 'primary' and the 'secondary' rules of *jus naturale* and *jus gentium*(19), or, confining themselves to the latter, they sought to draw a contrast between *jus gentium primaevum* and *jus gentium secundarium*(20); but the tendency grew in favour of a doctrine of simplification, which ignored such subdivisions as foreign to the original texts(21). As this tendency spread, the common foundation of both *jus naturale* and *jus gentium* in the dictates of the natural reason of man also came to be emphasised more strongly(22). But what was primarily intended to be conveyed by such emphasis was only the simple fact of a line of division between those parts of the system of *private law* which were uniform and immutable, and those which were subject to change.

We accordingly find a number of jurists going to the length of maintaining that the whole distinction [between uniform or natural and variable or positive elements] had no application to *public law*, and that public law, on the contrary, was entirely and totally positive(23). The majority, however, took a different line. They ascribed to *jus publicum* [equally with private law] a mixed content drawn from all the three sources of *jus naturale*, *jus gentium*, and *jus positivum*(24). But as soon as a separation of these various elements was attempted, the category of *jus gentium* inevitably proved itself to be inapplicable to public law(25). The result was —in the sphere of the philosophy of law and of political theory as well as in the legal treatises of jurists who included public law in their scope—that the tripartite division of law yielded more and more to a simple division between the categories of natural and positive law(26). Even when the Roman conception of *jus gentium* was actually retained, it usually lost any separate and independent significance; and it receded altogether into the background as an effective element in the constitution of the State(27). Thus there was gradually developed a theory of pure Natural Law,* in which

* I.e. in the sphere of public law, the element of *jus naturale* was left alone, or 'pure' (the element of *jus gentium* having almost entirely disappeared), to confront the element of *jus positivum*.

§ 14. The natural-law conception of the State

the conception of *jus gentium* only appeared, in the entirely changed sense of international law, as the particular form of Natural Law which was valid among sovereign States (28).

It is astonishing to find this theory of pure Natural Law made to cover all the fundamental relations involved, and to decide all the fundamental questions raised, in the whole of the life of the State. Yet its adherents were unanimous that the transition from a state of nature, exclusively controlled by Natural Law, to the conditions of political life, had always been made in obedience to immutable natural rules, and that the union of men in a political society, and the erection of a political authority, had always taken place in virtue of the same eternal principles. The first product of positive law, and the first occasion for the play of human will, which they consented to admit, was merely the choice of a particular form of State (29). Positive law being denied any capacity to affect or disturb the foundations of Natural Law, the solution of every fundamental problem in regard to the relation of the community to the individual, or that of the Ruler to the People, was accordingly left to the scope of a Law of Nature which sat high enthroned above the whole of historically established law. Now the primary practical object pursued by the theorists of Natural Law was the delimitation of an area within which objective Right* should be withdrawn from the caprice of the legislator, and subjective Right should escape the attacks of the State's authority (30); and the investigation of the limits of this area immediately entailed a far greater latitude of discussion on questions of public law than had ever previously been possible in the sphere of civilian theory (31). It was thus with a new and unprecedented force that the theory of Natural Law was able to enter the domain of public law, and to impose its claim to measure existing institutions by the irrefragable rule of Reason (32). And it was preeminently in *that* domain that the exponents of this theory came more and more to regard their ultimate task as consisting in the discovery of a rational ideal, which, if it could never be fully

---

* The same word *Recht* means (*a*) a system of law existing objectively as an external norm for persons, and (*b*) a system of rights enjoyed by those persons, as 'Subjects' or owners of rights, under and by virtue of that norm. The same thing is both a system of law outside me, when I look at it objectively, as obligatory upon me, and a system of rights inside me, when I look at it subjectively, as belonging to me and as giving me a legal position. Objective Right is what we call Law; subjective Right is what we call rights. But the two are different sides of the same thing, like the obverse and the reverse of a coin.

realised in actual life, was none the less to be made the object of a constant effort at approximation (33).*

4. In the theories about the nature of the State, which developed under the influence of this intellectual movement, there were contradictory elements, which conflicted seriously with one another; but the natural-law theorists were all agreed in making a definite break with the political ideas which had originated in the Middle Ages. The theocratic idea waned (34). The State was no longer derived from the divinely ordained harmony of the universal whole; it was no longer explained as a partial whole which was derived from, and preserved by, the existence of the greater: it was simply explained by itself. The starting-point of speculation ceased to be general humanity: it became the individual and self-sufficing sovereign State; and this individual State was regarded as based on a union of individuals, in obedience to the dictates of Natural Law, to form a society armed with supreme power.

II. *General view of Sovereignty in natural-law theory*

1. Two necessary attributes are thus presented [in this natural-law system of political theory] as determining the conception of the State. One is the existence of a society (*societas civilis*), directed to the objects which compel men to live together: the other is the existence of a sovereign power (*majestas, summa potestas, summum imperium, supremitas*, etc.), which secures the attainment of the common end. Both of these attributes recur in every definition of the State (35). But it was the second which, as soon as Bodin had taken his decisive step, came into prominence; for while the State shares the character of a purposive society with other forms of association, the attribute of sovereignty is its peculiar and specific criterion. The philosophical theory of the State thus becomes increasingly, and essentially, a theory of sovereignty (36).

Sovereignty ('majesty', 'supremacy', etc.),† in the theory of Natural Law, not only means a particular form or quality of political authority; it also means political authority itself, in its

---

* I.e. the theorists of Natural Law concentrated on the constitutional side of law (= public law), and attempted to lay down the 'natural' or proper form of constitutional law for all States, or rather to enunciate an ideal form which all States should seek to attain. We may say that this tendency is particularly illustrated in Vattel's *Droit des Gens, ou principes de la loi naturelle*, especially in Book I.

† *Majestas* is the usual Latin word for sovereignty, and 'majesty' is often used by Gierke as synonymous with sovereignty.

§ 14. *The natural-law conception of the State*

own essential substance (37). The word 'sovereignty' becomes something in the nature of a magic wand, which can conjure up the whole sense and content of the State's general power. The original negative conception—the conception of a power which is not externally subject to any *Superior*—is made to assume a positive form by being as it were turned 'outside in', and used to denote the relation of the State to everything which is within itself. From the quality of being the 'supreme' earthly authority [i.e. the quality of being simply the *highest* authority], there is deduced the whole of that absolute omnipotence [i.e. the quality of being the *only* authority, and therefore unlimited and all-powerful] which the modern State demands for itself. [Nor is this creed the monopoly of one side.] The champions of popular sovereignty vie with the defenders of monarchism in exalting its claims.*

It is true that all sorts of differences arose about the extent and content of this exclusive power. Different conceptions of the end of the State necessarily entailed different conclusions about the extent of the rights of 'majesty' which served as the means of its realisation; more especially, the ecclesiastical limitation of the end of the State to the secular sphere involved a large reservation in favour of ecclesiastical authority. Different views about the efficacy, and the extent, of the legal limits which were regarded as binding even on the supreme power also produced a variety of different interpretations of the maxim that sovereignty was a *potestas legibus soluta*, an 'absolute' plenitude of power. With these, in turn, were connected the controversies which turned on the possibility of a division, or multiplication, or limitation of 'majesty'—controversies which raised the question whether the legal ideas which any such possibility involved were really consistent with the logical presupposition of the unity, indivisibility, and inalienability of the supreme power.

On one point, however, there was general agreement. Whatever the form it took, this right of sovereignty was a right which was given and inherent in the very conception of the State. On this it followed that the origin of 'majesty' (though there might be a number of explanations of its precise mode) was always ascribed to one single general cause—the original act of State-creation, in obedience to Natural Law, which was anterior and superior to the process of historical legal development. When sovereignty was

---

* E.g. Rousseau may be said to vie with Hobbes in exalting sovereignty, though his sovereign is the General Will, and not a single Leviathan.

regarded as an *inherent and original right* of the State, there could be no need to explain it by any particular title of acquisition. When it was regarded as an *indestructible right*, it was secure against the assault of any legal title of more recent origin by which it might be confronted. And it was the *whole* of the substance of sovereignty which was thus secured and protected. Being a right which was both all-inclusive and *sui generis*, sovereignty must necessarily embrace each and every particular right of control which belonged to the nature of the State. In terms of adulation, it was compared to the inexhaustible ocean, which receives again into itself all its own effluences: it was celebrated as a sun, the source of universal light and heat, whose radiation never diminishes the eternal central fires (38).

2. But the more sovereignty was exalted, the hotter raged the dispute about its 'Subject' or owner (39).* Here again the ultimate decision was sought on the basis of Natural Law. Though there was a general agreement that a variety of constitutional forms had been produced by positive law, the fundamental issue of the ownership of sovereignty was none the less regarded as prior to the historical differentiation of constitutions. In all forms of State indifferently, a distinction was drawn between the Ruler and the body of the Ruled: the legal basis of the Ruler's authority was regularly ascribed to a previous devolution of its own authority by the body of the Ruled; and in this way it was easy to produce a single formula, equally applicable to monarchies and to aristocratic or democratic republics, which expressed, in terms universally valid, the relations always existing between Ruler and People under the system of Natural Law. From this point of view it was regarded as a secondary question—a question of mere historical title, irrelevant to the deeper question of principle—whether it was a single person, or a privileged assembly, or an assembly of all deciding by majority-vote, that held the position of Ruler in any actual State (40). Even the controversy about the possibility of a mixed constitution (though falling within the scope of Natural Law, in

* As we saw above, *Recht* in general is both 'Object' and 'Subject'. Something similar is true of my own particular element of *Recht*. My right of property in land has an 'Object'—the piece of land I own, which is the objective expression of that particular right. It has also a 'Subject'—myself as owner, which is the subjective expression. Wherever 'Subject' is used in the following pages (generally, for the sake of clarity, with the addition of the words 'or owner'), this is its sense. From this point of view 'subject' in our English sense ('the King's subject') is the 'Object' of sovereignty. When the word 'subject' is used with a small 's', the reader is asked to take it in this latter sense.

§ 14. *The natural-law conception of the State* 43

virtue of its bearing on the nature of the State's authority) was treated as posterior and secondary to the settlement of the fundamental issue of the 'Subject' of sovereignty—on the ground that it only related, after all, to the internal structure and composition of the Ruling authority (41). The primary question on which debate always turned was purely that of the positions to be accorded to People and Ruler on the basis of Natural Law.

On this question, as we can readily understand, it was the figure of the Monarch which presented itself first to the minds of most thinkers. But we have to remember that, just as the champions of monarchical claims expressly allowed that the 'collective' Ruler in a Republic possessed the same plenitude of power which they ascribed to the Monarch (42), so the opponents of princely absolutism equally attempted to limit both monarchy and democracy. Having ascribed certain overriding powers to the body of the People under a monarchical system, they proceeded, logically enough, to argue that even in a purely democratic State such overriding powers, belonging as they did to the whole body of the People, were distinct from the ordinary rights belonging to the majority of the assembly which was vested with Ruling authority (43). We can thus understand how the natural-law theory of the State came to be radically divided into the two sharply contrasted schools of 'Popular Sovereignty' and 'the Sovereignty of the Ruler'—with the middle view of a 'double majesty'* intercalated (in a variety of forms) between the two (44). But there is also a further cleavage to be noted in the natural-law theory of the State. Among the adherents of simple sovereignty [whether of Ruler or People—as distinct from the advocates of 'double majesty'], a number of different shades of opinion may be distinguished, determined by the extent to which thinkers assumed the existence of some fundamental limitation—either of Popular Sovereignty, by an independent right belonging to the Ruler; or, conversely, of the Sovereignty of the Ruler, by some independent right belonging to the body of the people (45). Over and above this, we have still to note a third and final cleavage. The question arose of the extent to which the 'Subject' of Ruling authority (whether such authority was conceived as sovereignty pure and simple, or as 'secondary' sovereignty, or even as not being sovereignty at all) † could be

---

* The theory of *duplex majestas*, as we shall see later, means the theory of the conjoint sovereignty of both Ruler and People.

† Ruling authority may be sovereignty pure and simple, as in a pure monarchy or republic: it may only be secondary sovereignty, e.g. when a monarch

qualified and controlled by positive law (46); and, more particularly, how far, in such a case, a division of this authority among several 'Subjects', or a participation of several 'Subjects' in its exercise, could be regarded as possible (47).

III. *People and Ruler as separate personalities*

1. In the conflict of political theories People and Ruler thus came to be opposed as rival powers; and each of these powers, when once it had vindicated for itself any political right whatever, was bound to be regarded as a separate *personality*.* We have now to enquire what conceptions were held of the personality of the People on the one side, and of that of the Ruler on the other; and then we shall have to consider whether, and if so how, it was found possible to transcend the dualism of the two by a conception of the one personality of the State.

It was universally held, until Hobbes dealt a death-blow to the idea, that the People possessed a separate personality. Thinkers were agreed that the People had originally owned political power, whole and undivided, and had subsequently, by a contract, subjected itself to a Ruler (48). But to possess the capacity for such an act, the People must already have been—before the erection of such an authority, and independently of its existence—a definite 'Subject' or owner of rights (49). In the view of all the upholders of the theory of contract in this period [i.e. before Hobbes], the institution of a government did not imply that the People thereby surrendered every political right, but only that it renounced its sole possession of rights. To the believers in Popular Sovereignty, the People still remained, as much as before, the 'Subject' or owner of 'majesty'; to the exponents of the theory of 'double sovereignty', it was still the 'Subject' of the greater of the two 'majesties'; to the advocates of the theory of a limited sovereignty of the Ruler, it continued to be the 'Subject' of the rights which limited 'majesty'; and even the champions of the absolute power of the Ruler reserved for the People at any rate two things—a claim to the due fulfilment of the contract of government, and the

owes his ruling authority to the primary sovereignty of the people, or exercises it subject thereto: it may not be sovereignty at all, if the Ruler is a mere delegate or commissary.

* A right involves a 'Subject'; a 'Subject' of a right is a person; and a person has personality. If there are State-rights, there must be some person, with a personality, as their 'Subject'. Is that person the People, or the Ruler, or can it be something above both?

§ 14. *The natural-law conception of the State*

right of resuming possession of 'majesty' in the event of its alienation(50). It followed, that, even after the State had already been formed, the People still preserved, to some degree or other, a personality of its own, which must of course be the same as its original personality(51).

But if it thus existed before any political authority, and independently of such authority, the personality of the People was inevitably bound to be conceived as being of the nature of a purely *collective personality*. It is true that it was the universal habit of thinkers—using terms such as *universitas*, *communitas*, or *corpus*, and calling in aid the [Roman-law] theory of the Corporation—to explain the personality of the People as a corporate [and not a collective] unity. This was the case with the Monarchomachi, among whom we find Junius Brutus [the author of the *Vindiciae contra Tyrannos**], like Althusius afterwards, making an extensive use of the theory of the Corporation(52). The idea of the People as a corporate unity also appears in the theories of double sovereignty(53), and in the cognate theory of Grotius(54); it is used in the works which advocate the doctrine of the limited sovereignty of the Ruler, and especially in the ecclesiastical theory of politics developed by Soto, Molina and Suarez(55); and it may even be traced in the writings of the absolutists, so far as they deal with the rights of the People(56). But though the writers of our period [1500–1650] thus brought the popular community under the head of the conception of Corporation, they steadily followed a line of thought which tended to the dissolution of corporate existence, in all its forms, into partnership connections with a merely collective unity; and while they borrowed from the theory of the Corporation, they borrowed only those principles which fitted into this tendency. This explains why they had no objection to describing the popular community as a *societas*, and believing that it actually was a *societas*, at the same time that they also applied the theory of the Corporation(57).† If, on the other hand, the conception of 'partnership' was taken seriously, and if it was genuinely applied to the community of the People, the internal substance of this community was bound to dissolve itself into a mere system of reciprocal rights and duties of individuals. Even the thinkers who

* On the authorship of this work see E. Barker (essay in *Church, State and Study* on the 'Huguenot theory of politics', and *Cambridge Historical Journal*, 1930).

† We have here to distinguish the *universitas*, or corporate unity, from the *societas*, or partnership, in which the members remain distinct, in spite of their connection, and the unity is thus 'collective' rather than corporate.

clung to the doctrine of Aristotle, and sought to lay particular emphasis on the natural growth of civil society, could oppose no permanent barrier to this process of dissolution (58). When the theory of the social contract triumphed, and the unity of the People was referred to a contractual act, it became entirely impossible to escape from the circle of individualistic ideas (59).

There were, indeed, some of the natural-law theorists who attempted, in spite of their individualistic premises, to attain the idea of a Universal which existed in its own right, and to believe in a Whole which depended only upon itself. The ecclesiastical writers on the philosophy of law, in particular, sought to prove that the community of the People, though it was freely created by individuals, did not derive its rights from them (60); but in defending such a paradox even the ability of a Suarez could only produce an ingenious *jeu d'esprit* (61).* In the philosophy of these writers, equally with the rest, a sovereign Universal which proceeded from the contractual act of autonomous individuals was bound to remain at the level of an aggregate of individuals (62). If the conception of a social contract was pushed to its logical conclusion, any right belonging to a community was necessarily reduced to the collective rights of a number of individuals (63); and the internal nexus of the popular community became nothing more than a network of contractual relationships between its various members (64). In the writings of Althusius we already find the idea of mere 'social' connection [or, in other words, the idea of simple 'partnership'] extended to the whole of the State, and this in spite of the fact that he lays more emphasis than any other writer upon its corporate character (65). Grotius, too, may be said to fill the formal mould of Corporation with the actual ore of *societas* (66). Yet it is obvious that, if you limit the internal nexus of a community to a mere matter of reciprocal rights and duties among all its individual units, you can only give the People the unity which it needs, in order to be a 'Subject' of rights, by assuming a merely external form of association between its members.†

It is thus a purely 'collective' interpretation of the personality of the People which really predominates in the natural-law theory of the State. The People is made co-extensive with the sum of its constituent units; and yet simultaneously, when the need is felt

* Gierke seems unjust to Suarez in this remark. See the translator's notes appended to notes 60 and 62.

† And therefore you cannot really speak at all of a Corporation, which is something transcending any mere external form of association.

§ 14. *The natural-law conception of the State*

for a single bearer (*Träger*) of the rights of the People, it is treated as essentially a unit in itself(67). The whole distinction between the unity and the multiplicity of the community is reduced to a mere difference of point of view, according as *omnes* is interpreted as *omnes ut universi* or as *omnes ut singuli*(68). The eye resolved upon 'reality' refuses to recognise, in the living and permanent unity of the existence of a People, anything more than an unsubstantial shadow; and it dismisses as a 'juristic fiction' the elevation of this living unity to the rank of a Person(69).* On the basis of this logic the common will was dissolved into a mere agreement of individual wills(70); and thus the co-operation of every individual came to be regarded as inherently necessary, if the popular community was to act directly and immediately as such(71).† Somewhat inconsequentially, this demand for unanimity was only sustained in regard to two points—the original constitution of civil society, and the subsequent alteration of certain of the original articles on which its existence depended(72); and on other points majority-decision was regarded as adequate(73). But this required a further fiction [in addition to the original 'fiction' that the People was a Person], in order to justify the identification of majority-will with the common will of all(74).

A similar difficulty arose in regard to the representation of the People. Any capacity for acting in lieu of the People could only be ascribed, from the general point of view with which we are dealing, to a procuratorial power conferred collectively by all individuals. Once more, therefore, recourse was had to a fiction—the fiction of the bestowal of such procuratorial powers in and by the act of election‡—in order to justify the assumption (which actual facts made inevitable) that it was possible for the popular

---

* The reader may possibly sympathise with 'the eye resolved upon reality'; and he may thus be led to doubt whether what Gierke calls the *Daseinseinheit des Volkes* is really a substance, in the sense of a being or person. The unity of existence present in a People may be argued to be the unity of a common content of many minds, or in other words of a common purpose, but not the unity of a Group-Being or a Group-Person.

† In other words all the members must pass a unanimous decision, if the community was to act otherwise than through some 'organ' or agency.

‡ It may be doubted whether the bestowal of procuratorial powers in and by the act of election should be regarded as a fiction. In England, Edward I actually and expressly required that representatives should be given *plena et sufficiens potestas pro se et communitate...ita quod pro defectu hujusmodi potestatis negotium praedictum infectum non remaneat* (Stubbs, *Select Charters*, 9th ed., pp. 481–2). The English clergy were using *literae procuratoriae* early in the thirteenth century; cf. E. Barker, *The Dominican Order and Convocation*, pp. 48–50.

community to be 'represented' in the exercise of its political rights by an assembly of Estates (75). The thinkers who strictly adhered to the logic of their premises proceeded to contend that the People itself still enjoyed, as against its own representatives, the position of the head of a business (*Geschäftsherr*) (76). Althusius in particular, although he applied the idea of the representative constitution at every point,* attempted none the less to protect the sovereignty of the community from the danger of being absorbed by its own representatives (77). But even when, in actual fact, nothing at all survived in the way of direct and immediate rights of the People, the view continued to be maintained, as a matter of theory, that the collective unity of the whole People still continued to be the true 'Subject' or owner of popular rights, over and above any assembly of Estates which was actually entitled to exercise such rights (78).

2. A separate personality of the Ruler, distinct from that of the People, was generally recognised as the 'Subject' of the rights of government. Such a view was obviously entailed both by the theory of the Sovereignty of the Ruler and by that of a double sovereignty; but even the pure theory of Popular Sovereignty, as long as it continued to include the idea of a contract of government,† which was first overthrown by Rousseau, was necessarily committed to the admission of an independent personality belonging to the Ruler (79). Without such a personality, it is obvious, a permanent relation of contract between Ruler and People was inconceivable. But this personality of the Ruler necessarily varied in character, according as the right to rule was assigned to a single person, or vested in a body of persons (80). Moreover, if the possibility of a mixed constitution were admitted, the personality of the Ruler might be divided into a number of personalities; or short of this, if a single constitutionally limited Ruling authority were allowed to be possible, that Ruling authority might find at its side another 'Subject' [in the shape of the authority enforcing the constitutional limits] which had a conjoint right to the exercise of

---

* I.e. holding a federal idea of the State, Althusius applied the idea of representation both to the federal State as a whole and to the units of which it was composed.

† Gierke distinguishes between *Gesellschaftsvertrag* (*pacte d'association*), or the contract of each with all, which creates a State in the sense of a political society, and *Herrschaftsvertrag* (*pacte de gouvernement*), or the contract of such a society with a person or body of persons, which creates a State in the sense of a government.

§ 14. *The natural-law conception of the State*

Ruling power (81). If, in any of these ways, a body of men were vested with the right, or with a conjoint right, to the exercise of Ruling authority, the conception of a collective personality [already applied to the People as distinct from the Ruler] was applied once more to meet the case of such a body. Thinkers accordingly spoke of the right of government as belonging to 'several' or 'many'; and they described a republic, for example, as 'the government of many' (82). But they insisted at the same time that the right of government belonged to these 'several' or 'many' only when acting in conjunction (83); and they argued accordingly that although an artificial unity here took the place of the natural unity inherent in the nature of monarchy, it was still a case of a *single* Ruling personality (84). The distinction between *omnes ut universi* and *omnes ut singuli*, which had been applied to the People, was also generally applied to this case of a body of Rulers; and the individual Optimates of an aristocracy, or the individual citizens who possessed the suffrage in a democracy, were declared to be subject to the community which they collectively constituted (85). This community, we may note in passing, was always identified with the majority of its members; in a word, the majority *was* the community (86).

When thinkers thus insisted on connecting the 'Subject' or owner of the legal exercise of Ruling power with the visible fact of an assembly of individuals, they could not escape a merely collective conception of such a 'Subject' of power (87). When, on the other hand, a *single* person was vested with Ruling power, the conception of his natural personality was accepted as adequate (88). The monarch for the time being was thus regarded as owning, by way of private proprietary right,* the whole of the powers which constituted the right of the Ruler, as distinct from the right of the People. It is true that a distinction was drawn, in regard to the 'Objects' covered by the Ruler's rights, between (1) the area of such rights and duties as were derived from the title of being the Ruling authority and (2) the sphere of the private rights of the Monarch [as a natural person]; but, in dealing with the problem of the 'Subject' or owner of rights, theorists stopped at the simple fact of the physical unity of the one individual. The natural-law theory of the State made very little use of the idea that the Monarch

* The authority of Loyseau, *Traité des Offices*, may be claimed for this view. Monarchs, he writes, *ont prescrit la propriété de la puissance souveraine, et l'ont jointe à l'exercice d'icelle* (II, ch. II, §§ 25–6).

played the part of two persons; and even the question of the continuity of the Ruler's personality in the event of a change of the occupant of the throne (a question which might seem to involve the use of that idea) was constantly befogged by the introduction of the notion of simple hereditary succession to the whole aggregate of rights(89).* Grotius, indeed, made an effort to draw a distinction in principle between the acts of a king as king and his acts as a private individual(90); but on the whole we may say that it was only found possible to distinguish the public sphere of the Monarch from his private sphere when they were both made to take their place by the side of a concurrent right of the general community of the People(91).†

IV. *Attempts to eliminate the dualism of People and Ruler The idea of a single State-personality*

1. The dualism of the two personalities—that of the Ruler and that of the People—was an obvious survival from the medieval State, with its system of Estates confronting the King; but it was in marked contradiction to the unitary tendency of the modern State. A movement was thus bound to make itself felt among the theorists of Natural Law in favour of obliterating the old antithesis by the development of a conception of the single *personality of the State*. In a variety of ways some approach was actually made to such a conception. Unable, however, to transcend the limits of an individualistic system of thought, the thinkers of the school of Natural Law never really succeeded in attaining a true idea of the personality of the State. They could only achieve, at the most, a one-sided exaggeration, either of the personality of the People, or of that of the Ruler.

The idea of the State as an *organic whole*, which had been bequeathed by classical and medieval thought, was never entirely extinguished. But the natural-law tendency of thought was hardly qualified to achieve the construction of an organic theory, or to crown it by the discovery of an immanent group-personality. The comparison of the State to an animate body regularly continued

---

* The allusion is to the regular succession of a private heir, under Roman private law, to the *whole* estate—*per universitatem successio*.

† If you banish the community, and leave the king isolated, you then confuse the two 'personalities' of the king—the public and the private—in the blaze of his solitary glory. If you admit the community by the side of the king, you can say that he stands in two relations to it—the public and the private.

§ 14. *The natural-law conception of the State* 51

to be drawn; and in this period too* [as had been done before in the Middle Ages] it was drawn out in detail, with a greater or less degree of good taste, by a number of writers. A distinction was made between the head and the members of the 'body politic': descriptions were given of the structure and functions of its internal organs: the differentiation and the harmonious connection of the several parts were shown to issue in a living unity of the Whole (92). The rule of the soul over the body was also adduced to illustrate the living unity of society; and the idea of a spiritual force thus informing the social body was then brought into connection with the notion of a single and indivisible sovereignty (93).

Various and contradictory as such pictures were, there could yet be extracted from them an idea which was capable of juristic formulation—the idea of a group-being, distinct from the sum of its members, which was vested as a whole with legal authority over its parts. So interpreted, the conception of the social organism was not only used by writers, such as Gregorius Tholosanus (94), who continued to maintain the natural origin of the political community: it was also dovetailed into the theory of a social contract, as an element which served to counteract, in some degree, the individualistic premises of that theory. It is in the ecclesiastical systems of Natural Law, which culminated in the theories of Molina and Suarez, that we find the most vigorous attempts to use the idea of the organic nature of the State in order to vindicate for the social Whole, when once it has been called into existence, a power of control over its parts which, notwithstanding its contractual origin, is none the less independent of the wills of individuals (95). [Such ideas were not confined to these Catholic writers.] We also find Althusius turning his original *consociatio*, which he has constructed purely on the basis of partnership, into a *corpus symbioticum*, and holding that the organic unity of this body explains the authority of the community over its members (96). Grotius, too, emphasises strongly the character of the State as a composite body, with its own independent system of life (97); in particular, he gives an admirably exact expression to the idea of the corporate 'organ', in the action of which the whole body itself is simultaneously active (98). † In fact, there was hardly a single

* The period from 1500 to 1650. For the use of this analogy in medieval thought, see *Political Theories of the Middle Age*, pp. 24 *seq.*

† Grotius argues that just as the body is the general and the eye the specific 'Subject' of vision, at one and the same time, so, at one and the same time, the

system of political theory which entirely escaped this 'organic' tendency of thought; and even the cause of monarchical absolutism was made to profit from the arguments which it supplied.

But the thinkers of our period, like those of the Middle Ages, never took the really decisive step. While they recognised an invisible unity as the internal principle of life in the body politic, they never conceived it as being the true Ruling personality. The organic theory was never applied to the problem of the 'Subject' of sovereign power. The organic being of the State stopped short, as it were, at the neuter gender; and an organic interpretation was only used to explain the objective connection of the parts of a Whole and the system of control involved in that connection.* As soon as the issue became that of finding personal 'Subjects' for this system of control [there was never any admission that an organic Group-person was such a 'Subject', but] the stage was at once again occupied merely by individuals, or by assemblies of individuals. An organism of this nature, destitute of any Ego, was after all only a simulacrum of a living being. In spite of all assertions to the contrary, it was no more than a work of art, counterfeited to look like a natural body; a machine, invented and controlled by individuals. Here again Hobbes—anticipated, it is true, by similar suggestions in previous writers (99)—only pushed the premises of the natural-law school to their ultimate logical conclusions. He began by comparing the State, that great Leviathan, to a giant's body; he proceeded to expound, in the minutest of detail, its analogies with a living being (100); but he ended by transforming his supposed organism into a mechanism, moved by a number of wheels and springs, and his man-devouring monster turned into an artfully devised and cunningly constructed automaton (101).

In this position of affairs, it became impossible to vindicate unity for the personality of the State except by vesting it exclusively in *one or other of the constituent parts* of the body politic [the People, or the Ruler].

2. The advocates of popular sovereignty attempted to represent

body politic is the general and the Ruler the specific 'Subject' of political authority.

* I.e. the organic analogy was applied (1) to the impersonal fact of the connection of parts (as in an organism), and (2) to the equally impersonal fact of a system of common control for maintaining that connection (again as in an organism); but it was not applied (3) to the personal factor of a controlling group-personality (such as also appears, on Gierke's view, in an organism).

§ 14. *The natural-law conception of the State*

the personality of the People as the one and only bearer (*Träger*) of all political rights. Among the Monarchomachi the express identification of 'People' and 'State' is frequent. They ascribe supreme authority to the *respublica*, or the *regnum*, in just the same sense in which they speak of the 'majesty' of the *populus*, or of the *universitas populi*, or of the *universitas civium et subditorum*(102). In the same way, and without any idea of suggesting a difference between the two terms, they sometimes describe particular rights of government as rights of the People, and sometimes as rights of the State(103); they speak of public property as the property of the People, *or* the State(104); they treat decisions of the sovereign community as expressions of the will of the People, *or* the State(105). In Althusius, the *respublica* is consistently identified with the *universitas populi*(106). Salamonius, if he actually speaks of a *persona civitatis* as superior to the *persona principis*, ascribes this *persona* to the sovereign People(107). Such interchange of terms was not, however, enough to make a personified popular community into a real State-personality which served, by its own inherent nature, as the active and effective 'bearer' of the will of the commonwealth. The community of the People, as it was understood in natural-law theory, was never anything more than the sum of its individual members regarded as a single unit; and on this it followed that a Ruler vested with the exercise of State-authority was related to that community, not as a constituent element included in it, but as the bearer of a power confronting it from without(108).

So long as the principle was maintained that the State owed its origin, not to the original foundation of civil society, but to the conclusion of a subsequent contract between that society and the bearer of Ruling power, the 'Subject' of political rights was necessarily doomed to be a divided and dual 'Subject'. Thinkers might limit the rights of the Ruler ever so rigorously; they might even degrade him to the position of servant of the People, and threaten him with punishment and deposition if he went beyond his appointed sphere; they could not escape the logic of their principles. The contractual relation must always involve a duality of persons; a personality of the Ruler must always emerge by the side of the personality of the People, equally essential to the existence of the State(109). It was only with the elimination of the last traces of a contract of government that it became possible to banish entirely the idea of the personality of the Ruler, and to confine the personality of the State, without qualification or reserve, to the sovereign community of individuals. But this was a height of radicalism which was never attained before the appearance of Rousseau's *Contrat Social*(110).

3. The many adherents of the theory of a double sovereignty, like the advocates of popular sovereignty, assumed an essential identity of 'State' and 'People'; but they were even less able, on the basis which they had adopted, to attain the idea of a real unity of the personality of the State. It is true that they always described the State (*Respublica, Imperium, Regnum*) as the 'Subject' of *majestas realis*, and that they never ascribed to the Ruler anything but a *majestas personalis*(111). These phrases may lead us to think, at the first glance, that they really proclaimed the idea of the sovereignty of the State; and there was, indeed, some dim inkling of that idea in their philosophy(112). But when they come to expand their doctrines in detail, any vestige of such an idea at once disappears. The terms they use may make it seem possible for them to interpret the two 'majesties' as only two different forms of the exercise of a single right; but they never attempted such an interpretation. They treated the two 'majesties' as separate spheres of authority, and they made them unequal in scope and range. Their origin was assigned to an act by which the People disengaged *majestas personalis* from its own originally complete and exclusive 'majesty', and conferred it upon a Ruler, while reserving *majestas realis* for itself; and the relation between the two was conceived as determined by the contract which was then made between the two separate possessors.

The theory of double 'majesty' thus involved a double 'Subject' of rights; and it was therefore impossible for its advocates to find any way of treating the State as the one and only 'Subject' of State-authority, or of interpreting the Ruler as the constitutionally appointed chief 'organ' of that 'Subject'. They used the word 'State' [just like the advocates of the theory of popular sovereignty] simply to denote the personified People, which confronts the Ruler as a multitude of individuals connected together in a collective unity. To this collective body, which is indifferently described as *respublica* and *populus*, the higher of the two sovereignties is ascribed(113); to it are assigned the various powers comprised in that sovereignty(114); the possessions of the State are treated as its property(115); it is conceived as entitled to exercise, either in a primary or a representative assembly, a supreme authority to which the right of the Ruler is subject(116). At the

§ 14. *The natural-law conception of the State* 55

same time, however, the Ruler is made to enjoy, in the shape of *majestas personalis*, a State-authority which is independent when acting in its own sphere; and this authority, with all the powers of government and the lucrative rights which it comprises, is treated as his by right—a right derived, it is true, from contractual acquisition, but yet, in virtue of that very title, a personal and private right (117). Different limits were often ascribed to the authority of the Ruler (118); but these differences do not affect the truth of two propositions. In the first place, no limitation of *majestas personalis* could ever deprive its 'Subject' of the position of a separate Ruler-person. In the second place, no extension of his derivative sovereignty could ever elevate the position of the Ruler-person into that of a true State-personality, so long as there still loomed in the background, even in the most shadowy of outlines, the form of a more original and a higher sovereignty belonging to the collective body of the People. This self-contradictory theory accordingly perpetuated the old dualism in regard to the nature of the 'Subject' of public authority; it failed to incorporate the Ruler in the People, and yet it was forced to regard State-personality as resident in the People (119). The opponents of the theory objected to it, with justice, that in spite of its logical *tours de force* it never succeeded in rising above the simple idea of popular sovereignty (120).

4. The theory propounded by Grotius, of a double 'Subject' of sovereignty [as distinct from a double sovereignty], approached much closer to the conception of the sovereignty of the State. Leaving supreme power single and undivided, Grotius assumes two 'bearers' of that power: recognising only a single 'majesty', which permeates the whole body politic as the soul permeates the body, he maintains that, just as the whole body and the eye are simultaneously 'Subjects' of the power of vision, so, in the State, there are two simultaneous 'Subjects' of supreme authority. The whole State (*civitas*, i.e. *coetus perfectus*) is itself the *subjectum commune* of authority: the Ruler (*persona una pluresve pro cuiusque gentis legibus et moribus*) is the *subjectum proprium* (I, c. 3, §7). But even Grotius, though he formulates the sovereignty of the State in terms which appear to be free from ambiguity, fails none the less to attain a true conception of the single personality of the State. While he tended towards an organic conception of the State, he was also deeply immersed in the individualism of the School of Natural Law; and his individualism prevented him from interpreting the immanent unity of a commonwealth composed both of head and

of members in terms of a single living personality. A 'person' was always for him either a natural individual, or a sum of individuals who were only held together in the way of a partnership, and could only be regarded as a unity in virtue of a fiction; it was nothing more. His *subjectum commune* turns out, in the end, to be simply the aggregate of the People. Whenever the rights of the State have to be distinguished from those of the Ruler, he can only think in terms of the body of the Ruled confronting the Ruler as the other party to the contract of government; and he accordingly employs the terms *universitas* or *populus* as synonymous with the terms *civitas* or *regnum*, in the purely collective sense to which we have already referred(121).

This explains why the sovereignty of the State of which Grotius writes never becomes anything more than a bloodless category. Refusing to recognise a real sovereignty of the People as always and everywhere present, and only consenting to admit the existence of popular sovereignty where the People itself was constituted Ruler by positive law(122), he was condemned to see his doctrine of the sovereignty of the State—proclaimed as universally and eternally valid, but in reality only allowed to exist in the one form of popular sovereignty—inevitably dwindling into an empty shadow. It only amounted, in the last analysis, to the notion that the original sovereignty of the community, which had once actually existed under the inchoate conditions of primitive civil society, continued still to enjoy a sort of conceptual existence even after it had disappeared *de facto* with the erection of a State-authority. Grotius uses this notion to prove that an alteration of the form of the State does not extinguish its previous rights and duties, and, more particularly, that a change from popular to monarchical rule, or *vice versa*, does not interrupt the continuity of the 'Subject' of public right(123). But as soon as he goes into any detail, even on this simple issue, we begin to see clearly how far he is from any approach to the conception of a single State-personality(124). Nor does he, in the rest of his argument, even when he is dealing with questions in which we should definitely expect some use to be made of the idea, ever recur at all to his *subjectum commune*(125). It disappears entirely in favour of the *subjecta propria* which are depicted as possessing *dominium*, or as sharing in *condominium*, according to the particular constitution which he has in view at the moment. We are always confronted, throughout his work, by the figures of individuals, or of collective bodies of individuals, acting

§ 14. *The natural-law conception of the State* 57

externally as the 'Subjects' of international rights(126), and internally as the 'Subjects' of State-authority(127). He allows, indeed, that an active personality of the People *may* still continue to exist by the side of the sovereign personality of the Ruler; he even allows that the personality of the Ruler *may* be merged, in the whole of its range, or in part of its range, into the personality of the People; but whether any of these possibilities is actually realised is made to depend entirely on the way in which the fortunes of the original sovereignty of the People have been affected by the accident of a particular method of acquiring Ruling power. On the one hand, the People may have retained, or recovered, the supreme power; and in that event, the People will be both the *subjectum commune* and the *subjectum proprium* of majesty(128). On the other hand, the Ruler, by an act of conquest, or through a contract of submission, may have acquired State-authority to as full an extent as it ever belonged to the People itself (*'imperium ut in populo est'*); and in that case such authority will be his personal and inalienable right, which he possesses *jure plenae proprietatis*, and of which he can freely dispose, as his own *patrimonium*, both *inter vivos* and at death(129). In a patrimonial State of this kind the personality of the People may still appear in the guise of a *subjectum commune*; but it has obviously lost any footing in the world of real life.

The general view of Grotius, however, is based on the assumption that, in spite of the transference of supreme power to the Ruler, the body of the People still continues to enjoy extensive rights in the State. Even a conqueror, he argues, may content himself with the appropriation of something less than absolute right, and he may thus only acquire *imperium ut est in rege vel in aliis imperantibus*(130). When a Ruler has been installed in virtue of a contract, there is a definite presumption in favour of a reservation of popular rights(131). In any case of doubt, it is not the full right of property, but only a right of usufruct, which properly belongs to the Ruler; and in such a case the People has a right of property in the authority(132), the territory(133), and the possessions(134) of the State. Special constitutional provisions may limit the authority of the Ruler even further: for instance, its exercise may require the co-operation of the People, or of some smaller assembly; or again, it may be initially assigned for a limited period, or it may be subject to a 'resolutive condition'(135).* But none of these

---

* 'A condition on the happening of which a contract or obligation is terminated', *N.E.D.*

possibilities really affects the existence of the sovereignty of the Ruler; and therefore none of these possible rights of the People really secures any effective sovereignty, either in whole or in part, for the *subjectum commune* of sovereignty (136)—though there is always the possibility that, as a result of the institution of a genuine *forma mixta*, the supreme power may itself be actually divided among a number of 'Subjects', and, more particularly, between king and People (137).* It follows that, even in the theory of Grotius, if we leave aside pure democracy and the pure patrimonial State, a dualism between two personalities is constantly reappearing; and indeed we may even say that it is definitely accentuated, by the wider application which he gives to the idea that the right to State-authority may be of the nature of a right of private property.† His doctrine of the *subjectum commune et proprium majestatis* thus remained essentially barren. It found a few adherents (138); but on the whole we may say that it was regarded as a variety of the theory of popular sovereignty, which was not without its own risks, and which was accordingly attacked and rejected along with that theory (139).

5. We may now turn to the advocates of the theory of the Sovereignty of the Ruler. We should expect them, *a priori*, if they attempted to attain the idea of a single State-personality, to identify it entirely with the personality of the Ruler; and we actually find them agreed in regarding the Ruler as the one and only 'bearer' of the active life of the State—the force which united, animated, and organised the whole body politic—the visible representative of the State itself. Yet as long as they recognised a personality of the People as existing at all by the side of that of the Ruler, they could not possibly deny that this had also its share in the representation of the State. The result was twofold. Not only did they tend, in treating of popular rights, to set the People over against the Ruler as a separate 'Subject' of these rights. In the very act of making this antithesis, they often went further still, and they even described the People as being the 'State' itself.

* In other words, the People, as a *subjectum commune*, remains without any effective sovereignty; but as a *subjectum proprium* it may enjoy, under a mixed constitution, a share in effective sovereignty. We may add that in a pure democracy it may also enjoy, in the same capacity, the whole of such sovereignty.

† The reference is to Grotius' conception of the Ruler as able to acquire, by conquest or contract, a personal and alienable right, *jure plenae proprietatis*. This opposes the Ruler even more definitely, as a still more independent authority, to the People in its capacity of the 'common Subject' of sovereignty.

§ 14. *The natural-law conception of the State*

This being the case, it was inevitable that every attempt to qualify the Sovereignty of the Ruler should prove an insuperable obstacle to the attainment of any conception of a single State-personality. (1) If, in accordance with a theory which had been inherited from the Middle Ages (a theory still held by many writers down to the days of Bodin, and defended even later, in spite of their acceptance of the strict conception of sovereignty, by the ecclesiastical theorists on Natural Law who were inspired by Molina and Suarez), the very nature of the State was held to involve a *limitation*, by the reserved and inalienable natural rights of the originally sovereign People, upon such sovereignty as had been alienated to the Ruler, it followed *ex hypothesi* that the collective body of the Ruled confronted the Ruler, at a number of points, as the true and proper State-personality (140). (2) The same result [of a dualism between Ruler and Ruled] was also possible, to say the least, if the idea was accepted of a contract of government made upon mutual terms, and if accordingly another form of *limitation* of the Ruler's sovereignty—i.e. a limitation by the constitutionally determined rights of the People—was recognised as binding upon him (141). (3) Finally, turning to the theories which rejected any idea of a *limited* sovereignty, but admitted, in lieu thereof, the possibility of a mixed constitution, with a *division* of sovereignty between several 'Subjects' and, more especially, between king and People, we observe a still deeper contradiction. Such theories extended the dualism of the State-personality, which it was their fundamental object to avoid, until it affected and divided the personality of the Ruler itself (142).

In opposition to all these tendencies, the systems of thought inspired by the logic of strict absolutism attempted to concentrate State-personality in a single person, either individual or collective. The primary aim of Bodin was to attain, by the unqualified rejection both of limited and of divided majesty, a Ruler-personality which included and absorbed the whole conception of the State (143). But even Bodin himself failed to take the last and decisive step. Clinging to the original sovereignty of the People, he vindicated for it, even after it had alienated State-authority, the ownership at any rate of State-property; and on this point he opposed the *respublica*, as the properly qualified 'Subject' or owner of such property, to the *imperans* (144). In the same way, but, in some respects, to an even greater degree, there appears in the theory of Gregorius Tholosanus, and in the theories of other advocates of the unlimited authority of the Ruler, a personality of the People, which takes its place, under the name of *respublica*, by the side of the personality of the Ruler(145). Arnisaeus was the only writer who assumed the total absorption of the *respublica* in the Ruler; but in spite of that assumption he treated the *societas* of the Ruled as a separate 'Subject', for which he reserved the name of *civitas*(146).

6. Thus the old dualism was not entirely vanquished, even by those who sought to exalt the Sovereignty of the Ruler; and it was therefore an event of the first importance when Hobbes, boldly demolishing what had hitherto been the foundation of all natural-law political systems, went at last to the root of the matter. He substituted for the two original contracts* a single contract by which each pledges himself to each to submit to a common Ruler, who, on his side, takes no part in the making of the contract(147). This assumption destroyed, in the very germ, any personality of the People. According to Hobbes, there has never existed, at any time, a *societas civilis* based simply upon itself. The personality of the People died at its birth(148). But just as there has never existed an original right of the People, so, when the State has been formed, it is equally impossible to think of any right of the People, even of the most modest description, as either surviving by reservation [since there was nothing to reserve], or as introduced *de novo* by contract, since a relation of contract between Ruler and People is inconceivable(149). With a logical inevitability all public right is absorbed, in every possible form of State, by a Sovereignty of the Ruler which is absolutely unlimited and illimitable, irresponsible and omnipotent, free from all obligation of law and duty, the engulfing reservoir of all rights both of individual subjects and of the aggregate body they form(150). Intolerant of any division, and thus excluding any mixed form of government, this authority is necessarily concentrated, in all its plenitude, at a single centre(151). Its 'Subject' can only be either a single and self-subsisting individual, or a sum of individuals united in a visible assembly and armed with the power which a majority has to control a minority(152).

There is thus, in Hobbes' view, a physically perceptible Ruler-personality, which is to be found everywhere. In it, and in it alone, he next proceeds to argue, the whole State also attains personality(153). For the unity of this artificial body wholly depends upon an agreement—an agreement attained, under the inevitable

* The contract of society and the contract of government.

§ 14. The natural-law conception of the State

compulsion of the command of Natural Law, in the contract which created the State—that the authority, the will and the action of the *unus homo vel unus coetus* shall count as the authority, the will, and the action of each and every subject(154). The Ruler thus appears as *persona representativa*: it is he who *personam omnium gerit*; whose *persona cunctorum civium persona est*; in whom *tota civitas continetur*(155). No personality of the community can stand by his side: apart from him, the community is a loose heap of individuals, a disunited multitude, and therefore in no sense a *universitas*(156). The personality of the State, like that of any other body, cannot be any other than single; its Ruler is more than the head, he is the very soul, of the body of this Leviathan; and as such he represents its personal identity, which only exists in him(157). In this way there arises, out of the artificial life (*vita artificialis*) of the great automaton (*homo artificialis*), an artificial person (*persona artificialis*) which, under the technical designation of *persona civitatis*, becomes the centre of public law(158).

This was the solution provided by Hobbes for the riddle which so many thinkers had so long attempted to solve(159). Basing himself upon arbitrarily assumed premises, but wielding a remorseless logic, he wrested a single State-personality from the individualistic philosophy of Natural Law. He had extended the idea of Natural Right until it meant the right of all to everything, and he had done so in order that it might perish, as a right of all, from the very abundance of its own strength, and then, surviving only in the form of a *jus ad omnia* left in the hands of a single man, or a single body of men, might proceed to convert itself into mere naked power. He had made the individual omnipotent, with the object of forcing him to destroy himself instantly in virtue of his own omnipotence, and thus enthroning the 'bearer' of the State-authority as a mortal god (*Deus mortalis*). In this materialistic and mechanical consummation the natural-law theory of the State seemed to have reached the end of its development. But instead of falling into the sterility of premature death, it drew a new and unexpected vitality from the very crisis which threatened its life. In the march of its onward movement in the future, it might sometimes be constructive, and sometimes critical; but it was always to remain dependent on the system of thought constructed by Hobbes. And the element which was to prove itself most fertile in its future progress was to be the idea of a single State-personality which he had managed to attain—even though that idea, as it stood in his presentation, was purely external and formal.

CHAPTER I: SECTION V, §15

THE NATURAL-LAW THEORY OF ASSOCIATIONS
(*DIE ENGEREN VERBÄNDE*)

There were two ways in which the conception of the State expounded by natural-law thinkers was bound to exercise a determining influence on the theory of other associations. On the one hand, their theory of Sovereignty drew an insuperable line of division between the State and all other groups. On the other hand, their theory of Contract tended towards the inclusion of the theory of the State in a general theory of Society, which permitted associations other than the State to appeal to a similar origin and to claim a similar justification. According as one or the other of these two directions was predominantly followed, there arose divergent tendencies which led to opposite results.

I. GROUPS WITHIN THE STATE

(1) *The unitary or centralist interpretation*

If we turn our attention first to the local communities and corporate groups contained in the State, we find the exponents of the theory of Natural Law agreed that the fact of their subjection to State-sovereignty distinguished them from the State by a genuine logical criterion. The question still remained—How far, in spite of this subjection, could they be regarded as retaining a common life of their own? The answer to that question depended on the view which thinkers held of the nature of sovereignty and of its relation to the processes of group-development.

1. On the whole, the theorists of Natural Law were driven by the tendency of their time to deny that local communities and corporate bodies had a social existence* of their own. So far as it moved in this direction, the natural-law theory of associations was far less favourable to such bodies, on the fundamental issue at stake, than was the positive-law theory of Corporations [which had been expounded by the civilians]. It must be admitted, how-

---

* Social existence = existence in the area of voluntary society, as distinct from political existence, which = existence in the area of a State, as 'institutions' chartered by it.

§ 15. *The natural-law theory of Associations*

ever, that the exponents of natural-law theory, when they came to suggest a practical policy, adopted this positive-law theory; and some of them even advocated a favourable treatment of corporate institutions.

It was a factor of decisive importance, to begin with, that the smaller communities contained in the State were never allowed to appear as having a birthright in Natural Law. It is true that those who maintained the theory of the organic origin of the State did not suppose the *societas civilis perfecta* [i.e. the State] to have issued immediately from an act of union between individuals. They believed that it had developed gradually, through an ascending series of other associations. But there was a general agreement that, after the State had once been formed, the Family alone continued to enjoy a right of existence derived from this original process of free social development. So far as other associations were concerned, thinkers were ready to allow that there had been a progressive widening of the original family-community, first into the local community, then into the city, and finally into the greater kingdom; but they still remained tied to an abstract scheme of thought, deduced from the conditions of the ancient City-State, which made the local community merely a preliminary stage of the civic community, and treated the civic community as the perfect realisation of the idea of State. The Family and the State were therefore regarded as the only societies which possessed a basis in Natural Law. So far as writers on politics dealt at all with the Family in connection with their theory of the State, they treated it as one of the natural bases of the State, describing it as a *societas privata* or *domestica*, and dividing it into the three societies of husband and wife, parents and children, and master and slaves (1); but they hastened to set over against it at once, as the *societas politica* or *civilis*, a community armed with sovereign power (2). Local communities and corporate bodies, as distinct from the Family, were regarded as only arising after the constitution of a system of political order, and within the limits of that system. They were useful, but not indispensable, divisions of the body politic; they had no place in the general natural-law scheme of civil society; they were only the particular institutions of a particular State, based on its positive law (3). This was the general tendency of all natural-law theory; but when the idea of a Social Contract was emphasised, and the sovereign State was directly based on the conclusion of a contract between individuals, the tendency became even more marked to relegate any corporate articulation of the State to the sphere of mere positive law (4).*

Deprived in this way of the sanction of Natural Law, associations were unable to vindicate an inviolable right of existence against either the State or the Individual. With the sacred and indestructible rights of the sovereign community confronting them on the one side, and the no less sacred and indestructible rights of the individual personality confronting them on the other, it became a question of mere utility what measure of rights they ought to be granted. The way was clear for attempts to demolish the traditional historic rights of intervening groups, in order to realise the ideal law of Reason and its rational system of rights.

[a] So far as their relation to the State was concerned, associations automatically lost any claim to possess an inherent social authority of their own the moment that the absolutist conception of sovereignty began to be seriously pressed. If the whole range of power required for the guidance of civil society was to be found in a single and indivisible 'majesty', the authority of the State must necessarily be exalted into being the one and only manifestation of that power of the Whole to control its members which belonged to the nature of human society; and on that in turn it followed that any association contained in the State could never be allowed to enjoy an inherent and independent existence in the sphere of public law, but could only do so, at most, in the sphere of private law.†

Even Bodin himself, in spite of his preference for a vigorous activity of corporate life, was unable to escape this logical consequence of his own conception of sovereignty. His full and searching enquiry into the corporate articulation of the State, with its advantages and disadvantages (III, c. 7), begins with a distinction and definition of the *collegium*, the *corpus*, and the *universitas*, which became a model for many subsequent writers. A *collegium* is the legal union of two or more persons of like status: a *corpus* is the union of several colleges: a *universitas* is a local com-

* 'Corporate articulation' of the State means a system (such as Althusius depicts) in which the State is a *communitas communitatum*—a body of which the parts are not individual atoms, but corporate limbs and members all fitly joined and knit together. The Fascist idea of the 'corporative state' is an attempt to translate this idea into practice.

† I.e. an association could not enjoy inherent rights as against the State, and as a matter of *Staatsrecht*; it could only enjoy such rights (if at all) as against individuals, and as a matter of *Privatrecht*.

§ 15. The natural-law theory of Associations

munity (*omnium familiarum, collegiorum et corporum ejusdem oppidi juris communione sociata multitudo*); while in the *respublica* there is added, to the attributes of a *universitas*, the further and higher attribute that it embraces and protects with its sovereignty (*imperii majestate*) all individuals and associations (no. 327).*

The three species of the 'more imperfect' associations arose, in Bodin's view, at a time long before the foundation of the State, and as the result of an imitation (which was itself due to man's social instinct) of the original and natural society of the Family: they continued to exist in the State as elements in its life which, without being, like the Family, necessary or indestructible, were none the less exceedingly useful; and the earliest founders of States accordingly regarded them as the strongest supports of their newly created system of order (nos. 328–9). Any thinker who considers the historical sequence of development which runs through *familia, collegium, corpus, universitas, civitas* and *imperium*, and who refuses to believe that a commonwealth can permanently exist *sine caritate et amicitia*, will never approve the views of those who treat all corporate articulation of the State as something that may be dispensed with (no. 342). It is true that corporations involve a risk of disorder; but to advocate the elimination of all corporations on that account is to overlook the fact that it is only *collegia perperam instituta* that ever threaten any danger. In view of that possible danger, it is good to be cautious in sanctioning the existence of all societies. More especially, the practice of religious confessions which are of foreign origin should only be allowed in exceptional cases. But the suppression of all *collegia* is a symptom of tyranny (nos. 342–4). The best constructed kingdoms find their firmest support in *collegia et corpora*; such bodies produce most readily the contributions which are needed for the general well being (nos. 345–6).

Holding such views, Bodin is even willing to argue in favour of a system of Estates with regular meetings, in order that a king may learn the wishes and grievances of each of these bodies and increase his prestige by the advice and the grants which he receives from their general assemblies. In particular, he recommends a system of provincial diets, and advocates its general introduction into France, adducing in its favour not only the example of Switzerland, but also (and especially) that of Germany, with its free towns

* The *numerus* is the number given at the *side* of the page in the later editions of the *De Republica*.

and its ten circles. He holds, however, that due proportion should be observed in regard to the number of groups and assemblies. Indiscriminate permission of all can only lead to anarchy; and a limitation of guilds, for example, has been everywhere found necessary (nos. 346–7). In spite of his enthusiasm for decentralisation and self-government, Bodin still regards all corporate institutions as nothing more than voluntary creations of the sovereign, which he can modify at will. In his view, the very nature of sovereignty necessarily involves the corollaries that the sovereign can no more be bound by law in dealing with *universitates collegia et corpora* than he is in dealing with individuals; that he can abrogate *ex aequitate* any law he has passed in regard to them, and withdraw any privilege he has granted; and that he never legally needs the co-operation of the assemblies whose advice he consents to receive (I, c. 8, nos. 85–99). It follows that the existence of all *collegia* and *corpora*, like that of all *universitates*, depends on a concession made by the State; they are *coetus in Republica jure sociati*, i.e. *summi Principis beneficio et concessu, sine quibus corporum et collegiorum jus ac nomen amittunt* (III, c. 7, no. 331). Only such authorisation by the sovereign power can produce the *legitima consociatio* [or lawful right of assembly] which is involved in the idea of an association, and which not only includes the right of meeting, but also the right of determining the time, place, character, and agenda of such meeting (*ibid.*). Indeed, the authorisation of the sovereign is the source of *all* corporate authority whatsoever (no. 332). It is usually granted *ad hoc* in each particular case; and the amount of rights conveyed in the grant is variously adjusted, according as religious or secular associations are in question, and, in the latter case, according as official or unofficial 'colleges' are concerned (nos. 330–2). In any and every case, the exercise of any governing authority by a 'college' is only possible in virtue of its being directly conferred by the State; and it must always be subject to supervision by the higher authorities of the State.

Bodin's conception of all corporations as State-institutions becomes most clearly apparent, when he proceeds to treat of the collegiate magistracies (*collegia magistratuum et judicum*) as the most distinguished corporations in the State, and to ascribe to them, and to them alone, a *jurisdictio et imperium* of their own(5), while other corporations are only allowed a power of decision in internal affairs and a modest power of discipline over their members(6).*

* In the France of Bodin's time, the collegiate magistrates were partly (1) financial boards, e.g. the *trésoriers de France*, who formed a *collège* in each

§ 15. *The natural-law theory of Associations*

This tendency of Bodin to lump together collegiate magistracies and general associations will also serve to explain why he refuses to regard an independent capacity for owning property as an essential attribute of a corporation. He admits that '*aliquid commune*' belongs to every *consociatio*; but it is enough for him if a law, or a particular disposition of the sovereign, assigns regular revenues to meet the cost of managing such common affairs as each may happen to have (7). We begin to discover that the possession of a personality of its own has ceased to be, in any sense, a necessary part of the idea of a corporation. It is only a possible accretion. It is a further illustration of Bodin's general attitude that, when he comes to deal with the offences of corporations and the punishment of such offences, he never pays any regard to the idea that associations may have an inherent right of existence (8).

We may trace a similar view of the relations of the corporation to the State in other political writers who adopted the strict absolutist conception of sovereignty. Gregorius Tholosanus, on the whole, follows Bodin's line; but we may already detect, in his various political writings, a bias which is even more inimical to the liberty of corporations (9). Bornitius elaborates, with even greater logic than Bodin, a theory of *collegia*, *corpora*, and *universitates* which makes them mere State-institutions (10). Arnisaeus regards associations as mere divisions (*classes*) created by the State among its subjects for the easier exercise of its governing power (11). Even the theorists who sought to modify the absolutist conception of sovereignty were apt to regard local communities and corporate bodies as no more than administrative institutions—useful in certain circumstances, but dangerous unless they were rigorously limited—which the sovereign could create, transform or abolish in the light of his own free judgment of their utility (12). Besold took more of a middle line, attempting to reconcile the new political doctrine [of sovereignty] with the old Roman-law theory of corporations (13). The regular teachers of Natural Law were less friendly to associations; and if they thought it worth while to mention them at all, they always refused to allow that they possessed any inherent group-authority (14). The ecclesiastical writers on Natural Law were especially influenced by the current

---

financial district or *généralité*, and partly (2) judicial bodies, such as the *Parlement* of Paris and the provincial *parlements*. Within these judicial bodies there were sub-colleges, e.g. the *maîtres des requêtes* formed a *collège*, with a corporate organisation and a corporate character, inside the *Parlement* of Paris.

tendency in favour of centralisation(15); and Suarez is conspicuous among them for his emphatic insistence that any power of action which goes beyond the limits of pure private law is reserved entirely for the State(16). He is thus led to reject entirely the conception that associations have a genuine power of self-government, and he seeks to refer any power of making decisions which they may enjoy either to an act of authorisation by the sovereign, or to a private contract made between the individual members(17). He applies the same fundamental principle to his interpretation of customary law, which he regards, with the aid of a series of forced assumptions, as a *lex tacita*(18). Similarly, in treating of the right of taxation, he refuses to admit the validity of any tradition or privilege which can have the effect of calling in question the unique authority over taxation which belongs exclusively to the State(19). He applies the same system of strict centralisation to the Church [e.g. in regard to its relations to religious orders and other religious associations], when he elevates it to the dignity of a sovereign spiritual State(20).

[b] If associations were thus denied any public authority, and all such authority was vindicated exclusively for the State, it became impossible to hold that they had any inherent existence of their own as against the *Individual*. In effect, the absolutist theory of the State tended towards a view which reduced all rights of corporations, so far as they were not derived or reflected from the sovereignty of the State, to the level of a system of partnership based upon individual rights. From this point of view corporations, like families, were often brought under the rubric of private 'societies' or companies(21); and Busius openly holds that the rights of *collegia et corpora* are only a matter of *jus societatis* with certain modifications(22).* There was indeed some tendency to recur to the traditional [Roman-law] theory of corporations when it came to a closer examination of deviations from the normal contract of partnership, such as hospitals or sanctuaries(23); but the peculiarities to be found in such cases were treated as being of the nature of mere external accretions. Even when thinkers really attempted to face the fundamental question, 'What personality of its own does the corporate Whole possess?' they generally gave the most superficial of answers, sometimes contenting themselves with a distinction between the 'collective' and the 'distributive'

* Society (*societas, Sozietät, Gesellschaft*) in this context means the simple business partnership of individuals united by a private contract.

§ 15. *The natural-law theory of Associations*

enjoyment of rights by a body of persons (24), and sometimes taking refuge in a conception of the corporate Whole as a 'feigned' individual (25).

On the whole the tendency ran in favour of a merely collective conception of associations. Attempts were made, for example, to explain the validity of the majority-principle by supposing that, for certain purposes and in certain cases, it was possible to identify *plures* with *omnes* (26). Those who took this view were enabled by it to interpret the regularly made decisions of corporations as contractual agreements [made by *all* the members] (27), and even to base their theory of the delicts of corporations on a similar view (28).*
[We may cite an even more striking instance of such ingenuity of interpretation.] By applying the idea of partnership to the village community some of the ecclesiastical writers on Natural Law even found themselves able to make a vigorous defence of the Fellowship principle in regard to the legal position of village commons (29).†

Suarez [did not apply the idea of partnership so indiscriminately. He] drew a clearer distinction between the rights of a mere community and those of a corporation. He distinguished the *communitas imperfecta*, which was not organised as an independent unit, from the *communitas perfecta*, which was competent to develop and exercise a community-control of its members; and on the basis of this distinction he included local communities and corporate bodies, 'imperfect' though they might be when regarded as parts of the political whole, among the *communitates* which, regarded in themselves, were 'perfect' (30). But Suarez himself, when he comes to investigate the real essence of corporate groups, remains in a state of vacillation. He hovers uncertainly between the idea of a multiplicity of persons, reduced by contract into a unity, and the fiction of a separate personality (31).

---

* If *plures* = *omnes*, then (1) a majority-decision = a contractual agreement of all, and (2) a majority-decision to pursue a course of conduct which results in a delict = a contractual agreement of all to commit that delict.

† If you apply the idea of partnership to a village, you can insist that all the villagers, as partners, are something of a Fellowship, with 'common rights'. (On the other hand, it will also be possible for a Fellowship which regards itself only as a partnership to wind up the business, and to distribute the common property among the existing partners.)

(2) *The federalist interpretation, especially in Althusius and Grotius*

In opposition to this trend towards centralisation and the absolute State there arose, among some of the adherents of the School of Natural Law, a federal theory. Developing the idea of the Social Contract to its logical conclusion, they sought to place associations generally on the same natural-law basis as the State itself; and they attempted accordingly to vindicate for them, even when they were included in the State, an independent sphere of action which belonged to them in themselves.

The way was prepared for this view, in the course of the sixteenth century, by the claim (which had been advanced in practice in the Wars of Religion, and was defended in theory by the Calvinistic advocates of popular sovereignty) of a right of resistance of particular provinces against a tyrannical political authority. In this connection the theory propounded by Hubert Languet exercised a deep and particular influence. Provinces and cities, he held, were appointed to superintend [along with, and even in lieu of, the national Estates and magistrates] both the pact between the nation and God and that between Ruler and People.* They were therefore entitled, and even obliged, to offer armed resistance to the Ruler who broke his contract; and in the last resource they could even renounce their allegiance(32). The success of the Revolt of the Netherlands gave the seal of historical approval to these views. Two things combined to make it easy for a general federal theory to develop from this beginning. The genius of the constitution of the Calvinistic churches was favourable to it; and the political institutions of the Netherlands, as well as of Switzerland and Germany, supplied no inconsiderable ground of positive law in its support.

It was the work of Johannes Althusius to give logical unity to the federal ideas that simmered in the ecclesiastical and political circles in which he lived, and to construct an audacious system of thought in which they all found their place(33). Althusius has a firm grip of the idea that the differentia of sovereignty provides a clear line of division between the idea of the State and that of all

---

* More exactly, the Ruler is included in both of these pacts—(1) that in which, as *co-promissor*, he is bound, along with the nation, to God, and (2) that in which, as a single *promissor*, he is bound to the People. The first pact, therefore, is not so much 'between the nation and God', as between the nation, *plus* the Ruler, and God.

§ 15. *The natural-law theory of Associations*

other associations. Just as he insists that only a federation can stand above States, so he denies that any part of a political whole, when once that whole has become a State, can ever possess the attribute of political authority. But while he regards *majestas* as the highest power on earth, he none the less brings it under legal limits; and while he recognises it as a unity which is absolutely indivisible and inalienable, he refuses to make it the one and only manifestation of that power of a community to control its members which is always involved in the very existence of human society. On this basis, he vindicates for associations a sphere of right which belongs to themselves, and an organic place in the structure of civil society. So far, we may say that he is in agreement with the original core of medieval thought(34). But while medieval federalism started from the unity of the Whole, Althusius takes his stand entirely on the basis of natural-law Individualism. He derives all social unity from a process of association which proceeds, as it were, from the bottom upwards. He regards the contract of society [i.e. the principle of partnership] as the creator of the whole system of public law and order [both in the parts, or earlier stages, of the State, and in its total and final structure].

In the very beginning of his *Politica* he sketches a general theory of association (*consociatio*), which he then proceeds to apply to all forms of society, including the State. He regards the juridical basis of social life as consisting, in every case, in an expressed or tacit compact. By that compact a common life is brought into existence; the means and the powers required for that common life are pooled; and a ruling power is instituted, capable of administering all the affairs which have been made, in this way, a common concern. Within this general framework, he distinguishes five species of association (*species consociationis*), each with its special functions, and each, therefore, with a special area of action and an independent authority of its own. They are the Family, the Fellowship (*Genossenschaft*), the local community (*Gemeinde*), the Province and the State. In this ascending series of groups, each higher stage always proceeds from the one below; and thus it is associations, and not individuals, which are the contracting parties in the formation of the higher and larger groups. More especially, it is the provinces or local communities which conclude the contract of society that founds the State; and they surrender to the State in that act (just as the groups on which they are based have similarly surrendered to them) only such part of their rights as is definitely required for the purposes of the higher community. The existence of the State is thus compatible with the survival of a series of concentrically arranged groups, intervening between the individual and the general community, each of them a unit sanctioned by Natural Law, and all of them supporting and sustaining the greater whole. The social life which these groups enjoy is not bestowed on them by the State: it is a life which proceeds from themselves. In fact, they give rather than receive: they are the source of the broader forms of social life; and while they are capable of living apart from the State, the State cannot live apart from them. They have therefore rights of their own which belong inviolably to them in their own particular area, even if their inclusion in a greater whole involves a number of limitations upon their freedom. They can themselves resist tyrannical attacks upon those rights by force of arms, even though this may involve a conflict with the authority of the State; and their officers are not only entitled, but also obliged, to protect them in their rights, and to offer active resistance to any encroachment upon them by the supreme Ruler. In case of need, particular territories may even secede, and either submit to another Ruler or declare themselves independent; for since *regna universalia* have been founded by the joint action of *familiae, collegia, pagi, oppida, civitates et provinciae*, each of these constituent units recovers its original liberty in the event of a breach of their contract of union.

In conformity with these ideas, Althusius holds that it is necessary to follow a method of expounding political theory which corresponds to its subject-matter, and proceeds from the lower to the higher. He therefore gives a detailed account of the rights of [lesser] associations before he treats of the State. He begins with the simple and private association (*consociatio simplex et privata*) which unites men in pursuit of some particular common interest. This private association is depicted as having two phases or stages. The first is the natural and necessary union of the Family, including both the narrower circle of the household and the wider circle of the kin-group. The second is the Fellowship (*consociatio collegarum*). Althusius describes the Fellowship as a civil and voluntary union, constituting a social body: he traces it through its various manifestations, from ecclesiastical and secular *collegia specialia* to the *collegium generale* composed of a whole Estate; and he vests it with corporate autonomy and self-government(35). Having established this basis, he now proceeds to the composite

§ 15. *The natural-law theory of Associations*

public association (*consociatio mixta et publica*), which unites the simpler groups in a general or universal scheme of life (or, as he terms it, *politeuma*), and which is therefore also called by the name of *universitas*. In this category—which may also be called by the name of *consociatio politica* or political association—Althusius is able, with the aid of a distinction which he draws between its 'particular' and its 'universal' form, to include both the local community and the State (36).

In dealing with 'particular political associations', he begins with a full account of the local community—the *universitas* in the narrower sense of the word, in which it refers to rural and municipal bodies. Here he first gives a sketch of the general institutions common to both of these bodies; and he then proceeds to treat of the peculiar features of rural and urban communities—first of all treating the development of the *universitas rustica* in its three phases of the *vicus*, the *pagus*, and the *oppidum*,* and then dividing *universitates urbanae* from one point of view into 'free', 'provincial' and 'mixed' cities,† and from another into 'mother-cities' and 'colonies'. The general principle which he asserts is that all these microcosms of the political community, rural and urban alike, should be regarded as possessing a large area of authority in their own right, though he admits that the co-operation of the higher authorities is required for the acts of small and dependent communities. Leaving these lower stages of *consociatio politica particularis*, Althusius now turns to the higher stage of the *universitas provinciae*. His picture of the Province, which professes to be based on the principles of Natural Law, is actually based on the model of the German territorial principality; and this will explain why he can both allow it a very large measure of independence, and yet, at the same time, make its governor the holder of an office conferred by the *summus imperans* of the whole realm.

Upon this basis Althusius begins his account of the State. It is a *universalis publica consociatio* produced by a contract of union between 'particular' communities; and it displays its essential principle in the form of a 'majesty' which embraces all these communities. We have already noticed the importance which he

---

* We may translate the terms into the English equivalents of 'village', 'hundred', and 'country-town'.

† The free city is a direct member of a federation, on the same footing as a province: the provincial city is included in a province: the mixed city will somehow combine both characteristics.

attaches to this essential attribute of the State (37). But in every other respect he is inevitably impelled, by the very genius of the federal system which he has developed with so rigorous a logic, to advocate and to apply the principle that associations are in their essence on a level of full equality with the State. In fact, his general theory of corporate bodies already contains in the germ the whole of his theory of the State. At each of his various stages of association, the contract of society [by which each stage is produced] already displays its power of developing a common life, in virtue of which the participants in that life constitute a single body, and count as a single person. In every stage this development results in a power of the whole over its members; and although at the stage of the Fellowship, as well as at the prior stage of the Family, this power is still only a *potestas privata*, it rises to the dignity of a *potestas publica* when we come to territorial associations—with the one qualification that it is kept within definite bounds in local communities and provinces, as a *potestas publica limitata*, by the authority of the higher *potestas publica universalis*. In every stage, again, the authority of the whole over its members has to be regulated by *leges directionis et gubernationis* (over and above the *leges communicationis*);* and this involves, from the first, a distinction between Rulers and Ruled. In every stage, however, authority is only a mode of service and a form of care for the welfare of the community; and obedience is simply a return for the provision of defence and protection. At every stage, therefore, it is the community of the Ruled which is the true 'Subject' or owner of the common authority, in virtue of that divine order of the world which is *ex hypothesi* revealing itself naturally in the whole of this natural-law system; and as the true 'Subject' of the common authority the community is superior to the officer entrusted with its actual exercise. Just as, in the State, 'majesty' is inalienably and inviolably the property of the People, so, in the Fellowship, the elected committee of management is necessarily *major singulis, minor universis collegis*. In the same way, the government of a local community, whether such government be an individual or a college, possesses a *jus in singulos, non in universos cives*; and the chief officer of a rural community is therefore subordinate to the com-

* The *leges communicationis* deal with the pooling of means and forces required for the common life; the *leges directionis et gubernationis* deal with the ruling power necessarily instituted for the administration of all the affairs which, in consequence of such pooling, have become the common concern.

§ 15. *The natural-law theory of Associations*

munal assembly, as the urban magistrate is subordinate to the civic representatives, and these are in turn subordinate to the whole civic body. Similarly, again, when we come to the Province, the deputies of the various corporate Estates (which should properly include, in every case, a fourth 'Estate of husbandmen or peasants' as well as the clergy, nobility and towns)* form an assembly of provincial Estates: the assent of this assembly is necessary before the territorial prince, or head of the province, can declare any war, impose any tax, proclaim any law, or undertake any other measure of importance; and the assembly has also a right of resistance and revolt against any governor who fails to discharge his duty.

So perfect a parallelism between all associations and all stages of development reduces the theory of the Corporation and the theory of the State to the position of mere aspects of a single and uniform theory of all Society. It is true that Althusius, following the jurisprudence of the civilians closely, allows a number of propositions drawn from the traditional Roman-law theory of corporations to find a place in his theory of politics. But these propositions acquire a fundamentally new significance by being incorporated into a system based on the principles of Natural Law. They are all made to fit into the general idea of a contract of society, proceeding steadily upwards from the individual to the State through an uninterrupted series of progressively higher and progressively broader social formations. There is thus no contradiction—on the contrary, there is full and absolute agreement—between Althusius' system of political ideas, as it has just been described, and his juristic theory of associations, as it has been explained in a previous section (38).† Whether we look at his views in terms of political theory, or in terms of jurisprudence, the result is the same. Any difference in kind between public and private law, between the commonwealth and a company, between the general will and an agreement of different wills, disappears. The one conception of the 'society' or partnership, founded on individual rights, is made to cover the whole of Group-life. Dividing itself first into the two varieties of the *societas bonorum* and the *societas vitae*, and then proceeding to lump together, as all belonging to the latter of these varieties, the Family, the Fellowship, the

---

* In Sweden there were four Estates—clergy, nobility, burghers and peasants.

† Gierke here refers to vol. IV, pp. 178 *seqq.* of his *Genossenschaftsrecht*, which is not included in this translation.

local community and the State, this partnership conception is stretched so far that it has to include simultaneously both the simple business company and the genuine corporate group. In each and every case, the union of men for the purposes of a common life is regarded as producing a living Group-person; and yet in the issue none of these Group-persons proves itself to be anything more than a collective sum of associated individuals. The Teutonic idea of the freedom of corporate bodies is introduced into the sphere of the Law of Nature; an inherent existence is vindicated for associations over against the State; and yet, in spite of every effort to attain the idea of a true and organic Group-being by the use of the Teutonic conception of 'Fellowship', there is a final failure to make either the State or the corporation a whole which is really one, and can assert itself against the individual in the strength of its own inherent existence.

In the exposition of a general theory of society based on the principles of Natural Law, Althusius had shown himself far in advance of his age; but some degree of approximation to his system of thought was really inevitable for every thinker who seriously believed that the State was derived from a contract of society. If a contractual agreement between individuals had power enough to produce a sovereign commonwealth, it must also possess the power of producing Fellowships and local communities. The State, by its positive law, might make the formation of corporate bodies subject to its previous consent: it might, by the same means, limit the right of such bodies after they had been actually formed; but the essential source of the existence of associations and their particular form of common life remained an act of voluntary agreement among the members themselves. Associations too had a basis in Natural Law: they were coeval with and akin to the State; and like individuals they might be regarded, not as the creatures, but rather as the living limbs, of the ultimate social Whole. There were some political theorists who, following this line of thought, described any State which transcended the bounds of a simple City-State as a *respublica composita* (39). There were others who, adhering either wholly or in part to the federal scheme of Althusius, interposed a gradually ascending series of associations between the individual and the State (40). A similar point of view was occasionally adopted even by writers whose general political tendency showed a definite hostility to corporations (41). But whatever the particular point of view, individualism was the general basis; and whenever the question arises, in any of these connections, 'What

§ 15. *The natural-law theory of Associations*

is the inward essence of a community?' the individualistic premises of the argument always lead inevitably to the obvious answer, 'It has the character of a partnership' (42).

It was a factor of primary importance that Grotius gave his adhesion, on some essential points, to the federal theory. Like the followers of that theory, he held that the various elements in the structure of civil society were based on the same natural-law foundation of contract as the State itself. In the second book of his *De Jure Belli et Pacis*, where he deals with the different titles to the acquisition of property (*dominium*) and authority (*imperium*), he makes a division, in the course of the fifth chapter, between three primary methods of acquiring a right over another person. The first is procreation, which is the basis of parental right: the second is contract, or *consensus*: the third is delict, which explains the imposition of slavery on persons or peoples by way of punishment. The second (or contractual) basis of the acquisition of *jus in personas* is further divided into *consociatio* and *subjectio*. From the contract of *consociatio* Grotius derives first marriage (§§ 8–16), and then all the other forms of *consociatio*, both *publica* and *privata*. Under the head of 'public associations' he includes both the *consociatio in populum* and the *consociatio ex populis* [i.e. the federation]; but while giving the State [whether federal or unitary] a special position under this head as *societas perfectissima*, he also includes under it the *societas inter populos* [i.e. international organisation] (§§ 17–25) (43). The contract of *subjectio* he makes the basis both of the rights of the master under the system of private law (in the matter of slavery and adrogation*) and of the rights of the Ruler under the system of public law.

This scheme is in some respects opposed to that of Althusius. Grotius recognises that there are other methods besides *consensus* by which power can be initially acquired. Again [even in the sphere of *consensus*] he holds that *subjectio*, as well as *consociatio*, has the effect of imposing an original obligation; and he proceeds, upon this basis, to make a general division of all forms of social grouping into *societates sine inaequalitate* and *societates inaequales* (44). But while, in both of these ways, he lays a broader foundation than his predecessor, the theory which he builds upon it is still a general natural-law theory of society at large, in just the same way as that of Althusius. It embraces the whole area of legal connections between persons, whether under private or under public

* Adrogation is 'the adoption of an independent person, reducing him to a dependent status (*filius-familias*)'.

law: it includes the theory of the State as simply a part (if the final and culminating part) of its general range. It is a theory of society which permits associations to enjoy an inherent and independent common life as against the State: indeed it may even be said to make the body politic itself nothing more than a *societas immortalis et perpetua* composed of parts which are commonwealths themselves. None of these parts can be separated from the Whole against its will: any of them may leave it, in case of need, by its own unilateral act. This involves a *jus partis ad se tuendam* which is prior to the *jus corporis in partem*; and Grotius justifies such priority by the significant argument '*quia pars utitur jure quod ante societatem initam habuit, corpus non item*' (45).

But every society, including the State, is regarded as deriving its existence, in the last resort, from the Individual; and none of them rises above the level of a system of relations established by agreement between the owners of individual rights. Grotius is no more able than other thinkers to establish a firm and logical line of division between partnership and corporation. Every local community or Fellowship, like the State itself, is simply a species of *societas* (46). If, notwithstanding, there appears on the scene a Whole, which is comparable to a natural body, with a unity that continues through all the change of its members (47), the appearance of such a Whole is attributed solely and simply to the effect of those provisions in the contract of society which were designed to secure this object. We have already noticed a primary principle which Grotius enunciates in this connection. He ascribes the validity of the majority-principle to an agreement (which, he holds, is to be assumed in every case) that the majority is to count as equal to the Whole in dealing with the affairs of any association (48). For the rest, we can only say that he makes all the rights and duties of corporate bodies depend upon a mere difference between the 'collective' and the 'distributive' aspect of a group of individuals.* This is made to explain why the same associated

* Summarising the argument of Gierke at this point, we may say (1) that a whole only emerges for Grotius when, and in so far as, there is a specific agreement that the whole shall act; (2) that he believes in an original specific agreement, in all groups, empowering the majority to act for the whole in dealing with group-affairs; (3) that if it be asked what group-affairs are, the only answer he gives is that they are all those affairs which can be brought under a collective point of view, as contrasted with a distributive—i.e. they are affairs that belong to all *ut universi*, as contrasted with affairs that belong to all *ut singuli*.

§ 15. *The natural-law theory of Associations* 79

individuals who possess rights *ut universi* have no lot or share in those rights *ut singuli*: it is made to explain why the debts of the *universitas*, on the principles of Natural Law, cannot be a ground for the liability of *singuli*(49): it is made to explain why, in the matter of delicts, the guilt of the community cannot be presumed of the individual members when regarded as individuals(50). But while the *universitas* thus receives some measure of recognition as a separate person, it really remains throughout an aggregate of individuals, which is only integrated into a unity in certain definite legal connections(51). As soon as we reach the point at which this artificial and juristic mode of thought ceases to be applied, we find at once that it is only individuals who really and truly exist(52).

(3) *The interpretation of Hobbes*

We have seen from the preceding argument, first that there was a current, arising from the natural-law theory of Sovereignty, which made strongly towards the absolutism of the State, and secondly that there was also a strong counter-current, proceeding from the natural-law theory of Contract, which made in the opposite direction. We have now to notice how Hobbes, once more,* defeated this opposing tendency by using against it its own argument of Contract(53).

Hobbes applies his own theory of contract not only to the State, but also to all other groups. His general view of associations is that they are partnership bodies, analogous to the State, which owe their existence to contract. Starting from the category of 'System', in the sense of a union of a number of persons for an object common to them all, he draws a distinction between systems which are *regularia* and those which are *irregularia*, using as his criterion the fact of the presence or absence of a 'representative person'. The regular systems are then subdivided into *Systemata absoluta sive independentia*, which are subject to no authority but their own 'representative person', and *Systemata subordinata*, which are subject—not only as regards their members, but also as regards their 'representative person'—to the authority of the State. The

---

* 'Once more'—because, as we have already seen at the end of § 14, Hobbes used the doctrine of Contract against the cause of popular sovereignty which it had hitherto been used to support, just as here he is shown to have used the same doctrine of Contract against the cause of Group-rights which it had hitherto served to vindicate.

first of these two subdivisions includes only States. The second subdivision may again be subdivided into *corpora publica* which '*ab auctoritate summae potestatis civitatis constitutae sunt*', and *corpora privata*, which '*ab ipsis civibus vel auctoritate aliqua extranea constituuntur*'. All *corpora privata* are *licita*, provided that *a civitate probantur*: otherwise they are *illicita*. *Systemata subordinata* may also be subdivided, from another point of view, and according to the nature of the object pursued, into *provinciae, oppida, universitates, collegia* and *ecclesiae*. Three other subdivisions may also be added to these five—great merchant companies possessing monopolies (*collegia mercatorum ad regulanda negotia*): *Systemata subordinata pro tempore praefinito constituta*, such as, e.g. assemblies of deputies convened by the King in order that he may take counsel with them, '*tanquam cum una persona cives omnes repraesentatura*'; and finally Families, in so far as the State has left them with a personality of their own.*

We now come to *Systemata irregularia*. They are either unions (*foedera*) which have no *unitas personae*, or assemblies (*concursus*) without any definite organisation or system of mutual obligation. It depends on the purpose of the individuals concerned whether they are allowed or forbidden. In general, special combinations and unions for mutual protection among the citizens of a State are superfluous and questionable, because the State *civium omnium foedus commune est*; and therefore they are forbidden as *conjurationes vel factiones*. The simple act of assembling for a legal and overt purpose, e.g. for a festive procession or a theatrical representation, is in itself permissible; but even this ceases to be allowable if a greater number than the object requires are gathered together, or if the State issues a prohibition.

According to these views, the *existence* of associations depends essentially on the same natural power of association which also created the State. True, any liberty of association [i.e. the right to create associations] only exists in so far as the State allows it to do so; nor can we speak of any independent right of groups, as against the State, any more than we can speak of such a right of individuals. But the life of *Systemata subordinata* is not a derivative life, which proceeds exclusively from the State; we may rather say that such bodies, like the State, have to some degree their own necessity or utility(54). On the other hand, while the *existence* of

* So far, in other words, as they are left by the law in the position of the Roman *familia*, with the *paterfamilias* as its representative person.

§15. *The natural-law theory of Associations*

a group can thus proceed from a force which is inherent in its members, it is impossible for a group to generate from itself any *authority* to control those members. In the act of making a political contract, all individuals transferred to the Ruler unconditionally all power of every sort; and while they may still possess a capacity of combination for particular objects, even after they have made that transference, they have no longer any power to bestow. It follows that the powers of corporate bodies, so far as they enjoy any powers, are really powers of the State, which it has entrusted to them. Following this line of argument, Hobbes insists that the whole of the *potestas* of subordinate Group-persons is a power derived from, and determined by, the State. He refuses to allow that any man can represent any section of the People further than the State (*cujus persona cunctorum persona est*) thinks fit that he should. He holds that the powers belonging to any agent of a corporate authority are determined, not by a commission proceeding from the community [i.e. the corporate body], but partly by precepts or charters issued by the sovereign, and partly by the general laws of the State (55). Otherwise there arises a State within the State (*civitas in civitate*), and the unity of the State is rent in two. It follows that the 'system' and its members are alike immediately subject to the authority of the State: '*Systema et membrum concives sunt*'. It follows again that, while the sovereign is judge in his own case in any *systema absolutum*, disputes between a *systema subordinatum* and one of its members must be settled in the courts of the State. In the same way claims of the 'system' against its members must be made effective by the process of an ordinary action at law, and not by the exercise of any compulsory power supposed to belong to the 'system' (56).

With the authority of the corporation thus absorbed in that of the State, Hobbes is able, as he proceeds with his argument, to fit both State and association into the same framework of a general theory of Society at large, without any sacrifice of his cardinal principle of political absolutism.

In his theory of corporations, as in his theory of the State, the central conception is that of the unity of group-personality. He regards the essence of every *Systema regulare* as consisting in the *persona civilis* (or *artificialis*) which is created by the appointment of one man, or one body of men, to be the *persona repraesentativa* of a multitude. The basis of this view is a general theory of 'persons, authors, and things personated', which comes in the sixteenth chapter of his *Leviathan*. According to that theory, a person is one who acts. One who acts in his own name is *persona propria sive naturalis*; one who acts in the name of another is *persona ejus, cujus nomine agit, repraesentativa*. In relation to the representative person, regarded as *actor* or agent, the person represented is *auctor* and the right to act is *auctoritas*. In virtue of such *auctoritas* the action of the *actor* is reckoned for legal purposes as being the action of the *auctor*, except that, when the authority is only a pretended and not a real authority, the *actor* himself incurs a personal obligation. Only *aliquid quod intelligit* can be a person; but what is represented (*cujus persona geritur*) need not possess intelligence. In that case, however, it cannot be an *auctor*. Thus when an inanimate thing, such as a church, a hospital, or a bridge, is personated, the rector, master, or overseer is the *persona repraesentativa* of that thing: but it is not the thing personated which is here the *auctor*—it is the owners, or governors, of that thing. In the same way, it is not the child, but the State, which is the *auctor* of the representative personality of the guardian. Similarly, when the gods of the heathen were personated in times past, the necessary *auctoritas* proceeded from the State. On the other hand, a multitude of men may form a single person [without any intervention of the State] by acting as *auctor* and giving an 'authority' to represent them into the hands of one man or person. Here, as Hobbes says, 'it is the "unity" of the representer, not the "unity" of the represented, that maketh the person "one", and "unity" cannot otherwise be understood in multitude'. But since each individual, in such a group, is *auctor* of the common *actor*, the words and acts of this *persona repraesentativa* are considered as the words and acts of all individuals, taken singly. If it be an assembly of men, and not a single man, who is authorised as *actor* or *persona*, '*tunc vox partis majoris accipienda est pro voce personae*'; otherwise this *actor* or 'person' would be mute, as is indeed actually the case when the voting is equal.

In this way, and by this delegation of the power of decision to a representative, there arises the artificial personality of *corpora fictitia*, in which '*homo vel coetus unus personam gerit omnium*'. There is no intrinsic difference between the personality of the State and that of other groups, except such as arises from the subjection of the latter to the power of the former. But that one difference is the parent of others. In contrast with the all-embracing representation of his subjects by the Ruler, the representation of the members of a *systema subordinatum* is in every case limited to *certis rebus a civitate determinatis*. Again, a subordinate group-personality [just as it may be limited in the range of its purposes] may also be limited in its duration; and Hobbes accordingly ascribes a temporary *persona cives omnes repraesentans* to an assembly of popular representatives convoked by a monarch. In the same way, he speaks of a *persona totius familiae* as vested in the *paterfamilias* [for the time being].

In dealing with associations, as in dealing with States, Hobbes draws a clear line of division between monarchical and republican constitutions. The absolutist tendency of his thought leaves no room in associations, any more than it does in the State, for a plurality of organs, with a constitutional division of functions. The *persona Systematis* is therefore, in every case, either *unus homo* or *unus coetus* (57). On one point, however, Hobbes admits a difference between the legal implications of government by a single man, and those of government by a single body of men. The point turns on the effect of acts undertaken by a representative person which go beyond the limits set to his *auctoritas* by the law and the constitution. Any action of a representative person which is *intra limites* is a '*factum uniuscujusque hominis eorum qui Systema constituunt*'; but no man carries any 'person' other than his own if he undertakes action which is *ultra limites*. It follows that the unauthorised action of a single man who represents a system is, in every case, his own action, and his own action only. It cannot be ascribed to the system, and it cannot be ascribed to any of its members. But if the 'person' representing the system be an assembly, a different result is involved. Any action of that assembly which goes beyond the bounds of its competence is also an action of the system itself, as a whole, because the system is identical with the majority [of voters in the assembly]. Not only so, but it is also an action of every individual who co-operated in it, though it is not an action of those who opposed it, or of those who were absent when it was undertaken. Hobbes applies this view particularly to delicts. He regards the delict of a single representative governor of a 'system' as only the delict of a single person, on the ground that no power of representation can give the representative a right to commit unauthorised actions; and he therefore holds that this single person alone is subject to punishment. On the other hand he regards the delict of a representative assembly as being simultaneously a delict of the *totum Systema* and a delict of the individual offenders (58).

Corporal punishment must therefore be inflicted on the individuals who joined in the act; but since individuals only can be punished in that way, the system itself must also undergo, in addition, any punishment of which *coetus capax est*. A *dissolutio Systematis* may therefore be pronounced against a *corpus fictitium*, as a form of capital punishment; or a fine may be levied upon any funds which it may possess.

It is not only to delicts, but also to debts, that Hobbes applies this distinction. If an individual who represents a system contracts a loan, only he should incur liability and repay the loan, '*vel ex communi thesauro vel ex pecunia propria*'. He cannot make others liable for his debt; and thus the creditor can only sue the *persona Systematis contrahens* who confronts him visibly as a natural person. If, however, a *coetus* is the borrower, all who have voted for contracting the loan are severally liable, when the creditor is an *extraneus*; but when the debt is owed to a member, *solus coetus ipse*, i.e. *ipsum Systema*, must answer for it. If it cannot answer, because there are no common funds, then the creditor, who is himself a member of the *coetus*, must put the loss down to his own account; for he must have been aware, at the time when he lent the money, even if he voted against its being borrowed or were absent from the voting, that he was also incurring a debt in his capacity of member (59).

It is obvious that these deductions, some of which are not very illuminating, are based upon an extremely individualistic point of view. Every form of group-personality is dissolved into representing and represented individuals. Whenever an individual is vested with any right, or charged with any duty, by his own act or by the act of others, *he* is involved with the whole of his personality. Where groups are in question, it is only by the *tour de force* of identifying an assembly with the changing majority of the individuals who compose it that Hobbes is able in some degree to disengage the idea of a corporate 'Subject' of rights and duties from the individual members of the group. With all its imperfections, however, the atomistic and mechanical construction of *Systemata subordinata* which appears in his theory has a historical significance of its own. He was the first to introduce into the theory of Natural Law a conception of Group-persons, which was not simply borrowed from the civilian or Roman-law theory of corporations, but was genuinely deduced from the actual principles of Natural Law; and he was the first to make such a conception the pivot both of public law and of the law of corporations.

§ 15. *The natural-law theory of Associations*

II. GROUPS ABOVE THE STATE

When we come to associations which transcend the State, we find the natural-law theory of Sovereignty incompatible with any idea of a *Super-State* [i.e. any idea of an international or federal political system], but compatible with the idea of a *social bond of connection between States* [i.e. the idea of a free partnership].

The medieval idea of a world-monarchy was an idea foreign to the thinkers of the School of Natural Law. They left to the publicists of the Holy Roman Empire the task of continually re-invoking, on reams of paper, the unsubstantial ghost of the old *imperium mundi*(60), but they made the indestructible germ of that dying system of thought yield the new and fruitful idea of *international society*. After the end of the sixteenth century, it became the habit of thinkers to explain the obligatory force of *jus gentium* by a *societas gentium*, in which the original and inextinguishable unity of the human race was supposed to have survived, even though sovereignty had passed to the separate nations(61). It must be admitted that the lack of any clear distinction between partnership and corporation prevented a clear conception of the character of this society of States. On the one hand, a tendency continually reappeared to harden international society into a world-State, and to arm it with the authority of a Super-State organised on Republican lines(62): on the other, the stricter advocates of the theory of sovereignty rejected *in toto* any idea of a natural community uniting all States together(63). But the doctrine which held the field, and determined the future of international law, was a doctrine which steadily clung to the view that there was a natural-law connection between all nations, and that this connection, while it did not issue in any authority exercised by the Whole over its parts, at any rate involved a system of mutual social rights and duties(64). From this point of view international law was conceived as a law binding *inter se* upon States which were still in a state of nature in virtue of their sovereignty, and binding upon them in exactly the same way as the pre-political Law of Nature had been binding upon individuals when they were living in a state of nature. The tendency of contemporary thought, which regarded all positive law as the product of State-legislation,* deprived inter-

* In the view of Gierke, expressed in his work on Althusius (see Appendix II), law is not produced by the State. It is the result of the common conviction of a human community (whether such conviction be manifested directly by usage, or declared by an organ of the community appointed for that purpose) not that there *shall* be, but that there already *are*, necessary limits to freedom. From this point of view positive law is not, in its essence, the product of State-legislation.

national law of any positive character, but gave to it, in exchange, the sanction of pure Natural Law.

If the theory of Natural Law were to remain true to its conception of sovereignty, it could never admit a federal combination of particular States [any more than it could admit a general society of all States] to the position of a Super-State. The conception of the federal State, which was derived by Besold and Hugo, as we have had occasion to notice elsewhere,* from the positive public law of the Holy Roman Empire, could not grow on natural-law soil; indeed we may even say that it has only maintained its existence in modern thought by dint of a constant and bitter struggle with Natural Law. The natural-law theory held rigorously to the principle that it was only the Whole *or* the part [of a federation] which could ever be a State, and that both could not be simultaneously States. A federation must therefore be a case either of a single unitary State with a corporative structure, or of a system of contract between sovereign States resting on the same basis as international law (65). But when the natural-law theorists proceeded to apply this idea—treating Germany as a unitary State, and then placing the United Netherlands, the Swiss Confederation and the Hanseatic League, along with the loosest of confederations, under the same indiscriminate rubric of *foedus* or contract—they found themselves enabled, by the very elasticity and ambiguity of their conception of partnership, to glide insensibly into the use of terms and ideas drawn from the law of corporations (66).† Grotius even goes so far as to draw a distinction of principle between mere contracts of confederation and organised unions of States—distinguishing further, among the latter, between a union of States under a common head and a federation of States which has been transformed, by a *foedus arctissimum*, into a *Systema civitatum* or *Corpus confoederatorum* (67). Whether the inviolability which he vindicates for the sovereignty of the several States (each of which is to remain in itself a *Status perfectus*) can in any way be combined with their inclusion in a union of so corporate a character is a question which is left unanswered.

* Gierke is referring to a section of his fourth volume which is not translated here (§ 12, p. 228).

† I.e. starting from the idea that a federation is only a contract or partnership, but then proceeding to obliterate the line between partnership and corporation, they are able to treat a federation of partner States as if it had corporate unity, and were thus itself a State.

III. GROUPS PARALLEL WITH THE STATE

The Church

It was equally impossible for natural-law theory, if its conception of sovereignty were pushed to a logical conclusion, to recognise associations as able to exist *side by side* with the State. If the *potestas summa et absoluta* ascribed to the State was to be a real fact, all other associations must necessarily be contained in the State, and they must necessarily be subject to its power.

But what was to be said, in that case, of the relation of the State to the Church? Here the School of Natural Law had to face the great problem whether the Church was to remain outside its general scheme of ideas, or whether it was to be included, like other bodies, within the limits of that scheme.

From the Catholic point of view, the Church stood outside the domain of Natural Law. The Catholic doctrine of Natural Law, equally with all positive jurisprudence which was coloured by Catholic tendencies, maintained the medieval theory of the two swords;* and it therefore set the Church, as a spiritual State which was independent and complete in itself, over against the secular State. In the natural-law systems of the Dominicans and the Jesuits, the relations between the State and the Church were made to depend entirely on the fundamental distinction which they drew between a human structure created by contract in virtue of Natural Law and a divine and supernatural institution. The Church was regarded as the original and innate 'Subject' of an inherent sovereign authority which, by the dispensation of God, was monarchical in character and universal in scope, and was vested immediately by Him in the person by whom it was exercised at any given moment(68). As the higher of two separate sovereignties, this spiritual authority was superior to the political, and therefore political sovereignty was fundamentally not sovereignty at all. Political sovereignty might indeed seem to be safeguarded by a formula, commonly used by the more moderate curialists after the days of Bellarmine, which makes the primacy of the Church express itself, where it touches the secular sphere, only in the form of *potestas indirecta*; but the safeguard is more apparent than real(69). True some voices were raised, even in the sphere of Catholic doctrine, in opposition to the theory of ecclesiastical supremacy. It was argued that the State possessed a *jus*

* I.e. it distinguished the two independent spheres of *spiritualia* and *temporalia*.

divinum analogous to that of the Church, and the idea of the subordination of its authority to that of the Church was accordingly rejected. But even so the Church was always regarded as a separate spiritual State, a *politia* or *societas perfecta*, with a sovereign power co-ordinate with that of the State. There were two separate powers; each of them was independent in its own sphere; and the two were simply connected by mutual alliance (70).

On the Protestant side too, after the early ferment of the Reformation had subsided, the old medieval idea of two *potestates distinctae* continued for some time to survive, and to hold unchallenged sway in theory. There was only one difference. Holding, as they did, that the one universal invisible Church was not a legal institution, and believing, accordingly, that the Church only manifested itself as a legally organised association in the form of a territorial Church, Protestant thinkers were free from any idea that the possession of the two powers could be divided between two separate external authorities (71).

In the Lutheran Church, the view which came more and more to prevail was to the effect that the one divinely appointed authority [the Prince] was called to the exercise of *regimen* in things spiritual as well as temporal, but that he possessed the two powers by different legal titles, and was bound to exercise them according to different laws, through different organs, and subject to different limitations imposed by the rights of the general community. In this view the State and the Church appeared as separate social organisms, with sovereign powers of different origins; only they were united, just as two States may be joined under a system of personal union, by having a common head. This point of view found juristic expression in the episcopal system and the theory of the three Estates* (72).

A more definite breach with the medieval system of canon law was marked by the theory which triumphed in the Reformed Church of Calvin. Based on the congregational principle (*Ge-*

---

* We may call the Lutheran system one of 'qualified parity'. There is parity, in the sense that Church and State are on a parity as social organisations, with different sovereign authorities corresponding to their different character as organisations; but the parity is qualified, and highly qualified, by the union of the two authorities in one hand. The episcopal system, in which the prince is *summus episcopus*, is a juristic expression of this qualified parity: the system of the three Estates, in which the clergy are a separate Estate, but have to act with the other two in a single State under the supreme authority of the prince, is another juristic expression.

§ 15. *The natural-law theory of Associations*

meindeprinzip), Calvinism none the less continued to hold, like Lutheranism and Catholicism, the theory of the double 'polity'; but unlike the Lutherans, the Calvinists vested the united exercise of the two powers not in the Head, but in the whole Body, of the community. They regarded the People as possessing both a temporal and a spiritual sovereignty, which were in some sort coordinate with one another, and they made each of the two separate sovereignties issue in a corresponding series of group-organs (73).

We have noticed, in its various phases, the idea of dualism between Church and State. It was impossible for the theory of Natural Law, as it moved onward to its culmination, to assimilate such an idea. On the contrary, it found itself forced, by the sheer necessity of keeping its logical system intact, to press the Church, like other bodies, into the common mould of its theory of the State. The task was the easier because the development of the Protestant system of the State-Church had already provided the theorist with a basis in actual fact. The Church had already been incorporated into the State in practice. It only remained to incorporate it also in theory. Such incorporation of the Church in the State was most readily achieved by those who held the purely 'territorial' view of the Church.* From the beginning of the Reformation this view had always found supporters; and it naturally became an obvious axiom of political theory as soon as thinkers grasped, and pressed to its logical conclusions, the conception of sovereignty which made it the one and only form of social authority. This territorial view eliminates not only the conception of a spiritual State, but also any conception of a spiritual authority. For it there is no other

---

* Gierke uses, in the following argument, a distinction between three forms of ecclesiastical organisation which is common in German thought. (1) 'Collegialism' ('formulated', according to the *New English Dictionary*, 'under the name by Pfaff in 1742') is the theory 'that the (or a) visible church is a purely voluntary association (*collegium*) formed by contract, in which the supreme authority rests with the whole body of the members; and that the civil magistrate has no other relations to the church than those which he has to any other association within his territories'. (2) 'Episcopalism' is the theory 'which places the supreme authority in the hands of an episcopal or pastoral order: if this authority is in practice exercised by any recognised head of the church, it is only as the delegate of this order as a whole, and with their consent'. (3) 'Territorialism' is the theory 'which places the supreme authority in the civil power': its motto is *cujus regio, ejus religio*. In England Nonconformity may be said to represent 'collegialism', and Anglicanism a mixture of 'episcopalism' and 'territorialism', with the proportions and the continuance of the mixture both in dispute.

authority, even in ecclesiastical affairs, than the unique and indivisible majesty of the State (74). As an invisible community, the Church is a kingdom by itself. In its external and legal manifestation, it is a State-institution; spiritual office is a particular sort of State-office; and spiritual property is State-property devoted to a particular object*(75). Views of this general character are compatible with very divergent conceptions of the limits to which the authority of the State should be subject in the area of religious life. The territorial system can equally find room both for theories of religious persecution and for theories of liberty of conscience (76). But the issue between persecution and toleration is not a question of the boundary to be drawn between Church and State. It is only a question of the boundary to be drawn between the State and the Individual.

Meanwhile the purely territorial system came into collision with the natural-law doctrine of the contract of society. If such a contract could produce social bodies, why should not a religious association be the product of a 'league and covenant' between believers? The question did not stay long for an answer. As early as the seventeenth century we already find thinkers of the School of Natural Law holding the view which has since been given the name of 'collegialism'. It is a view of the Church as based on a separate ecclesiastical contract of society. It is a view which makes it one of the associations contained in the State.

At first this view can hardly be said to have come into actual conflict with the 'territorial' system. On the contrary, it rather served as a foundation and support for territorial ambitions. We have to remember that a formula had already been found, applicable to all the associations contained in the State, which made it possible to combine two different ideas—the idea that they derived their existence from a voluntary contract of union, and the idea that they derived their authority from the authority of the State. On this basis, it was easy to assume that there was also a religious contract of union, and that this contract, like other similar contracts, could indeed produce a society, but not an authority. This line of thought may be traced particularly in Grotius' work *De Imperio summarum potestatum circa sacra* (77), which sketches a collegial-territorial system of Natural Law for the Church. This

---

* The reader may find some interest, from this point of view, in Paley's *Moral and Political Philosophy*, Book VI, c. x, 'Of Religious Establishment'. E.g. to Paley the clergy are 'a class of men set apart by public authority', and maintained 'from revenues assigned by authority of law'.

§ 15. *The natural-law theory of Associations*

system, we have to admit, does not altogether square with Grotius' general theory of corporations, as it was described a few pages back. On the contrary, the *De Imperio* shows a far less liberal attitude to the rights of associations, though the writer seeks to conceal his departure from his earlier views by making an artificial distinction between the various species of social authority. In the scheme of ideas which he now propounds, all *regimen* is either *directivum* or *constitutivum*. (1) The first form of *regimen* imposes no sort of obligation: at the most, it either gives advice, *qua suasorium*, or it enunciates some existing obligation, *qua declarativum*. (2) *Regimen constitutivum*, on the other hand, is a real source of obligation; but it can only impose that obligation either *ex consensu* or *ex vi imperii*. (*a*) *Regimen ex consensu* arises from the binding force of contracts. In the first instance, therefore, it can only bind the consenting parties; but secondarily, and indirectly, it may also bind those who are not consenting parties, if and provided that they too are members of the *universitas*, and if the *major pars* of this *universitas* makes a decision which is necessary for its maintenance or improvement. Even so, the obligation does not arise from any *superioritas* of the majority, '*sed ex illa naturae lege, quae vult partem omnem, quae pars est, ordinari ad bonum totius*' (78). (*b*) *Regimen ex vi imperii* [as distinct from *regimen ex consensu*] '*obligat ex vi intrinseca supereminentiae suae*'. It is either *supremum* or *supremo inferius*. The latter species may again be subdivided. It is either *ex supremo emanans* (in which case it is sometimes only *obligativum*, but sometimes also *coactivum*), or it is *aliunde ortum habens*. But it is only the paterfamilias, and (to a less extent) the guardian and the teacher, who possess an intrinsic *imperium* which is not derived from the sovereignty of the State [i.e. which *aliunde ortum habet*].

In accordance with this scheme, Grotius invests the *Ecclesia* (as a *coetus* which is not only permitted, but also instituted, by the law of God) with all natural rights of a *universitas legitima*, including the right to exercise a *regimen constitutivum ex consensu*; but he will not allow it a *regimen imperativum* (79). To the clergy, as distinct from the Church, he refuses to allow even an *imperium constitutivum*: they have merely a faculty of *directio*, such as belongs to a physician (80). All real authority, in ecclesiastical as well as in civil matters, is reserved for the political sovereign; and his *summa potestas* must necessarily, on the principles of Natural Law, and by its very nature as a unique and universal authority, embrace things sacred as well as profane (81). Similar views had been developed by other writers previous to Grotius (82); but it was an almost contemporary writer, Conring, who expressed most vigorously the general idea that the Church is no separate State, but a corporation contained in the State(83).

Collegialism, however, was destined to become the definite enemy of territorialism, as soon as thinkers began to argue from the doctrine of a contract of society to the existence of an inherent social authority belonging to associations. In that case the authority of the Church, like that of other associations, could be regarded as a corporate authority, subject indeed to political sovereignty, but none the less rooted and grounded in the very fact of ecclesiastical society, and independent in its own area. Gisbert Voet was the first to erect a complete system of natural church-law on this basis(84). He explains the existence of the visible Church as being entirely due to a voluntary contract of union(85). True to the constitutional ideal of the Calvinists, he regards the particular congregation, under its own presbytery, as the primary form of the Church, produced by a covenant made between individual believers; and he proceeds to interpret the larger ecclesiastical groups, organised in an ascending series of different synods, as later formations due to a contract of union (*combinatio, unio, et incorporatio*) between a number of congregations(86). He ascribes to the Church thus constituted a spiritual authority, in regard to doctrine, ritual, and discipline, which proceeds directly from its natural power over its own body (*corpus suum*)(87). He admits that, so far as positive law is concerned, the relation of the Church to the State is determined in a variety of different ways, according as such law varies from State to State(88). He allows, again, that owing to a stress of circumstances due to the Papacy, the true Church has been forced in a number of cases to hand its authority over to the secular government(89). But he holds, none the less, that according to divine and natural law all that the State can properly do is to exert over the Church a supervision which issues from the nature of its political authority, and the Church itself must always retain its own separate spiritual authority(90). He utters a warning against the total surrender of the ecclesiastical commonwealth to the State. He protests against the treatment of Church property as the property of the State; and he thus applies in the sphere of the law of property [as well as in regard to doctrine, ritual and discipline] his general idea that the Church is an independent corporation, depending upon itself(91). It is little wonder that his book was instantly stigmatised by the adherents of territorialism as a backsliding into papalism(92).

CHAPTER II

THE PERIOD FROM THE MIDDLE OF THE SEVENTEENTH TO THE BEGINNING OF THE NINETEENTH CENTURY

SECTION I

THE NATURAL-LAW THEORY OF SOCIETY DURING THE PERIOD OF ITS ASCENDANCY

§§ 16 to 18

CHAPTER II: SECTION I,* §16

THE GENERAL THEORY OF THE GROUP (*VERBANDSTHEORIE*) IN NATURAL LAW

I. *The vogue of Natural Law and its individualistic basis*

After the middle of the seventeenth century the influence of natural-law speculation steadily grew in depth and in extent. The doctrines of the Law of Reason not only acquired an intellectual supremacy over every department of jurisprudence: they also began to translate themselves into fact. Advancing irresistibly on their triumphant progress, they only came in sight of the limits of their power at the moment when, in the general European revolution of 1789, they also achieved the realisation of all the high hopes which they had inspired. To trace effectively the development, during this period, of the views entertained in regard to the legal nature of Groups, we must henceforth endeavour to follow the history of the natural-law theory of Society not only in its inward growth, but also in its external operation.

We may first of all glance at the general theory of the Group which was held by the School of Natural Law. We have already seen that there had arisen, on the soil of the doctrine of Social Contract, a general theory of society which included the State and all other human groups in its scope, and interpreted them all in the light of a single principle. This general theory of all forms of *societas* was now expounded in detail, and it became the more influential as thinkers occupied themselves more with attempting to elaborate Natural Law into a regular system of doctrine—an ambition which was nowhere pursued more ardently than in Germany. Even when no such attempt was made—when thinkers confined their attention to the State, or when [though dealing also with other groups] they assigned to the State alone an inherent right of existence—it was still their regular habit to raise the fundamental issues of principle in which the problem of Group-life as a whole was involved. The very rebel who followed a line antagonistic

---

* Gierke gives at this point, in the German original, a list of the works to which reference is repeatedly made in this section. For this list, see below, pp. 409–417.

to Natural Law was forced to define his position in reference to the general axioms of this dominant social theory.

The development of the general natural-law theory of Groups proceeded along many divergent lines, and it was attended by lively differences of opinion. But the guiding thread of all speculation in the area of Natural Law was always, from first to last, individualism—an individualism steadily carried to its logical conclusions. Every attempt to oppose this tendency was necessarily a revolt, on this point or on that, against the idea of Natural Law itself. Many of these attempts meant nothing more than an obstinate adhesion to the crumbling intellectual system of the past; some of them contained the germs of a future philosophy; but none of them, at the moment, possessed either the lucidity, or the vigour, which would enable it to withstand the progress of the general individualistic tendency.

II. *The priority of the individual to the community, and the consequent views of law and property*

The fixed first principle of the natural-law theory of society continued to be the priority of the Individual to the Group—a priority all the more readily assumed because the state of society was universally held to be derived from a previous state of nature, in which it was supposed that no real group had existed.

According to the view which more and more held the field, the individual in the state of nature had been his own sovereign. Men were originally free and equal, and therefore independent and isolated in their relation to one another. But how could this assumption be reconciled with the postulate, which lay at the root of the whole of Natural Law, that a valid law already existed in this self-same state of nature? Was it possible to conceive a system of law as having authority, unless it limited individual wills? And could individuals be limited and bound by a common law, unless they were at the same time united in a community?

The solution of this problem was a matter of decisive importance, not only for its bearing on men's conceptions of the primitive condition of humanity, but also for its effects on their interpretation of the contemporary world. The view was becoming more and more prevalent that, after the foundation of civil society, the authorities vested with the possession of sovereignty still continued to remain, in their sovereign capacity, in the same state of nature in which sovereign individuals were supposed to have been before.

§16. *General theory of the Group in Natural Law* 97

The first conclusion drawn from this view was that sovereign States were to be regarded, in their relations to one another, as 'moral persons'* still remaining in a state of nature, and therefore subject to the continuing validity of the pure Law of Nature, which thus became a system of international law (1). In this way the question originally raised in regard to the state of nature—'How could a system of law be possible among completely free and equal individuals?' recurred again as a fundamental question of international law. Nor was this all. There was also the question of the relations of the political sovereign to his subjects. Remaining as he did in the freedom of the state of nature, he was held to be unrestrained by any limits of positive law; but he was also held to be obliged by the Law of Nature (2). We can see how the profoundest issues of public law [internal as well as international] depended on the possibility of reconciling sovereignty with legal obligation.

All difficulties disappeared if once thinkers consented, with Hobbes and Spinoza, to explain away Natural Law into the natural rule of the power of the stronger over the weaker, and to regard the state of nature as a war of all against all (3). A natural law of that order erected no barriers against the play of will, and founded no community. But such Natural Law was no law at all: it only sailed under the name of law like a ship under false colours, to conceal the bare piratical idea of power. If he were subject to no other law than a Natural Law of this description, the sovereign Ruler of actual contemporary life (equally with the sovereign individual of the primitive state of nature) was really released from any legal obligation at all. Public law disappeared, so far as his relations to his subjects were concerned: international law equally disappeared, so far as concerned the mutual relations of States (4). Unless the theory of Natural Law was willing to lay the axe to the roots of its own existence, it was precluded from following the line that Hobbes and Spinoza indicated (5).

It is not surprising, therefore, to find that the prevalent doctrine in the School of Natural Law insisted firmly on the genuine *legal* character of such law, and regarded its binding obligation as coeval with the state of nature. The followers of this doctrine would

* Moral person (*persona moralis, personne morale*) simply means a non-physical person—a person such as exists in the world of men's thoughts (and particularly in the world of their legal thought), but not in the world of physical nature. No ethical connotation is involved, but it is the danger of the term that an ethical connotation may be imported. Rousseau's theory, that the general will of the moral person of the community is always right, does not escape this danger.

not even consent to turn an ear to the teaching of Thomasius, who held that the Law of Nature had only a power of inward obligation, and thus turned it into a mere moral imperative (6). They always insisted that the Law of Nature had the full power of external obligation (7). But they began to diverge, and to diverge very widely, when they tried to find a way of explaining the existence of this external obligation without sacrificing at the same time their belief in natural liberty. The simplest way of producing an external control* which was compatible with the full sovereignty of the earthly Ruler was to find it in God Himself. Now it is true that there was lively controversy about the relation of *jus naturale* to God, and whether its origin was to be ascribed to His Will or His Being;† but any appeal to Divine authority was not a matter of such practical moment in connection with *jus naturale* as it was in connection with another issue—that of the importance to be assigned, and the scope to be given, to the *jus divinum* derived from immediate divine revelation.‡ Even if the Divine Will was considered to be the ultimate source of Natural Law, and God was held to be the legislator who formally enacted it, the Reason of man was still regarded as the only source from which knowledge of this law could be actually gained, by way of a natural or rational revelation running parallel to the process of religious revelation proper (8).

* Natural Law, it was argued, is binding not only *in foro conscientiae*, but also *in foro externo*. It is an external control, which has the power of imposing external obligation. But how can there be an external control which is really compatible with the natural liberty of the Ruler, who remains in the state of nature? One answer, here discussed, is to the effect that the external control of Natural Law is really an external control imposed by God, whose law is always above our liberty.

† The controversy is the same as that waged between the medieval Realists, who held that Natural Law was the dictate of Reason, grounded on the Being of God, and the medieval Nominalists, who held that it was simply the command of God, founded upon his Will. Cf. *Political Theories in the Middle Age*, pp. 172–4.

‡ We may remember in this connection St Thomas' distinction of the various '*leges*'—the *lex aeterna* by which God Himself acts: the *lex naturalis*, which is the detection by human reason of His eternal plan: the *lex divina*, which is the law He has directly revealed to men in the Scriptures; and the *lex humana*, or positive law of human societies. The controversy about the extent to which *lex divina*, or Scriptural law, was an external rule that imposed itself on the State was a controversy of more practical importance (Gierke suggests), in the period after the Reformation, than the more academic controversy about *jus naturale* and its origin in the Being or Will of God. The one touched statesmen and clergy, we may say: the other only affected the professors of Natural Law in the Universities.

§16. General theory of the Group in Natural Law

The idea of a transcendental source of natural-law obligation receded still further into the background if the Law of Nature was ascribed not to the Will of God, but to his Being, or if, again, He was only invoked as the author of the Reason which itself determined the rules of such law(9). Much the same may be said of another assumption, which was made by a number of thinkers—that Natural Law had an external sanction in the Divine threat of penalties for its breach; for here again all that was meant was [not a direct intervention of God, but only an inevitable] retribution which manifested itself in the natural course of affairs(10).

We thus see that the appeal to Divine authority in order to secure a legal validity for the Law of Nature resulted in little more than the provision of a formal basis for it; and those who never introduced the name of God at all were able to secure the same result almost equally well [by contenting themselves with human reason as the formal basis of Natural Law](11). If, therefore, the power of the Law of Nature to impose obligation *in foro externo* was not to remain a mere phrase, it had to approve itself as an actual fact in the current relations between man and man [apart from any Divine intervention].* This was the line actually taken in the prevalent theory. All living beings who came into contact in the state of nature were supposed to have a claim upon one another to the observance of Natural Law; and the claim was held to be guaranteed by a power of using coercive measures, which, under the conditions of the state of nature, must necessarily take the form of self-help. According to this view each individual, in the original condition of humanity, had been the guardian and enforcer of Natural Law as against every other individual(12). This view was extended to cover the relations of State to State under international law; it was even extended to cover, in some degree, the relations of subject to sovereign under public law. In both cases [that of State *versus* State, and that of subject *versus* sovereign] there was supposed to be a right, which could be enforced by the method of self-help, to the due observance of the limits imposed by the Law of Nature(13). Two results followed, or seemed to follow, from this general view. On the one hand, it appeared as if Natural Law possessed that quality of being enforceable, in

---

* Since God was not really regarded by the thinkers of the School of Natural Law as giving that law the power of binding *in foro externo*, it must be shown that Natural Law carried in itself such a power, which could be seen at work in the relations of man to man, apart from God, or from any intervention by Him.

which, from the days of Thomasius onwards, the distinction of law from morality had been more and more made to consist; and on this, in turn, it appeared to follow that it carried in itself a full power of imposing obligation(14). On the other hand, so long as any idea of external enforcement by a superimposed authority continued to be excluded, the nature of the legal obligation imposed by Natural Law seemed compatible with the notion of a sovereign and absolute liberty.

But the question at once arose whether it did not necessarily follow, if natural legal obligation were once admitted to be a primordial fact, that you had already, in that very assumption, introduced the fact of *community* into the regime of the state of nature. It was difficult to answer the question with a simple negative. It is true that the prevalent doctrine in the School of Natural Law made law the source of community, and not community the source of law(15). But even if that were admitted, the question might still be asked whether a system of law could exist, even for a single moment, without giving effect to the community-creating power which was inherent in its nature. And yet the whole natural-law body of thought was based on the opposite assumption—the assumption that *status naturalis* was the very antithesis of *status socialis*.

A favourite method of escaping from this dilemma was found in the conception of *socialitas* which had been propounded by Grotius. The advocates of the principle of 'sociability' held that the Law of Nature commanded sociable behaviour, and they therefore believed that the state of nature, if it were not yet a state of society, was at any rate a state of sociability(16). They represented this state as a state of common intercourse, but intercourse so formless, and so insecure, that the conception of a *societas* was entirely inapplicable to it(17). Yet it contained already, from the very first, the germ of society; and the antithesis between the natural and the civil condition thus lost its edge. The transition to civil society no longer appeared as a break-away from Natural Law, but rather as a further development and strengthening of its principles. Two consequences ensued. In the first place it became possible to hold the theory that all positive law either was, or at any rate should be, informed by Natural Law*(18). In the second place,

---

* This followed upon the idea that civil society, and therefore the positive law belonging to it, were developments and corroborations of an original sociability and the original natural law belonging thereto.

§16. General theory of the Group in Natural Law

a basis was provided for a school of legal thinkers (such as we find more particularly in Germany), who, starting from the idea that the creation of society was a stage in the evolution of Natural Law itself, proceeded to add to 'pure Natural Law' —which they interpreted as strictly as ever in an individualistic sense—a separate and subsequent body of 'social natural law'*(19).

It is obvious that all such attempts to find a half-way house involved no real surrender of the idea that individual isolation was prior to social cohesion. But the strict individualistic school would not accept even the appearance of a concession to the idea of community which was involved in these attempts. Under the influence of the philosophy of Hobbes, the view continued to be urged that the state of nature did not contain even the germ of community; that the formation of society was a 'break-away', dictated by reason, from the natural order of human relations; in a word, that society began in an act of artificial institution, and as a conscious departure from nature(20). In England, the influence of Locke secured an increasing acceptance for the theory that the original condition of man was unsocial—an acceptance due to the fact that he used it to support the rights of individuals to liberty of action(21). On the Continent, Rousseau's theory spread like wildfire. In that theory the state of nature, as a state in which the liberty and equality of men were still unlimited by any social fetters, was elevated to the splendour of a lost paradise:† community was regarded as a necessary evil; and all social institutions were allowed a right of existence only in so far as they were directed to the restoration of the liberty and equality of the state of nature, which the world had suffered so much by losing(22). In Germany also, similar views were widely disseminated during the second half of the eighteenth century(23). They attained their theoretical zenith in the early teaching of Fichte, who derived the

---

* On this basis we get (1) the pure state of nature, with its pure natural law; (2) the state of non-political society (which develops from the state of nature under the impulse of natural law), with its social natural law; and (3) the state of political society, with its system of positive law.

† Gierke's account of Rousseau has to be modified, partly by a distinction between the theory of his *Discours* of 1753 and that of his *Contrat Social* of 1762, partly (and consequently) by a recognition of the superiority which, in the latter, he assigns to the civil State in comparison with the state of nature. See Bosanquet, *Philosophical Theory of the State*, and Vaughan, *The Political Writings of Rousseau*.

whole system of law from the conception of the Ego and its absolute liberty(24).

In Fichte's view the 'relation of Right' (*Rechtsverhältniss*) arises among human beings when the Ego, in the process of becoming self-conscious, has passed beyond the stage in which it places itself in the world of sense as the sole original cause and demands for itself unfettered activity and an absolute power of coercing others. It now proceeds, in the light of its own self-consciousness, to take for granted the existence of other reasonable beings outside itself; it ascribes freedom to them as well as to itself; and it finds that it must, as the price of remaining self-consistent, and in order not to contradict either its own liberty or the liberty of others (which it has deduced from its own), proceed to limit its liberty by the idea of the liberty of all other persons(25). On this basis 'original Right' (*Urrecht*) is co-extensive with the sovereignty of the Ego(26); and natural 'Law' (*Gesetz*) is not obligatory, but only permissive, in the sense that it offers advice in regard to the action which the Ego should properly take *if* it would correspond to its own notion(27). It depends on the free decision of individuals whether they will follow this 'problematical' (i.e. conditional) rule: whether they will found a 'community', by declaring self-imposed limits and agreeing to their observance; whether, finally, for the purpose of guaranteeing these limits, they will institute a coercive law which operates mechanically(28). But just because he thus starts from the omnipotence of the Individual, Fichte is unable to regard Natural Law as law in the proper sense. It is only the power of the State, he argues, which gives reality to the rule of law. Conversely, he adds, it is only the law of Reason which the State can confirm as real law. 'The State becomes man's state of nature; and its laws should be no other than the realised law of nature'(29).

Kant is equally unable to transcend the limits of an individualistic point of view. [There are, it is true, some higher elements in his thought.] He bases law, along with morality, on the 'categorical imperative', which is an *a priori* datum involved in the law of thought(30): he believes in an *a priori* existence of the idea of the civil or social state, which is as early as the state of nature itself(31): he assumes an enforceable legal obligation to enter into membership of a legal community(32). But [his fundamental basis is individualism:] he makes the autonomous individual prior—in idea, if not in time—to any form of community(33); and he regards contract as the only legal method of producing a legal nexus

§ 16. General theory of the Group in Natural Law

between human beings (34). If, like Fichte, he attributes no more than a provisional validity to the pre-political Law of Nature, he also, like Fichte, holds that the State, as an organisation intended for the purpose of giving a peremptory form to law, is bound to accept and confirm the substance of a pre-existent law of Reason; and he believes that the norm or standard of this law of Reason must still continue to be the inherent and inalienable claim of the rational individual being—regarded as an end in himself—to enjoy liberty, equality, and independence (35).

This belief that the primitive system of legal relations need not be associated with the existence of any community was also reflected in the development of theories regarding the origin of *property*. Thinkers still retained the traditional assumption of an original community of possessions; but while the Middle Ages had believed that this *communio primaeva* had issued in a positive system of joint-property, the School of Natural Law interpreted it as being only a *communio negativa*, similar to the present system of common enjoyment of air and sea, and signifying, therefore, not so much community of property as the entire negation of property (36). This idea of a 'negative community' of property in the state of nature was one which could be, and was, increasingly turned to account for the purpose of justifying, as consonant with Natural Law, the limits imposed upon private property in the civil state*(37). But unlike positive community of property, from the division of which a system of severalty must necessarily emerge, mere negative community could never be represented as the origin of private property (38). On the contrary it tended to give free scope to the development of theories which derived private property (like all other rights) from the primitive right of the Individual. Following this line of thought, Locke argued (and his argument was a landmark in the history of thought) that property already existed, in the pre-social state, as the result of individual labour or occupation; and he was thus able to reckon it, along with liberty, as one of the natural-law rights which civil society found already existing when it appeared on the scene, and which it could not touch or modify (39). From the days of Locke onwards the theory of the pre-social origin of property found an increasingly

---

* E.g. to take an example which Gierke cites from Pufendorf in his note, the right of the State to unclaimed property, and its *dominium eminens* over all property, might be regarded as derived from, and as relics of, the original 'negative community'.

large measure of support(40). On the one hand, it received the homage of Rousseau himself (41); on the other, Justus Möser made it the basis of his conservative theory of history and society (42). With some reservations, it was adopted also by Kant(43). But an older theory, which supposed property to have been created for the first time by the emergence of political authority, still survived. Not only was it still upheld by the opponents of natural-law individualism(44): it was even advocated by some of the exponents of that system of thought, who attempted to give it a new basis by arguing that the real source of private property was a 'contract of property', which they held to be included in the general 'contract of society' (45). Fichte in particular, arguing upon this basis, arrived at a system of economics which may almost be called socialistic*(46).

Though the priority of the Individual to the Community was thus emphasised with an ever increasing intensity, there were never wanting representatives of an opposite view, which started from the assumption of *primitive community*. This view, however, generally took the form of a theological reaction against the secular theory of Natural Law; and all the attempts of theologians to derive civil society from the original communion of man with God, or from a primitive community of men which had been established by God, were inevitably driven from the field by the victorious advance of individualistic theory(47). This was the more inevitable because the advocates of such views could not even preserve their own loyalty to their principles. As they developed their theory of society, they deserted their own side, and went over to the view that the community was derived from the individual(48). Leibniz himself, although he started in principle from the idea of the Whole, failed to escape from this temptation(49). The first attempts at an historical conception of social evolution led to vigorous attacks on many of the fictions of the Natural-Law School; but in their immediate results such attempts were even less effective [than the arguments of the theologians] in destroying the foundations of individualism. Montesquieu never transcends the idea of society as the product of intelligent individuals(50). Justus Möser attacks the revolutionary demands of the law of Reason; but in his own theory he derives civil society from a contractual union between independent landed properties, and from the subsequent contracts

---

* On Fichte's economics see W. Wallace, *Lectures and Essays* (Part II, no. VIII), 'the relations of Fichte and Hegel to Socialism'.

§ 16. General theory of the Group in Natural Law

made with fresh individual entrants(51). Vico and Ferguson, too, never really break with the idea of a non-social primitive condition(52). Herder was the first to declare that the 'state of society' was man's 'state of nature'; but even Herder limits this natural society to 'Family organisations'. Nature has ended her work with them; and when it is necessary to go still further, reason and need now lead men on, and freedom takes its beginning(53).

It was a matter of no little importance that the idea of the simultaneous origin of the community and the individual was never entirely extinguished. But, at any rate for the time being, the broad and sweeping current of individualistic ideas was not stemmed in its course by that survival.

III. *The natural-law view of the source of Group-authority*

From the premiss that the individual was prior to the community the prevalent theory of this period immediately proceeded to draw the conclusion that the community derived its origin from the individual. If that premiss were really held—if, in other words, the state of nature was really conceived to be a non-social state—it was impossible to avoid this conclusion, unless the idea of *supernatural co-operation* were introduced into the process of social evolution. Attempts were constantly made to use the idea of divine intervention in order to refute the theory that social authority was derived from individual sovereignty. Among the adherents of the doctrine of the original sovereignty of the People, for example, we find something of a tendency to develop the view —which had been originated by Suarez and Molina—that while the *existence* of civil society may be allowed to be the work of individuals, the *power* of the associated community over its members proceeds from God(54). From another point of view [which may be traced in Bossuet and Fénelon] the community itself, as a simple fact of social union, is held to possess no sovereignty, and sovereignty is represented as arising only when a divine commission is directly given to the Ruler—so that the final constitution of political society [as including both a community and a sovereign] is based on an act of divine institution(55). Horn developed these theocratic ideas still further, and with a more rigorous logic. Basing himself on the premiss that individuals alone existed in human life, he entirely denied the possibility of producing a social Whole by any human means; and he therefore derived social authority from an act of divine intervention, by which one individual was elevated above the rest, and equipped with sovereign omnipotence (56).

If, on the other hand, the existence of an *original community* was made the basis of argument, it is easy to see how political authority, like all other forms of Group-authority, could be conceived as the continuation of a naturally given social authority [inherent in the original and naturally given community], which limited the individual from the very first, and could only be reformed or transformed [but never eliminated] by the claims of human liberty. Some sort of advocacy of this view, more or less clearly expressed, was never entirely absent (57).

But the dominant tendency of the age was neither favourable to theocratic ideas, nor ripe for historical explanations in terms of organic continuity. More and more widespread, therefore, was the triumph of the idea, inseparable in its nature from the theory of a social contract, that a previous sovereignty of the individual was the ultimate and only source of Group-authority. This was a point on which natural-law doctrines of the most divergent kinds were all unanimously agreed. For all of them alike, political authority was the product of a fusion of so many original individual authorities, whether the fusion was regarded as total, or as limited to certain points. For all of them, therefore, the community was only an aggregate—a mere union, whether close or loose—of the wills and the powers of individual persons. This was the basis on which Hobbes and Spinoza erected their thoroughgoing theories of absolutism (58): it was also the basis on which Althusius and the Monarchomachi, like Locke and Sidney afterwards, erected their theories of popular sovereignty (59): it was equally the basis of the theories which attempted to steer a course more or less midway between absolutism and popular sovereignty—the theories we find in Grotius, Huber and Pufendorf, and their disciples, and among all the most influential of the German systematisers of Natural Law (60). Rousseau argued, with all the force of his fiery eloquence, for the derivation of political authority from the individual (61). He tried hard to refute, by the aid of new reasons, an old argument often alleged against this theory—the argument that the right of life and death enjoyed by the State could not possibly have arisen from a devolution of individual rights, because the individual himself enjoyed no right of self-murder (62); while Beccaria, taking an opposite line, was bold enough to use that argument in support of the first attack delivered on the principle of capital punish-

§ 16. *General theory of the Group in Natural Law*

ment*(63). Towards the end of the eighteenth century it had almost become an undisputed axiom that the origin of all social authority was to be found in the contributions of power and of will which had been made for that purpose by free and equal individuals(64). It is significant that two thinkers of such different tendencies as Möser and Sieyès could agree in identifying the original creation of society with the constitution of a business partnership†(65). Fichte, too, until the days of his conversion [to a belief in the Group and in Group-authority] was a rigorous upholder of the individualistic basis(66); and Kant also never escaped from the idea that the whole of the right of civil society over its members was only the sum of the rights transferred to it by individuals(67).

IV. *Natural Law and the idea of contract as explaining the origin of Groups*

If this were the case, it followed automatically that the only legal method of bringing a community into existence was the free act of individual wills. How could there be any valid machinery, except that of free agreement, by which the inherent sovereignty of the individual could be abolished, or even transferred? It was this process of thought which turned the hypothesis of an original social contract into an accepted dogma of Natural Law. The theory of Contract assumed various forms; but there was a general agreement among its advocates that the basis of civil society was a legal transaction, by which previously free and equal individuals had alienated their right of self-sovereignty in favour of a group which they had themselves created. The prevalent theory in the School of Natural Law continued to represent the transition from the state of nature to the social state in two stages. In the first, a contract of union had substituted social cohesion for individual isolation. In the second, a contract of subjection had abolished the previous equality of all, and constituted a Ruler(68). No great change was made in this theory when Pufendorf intercalated the

---

* Molina deals with the point raised by Beccaria, and provides an answer; see note 60 to § 14.

† Contrast the famous passage in Burke's *Reflections*—'the State ought not to be considered nothing better than a partnership agreement, in a trade of pepper and calico, coffee or tobacco, or some other such low concern, to be taken up for a little temporary interest, and to be dissolved by the fancy of the parties'.

act of making a constitution between the two contracts(69), or when other writers, again, proceeded to transform this act into a formal constitutional contract*(70). The extremer forms of the theory, which assumed a single original contract, and made the State spring, directly and ready-made, from one act of agreement between all its members, had only the effect of attaching still greater importance to the immediate action of individual will. On the one hand, Hobbes and Spinoza, assuming a single contract of *subjection*, ascribe its conclusion to the deliberate act of all individuals(71); on the other, Rousseau, proclaiming the theory of a single contract of *society*, makes it entirely unnecessary for the community, which has already achieved its unity in and by that contract, to undertake any further action for the completion of the civil State(72).

Important differences between the various theories of contract were created by different conceptions of the *motive-forces* which were supposed to have determined men to surrender their natural freedom. [But these motive-forces were never regarded as primary factors.] So long as the root-idea of contract was maintained, any force (however powerful it might be, and whether it were regarded as internal or external), which impelled men to create a society, could only appear as one of the remoter causes of the civil state; and the legal basis of that state was still made to reside exclusively in a deliberate agreement of wills. Thinkers who believed in an internal force might recognise a social instinct as innate in man, and seek to ascribe the final cause of the State to God or Nature; but they still made its legal existence depend upon free consent(73). Those who believed in an external force might regard man as naturally an anti-social being, who could only be compelled to enter a community by the pressure of external necessity; but they held, none the less, that the community only acquired a power of obliging its members when there had been a decision of individual wills to that effect, and they sought accordingly to represent the making of the contract as an act which, in spite of the compulsion of circumstances, was itself juristically free(74). The same was true of the views which attempted to reconcile these two alternatives(75). It was also true even of Kant. He believed, indeed, in the existence of a duty to enter a legal community, arising from the rational

---

* This involved three contracts—the contract of society (*Gesellschaftsvertrag*); the constitutional contract (*Verfassungsvertrag*); and the contract of government made thereunder with the Ruler (*Herrschaftsvertrag*).

§16. *General theory of the Group in Natural Law* 109

imperative, 'that the state of nature should be transformed into the civil state': he even allowed the use of compulsion by each against each with a view to enforcing this duty; but he held, all the same, that the formal consent of all individuals was the indispenssable juristic method by which the foundation of civil society must necessarily be set in motion (76). The general tendency of thinkers was towards unqualified voluntarism. Regarding the institution of the social state as a free act of human will, they distinguished it more and more from the motive-forces which lay behind it (77), and they imported into it, more and more, the element of conscious calculation (78).

If we turn to consider the *efficacy* of the original contracts we find, once more, an absence of general agreement. In two directions we find the efficacy of contract depreciated. Those who regarded contract as explaining the existence of the State, but as incapable of explaining its authority, refused to admit that the force of individuals was adequate by itself to produce a completely equipped community (79). Those who continued to attach importance to the idea that a community was an original [and naturally given] fact sought to whittle down the creative force of an act of contract until it became a mere power of modifying [the original and natural community] (80). But such moderate views were increasingly forced to give way to the more rigorous doctrine which made the original generation of the community depend wholly and entirely upon contract (81).

The majority of the natural-law theorists regarded the original contracts which they postulated as *historical facts*, of which, by the mere play of accident, no historical evidence had been preserved. The most they were willing to allow was that sometimes primitive man, instead of making a definite contract, might have made tacit agreements of union (82). They also admitted the possibility of societies which had been, in the first instance, founded and held together by force; but they held that such societies only attained stability through the subsequent assent of their members, either tacit or express (83). But side by side with these views another began to make itself felt, which Kant was the first to express in clear terms. According to this view, the political contract had not the historical reality of 'fact': it had only the practical reality of 'an idea of reason'.* It was an *a priori* idea in the light of which

---

* In other words, Kant holds that contract is not the chronological antecedent, but the logical presupposition, of the State. The thinker who wishes to

alone the State could be understood, and by which alone 'its legal justification could be conceived' (84). The distinction drawn by Kant disentangled the problem of the historical origin of the State from the natural-law fiction [of its origin in a contract]; but it only did so at the cost of entangling the problem of the philosophical explanation of the State's legal basis (and entangling it more deeply than ever) in the meshes of individualistic fictions.

When we turn to consider the question of the *continuation* [i.e. the continuing validity] of the original contracts, we find the progress of individualistic views once more reflected in the development of natural-law theories. The demand for original unanimity [in the first formation of the State] began to be pressed more rigorously. An increasing emphasis was laid on the necessity of explaining all majority-decisions by an original unanimous agreement that they should be valid (85), until finally it came to be doubted whether such decisions had any obligatory quality at all (86). [The progress of individualistic views, which appears in such insistence on individual unanimity in the *first* formation of the State, was also reflected in the development of natural-law theory in regard to the *subsequent* validity of the original contract.] At first, thinkers had been content with the idea that later generations were bound by the contracts of their predecessors; but the fiction of fresh contracts [renewing the original contract in each generation] soon came to be regarded as necessary in order to explain the social obligation of each new age (87). At last a point was reached when the individual was not only assured freedom of entry into the State [by being made a party to a fresh contract when he reached maturity], but also freedom of exit; and each group of individuals was thus given the right of creating a separate autonomous society (88). Here the theory of contract had touched an extreme where, by denying to the will of yesterday any authority over the will of to-day, it condemned itself to suicide.

It was in connection with the State that the theory of contract had been developed. But it came more and more to be applied to all human associations, so far as they could not be regarded as merely creations of the State itself (89); and thus the existence of the Church, like that of local communities and corporate bodies, was ascribed to a special contract of society made for that pur-

understand the State must regard it 'as if' it had been formed by contract: the statesman who wishes to guide it properly must regard his position 'as if' it had been derived from contract.

§16. *General theory of the Group in Natural Law*

pose(90). Only in the sphere of Family-life, and only in the shape of the household community, was it possible still to trace a survival of naturally developed and necessarily binding obligation(91). But even in the sphere of the Family itself the admission that there could be a society which was independent of the will of its members was finally limited to the relation between parents and children under age. When once the age of majority had been attained, a contract of partnership was held to be necessary; and the full logic of the conception was particularly, and increasingly, applied to the institution of marriage(92).

Opposition to the doctrine of contract was never entirely absent; but it was partly based on theocratic assumptions, which had now lost their vitality(93). There was little profit to be gained from Horn's penetrating criticism of the theories of contract(94), when the critic himself, caught in the toils of a crude individualism, at one moment refused to allow any source of a genuine political authority other than a direct commission of divine 'majesty' to an earthly lieutenant(95), and then at the next, when he dealt with republics, was ready to make a mere contract between individuals the basis of something which in every way resembled a genuine political authority(96). The doctrine of contract was more seriously threatened by the continued existence of the older theory of the natural origin of the State(97). But it was only by slow degrees that a fresh philosophical outlook and a broader historical knowledge were applied to this theory(98); and meanwhile the very leaders of the movement which was to produce an organic conception of historical evolution contented themselves with modifications of the theory of contract, and never attempted to reject it entirely(99). In much the same way, the opposition which was offered to the contractual theory by those who attempted a more realistic treatment of the State was in its beginnings no more than tentative(100). Hume himself, vigorously as he argued against the idea that actual political obligation depended on a legal basis of contract, none the less retained a belief in the existence of an original contract(101).

V. *The natural-law view of the purposes of Society and its various Groups*

If all forms of common life were the creation of individuals, they could only be regarded as *means to individual objects*; for how could individuals ever have come to such a pass, as to sacrifice their natural liberty and equality to an object that lay outside or above themselves?

The view we should thus expect was that which was actually held by the theorists of the Natural-Law School. They agreed in holding an individualistic theory of all social purposes, and, in particular, they always regarded the end of the State (differently as they might define it) as consisting in the attainment of some good which the individual sought to attain for himself, but could not actually attain so long as he lived in isolation(102). They were equally agreed in believing that the end of any community also limited its *sphere of authority*, and, in particular, that the end of the State limited the extent of political authority; for it had to be assumed, on their principles, that in every contract of partnership each individual transferred to the partnership only such rights as the end of the partnership necessarily involved(103). If, in spite of this large measure of agreement, they differed widely from one another when they came to determine the actual *relation between Society and the Individual*, the difference was due not only, or so much, to any difference of views about the end of society, as to a divergence of opinion about the amount of the authority which was indispensable to the attainment of that end.

So far as any theories were developed, on the basis of the doctrine of contract, which were favourable to *the complete absorption of the individual in society*, they rested on the assumption that there was no other way for the individual to attain the enjoyment of the end of his life than by an absolute legal surrender of himself. But it was only Hobbes who pushed this paradox, which he had himself invented, to its extreme limits; and even he made some reservations in favour of the individual(104). Spinoza, using the same basis as Hobbes, drew very different conclusions, seeking to build upon it a theory which made the spiritual and moral liberty of the individual the final end and controlling limit of the State's authority(105). Rousseau starts, like Hobbes and Spinoza, from the idea that the surrender of all individual rights to the community is the only logically conceivable, and the only legally valid, means of achieving an individualistic purpose, which consists, on his view, in restoring the lost liberty and equality of all(106); but though he starts from the idea of surrender he succeeds in ending his argument, by dint of a series of sophisms, in a conclusion which seems to guarantee the indestructible rights of man(107).

But the prevalent doctrine of Natural Law assumed, as a matter

§ 16. *General theory of the Group in Natural Law*

of course, that the individual surrendered *only a part of his original rights* into the common stock of society; and the advocates of that doctrine increasingly made it their chief endeavour to provide the individual with a guarantee against the abuse, or even the extension, of the social authority which he had called into being. More and more emphasis was laid on the fact that the purpose of all social institutions was limited to the development of individual persons. Even the thinkers who still maintained that the purpose of the State had a general or public character proceeded without hesitation, after elevating the idea of *salus publica* to the position of the supreme standard of political life, to identify it with the mere fact of the prosperity or happiness of individuals(108). But the victory lay more and more with a trend of thought which definitely refused to acknowledge that Society had other than limited purposes, or that the State itself had any but particular and strictly defined objects. With the purpose of the State thus confined to the provision of external and internal security, or to the realisation of a scheme of legal order(109), the sovereign commonwealth was reduced, in the last analysis, to the level of an insurance society for securing the liberty and the property of individuals(110).

At the same time, and in close connection with this trend of thought, the theory of the Rights of Man grew into a great and spreading tree. The supposition that individuals, on their entry into civil society, were only willing to surrender the smallest possible part of their freedom, was now associated with the doctrine that certain of the original rights of the individual were inalienable and intransferable, and could not, therefore, be effectively surrendered, even by an express act of contract(111). In this way a distinction came to be drawn between inherent and acquired rights. Acquired rights, it was argued, were subject to the system of positive law, which depended for its existence on the State; but inherent rights were based on the pre-social Law of Nature, and since that law was still valid to protect them, they were immune from any invasion by legislative action(112). The theory of rights of man which were thus inviolable by the State itself was used by Thomasius and his successors in the struggle for freedom of conscience(113). It was developed by Locke and the political economists in the interest of economic liberty(114). It was expounded by Wolff in the academic form of a doctrinaire theory(115), and erected by later thinkers into a definite and rigid system(116). Finally it became, after the French Revolution, the essential core of the whole of the doctrine of Natural Law(117). In the heart of social life itself the individual had now a sphere reserved for him which was itself immune from society; and this Sovereignty of the Individual was obviously more original, and more sacrosanct, than any possible Sovereignty of Society, which could only be derived from *him*, and could only serve *him* as a means.

But it must be admitted that individualism was always liable to transform itself into social absolutism, just as social absolutism was equally liable to transform itself into individualism(118). These imagined contracts could be made to include whatever was needed to suit the practical tendencies of the age. An individualistic basis of thought did not prove itself then, any more than it does now, an effective barrier against socialistic or communistic aspirations(119).

Only occasionally does there ever appear, during the period of which we are treating, any inkling of what we may call the higher view. This is a view which makes both Society and the Individual contain in themselves their own end and object, so that neither can ever sink into being a mere means to the other, though either is meant for the other. It is a view which regards the juridical organisation of a community as ceasing to be true to its own 'Idea', unless it assigns equally original, and equally sacrosanct, spheres to the commonwealth as a whole and each individual member, and attunes their several spheres in concord and harmony(120).

VI. *The natural-law view of the Being of Groups*

We may now turn, in conclusion, to enquire into the natural-law conception of the Being, or essential nature, of Groups; and here we can really see how a logical individualism is inevitably impelled to annihilate any idea of the independent existence of the group. If civil society in general was merely the result of a contractual act, whereby individual rights were pooled in order that individual objects might henceforth be socially pursued, such society must, in the last analysis, resolve itself into an aggregate of mere legal connections between individuals. No group could be anything more, upon this basis, than a simple nexus. This legal nexus might be depicted as loose or intimate, simple or complicated, temporary or permanent; but however it might be depicted, it was constituted by the same elements of thought which were to

§ 16. General theory of the Group in Natural Law

be found in the *societas* or partnership based upon individual rights. In this respect there was no difference to be traced between the various groups in the successive stages of group-life, culminating in the State. The State itself simply formed, as the *societas perfectissima*, the highest stage of a uniform ascending series.

None the less, the theory of Natural Law did not entirely abandon the traditional conception of Group-personality. [It could not afford to do so.] There was too urgent a practical need for some embodiment of the social Whole as a single unity, constant through all the changes of its individual members, and capable of holding a legal position of its own. The consequence was that the point of view we have just described [which treats a group as merely a legal nexus between individuals] was only adopted to be dropped again instantly; and the 'legal nexus' was always being transformed into a 'legal Subject' of rights. We have already seen that Hobbes had indicated the way by which this ascent from individualism to the idea of the personality of a community could apparently be made. His theory was the point of departure from which the further development of the natural-law theory of the Group-person mainly proceeded.

There was only one writer who remained true to individualism to the very end, and was audacious enough to deny altogether the fact of Group-personality. This was Johann Friedrich Horn. Only the Individual, he argues, has any real existence. No union of men is anything more than a *multitudo singulorum*. Even a society which is united enough to form a State is not, in reality, a Whole. It does not constitute, in any way, a *totum*: it is only a sum of persons, which, as such, '*nullam seriem Rerum intrat, et ideo affectiones Entis non sustinet*' (II, c. 1, §18). Suppose you take a multitude of this sort; suppose you call it by the name of '*civitas*', and then describe it, under that name, as the '*materia*' of a '*corpus*' which is composed of '*membra et partes*'; suppose you then introduce the term '*respublica*', and use that term to denote the '*forma*' which permeates, inspires, and vitalises this body. All you have done is only a matter of pictorial expression, which you have used '*per analogiam et similitudinem*'; and strictly speaking the language you ought to have employed is that of '*quasi-materia*', '*quasi-corpus*', '*quasi-pars*' and '*quasi-forma*' (I, c. 1, §1; II, c. 1, §1). It is inconceivable, therefore, that a community, as such, should ever be the 'Subject' of rights over individuals. Least of all can political authority belong to the popular community, either originally or subsequently; either in substance, or in exercise; either in whole, or in part(121). Only in a monarchy can a single 'Subject' of political authority ever be found; and there one man, as the lieutenant of God, becomes the bearer of a transcendental 'majesty' which extends over all individuals (II, c. 1, §§4 sqq.). In a republic a 'Subject' of majesty is absolutely indiscoverable. Any *universitas* which it is possible for thought to conceive is nothing but a plurality of *singuli*; and a plurality of 'Subjects' contradicts the conception of indivisible majesty(122). A republic is therefore only a simulacrum of political unity, produced by an imitation of monarchy; and what exists there in reality is only a nexus of *mutuae obligationes singulorum*, founded on a *commune pactum*(123).

This utter denial of the existence of group-unity did not meet with the approval which it enjoys to-day(124). It is true that a number of political thinkers, who limited themselves to describing the relations between Ruler and Ruled, omitted the idea of State-personality from their theory of the State [and, so far as that goes, such writers may be said to agree with Horn]. But their attitude was simply negative; and they were far from intending to make any attack in principle on the idea of a common or group 'Subject' of rights. When real attempts were made to expound a genuine legal philosophy of the nature of social groups, there was a general agreement in assuming the existence of a social Whole which stood above individuals; and differences only began to appear when it came to the actual interpretation of the unity ascribed to this Whole. These differences mainly depended on the extent to which thinkers adopted a Representative or a Collective view of the unity of the Group-person. Both views were compatible with the general framework of the individualistic system; but while those who held the Representative view only sought to fit the idea of a Ruling authority into the scheme of rights of individuals, those who held the Collective view attempted to bring the idea of Fellowship itself under that scheme.

In the thorough-going systems of absolutism the procedure of Hobbes was followed, and the principle of Representation was adopted. The essence of Group-personality was made to reside in the fact that, by virtue of a cession of the powers and wills of all, the Ruler represented each and all of his subjects as a *persona repraesentativa*(125). But even in this connection the principle of Collectivity had to be introduced as a second line of defence. It is true that this principle, even when it was allowed to appear, was

§ 16. *General theory of the Group in Natural Law*

never held to possess a creative or constituent character:* and in regard to monarchically organised societies, it was never allowed to appear at all. But it was applied, as a sort of supplement to the principle of Representation, in order to meet the case of republics, and also of corporate bodies in which an assembly was appointed to act as *persona repraesentativa*. Proceeding on the traditional distinction between *plures ut universi* and *plures ut singuli*, and adding to it the doctrine of the legal equivalence of *universi* and *major pars*, the thinkers of the absolutist school adopted, in order to meet such cases, the idea of the unity of a Collective person, and they made that person the 'bearer' of an ownership of rights. It is obvious that this idea of collective personality was bound to play a greater part in the theory of Spinoza, who regarded democracy as the normal form of the State (126), than it could in that of the orthodox champions of monarchical absolutism (127).

In opposition to the principle of Representation adopted by the absolutists, we find the majority of the natural-law theorists—under the influence of a conception of Groups which was fundamentally a 'Fellowship' conception, such as naturally flowed from the dominant form of the theory of social contract—maintaining the view that all Group-persons were Collective unities, produced by the action of individuals in associating themselves together to form a community. But they too found themselves more and more forced to introduce the idea of Representation, as a constituent factor which was needed to explain the development of Group-unity into a full and complete personality. Huber, for example, starts from the view that the act of association, with the added aid of the majority principle, is capable of producing a Group-person (128); but he proceeds to make the full completion of the unity of this Group-whole depend on a further act which devolves representative authority upon a Ruler (129). Arguing upon this basis, he ascribes the difference between the full and complete personality of the State, and the less complete personality of the *universitas*, to the fact that the representation [of the community]

* I.e. the principle of Collectivity (the idea that the Many can collectively form a unity) was never, in any case, regarded by the absolutists as producing sovereignty. They would not allow that a collective Whole possesses, by the fact of its existence, an inherent sovereignty over its members. They held that, if sovereignty was to exist, there must always be a Representative of the Whole, and they believed that the presence of this Representative could alone produce sovereignty. But they admitted that this Representative might itself be collective—as in a republic, or, again, in a corporate body governed by an assembly.

by the political authority is not subject to the limitations which hold good, both in respect of contracts and of delicts, for representation [of other groups] by other forms of group-authority (130).

The views of Pufendorf: the persona moralis

Pufendorf tried to unite the two ideas of Collective and Representative unity, and he did so by seeking to bring every *societas*—be it State, Church, local community, corporation or family—under the general conception of *persona moralis composita*. Disagreeing with Hobbes [who held that no community could even exist without Representation], he held that this conception of the 'composite moral person' had a constituent or creative character, in the sense that it explained how individuals could unite to form a community possessing the capacity for a common rule of law and a common will (131). Here was a Fellowship basis; but a real person had still to be brought into being upon that basis.* To this end (and here he approximated, after all, pretty closely to Hobbes) Pufendorf went on to postulate the subjection of the powers and wills of all to the power and will of a single man or body of men, to the end that the sum of associated individuals should be represented by a 'person' who could act as a single unit (132). He believed that he could, in this way, interpret the fact of Group-personality in terms which made it belong to the same general category as the fact of individual personality. But the method by which he arrived at this general category [including alike both Group-personality and individual personality] depended upon a preliminary distinction. He distinguished the conception of legal personality, to which he gave the name of *persona moralis*, from the conception of natural personality. He held that the legal world was a world not of physical, but of mental factors—or rather, in view of the fact that it was the moral aspect of these mental factors which was really in question, it was a world of moral factors, or *entia moralia* (133). He regarded these *entia moralia* as being, in themselves,

---

* In Pufendorf's view, a community can exist on the basis of the conception of a composite moral person. This means that it exists on a Fellowship basis, without any need for the idea of a Representative ruling authority to constitute or create it. In other words, it is brought into being by the mere conception of the composite moral person, which has thus 'a constituent or creative character'. But in order that this person may become 'real', Pufendorf goes on to introduce the idea of a Representative ruling authority, in the person of which the community attains 'real' personality. He has not, after all, attained the idea that the composite moral person is 'real' in and by itself.

§ 16. General theory of the Group in Natural Law

only attributes (*modi*) which were ascribed by rational beings to physical objects and movements, in order that they might operate with a directing and moderating influence on the freedom of human will, and so regulate human life harmoniously (134).* Now these *entia moralia* stood to one another in the relation of superior and inferior. That relation could best be depicted by our minds, always prone to think in material terms, '*ad normam entium physicorum*'. Accordingly, although all 'moral beings' were, properly speaking, only *modi*, we applied the category of *substantia* as well as that of *modus* in trying to think about them. We regarded some of them as being *substantiae*, which supported (or 'subsisted' under) others, in the sense of being their basis; and we regarded these others as being *modi*, which 'inhered' in those *substantiae* (135). In this way there emerged, as '*entia moralia ad analogiam substantiarum conceptae*', the *personae morales* attributed to human beings under a system of legal order (136). Since the attribute of being a 'Subject' of rights is ascribed to human beings not only as individuals, but also as groups, these *personae morales* may be either *simplices* or *compositae* (137). The *persona moralis simplex* is the individual—not the individual in his totality, as revealed to the senses, but the individual *sub modo*, that is to say in so far as a definite *status moralis* is attributed to him (138). This is the reason why one individual can represent several persons (139). A *persona moralis composita* [as distinct from a simple moral person] is present when a single will, and with it a definite sphere of rights, is ascribed to a multitude of individuals duly and properly united (140). It follows that individual persons and Group-persons have both the same sort of existence [i.e. a moral existence]; but both of them are distinct from *personae fictae*, those '*simulacra et umbrae personarum moralium*' (for they are nothing more) which only exist in semblance or jest, without having any legal effect attached to them (141).†

---

* If you take a physical object (e.g. a natural person, regarded as a physical body), or a set of physical objects (e.g. the natural persons who move together in a group), and then proceed to ascribe to that object or set of objects the attribute of personality, this attribute will operate on your free will, because you will respect the object or set of objects as having the attribute of personality; and it will also introduce into human life the harmony which comes from such respect being paid.

† The argument is that the attribute of being a person can only really inhere in an appropriate substance: e.g. Caligula could give the 'person' of a senator to a fool, but not to a horse; and the 'person' of a senator, as given to a horse, is *ficta*, and only exists in semblance or jest.

It cannot be denied that Pufendorf, in enunciating these conclusions, is entering into a new world of thought. And yet the individualistic basis of his thought prevents him from achieving anything more than a purely formal assimilation of the group-person to the individual. As long as it was merely a question of employing a formal concept, Pufendorf could drive firmly home the principle that the corporate person must be conceived as a 'Subject' of rights, which willed and acted with the same unitary quality as a single person (142). But as soon as the real substratum or basis of these attributes [of willing and acting] had to be defined, difficulties began to appear. Behind the *persona moralis simplex* there stood, after all, the living natural person of the individual, drawing to himself, as *persona physica*, the attribute of personality (143); but the *persona moralis composita* had to find its basis, not in a real Whole, or a living community, but in the artificial outcome of contracts by which individuals had bound themselves to one another (144). Even the validity of majority-decisions was made by Pufendorf to depend merely on an agreement made to that effect (145). A unity thus interpreted in terms of the rights of individuals was in the last analysis only a deceptive sham: closer examination reduced it to fragments, and resolved it into a mere sum of legal relations between individuals.

But if Group-unity was thus reduced to a sum of legal relations, it became inevitable that the two different kinds of legal relations on which it depended—the relation of the Representative person to the body represented, and the Collective relation involved in the obligation of partnership—should each of them seek to vindicate its own separate and independent significance. This was exactly what happened in Pufendorf's theory. Springing as they did from different contractual origins [the one from the contract of subjection, and the other from that of society], the two relations were also made to issue in different results. (1) Where Group-personality was due to the representation of all by a single person, it became engulfed in the personality of this representative; and the *persona composita* thus dwindled into a *persona simplex* whenever a single man was constituted as Ruler (146). (2) Where an assembly had to represent the Group, that assembly—in and by itself, and without any regard to its representative function—was made to appear as a *persona composita*; and here the term signified nothing more than the union of the many members of the assembly, associated together on a basis of partnership, to act as a single

§ 16. General theory of the Group in Natural Law

body(147)....Such contradiction was fatal in its very nature to any successful combination of the ideas of Collective and Representative unity in a new and consistent system of thought.

Here we touch the secret of the peculiar fate which befell the original genius of Pufendorf. His theory of *entia moralia* ceased to be used by his disciples as the foundation of a general philosophy of Law, and it was only applied as a way of explaining a number of legal phenomena which obstinately refused to be brought into line with the facts of the material world(148). The result was that the conception of the *persona moralis* gradually lost the general significance which had been given it by Pufendorf. Thomasius and Titius still followed the master's line of thought(149); but Hert, Gundling and Schmier entirely dropped any reference to the immaterial nature of personality. Applying the term *persona moralis* only to Group-personality, they substituted for Pufendorf's distinction of the *persona moralis simplex* and the *persona moralis composita* a new distinction between the *persona physica* and the *persona moralis, composita, seu mystica*(150). In later writers we find the expression *persona composita* almost vanishing altogether(151); and the term *persona moralis* is made the regular technical term employed in treatises on Natural Law to designate the Group-person(152). This usage was not affected by the fact that many of the exponents of Natural Law, such as Wolff and Daries, gave a new and vigorous expression to the distinction which Pufendorf had drawn between the legal and the physical personality of the Individual(153). In the end the origin of the adjective 'moral' passed entirely into oblivion, and its real sense was forgotten.

With it there also disappeared those tendencies towards the transcending of mere individualism, which were obviously implicit in the conception of a 'composite' person. The more the physical person gained in reality, the more the moral person was bound to lose. It now stood by the side of the living individual as an abstract mental scheme, which had the one merit of enabling thinkers, when they were dealing with certain species of legal connections between individuals, to provide a single centre on which such connections could converge. Here the two constructive elements of individualistic social theory [the Representative and the Collective] proceeded again to diverge widely from one another, as we have already seen them diverging in the theory of Pufendorf. Among his immediate disciples, we find the possibility of a purely Collective form of Group-unity again receiving particular emphasis, though they also continued to maintain, from the other [or Representative] point of view, that full and complete unity was only made possible by the addition of a representative authority (154). There was one thinker, Hert, who succeeded in developing upon this basis an extreme and peculiar theory. On the one hand, he extended the conception of the moral person *usque ad infinitum.* On the other, he refused to recognise any community except the State as a Group-person inherently capable of will and action.

[We may take the latter side of his theory first]. He begins by admitting that the contract of union of *singuli cum singulis* is in itself sufficient to produce the result '*ut paciscentes fiant una quasi persona seu unum corpus*'. But he hastens to add that it is the contract of subjection which first animates this '*rudis et indigesta moles*', and produces an '*anima in corpore*' by transferring the powers and wills of all to a *summa potestas* (155). It follows on this that any group other than the State can only develop a common life as a part of the State, and in virtue of a representative authority derived from the sovereignty of the State (156). [On the other side of his theory] we find Hert laying it down that the Group is only one of a number of cases in which the conceptions 'man' and 'person' are not co-extensive. He reduces all these cases under two heads, to each of which he devotes a separate essay—one of them entitled '*de uno homine plures sustinente personas*' (157), and the other '*de pluribus hominibus personam unam sustinentibus*' (158). Appealing to the original sense of the word '*persona*',* Hert argues that all that is really involved, under either head, is a peculiar method of allocating the 'rôles', or parts, which men have to play on the legal stage. On the one hand, the [natural] personality of a single man may be divided among any number of rôles [and thus become any number of legal persons] (159): on the other, a number of men may be united together, if need requires it, in a single personality (160). It is plain from the heterogeneous nature of the legal examples which Hert accumulates to illustrate such union that no genuine community can be made to exist on this basis, but only, at most, a formal unity. True, he distinguishes two categories of *unitas personarum* [i.e. two different ways in which a number of men may form a single legal person], according as the source of

* In Latin, an actor's mask, and so the rôle or part played by an actor. On this basis one man may wear a number of 'masks', in the sense that he carries a number of legal personalities, and *per contra* a number of men may wear a single mask, in the sense that they carry a single legal personality.

§ 16. General theory of the Group in Natural Law

such unity is only a legal fiction, or an actual contract. But when we find the second of these categories made to include the *civitas* and the *universitas* equally with marriage, the nexus between *correi debendi et credendi** and the position of joint-feoffees, we can clearly see that his aversion from the idea of a '*persona ficta*'† is only based on the absence of any true conception of a Corporation.

Gundling went further still in the same direction. On the one hand, he made the personality of the State consist only and exclusively in the Representative personality of the Ruler (161); on the other, he interpreted the *universitas* as a purely Collective person (162)—rejecting the view that a 'fiction' was necessary in order to explain the existence of such a person, or its capacity for expressing a will (163), and rejecting it all the more emphatically because he pursued a rigorously Collective interpretation of Groups to its extremest logical conclusion (164). In much the same way as Gundling we also find other writers attempting to distinguish between the Representative personality which the State acquires in the person of its sovereign Ruler and the simple Collective personality [of other Groups] (165).

That distinction assumed an acuter form when it came to be connected with another and more general distinction, which had long been drawn in the theory of Natural Law—the distinction between the *societas aequalis* and the *societas inaequalis*. This connection appears particularly in the theory of J. G. Boehmer. According to him, the Being of a *societas aequalis* is limited entirely to the Collective unity of its associate members; but when a *societas inaequalis* comes into existence, there appears along with it—superimposed on the 'Fellowship' basis originally present in such a society no less than in the 'equal society'—a Representative unity in which Collective unity now disappears (166). This line of theory, or something very like it, attained a general vogue (167); and it came to be the regular opinion, among those who adopted this view, that the addition of a Ruling authority produced a fuller and completer unity, and that a higher degree of Group-personality

---

* A body of persons who are joint-debtors or joint-creditors.

† Strictly speaking Hert is not averse from the idea of a *persona ficta*. On the contrary, he applies it to a number of cases of Group-unity (see the beginning of the last sentence of note 160). But he will not accept it as explaining *all* cases of Group-unity, preferring to use the idea of a collective contract of union as a general line of explanation.

was thus attained in the *societas inaequalis* than was possible in the *societas aequalis* (168). At the same time, however, the drawing of this fundamental distinction between unequal and equal societies tended also to erect an increasingly insurmountable barrier between the State and the Corporation (169).

The atomistic conception of the nature of associations in eighteenth-century Germany

There ensued a progressive disintegration of the natural-law conception of Group-personality. The denotation of the term '*persona moralis*' came more and more to be limited to the Collective form of unity constituted by the *societas aequalis*. The more real and active form of unity, which showed itself in the *societas inaequalis*, ceased to be regarded as the result of an internal development of the personality of the Group-whole; it was treated as being the completion of an imperfect Collective person, from without, by a 'Subject' or owner of Ruling authority who was superimposed upon it. This meant that the moral person disappeared from the interpretation of the relation of Ruler and Ruled, and only survived for the interpretation of the relation of Fellowship (170).

This was not all. The increasing rigour with which the conception of purely Collective unity was applied also meant that the moral person gradually lost any real existence of its own [even in its own field of the Fellowship or 'equal society']. The supposed person dwindled down into a mere shorthand description for any sum of individuals which was in any way possessed of social rights or duties. Thus attenuated, the conception only retained, in the last analysis, a sort of technical value for purposes of external application; in other words, it was a term of art which made it possible for several persons to be treated as being a single person, in an area of action common to them all, as regarded their external relations to some 'third party'. Internally, the conception was useless; for if this unity of the moral person was really nothing but a Collective aggregate or sum, it had to be dissolved again into a multiplicity of different persons before legal relationships could be conceived as existing in it. In this way we find a general theory of society developed [in eighteenth-century Germany] in which the conception of the moral person is only applied to the external relations of a society, while its internal life is interpreted, with the aid of conceptions drawn from private law, in terms of *societas* and *man-*

§ 16. *General theory of the Group in Natural Law* 125

datum,* and is thus reduced entirely to a matter of mutual obligations between so many individuals. On the logic of these principles the State could only act as a Whole, and display the quality of a moral person, in the external area of international law. In the sphere of internal public law, it resolved itself into nothing more than a number of legal relations—the relation between Ruler and subjects; the various relations among the subjects themselves (171). Only in one connection was the conception of the moral person applied to internal public law. If the State as a Whole was not a moral person, parts or elements of it were allowed that quality. When the Ruling authority in the State, or some form of subordinate political authority, was ascribed to a body of persons acting in conjunction, or when, again, the body of the People, as a separate entity, was argued to have rights against the Ruler, such bodies were treated as moral persons. The same general philosophy was equally applied to all forms of Groups other than the State; and theorists were thus content to stop short at a conception of *societas* which made it a moral person externally, and internally only a nexus of reciprocal rights and duties.

All this meant the disappearance of any clear line of logical division between the genuine corporation and the mere 'society' or partnership. Internally the law of partnership was made to explain every form of human community, including the State; externally every form of group-relation, including the mere relation of joint-owners of property, was vested with a moral personality (172); and the view continued to be advocated that such personality was equally present, in just the same way, whether a number of individuals were united to form a single 'person', or, conversely, a number of 'persons' were carved out of one individual (173). It is true that this atomistic scheme of ideas was not applied by all thinkers without qualification (174); but it is equally true that it forms the essential basis of the great theories of Natural Law which exercised influence in Germany during the course of the eighteenth century. It dominates entirely the theory of Wolff (175). It is no less evident in that of Daries (176). It is elabor-

* *Societas* and *mandatum* are both, in Roman law, forms of consensual contract between individuals. *Societas*, or partnership, could be used, as we have already seen, to explain the State in the sense of a political society: *mandatum*, or agency, to explain the State in the sense of a Government. To Gierke they are both inadequate 'private-law' notions. The true State is more than a partnership of individuals, and cannot be explained in terms of *societas*: the true Government is based on something more than a *mandatum* given by individuals.

ated with laborious care, and with no small measure of juristic ability, by Nettelbladt, whose comprehensive theory of *societas* may well be termed the most mature product of the whole of this movement of thought.

In Nettelbladt's theory the entire world of human groups is depicted as developing, in an uninterrupted series, from the one conception of *societas*; but that conception itself—in spite of the differentiation of form through which it passes, and the constant enrichment of content which it acquires, in the course of his exposition—never gets beyond the limits of individualism(177). At every stage the internal life of the Group appears as a sum of individual obligations; at all stages alike—the Family, the Corporation, the local community, the Church, the State—there never emerges any idea that a community has its own law of being, even in contexts where it is impossible to avoid contrasting the Individual with the Whole to which he belongs(178). Yet Nettelbladt persists in regarding a plurality of persons, when it confronts another 'Subject' of rights in its collective capacity, as constituting a moral person. The moment that the views, the wills and the powers of a number of persons are thus directed externally to some identical object, those persons are held to constitute a single person in relation to that object, and to become a *persona moralis*; and on that basis, 'what is not one being deemed to be one' ('*non unum pro uno habetur*'), they are treated as being equivalent, in the sphere of their common rights and duties, to a *persona singularis*(179).

Achenwall's theory of society is based on a similar foundation. He does not reject entirely the idea of a Group-whole, of which individuals are the constituent parts(180); but like other thinkers of his time he ends by reducing the rights of associations, in their internal life, to a mere aggregate of contractual relations, formed between the associates acting as separate units(181); and like them, again, he will only allow this Collective unity to be conceived as a 'moral person' when it is acting externally, i.e. when it is dealing with non-members(182). Scheidemantel, starting from the same assumptions, comes nearer to the idea of a true Group-being composed of individual units(183). Generally, however, we may say that the end of the eighteenth century witnessed an irresistible movement towards the disintegration of the idea of Group-personality in the theory of Natural Law.

This is particularly evident in the controversy, which became

§ 16. General theory of the Group in Natural Law

increasingly vigorous, in regard to the basis and justification of the majority-principle. Those who held the Individualistic theory of Society were agreed that the common will of a 'moral person' must essentially mean a unity of *all* the wills of *all* the associated individuals, and that any identification of majority-will with group-will could therefore only be based on a precedent agreement of all individuals to that effect. The older School of Natural Law had regarded such a precedent agreement as an institution which was demanded by the very nature of Group-personality, and was therefore always to be presumed (184). But a new view began to gain ground, which ran in the opposite direction. According to this view, the principle of unanimity was the rule which issued, and must always continue to issue, from the nature of society; and decision by a majority-vote was an exception to this rule for which a special justification was necessary (185).

The appearance of this view marked the disappearance of the last trace of internal group-unity: the 'moral person' was finally degraded into a noun of assemblage, and the common will into a sum in arithmetic. Thus we find A. L. Schlözer hardly using at all the idea of Group-personality, but expounding, with a stiff pragmatism, a point of view which leads to the conclusion that any collective unity is only a sum of individuals (186), any common will can only be regarded as a 'sum of all particular wills' (187), and any organisation of wills can only exist on the basis of representation of individual wills by a 'foreign' individual will contractually empowered to that end (188). In the same way Christian von Schlözer, in his treatise *De jure suffragii*, resolves the common will into an agreement of individual wills; and he therefore attacks the view that the majority-principle derives its origin from the unity of the Group-personality, arguing that the description of a society as a *persona moralis* is only a metaphor, from which no conclusions ought to be drawn, and contending that the nature of any *societas* ought to be properly investigated before it is thus compared with a person (189). Hoffbauer equally assumes a purely Collective view of the 'moral person' (190). He reduces group-will, where 'equal societies' are concerned, to a union of all individual wills (191), and where 'unequal societies' are in question, to a submission of all other wills to the will of the Ruler appointed to represent those wills (192). Wilhelm von Humboldt goes furthest of all: he demands an express enactment of the legislator, 'that any moral person, or society, should be regarded as nothing more than the union of the members at any given time' (193).

*English and French theory in the eighteenth century:
Locke and Rousseau*

Meanwhile, in England and in France, the resuscitation of the theory of popular sovereignty had produced an attempt to give a more living content to the idea of Collective personality. Here the distinction between *societas aequalis* and *inaequalis* was dropped; and it thus became impossible to explain the development of Group-unity into a Being possessed of authority by referring that development to the institution of a Ruler who stood outside and above the community. If, under such conditions, there was to be any Group-unity which had the capacity of will and of action, and could be depicted as the 'Subject' of political authority, such unity had to be found not in a uniting Representative Ruler, but in the united community itself. The only question which then arose was whether it was possible—and if so, how it was possible—to raise the conception of Collective unity (the only conception possible as long as thought was confined to the limits of natural-law individualism) to the required degree of intensity.

In dealing with this problem, Locke marks but little advance. Although the community, on his own principles, is nothing but a partnership of individuals who remain individuals, he yet makes it also, at the same time, a single body(194). His treatment of the majority-principle is a good illustration of his method. On the one hand, he seeks to derive it from the nature of the community as a single body. All bodies, he argues, must be moved by a single power in a single way; in the body politic, the only motive power discoverable is the superior power possessed by the majority; therefore the identification of majority-will with the will of the whole is a consequence of the Law of Nature and Reason(195). On the other hand, and in the same breath, [recurring to the idea of partnership,] he thinks it necessary to suppose a contractual agreement of all individuals to submit to the future resolutions of a majority, and he makes this agreement the legal basis of the validity of such resolutions(196).

Rousseau occupied himself far more seriously with the problem of raising Collective unity to the dignity of a living and authoritative Group-person. It was a problem which was particularly pressing for him, because he rejected absolutely any idea of Representative unity. He asserts again and again that the social contract produces a moral body equipped with authority over its members; that such a body, like the natural body, is a single and

§ 16. *General theory of the Group in Natural Law*

indivisible whole; and that it possesses an Ego, a life, a will of its own (197). He makes this real Group-being, under the name and style of a 'moral person', the one and only Sovereign, which not only stands on a level with actual individuals in all its external relations, but is also the genuine 'Subject' of political authority internally (198). But vigorously as he sought to depict the substantive existence of this sovereign Group-person, Rousseau was unable to escape from the trammels of a view which made it, after all, only a sum of individuals united in a single aggregate. But how could a contract between individuals conceivably produce anything which was not itself a mere matter of individuals? Rousseau attempts to meet the difficulty. He argues that the associated individual wills blend together in a general will (*volonté générale*), which is no longer the will of all (*volonté de tous*). But all the dialectical arts which he uses in order to prove that the general will is different from the will of all fail to turn it into a genuine common will. In the last resort the whole distinction comes to this —that the will of all is the sum of individual wills, including all their actual variations from one another, while the general will is to be found by adding the concordant motives of individual wills, and excluding all their dissonances (199). The innate character of this general will is not even sufficient to produce the principle of majority-rule; and if majority-rule is to be substituted for it, it must be stipulated for in an agreement—though it is only fair to add that Rousseau regards such an agreement as indispensable (200). The supposed general will is thus, after all, no more than an average of individual wills, to be found by the use of a ready-reckoner. Only a miracle can enable it to show the higher qualities which Rousseau poetically credits it with possessing (201).

[Just as the general will stays at the level of an average of individual wills, so] the sovereign Group-person never rises beyond the sum total of individuals who constitute the society at any given time. The same persons who are governed, in their capacity of subjects, also constitute the sovereign in their other capacity of citizens (202). Each is, in part, the joint-owner of a sovereign authority to which, at the same time, the whole of himself is subject* (203). Corresponding to this double position [of subject and

---

* Compare the epigram of a French writer: 'The modern Frenchman looks with pride at his face in the glass as he shaves in the morning, remembering that he is the thirty millionth part of a tyrant, and forgetting that he is the whole of a slave'.

citizen], in virtue of which the individual can contract with himself and owe obedience to himself, there is a double series of obligations which the social contract creates for the individual (204). But while the individual thus incurs obligations, it is inconceivable that the sovereign community should be bound, either by the social contract itself, or by any other sort of law (205). It can undertake obligations, in the same way as an individual, in reference to third parties (206): it can never oblige itself, as a Whole, to any of its own members (207). By its very nature,* this sovereign moral person manifests itself totally, and manifests itself exclusively, in the assembly of all (208). It manifests itself totally in that assembly, in the sense of being so identical with it that each new assembly cancels the whole of the previous political and legal situation; and each new assembly, therefore, unless it prefers an alteration of that situation, or a modification of it, has to give it the validity which it would otherwise lack by an act of express or tacit confirmation (209). [As it manifests itself totally in the assembly, so also the Sovereign manifests itself exclusively in that body.] In it, and in it alone, can the Sovereign show itself a being which acts and wills (210). Any form of 'Representation' of the sovereign Collective being is incompatible with the very conception of that being (211). The moral person is so entirely bound up with a visible aggregation of individuals, that no idea of any 'Organ', through which the invisible but living unity of a social body attains an active expression, can ever possibly emerge (212).

But in spite of his theory of the primary assembly, Rousseau is forced to provide some sort of permanent organisation for the community, and to fill in some way the void which he has created by abolishing the Representative unity involved in the existence of a Ruler. He therefore devises an ingenious system by which the sovereign moral person creates, in the shape of an administrative body (*gouvernement*), a second moral person—subservient to itself, but yet possessing a life of its own; acting with a delegated and dependent authority, but acting none the less (213). But this secondary moral person turns out, once more, to be only a Collective unity, composed of individuals, and never transcending the individuals who compose it (214).

The theory of Rousseau exercised a great influence on the natural-law theory of Group-personality (215); but even in France,

* By its very nature—as being one with *all* its members, from whom it can never separate itself, even for the purpose of obliging itself.

where it passed into the programme of the Revolution, it was considerably modified, mainly in the direction of bringing it more within the bounds of political possibility. It was Sieyès who, more than any other writer, gave to Rousseau's theory the popular form in which it long continued to inspire the political doctrines of Radicalism. Like Rousseau, he identified the moral personality of the social body with the sum of its individual members, regarded as a single aggregate (216); like him, he identified the common will with the will of all (217); like him, again, he identified the will of all with the will of the majority, in virtue of an agreement of all supposed to have been made for that purpose (218). But Sieyès restored the idea of Representation which Rousseau had rejected; and he therefore regarded a Collective unity as not only operative in a primary assembly of all its members, but also willing and acting through its appointed representatives (219). He was thus able to eliminate from the State the idea of a separate moral personality of the Government, which had been introduced by Rousseau—substituting, in its place, a scheme by which a variety of different bodies represented the sovereign community (220).

Fichte and Kant

In Germany, the writers who clung to the theory of the Sovereignty of the Ruler adopted only isolated elements of Rousseau's doctrine (221). Fichte, however, as a professed adherent of Rousseau's theory of Popular Sovereignty, attached himself also to Rousseau in his speculations on the nature of Groups; but as he was pledged to an even still more drastic form of individualism, he employed an even more artificial method of arriving at a real social Whole—only to remain, in the end, even further removed from any idea of a real and living Group-being. In Fichte's view, a civil society is simply an aggregate of so many associated individuals. But it is only with a part of their personality—not with their whole being or their entire selves—that individuals combine to form this 'protecting body' or insurance society. So far as they are included in it, they now constitute, in their association with one another, the sovereign 'Subject'. Each person is thus, from one point of view, a 'partner in sovereignty'; but each still remains, from another, a 'free individual' (222). Nevertheless, Fichte proceeds to argue that the State is a single 'body' and a 'real united Whole'. With the conclusion of the contract of union, all in their particularity are henceforth confronted by all in their association; and all in their association are a real, and not an imaginary Whole—they are a true universal (*Allheit*) in the sense of a *totum* 'which is one by the very fact of the case', and not a sum total of units (*Alle*) in the sense of a mere *compositum*. This Whole is the other party to the contract; and it receives its consummation from the fact that each individual makes a contract with it, pledges himself to protect it, becomes a part of it, and identifies himself with it. 'In this way,' Fichte writes, 'by means of contracts of individuals with individuals, the Whole comes into existence, and it is then consummated by the fact that all individuals [as such] proceed to contract with all individuals as a whole'. But how is this transformation of multiplicity into unity really achieved? Simply by a process of abstraction. The act of union, Fichte argues, is not directed to the protection of this or that determinate individual; since each person may, or again may not, be the first to be attacked, it is directed to the protection of all indeterminately. Now 'this indeterminacy, this uncertainty which individual will be the first to suffer attack, this consequent wavering of the imagination, is the bond of union, and the reason why *all* coalesce into *one*' (223).

A Whole thus constituted cannot possibly be a living being. Fichte may compare it, as he repeatedly does, with the organic structure of a natural product; but all he gains from the comparison is the idea of a reciprocal relation of parts, and not that of a living unity of the Whole. He thinks it most appropriate to compare the State to a tree, in which each single part has consciousness and will. Every part of a tree, however much it may want its own self-preservation, is compelled to will the survival of the tree, because its own survival is only possible on that condition. Strictly speaking, the tree itself is 'nothing to the part but a mere idea, and an idea cannot be injured. But the part really wishes that none of the parts, whichsoever it be, should be injured, because, if any be injured, it must suffer itself simultaneously. It is otherwise with a heap of sand, where it may well be a matter of indifference to one part, that another should be parted from it, or trodden underfoot, or scattered'. Throughout the course of his subsequent exposition of the organic nature of the social Whole, Fichte never departs from this general view. The parts of such a Whole, like those of a tree, are only what they are in virtue of the connection of the Whole, and the life of each part is therefore conditioned and determined by the life of every other part; but this life of the parts is all that constitutes the life of the Whole, and the only unity that

§ 16. *General theory of the Group in Natural Law*

exists is the common factor of reciprocal interdependence present in every part(224).

If the 'organic Whole' is thus left as an abstract conception, it can have no effective personality of its own. Fichte, it is true, sometimes places 'mystical', 'moral' or 'juridical' persons by the side of 'physical' persons; but all that he means by these terms is relations of connection between individuals(225). To the State, as a whole, he never applies the category of 'person' at all. Even in the sphere of external relations, he does not employ the idea of State-personality: he derives public international law, no less than private, from the legal relations which arise as the result of contracts between individual citizens of different States. 'A relation between States is always based on a legal relation between their citizens. The State *per se* is an abstract conception: only the citizens, as such, are real persons'(226). In its internal life, the body politic is ruled, in Fichte's view, by 'common will', which he derives, in the same way as Rousseau, from the united wills of all, by the process of making each will shed its particularity, and adopt as its only object the rule of right which is common to all(227). In one respect, he goes even beyond Rousseau: he rejects the majority-principle, opposing to it, with an eager advocacy, the principle of unanimity, and only making the limited concession that an overwhelming majority may be allowed, in special cases, to enjoy the right of declaring dissentients to be non-members(228). He follows Rousseau generally in thinking that the true realisation of the general will is only possible in a primary assembly of all the citizens(229); he departs from him in admitting that, within certain limits, the representation of the general will by duly appointed deputies may not only be possible, but even necessary(230). But he never abandons the principle that the community must always hold the position of a sovereign principal, which can always override the 'presumptive common will' of its agents by a declaration of its own actual common will(231). He is so far removed from any idea of a corporate 'Organ' that he even insists on excluding all persons who hold political office—whether popular representatives or administrative officials—from membership of the community; and he treats such persons as mandatory agents of the remainder which is left when they have been subtracted from the body of the whole(232). In his later writings Fichte considerably changed his original theory, and advanced towards a really organic view of society(233). But he never broke away altogether from his previous system of ideas; and the 'higher view of the State', which he preached in his later days, never reached the stage of a definite expression in terms of juristic ideas (234).

This mixed view of the nature of the Group, half individualistic and half collective, was one which even Kant was unable to transcend. Limiting the conception of personality entirely to the individual, in his capacity of a free rational being (235), Kant leaves no room for any real Group-personality. Occasionally, it is true, he applies the term 'moral person' to denote a complex of individuals. While he is singularly silent, in treating of corporations and charitable and other foundations, about the question of their personality (236), he regards the relations of States under international law as a relation of 'moral persons' (237); and in the sphere of internal public law he treats a number of bodies as separate 'moral persons'—e.g. the bodies which exercise the three different 'powers'; public boards; the People itself (238). But what he means by this term, which he never explains in any detail, is obviously nothing more than a sum of individuals regarded as a single aggregate. In particular, his conception of the People is only a Collective or 'Bracket' conception (*Sammelbegriff*), which may be used to signify either the aggregate of the State's subjects, or the aggregate of its active citizens, and may therefore be either contrasted or identified with the idea of the State, according as it is used in one or the other sense (239). He may proclaim that in the ideally rational form of State, which is the only legitimate definitive form, sovereignty belongs to the People: the fact remains that the sovereign People is nothing more than a mere sum total of associated individuals, just as it had also been for previous thinkers (240). In his view, as in theirs, the general will which is the true Ruler is produced by a union of all individual wills, and appears in the form of an agreement between them all (241); and thus the political methods of majority-decision and representation, which are indispensable in all large States, can only be justified on the ground of their having been adopted 'with *universal* assent, and therefore by means of a contract' (242).

But here again, as we have seen before, Kant finds a way of depriving his theoretical individualism of any practical importance. By pressing his distinction between *homo phaenomenon* and *homo noumenon*, and by making the individual co-operate in the creation of the general will 'only in his pure humanity' as *homo noumenon*— i.e. only in so far as 'pure reason, which lays down the rule of

§ 16. *General theory of the Group in Natural Law*

right', displays itself in him (243)—Kant really eliminates personality from his scheme. He depersonalises the Individual, in his capacity of joint sovereign, into an abstract rational being; he depersonalises the Group-will into an objective content of will issuing from abstract reason (244). He loses any conception of a living 'Subject' of the common sphere [of social authority]; he substitutes in its place the idea of an impersonal will of law—a will remote from actual concrete wills; a will of which individuals are instruments; a will in whose service these instruments have to work, under a system of strict dependence, at a task which is common to them all.

General Retrospect

Looking back at the development of the natural-law views of the being and essence of groups, we can see that stone upon stone has crumbled away from the theory of Corporations which had been built up by the Roman lawyers and the canonists. The collapse of that theory becomes complete when Natural Law expressly rejects, and ends by banishing altogether, the conception of the *ficta persona*. In the general theory of society which takes the place of the old theory of Corporations, the School of Natural Law uses the conception of the 'moral person', for which it claims a higher degree of reality, to fill the gap created by the disappearance of the fictitious person; and it attempts, but owing to its fundamental individualism it attempts in vain, to give a real existence to this moral person. In its treatment of the formal structure of the social connections between individuals, the School of Natural Law adopted the contractual scheme of *Societas* and *Mandatum*, and it broadened and deepened this scheme, in many directions, with the aid of conceptions derived from Teutonic ideas of Fellowship and Kingship (*Herrschaft*). But imprisoned within the limits of that contractual scheme, it was never able to attain the idea of the inherent and independent existence of a social Whole. It could only achieve its doctrine of the moral personality of groups by combining, in one way or another, two different conceptions—the conception of Collective and that of Representative unity; and on either conception the Whole is no more than the associated individuals of which it is composed. The existence of the 'moral person' is thus only a fact because it coincides, and to the extent that it coincides, with the existence of individuals; and the unity of will and power in a Group-person is only a reality because, and only a reality in so far as, individuals are actually willing and acting as one, either on the Collective basis of unanimous agreement, or the alternative basis of Representation by a single person or body.

On such a view, the 'fictitious person' has indeed disappeared; but with it there has also disappeared any 'person' of any sort which is in any way separate from individuals. The Being of each Group is reduced to the mutual legal relations of its members; and the 'moral personality' is only a formal conception which serves to indicate, as a shorthand expression, certain legal results involved in these relations of connection. In such a circle of ideas, a Group-being with a single life of its own is something inconceivable; and a purely mechanical view of society is the inevitable result. Occasionally, even in the strictest individualistic systems of Natural Law, the traditional organic metaphors and similes continue to be adduced (245): they are even used to some extent (as we have already seen in dealing with Locke, Rousseau and Fichte) as technical terms of art for the purpose of expressing the nature of group-unity (246). But Hobbes, in referring to the 'artificial life' of automata, had already built a bridge by which it was easy to pass from the conception of social organism to that of social mechanism. The precedent he had set was not neglected; and we often find that even when society is formally ranked as a moral body by the side of natural bodies, it is really regarded as merely an artificial imitation of the living organism (247). For Locke and Fichte, and even for Rousseau, the social body is in the last analysis only a mechanically constituted Whole, with a life which only resides in the life of its parts (248). It is hardly surprising, therefore, that as the doctrine of Natural Law developed, modes of expression derived from an organic point of view often disappear entirely, or sink into an empty form of words (249); and the analogy of an artificially constructed machine more and more takes the place of the natural body in the interpretation of the social Whole (250).

It was impossible for the idea of an organic Group-being to disappear entirely, so long as the individualism of the School of Natural Law was still confronted by any really vital philosophy which made the Whole its basis and starting-point. But that idea was seldom, if ever, developed clearly to its ultimate results, and still less was it ever expressed in any juristic form. Least of all was any attempt ever made to conceive in terms of personality the living unity immanent in an organic Group-being. Even the thinkers who were most opposed to a purely individualistic interpretation of society evaded entirely the question of Group-personality(251). There were others who only attained the conception of a moral person to fall back instantly on the idea of a merely Representative or merely Collective unity(252). Even Leibniz, unable to rise to the conception of the personal existence of the group, was content to crown his nobly planned edifice with a shadowy *persona ficta*(253). Nor is there, in any of the social theories of the eighteenth century which prepared the way for an organic view of historical development, anything more to be found than the merest germ—the dormant and undeveloped germ—of a legal interpretation of the living Group-personality(254).

CHAPTER II: SECTION I, §17

THE NATURAL-LAW THEORY OF THE STATE

I. GENERAL VIEW

The general natural-law theory of Society culminated in a 'natural' theory of the State. Within that theory, the subject of natural public law, under the name of '*jus publicum universale*', gradually vindicated an independent position as a branch of study distinct from 'Politics'*(1).

So long as the State was simply treated as *societas perfectissima*, and so long as its theory was simply regarded as an illustration (if the best and completest illustration) of the general conception of *societas* already described in the previous subsection, the ideas which found most vigorous expression in natural-law theories of the State were merely the general ideas about the nature of Groups with which we are already familiar; and these general ideas were freely applied, whether their ingredients were consistent with one another or contradictory. But a new situation arose, and thinkers were confronted by fresh intellectual problems, as soon as they turned to face the conception of Sovereignty (which still continued to be the essential core of the theory of the State), and attempted to bring it into harmony with their conception of *societas*.

* Natural public law is what we might call 'general first principles of constitutional law'. Politics (*Politik*), as distinct from it, means the practical study of political methods and institutions.

These problems arose from the fundamental difficulty of uniting a traditional conception of sovereignty—which at the bottom nobody wished to disturb, or indeed, in view of the political trend of the age, could think of disturbing—with the general idea of the Law-State (*Rechtsstaat*) which was inherent in the essence of Natural Law. If, on the one hand, the logical evolution of the conception of sovereignty were permitted to run its course freely, it inevitably followed, however much the dictates of God or of Reason might still be exalted above the authority of the State, that the internal system of political relations was deprived of any of the attributes of a genuine system of law. On the other hand, if Natural Law were not to annihilate itself utterly in the way indicated by Hobbes, it was bound to retain the Teutonic conception of the State as a system of legal relations. It was the latter of these tendencies that actually showed itself strongest; and the whole of the natural-law theory of society shows an increasingly conscious and vigorous effort to interpret the State, like every other *societas*, as a system of reciprocal legal rights and duties. But the conflict between the idea of sovereignty and that of the Law-State involved a number of compromises or concessions, which could only be made at the expense of strict logic. First and foremost, owing to the growth of an idea which we have already had reason to mention—the idea that there was a part of the original sovereignty of the individual which had not been surrendered in the contract of civil society, so that a sovereign Individual still remained to confront the sovereign State—it became possible to maintain that the individual citizen had his own inherent rights, which stood over against the authority of the State. In the second place, and on the same basis of argument, it could also be maintained (as we shall have to show later on) that in the area of their mutual relations all groups had their own inherent rights, which were not abolished by the fact of inclusion in a higher sovereign group. Finally (and here we touch the only point specifically relevant to our present theme, which is that of the internal structure of the State in itself), it came to be held, in defiance of the logical demands of the conception of sovereignty, that political authority was by its nature divided, in one way or another, into a number of independent spheres of right belonging to a number of different 'Subjects'.*

* The first point raised in the latter part of this paragraph touches the relation between the State and the Individual, and the limitation of State-sovereignty by individual rights. The second turns on the relation between the

§ 17. *The Natural-Law theory of the State*

Prima facie, the adherents of the School of Natural Law may seem to have found the clue to the solution of this fundamental antinomy [between the idea of sovereignty and that of the Law-State] in the conception of State-personality which they finally succeeded in attaining. This would have really been the case if only they had conceived the State [not merely as a 'moral person', but] as a living Group-person. On that basis, it would have been an easy step to explain the apparent antinomy between the idea of a united and indivisible sovereign power and the idea of a constitutional division of powers by drawing a contrast between the unity of the State-personality and the plurality of its organs. But the idea of a true Group-being could never be elicited from the natural-law conception of Group-personality, as that conception had actually developed on the basis of individualism. The natural-law *persona civitatis* might be depicted as 'Representative' or 'Collective': in neither case could it ever transcend the category of Individuals; in neither case could it ever possess an inner being which could be formulated in juristic terms. Under these conditions each new attempt to give a more definite expression to the personality of the State as a Whole only meant a new obstacle to the development of the theory of the constitutional State. It is not a mere accident that we should find the advocates of the theory of absolute sovereignty laying the greatest emphasis on the idea of State-personality, or that a tendency to the doctrine of constitutionalism should always go hand in hand with a tendency to eliminate that idea.

In the light of these considerations, it is easy to see that the controversy about the 'Subject' of sovereignty, which still continued to agitate men's minds, could hardly be settled by simply admitting the principle (first propounded by Hobbes, and never forgotten afterwards) that the State-personality, in itself, was the real 'Subject' of sovereignty.

State and the Group, and the limitation of State-sovereignty by Group-rights. The third concerns the limitation of the State in its own internal character, apart from any question of its relations to Individuals or Groups. Since the general theme of the present passage is that of the accommodation of the idea of sovereignty to the idea of the Law-State, Gierke remarks that the third point is the only one which is specifically relevant to this general theme. In other words, the system of division of powers attempts to make sovereignty a legal structure in its own inner nature, and thus seeks to effect a real reconciliation of sovereignty and Law; while to let the Individual, or the Group, 'contract out' of sovereignty, in the sphere of inherent rights, is still to leave sovereignty, in the rest of its range, unlimited by Law.

We may admit that the formal conception of State-sovereignty which was attained by the use of this principle was not altogether without value. But we must also recognise that this conception was not suited, in its actual implications, to lift thinkers above the alternatives of the sovereignty of the Ruler and popular sovereignty. Its effect was rather the opposite. Failing to provide any firm foundation for the views of theorists who sought to mediate between these alternatives, the conception of State-sovereignty as inherent in the personality of the State was mainly used as a cloak for doctrines of the unlimited sovereignty either of Ruler or of People. Being a purely *formal* conception, it was entirely devoid of any substantive internal content; and it could not, therefore, be developed into a concrete and actual conception of sovereignty, as resident in a whole Group-being which manifested itself in every one of its parts. This will explain why the advances that had already been made in this direction [i.e. in the direction of the idea of the sovereignty of the whole Group-being] now found themselves doomed to suppression. The theory of a 'double majesty', which had once held sway [and which had made both King and People sovereign, thus vesting sovereignty in the *whole* body politic], was no longer defended by any thinker. If it was mentioned at all, it was only by the advocates of the sovereignty of the Ruler, and only for the purpose of rejecting it as a deplorable error (2). The theory of the *subjectum commune* of 'majesty' [which made the whole body politic the general or 'common' Sovereign, acting through the Sovereign 'proper' as its organ] only survived in a few scattered writers; and it failed to yield them the results for which they hoped even when they sought to combine it with the conception of the moral personality of the State (3). The few who adopted this theory transformed it so utterly, in order to save the reputation of its author [Grotius], that it lost any particular meaning (4); but the majority of writers simply rejected it altogether, as running dangerously near to the theory of popular sovereignty (5). The two opposing theories of the absolute sovereignty of the Ruler and the absolute sovereignty of the People were thus left alone in the field; and thinkers who sought to advocate the cause of constitutionalism found themselves faced by the difficult task of attempting, with the aid of no better tool than one or other of these theories, to wrest some soil from the hard ground of sovereignty, in which a theory of constitutional rights might be made to grow.

§ 17. *The Natural-Law theory of the State*

II. THE THEORY OF THE SOVEREIGNTY OF THE RULER

At first, as we should naturally expect from the general historical development on which the events of the Thirty Years War had set their seal, the victory lay with the theory of the sovereignty of the Ruler. The advocates of that theory were agreed that the State, as the 'Subject' of supreme authority, was to be identified with the Representative personality of the Ruler. Except for Horn, whose attempt to treat the monarch as the only possible 'Subject' of real political authority was universally rejected (6), they all maintained that the Ruler might be either a single or a collective person, according to the form of the State; but they did not believe that any difference in the scope and the content of his sovereignty was created by this distinction (7). On the other hand, they refused to allow that the People, as such, had any share in sovereignty, after the State had once been formed (8); and even in regard to democracies they drew a sharp distinction between the sovereignty of the community, in its capacity of constituted Ruler, and the original sovereignty of the People, which was supposed, in all forms of State alike, to have come to an end with the transformation of civil society into a State (9).

The question, however, remained, whether there did not still continue to exist a Collective personality of the People which [if it was not the 'Subject' of sovereignty] was, or at any rate might be, a 'Subject' of popular rights as against the Sovereign.

On the absolutist side, which followed the line of Hobbes, and pushed the conception of a single and unique State-personality to its logical conclusions, the question was answered in the negative. It was held that the People only became a person in the Ruler: apart from him, it was but a disunited multitude. As a governed community, the People was therefore destitute of any capacity for rights; and conversely, the instant it was recognised as a 'Subject' of rights, it also acquired, by that very fact, the position of Ruler. A difference of opinion arose, however, when it came to the drawing of conclusions from these premises in regard to the possibility of a constitutional State. The stricter school of absolutists held the view that a system of constitutional law legally binding upon the sovereign was a thing which was utterly inconceivable. The extremist theories of Hobbes were, indeed, rejected: a sphere was reserved to the individual, beyond the reach of the State: the authority of the State was held to be subject to a fixed standard of action, whether derived from Divine command or from the command of Reason; but any limitation imposed by positive law was held to be incompatible with the essence of sovereignty. This was the reason why the conception of a constitutionally limited Monarchy was regarded [by the absolutists] as particularly objectionable. There might be differences of opinion among them in regard to the propriety and the real character of other historical developments of a constitutionalist type; but there was a general agreement that a Monarchy which was constitutionally limited was not a Monarchy at all. This was the line taken by Spinoza(10); by the advocates of absolute monarchy in England(11) and France(12); and by many of the political thinkers of Germany(13). On the whole, however, this drastic theory of the sovereignty of the Ruler was prevented from finding a footing in Germany by its incompatibility with the legal situation which actually existed in that country; and a more moderate opinion prevailed which, while it kept to the general principles of the absolutist doctrine, admitted, in one way or another, the existence of constitutional limitations on sovereignty. Horn himself, vigorously as he rejected any diminution of regal majesty by popular rights, admitted that there were differences in the *modus habendi majestatem*. Even in the case of absolute monarchy he assumes a difference of degrees, according as there is a *dominatus* with an *exercitium absolutissimum* of 'majesty', or a *regnum absolutum* with a less drastic exercise of ruling power, or a dictatorship limited in point of time; and by the side of these absolute forms he also recognises a limited monarchy, in which the monarch is under a contractual obligation, in exercising his 'majesty', to observe certain conditions, or even (it may be) to take the advice of certain persons. He does not, however, regard the fulfilment of such obligation as a matter which admits of any form of legal sanction(14).

But the writer who took the greatest pains to prove that supreme authority was not necessarily unlimited was Pufendorf(15). [There are, indeed, some elements in his theory which run in an opposite direction.] He regards the personality of the People as absorbed entirely by its representation in the person of a single Ruler or body of Rulers. In other words, he makes the *persona moralis composita* of the State manifest itself so fully, and so exclusively, in the Sovereign, that everything which the Sovereign, as such, may will or do must be counted as the will and action of the State; while anything that one man, or many, or all, may will or do apart

§ 17. The Natural-Law theory of the State

from the Sovereign, must be counted as a private will or a private activity—or rather, not an 'activity' [since the word implies some unity], but a multiplicity of activities (16). He is thus led to follow Hobbes in denying that the governed community can possibly have any rights against its governor; though, unlike Hobbes, he makes individual subjects enjoy rights against the government, which are real, if imperfectly guaranteed, rights (17). But Pufendorf [also leaves room for the principle of constitutional limitation. He] incorporates in his theory (primarily with reference to monarchy) the idea of differences in the *modus habendi* of 'majesty'. Over against the patrimonial 'mode' or form, under which political authority is *in patrimonio imperantis*, he sets what he regards as the normal form, under which the Ruler for the time being enjoys only a right of usufruct in political authority, so that he cannot by himself dispose of the substance of political rights either *inter vivos* or by will (18). Moreover, he recognises that, side by side with the *imperium absolutum*, which is only limited by the rules of Natural Law, it is possible to conceive an *imperium limitatum*, where the king is limited by a constitution in exercising his sovereignty, and where he needs the assent of the people, or of an assembly of representatives, for some of his acts of government. In spite of these limitations, he argues, the supreme power still remains with the monarch, undivided and unmutilated; nor is any disintegration of the unity of the State's will involved in them, since it still continues to be true that '*omnia, quae vult civitas, vult per voluntatem Regis, etsi limitatione tali fit, ut, non existente certa conditione, Rex quaedam non possit velle aut frustra velit*'. The assent of the People, or the Estates, is therefore not the *radix*, but only the *conditio sine qua non*, of the exercise of political authority; and such right of assent confers no share in that authority upon either People or Estates. Even a *clausula commissoria*, which has the effect of making the monarch forfeit his authority if he transgresses its limits, fails to alter the situation: only a *conditio potestativa* is contained in such a clause, and the cognisance of the question, whether that condition has come into play, will be a matter of *nuda contestatio*, and not of judicial decision.* On the other hand, if the unity of the State is not to be

---

* In England, we might say that the Bill of Rights is a *clausula commissoria* for succeeding monarchs: if any of them violates its terms he forfeits the throne. But the Bill only recites the condition on which this *may* happen (*conditio potestativa*); and the question whether the condition on which this may happen has actually and really appeared is not a question for a court (none is provided in

disintegrated and the essence of monarchy destroyed, the monarch should never be obliged to allow the positive substance or object of his volition to be imposed upon him by a foreign will. He must accordingly preserve full liberty to summon or dissolve the assembly of the People or the Estates, to lay proposals before it, and to accept or reject its decisions; and he may also, in the interest of the public welfare, amend the fundamental contracts on which the State is based, if they are leading to its dissolution (19).

Pufendorf's theory attained an extraordinary vogue. It continued, in its main lines, to determine the character of the natural-law theory of the State till the middle of the eighteenth century, and even later. It was adopted, almost unchanged, by Thomasius (20), Titius (21), Gundling (22), and others of his disciples (23). It also received the allegiance of both the Cocceji (24), Stryck (25), Ickstatt (26), Kreittmayr (27), Heincke (28), and other advocates of the absolute authority of the territorial prince (29). It was pushed in the direction of absolutism, and given a more rigorous form, by J. H. Boehmer (30). Conversely, there were other writers who modified it in the opposite direction, and sought to give a wider scope to the doctrine of constitutional limits (31). In particular, a number of writers disagreed with Pufendorf's admission of the patrimonial form of State, regarding it as logically inconsistent with his other ideas, and holding that it could never be possible for a Ruler to dispose of the substance of the State without the assent of the People (32). On the whole, however, we may say that the general fate which befell Pufendorf's views was that his theory of sovereignty was accepted, so far as its practical results were concerned, but its ingenious basis [which reconciled popular consent with sovereignty by making it the *conditio sine qua non* of the exercise of sovereignty] was sacrificed, and the old antithesis between the rights of the Ruler and the rights of the People was re-introduced.

This antithesis, and with it the conception of a Collective personality of the People as still continuing to confront the Ruler, was steadily maintained by the thinkers who, while professing the general theory of the sovereignty of the Ruler, were mainly influenced by constitutionalist tendencies. Critics might censure, and censure with good reason, the disintegration of the unitary personality of the State which was involved in such a position: the

the Bill), but for mere assertion (*nuda contestatio*) by Parliament or People. Blackstone says much the same in his *Commentaries*, I, pp. 211–14. But Pufendorf was writing, of course, before the Bill of Rights.

§ 17. *The Natural-Law theory of the State*

fact remained that, so long as Natural Law was the basis of thought, it was only possible to safeguard the conception of popular rights, while rejecting the theory of popular sovereignty, at the price of admitting a dual existence of two personalities—the personality of the Ruler and that of the People. Even the strict absolutists themselves had to recognise, if once they admitted the theory of contract, that the People must possess, at the very least, some dormant or latent form of personality; for as soon as they argued in terms of contract, they were not only bound to make the original sovereignty of the community the premise of their argument—they were also bound to acknowledge that sovereignty might possibly revert to the community in which it began (33). A complete break with the whole theory of contract was necessary before the idea of the personality of the People could be entirely eradicated (34). But if it was possible for the People to exist for a single instant *in the absence* of a Ruler, there was no logical objection to the idea that it should also continue to exist, as a personality, *side by side* with the Ruler. [Not only was there no logical objection against the idea; there was also a logical argument in its favour.] It was obviously far more consonant with the idea of contract to hold the view that, after the conclusion of the contract of subjection, the community still confronted the sovereign as a party to that contract, than to profess the theory that the community itself expired in the act of concluding the contract, and that the contract produced rights and duties for individuals only. These considerations will explain why the old conception of political relations, as relations of contract between Ruler and People, always continued to persist. The *persona civitatis* was held to be merged in the *Imperans*, but the governed community was none the less regarded as a separate collective person, for which certain rights were in every case reserved, from the very first, by the terms assumed to be contained in the original contract, and to which more extensive rights might be granted [in particular cases] by express constitutional provisions to that effect.

It is along these lines that Huber attempts a general interpretation of the constitutional State, which deserves particular attention. He begins by postulating that in every State the Ruler, and the Ruler only, is vested with 'majesty', and that no difference in the form of the constitution, or in the method of its acquisition, or in the *modus habendi* under which it is exercised, can vary or alter this majesty (35). But he proceeds to argue that in every State the right of the Ruler is confronted by two other sorts of rights—the rights of individuals, and the rights of the popular community—which bind and limit the supreme authority, though they do not affect its essence (36). The source of popular rights is the *leges fundamentales*, which, however, are really 'contracts', and not 'laws' (37). Some of these rights exist in all States: they are the results of the self-evident terms of the original contracts (*leges fundamentales tacitae*) (38). Others may be either originally reserved, or subsequently secured, by express agreements to that effect (*leges fundamentales expressae*) (39); but rights of this latter order cannot go beyond a certain point, unless a system by which the People participates in the office of Ruler has taken the place of a system of limitation of the Ruler's rights (40). Huber accordingly assumes that there are always two 'Subjects' of political rights. On the one hand there is the personality of the State, which he identifies, in exactly the same way as the absolutists, with that of the Ruler (41): on the other, as he expressly contends, the People also *jus personae retinet*, and continues to be a *universitas* (42). In developing his theory Huber delivers a vigorous attack on every kind of absolutism, popular as well as monarchical, in every kind of State (43). But if he is consistent in that respect, he fails to reconcile the inherent self-contradiction which clearly reveals itself in his theory when it comes to be applied to democracy (44).

In much the same way we find the German political writers who attempted to find an independent basis for the rights of the local Estates of the German territorial principalities (*Landstände*) still holding to the idea of a contractual relation between the prince, as representing the 'State', and the 'People', as represented by the Estates (45). The conception of sovereignty was severely limited by many of these writers (46); and Leibniz, too, though he failed to transcend the traditional doctrine in his view of State-personality [as resident only in the Ruler] (47), attempted to broaden the whole basis of argument for constitutional limitations on the Ruling authority. He delivered a vigorous attack on the academic conception of sovereignty; and arguing that all human relations are necessarily conditioned [and therefore cannot be 'absolute'], he rejected any idea of absolute sovereignty in favour of a conception which made it no more than relative (48).* For the time being, Pufendorf's doctrine triumphed over that of Leibniz; but there

* In other words he held that there is no absolute sovereignty, free from and unrelated to conditions of time and place; there is only a relative sovereignty, which exists under and subject to such conditions.

were many of Pufendorf's disciples who had already begun to revolt against the complete absorption of the People in the Ruler (49). Hert, Schmier, Heineccius and other writers, while following Pufendorf in other respects, recur to the idea that the State must include a collective personality of the People as well as the sovereign personality of the Ruler (50). Occasionally, too, we find writers [who start by assuming that the Ruler is the only 'Subject' of rights] slipping imperceptibly over into the idea of rights of the People [which implies that the People is also a 'Subject' of rights]; nor indeed was it easy, when it came to the point, to maintain intact an artificial interpretation of the State which limited the Ruler by the Group-will, and yet, at the same time, left no 'Subject' of will other than the Ruler.*

By the middle of the eighteenth century we can trace a general change in the theory of Natural Law, which makes it more favourable to the principle of popular rights. It is a change which naturally accompanies the disintegration of the conception of State-personality, and the consequent weakening of the conception of sovereignty, which we have already described. In the writings of Wolff [1740–50] the sovereignty of the Ruler almost ceases to appear as a definite antithesis to the sovereignty of the People. He holds that the People is free to choose whether it will retain in its hands the right of controlling its members, which the contract of society creates for the community that it constitutes, or whether it will devolve that right in one way or another—either on one person, or on several; either wholly, or in part; either unconditionally, or on such conditions as it chooses to impose; either revocably, or irrevocably; either for a time, or for life, or with rights of succession; either in substance, or merely *in exercitio* (51). If the People decides upon devolution, the rights of any governing person or body must be entirely determined by its will, as declared, tacitly or explicitly, at the time of such devolution (52); and Wolff is thus able to assume, as an obvious truth, that constitutional limitations may be imposed on a political authority, and that a constitution may be

* The gist of this paragraph is that democratic ideas survived, or were enunciated afresh, in the German theory of the first half of the eighteenth century. This is illustrated by (1) advocacy of the rights of Estates; (2) Leibniz's theory of sovereignty as relative; (3) the tendency of some of the followers of Pufendorf to admit the idea that the People is a personality side by side with the Ruler; and (4) the tendency of some writers to proclaim the idea of rights of the People, and therefore, if only by implication, to make the People a legal 'Subject' of constitutional rights side by side with the Ruler.

interpreted as a relation of contract between Ruler and People(53). Nettelbladt, following a similar line of thought, derives the whole of the system of internal public law from a contract made between the initially sovereign community and one or more 'Subjects' vested with ruling sovereignty or parts of it(54); and he admits that reservations or conditions may be freely imposed when the contract is being made(55). Only in the sphere of external affairs will he allow that the moral personality of the State is absorbed and contained in that of the Ruler(56): in the field of internal affairs he holds that the People has always and everywhere its own separate moral personality(57); and he even supposes a third moral personality, beside those of Ruler and People, wherever a popular assembly is to be found(58). Hoffbauer expounds an exactly similar view(59), except that he limits the hypothesis that an assembly of Estates may have a personality of its own, distinct from that of the People, to cases in which the members of such an assembly are not bound by *mandats impératifs*(60). Even the writers who laid more emphasis on the sovereignty of the Ruler and the need of its being inviolable were now willing to accept, without any demur, the idea of the Constitutional State, in which Ruler and People stood to one another in the relation of parties to a contract. We find a theory of this sort, with all the consequences which it entails, in the writings of Daries(61), Achenwall(62), Scheidemantel(63), and A. L. von Schlözer(64), who are even ready to face the revolutionary consequences which must ensue in the event of a breach of the political contract(65).

In the course of this conflict between absolutist and constitutionalist tendencies, the controversy in regard to the real nature of the relation between Ruler and People came to be connected more and more closely with another controversy, which turned on the various forms that the 'Subject' of ruling authority itself might take. This latter controversy was concentrated on the one question, whether a mixed form of State was at all conceivable, and whether, if that were the case, such a form was objectionable, or admissible, or even ideal. But before we address ourselves to this question, we must pause to consider the attitude to the problem of State-personality which was adopted by the advocates of the renascent doctrine of Popular Sovereignty.

§ 17. *The Natural-Law theory of the State*

III. THE THEORY OF POPULAR SOVEREIGNTY

For a century past [i.e. from 1641 onwards] the doctrine of the sovereignty of the People had remained a living force in England alone. But while the English advocates of that doctrine were eager in insisting that the People possessed the final authority in the State, and possessed it as an inalienable property which might be recovered at any moment, notwithstanding any positive law to the contrary, they never went to the length of breaking entirely with the idea of a contractual relation between People and Ruler; and they did not hesitate, therefore, to dissolve the single personality of the State (so far as such an idea was ever present to their minds) into a plurality of 'Subjects' of rights.* Sidney, for example, is concerned to prove the identity of the sovereign personality of the People with the Parliament which is its plenary representative (66); but he interprets the relation of People and Government, none the less, as a relation of contract (67)—though he also maintains that the presence of a contract can never deprive the People of its superior position, or take away its sovereign right of final decision in the event of a difference of opinion (68). Locke equally seeks to retain the idea of the contractual character of the constitution (69); and so far as he transcends it at all, it is only in his contention that the People possesses, in virtue of its inalienable sovereignty, a power of adjudicating finally upon the conduct of the other party to the contract, which makes the existence of all constitutional law depend, in the last resort, on the judgment of the community (70).

Rousseau was the first thinker to abolish every vestige of the idea of a contractual relation between People and Ruler. He began by assuming that a single contract of society (*pacte d'association*) contained the whole of the creative force which made the State (71); he then proceeded to argue that the social authority thus brought into being possessed perfect sovereignty after the pattern of the strictest absolutism—a sovereignty incapable of any alienation, any division, any representation, any limitation (72); and he concluded accordingly that it was impossible for the sovereign com-

---

* Gierke's contention is that English thinkers assume a single *persona civitatis* —the People (either *per se*, or as expressed in Parliament)—but then go on to assume a contract; and since a contract involves two *personae* at least to make it, they necessarily must end by assuming a plurality (or at any rate a duality) of *personae civitatis*, or, in other words, a plurality or duality of 'Subjects' of political rights.

munity, even if it wished, to vest any public authority in any other 'Subject' by way of contract, or to bind itself by contract to observe any limits upon itself (73). The erection of a government is merely a unilateral act of the sovereign: it is a free commission which can be freely revoked at discretion (74). The collective sovereign, when it makes its appearance as a civic assembly, is therefore above all law. The whole of the existing scheme of law collapses before it whenever it meets; it can make a new constitution to take the place of the old; and if it prefers to make no change, it must deliberately decide to confirm the old constitution in order to give it a new title to existence (75). As with the constitution, so with the government: any right to their position which its members may have acquired disappears in the presence of the sovereign, which at its discretion can either renew, or bestow elsewhere, such power of agency as it may have given (76). This is, in effect, the declaration of a permanent right of revolution, and a complete annihilation of the idea of the constitutional State. Rousseau believes that he has purchased the perfect unity of the State's personality by paying this extravagant price (77). But since his idea of the personality of the State is simply a mechanical interpretation of the personality of the People, he is forced after all (as we have already observed) to introduce a further personality of the government into the body politic; and though he tries hard to conceal what has happened by degrading this second moral person to a subordinate position, he really fails, no less than other thinkers, to escape from a dualistic conception of the 'Subject' of political rights (78).

Rousseau's system of thought continued to be the foundation on which the whole revolutionary theory of the State achieved its further development. It was inconceivable that the sovereignty of the People should be exalted to a higher point in that theory: on the contrary, it was inevitable that it should be curtailed, as soon as there was any return to the ground of actual reality. Any thinker who admitted the possibility of the representation of the People, or believed in the need of a governing authority which was in any degree stable and independent, was bound to modify Rousseau's views. He must necessarily approximate to the idea of the constitutional State; he must curtail the omnipotence of sovereignty in its actual operation, even if he represented it as free from any limitation in principle; he must recognise the 'bearers' of the constituted powers of government as 'Subjects' of political rights, concurrently with the popular community, even if he expressly

§ 17.] *The Natural-Law theory of the State* 151

identified that community with the State itself(79). The theory of Fichte affords a good illustration of this compelling necessity. He was the purest exponent in German thought of the principle of popular sovereignty; but he also sought to find room for the idea of a constitutional law which was binding upon the People itself(80). The People, he holds, must necessarily devolve upon a government, whether monarchical or republican, an 'absolute positive right', which includes the ordinary course of legislation, jurisdiction and administration(81). It reserves, however, a constituent authority, together with a power of supervising the government and pronouncing on the legality of its actions(82). But if it wishes to exercise this reserved sovereignty, the People must again become the 'Community' (*Gemeinde*), in order that it may be able, in that capacity, to distinguish its will from the will of the supreme authority which it has constituted, and to revoke its declaration that the will of that authority is its own will(83)*. Here a difficulty emerges. A private individual cannot, and the government *will* not, summon the Community into being; and yet the Community must be a Community before it can declare itself such. Fichte meets the difficulty by supposing that 'the People is declared in advance, by the constitution, to be the Community in certain contingencies'(84). In small States, this emergence of the Community is made possible by a provision for periodic assemblies: in large States, it is achieved by the creation of a special authority, which has to establish the existence of a case of illegality, and to bring about, at the same time, the meeting of the Community. In large States, therefore, the People must choose special ephors,† and arm them with 'absolute negative power' in virtue of which they are able, by issuing an interdict that brings all the government of the State to a standstill, to introduce the deciding voice of the People itself, which thus re-enters upon its sovereignty(85). The decisions then made by the Community thus brought into being are 'constitutional law'(86). If, however, in spite of all the securi-

* The Community is prior to the People; and it only becomes a People when it constitutes a State, in which we may henceforth speak of People and Government. This People, however, must reconstitute itself back into a Community, if it desires (1) to alter the act which constituted the State (i.e. the constitution), or (2) to judge the legality of the acts of the Government (i.e. to pronounce whether they are in accordance with the constitution).

† The idea of the Ephorate, borrowed from Sparta, goes back to Calvin, and appears in the *Vindiciae Contra Tyrannos* and in Althusius: see E. Barker, *Church, State and Study*, p. 84.

ties which Fichte attempts to provide against such a contingency, the executive authority and the Ephorate should combine against the People, there is still in reserve the legal method of popular revolt for the purpose of giving effect to the real common will(87).

Fichte attempts in this way to construct a constitutional State, in which the People is sovereign, but the supreme authorities are none the less owners of rights secured to them under a contract [i.e. the contract by which the People devolves an 'absolute positive right' upon the government](88). But while he makes this division between People and Government, Fichte still seeks to preserve the idea of a single 'Subject' of political rights; and he does so by dissolving the People into a mere 'aggregate of individual subjects' so long as the Government continues to act constitutionally(89), and, conversely, by making the magistrates relapse into the position of mere private persons as soon as the People again becomes a 'Community'(90). The personality of the State is thus made to appear at one given point at each given moment; but a personality which is now here and now there, and which alternates somehow between People and Government, is a personality which has lost any substantive or continuous existence of its own. We are hardly astonished to find that any idea of the personality of the Group-being vanishes utterly from Fichte's philosophy in the later phase of his thought, when he abandons the principle of the actual sovereignty of the People(91).

Meanwhile [in the course of the eighteenth century] the theory of *constitutionalism* had also adopted the doctrine of popular sovereignty as its basis. This was due to the influence of Montesquieu. When he gave to the theory of constitutionalism the form which was to prove decisive for the thought of the Continent, he incorporated in it the idea, which he had borrowed from English thinkers, that supreme authority belongs in its nature to the associated community(92). But the principle of popular sovereignty never played any serious part in the theory of constitutionalism. It only served, as a rule, to satisfy a need which was felt by different thinkers with different degrees of acuteness. It enabled them to find, at any rate in the abstract, some single basic authority underlying the 'division of powers' which seemed to disintegrate the unity of the State; it provided a sort of primary 'Subject', over and above the secondary 'Subjects' who exercised the several 'powers' in co-ordination with one another. This explains why Montesquieu himself fails to draw any practical conclusions from his recognition of the basic

§ 17. *The Natural-Law theory of the State*

rights of the community, and why, so far from doing so, he entirely omits the conception of the unity of sovereignty (just as he omits the conception of the personality of the State as a whole) from the picture which he draws of the constitutional State (93). In many writers [of the constitutionalist school] the theoretical acceptance of popular sovereignty only produces a crop of political maxims, in lieu of any real juristic interpretation (94). Justi, attempting to reconcile the theory of constitutionalism with the unity of power and will demanded by the idea of the body politic, lays more emphasis than the rest of the constitutionalists on the indefeasible 'fundamental authority of the People' (95); but he is prepared, none the less, to divide the personality of the State, and indeed to divide it twice over. Not only does he make the 'supreme executive power', when once it has been erected, stand over against the People as a separate contracting party (96); he also suggests a division of this authority itself among a number of different 'Subjects' (97). In the theory of Kant, the principle of popular sovereignty is still retained, in its full integrity, as a theoretical basis (98), but it is transformed for practical purposes into a mere 'idea of the reason' [or logical presupposition]. As such, it ought to guide the possessor of political authority (99), but it involves no diminution of the formal rights inherent in a sovereignty of the Ruler which finds its justification [not in this 'idea' of the sovereignty of the People, but] in the fact of historical growth (100). Kant sketches, indeed, an ideal constitutional State in which popular sovereignty is nominally present; but no living 'Subject' of supreme authority is anywhere really to be found in this State. The 'bearers' of the different powers [legislative, executive and judicial] are supposed to govern, but each is subject to a strict legal obligation appropriate to its own sphere (101); and over them all, as the Sovereign proper, the abstract Law of Reason is finally enthroned (102).

The history of the theory of constitutionalism shows how a doctrine derived from the principle of popular sovereignty could produce almost the same results as the other [and apparently opposite] system of thought which started from the principle of the sovereignty of the Ruler. In the one case, just as in the other, the inviolability of sovereignty, and the unity of the personality of the State, are sacrificed, in order to attain the possibility of a constitutional law which is binding even on the Sovereign. In either case, the hotly disputed issue of the possibility of a mixed form of State becomes the centre of the whole argument.

IV. THE THEORY OF THE MIXED CONSTITUTION

Whether such a mixed form of State should be recognised, side by side with the three simple forms, was a question which had been constantly in debate from the Middle Ages onwards (103).

When the point of view adopted was that of the sovereignty of the Ruler, and when the conception of such sovereignty was pressed to its logical issue, the answer was inevitably in the negative. If, on the one hand, a mixed constitution was understood to mean the division of Ruling authority among a number of 'Subjects': if, on the other, indivisibility was reckoned as one of the essential attributes of sovereignty; and if, finally, Ruling authority was held to be identical with sovereignty—then, and upon these conditions, it was impossible to admit that such a mixed form could exist. But what, in that case, was the position to be assigned to existing constitutions, the actual fruits of historical development, which did not square with the logic of an exclusive sovereignty resident in a single person or a single body of persons? Some thinkers tried to answer the question by pointing to the possibility of a simple limitation of the supreme authority (104), or by attempting, in a way which went more to the root of the matter, to reduce the conception of the mixed constitution (*forma mixta*) to that of the moderate or limited (*forma temperata*) (105). But the more exactly the *amount* of the limitations compatible with sovereignty was defined, the more was such an expedient bound to prove itself ineffective. If, on the other hand, limited sovereignty was regarded as an impossible contradiction in terms, the opposite course had to be followed; and [instead of the mixed constitution being placed under the head of moderate or limited constitutions] any State in which the power of the Ruler was constitutionally limited had to be reckoned under the head of mixed States (106). [This was, in effect, to dismiss such a State to limbo.] But it was hardly possible, and least of all was it possible in Germany, that any success should long attend the violent methods of the thorough-going absolutists who simply abolished with a stroke of the pen, or treated as of no account, any constitution which contradicted their scheme of political theory.

So it was that the doctrine of Pufendorf won its way to general acceptance. According to that doctrine, division of powers is indeed a fact, but a fact which is only the basis of a monstrous and irregular form of State, and not of a *forma mixta* comparable

§ 17. *The Natural-Law theory of the State* 155

to the simple and unmixed forms. The very essence of the State is contradicted by any institution which vests several persons, or assemblies of persons, with independent rights of participating in political authority. 'Majesty', like the mind, is *unum et individuum*; and you can only distinguish its 'parts' in the same sense in which, when you are dealing with the mind, you distinguish the mental faculties. If, none the less, a division of majesty actually occurs, it is simply a case of a *respublica irregularis*; and a State of that kind is a diseased or 'perverted' State, like the perverted form of State described by Aristotle, with the one difference that the seat of the disease is here to be sought in the constitution itself, and not in the government only (107). The doctrine of the master was adopted, on this point as on others, by a number of his successors—among them Thomasius (108), J. H. Boehmer (109), Hert (110), Schmier (111), Gundling (112), Heineccius (113), and Heincke (114). In time, however, this idea of irregularity came to be modified. It was argued that 'irregularity' only signified a deviation from the strict academic pattern, and did not prevent the recognition of mixed constitutions as systems which might, under certain conditions, be active and even appropriate (115). Otto declares in so many words that *irregularitas* due to a *forma mixta* is not an evil, and that, in Germany for example, it is '*ad genium populi accommodata*' (116). Titius, again, on the ground that no inviolable rules are prescribed for the form of the State either by nature itself or by the *consensus gentium*, seeks to eliminate altogether the distinction of regular and irregular forms in favour of a distinction between *respublicae adstrictae* and *laxae* (117).

We find another school of thinkers attempting to reconcile the conception of the mixed form of State, under one designation or another, with the requirements of the conception of sovereignty, by the method of abandoning the idea of divided sovereignty in favour of the idea of an *undivided participation* in 'majesty' by a number of 'Subjects'. A view of this nature had already been suggested by Besold; and it gradually won a general acceptance, especially in regard to the application of the theory of the mixed constitution to Germany (118). We may notice particularly the serious attempt which is made by Huber to interpret the constitutional State, by the aid of this idea of undivided partnership, without sacrificing the unity of political authority. He regards any real *forma mixta* as inconceivable; the State, which is one body and one mind, cannot be the residence of a *triplex majestas*. On the other hand it is quite conceivable that several 'Subjects', and more especially a King and People or a King and Senate, should enjoy majesty in common (*communicative* or *simul*). Along with forms of the State in which majesty is only limited there may thus exist others in which it is *common*; and among the latter we may again distinguish between a complete *communicatio majestatis* (such as may be seen in Germany, Poland and Venice, where it is the basis of a formal *societas imperii*), and a mere *communicatio quorundam jurium majestatis*, which leaves the Ruler in possession of a *potestas summa, sed non integra* (119).

There were other writers who made similar attempts to preserve the conception of the mixed form of State while rejecting the doctrine of division of powers (120). It is obvious, however, that methods such as these could only have really secured the unity of the 'Subject' of political rights if the different 'Subjects' thus conceived as possessing rights in common had either been raised to the power of a new moral person, or depressed to the position of mere representatives of a State-personality which stood apart from and above them all. Neither of these courses was followed; and the 'Subject' of political authority thus remained divided and disintegrated. But if there were thus several 'Subjects' of sovereignty, it necessarily followed, however intimate the community of their relation with one another might be held to be, that *each* of them must somehow be allowed, at the very least, an 'unlimited share' in sovereignty*(121). [The facts of actual politics favoured such a conclusion.] If close attention were paid to the actual structure of mixed constitutions, and if the heterogeneity of the functions assigned to the several joint-possessors of sovereignty were taken into account—indeed, if regard were merely had to the way in which territorial sovereignty in Germany had definitely split away from imperial authority—it became impossible to deny the existence of an actual division of sovereignty, at least in regard to some part of the essential rights it involved (122). The result was a gradual process of reversion to the idea of divided sovereignty; and such reversion was not really postponed by the introduction

---

* An unlimited share is a share which is not limited to a part, but is a share in the whole (cf. 'unlimited liability'). Gierke's argument is that the theory of undivided partnership in sovereignty breaks down. There has to be a division of partnership into shares, with each partner taking his share. True, the shares of sovereignty may not be separate or discrete blocks of rights. They may only be non-separate and non-discrete shares in the whole system of rights. But that much, at the very least, they have to be.

§ 17. *The Natural-Law theory of the State*

of a theory which suggested that the various part-sovereigns, though each independent in his own sphere, only possessed a full and entire sovereignty when they acted in conjunction. This theory is expressed most clearly in Achenwall; '*In Republica mixta dantur plures personae, seu singulares seu morales, quarum cuilibet competit certa pars imperii, vel qua propria vel qua communis, independenter a reliquis; hinc plures singuli vel corpora, qui sibi invicem sunt aequales et liberi quoad partem imperii cuique competentem. Quamobrem in Republica mixta illi, inter quos divisum est imperium, non nisi junctim habent imperium plenum et absolutum*' (123).

We can now understand why, in spite of all the attacks delivered against it, the traditional theory still survived that the mixed constitution was simply a clear case of divided sovereignty (124). The objection that this meant the disintegration of the State might sometimes be met by the answer that the State itself remained, after all, the permanent 'Subject' of all sovereignty (125); but this plea of 'the Sovereignty of the State' could bear no fruit, and produce no result, so long as sovereignty itself continued to be treated as an object divided among a number of different ruling 'Subjects'. Nor was a more satisfactory solution to be found in the distinction between the 'substance' and the 'exercise' of majesty, which Leibniz made the basis of his theory (126).

But the theory of the mixed constitution began to acquire a wholly new vigour when the doctrine of constitutionalism associated it with the principle of a *qualitative division of powers*.* When political power began to be differentiated into a number of different powers which were distinguished from one another by their own essential character, it became possible to hold that a system which assigned these different powers to a number of differently constituted 'Subjects' was so far from being prejudicial to the interests of the State, that it might even be regarded as indispensable to its true perfection. As the English constitution gradually came to be considered the ideal, it thus began to be celebrated, from the days of Locke onwards, not only for the merits which it derived from its supposed mixture of the three simple forms of State [monarchy, aristocracy, and democracy], but also

* From this point of view the doctrine of constitutionalism required a mixed State to exhibit a division, not so much between different *quantities* of power divided among different sets of persons, as between different qualities or kinds of power—the executive, the legislative, the judicial—divided according to their *quality* among different authorities appropriate to their special requirements.

for the clear separation of the different powers which was consequent upon and determined by this mixture(127). Montesquieu openly declared that the union of the three powers in a single 'Subject' was the grave of political liberty, their separation from one another its guarantee, and their division among different authorities its proper canon and test(128); and it was because division of powers was most perfectly attainable in the mixed constitution that he assigned this form a pre-eminence over the simple forms(129).

When the theory of division of powers proceeded on the assumption of the sovereignty of the People, its adherents could meet the reproach that they destroyed the indivisibility of sovereignty with the reply that sovereignty itself [as distinct from the various 'powers'] remained undivided in the hands of the People. But the more the doctrine of constitutionalism was pushed to its logical conclusions, the less was it possible for it to invoke the sovereignty of the People. On the strict logic of that doctrine, the permanent sovereignty of the community was supposed to find its one and only expression in the legislative power, and this power was held to be exercised [not by the community, but] by its representatives; moreover, it was supposed to be only one among a number of powers which were all equally independent(130). We can trace the consequent reaction in Rousseau's attempt to prove the genuine and unimpaired sovereignty of the People. He has, it is true, no objection to a mixed constitution, in the sense of a composite structure of the governing body [a body distinct from the *État*, or sovereign people](132). After all, on his principles, the distinction between different forms of constitution is a little thing, a mere secondary distinction between different forms of *gouvernement*(131).*
But he attacks the doctrine of a division of powers [in the State itself] with all his power: it is, he argues, an intolerable dismemberment of indivisible sovereignty(133). And yet, if we regard the substance of his thought rather than the form in which it is expressed, we cannot deny that Rousseau himself is not entirely averse from the principle of the division of powers. Not only does he separate the legislative power as clearly as possible from the executive: he also advocates the exercise of the two separate powers by two different moral persons(134). He even goes to the length of refusing to allow to the People, as such, any capacity for under-

---

* The change in the order of the notes, here and elsewhere, is due to a change, in the translation, of the order of the sentences in Gierke's text.

§ 17. *The Natural-Law theory of the State*

taking an act of government: if it is ever called upon to do so, it must turn itself, in order to act, into a governing body, by the aid of a transformation which is little short of a miracle (135). Rousseau may emphasise as much as he likes the principle that legislation alone is really sovereignty, and that every other function of the State is a subordinate form of service; but he fails entirely, none the less, to prevent [executive] government from assuming the character of genuine political authority, or the governing body from acquiring the status of a 'Subject' of political rights (136). The advocates of the radical theory of popular sovereignty after his time came even closer than he did himself to the idea of a real and essential division of powers (137).

If radicalism could thus combine division of powers with popular sovereignty, the growing school of constitutionalism showed itself still more ready to succumb to the theory of Montesquieu, which combined the postulate of division of powers with the conception of the mixed form of State (138). From the middle of the eighteenth century onwards the exponents of the natural-law theory of the State, even when they still continued to profess a belief in the sovereignty of the Ruler, were seldom or ever averse from recognising a mixed form of State, with sovereignty divided, in one way or another, among a number of different 'Subjects' (139). In Germany, as elsewhere, the mixed constitution was gradually elevated to the dignity of a political ideal (140). It was advocated with especial ardour by Justi (141) and A. L. von Schlözer (142); and its vogue culminates in the theory of Kant, which derives division of powers directly from the rules of logic, and treats such division as an inviolable precept of the law of reason for every legitimate and really authentic State (143).

V. THE CONTRIBUTIONS MADE BY THE NATURAL-LAW THEORY OF THE STATE TO THE DEVELOPMENT OF PUBLIC LAW

This was the end of the natural-law theory of the State. Supporting the cause of the constitutional State, it ended, so far as its conception of sovereignty was concerned, in what was almost unconcealed bankruptcy; it ended, so far as the idea of the unity of the State-personality was concerned, in absolute disintegration. Not until the whole of the individualistic theory of the State evolved by the School of Natural Law had been transcended, and the conception of a living Group-being had been elaborated by a school of thought which followed the organic idea of historical evolution, was it possible to restore the idea of a sovereign State-personality.

Yet the School of Natural Law had rendered a real service. It had refined the idea of the unity of the body politic into that of a single *persona moralis*; and in doing so it had shed a definite and lasting light on a number of problems in public law which were capable of solution by a *formal* and technical conception of personality.

(*a*) The principle that a moral person was a unity, which continued to exist through all the changes of its parts, produced, or helped to produce, a theory of the continuity of public rights and duties; and it began to be generally assumed that the State remained the same identical 'Subject' of rights not only when there was a change of persons or territory, but also when there was an alteration in the form of the government(144). A further consequence followed. In cases of the division of an existing State, or the union of several existing States (such cases being held to involve merely 'alterations' of the political situation, as distinct from the complete extinction of a State), rules were laid down which secured the transference of the rights and duties of the old 'Subject' of rights to the new 'Subject' which had taken its place(145).

(*b*) The conception of the Ruler as Representative of the personality of the State was also useful. A clear distinction could thus be made between the Ruler as a 'Subject' of rights in his representative capacity, and the Ruler as a 'Subject' of rights in his private character. Where an assembly was recognised as Ruler (or as Joint-ruler), the natural-law conception of the *persona moralis* was applied to it; and the members of such an assembly who enjoyed the right of representing the State (or of joining in its representation) were held to do so as a Collective unity, and not as individuals. The rules of the law of corporations could thus be applied to the activities of the will of this representative Collective person, and they could be made thereby to regulate the willing and acting of the State itself(146). Even more important consequences could be drawn [from the conception of the Ruler as Representative of the personality of the State] where a single person was the bearer of Ruling authority. Here an identity was allowed to exist, either wholly or partially, between the representative *persona physica* of this individual and the personality of

§ 17. The Natural-Law theory of the State

the State; but two rôles or persons were distinguished within the *persona physica*—that of the Ruler, and that of the private individual (147). This distinction produced a number of consequences. It produced a separation in principle between the sphere of the King in public law, and his sphere in private law (148). It produced a separation between acts of government which were done by the Ruler as Ruler, and were therefore done by the State through him, and his private acts (149). It also supplied a principle which could be applied to acts done by officials in the discharge of their official duties; for though use was made of the private-law categories of *mandatum* and *ratihabitio** in order to explain the validity of such acts, it was also possible to take the ground that officials represented the Ruler as such—i.e. in his public, as distinct from his private capacity—and to argue accordingly that their acts were really acts of the State itself (150). Again the distinction between the person of the Ruler and that of the private individual automatically supplied the true principle for solving the old and vexed question, whether the successor was bound by the acts of his predecessor (151); though it must be admitted that there was always a tendency to confuse the issue again by introducing principles drawn from the private law of inheritance (152). Even the unlawful dictator ruling during an interregnum was gradually recognised as possessing, to some extent, a right of representing the personality of the State, which enabled him to bind the citizens by his acts (154); but the theory of Natural Law generally insisted on the need of legitimation of his *de facto* position by a subsequent act of confirmation (153).

(*c*) But it was in their treatment of State-property that the natural-law theorists developed their conception of the personality of the State furthest (155). They drew a distinction in principle between State-property and the property of the Ruler: they ascribed the ownership of State-property to the State itself, and vested the Ruler with nothing but a right of administration: they required the revenues accruing from the property of the State to be applied to public objects, and they made the alienation of such property depend on the consent of the People (156). There was, it is true, a great deal of difference of opinion in regard to the classification of the different elements included under the head of State-property (157). The demesne of the territorial prince offered a peculiar problem, and there were some thinkers who failed to

---

* *Mandatum* is an authorisation of the action of an agent in advance. *Ratihabitio* is a term used to signify a subsequent confirmation.

classify it precisely (158); but with the passage of time even demesne came to be included, without any qualification, in the general conception of State-property (159).

An increasing precision was also given to the distinction between the private-law right of the State to own particular objects and its public-law right of government over the whole of its political territory* (160). We must admit, it is true, that it was the theorists of Natural Law who developed an intermediate idea—that of the *dominium eminens* of the State, in the sense of its supreme or final ownership of everything; and it was they who applied that idea to justify the interference of the State with private property, especially in the way of confiscation and taxation (161). But while we make this admission, we must also note the gradual growth of another view of the matter, which was opposed in principle to including the conception of property at all in the area of the political rights of government (162).

CHAPTER II: SECTION I, §18

THE THEORY OF CORPORATIONS IN NATURAL LAW

I. ASSOCIATIONS CONTAINED IN THE STATE

The natural-law theory of society included its own particular theory of associations (*die engeren Verbände*); and this theory asserted itself with a growing independence, and with increasing success, against the traditional theory of Corporations to be found in positive law. The basis of this natural-law theory of corporate bodies was common to all thinkers; but the results produced by different thinkers differed, and differed widely, according as 'centralist' or 'federalist' tendencies were allowed to dominate thought.

---

* The story of the emperor Frederick I and the two jurists Bulgarus and Martinus is to the point. On a ride together they discussed the question whether the emperor had only *imperium*, or whether he had also *dominium*, over his territories. At the end of the ride the jurist who contended that he had both of these rights received the present of a horse. The other consoled himself by remarking, *Amisi equum, quia dixi aequum.*

§ 18. *The theory of Corporations in Natural Law*

(1) *Divergence of centralist and federalist views*

There was a difference, to begin with, between the different systems or schools in regard to the proper grading of associations on the principles of Natural Law. It is true that all corporate bodies alike were in some degree or another brought under the rules of Natural Law by all the different schools. As they were all included under the generic conception of *societas*, they must necessarily all have their place in the general scheme which had been elaborated for all 'societies', and which usually formed the preface to every account of the general natural-law theory of society. But this still left open the question whether, and if so, to what extent, the existence of intermediate corporate bodies between the Individual and the State was an integral part of the natural order of society, or an optional and arbitrary institution of positive law.*

(*a*) The balance of opinion inclined to the centralist view, which at most would admit only the Family—and not the local community (*Gemeinde*) or the Fellowship (*Genossenschaft*)—to a separate and distinctive position in the natural-law grading of associations. The majority of the natural-law theorists contined to follow the scheme of Aristotle; and in constructing a hierarchy of natural-law groups they accordingly made the State, regarded as a *societas perfecta* or *sibi sufficiens*, follow immediately upon the Family, with its three *societates simplices*† and its *societas composita* (the Household) formed by the union of the three(1). True, the local community [the 'village' of Aristotle] was treated in this connection as a stage on the road to the State; but in the State itself, when once it had come into existence, this community was only allowed the significance of a constituent part or division(2). The Fellowship, as a *societas arbitraria*, was banished altogether from the category of natural groups(3). The result was that the rights of corporate bodies (if we leave out of account the background of natural-law principles which was involved in the inclusion of such bodies under the general head of *societas*) were treated as merely a part of the

---

* Briefly the argument is that all the shades of natural-law theory agreed that Natural Law *applied* to all associations; but they were not all agreed that all associations had been *produced* by Natural Law. They were thus led to differ about the grading of associations—some saying that all associations were natural; others arguing that some associations, at any rate, were artificial in origin.

† That of husband and wife; that of parent and child; and that of master and servant.

system of civil rights which the State first brought into being. If any closer examination of the question was attempted, it was generally in connection with the theory of the position of the subject (*Untertan*), and it only meant the addition of some account of subjects when acting as groups to the general account already given of the position of individual subjects(4).

The centralist tendency in the natural-law theory of society was strongly accentuated in the theories which, following the lead of Hobbes, identified the formation of human society with the creation of the State, and supposed it to be achieved by previously isolated individuals through the conclusion of a single contract. On this basis it became impossible to regard any intermediate groups, of any description, as natural 'group-steps' standing between the Individual and the State [and leading up from the one to the other]. They could only be secondary formations which had come into existence within the State, and after it had been created. The natural-law system, as we find it in Spinoza, Rousseau, Justi, Fichte, Kant and many other writers, knows only the Individual and the State.

(*b*) In Germany, on the other hand, there was never entirely extinguished what we may call a 'federalist' point of view. Under its influence, thinkers were able to regard the Fellowship and the local community as natural group-steps in the process of political evolution, with a life and purpose of their own; and they could hold that these intermediate groups, even in a fully constituted civil society, had their own inherent existence, which was based upon, as it was also secured by, Natural Law. No exposition of this line of thought which was as bold or as logical as that of Althusius was ever attempted again; but the idea of a natural articulation of human society in a series of ascending grades remained active in more than one quarter(5), and Leibniz gave it a new and vigorous life(6). We may also notice another expression of this federal tendency. The more thoroughly the general natural-law theory of 'societies' was elaborated, the more inevitably was it impelled towards the idea that by Natural Law the Corporation and the State stood on a footing of equality(7). The most perfect expression of this tendency is to be found in the theory of Nettelbladt, which exercised a considerable influence. He made a radical distinction, both in natural and in positive law, between the rights of the individual and social rights. Basing the latter entirely on the one conception of a contract of society, he interpreted the whole world

§ 18. *The theory of Corporations in Natural Law*

of human groups—in all its ascending series of Family, Fellowship, local community, Church and State—according to a scheme which was common to the whole series, and yet left room for a large diversity (8). But there were many other systems, besides that of Nettelbladt, in which the natural-law theory of society was developed, with various degrees of definition, along similar lines (9).

(2) *The relation of the Corporation to the State*

(a) *Views inimical to Corporations.*

These differences of opinion about the proper grading of associations on the principles of Natural Law were important for their bearing on the general theory of the relation between the Corporation and the State.

If the corporative articulation of civil society was not derived from Natural Law, it must also be devoid of any sanction in Natural Law. It could only be a part of the system of positive law, which the State was free to determine by considerations of mere expediency. In that case local communities and Fellowships had no lot or part in those sacrosanct rights which, according to the theory of Natural Law, were derived immediately from the law of Reason, and were therefore above the reach of legislative discretion. Their 'person' was not, like that of the individual, inviolable by the State, and it was not invested with inherent rights. The obligation which they imposed on their members was not, like political obligation, a necessary and inevitable limitation of natural liberty. They were creations of historical law, but they had no rights under the Law of Nature.

In the age of Enlightenment,* the prestige of historical law increasingly paled before the splendour of the new ideal law; and the more it paled, the easier it was to advance from denying that corporations had a sanction in Natural Law to questioning whether they existed at all. Natural-law theory of this extreme order became a powerful ally of the practical policies which were directed to the destruction of the corporative system of Estates inherited from the Middle Ages. There were now two forces in the field—the State, with its passion for omnipotence: the Individual, with his desire for liberation. They had one thing in common, however hotly they might otherwise wage a frontier-war with one another. They could both use the weapons forged by the extremist

* The age of Frederick the Great, Voltaire and the Encyclopaedists.

natural-law theory to wage a joint battle against intermediate groups.

Even the most advanced of the absolutists did not, at first, demand the elimination of corporations: they only desired a strict limitation of their powers. The utility of a corporative articulation of civil society was not in dispute. But the whole structure of corporations, in their inner life and their external relations, was treated as a product of the State; and the State was urged to pursue a policy of asserting and using to the full its authority over them, in order to meet in advance the menace of group-formation and to remedy its existing abuses. Thus the legality of every association was made to depend on a government 'concession' (10): any meeting, including the regular meetings of members of recognised corporations, was supposed to require the permission of a higher authority (11); and all the more important activities of corporate life were made to involve the co-operation of the State (12). Where the positive law in force was contrary to the principles of Natural Law, there was no hesitation in assigning to the State a right to annul or remodel corporations on grounds of public welfare (13). In the same vein, the authors of constitutional Utopias in which the State was constructed on the basis of intermediate groups, instead of connecting their schemes with actual and historical corporations, attempted to secure a rational articulation of the body politic by a purely mechanical division of people and territory (14).

After the middle of the eighteenth century, and more particularly in France, the attack on the principle of corporate life was transformed into a regular war of annihilation. In 1757 Turgot formulated, in its extremest form, the idea which had been developed by the School of Natural Law, that 'moral bodies'—in contrast to individuals, who had rights which were sacred even for the whole community—had no rights at all as against the State (15). Rousseau, who held that the natural right of association had been exhausted and abolished in the act of concluding the political contract (*le pacte d'association*), rejected entirely any idea of the corporative articulation of the State, on the ground that it was a falsification of the general will (16); and he made it an object of policy that all separate societies in the State should be eliminated (17). Revolutionary theory afterwards never escaped from this circle of ideas. The actual policy of the Revolution itself, as is well known, went far towards the achievement of an atomistic ideal, for which the absolute monarchy of the *ancien régime* had already

§ 18. *The theory of Corporations in Natural Law*

prepared the way. In the execution of that policy the natural-law theories which were inimical to corporations played a leading part. They are to be heard, in every note of their whole gamut, during the famous debates of the French National Assembly on the confiscation of Church property (18). The older ideas of positive jurisprudence still found a vigorous expression, even in that body (19); but they were overwhelmed in the flood of natural-law arguments, some based on the idea that rights of corporations, in the sense of rights separate from those of the State, were simply non-existent (20), and others on the view that any possible right which a corporation might possess, being without sanction in Natural Law, was bound to disappear before the sovereign rights of the State (21).

After the ruin of the old historical associations, the problem of reconstruction began to appear. It was recognised that some sort of intermediate groups, midway between the State and the Individual, were after all indispensable; and here a new division of opinion emerged in the camp of Revolutionary theory itself. There were some who exalted the merits of decentralisation, as against an exaggerated policy of unity, and argued that there ought to be room for the separate life of the parts as well as for the life of the Whole. But the conception of corporations current in the old law of France was still anathema; and no conception of associations was really permitted which did not square with the general principle that any division of the body of the State should be made by the State itself, and made for reasons of State. It is significant that Sieyès, who had begun as the most uncompromising advocate of Rousseau's point of view (22), afterwards became a champion of the inviolability of corporate property (23), and ended as an enthusiast for a system of self-governing municipalities (24); but it is also significant that he always guarded himself against any suspicion of a desire to restore the old system of corporations (25). The mechanical and mathematical divisions of the State which he suggested as the vehicles of communal life had indeed very little in common with the old corporations.

In Germany, as well as in France, the entry of Rousseau's ideas was accompanied by his spirit of hostility to the principle of corporate life. It is true that there was hardly a single writer of any repute who went to the length of advocating the complete elimination of intermediate groups. But from the middle of the eighteenth century onwards we find the adherents of the pure law of Reason denying that associations possessed an inherent right of existence, and advocating a view of their origin which made them entirely State-institutions (*Staatsanstalten*). Justi includes no corporative elements in his scheme of civil society (26). Scheidemantel attaches great importance to the 'societies' (*Gesellschaften*) in the State; but he denies altogether the principles of liberty of association and the right of meeting (27), and he subjects even authorised societies to permanent State supervision (28). He holds that a society can have rights and responsibilities of its own, so long as it remains within the four corners of the law; but in order that these rights and responsibilities may be kept in harmony with the aim of the State, he makes them depend on its influence and control to a degree which gives them a definitely permissive character, of the nature of a *precarium* (29); and not content with depriving associations of any sort of autonomy under public law (30), he would even place their property at the disposition of the State (31). He distinguishes public and private societies; but his general treatment of the various species of lawful societies shows a tendency to regard the State-institution as the ideal to which societies should as far as possible conform (32).

Fichte banishes the conception of the Corporation entirely, in favour of that of the State-institution (33). Kant's attitude to the old and historical rights of corporations shows a lack not only of sympathy, but also of understanding; and he does less justice to the importance of associations than any of his contemporaries. He begins by directing his attention exclusively to the institutional element in all permanent forms of union; and he accordingly puts the 'Corporation' and the 'perpetual Foundation' (*Stiftung*) on the same basis (34). Holding this conception of moral bodies, he denies that they have any right to independent existence; and he holds that the State has the right, at any time that it thinks proper, to annul them, and to confiscate their property on payment of compensation to their surviving members. He goes even further. Arguing that the appropriation of land to the exclusive use of subsequent generations, who succeed to it under particular rules to that effect, is invalid, and contending that any title to corporate possession hitherto existing has now lapsed with the change of public opinion, he refuses to recognise that the property of moral bodies is property at all. It is only a right of temporary usufruct; and thus the confiscation of corporate property by the State is only the removal of a 'supposed' or 'assumed' right (35). Nor is it merely as a matter of theory that Kant claims this competence for

§ 18. *The theory of Corporations in Natural Law* 169

the State. He obviously regards the dissolution of moral bodies as an actual and practical postulate of the law of Reason; and he is convinced that, in this as in all other cases, the law of Reason should break with the law of History, and should burst the bonds laid by the past on the present (36).

(*b*) *Views favourable to Corporations:*
especially in the theory of Nettelbladt.

If Natural Law thus supplied the driving ideas to a movement which was ultimately directed towards the engulfing of corporations in the State, we must not overlook the fact that other and different ideas also continued to flourish in natural-law social theory, and that the growth of such ideas served to prepare the way for a restoration of the liberty of corporations in a rejuvenated form.

To pursue the theory of a contract of society to its logical conclusions was necessarily also to arrive, as we have already had reason to notice, at the idea that associations had a natural right to exist independently of State-creation. As a *societas*, each corporate body was the result of contract; and all such bodies derived their existence, exactly in the same way as the State, from the original rights of individuals which formed the basis of contract. The State might forbid its subjects, wholly or partially, to form separate societies; but if and so far as it refrained from doing so, individuals were only making use of their natural liberty (and not employing a right which had first to be conferred by the State) when they associated with one another to attain common ends by common means. Positive law might limit corporations ever so strictly; but it could not destroy the sap of vitality which they drew from their roots in Natural Law, and it could not but leave them, to a greater or less degree, in possession of inherent rights of their own, even against the State itself.

Ideas such as these were assumed as axiomatic even by writers who were among the protagonists in the struggle against the independence of corporations. Hobbes himself had shown the way in this direction, by propounding the doctrine that the contract of society, though it could never produce a new *authority* after the State had once been erected, could still produce new *forms of association*. Pufendorf followed Hobbes closely in this respect. When he comes to treat of the *vincula peculiaria* which serve in most States to bind citizens together, over and above the general bond of political obligation, he first directs his attention to the *peculiaria corpora civitati subdita* (37). Among these bodies he treats the Family, and the Family only, as prior to the State; and he therefore holds that the Family has retained the right to everything which has not been specifically taken from it. The other associations are posterior to the State; and they fall into two subdivisions—*publica*, or those founded by the sovereign authority itself; and *privata*, or those which owe their existence to a contract (*ipsorum civium conventio*) or to some external authority. Private associations can only become *corpora legitima* with the consent of the State (38). Whatever right or authority they exercise over their own members depends entirely on the assent of the sovereign authority, and can never acquire an independent title as against that authority (*quicquid juris habeant et quicquid potestatis in sua membra, id omne a summa potestate definiri, et nequaquam huic posse opponi aut prevalere*). Otherwise there would be a State within a State (*alias enim, si daretur corpus limitationi summi imperii civilis non obnoxium, daretur civitas in civitate*) (39). The conclusions which Pufendorf draws from this subordinate position of corporations, especially in regard to the limits of the representative authority of their assemblies and officers, are similar to those of Hobbes (40). Otherwise, and apart from this limitation, he regards it as a characteristic inherent in the organic nature of the State that the body politic should be constituted by members which are also bodies themselves (41).

After Pufendorf, the distinction between *societates aequales* and *inaequales* begins to be used with a view to attaining conclusions similar to those which he had drawn (42). The equal society is defined as a society without social authority; unequal societies (with the exception of family groups under a paternal authority) are regarded as societies which can only be constituted by a political group with a Ruling authority [i.e. the State]; and the principle is thus attained that though a corporation may *exist* as an equal society in its own right, it can only possess any *authority*, of any kind, in the form of a fragment of State-authority with which it has been entrusted. Hert may be reckoned among the first who used the antithesis of *societas aequatoria* and *societas rectoria*, with a clear sense of its implications, to explain the relation between the Corporation and the State. He holds that the contract of society is capable of producing a body which is constant through all the changes of its members, and possesses a single personality; but he hastens to add that such a body can never have a 'mind' (*Seele*),

§ 18. *The theory of Corporations in Natural Law*

and thereby a capacity for will and action, until there has been instituted a supreme authority [which can give it such a mind and capacity]. Now the only example of such an authority is the political sovereign of the State, who has been instituted by means of the original contract of subjection; and the *universitas* must therefore be content to receive any organised form of authority which it possesses at the hands of that sovereign, and as a part of the State (43).

J. H. Boehmer erected this new doctrine of corporations into a formal system (44). He admits that liberty of association, which existed in the state of nature as an effect of natural liberty, has never been utterly extinguished in civil society; but he holds that it has been limited, and that in two ways. In the first place, *collegia* can now only be formed as *societates aequales*: they cannot, therefore, create an *imperium*: at the most they appoint a manager. If an association could create its own government, there would be a State within a State. A *collegium*, in its capacity of a moral person, is therefore subject to the authority of the State, and subject in the same way as its own individual members. In the second place [besides being subject in the same way], it is subject to an even greater degree. Where an association is concerned, a still stricter use of political control is necessary, proportionate to the greater power and the more serious menace presented by such a new person, composed of a number of individuals, when compared with ordinary individuals. On both of these grounds Boehmer would vest the State with a power over corporations sweeping enough to leave hardly a trace of the liberty of corporations which he has begun by admitting in principle. He argues that the bearer of political authority has to take proper measures, in his general policy, to prevent corporations from assuming an authority of their own, and thus becoming small States, or causing injury to the State in any other way. Moreover, the Ruler has also a number of rights of detail. He has a right, in the first place, to prohibit particular *collegia* at his discretion, and to deprive them thereby of the *jura personae civilis* (45). He can also issue an ordinance in advance, as was done in Roman law, proclaiming that no *collegium* will be tolerated in the State which has not been expressly sanctioned; and he is further entitled to create *collegia et societates* himself, as he may think fit, and in doing so to regulate their government, constitution and powers. The *collegia publica* he thus creates will henceforth be totally dependent on the authority of the State. More especially, they will be strictly limited in the management of property, since, whatever they possess, *auctoritate publica possident*(46); and the sovereign may even compel his subjects to become members, and to share in the burdens, of such bodies. Finally, he must also exercise a constant supervision of *collegia privata* (particularly the guilds, with their *monopolia et mores pessimi*), in order to prevent their taking any decision which is detrimental to the State; and he may also prescribe in advance definite limits to their action.

On such a view there can be no question of any independence of associations. The way is barred in both directions. Suppose, on the one hand, that a real and effective social authority is recognised as belonging to a local community or a Fellowship. In that case such authority cannot be exercised as an inherent right, because authority is excluded from the idea of *societas aequalis* [which is the idea constituting these bodies]; and it must therefore be exercised in the name and under the commission of the sovereign, as part and parcel of the authority of the State. Suppose, on the other hand, that a corporation acts in its own inherent right. In that case there is only a contractual obligation of the members [to accept its authority] and nothing more; and even so the State is still entitled to avail itself of its suzerainty over corporations to interfere and impose limits on their action, or to reserve the right of previous assent.* True to the logic of his ideas, Boehmer rejects altogether any idea of corporations legislating(47), or judging(48), or administering(49) for themselves. He even refuses to allow the validity of the conception of corporate office(50). If we add to this the defenceless position in which he leaves any privilege granted to corporations(51), and the strong inclination which he shows to hand over their property to the State(52), we cannot escape the impression that Boehmer has travelled from one pole to the opposite. Basing himself in theory on the idea of the liberty of associations, he comes to a practical conclusion in favour of their absolute subjection.

When the antithesis between *societas aequalis* and *inaequalis* had been developed to such a point, it became possible to use a natural-law basis of argument as a lever for ejecting the law of corporations entirely from the sphere of public law, and removing it into the sphere of private law. If public law were defined as the system of rules relating to government, and if, again, associations were held

* Briefly—if an association exercises *real* authority, it does not do so in its own right; and if it exercises authority in its own right, it does not exercise *real* authority.

§ 18. The theory of Corporations in Natural Law

to be incapable of producing any government, it followed that public law was concerned with associations not as active 'Subjects', but as passive 'Objects', and only dealt with them in so far as it dealt with the rights of governing authority over them; and on this it followed in turn that the rights which belonged to corporate bodies must be merely rights at private law. This is the line of argument followed by J. H. Boehmer. He explains the distinction between *jus privatum* and *jus publicum* by the fact that in the *status civilis* all *actiones* are either *privatae* or *publicae*, and therefore need different *normae*. He then classifies as *actiones privatae* the acts of *cives ut singuli*, the acts of *singula corpora ut privati*, and the acts of the *Princeps qua privatus*; while he limits the category of *actiones publicae* to the acts of *cives qua membra Reipublicae* and the acts of the *Princeps qua talis* (53). Logically enough, on this basis, he can only find a place for the theory of associations, in his '*System of General Public Law*', under the heading of 'the State's control of corporations and churches' (54). Titius goes further still; and he never mentions local communities or Fellowships or Churches except in connection with private law (55). The distinction between public and private law generally continued to be drawn on similar lines by later writers (56).

From another point of view, we find the distinction between 'equal' and 'unequal' societies helping to provide a bridge of transition from the natural-law theory of the contract of society to the Roman-law theory of corporations. It only needed a further development of the often expressed idea, that a group could not possess full personality until it acquired a representative Ruling authority, to bring the natural-law distinction of *societates aequales* and *inaequales* into line with the Roman-law distinction between *societas* and *universitas*; and when this had been done it became possible to argue that while the contract of society might produce a *societas*, or partnership, it was only the influence and action of a political authority that could explain the existence of a corporation, or *universitas*. This is the line followed by Huber, for example, when he develops the particular theory of *universitates* which forms part of his general theory of the State (57). He begins by describing the *universitas* as a body of persons, being neither a Family nor a State, who are united for the sake of a common advantage and provided with a definite system of government (*certus regiminis ordo*). He emphasises the element of *certum regimen* as the essential attribute which distinguishes a *universitas* from a *societas* (58); but he equally makes it a reason for requiring that, before a *universitas* can come into being, the sanction of the State, from which it receives a government of its own, must first of all be obtained. Nor is he content with arguing that a corporation only becomes such in and by this act of the State. He proceeds to make the definite permission (or 'concession') of the State a necessary element in the idea of the *universitas* (which, incidentally, at once excludes the Family and the State from that category); and he accordingly includes the fact of such permission in the more precise definition which he finally gives (*coetus...sub certo regimine permissu summae potestatis ad utilitatem communem sociatus*)(59). In explaining the relation of the Corporation to the State, he applies throughout the two ideas (1) that a corporation can act in its own right only within the sphere which it has in common with a *societas*, and (2) that the organised authority, which distinguishes a corporation from a *societas*, can only be exercised by its bearers in the name of the sovereign, and by virtue of a commission given and defined by that sovereign(60). Huber's exposition of the subject is repeated, sometimes in his very words, by Schmier(61)—and this in spite of the fact that, in an earlier passage of his treatise, he expresses his agreement with Boehmer as regards the recognition to be given, and the limits to be assigned, to the rights of association which spring from 'natural liberty'(62). Statements which approximate to Huber's point of view are also to be found in other writers (63).

In general, however, the adherents of the School of Natural Law, far from following the line of thought which we have just described, departed further and further, as time went on, from the Roman-law conception of an essential difference between *societas* and *universitas*. In particular, the German thinkers who applied themselves to the systematic construction of a natural theory of society were so far from accepting that conception, that they directed their main effort to attaining a homogeneous conception of all forms of society, which would obliterate any line of division between partnership and corporation. This tended also to eliminate the artificial distinction which had hitherto been drawn between equal and unequal societies. Such a distinction lost its significance as soon as it came to be held that the very simplest form of society already contained the elements of which *all* groups were composed, up to and including the State. At any rate it ceased to oppose any further obstacle to the rise of a more liberal view, which would be ready at need to broaden the basis of the inherent rights

§ 18. *The theory of Corporations in Natural Law* 175

theoretically recognised as belonging to associations in relation to the State.

The actual development of the natural-law theory of society corresponded to what we are thus led to expect. The emphasis which they laid on the homogeneity of all societies really led many of the exponents of that theory to adopt a more favourable attitude to the idea of the independence of corporate bodies. The status which Leibniz assigns to local communities and Fellowships in the general hierarchy of groups depends entirely on the assumption that they possess an inherent social authority; and though he introduces the distinction between equal and unequal societies, his view remains unaffected by it (64). Wolff definitely lays it down that the contract of society produces of itself, in every society, an initial *imperium* of the body over its members (*jus universis competens in singulos*); and he reduces the distinction between the *societas aequalis* and the *societas inaequalis* to the simple fact that in the former *imperium* remains with the body itself, and in the latter it is delegated by it (65). On this basis the autonomy of the body, and its jurisdiction over its members, are both conceived as inherent rights, necessarily issuing in some degree from the nature of a society (66); and the control of the State over corporations is regarded as derived, not from the fact that the authority of a corporation comes from the State, but from the general power of supreme control which belongs to the sovereign (67). We find similar views in regard to the basis of the authority of corporations, and that of the control of the State over corporate bodies, expressed by S. Cocceji (68), Heineccius (69) and Daries (70).

But the greatest exponent of such views was Nettelbladt; and he developed them into a comprehensive system, in which the idea of the liberty of corporations finds full expression. He was the first thinker who drew from the old axiom, that social entities had a sanction in Natural Law, the new conclusion that all societies, like all individuals, had inherent natural rights. In his view the basis of the existence of a *societas* is the union of a number of men to form a moral person, for the purpose of attaining a common object which is not transitory, and not concerned solely with rights of property, by means of a social constitution (an *interna constitutio*, which serves as the *politia societatis*). Such a *consociatio* may, he believes, arise naturally, or it may be created by a 'third party'; but it may be also produced by the free will of the members, and in that event the means by which it is achieved is a contract. In whatever way a society comes into being, it brings with it into the world certain rights of its own, so that henceforth we must distinguish within it between *jura personae moralis* and *jura singulorum*. Its own rights, being *jura socialia sive collegialia*, are derived *ex natura societatis*, and therefore *ponuntur posita societāte*; but in societies (as also with individuals) original and inherent rights may receive an addition in the shape of acquired rights, or *jura societatis contracta*. The 'substance', or essence, of *jura socialia* is the *potestas societatis*: the 'exercise' of such rights is the *regimen societatis*. Social authority (*potestas societatis*) can assume different forms in different kinds of societies: it may be *summa*, or it may be *subordinata*; and any original authority may also be further increased by the addition of acquired rights. In a voluntary *societas, quae sibi ipsi originem debet*, the primary 'Subject' of social authority is the *societas ipsa*: in a natural society, it is the 'Subject' determined by nature itself: in a *societas per alium constituta*, it is the *constituens*. It is possible, however, for social authority to be transferred, in substance or in exercise; and consequently, while it always belongs to its original holder as a perfect, unlimited and proprietary right, it may be vested in the subsequent holder as a right which is imperfect, limited, usufructuary and non-transferable. *Imperium*, or the *jus dirigendi actiones membrorum societatis* so far as the welfare of the society may demand the curtailing of liberty, is only a part of social authority. There is therefore no *imperium* without *societas*, as, conversely, there is no *societas* without *imperium*. *Imperium* includes the power of punishment. For the rest, the total authority exercised by any society includes three general powers—the directorial (*rectoria*), the supervisory (*inspectoria*) and the executive (*executoria*), besides such special powers as the object of a society may require (71).

When he proceeds to consider and classify the *species societatum*, and to draw, in the process, a distinction between the 'equal' and the 'unequal' species of society (72), Nettelbladt is obviously precluded, by the basis which he has adopted, from explaining the difference between these two species by the presence or absence of a social authority. Upon his view, social authority is equally present in both. [The difference between them must therefore be explained, not by the presence or absence of social authority, but by a difference in the residence of such authority.] In a *societas aequalis*, the authority does not belong to one of the members, or to a part of the members, who exercise it over the rest; it is the property either of the whole body itself (*penes omnes simul sumptos*) or of an *extraneus*. If the society has constituted itself, there is a presumption in favour of the rights of the members generally: if it had been constituted by a third party, the presupposition is in favour of that party (73). In a *societas inaequalis*, on the other hand, one of the members, or some part of the members, may properly exercise authority, either limited or unlimited, over the whole body; but it is also possible for a *societas inaequalis imperfecta* to exist, in which some of the rights of social authority remain with the whole body of the members (74).

The further development of Nettelbladt's argument leads him to the view, that the *jura socialia societatis* which are derived from the nature of a society may be held to include all the rights which we now describe by the name of 'internal rights of corporations' (75). This is a view which he still continues to maintain, as a general principle, when he comes to describe in detail the relations between associations and the State. But there are certain modifications [of this general view], which result from an application of the general principles of Natural Law regarding the subordination of *societates minores* to the *societas major* in any *societas composita*. The nature of these modifications differs considerably, according as the connection between a contained association [or minor society] and the body politic [or major society] is close or loose (76). In this connection Nettelbladt distinguishes five main kinds of *societates*.

The first is *societates publicae in sensu eminenti tales*, which are regarded as including 'colleges', such as Estates, which possess, in whole or in part, the State-authority itself (77). The second is *societates quae sunt magistratus*, that is to say collegiate magistracies or boards. These are bodies created by the Sovereign for the exercise of functions of government; and therefore the rights which any such body possesses (its *jura socialia*) are by the nature of the case, and apart from any question of their being taken over into his hands, the rights of the *Superior* (78). The third is *societates publicae stricte sic dictae*, which are constituted by the Sovereign for other objects of general and public welfare, and are only distinguished from magistracies by the lack of coercive authority (79). The fourth is *universitates personarum*, or in other words local communities and other communal groups, which are alike in drawing their origin from an act of State-authority, but which may, none the less, have very different constitutions (80). The fifth and last is *societates privatae in republica*, or voluntarily formed 'Fellowships', *quae sibi ipsis originem debent, sicque publica auctoritate interveniente non sunt constitutae*. Their creation is permissible—so far as their object is not in itself improper, or incompatible with the position of a subject—in virtue of *vis libertatis subditorum civilis*; but, at the same time, '*confirmatio seu approbatio Superioris utilis, non necessaria est*'. These 'private societies' possess a social authority of their own, in all matters of dispute, as soon as they come into existence; and this authority includes not only the general *jura socialia* already mentioned [i.e. *potestas rectoria, inspectoria* and *executoria*], but also the special rights which their particular object requires (81). But they still remain subject to State authority in any case of doubt. True, the Sovereign has no *jura societatis* by virtue of which he can control them: he has only the *jura in potestate civili contenta*; but the effect of this is that their own *jura societatis...eatenus subordinata sunt potestati civili, quatenus salus Reipublicae id requirit* (82). There are, however, two ways in which this normal position [of private societies, or voluntary Fellowships] may be varied. On the one hand, corporations may be *liberae*, and as such exempt from the general suzerainty of the State over corporations; they may even be *privilegiatae*, and as such own rights of political suzerainty themselves, as their own *jus proprium* (83).* On the other hand, and in the opposite sense, the political Sovereign may himself possess the *potestas societatis* in and over a corporation. Before he can possess it, however, he must have a proven and particular title to such power, as distinct from the general power which belongs to his position as Sovereign: he must have, e.g. a title arising from *delatio a societate*, or from *devolutio*. Even in such a case political authority and social authority must continue to be distinguished; and a clear line of division must always be drawn, even when they are personally united, between *jura majestatica* and *jura collegialia* (84).

There is hardly another system of Natural Law which can be said to contain so full or so logical an exposition of the theory of associations; but views of the same general character were very commonly held. Achenwall, for example, tries to distinguish between the inherent and the acquired rights of societies; and he seeks [in dealing with inherent rights] to show that associations have a social authority of their own (85). The same is true of Hoffbauer (86). He relies largely on the views of Nettelbladt; in par-

* E.g. a guild or fraternity may be *libera*; and a chartered company (such as the English East India Company) may be *privilegiata*, and exercise rights of political suzerainty as *jura propria*.

ticular, he repeats his division of societies into those which are 'public', and constituted by the State itself for political objects, and those which are 'private societies', created by the citizens of the State for the attainment of their own private objects. He proclaims an express 'right' of the citizens to unite in private societies, provided that their object is not in contradiction to that of the State, and to determine freely the constitution of such societies (87). There were other writers towards the end of the eighteenth century, and among them some of the sternest individualists of the time, who proclaimed liberty of association as one of the fundamental natural rights of the Individual, and espoused its cause against the encroachments of political authority. A. L. von Schlözer, for example, can write—'In the general society, individuals may emerge who are engaged in a similar effort to attain human happiness. A number of them will associate and form a group, if they believe that they can attain a lawful object, by that means, more effectively than each of them can attain it for himself.... The great society must not only allow such groups to arise; it must also protect them: the ideas and the acts of each guild are only a matter of concern to the general society, in the sense that they ought not to run counter to the civil contract' (88). W. von Humboldt was no less ardent a champion of the right of free association. When civic co-operation was really necessary, he argued, the free group was preferable to the political institution as a means of dealing with all objects other than that of public security, and, in particular, for the purpose of promoting the advancement of general welfare, religion and morality (89).

Side by side with this current of ideas inspired by Natural Law, we may also trace another movement of reaction against State-absolutism and against its enmity to corporations—a movement which was based on historico-political grounds. The notion had always survived that the well-being of the social system required, not only that the life of associations should be harmoniously co-ordinated with that of the Whole, but also that it should be free and independent within the limits of its own sphere (90). Montesquieu expressly advocates the preservation of privileged corporations and their mediatory functions in a monarchical form of State, because their destruction inevitably perverts monarchy into despotism (91). In Germany Justus Möser is conspicuous for his struggles on behalf of the liberty of corporations. In his historical review of the misfortunes of his country, he never fails to celebrate the strength and the vigour of the old Fellowship-life, or to lament the days of its suppression (92); and he draws the political moral, that a free and powerful community is inconceivable in the absence of a firm foundation in corporate life. In the strength of this belief, he espouses the general cause of liberty of associations against the dead level of legislative uniformity (93). He champions their independence: he even goes to the length of advocating the isolation of local communities, and of guilds and crafts, behind the barriers of their locality and class (94); and he recommends a fresh formation of Fellowships on the lines of voluntary association (95). 'Daily we see', he prophetically proclaims, 'what great things can be done by corporations, societies, fraternities and all such sorts of association' (96).

(3) *The natural-law conception of the internal nature of Corporations, as affected by the fact of their inclusion in the State*

If we turn, in conclusion, to enquire what was the natural-law conception of the *internal nature* of corporations, the answer is largely to be found in the account which we have already attempted to give of the natural-law theory of Groups in general. We have still, however, to trace the application of this general theory to local communities and Fellowships in one particular respect. How was that theory modified, when it was applied to these bodies, by the fact of their being included in the State?

In seeking to answer this question, we must begin by distinguishing two different tendencies in the natural-law theory of Groups—tendencies opposed to one another, and yet meeting or intersecting at a number of points. One of them led to the elimination of any idea of the real rights of corporations, in favour of a conception of the Corporation which made it purely an Institution (*Anstalt*): the other tended to encourage thinkers to reconstruct a belief in the inherent rights of corporations, by the aid of a conception of the nature of the social group which made it a Fellowship (*Genossenschaft*).

(*a*) *The Corporation as an Institution* (Anstalt).

A view of corporations as being of the nature of Institutions [and therefore State-created] necessarily ensued (in spite of all preliminary assumptions about the natural basis of *societates*), as soon as thinkers ceased to regard an act of agreement among its members as sufficient to explain how a *societas* could become a corporation, and began to argue that the only force which could explain the existence of a corporation was a Ruling authority imposed from above, and imposed from without, upon the *societas*.

This was the obvious tendency of a theory which had been developed in connection with the teaching of Hobbes. This theory involves two postulates. In the first place, the unity of a group's personality is made to depend entirely on the 'representation' of all its members by a single person or body of persons; in the second place, a 'representative' power of this order is held to be inconceivable, and inadmissible, so far as regards any group which is included in the State, except in the form of an emanation from the authority of the State. [On this basis, any corporate group with a single personality will be entirely a State-created Institution.] But even in the more moderate theory of Pufendorf, the institutional element [if it is not everything] still plays a decisive part in determining the nature of corporations. We may admit, indeed, that his *persona moralis composita* is made to involve, as the condition of its existence, a previous union already achieved on a voluntary basis, and held together by the internal ties between its members. But we must also notice that it only acquires the character of a genuine unity, able to will and act as such, by the addition of a representative Ruling authority; and so far as regards all *corpora civitati subdita*, this authority must proceed from the grant and concession of the State (97). At the same time it has to be added (as we have already had occasion to notice) that Pufendorf does not push his principles to their full and proper conclusion; and instead of keeping his [original] Collective and his [added] Representative unity in close connection with one another, he allows them to become detached. The result is that when he comes to treat of the property, the legal proceedings (*negotia juridica*), and the delicts of the *universitas*, he often falls back upon traditional views and expressions which really imply the principle of Fellowship (98).*

The disciples and successors of Pufendorf are under the influence of similar views [but some of them depart even further from the Institutional idea of corporations]. Going back to the idea that a Collective unity has a substantive existence of its own, and willing to allow that even a mere partnership already possesses a moral personality, they are more inclined than he was to apply a purely

* In other words, he leaves out of account the need of representation of the group, and assumes that, simply on its collective side, it can hold property, conduct legal proceedings, or commit delicts.

partnership view of corporations, at any rate in interpreting the legal position of corporate bodies in those connections where the presence or absence of a corporate authority is immaterial (99). This is particularly the case with Gundling and Hert (100); and we find both of them, therefore, more prepared than previous thinkers to abolish any real line of division between corporation and partnership (101).

Huber follows a different line. While interpreting the natural-law theory of society at large in the light of the traditional [Roman-law] theory of corporations, he also seeks to maintain a view of the Corporation which separates it clearly from other groups. He takes great pains to distinguish it from other forms of grouping—first from the State and the Family (102); next from the ordinary [voluntary] society or community (103); and finally from institutions which are without a constitution of their own (104), and from collegiate magistracies which have no particular and specific purpose (105). When, however, he comes to discuss the rights and duties of the Corporation [he seems to alter his ground; for here] he avails himself largely of a distinction between two totally different elements which he regards as being involved—the element of a 'society' or partnership which rests upon its own basis, and the element of an 'institution' which is imposed on that society. In explaining the rights and duties of the Corporation which fall within the area covered by the contract of society [i.e. the area corresponding to the first of these elements], he applies the idea of a purely Collective group-personality, using for the purpose the relevant doctrines [about *societas* or partnership] in the theory of the civilians (106). In explaining the rights which fall within the other area [i.e. the area corresponding to the element of the 'institution'], where the dominant notion appears to be that of a Whole superior to its individual members, he adopts the idea of a sphere of authority derived from, and delegated by, the sovereign power of the State (107). If we consider separately the two sorts of elements which are present in a Corporation, he proceeds to argue, we shall say that those of the first sort are not generically different from the elements present in a simple *societas* (108), and that those of the second sort are the same in kind as the elements present in any collegiate magistracy instituted by the State (109). If, however, the two are brought into union (a union which, it must be admitted, remains purely external), the product, in his view, is a structure which is *sui generis*—that of the *Universitas*. Views of a similar character, though not always so clearly or so definitely expressed as they are by Huber, may be traced in other writers, who seek to transplant into Natural Law the distinction drawn by positive law between the *societas* and the *universitas*(110). The ultimate result of such views is that the Corporation is treated as being at one and the same time a Fellowship, in the sphere of private law, and a State-institution, in the sphere of public law(111).

The same result was also attained, on the basis of pure Natural Law and without any reference to positive law, by thinkers such as J. H. Boehmer and his successors, who made the rights of corporations issue primarily from the conception of the *societas aequalis*, interpreted as a society which possessed no social authority. It was possible, along this line of approach, and by using this idea of the natural society of equals (in a heightened form which made it tantamount to a Fellowship), to find a source and a justification for such rules of the law of corporations as presupposed nothing more than a mere union of Many to form a One(112). [But this was all that was possible.] When it came to explaining the existence of a real corporation, with a real capacity for life and action—a thing which it was impossible to conceive in the absence of an organised group-authority—these theorists found themselves forced to take refuge, after all, in the idea of the State 'institution'(113).

A different situation arose if the assumption were made that even a *societas aequalis* did possess social authority, or if, again, it were admitted that a contract between subjects of the State might have [of itself, and without any intervention by the State] the effect of producing a *societas inaequalis*. But it is to be observed that even those who advocated the liberty of corporations most ardently on this basis were content to limit their actual application of the pure 'Fellowship' principle to the groups which they called by the name of 'private societies'. 'Public societies' were ascribed by these thinkers to an act of State-creation; and local communities were accordingly treated in their theory as essentially State-institutions(114).

The extremest form of a purely 'institutional' conception of corporations was that which finally appeared, as the basis of attacks on the very existence of all corporations, in the militant theory which spread from France over Europe(115). Hatred of the Corporation was primarily based on the revolt of the individual against the yoke of obligation imposed on him by his predecessors;

and an exclusive prominence thus came to be given to this factor of obligation, which the Corporation possessed in common with the 'Foundation' (*Stiftung*).* Many writers hardly drew any distinction at all between the Corporation and the Foundation(116); and Kant definitely treats the Corporation as only a secondary species of Foundation(117). Even among the most ardent panegyrists of free association there are some who frown on all true corporations, because they regard them as being, in the same way as 'foundations', a control of the living by the dead(118).

(*b*) *The Corporation as a Fellowship* (Genossenschaft), *especially in the theory of Nettelbladt.*

Turning to the other of the two tendencies we have mentioned, we have now to trace the emergence, in the School of Natural Law, of a 'Fellowship' view of the Corporation. The vogue of such a view depended on the extent to which the legal position of corporations was interpreted as the result of a voluntary contract of society.

Up to a point, as we have already shown, this Fellowship view was the inevitable result of the natural-law theory of society. The natural-law theorists always held that a simple contract of partnership possessed in itself a cohesive force (an element which was absent from the conception of *societas* entertained by the civilians) capable of holding individuals together in a unity which persisted in spite of any change of membership. This view attained increased significance when a Fellowship group of this nature [i.e. a group with a unity which was not affected by any change of membership] was recognised as something more than *one* of the constituent elements in a full and complete corporation, and was regarded as capable of being, by itself and without the addition of any other element, a real if imperfect 'Subject' of rights. Such a line was very generally followed in the German theory of Natural Law. Even Huber, in spite of his inclination towards civilian theory, recognised that a society could already be a moral person before it had attained the position of a *universitas*(119). The theory of Pufendorf, too, was more and more modified in a direction which led to the recognition of purely 'Collective' persons, side by side with those Group-persons which had attained their full development through the addition of a 'Representative' unity(120). Finally, we find a frank and unqualified admission (for which

* E.g. ecclesiastical foundations, or, again, economic foundations with exclusive rights, possessing some form of monopoly.

Hert and Boehmer had already set a precedent) that a *societas aequalis*, in spite of the absence of any social authority, is none the less a *persona moralis*(121). Here, at last, a purely Fellowship form of group-unity is really made to take its place, in general theory, by the side of the 'institutional' corporation. But this Fellowship form of group-unity still lacks the essential attribute of a genuine corporation. If it has the quality of being a moral person, it shares that quality indiscriminately with all forms of community in which the members can conveniently be regarded as possessing rights or duties 'jointly' (*insgesamt*)(122). It cannot develop into a Whole which is something more than its members. This Collective person, after all, is only what in Germany we nowadays call the 'joint hand' (*gesamte Hand*).*

But the natural-law theory of society had further conquests to make; and it eventually succeeded in building, on its own foundation of a voluntary contract of society, a real Fellowship possessing the rights of a full corporation. That achievement became possible as soon as the action of subjects of a State, in concluding a contract between themselves, was admitted to have the power of producing a social authority. Thinkers who made that admission were able—at any rate in dealing with Fellowships which were due to deliberate action—to broaden the rights of the simple *societas* into a comprehensive system of corporate rights without introducing any added element of State-'institution'. This will explain the rise of an influential Fellowship theory, which in Germany owed its foundation to Wolff, but which passed from him into almost all of the systematic treatises on Natural Law after the middle of the eighteenth century(123). The most elaborate statement of this theory is that which we find in the writings of Nettelbladt. His teaching has an added and special interest, partly because he supplements his statement of Natural Law, at every point, by a corresponding statement of positive law, and partly again because, in the course of adding this supplement, he steadily seeks to apply in detail the same general leading idea—the idea that the relation of the rules of positive law to Natural Law, which immutably fixes the principle of such rules, must be mainly of the nature of executive ordinance(124).† We shall thus be justified in using his doc-

* On the *gesamte Hand* see Maitland, *Collected Papers*, III, pp. 336–7. It is a form of 'joint ownership', stronger (in the sense of having less flavour of individual rights) than our English 'joint ownership'.

† In other words, positive law must be related to Natural Law much as 'statutory orders', or '*règlements d'administration publique*', are related to legislation.

trine, which may be regarded as typical, as the basis of our account of the [eighteenth-century] natural-law theory of the Fellowship.

We have already seen that Nettelbladt and the other writers of his way of thinking are under the influence of a view which resolves the existence of a group, in its internal aspect, into a sum of individual relations, and yet at the same time consolidates it, in its external aspect, into a *persona moralis* possessing rights and duties in the same way as an individual(125). In accordance with this view, they begin by assuming that the internal rights of corporations, so far as they possess inherent validity in relation to the State,* are entirely the result of contractual agreements. The basis of such rights is the original contract for the formation of a society, which already brings into being a more or less comprehensive social authority(126). The authority so created, though it actually contains all the elements of a genuine corporate authority, is juristically speaking no more than a contractually constituted sum of individual rights, and it therefore derives its power from a continuous act of assent on the part of the associated members(127). In itself, such authority belongs to these members only, in their totality(128); but it may be transferred, by a further contract, either in whole or in part, to a single or a collective person(129). If this is not done, and if the society thus remains a *societas aequalis*, all the members as a whole are still entitled to exercise social authority; and on this it follows, first that every exercise of such authority properly requires a fresh contractual agreement of wills among all the members, and secondly that, if a majority-resolution is allowed to count as *communis consensus*, or the action of representatives is reckoned as the action of *universitas ipsa*, this can only be the case in virtue of a previously made and unanimous agreement to that effect(130). In addition, there are also special contracts to be considered. A special contract is necessary to enable new members to be accepted, and to make possible the alteration of *personnel* which such acceptance involves(131): similarly the exclusion of previous members can only, as a rule, take place by way of a similar contract(132); and in the same way, again, the appointment and authorisation of the officers of a society always depends upon the conclusion of contracts to that effect(133).

None the less, and although it is thus constituted merely by

* There may be *some* internal rights of Corporations which are given by the State, and do not therefore possess 'inherent validity' in relation to the State.

contractual relations, a Corporation, in virtue of the union of powers and wills which is produced by the various contracts, becomes a single Group-person in its external relations; and as a *persona moralis*, it stands on a level with the Individual (although it is not in itself an Individual), and it is therefore included in the general scheme of the rights and duties of *singuli* (134). This last idea is one which we find particularly applied by Nettelbladt, and applied both in treating of natural and in treating of positive law. The method which he follows in dealing with *jurisprudentia socialis* [or the law of associations] is to begin by developing, in a first section, a general theory of associations, and then to proceed, in a second section, to a systematic exposition of the methods by which the law relating to the rights of individuals can be applied to 'societies'* (135). In his treatise on Natural Law, he begins this exposition with the theory of acts (*Handlungen*); and here he starts from the axiom that the *societas* has to be reckoned as the author of any *actio* which *volente societate edita est*. This, he argues, is the case [i.e. an act really has the will of a society as its author] (1) so far as concerns unequal societies, or equal societies not having any *potestas* of their own, '*quando superior harum societatum vi potestatis sibi competentis hoc vel illud fieri vel non fieri voluit*', and (2) so far as concerns a *societas aequalis* having power of its own, when any act '*ex concluso societatis fit vel non fit*' (136). Nettelbladt is thus led to insert, at this point, a detailed theory of the acts of corporations. In its course he not only succeeds in making the Law of Nature explain nearly every one of the maxims [in regard to the acts of corporations] which had been developed by the civilian lawyers in the course of centuries of effort; he even lays down subsidiary rules of Natural Law in regard to matters (such as differences of voting power, the greater weight of the *vota saniora*, and the method of taking divisions, or *itio in partes*) which, as he himself admits, essentially depend on positive law (137). In his other treatise, where he states the positive law on these matters, he has left himself little to add; but it is noteworthy that he pronounces the treatment of a *universitas* as a *minor* to be entirely a rule of positive law (138).

Other writers on the Law of Nature show a similar inclination for dealing in considerable detail with the theory of corporate

* Nettelbladt wrote both a *Systema* of general Natural Law, and a *Systema* of general positive [German] law. In both treatises alike, when he comes to treat of the law of associations, he follows the same plan—writing a first section on the general theory of associations, and then a second section on the application of the rights of individuals to associations.

acts(139). It has already been shown, in a previous section, that the fiction of a unanimous agreement in regard to the taking of future decisions was constantly used as a way of reconciling the validity of majority-decisions with the idea (still firmly held as a matter of principle) that any unity of a number of wills must necessarily possess a contractual character. It has equally been shown that majority-decision was steadily degraded to the position of a mere exception from the general requirement of absolute unanimity, which had come to be regarded as properly applying also to the acts of corporations [no less than to those of public deliberative bodies](140). Here we need only draw attention to the fact that natural-law theory was inevitably forced, by following this line of argument, to confine the majority-principle within the narrowest possible limits, and (more especially) to extend the scope and to emphasise the inviolability of the *jura singulorum* which were regarded as sacrosanct from the rule of number(141).

Returning now to Nettelbladt's exposition of the application of the rights of individuals to 'societies', we are next confronted [after he has concluded his theory of the acts of corporations] with a view of 'things' (*Sachen*) as the objects of corporate *dominium vel quasi-dominium*.* Here he introduces [in dealing with the natural-law aspect of the matter] the notion that a 'society' may own a property peculiar to itself (*dominium solitarium*), as distinct from any joint property of the members; and he argues that Natural Law itself can provide a basis for distinguishing such '*res societatum patrimoniales*' from '*res societatum in species sic dictae*', because it can supply the criterion, 'Does *usus* belong to the *tota societas*, or does

* Gierke's analysis of Nettelbladt's exposition of the rights of *societates* (as given in his two 'systems') is somewhat difficult. Roughly we may put it as follows. Gierke argues that the exposition shows a wavering between the idea of group-life and group-action as the life and action of the Whole, and the idea of such life and action as the life and action of all the individual members—with an inclination to the latter. He has already illustrated this argument with regard to (1) the acts or decisions of associations; and he now proceeds to consider in some detail (2) the property of such bodies, (3) their by-laws or *leges*, (4) their *negotia juridica*, and (5) their obligations. Under the last head he discusses particularly Nettelbladt's view that associations have no obligation, and are not liable, in cases of delict.

His analysis next passes to (6) the rights of individual members against associations, (7) to the possibility of associations having possession or quasi-possession and (8) to legal remedies applicable to associations. Here the analysis seems to become a simple paraphrase, with less of a constructive argument running through it. The translator has not ventured to omit any part of the analysis; but he confesses that it runs into detail.

it belong to the *singula membra?'*(142). When he comes to deal with the positive-law aspect of the matter, all that he finds it necessary to do, in fitting the property of *universitates* into these two categories, is to pay attention to some few particular legal questions which arise(143).

He next deals with the *leges societatum* [or by-laws]. When he is dealing with the matter from the standpoint of Natural Law, he confines himself to the remark that, so far as regards *societates aequales cum potestate*, such *leges* or by-laws are no more than *leges conventionales*, because they are simply based on a *conclusum*; while, as regards societies with an *Imperans*, they are *leges proprie sic dictae*, because they are promulgated by the head of the society(144). When he deals with the matter from the standpoint of positive law, he goes more fully into the scope of *statuta universitatis*, which are made to include 'observances' or customary rules, regarded as tacit enactments(145).

From by-laws, he turns to the legal proceedings of corporations (*negotia juridica*), distinguishing them from the legal proceedings of individual members, and dividing them into *negotia publica* (which in turn may be subdivided into *interna* and *externa*) and *negotia privata*(146). In the same way, when he comes to expound a theory of the *obligationes societatum*, he distinguishes the obligations of individual members from those of the society itself; but all that he actually mentions under the latter head, when he is treating of the matter from the standpoint of Natural Law, is obligations arising in the course of legal proceedings [i.e. of civil litigation] (147). It is only when he is treating of obligations from the standpoint of positive law that he ever mentions obligations incurred in connection with delicts. This omission is to be explained by the fact that he regards the *universitas* as altogether incapable of *dolus* or *culpa*;* and he therefore pronounces not only against the possibility of the punishment of a *universitas*, but also against its duty to pay compensation, even when there is a question of some unauthorised act committed by all the members in their corporate capacity(148). Suddenly to deny intellect and will to a *universitas*, as Nettelbladt does in this connection, is to present the reader with a double difficulty—that of reconciling this particular opinion with

---

* On these terms, and the general problem of liability, see Pound, *Introduction to the Philosophy of Law*, c. III. The issue here raised, of the liability of groups in case of delict, may remind the English reader of some of the problems of Trade Union law.

the rest of his views, and that of understanding the opinion itself, in the form in which he proceeds to express it. Suppose, we are told, that an illegal act has been committed on the part of *omnes singuli*. Then, in so far as these *singuli, in iis quae tangunt finem communem, sunt ut unus intellectus et una voluntas*, the illegal act—though it cannot be reckoned as *factum universitatis, cujus auctor debet esse universitas*—must still be reckoned as *factum tale singulorum ex universitate, cujus coauctores sunt omnes qui constituunt universitatem* (149). [This is a perplexed saying; and] in view of the general perplexities in which he becomes involved, we can readily understand why most of the writers on Natural Law were far from sharing Nettelbladt's radical dislike of the idea of corporate delicts (150).

In dealing with rights, as well as in dealing with duties [or obligations], Nettelbladt attempts to distinguish sharply between the sphere of the community and that of individuals, pitting against the rights of any *societas*, whether inherent or acquired, the *jura singulorum* which the society cannot touch. His natural-law theory of the rights of individual members, which came to exercise a considerable influence, proceeds upon the principle that such separate rights of individuals are always present *si membra societatis, quoad punctum definiendum, ut una societas considerari nequeunt*. This, he contends, is not only the case (1) when a legal question lies altogether outside the *nexus socialis sociorum*: it is also the case (2) when, though that *nexus* is present, there is either (*a*) a question of some right of a member which is something more than that of joining in the exercise of a right belonging to the Fellowship, or (*b*) a question of a superior or separate right of a member, or of a class of members. He accordingly enumerates a list of *jura singulorum*, including

(1) all rights acquired by voluntary actions which are undertaken outside the area of the society;

(2) any right acquired by a *titulus specialis*, even though such a right may affect the society, e.g. *potestas, jura directoralia*, and *officialium jura officiis cohaerentia*;

(3) the right to appear and vote in meetings;

(4) a right of user of the *res societatis in specie sic dictae*.*

He adds, however, that all this is true with the reservation, *quatenus omnia haec jura salva obligatione, qua socius societati obstrictus*

---

* It would appear that no. 1 in this list corresponds to no. 1 in the preceding sentence; no. 2 corresponds to no. 2*b*; and no. 3 and no. 4 to no. 2*a*. (The right to attend meetings and vote, and the right of user, are rights of the individual *qua* individual; and they are thus 'something more than joining in the exercise of a right belonging to the Fellowship'.)

est, exercentur (151). When he expounds the positive law of the matter [in his other treatise], he assumes the validity of these general natural-law principles, and he only indicates some peculiar features in the rights of *universitates* [under positive law] which differentiate such rights from those of private persons (152).

He next treats of possession and quasi-possession by societies. Possession *de facto*, he holds, is certainly as much possible for a society as it is for a *persona singularis*; but it is always necessary to distinguish the case in which individuals are *de facto* possessors on their own account from that in which they enjoy such possession *societatis nomine*. Where the possession is possession *de jure*, it is again true that the rules which hold good for *singuli* are equally applicable to societies, both in regard to *jus possidendi* and in regard to *jus possessionis** (153). In dealing with possession in his treatise on positive law, Nettelbladt repeats these general principles (154), supplementing them by a careful exposition of the rules about acquiring and losing possession in cases where the other party is a *universitas* (155).

Finally he treats of *remedia juris in applicatione ad societates*. In this connection he develops a theory both of the peaceful settlement of disputes by compromise, conciliation and arbitration, and of their forcible decision by war or reprisals (156). He also propounds a theory of judicial procedure (*Gerichtshilfe*), dealing first with the power of a society to decide, in cases of dispute, in regard to rights and duties belonging to its members as members (157), and then with the position of societies when they are parties to a case (158).

It is obvious that Nettelbladt's general natural-law theory of associations represents a vigorous reaction of the German conception of Fellowship, which had never been utterly submerged, against the foreign conception of the Corporation. In his theory the *persona ficta*, affixed to the group by an act external to itself, has disappeared; and there appears instead an internally united group, shaping itself by its own power into a Whole, with a capacity both for the enjoyment of rights and for action, and yet, at the same time, assuring to each individual member his own separate sphere of activity in the community. And yet we have to confess that the corporate body so constituted is prevented by its indivi-

---

* The distinction between *jus possidendi* and *jus possessionis* is a distinction between having a legal title to possess, and having the right which arises from being in possession whether or no there is a legal title to possess.

dualistic structure from rising to the stature of a substantive Group-being. It is not distinct in kind, but only in degree, from any casual society or community. It is significant that Nettelbladt is unable to give any definition of the idea of a *universitas* other than that it involves a *societas plurium quam duorum** (159).

[Just as the natural-law theory, as it appears in Nettelbladt, seeks to abandon the Roman-law notion of the corporation, and to return to the German idea of the Fellowship, so] from another point of view, we may admit that it also breaks away from the Romanistic conceptions of *societas* and *communio* [partnership and co-ownership], and gives new life and vigour to the German conception of the 'joint hand' (*Gesamthand*).† The division of every system of common interest into separate spheres belonging to the several members is no longer regarded as necessary; on the contrary, there are seen to be various ways in which a fusion of individual spheres of interest into a single common sphere may be achieved. But our admission must at once be qualified. Natural-law thinkers were unable to express such a union of persons [in a common sphere of interest] by any legal conception other than the self-same notion of *persona moralis* which they also used to explain the 'Subject' of full corporate rights. They invoked this *persona* everywhere. They vested the community of husband and wife, the community of parents and children, the community of master and servants, with 'moral personality': they even regarded the family-community [which included all these three communities] as a moral person composed of a number of members which were moral persons themselves (160). Starting from the basis thus provided, Nettelbladt allows himself to glide imperceptibly into a Fellowship conception of the broader family-group [i.e. the 'House', including all the members of a princely or noble family]; and then

---

* The point of view of this paragraph regards the Group in itself—'Is it a Roman *universitas* or a German Fellowship?' The point of view of the next regards the Group in relation to property—'Is its property a matter of Roman *societas* and *communio*, or of German *Gesamthand*?'

† 'The intimate conjunction of two things, so that they are no longer separable (e.g. *A*'s gold and *B*'s silver to produce electrum)...sometimes produces co-ownership in the whole (*communio*)' (Poste's edition of the *Institutes of Gaius*, pp. 166–7). The difference between Roman co-ownership and the German *Gesamthand* may be roughly said to be the difference between (*a*) two or more persons each laying a hand on the same thing at the same time, and each saying, 'This is mine—up to such and such a point, though it is yours beyond', and (*b*) two or more persons laying joint hands on a property, and saying, 'This is ours, in the sense that it belongs to all of us'.

The Period from 1650 to 1800

[leaping from Fellowship to corporation, because the elastic idea of the moral person can easily be stretched to that further point] he finds himself enabled to take the rules of law relating to the rights of corporations and to apply them to the aristocratic House and the House-property belonging to the 'line' (161). Without further ado, the idea of their being separate moral persons is next applied to all the collegiate or collective organs which act on behalf of a group, and even to all the sub-groups which exist within it (162); and, finally, no objection is taken to the idea of extending a moral personality (uniting, or supposed to unite, the various parties concerned) even to cases of mere profit-making companies, or of simple co-ownership, or indeed of any other matter of common rights or common duties (163).

The distinction which properly separates a system of common relations from a system in which there is a common 'Subject' of rights was thus completely obliterated. All this tended, in no small degree, to encourage a return to Germanic conceptions of law, and to promote a more realistic treatment of the actual factors in our own domestic legal institutions; but the price which had to be paid was the sacrifice of a true conception of Group-personality (164). Only by the use of artificial arguments was it possible for this uniform theory of all societies to conceal (and then only partially) the contradictions which followed on the fitting of dissimilar things into the same Individualistic-Collectivist mould. We can trace this result [i.e. the concealing of contradictions by the use of artificial arguments] at various points.* First of all, in order to make the

---

* Gierke is here arguing that a theory which makes a Group a Collection of Individuals (under the name of *persona moralis*), and which has thus both a Collectivist and an Individualistic basis, will necessarily be inconsistent; will betray its inconsistencies when it tries to get all sorts of groups into its scheme; and will be driven to seek to conceal its inconsistencies by doing violence to one or other of its bases. (1) It will do violence to its Collectivist basis (i.e. its idea that a Group is a collective body over and above the individual members) when it tries to fit into its scheme a case of individuals owning property by 'joint hand'; for here it will make concessions to the rights of individuals which really contradict that basis. (2) It will do violence to its Individualistic basis (i.e. its other idea that a Group is only a number of individuals) when it tries to fit into its scheme the case of a corporation; for here it will make concessions to the rights of corporations which really contradict *that* basis. (3) It will do violence to both its bases when it tries to meet a case which cannot be met at all by the idea of a Collection of Individuals (in whatever way that idea may be interpreted); for here it will introduce another person, a *persona repraesentativa*, who is something more, and something above, the Collection of Individuals described under the name of *persona moralis*.

conception of the Collective person applicable to cases where there was merely a question of 'joint hand', this would-be uniform theory had to make concessions to the rights of individuals which ended in cancelling any idea of a Group-person as something distinct from the individual persons who composed it (165). Secondly, in order to combine the fact of corporate unity with its conception of the merely Collective person, the theory had to find room for principles [about the rights of Corporations] which could only be reconciled by dint of a violent interpretation with its basic idea of a Whole as something simply constituted by the addition of Individuals (166). Finally, in cases where it was forced to postulate a Group-unity which was independent of the sum of the members for the time being, the theory was forced to go altogether outside the bounds of the *persona moralis*, and to set over against it a *persona repraesentativa*, as an 'institutional' unity [i.e. a unity not inherent, but due to State-institution, and thus] created by act of commission and delegation (167).

To pursue this line of thought to its logical conclusions was, in the last result, to end by producing a total dissolution of all forms of group-existence. Curiously enough, it was the exponents of the principle of liberty of association who were most inclined to degrade the whole theory of the rights of associations into a mere form of the rights of individuals. Möser [though he was an apostle of associations] refused to acknowledge any distinction between partnership and corporation (168); and the theory of Natural Law generally ended with what we may call the evaporation of the 'moral person' into a mere terminological figure of speech (169). William von Humboldt illustrates most clearly the final consummation of this trend of thought. Concerned to substitute, wherever he can, true 'bonds of union' for the 'fetters' forged by contemporary law—to remove all permanent checks on the free individual, to make marriage freely dissoluble, to prevent legal obligations from tying the hands of future ages, to limit testamentary dispositions—he directs his ardour against 'the societies which are generally called by the name of moral, as distinct from physical, persons' (170). He argues that all moral persons have, at the very least, the same disadvantages as wills and testaments. They always involve a unity which is independent of the sum of their members and which continues over a long period of years. It is true that many of the disadvantages which they produce in Germany are only the result of their possessing exclusive privileges, which are not inherently connected with them, but in virtue of which they often become, in effect, 'political bodies'. But apart from such added privileges, and considered only in themselves, 'they bring in their train a considerable number of inconveniences. And yet their disadvantages only arise when their constitution compels all the members to use the common resources in a way they do not wish, or when, by requiring unanimity, it really forces the majority to obey the minority'. Otherwise, 'societies and associations are the surest means of fostering and advancing human development'. The best course would be that the State should simply enact 'that any moral person, or society, should only be regarded as a union of its members for the time being, so that nothing should hinder them from deciding at their discretion, by a majority of votes, on the use to be made of common powers and common resources'. Such an enactment, however, must not be allowed to involve—what has often happened where the clergy are concerned—that the members are turned into mere tools.* As for the legal regulation of all such unions—'the principles of testamentary dispositions and contract are adequate'(171).

II. GROUPS ABOVE THE STATE

International society and federations

The contradictions we find at work in the natural-law theory of corporate bodies are reflected in its treatment of super-State Groups.

The problem of the extent, and the nature, of international society still continued to be met by a variety of solutions. If the state of nature were conceived as an absolutely non-social state; and if, again, international law were regarded as simply the Law of Nature, still continuing to prevail between States because they were *personae morales* who still continued to remain in a natural state of liberty and equality—then the logical result was a total rejection of any idea of a general 'society of States'. For a time it appeared as if, owing to the prestige of Pufendorf, a view of this sort would actually hold the field(172). In the long run, however, the opposite theory triumphed. Assuming [not an original non-

---

* If a group is given liberty, by an enactment of the State to that effect, to determine freely its policy from time to time, without being restricted by the dead hand of the past, it should not use its liberty to turn its members into the tools of a particular policy, as ecclesiastical groups have often done.

social condition, but] an original community of all mankind, thinkers argued that the state of nature which continued to prevail among States must necessarily be a state of natural society. Even when they made the solitary individual their starting-point, they could still attain the same result. They could proceed to add, to their postulate of the solitary individual, the idea that the creation of a social condition was none the less to be regarded as a stage in the development of Natural Law; and they could then argue that Natural Law [in the course of its development] dictated, or at any rate postulated, a society of Nations. With this conclusion there generally went hand in hand the recognition of a body of positive international law, which was held to be due to a further development of 'natural' international law, among the society of Nations, through a process of express or tacit consent. The conception of a universal society of States was successfully vindicated by Mevius, by Leibniz, and by other opponents of the theory of Pufendorf(173): it was also maintained by Thomasius(174); and it was finally restored* in its integrity by Wolff and his successors(175). With the aid of the natural-law category of *societas aequalis*, an attempt was made to qualify the nature of this international society by adding the idea that the original liberty and equality of all the sovereign *personae morales* remained intact, notwithstanding the existence of a 'social' obligation(176). On the other hand we also find Wolff, and other writers, reviving the idea of a *civitas maxima*, and holding that every State, in its capacity of a citizen of this great City, was subject to a real group-authority(177).

The existence of particular societies of States [or federations] was also recognised by all the writers on Natural Law. [It is true that the idea of a real federation found little favour.] After Pufendorf had once rejected the notion of a 'composite State', in the form in which it had been developed on the basis of the positive law of the Holy Roman Empire, it became the orthodox, and we may almost say the unquestioned, view in the School of Natural Law that a State which stood above other States was an impossibility(178). [But other and lower forms of federation were allowed to be possible.] Not only was it admitted that relations of partnership between different States might eventually grow out of simple alliances(179); a distinction also began to be drawn between *foedera simplicia*, or mere leagues, and *systemata civitatum* which had

* Gierke is thinking of the medieval view of a single '*humana civilitas*' when he speaks here of 'restoring', and, a few lines later, of 'reviving'.

the effect of permanently uniting a number of States in a single *corpus*. These 'systems of States' were then further divided into 'unions' and 'confederations'. The term 'union', in its original connotation, was confined to a personal union(180); but the conception began to gain ground of a real union, under which some two or more States, in addition to having a common Head, had also pooled their rights of sovereignty(181). 'Confederations', or *corpora confoederatorum*, were interpreted as being Leagues of States (*Staatenbünde*) in which the sovereignty of the several States remained intact, and was only 'exercised' in common, and that, moreover, only to a limited extent—with the result that, though the whole might appear to be a State, it never really was so (182). Pufendorf applied this line of interpretation rigorously, and absolutely refused to admit the validity of majority-decisions in any form of confederation(183). But there were many who took a different line. Though they accepted the natural-law conception of the *societas aequalis* as applicable to confederations, they were none the less prepared to admit that a confederation possessed some 'social authority' of its own; and while they differed about the extent of that authority, the general result of their views was to render possible some approach to the full federal form of State (*Bundesstaat*)(184). Nor was this all. If only they cast a glance at the Holy Roman Empire, thinkers had to confess that at any rate in actual life, if not in theory, there were intermediate formations to be found, which lay mid-way between the federal form of State and the unitary State with autonomous provinces; nor could even a Pufendorf abolish those intermediate formations by declaring them 'monstrous' and 'irregular'*(185). In such cases, just as in the analogous case of the theory of the mixed constitution, the irregular forms gradually came to be treated as justifiable exceptions from the rule(186).

Finally, the conception of the federal State was again admitted to a regular place in orthodox natural-law theory. Leibniz(187) and Montesquieu(188) had already defended it to some extent: Nettelbladt restored it fully to its position(189). He made a definite

---

* Gierke's point is that thinkers were not only forced to go beyond Pufendorf's category of the confederation, and to make an approach to the federation proper, but they were also forced to recognise the *de facto* existence of a form of State which was something more than a federation, though something less than a decentralised unitary State. This intermediate form was the Holy Roman Empire, as it existed down to 1806.

distinction between all unions, or systems, and the *respublica composita* proper, in which both the whole and the part were States(190); and he found it possible, on this point as on so many others, to elicit principles from Natural Law which were curiously and admirably in accordance with the actual positive law of Germany(191).

III. GROUPS WITHIN THE STATE

The Church

When we turn to conceptions of the Church and its relations to the State, we find the natural-law theory of society exerting an overwhelming influence, and bringing under its spell, to an ever increasing degree, the whole of the literature of ecclesiastical law. The natural-law theory of the Church may thus be appropriately treated, not as a separate theme, but in its connection with the positive-law doctrine [of churches and their rights] to be found in ecclesiastical law (192).

[The section which was to have dealt with the natural-law theory of the Church after 1650, and which would thus have completed the sketch given in §14, III, was never published.]

APPENDICES

I. TROELTSCH ON NATURAL LAW AND HUMANITY
   AN ADDRESS DELIVERED ON THE SECOND ANNIVERSARY OF THE GERMAN HOCHSCHULE FÜR POLITIK, OCTOBER 1922

II. GIERKE'S CONCEPTION OF LAW

APPENDIX I

ERNST TROELTSCH

THE IDEAS OF NATURAL LAW AND HUMANITY IN WORLD POLITICS*

§. 1. The contrast between German thought and the thought of western Europe, 201. §. 2. The common European tradition of Natural Law, 205. §3. The tradition of Natural Law in western Europe since 1789, 208. §4. The development of German thought since the Romantic Movement, 209. §5. German idealism and nineteenth-century realism, 213. §6. Qualifications of the contrast between German thought and the thought of western Europe, 215. §7. The problem of modern Germany, 216. §8. The new historical attitude required in Germany, 217. §9. The new ethical attitude required, 219. §10. Spenglerism and Socialism, 220.

§1. *The contrast between German thought and the thought of western Europe*

Above the practical and temporary questions with which we are confronted to-day, there rises the theoretical and permanent problem of the difference between the German system of ideas—in politics, history and ethics—and that of western Europe and America. The latter of these systems has its marked internal discrepancies, and there are points at which it occasionally approaches the German system of ideas; but it unquestionably possesses a logical unity of its own. We only need read James Bryce's great book on *Modern Democracies* to be convinced of this fact. Similarly, in spite of all the intellectual differences which are so marked a feature in our own life, there is also a logical unity in our German system of thought. It is a unity which every foreigner immediately feels, even if he cannot define it. If he is unfavourably inclined towards us, he recognises it instantly, with a sort of instinctive aversion, as something alien; while conservatives in all countries, and especially in northern Europe (though we have to remember that northern Europe is largely under the intellectual influence of Germany) feel a natural kinship with it. If you enter into conversation with the Dutch or the Scandinavians, you soon learn much which is valuable and instructive in this respect; and in the field of scholarship the works of Kjellén† supply clear evidence of the affinity. One thing which is obvious, from the very start, is that our world of ideas is confined to a

---

* Humanity (*Humanität*) means the unity of mankind, or what Dante calls *humana civilitas*. The idea that all men form a single society is naturally associated (as it was by the Stoics and by medieval writers) with the idea of a single Natural Law common to that society. (The division of Troeltsch's essay into sections, and the headings of the sections, are due to the translator.)

† The reference is to R. Kjellén's *Die Groszmächte vor und nach dem Weltkriege*, a descriptive work of political geography.

much smaller area and a far smaller population. That is the real reason why German propaganda was ineffective during the War. Even if we had possessed more adroitness, and a greater psychological gift for understanding other peoples, we could not have bridged the gulf. Neither side had the power—to say nothing of the inclination—to understand the other; and of the two sides, ours was the one which was both isolated and numerically inferior.

The same contrast also appears, in an acute form, in our own internal political struggles. It supplies telling catchwords to those who seek to interpret the obvious fact of a real and practical struggle, between the different classes and interests in the nation, as a conflict of moral and theoretical principles; who desire to transform the clashes of interests which have arisen from purely natural causes into a 'spiritual conflict', and hope, in that way, to produce acute and fundamental divisions. The designation of 'western' has thus come to be applied (as it is in Russia) to all movements in favour of democracy, or pacifism, or national self-determination, or a League of Nations, or the attainment of international understanding; and such movements are then opposed to the specifically 'German' way of thought, with its historical and organic character. This is simply the old external contrast reappearing in a new and internal form; and it is applied by the very same means which were used by the propaganda of the Entente in the War. The war-cries which then divided the nations are being imported to-day into our midst.

The fundamental difference between the two worlds of thought is thus clear enough in actual fact. It is something which can everywhere be felt. But what is the origin of the difference? What is the genuine essence of the thought of western Europe, and what is the essence, in contradistinction to it, of the German scheme of thought? In answering such questions, we are brought up against the conceptions of Natural Law and Humanity, with the notion of Progress now added as the modern corollary of both. These conceptions, in turn, are closely connected with all the fundamental ideas of the general culture and the religious life of Europe. Their original roots go far deeper than the revolutionary zeal of modern times: they run down into the spiritual development of some thousands of years, though they have been made to assume very various forms in the course of their long history. The attitude we adopt towards these conceptions determines the parting of the ways. In Germany we are unprepared, and disinclined, to understand this divergence; we are even unable to comprehend properly the terms 'Natural Law' and 'Humanity', by which the divergence has just been suggested; and our failure is answered, on the other side, by a misunderstanding and misinterpretation of our ideas, which is if anything still more drastic. We must therefore go deeper into the matter in the course of our argument; and first of all we must explain the significance attached in western Europe to the terms 'Natural Law' and 'Humanity', which have now become almost incomprehensible in Germany, and have lost altogether their original life and colour.

It is essential to remember, in dealing with these terms, that we are dealing with something more than merely modern, or merely west-European, conceptions. We are face to face with ideas which are both of great antiquity (they go back to classical and Christian thought) and of general European scope; ideas which are the basis of our European philosophy of history and ethics; ideas which have been closely connected, for thousands of years, with theology and humanism. Remembering the age and range of these ideas, we can understand the innumerable applications and modifications which they have undergone, and the far-reaching practical effects which they have produced. German conceptions, in comparison, are new and modern; they are inchoate—uncorroborated by the process of world history—undigested in theory. The force of conservatism and the weight of numbers are both on the side of the tradition of western Europe. This may seem paradoxical, all the more as German thought professes to be essentially progressive, democratic and favourable to the cause of revolution. But it is just this paradox which we have to master and understand.

In the first place, the contrast of 'conservative' and 'revolutionary' is one which has to be banished from the whole problem. It has only come into existence as the result of very recent complications: it is only in German thought that it is regarded as fundamental; and the reason why we take that view is that the modern democratic movement—which flows inevitably from the increase of population and the education of the masses—has only just begun to assert itself among us, and has done so in a series of revolutions. In its own nature, and apart from these temporary conditions, democracy may well assume a conservative form. American democracy, in its political and social aspects, tends to issue in the strictest conservatism; it regards its principles as the eternal and divine commands of morality and of law. The same is also true, if to a less extent, of English democracy as it has developed since 1832; it shows, as we all know, a fundamentally conservative character. Even the French regard the glory of their Revolution as the final victory of the eternal moral order of mankind, and worship it as a sempiternal dogma which is the salvation of all humanity. The real revolutionary element, in all these three countries, has transferred itself to the sphere of social and Socialistic movements; and the political constitution of the democratic type is now left to wear its historical nimbus and to show its fundamentally bourgeois character. The revolutions to which democracy owes its origin belong to a far distant epoch; and they are already sanctified by history. This is the reason why it is much more difficult for Socialism to assert itself in these countries than it is in ours.

German thought, on the other hand, whether in politics or in history or in ethics, is based on the ideas of the Romantic Counter-Revolution. This was a movement which began by seeking to clear away the postulates of west-European thought, along with the scientific basis of mathematico-physical principles on which they rested. It proceeded to erect, both in the sphere of the State and in that of Society at large, the 'organic' ideal of a group-mind (*Gemeingeist*)—an ideal half aesthetic and half religious, but instinct throughout with a spirit of antibourgeois idealism. Finally, on the basis of this ideal, and in order to give it form and substance, Romanticism sought to remedy the political disunity of Germany by the erection of a powerful unitary State. As Germany pursued the complicated course of its intellectual and political history, during the nineteenth century, the thread of this guiding idea, as we shall see, was again and again interrupted, and it was repeatedly entangled in compromises which sometimes ended in making it entirely untrue to itself. None the less, it is this German system of Romantic thought which is really responsible for producing the differences—differences that cut so deep, and may be traced in so many directions—between the two opposing camps.

Here we touch the core of the contrast. We begin to see, on the one side, an eternal, rational and divinely ordained system of Order, embracing both morality and law; we begin to see, on the other, individual, living, and perpetually new incarnations of an historically creative Mind. Those who believe in an eternal and divine Law of Nature, the Equality of man, and a sense of Unity pervading mankind, and who find the essence of Humanity in these things, cannot but regard the German doctrine as a curious mixture of mysticism and brutality. Those who take an opposite view—who see in history an ever-moving stream, which throws up unique individualities as it moves, and is always shaping individual structures on the basis of a law which is always new—are bound to consider the west-European world of ideas as a world of cold rationalism and equalitarian atomism, a world of superficiality and Pharisaism. All this needs, and must duly receive, an explanation in greater detail. We shall accordingly sketch the main lines of the common European tradition; and then we shall first of all trace the development of that common tradition into the political and moral ideology of western Europe, and afterwards seek to follow the course of German romantic ideology, through the various phases of its evolution, until we come to the historical realism of the present day.

There is one fact which must not be forgotten in this connection. It is the Germany of Protestantism and Lutheranism, of Classicism and Romanticism, which presents us with difficulties of interpretation. Catholicism* stands much closer to the common tradition of Europe: it can understand that tradition better: it can come more easily to an understanding with its modern developments. There are, indeed, some elements in Catholicism—elements which go back to the medieval system of Estates, or are derived from medieval mysticism—that connect it in some degree with Romanticism, and have produced a deceptive appearance of its special affinity to that movement. But the real genius of Catholicism is severely rational, and it is directed, as such, to Natural

* So far as I follow Troeltsch's thought, he is drawing a distinction between the two Germanies—that of the Lutheran north, and that of the Catholic south and west.

Law and the idea of a common Humanity based on the rational and religious unity of all mankind.* It is this tendency that constantly reappears as the main characteristic of the Catholic system of legal and political ideas. It is a tendency which is still of practical importance to-day, and really determines the policy of Catholicism.

§2. *The common European tradition of Natural Law*

The ideas from which our argument starts are the ideas of a Law of Nature, of Humanity, and of Progress. They are ideas which are closely connected with one another, alike in the common tradition of Europe at large and in the scheme of thought peculiar to western Europe; but of the three it is the idea of Progress which is being particularly applied, and has been especially elaborated, in connection with modern life. The origin of this general philosophy is to be found in the later period of classical antiquity—in the Stoic theory of Greece and Rome, and especially of Rome; in Cicero and in certain elements of Roman Law; and finally, and above all, in the combination of these factors with Christian ideology to form the Christian system of Natural Law. The fundamental conception is that of the dignity of the common element of human Reason, as it appears in every individual; and this conception, in turn, goes back to that of a 'common law', pervading all nature and the whole universe, and proceeding from a divine principle of Reason which expresses itself increasingly in the successive stages of created beings. The true nature of man is assumed to be the divine Reason operating in him, with its sovereignty over the senses and affections. Several conclusions are directly derived from this assumption. It explains the claim which the individual makes, and the duty which he admits, that Reason should be acknowledged to be the Natural—which is also to say the Divine—Law. Again, it provides the foundation of all human legal institutions, which thus become directly identical, in the last analysis, with moral principles. Finally, it furnishes the ideal of a single organisation or society of all mankind.

The general background of these ideas is Pantheism, which first in Rome, and then, and above all, in Christianity, passes into Theism and a belief in an overruling Providence. The whole system of thought is innocent of any revolutionary intention; but it implies, none the less, a radical renunciation of the empirical world of actual fact. In the beginning, in the golden age, men started with liberty, equality, fraternity. The almost invincible force of human affections and passions led to struggle and self-seeking. But that self-same Reason which is the source of the dignity of individuals maintained itself in the face of these consequences, and created the necessary means for their repression—law, force, authority and property. This result once achieved, it now becomes the ideal of Natural Law to achieve a rational organisation of all

* Catholicism believes not in a diversified world of 'unique individualities', but in a single *respublica Christiana*, amenable to a single law.

these means which shall be compatible with the natural rights that belong to the dignity of man. This leads to the idea of a cosmopolis, or world-State, in which all men are at one, and which is best organised as a monarchy, because monarchy is the reflection and mirror of the divine government of the world.

The whole of this system of ideas was adopted by Christianity as a necessary supplement, or complement, to its own other-worldly and eschatological ethics, which stood helpless before the practical problems of actual society. The Christian doctrine of inherited sin made the system still more conservative in character: it made the means of repression provided by positive law appear to be far more sacrosanct, and even divine. While positive law was thus consecrated, natural rights were also attenuated. The realm of Natural Law was overshadowed and dominated by the Kingdom of God, or the Church; and in this way, and on the assumption that nature could never be free from the taint of sin, the natural-law principles of autonomy and rational self-realisation were kept within definite limits and prevented from going too far.

It was this combination of Stoic theory with Christianity that produced the Christian system of Natural Law which held sway for a thousand years, and dominated the theology, the jurisprudence, the political theory, the politics, and the history of the Middle Ages. We may admit that the influence of medieval society (which was based on the institution of different corporate Estates) led the Christian system of Natural Law to ally itself with a theory of the organic differentiation of the social Whole into unequal parts, associated together on a principle of division of labour which assigned different functions to each.* But this theory could, with the help of Aristotle,† be treated as a necessary consequence of the order of nature, and thus be interpreted as part of the essence of natural ethics and natural law; and by its side, and under its cover, the purely individualistic ideas of Natural Law still survived in their full vigour. Nor did they only survive in theory: they also asserted themselves actively, in all sorts of radical revolts among the various 'sects',‡ until they culminated in Ockham's theory of the State and the Jesuit views on the right of revolution. There are always two separate inspirations—the organic and the individualistic—in the 'natural' social theories of the Middle Ages; and however closely they

---

* I.e. the three Estates of clergy, nobility and commons were held to form a 'body politic', or political organism, which started from the principle of the inequality of the different parts, and of their contributing different and unequal functions to the common life of the organism.

† Aristotle's theory of κοινωνία assumes that it is naturally based on the existence of various mutually complementary parts, which attain a higher and more self-sufficient life by exchanging their different products.

‡ In his *Soziallehren der Christlichen Kirchen* (II, §9), Troeltsch traces the social ideas of the various dissident or nonconformist 'sects' of the Middle Ages.

may be connected in theory, it is always a question which of the two will actively come to the front.

It was on the basis of this Christian system of Natural Law that there developed the modern and secular system of Natural Law which we find in the writings of Bodin, Grotius, Hobbes, Pufendorf, Althusius and many less famous thinkers. Their object was partly to explain the absolutist governments which had been produced by the movement of events, and partly (at a later stage) to justify the emancipation of the citizen from such governments, and to proceed to the erection of new political ideals upon that basis. The double aspect of Natural Law still persisted. On the one hand, it was argued that the very nature of a community inevitably involved Rule and Sovereignty, and that it was necessary for a power to exist which could introduce order among sinful men—indeed it was even argued that the rights of the people had been absolutely transferred to such a governing power; and such arguments were supported by theological doctrines about the rights of 'the powers that be' and the designs of Providence. On the other hand, the movements opposed to absolutism sought comfort and countenance in ideas of inherent and indestructible human rights which were based upon the divinely appointed order of the Universe. In the course of developments such as these many new movements of thought naturally made themselves felt. The Humanistic revival of classical learning, and the new growth of atomical natural science, provided a variety of new ideas and methods. But the old terminology, and the old basic ideas, still persisted; and such new movements as appeared are almost exclusively to be found on the radical and progressive side—the side which had transcended the natural right of absolutism in favour of a popular and radical doctrine of the natural rights of man, and which came, in process of time, to be called the School of Natural Law *par excellence*. Here the doctrine of inherited sin has crumbled away; and its place has been taken by a convinced optimism in regard to human nature and reason and a belief that, if left to themselves, men will follow the lead of their natural interest in the community, and will solve every problem rationally by the standard of utility. The disintegration of the Church into separate churches and sects, coupled with a new spirit of religious individualism, removes the control of public life by the Church, and issues in demands for freedom of conscience and the separation of Church and State. The natural sciences bring into the common stock the analogy of their own fundamental atomism and of the natural rational laws by which atoms are organised. In all these ways the idea of a steadily moving Progress, and the ideal of a rational self-development of Society and the State, are evolved from the old and predominantly conservative Natural Law of the Church.

§3. *The tradition of Natural Law in western Europe since* 1789

Secular and progressive as it may be, this new Natural Law still continues, none the less, to find its basis in God's ordinance. It is closely connected with rationalistic theology: it can even be the ally of Calvinism, in the extremer forms of that doctrine. With all its zest for progress, the theory still remains moderate: it retains a conservative and bourgeois character. Even in the writings of Rousseau, where the idea of Natural Law finds its most revolutionary application, it has still a profoundly religious basis; and indeed—as a force impelling men in the direction of political institutions which are simple, clear and austere —it is sharply contrasted with the so-called 'progress of civilisation'. Not until the days of the French Revolution do we find the idea of Natural Law directed along the line of pure and radical Progress, and pressing towards the goal of absolute popular Sovereignty within the area of a great modern State; and the French Revolution, for that very reason, marks a break with the Church and the whole of the past. In the Anglo-Saxon world, the new idea of Natural Law is essentially a demand for personal liberty, the free choice of rulers, and the people's right of controlling the conduct of affairs by the rulers they have chosen: in France, it is a proclamation of the theory of direct self-government, the principle of political equality, and the participation of all its members in the control of the State. A deep division is here involved—the division between democracy proper and a system which should be designated as Liberalism rather than democracy. Besides this cleavage, and in addition to it, the practical application of this new natural-law idea of Humanity has produced, in the course of time, a great number of other antinomies and problems, which have not only gradually cooled the original ardour of its adherents, but also make any theoretical exposition of the idea to-day exceedingly difficult, complicated and self-contradictory. The difficulty can be traced in the discreet and quietly elegiac exposition of James Bryce, a widely travelled observer equally versed in theory and affairs. He is conscious throughout his book (*Modern Democracies*) that he is describing the main political forces behind a development extending over a century and a half, and covering the greater part of the world, as far afield as Australia and New Zealand. This is the ground of his confidence in the type of government he describes and in the permanence of the type. On the other hand, the jurist Laski,* in his *Foundations of Sovereignty*, believes that the modern idea of parliamentary democracy is in a state of collapse; but what he is really attacking in that idea is the relics of the old natural-law theory of absolutism, and he is attacking them in the cause of a higher Humanity and real Progress.

In spite of what has been said about its antinomies and its problems, this general body of thought remains something in the nature of a consistent whole; and if it is challenged in its fundamental principles,

* H. J. Laski, Professor of Political Science in the London School of Economics.

or has to face an opposition which menaces it politically, it can be rallied together in some sort of unity to meet the challenge. The reaction against it which appeared in Positivism has made no essential change in its nature. Positivists, in the last resort, are equally anxious for the unity of mankind, and they equally desire its organisation on the basis of natural laws, with due recognition of the individual's human rights and his claims to happiness. Socialism itself, in western Europe, is willing to dress its demands in the terminology of Natural Law and Humanity: it simply extends the demands for political equality and liberty to the economic sphere; and it expects the consummation for which it longs, and the coming of an ideal condition of all mankind, from the operation of the general laws of the order of the world. We need not be astonished, therefore, to find that this system of ideas, in spite of its imperfections, and notwithstanding its divisions, was able to form a common front in the hour of need against German ideology, or that it could evoke, to meet the challenge of 'German barbarism', the enthusiastic instincts of all who believed in universal ends common to all mankind—in Humanity, the cause of Natural Law, and the moral rules of Nature. Pacifism, and a belief in a League of Nations, which very naturally came to be used in their own interests by those who were originally impelled towards them by their genuine convictions, are tendencies which readily originate in this general scheme of thought:* they can be viewed as the dictates of God, of Nature, of Humanity. Another result, which follows as readily, is a gospel of liberty which would bring enslaved and backward peoples, with or without their own consent, under a régime of self-determination and self-government, and which seeks to ensure, by reward and punishment, the maintenance of that régime. It was only the other day that a judge of the Supreme Court of the United States, C. E. Hughes, delivered a course of lectures to students, describing democracy as the form of constitution which, if it was the most difficult, and if it made the greatest moral demands on its members, was yet the form dictated by God, by Nature and by Humanity. In his introduction to the German translation of these lectures, D. J. Hill, the former American ambassador in Berlin, makes the characteristic remark, that the lecturer never mentions the essential premiss on which his lectures are based—the natural and divine foundation of the rights of man—simply because it is self-evident to all Americans.

§4. *The development of German thought since the Romantic Movement*

The intellectual thought of Germany originally shared in this general system of ideas, or at any rate it shared in the conception of a Christian Law of Nature which was the basis of the system. It goes without saying

* I.e. the peoples of western Europe, who held convictions about a Law of Nature and Humanity, were impelled by those convictions towards a belief in a League of Nations and a gospel of Pacifism; and they naturally used that belief and gospel to support their own side in the War ('the war to end war').

that the Germany of the Middle Ages was no less dominated by the idea of a Christian Law of Nature than the rest of western Europe; and even to-day the idea of that Law still persists in the ranks of German Catholicism. Luther, too, and the older and orthodox form of Protestantism generally, shared this inheritance; but an excess of emphasis on original sin, and a corresponding excess of emphasis on mere authority—the authority of the powers created by historic development, and thus, as it were, legitimised by Providence—invested Lutheran doctrine with a peculiar tinge of authoritarian conservatism, which the close connection of Church and State in the Lutheran system served to strengthen. The result was that, for practical purposes, the natural-law ideas of western Europe only affected Germany in the sadly attenuated form of enlightened despotism; and even the theoretical protagonists of that law, such as Wolff and Kant, proclaimed its principles with considerable reservations—reservations in favour of the actual historical environment which, as it impinges upon those principles, gradually subjects them to a rational process of modification.

The peculiarity of German thought, in the form in which it is nowadays so much emphasised, both inside and outside Germany, is primarily derived from the Romantic Movement, which itself is simply a development, a *progressio ad infinitum*, of the classical spirit of antiquity. Romanticism too is a revolution, a thorough and genuine revolution: a revolution against the respectability of the bourgeois temper and against a universal equalitarian ethic: a revolution, above all, against the whole of the mathematico-mechanical spirit of science in western Europe, against a conception of Natural Law which sought to blend utility with morality, against the bare abstraction of a universal and equal Humanity. Confronted with the eruption of west-European ideas of Natural Law, and with the revolutionary storms by which they were accompanied, Romanticism pursued an increasingly self-conscious trend of development in the opposite direction of a conservative revolution. In the spirit of the contemplative and the mystic, the Romanticists penetrated behind the rich variety of actual life to the inward forces by which it was moved, and sought to encourage the play of those forces in a steady movement towards a rich universe of unique and individual structures of the creative human mind. From this point of view Romanticism too connects itself naturally with historic tradition—not, it is true, with the theological and scientific elements in that tradition which magnified the idea of Natural Law, but rather with mystical and poetical tendencies,* which were entirely free from the influence of any such idea. The thought of Romanticism is directed to the particular, the positive: to what is eternally productive of new variety, constructive, spiritually organic: to plastic and super-personal creative forces, which build from time to time, out of the material of particular individuals, a spiritual Whole, and on the basis of that Whole proceed from time to

* I.e. the historic tradition of Romanticism goes back to the German mystics, and to the old Teutonic poetry of the Volsungs which inspired Wagner.

time* to create the particular political and social institutions which embody and incarnate its significance.

Here we touch the essence of the peculiar form which German Romanticism assumed. Writers such as Wordsworth† and Byron, Victor Hugo and de Vigny, and more especially Leopardi, use the old Stoic conception of Nature, and measuring thereby the claims for happiness made by the modern spirit they arrive at pessimism and *Weltschmerz*. Schopenhauer was the only thinker who followed that line in Germany. German Romanticism in general derived from its conception of individuality a new principle of reality, of morality, and of history. The decisive factor in this connection was a feeling, half mystical and half metaphysical, which interpreted the idea of individuality as meaning the particular embodiment from time to time assumed by the Divine Spirit, whether in individual persons or in the super-personal organisations of community-life. (1) The basis of Reality was regarded as consisting, not in material and social atoms on a footing of equality with one another, or in universal laws of nature by which these atoms were combined, but in personalities constantly moving to different specific forms, and in plastic forces constantly at work on a process of individualisation. (2) This in turn resulted in a totally different view of Humanity. Instead of ideas of the equal dignity of Reason everywhere, and of the fulfilment of universal law, we have the conception of a purely personal and unique realisation of the capacities of Mind in every direction, primarily in individual persons, but secondarily also in communities themselves. (3) The result of that conception, in turn, was a different theory of Community. Contract and rationally purposive construction were no longer regarded as the factors which created the State and Society out of individuals. The true factors were rather to be found in super-personal spiritual forces, radiating from individuals who laid the foundations of social life;‡ in the National Mind (*Volksgeist*); in the 'Idea' of the Good and the Beautiful. (4) Along with this different idea of Community there goes a different ideal for mankind in general —not the ideal of a final union of fundamentally equal human beings in a rationally organised community of all mankind, but the ideal of a wealth of national minds, all struggling together and all developing thereby their highest spiritual powers; in a word, the ideal of a mirror of God presented by a number of national Minds, all lifted above the world of utility and material welfare. (5) Add these factors together, and you substitute the idea of Development for the old idea of Progress. You abandon a world where men are always seeking, on the basis of equality and by a mere process of incessant climbing, to increase

* '*Jeweils*', which I have translated by the phrase 'from time to time', recurs again and again in Troeltsch's argument. It implies a constant genesis, or re-genesis—as opposed to creation once and for all.

† An English reader naturally feels that Wordsworth, who wrote the *Ode to Duty* and *The Happy Warrior*, has here fallen into the wrong company.

‡ Compare Carlyle's teaching in *Heroes and Hero-worship*.

the range of reason, well-being, liberty and purposive organisation, until they attain the goal of the unity of mankind. You enter a world in which there is a hierarchy of qualitatively different cultures—a world in which the people that from time to time enjoys the hegemony hands on the torch to the next; a world in which all peoples must be put together, as mutual complements to one another, in order to represent the totality of the life-process. (6) The basis of the whole scheme of thought is ultimately a metaphysic in which individuality, plurality and pantheism are combined. It is a metaphysic which stands in sharp contrast to the pantheism of the Stoics, with its monistic trend, its identification of morality with material well-being, its reference of everything to a single law: it is a metaphysic which equally stands in contrast to Christian Theism, and also to naturalistic Deism. Here we ultimately come upon the final and deepest difference between Germany and western Europe; and it is a difference which perhaps goes back as far as the days of Master Eckhard and Leibniz.*

The general system of ideas we have just described was developed by our classical philosophers and their contemporaries—Hegel and the Historical School; and it was developed on every side, as a new philosophy of nature, history, ethics, aesthetics, religion and politics. It is as a philosophy of politics, in particular, that its influence has been most permanently important, both for international relations and in the general divergence of views which it has helped to produce. (1) When the State becomes the embodiment and expression of a particular spiritual world as it exists at a given time, the justice and law it enforces also become particular and positive. Law ceases to be a mere non-spiritual product of authority: it becomes the peculiar expression—the expression at a given time, conditioned by the circumstances of that time—of a world of ideas engaged in the process of organising itself in an external and legal form. The result of this view is a total and fundamental dissolution of the idea of a universal Natural Law; and henceforth Natural Law disappears almost completely in Germany. Law too, like other things, becomes something particular and positive, which only belongs to a given time and period. (2) Not only so, but morality proper—morality in the strict sense of the word—becomes altogether a matter of the inner self, in its own particular spiritual substance. The moral code is distinguished not only from the rules of Law, but also from the demands and requirements of social well-being. This conception served as a solvent to the combination of law, morality and social well-being which was prevalent in western Europe, and which, indeed, went back through the Middle Ages to Stoicism. It made Law something which lay outside the bounds of morality. (3) In addition, however, to this development, there was also another, which was its

* In other words, it was not, after all, Romanticism and Hegel which first divided Germany from the West: it was the mysticism of Eckhart (A.D. 1300), and the philosophy of Leibniz (1700), with its relativism and its doctrine of immanence.

converse. This de-moralised Law was associated, in virtue and in consequence of a basic philosophy of Pantheism, with the idea of a spiritual and divine essence inherent in the community.* This meant a deification of the actual particular State; and this deification not only excluded the possibility of any revolutionary impulse, or indeed of any human initiative which was merely a matter of 'personal accident'— it ultimately resulted in the mystical elevation of every State, even the State which was actually as imperfect as it could be, to the position of a sort of deity. (4) The whole of this line of argument assumed the inequality of individuals; and this inequality, even if it did not result in the individual being treated as a minor, or divested of his autonomy, involved at any rate the necessity of a system of social grades, social complements, and a social hierarchy. It placed leadership in the hands of great men, from whom the spirit of the Whole essentially radiated, and by whom it was organised. The result was an aristocratic bias and a pyramidal system of graded Estates, utterly repugnant to all the ideas of western Europe about political equality, and only artificially connected with the ideas of organic social unity which the Middle Ages had sought to formulate in Aristotelian terms.† Viewed in its results, the contrast between Germany and western Europe is complete and all-pervading. On the other hand, we have to admit that there is no real difference between them in regard to the value to be assigned to the free personality itself. And we must also admit that criticism of German thought, on the ground of its break with historic tradition, can only be properly applied with any rigour after allowance has first been made for the novelty of the German conception of the philosophy of history, as compared with the somewhat mechanical view of history which is connected with the Christian and secular doctrines of Natural Law.

§ 5. *German idealism and nineteenth-century realism*

It was not fated that this German system of ideas should be given the opportunity of a free and unprejudiced development, in the course of which it could correct and purify its principles by actual trial and experiment. It was only a handful of the great men who belonged to the age of the War of Liberation that could work and think in these terms. There came, after 1815, a return of the old enlightened despotism; and for want of a better object, that despotism was made the legatee of the new system of ideas. The result was a certain narrowing and hardening of the system. Then there arose the necessity, before anything else could

* I.e. *Recht* is *Volksrecht*: *Volksrecht* is the product of a *Volksgeist*: the *Volksgeist* is an embodiment and 'objectification' of the Eternal Mind. Thus Law is 'associated with the spiritual and divine essence of the community'. Because it is the expression of *mens populi*, and *mens populi* is an expression of *mens Dei*, it attains a sort of divinity.

† The use of Aristotle's theory of 'genesis', proceeding through successive stages or degrees, to foster the idea of a social *Stufenfolge*, is explained in Troeltsch's *Soziallehren der christlichen Kirchen*, pp. 270 sqq.

be done, of constructing from the resources of the German spirit and of German culture a new and united Germany: there came contact and struggle with a new wave of west-European thought: there came the disillusionment of the old belief in spiritual forces, after the collapse of the revolution of 1848: there came, ultimately, the realism of the Bismarckian epoch, engaged in a struggle with a sea of troubles, and seeking to wrest from that struggle the realisation of political unity. The result of all these factors was the conversion of the original idealism into a stern realism. It is true that the fundamental ideas of Romanticism still continued to be held; nor was there any return to the Law of Nature and the ideas with which it was allied. But the conception of a wealth of unique National Minds turns into a feeling of contempt for the idea of Universal Humanity: the old pantheistic deification of the State becomes a blind worship of success and power; the Romantic Revolution sinks into a complacent contentment with things as they are. From the idea of the particular law and right of a given time, men proceed to a merely positive acceptance of the State: morality of the spiritual order, transcending bourgeois convention, passes into moral scepticism; and the urgent movement of the German mind towards a political form and embodiment ends merely in the same cult of imperialism which is rampant everywhere. Caught in an obscure welter of motives, thought turned readily in the direction of Darwinism—a philosophy which, distorted from the ideas of its author, was playing havoc with political and moral ideas in western Europe as well as in Germany. Henceforth the political thought of Germany is marked by a curious dualism, which cannot but impress every foreign observer. Look at one of its sides, and you will see an abundance of remnants of Romanticism and lofty idealism: look at the other, and you will see a realism which goes to the verge of cynicism and of utter indifference to all ideals and all morality; but what you will see above all is an inclination to make an astonishing combination of the two elements—in a word, to brutalise romance, and to romanticise cynicism. One especially dangerous method for the making of such combinations was offered by the later phases of the teaching of Nietzsche. In himself, Nietzsche was essentially and thoroughly sympathetic with the very trend of development in German thought of which we have already spoken; but his peculiar combination of romanticism and materialism led none the less to his lending the brilliance of a fine poetic diction to aid the sad confusion into which that trend was falling. By the side of Nietzsche we may also place the philosophy of Marxism, itself a child of the romantic philosophy of history, but a child which attempted to banish the spiritual and moral elements in its parent, and largely borrowed its own ethics (so far as such an element can be attributed to it at all) from the revolutionary theory of Natural Law current in western Europe. Bismarck, Nietzsche and Marx—these are the three who, in their different ways, have at once fostered and dissipated the movement of the ideas of romanticism. Fundamentally, however, the stream is still there: it is still a flowing river; and to-day we can hear once more the great murmur of its waters everywhere.

§6. *Qualifications of the contrast between German thought and the thought of western Europe*

The differences between Germany and western Europe are now clear and intelligible. But it is only in a purely theoretical and extreme formulation that they appear to be so clear-cut. In actual life pure theory is never sovereign; and peoples are much more akin in reality than they are bound to appear in the light of theories. What is true of the theories themselves is equally true of their development. Here that development has been sketched entirely as a matter of the logical evolution of principles. In actual life, the growth and development of these theories is inevitably connected with the concrete needs and the active interests of the practical position at the time. The idea of Natural Law itself, in the ancient world, sprang from a strong current towards individualism which was inherent in the actual social life of a universal empire; and each new development of that idea was produced in its turn by the practical necessities of the general conjuncture of affairs in each new phase of history. In the same way, but to an even greater degree, German theories were originally the product of the idealism of a small cultural *élite*, destitute of a State, and therefore intent on the things of the mind; and the changes which they underwent were due to a practical impulse towards their political embodiment, which was itself developed in the course of great European conflicts. It is not a simple matter of two logical alternatives, of which one is adopted here and the other there, and either is then developed on its own basis, with the primary purpose of satisfying the demands of consistency, in order that they may be pitted as rival systems and engage in an opinionated struggle against one another. It is rather a question of systems of thought which are connected with actual situations and actual needs, and which, because they are thus connected with real life, are generally defended not only on grounds of theory, but also, and indeed primarily, on the ground of their practical effects and advantages. This is a point which Bryce explicitly makes in dealing with the thought of western Europe: but the same line of argument is equally, or even more, common in Germany. Here too we find practical arguments used; and here too appeals are made to the actual psychological nature of the nation, the unique character of the historical destinies of Germany, and the difficulties of political geography which she has had to encounter. Paul Joachimsen, in an excellent essay on *The Psychology of the German State*, has recently illustrated this practical method of approach.

Nor must we forget that the differences of which we have spoken are, in the last analysis, less mutually exclusive than they appear at first sight to be. Both systems postulate the idea of the autonomy of man and of personality: both postulate that critical attitude towards experience and tradition which was the product of the Age of Enlightenment. It is true that this ideal of the autonomous personality is only a sort of common ingredient in two different systems which still remain fundamentally different: it is also true that any attempt to develop this ideal logically involves some difficulties for both. But from our present point of view—which is that of seeking to understand the purely theoretical elaboration of which the contrast between Germany and western Europe is capable, and the actual use which was made of it, for purposes of propaganda, in the Great War—we must forget the practical qualifications of the contrast, and neglect the internal contradictions and limitations in either of the opposing views. So regarded, the two systems confront us purely as systems, and either seeks to vanquish the other as a code of ethics and a school of philosophy. The most definite formulation, the clearest differentiation, are then the methods attempted, with the object of mobilising every moral instinct against the opposing side.

§7. *The problem of modern Germany*

If we would simply understand these differences, we are thus entirely justified in treating them on this ground of pure theory, and in this concentrated form. On the other hand we are bound, as soon as we rise above the immediate objectives of war, to regard any understanding we have attained as simply a preliminary basis, on which our wills can then proceed to adopt an attitude and make a decision in regard to these differences—or even to build a bridge and attempt a reconciliation between them. But the fundamental question to which we naturally come in the last resort is this: 'Who is in the right in this conflict of views?' Perhaps we ought to restate the question; and remembering that on this issue, more than on others, it is impossible to be lifted above the strife in a temper of complete dispassionateness, and that each of us is bound, after all, to judge the issue primarily from the point of view of his own nation and its history, we ought to ask, 'To what extent are we perhaps compelled by this conflict to correct our German theories, since it has undeniably dealt them some shrewd blows, on some of their essential points, and since we cannot possibly evade our difficulties by any sort of appeal to Kant and the German Age of Enlightenment?' For a glance at the great main features of our development will teach us, beyond any shadow of doubt, that in all our views of history and politics and ethics we bear the stamp and show the influence of the post-Kantian period, far more than we do of the period of Kant. Indeed it is as clear as anything can be that it was really the post-Kantian age which first revealed the wealth and the depth of the historical approach to reality.

We need not enquire whether such self-analysis and self-criticism can have any effect on the general position of international affairs. That is a separate and independent question; and that field is still predominantly one of conflict and the deliberate fanning of the flames of difference. What we have really to face is a problem which springs from ourselves, and has its roots in our own actual duty of self-analysis, at this tragic hour of our national destiny and in the stress of the spiritual crisis which it imposes upon us. Our primary concern is not with propaganda and apologetics for the world outside: it is with order and clarity at home, and among ourselves.

§8. *The new historical attitude required*

We can only find a solution of this problem if we apply two standards of judgment. We may ask, first of all, whether our theories actually justify themselves by providing a clue to the meaning of history; we may ask, in the second place, how they stand related to the fundamental demands of ethics. Let us attempt, in conclusion, to give the briefest of answers to our final problem, along each of these lines of enquiry. A full answer can only be given after a long effort of investigation by our historical and moral sciences. That is the new labour that confronts us; it is the duty laid upon us by the spiritual disturbances which the War has produced. All that can here be attempted is some indication of the main lines on which such an effort must proceed, if ever we are really to solve the grave questions which have been raised by the world-propaganda against us.

Pursuing first the historical line of enquiry, we may fairly urge that German theories, in virtue of the very idea of individuality which has formed their basis, have contributed in a remarkable degree to historical investigation and the understanding of history. They have taught the world the nature of historical thought: they have created the historical sense, as a specific and definite thing. This is the advance which they mark on the historiography of the Age of Enlightenment, and on the later historians who wrote in the spirit of Positivism or *belles lettres*. It is the lesson which we can learn from an English work, by Gooch, on 'Modern Historiography',* though the work does not appear to have evoked any great amount of sympathy in England. But this same idea of individuality has also produced some consequences which may well give us pause. In its permanent effects it has been altogether disastrous to the conception of universal history. It dissolved and disintegrated that conception: it enslaved it to notions of 'relativity': it transmuted it either into specialisation, buttressed by 'method', or pure national introspection. In this respect the tendency of the Age of Enlightenment was something greater and broader;† and this tendency has survived in western Europe to a greater extent than it has with us. Romanticism itself, like contemporary classicism,‡ had been ready enough to think in terms of universal history; but there came a change. The increase of specialist research; the abandonment of the philosophy of history which

---

* The reference is to *History and Historians in the Nineteenth Century*, by G. P. Gooch, 1913.

† Compare, for example, Gibbon and Giesebrecht—*The Decline and Fall of the Roman Empire* (vol. 1, 1776) and *Die deutsche Kaiserzeit* (vol. 1, 1855).

‡ E.g. the 'classicism' of Winckelmann's work on Greek Art and Wolf's *Prolegomena to Homer* (circiter 1770–95).

had once held sway; the complete detachment from any sort of philosophy in a school of research which sought the particular, and immersed itself, either from *parti pris* or under the weight of learning, in pure detail—all these causes turned most of our historiography into the paths of materialism or complete relativity.

What was needed, in the face of such a development, was a return to a way of thinking, and a way of feeling about life, which was not merely 'historical', but 'universal-historical'. It will be one of the great tasks of the future to attain such a way of thinking and feeling. We may even say that thought and feeling of this nature are always essentially present wherever there is an impulse towards history, and they can only be repressed by the pressure of special circumstances. But if you want universal history, you must have some notion of the future and its goal;* for only in the light of such a notion can the record of man be drawn together into a unity. How far that is possible, and in what sense it is possible, is one of the great burning questions of the day. The attitude towards history which is merely specialist, or for that matter merely contemplative, has to be transcended: the image of Clio has to be made to face, once more, towards the great and universal problems of the future. The rigour, the width of equipment, and the devotion of research into what has happened (*Gewesenes*),† must be combined with the will that acts and shapes the future; and this active will of the historian must not only penetrate into the being of his own particular nation, but it must also rise to a view of the being of that nation as connected with the being and the development of the whole World. Here again western Europe has certainly preserved, at any rate among some of its representatives, a greater degree of active vigour and practical sense.

Last of all, and most of all, the problem of attaining a harmony of culture in our generation requires us to pay a much greater regard to the great world-forces in politics and ethics which dominated the nineteenth century, and primarily to the developments which sprang from Natural Law and the idea of Humanity. These developments will, and must, play their part in determining the ideal which must underlie any future harmony of civilisation; and they will do so because they are inextricably connected with a certain intellectual maturity, a certain stage in the increase of population, and certain religious and philosophical elements in our modern phase of civilisation. They will also have a decisive influence on what we actually are, as well as on our ideals of what we should be. These are matters which have indubitably been neglected by our German historiography, or at any rate treated with an ill-advised antipathy, which astonishingly combines an exaggerated romanticism with a habit of reliance on Prussian militarism for the support of law and order. A change is possible without any rejection of the essence of German ideas: on the contrary, a change would

* 'True history', we may say, 'is teleological history'.

† Compare Ranke's saying about History, in the preface to his first work, *Er will bloss zeigen wie es eigentlich gewesen.*

only mean a return, in many respects, to an earlier, broader and more candid treatment of history. It would also restore a new contact with the thought of western Europe, at a number of points on which there was once a large measure of agreement between it and our own classico-romantic age (1770–1800); and on one point in particular—that of the so-called 'Rights of Man'—it would aid us in correcting a certain one-sidedness, which was already fraught with serious consequences in that age, and is even more serious to-day in view of the universal diffusion of Western ideas which has since ensued. But we need not, in changing our attitude, forego altogether any criticism of the ideas to which we turn—the less, as such criticism is already being applied to them at many points in western Europe itself, where it is generally current in the form, not indeed of Marxian Socialism, but at any rate of socialistic ideas. We may even say that the best elements of German thought have in many respects a close affinity with such criticism, so far as it is directed to something more than economic interests and struggles, and so far as it has regard to problems of spiritual life and the deeper foundations of social well-being.

§9. *The new ethical attitude required*

When we turn to our second, or ethical, line of enquiry, we have to begin by insisting once more on a fact to which we have already referred. If the classico-romantic spirit is closely connected with German historical thought, it also marks an extraordinary advance, if we look at its general tendency, towards a free, personal, and individual ethic.* In order to feel the aesthetic invigoration and emancipation which such an idea of morality can inspire, we must read the Edinburgh Rectorial Address in which Mill expressed his desire that something of the spirit of Humboldt might fall on the 'gentleman' trained by Puritanism and business†—a suggestion afterwards rejected by Herbert Spencer, as derogatory to the natural sciences and empirical observation. An ideal such as that of Humboldt is indeed a real emancipation, when we set it over against ideas of morality which are simply those of a religious confession, or of middle-class convention and social position, or of bare and abstract rationalism. The same is true of the organic conception of the community which is connected with such an ideal. The conception that a community has a unity of life, pervading its different parts, which is directed to the well-being of the whole and determined by the individuality of the whole, is surely something richer and more living, from a purely ethical point of view, than any conception of 'contracts' and 'controls' intended to secure a common diffusion of prosperity.

* Because it starts from the conception of individuality (p. 211 supra), and because it postulates the idea of the autonomy of man and of personality (p. 215).

† In the *Essay on Liberty* also, c. III, Mill cites Humboldt's *Sphere and Duties of Government*, and states, as a theory of which 'few persons, out of Germany, even comprehend the meaning', his ideal of individuality of power and development.

And it provides as surely, from the same ethical point of view, a higher principle of conduct than the opposing idea of Equality, which always tends to result in a tangle of radical contradictions, or else in banal superficialities.

Yet when all is said, the moral philosophy of Romanticism has its defects. The idea which it presupposes, and yet only allows to emerge in one particular form—the idea of the fundamental personal liability, the responsibility, the autonomy of Personality—is one which ought to have been given a very much greater prominence than it ever received in Germany, especially in the later transformations and political perversions of the spirit of Romanticism. The theory of the Rights of Man —rights which are not the gift of the State, but the ideal postulates of the State, and indeed of Society itself, in all its forms—is a theory which contains so much of the truth, and satisfies so many of the requirements of a true European attitude, that we cannot afford to neglect it; on the contrary, we must incorporate it into our own ideas. The same is true of the theory of Associations, as possessing their own individual unity of life, which has now become so important a factor in our view of Society and the State.* We must not allow that view to be petrified by tradition and custom and national self-esteem: we must not allow it to leave out of account other States and peoples and communities, or the need of an ordered system of relations with them. The wider horizon of 'the parliament of man and the federation of the world' must include all the elements of which we have spoken, as moral necessities and postulates; and while we recognise the obstacles which actually confront these postulates, we must none the less cling to them as our ideal. At the heart of all the current ideas about a League of Nations, the organisation of the world, and the limitation of egoisms and forces of destruction, there is an indestructible moral core, which we cannot in its essence reject, even if we are painfully aware, at the moment, of the difficulties which it presents and the abuse to which it is liable. We may see the difficulties and the abuse clearly: we may seek, with all our strength, to overcome them; but what we cannot do, and must not do, is to deny the ideal itself in its own essence, in its ethical significance, in its connection with the philosophy of history.

§10. *Spenglerism and Socialism*

We have sketched a programme of self-analysis for the historical, political and ethical thought of Germany; but it is no more than a mere indication of the directions along which the effort has to be made. Such a programme can only be achieved by the labour of generations, and by the gradual formation of a common resolve, among our leading

---

* Troeltsch is contending that just as German thinkers ought to give a deeper sense, and a wider scope, to the idea of individual personality which Romanticism implied, so they ought to generalise (and not confine to Germany) the idea of Group-personality which it also assumed.

thinkers, to work together for its realisation. We are not required to retrace the whole of the path we have trod, or to renounce the quality of our national spirit: we are only asked to recover ideas which we have allowed ourselves to lose, and to develop and adapt the thought of our stock to the vastly altered condition of the modern world. At the moment we are still very far from being of one mind in regard to the assumptions on which we ought to proceed. When we look at a book such as Spengler's *Decay of Civilisation*, which is fundamentally inspired by Nietzsche, and reflect on the enormous impression which it has made, we have to admit that the current is flowing in the opposite direction to that which has just been suggested. It is encouraging men to formulate, in their extremest form, all the deductions which can be drawn from Romantic aestheticism and Romantic ideas of individuality to foster the cause of scepticism, of amoralism, of pessimism, of belief in the policy of force, of simple cynicism. 'Decay' is indeed a consequence which follows logically on such a basis; for with such ideas in their minds men simply cannot exist, or fight the battle of the future. Spengler's book is an absolute confirmation of the reproaches which western Europe brings against us: it is nothing less than a hauling down of the flag of life in the course of man's perpetual struggle to keep it flying. He who desires to survive—and our nation *does* desire to survive—can never go that way. Our duty to our German traditions is not to push them to an extreme and one-sided conclusion—surrendering, in the process, the relative merit of strict and scholarly accuracy which they possess—but to bring them into new contact with all the great movements in the world about us.

But it would also be an error, and an error in the reverse direction, to believe that socialist theory, and the socialist interpretation of history, are on the right track. It is true that the German theory of Socialism, in its Marxian form, is a combination of elements. It unites a theory of history which was formed by Romantic philosophy, and which makes history a process of constant individualisation, with the principles of a democratic and humanitarian cosmopolitanism. The first of these elements is responsible for anything which Socialism can offer in the way of a realistic view of history and evolution, or of spiritual suggestion and constructive social power: the second is the source of the whole of its gospel of world-revolution, world-salvation, the cause of Humanity, the universal organisation of all mankind. But if Socialism is a combination of elements, it is a defective combination. The first of its elements has been utterly desiccated by a barren economic materialism, and the atheism which goes along with it; and the union between its two elements is so external, and so artificial, that they are continually breaking apart. Socialism is a compound which is always dissolving into its component parts—a rigorously determinist idea of evolution, altogether barren of controlling ideas; and a totally unhistorical passion for revolution, to be achieved in the name of Humanity and Equality. When the socialist feels that he must enunciate principles, he naturally lays his emphasis entirely, or almost entirely, on the second of these factors. When that happens, socialistic principles become practically indistinguishable, in spite of the Socialist challenge to the bourgeoisie, from the bourgeois philosophy of the West; and the individualistic and utilitarian basis of that philosophy, in particular, is simply adopted wholesale. The distinction between German Socialists and the peoples of western Europe is thus practically reduced to the fact that the latter, with the proud confidence of great nations, feel themselves to be representatives of great national positions of leadership, while the former simply follow in their wake, failing to bring their own nation into any touch with the problems of the future, and failing equally, as a result, to pay any real attention to the peculiar political conditions of its life.

Neither the doctrines of Spengler nor the doctrines of Socialism are the new gospel that we need. They are rather the Scylla and Charybdis between which we must steer our course. We must make for the open sea of fresh, unprejudiced, far-seeing thought upon all these issues, remembering that, if they are in themselves the oldest objects of human action and human thought, the answers they ask for from us to-day are new.

APPENDIX II

GIERKE'S CONCEPTION OF LAW*

The development of natural-law ideas in regard to the relation of the State to Law attained its culmination at the end of the eighteenth century. After that time we can begin to trace a process of collapse and disintegration in the whole of the natural-law system of thought.

In Germany the theory of Natural Law disappears before the new world of ideas introduced by the Historical School. It was the achievement of that School to transcend, at last, the old dichotomy of Law into Natural and Positive. Regarding Law as a unity, and conceiving it as the positive result and living expression of the common consciousness of an organic community, the thinkers of the Historical School refused to content themselves with merely continuing to emphasise one or the other side of the old antithesis: they sought and achieved a synthesis of both in a higher unity. The factors which determined their conception of the relation of the State to Law were factors equally derived from the Natural and the Positive Law of the older doctrine. In the new view which they attained, Law ceased to be regarded as partly anterior and superior to the State, and partly produced by and inferior to it. Law and the State were held to be so intertwined that they were regarded as coeval with one another; as intended to supplement one another; as dependent upon one another.

The philosophical elaboration of this idea has not yet been fully achieved. Meanwhile there has been an abundance of criticism, from all sorts of quarters, some of it devoted to discovering the errors of the Historical School, and some of it even to calling in question again the very foundations of the historical view of Law. So far as the problem of the relation between Law and the State is concerned, we can detect in the chaos of modern opinion two particular currents of thought, opposed to one another, but united together in opposition to the historic-organic idea of Law. On the one hand, there has been a period during which conceptions of an abstract Law of Nature pressed once more to the front, and menaced the very idea of the State. On the other hand, there is now a current of thought, which is gradually gaining volume in Germany,† that threatens to undermine all the foundations of Law. It recurs to the old ideas of Positive Law, but it abandons the notion of Natural Law which used to be the complement of those ideas. In this last and newest way of approach, the idea of Law ultimately vanishes altogether. So far as its content or substance goes, it is en-

* Translated from his *Johannes Althusius*, Part II, c. VI, §iii.

† These words were originally written about 1880. They are repeated in the later editions.

gulfed in the idea of Utility; so far as its power or efficacy is concerned, it is engulfed in the idea of Force. If this way of approach should prove victorious, the only merit of the Historical School will have been its rejection of Natural Law; and the ideas of Natural Law, reduced to an idle play of the human imagination, will have pursued in vain their many centuries of evolution.

But if there is to be a true Law in the future—a Law which is not a mere *décor* of traditional well-sounding names, but the genuine expression of a specific, unique and intrinsically valuable idea of the mind of man—a different historical perspective reveals itself to our eyes. In that perspective, we can see that the idea of Law has won real and permanent conquests from the development of Natural Law; we can see that the Historical point of view, far from surrendering those conquests, has only generalised and diffused them; and we may confidently believe that these conquests will never be lost in the future, whatever changes or improvements may be made in men's conceptions of Law. On such a view the sovereign independence of the idea of Justice, secured before by the old conception of Natural Law, will still continue to be firmly secured by our new conception of Law as something thoroughly positive—no matter whether the idea which opposes that conception be the idea of social utility, or the idea of collective power.*

If Natural and Positive Law thus coincide in their essence, the relation of Law and the State will no longer be conceived in two opposite ways, as it was in the older theory; and the ideas which found expression in opposite points of view may now be united in one. We shall no longer ask whether the State is prior to Law, or Law is prior to the State. We shall regard them both as inherent functions of the common life which is inseparable from the idea of man. They will both be primordial facts: they will both have been given, as seeds or germs, coevally with man himself: they will both appear, as developed fruits, simultaneously with one another and in virtue of one another. We shall regard the State, and all other organised forms of collective power, as no mere product of Law; but we shall hold that every form of power, from the lowest to the highest, can only enjoy a sanction, and receive its consummation, when it is stamped and confirmed by Law as being a legal power. Conversely, we shall regard all Law as needing the sanction and consummation of power; but we shall not count the State, nor any other human power, as the maker and creator of Law.

Law, which is, in its essence, a body of external standards for the action of *free* wills, cannot itself be made of the substance of will; for if will is made the standard for wills, the logically inevitable result must always be that will turns itself into power. If there is to be an obligatory external standard for the action of will *in general*, and not merely for the action of this or that *particular* will, such a standard must be

* 'Social utility' and 'collective power' seem to represent the creeds of Socialism and Radical Democracy.

rooted and grounded in a spiritual force which confronts the will as something independent. That force is Reason. It follows that Law is not a common will that a thing shall be, but a common conviction that it is. Law is the conviction of a human community, either manifested directly by usage or declared by a common organ appointed for that purpose, that there exist in that community external standards of will —in other words, limitations of liberty which are externally obligatory, and therefore, by their very nature, enforceable.

It is true that the State, in its capacity of legislator, not only shows itself active, over a large and important field, as the 'bearer' and the corroborator of this conviction of Right (or Law), but also consummates every development of such conviction (1) by the issue of a command and (2) by the use of compulsion. But (1) the action of the common will in commanding obedience to what *is* Law is not an action which *creates* Law: it is only an action which sanctions Law. Similarly, (2) the fact that a supreme power is needed, in order to realise fully the compulsoriness demanded by the nature of Law, does not prevent Law from still being Law even though, in a particular case, compulsion is lacking, or can only be imperfectly applied, or is altogether impossible for want of a higher power which is capable of using it—provided only there really is a common conviction that compulsion would be right if it were possible, or if a competent authority were in existence.

On this basis, we may, indeed, hold that the State is more than a legal institution, and exists for more than the purpose of Law; but we shall also hold that the purpose of Law is pre-eminent among all the purposes of the State's existence—just because the full consummation of Law requires the presence of a sovereign power—and we shall therefore regard the legal purpose of the State as its essential purpose, which cannot for a moment be abstracted from our idea of its nature. Conversely, we may, indeed, regard Law as intended primarily to serve the purposes of the State's life; but we shall also consider its objects as far from being exhausted by, or limited to, such service. There is indeed one admission which we shall have to make on such a view. If we place the State neither above Law, nor outside it, but *in* it, thus confining the liberty of the State within the bounds of the system of Law: if, again, we set Law neither above the State, nor outside it, but *in* it, thus allowing the formal omnipotence of the sovereign authority to assert itself even against Law—then there will be a possibility of contradiction between the Matter and the Form of Law*, the actual and the ideal. But to deny the possibility of such a contradiction is to deny the very idea of Law.

A deep element in the spiritual nature of man longs for the union of Law and Power—of Right and Might. Division between them is always

---

* The Matter is what is actually expressed by the sovereign authority in its enactment: the Form is the ideal of Right which ought to shape and control such enactment.

felt to be something wrong. This feeling is the best evidence that Law may exist without Power, and Power may exist without Law. But it is also the source of a healing and reconciling influence, which is always tending to bring us back to a unity of Right and Might. The human conscience cannot permanently endure the separation of the two. Right which cannot establish itself vanishes at last from the common conscience, and thereby ceases to be Right. Might which exists without Right, if it succeeds in maintaining itself, is felt at last by the general conscience to exist as of right, and is thus transformed into Right.

In a note appended to later editions Gierke adds:

The statement of the author's own views on the relations of Law and the State, and his animadversions on the Power and Utility theories, make the concluding remarks of this chapter depart from the spirit of historical analysis to a greater degree than the occasional remarks at the end of the previous chapters of this work. This may appear to be open to criticism. The author would plead in excuse that he was dealing with a matter which lay close to his heart.... I still live to-day in the conviction that our legal theory and our legal life can only thrive on one condition—that 'positivism' should somehow learn to preserve for the idea of Law that original and independent title to existence which was vindicated for it by the School of Natural Law. I regard as mistaken all the attempts to resuscitate Natural Law into a bodily existence, which can only be the existence of a simulacrum. But the undying spirit of that Law can never be extinguished. If it is denied entry into the body of positive law, it flutters about the room like a ghost, and threatens to turn into a vampire which sucks the blood from the body of Law. We have to accept together both the external experience which testifies that all valid Law is positive, and the internal experience which affirms that the living force of Law is derived from an idea of Right which is innate in humanity; and when we have done that, we have to blend the two experiences in one generic conception of the essential nature of Law. The method of achieving this object is a matter on which agreement cannot so easily be found. But many who seek to attain it by other means will agree with me about the end which we have to attain.

CONTENTS

PART II

V

GIERKE'S NOTES

§ 14. The Natural-Law Conception of the State	229
§ 15. The Natural-Law Theory of Associations	269
§ 16. The General Theory of the Group in Natural Law	288
§ 17. The Natural-Law Theory of the State	333
§ 18. The Theory of Corporations in Natural Law	367

VI

LISTS OF AUTHORITIES

A. 1500–1650	401
B. 1650–1800	409

VII

INDEX 418

V
GIERKE'S NOTES

§14. THE NATURAL-LAW CONCEPTION OF THE STATE

1. After the sketch given in my work on 'Johannes Althusius and the natural-law theories of the State', the only matter on which I need to go into detail here is the relation of the natural-law doctrine of the State to particular problems which are of special importance in the history of the theory of the Corporation; and for the rest I shall content myself with giving references to that work.... I have not worked through the large body of literature which has appeared since the completion of this subsection. But I may refer to the Addenda to the second and third editions of my work on Althusius for an account of my attitude to views differing from my own which have been put forward since I first wrote.

2. This is the case with J. Oldendorp (1480–1561), *Juris naturalis, gentium et civilis isagoge*, Cologne, 1539 (*Opera*, I, pp. 1 sqq.); N. Hemming (1513–1600), *De lege naturae apodeictica methodus*, Wittenberg, 1652 (also printed in Kaltenborn, II, pp. 26 sqq.); G. Obrecht, *De justitia et jure*, in *Selectissimae disputationes*, Strassburg, 1599, no. 1; B. Winkler (1579–1648), *Principiorum juris libri V*, Leipzig, 1615 (Kaltenborn, II, pp. 45 sqq.); B. Meiszner, *De legibus*, Wittenberg, 1616; John Selden (1584–1654), *De jure naturali et gentium, juxta disciplinam Ebraeorum*, London, 1640. See also Bolognetus (1539–85), *De lege, jure et aequitate*, in *Tract. Univ. Jur.* I, fol. 289–324. *Early works on Natural Law*

3. See Franciscus Victoria (Dominican, †1546), *Relectiones tredecim*, Ingolstadt, 1580; Dominicus Soto (Dominican, 1494–1560), *De justitia et jure*, Venice, 1602 (first published 1556); F. Vasquez (1509–66), *Controversiarum illustrium aliarumque usu frequentium libri III*, Frankfort on the Main, 1572; Gregorius de Valentia (Jesuit), *Commentarii theologici*, Ingolstadt, 1592, II, Disp. 1; Balthasar Ayala (1548–84), *De jure et officiis belli*, Antwerp, 1597; Ludovicus Molina (1535–1600), *De justitia et jure tomi VI*, Mainz, 1614 (and also in 1602); Leonhardus Lessius (Jesuit, 1554–1623), *De justitia et jure libri IV*, 3rd edition, Antwerp, 1612 (first published in 1606); Cardinal Robert Bellarmine (1542–1621), *De potestate summi pontificis in rebus temporalibus*, Cologne, 1611 (first published in 1610); Johannes de Lugo (Jesuit), *De justitia et jure*, ed. nova, Lyons, 1670. *Ecclesiastical writers on Natural Law*

4. F. Suarez (Jesuit, 1548–1617), *Tractatus de legibus ac Deo legislatore*, Antwerp, 1613 (first published in 1611).

5. Hugo Grotius, *De jure belli ac pacis libri tres*, 1625; the edition used by the author is that published at Amsterdam, 1702.

6. See Machiavelli (1469–1527), *Il principe* (first published in 1515), and the whole body of literature written about and against him.
See also the numerous 'Mirrors of Princes' and cognate writings, such as: G. Lauterbeck, *Regentenbuch*, new edition, 1559; Osorius, *De Regis institutione*, Cologne, 1572; Waremund de Erenbergk (Eberhardt von Weyhe), *Aulus-politicus*, 1596; Hippolytus a Collibus, the *Princeps* (1592), and the *Consiliarius*, the *Palatinus* and the *Nobilis*, edited together, with additions, by Naurath, *Political writings on practical questions*

Frankfort, 1670; Mambrinus Rosaeus, *Institutio principis christiani*, Strassburg, 1608; Tympe, *Aureum speculum principum*, Cologne, 1629 (first published in 1617); Georg Engelhardt von Löhneys, *Hof-, Staats- und Regierkunst*, 1622; Carolus Scribanus, *Politico-Christianus*, Münster, 1625; Ambrosius Marlianus, *Theatrum politicum*, Danzig, 1645; Saavedra Faxardo, *Idea da uno principe Cristiano*, 1649.

See also the writings on *arcana reipublicae*, such as: Clapmarus (1574–1604), *De arcanis rerumpublicarum libri VI*, Jena, 1665 (first published in 1605); G. Obrecht (1547–1612), *Secreta politica*, Strassburg, 1644 (previously published in 1617). In addition, we may cite: Oldendorp, *Von Rathschlägen, wie man gute Policey und Ordnung in Stedten und Landen erhalten möge*, Rostock, 1579; Ferrarius, *De republica bene instituenda*, Basle, 1556, translated into German by Abraham Saur, Frankfort, 1601; Melchior ab Ossa, *Testamentum*, Frankfort, 1609; Zech, *Politicorum libri III*, Cologne, 1600; Gentillet, *Discours sur les moyens de bien gouverner*, 1576; Jacobus Simananca, *De republica libri IX*, 3rd edition, Antwerp, 1574; Lipsius, *Politicorum libri VI*, Antwerp, 1604; Loys de Mayerne, *La monarchie aristodémocratique*, Paris, 1611; J. A Chokier de Surlet, *Thesaurus politicorum aphorismorum*, Cologne (many editions); Jean de Marnix, *Résolutions politiques et maximes d'État*, Rouen, 1624.

Treatises on raison d'état

7. Botero, *Della ragione di stato*, Venice, 1559; Zinanus, *De ratione optime imperandi*, Frankfort, 1628; W. F. ab Efferen, *Manuale politicum de ratione status*, Frankfort, 1630; Wangenbeck, *Vindiciae politicae adversus pseudopoliticos*, Dillingen, 1636. The work of Hippolithus a Lapide, *De ratione status in imperio nostro Romano-Germanico*, 1640, belongs in its general tone and treatment altogether to the purely political school, and makes the dictates of *raison d'état* superior to the requirements of Law; but in dealing with German conditions the author distinguishes sharply between (1) the analysis of the existing conditions (which is treated from a purely historico-legal point of view in Part I), and (2) political maxims (which are suggested in Parts II and III).*

8. Petrus Gregorius Tholosanus (1540–91), *De republica*, Frankfort, 1609 (first published in 1586).

Arnisaeus

9. H. Arnisaeus († 1636), *Opera omnia politica*, Strassburg, 1648. Among his writings may be specially noted: *Doctrina politica in genuinam methodum quae est Aristotelis reducta* (first published in 1606); *De jure majestatis libri III* (first published in 1610); *De auctoritate principum in populum semper inviolabili* (first published in 1611); *De republica seu relectionis politicae libri II* (first published in 1615).

10 H. Conring (1606–81), *Opera*, Brunswick, 1730, vol. III.

Works on political theory not based on Natural Law

11. See B. J. Omphalus, *De civili politia libri III*, Cologne, 1565; Casus, *Sphaera civitatis*, Frankfort, 1589; Albergati, *Discorsi politici*, Venice (point by point against Bodin and for Aristotle); J. Stephanus, *Demonstrationes politicorum*, Greifswald, 1599; Melchior Junius, *Politicarum quaestionum centuria et tredecim*, Strassburg, 1631 (first published in 1602); J. Crüger, *Collegium politicum*, Giessen, 1609; H. Velstenius, *Centuria quaestionum politicarum*, Wittenberg, 1610; W. Heider, *Systema philosophiae politicae*, Jena, 1628 (1610); C. Matthias,

* *Ratio status*, or *ratio administrationis*, in its original sense, is concerned with the *ratio*, in the sense of the general principles and the particular requirements, of a State and its government. This is the sense in which e.g. Althusius uses the phrase. The idea of *raison d'état* or *Staatsraison* is a later development. Cf. F. Meinecke, *Die Idee der Staatsraison in der neueren Geschichte*.

Notes to § 14

Collegium politicum, Giessen, 1611, *Systema politicum*, Giessen, 1618; C. Gneinzius, *Exercitationes politicae*, Wittenberg, 1617–18; Diodorus of Tulden († 1645), *De regimine civili libri VIII* (in *Opera*, Louvain, 1702); Aaron Alexander Olizarovius, *De politica hominum societate libri III*, Danzig, 1651.

12. J. Bodin, *De republica libri VI*, ed. 2, Frankfort, 1591 (first French edition 1577, first Latin 1584). On the epoch-making importance of his theory, see the modern works mentioned in the author's work on Althusius, p. 351 n. 2. [See also J. W. Allen, *Political Thought in the Sixteenth Century*, Part III, c. VIII.] — Bodin

13. Among the writings of the so-called '*Monarchomachi*' there are pamphlets both on the Protestant and on the Catholic side which equally advocate the cause of popular sovereignty. — The Monarchomachi

(a) On the Protestant side, the work of Hotoman (1524–90), *Francogallia*, Frankfort, 1665 (first published at Geneva, 1573), has still mainly an historical basis. In the anonymous treatise [probably written by Beza, Calvin's successor in Geneva], *De jure magistratuum in subditos et officio subditorum erga magistros*, Magdeburg, 1578 (first published in French, and stated on the title-page to have been published at Lyons, 1576), the argument from Natural Law still plays a secondary part. Natural Law is the basis of argument in the following: Stephanus Junius Brutus (the real author was H. Languet (1518–81), or according to others P. Duplessis-Mornay), *Vindiciae contra Tyrannos*, Paris, 1631 (first published at Edinburgh [the real place of publication was Basle] in 1579); George Buchanan (1506–82), *De jure regni apud Scotos dialogus*, 2nd edition, Edinburgh, 1580 (first published in 1579); Lambertus Danaeus, *Politicae Christianae libri VII*, 2nd edition, Paris, 1606 (first published in 1596); John Milton (1609–74), *The Tenure of Kings and Magistrates* (1648–9), *Eiconoclastes, Defensio pro populo Anglicano* (1651), *Defensio secunda* (1654), in his Prose Works, London, 1848 (II, pp. 2sqq., 1, pp. 307sqq., 3sqq., and 216sqq.). [On the three Huguenot authors first cited by Gierke—Hotoman, Beza and Languet—see J. W. Allen, *Political Thought in the Sixteenth Century*; and on the authorship of the *Vindiciae contra Tyrannos* see E. Barker, in the *Cambridge Historical Journal*, 1931 and R. Patry, *P. du Plessis-Mornay*, pp. 275–82.]

(b) On the Catholic side there are the following: Marius Salamonius, *De principatu libri VI*, Paris, 1578 [originally published at Rome, in 1544; the writer seems to have been a Spaniard]; Boucher, *De justa Henrici III abdicatione e Francorum regno libri IV*, Lyons, 1591; Guilielmus Rossaeus, *De justa reipublicae Christianae in reges impios et haereticos authoritate*, Antwerp, 1592 (first published in 1590, with a preface dated 1589); Mariana, *De rege et regis institutione*, Frankfort, 1611 (first published at Toledo, 1599).

New works on the *Monarchomachi* are mentioned in the author's work on Althusius (especially Treumann, Rehm, Landmann and Gooch). See also A. Elkan, *Die Publizisten der Bartholomäusnacht*, Heidelberg, 1905 [a work valuable for its account of Hotoman, Beza and Duplessis-Mornay]; F. Atger, *Essai sur l'histoire des doctrines du contrat social*, Paris, 1906, pp. 100sqq. [Mention may also be made of G. Weil, *Les Théories sur le pouvoir royal en France pendant les guerres de religion*; G. de Lagarde, *L'Esprit politique de la Réforme*; A. Méaly, *Les publicistes de la Réforme*; J. N. Figgis, *From Gerson to Grotius*.]

14. See G. Barclaius (1577–1608) [really 1543–1605], *De regno et regali potestate adversus Buchananum, Brutum* [i.e. the author of the *Vindiciae contra Tyrannos*], *Boucherium et reliquos Monarchomachos libri VI*, Hanover, 1612 (first — Advocates of absolutism

published in 1600); T. J. F. Graswinckelius (1600–66), *De jure majestatis*, The Hague, 1642; Claudius Salmasius (1588–1653), *Defensio regia pro Carolo I rege Angliae*, Paris, 1651.

Althusius

15. Johannes Althusius (1557–1638), *Politica methodice digesta atque exemplis sacris et profanis illustrata*, 3rd edition, Herborn, 1614 (first published in 1603). [Recently reprinted, from the 3rd edition, with an introduction by C. F. Friedrich, Harvard University Press, 1932.]

Political text-books after 1600, based on Natural Law

16. See Otho Casmannus, *Doctrinae et vitae politicae methodicum et breve systema*, Frankfort, 1603; B. Keckermann (1571–1609), *Systema disciplinae politicae*, Hanover, 1607; J. Bornitius, *Partitionum politicarum libri IV*, Hanover, 1607, *De majestate politica*, Leipzig, 1610, *Aerarium*, Frankfort, 1612, *De rerum sufficientia in republica et civitate procuranda*, Frankfort, 1625; H. Kirchner, *Respublica*, Marburg, 1608; Z. Fridenreich, *Politicorum liber*, Strassburg, 1609; J. H. Alstedius, *De statu rerumpublicarum*, Herborn, 1612; Busius, *De republica libri III*, Franeker, 1613; M. Z. Boxhornius († 1613), *Institutionum politicarum libri II*, 2nd edition, Leipzig, 1665; G. Schönborner (1579–1637), *Politicorum libri VII*, 4th edition, Frankfort, 1628 (first published in 1614: a second-hand work, based upon this, is the *De statu politico seu civili libri VI* published at Frankfort in 1617); P. H. Hoenonius (de Hoen, 1576–1640), *Disputationum politicarum liber unus*, 3rd edition, Herborn, 1615; M. Bortius, *De natura jurium majestatis et regalium*, in Arumaeus, 1 (1616), no. 2; König, *Acies disputationum politicarum*, Jena, 1619; Adam Contzen (Jesuit, 1573–1635), *Politicorum libri X*, Mainz, 1620; Claudius de Carnin, *Malleus tripartitus*, Antwerp, 1620; Menochius (Jesuit), *Hieropolitica*, 2nd edition, Cologne, 1626; Werdenhagen, *Universalis introductio in omnes Respublicas*, Amsterdam, 1632; C. Liebenthal, *Collegium politicum*, Marburg, 1644; N. Vernulaeus, *Diss. politicae*, Louvain, 1646; Daniel Berckringer, *Institutiones politicae sive de republica*, Utrecht, 1662.

17. The reference is to Besold's *Opus politicum*, ed. nova, Strassburg, 1626.

Hobbes

18. Thomas Hobbes (1588–1679), *Elementa philosophica de cive*, Amsterdam, 1647; *Leviathan, sive de materia, forma et potestate civitatis ecclesiasticae et civilis*, Amsterdam, 1670 [in English, under the title of *Leviathan*, 1651]. On Hobbes see particularly F. Tönnies, *Thomas Hobbes der Mann und der Denker*, Leipzig, 1912. [See also A. Levi, *La Filosofia di Tommaso Hobbes*, Milan, 1929.]

19. Compare e.g. Schneidewin in *Comm. on the Institutes*, I, 2; Mynsinger, *Apotelesma* on l. 1 D. 1, 1; Rittershusius, *Instit.* I, 2, pp. 25 sqq.; Ostermann, *Rationalia ad Instit.* I, 2.

20. Compare Cantiuncula, *Instit.* I, 2; Vasquez, *Controv. illustr.* cc. 7, 10 and 54; Hunnius, *Comm. in Instit.* I, 2, *Coll. Instit. Disp.* I, *Var. resol. jur. civ.* I, 1, qu. 19 sqq.; Binnius, *Comm. in Instit.* I, 2; Sylv. Aldobrandinus, *In primum Instit. Just. librum Comm.* (Venice, 1567); J. F. Ozerius, *Comm. in libros Instit.* (Venice, 1562), pp. 37–8; Bachoven ab Echt, *Comm. in Instit.* I, 2, pp. 9 sqq., *Pandect.* pp. 16 sqq.; V. W. Forster, *Tract. Disp.* I; P. Busius, on l. 1 D. 1, 1; J. Harprecht, *Instit.* I, 2; Wurmser, *Exerc.* III, qu. 1; T. Schuminovius, *In I. libr. Instit. Just. catholica explicatio*, Brussels, 1663, 1, 2.

21. Compare Connanus, *Comm. jur. civ.* I, cc. 1–7; Melchior Kling, *Instit.* I, 2; Vigelius, *Decisiones juris controv.* IV, no. 6; Faber, *Jurispr. Papin.* I, 2, pp. 31–57, *Rationalia*, I, 1–4; A. Matthaeus, *Comm. in Instit.* I, 2; Ludwell, *Comm. in Instit.* I, 2; Schambogen, *Lect. publ. in Instit.* I, 2, qu. 1–7; G. Frantzke, *Comm. in Instit.* I, 2; Lauterbach, *Coll.* I, 1, §§ 22 sqq. Compare

also Duarenus, I, 1, c. 5; Cujacius, I, pp. 9 sqq., VII, pp. 14 sqq.; Diodorus Tuldenus, *Comm. in Instit.* I, 2; Petrus Ligneus, *Annot. ad Instit.* I, 2; H. Giphanius, *Instit.* I, 2; Cothmann, *Disp.* I, *thes.* 4–12, *Instit.* I, 2, *Cod.* I, 14.

22. More particularly, we find Ulpian's dictum about the participation of animals in Natural Law disputed, or explained as an unauthoritative mode of expression; and this leads to a rejection of the hitherto generally accepted doctrine that *jus naturale* (or *jus naturale primaevum*) is a law common to men and animals, while *jus gentium* is to be regarded as a law peculiar to men. On this basis the difference between *jus naturale* and *jus gentium* was explained simply by reference to the distinction between the 'absolute' and the 'conditioned' dictates of reason, or, again, between 'original' knowledge of the law of Reason and the knowledge which is 'acquired' in the course of historical development. See Corasius, on l. 1, §2, D. 1, 11; Connanus, loc. cit.; Forster, op. cit. no. 30; Bachoven von Echt, op. cit. p. 11; Ludwell, loc. cit. *Natural Law and Jus gentium*

23. See especially Connanus, *Comm. jur. civ.* I, c. 4. Compare also Boxhorn, I, c. 2, §§ 3–8, c. 3, §§ 15 sqq.; and the *Commentary* of an ex-professor of Jena on the *Codex*, I, 1–13, in G. A. Struvius, *Jus sacrum Justin.*, Jena, 1668, *Prooemium*.

24. See Hotoman, *Instit.* I, 2, pr.; Vultejus, loc. cit.; Giphanius, loc. cit.; Forster, *Tract. Disp.* I, no. 29; Wurmser, *Exerc.* I, qu. 3 (*jus publicum ex praeceptis naturalibus, gentium et civilibus collectum est*).

25. Thinkers who maintained the theory that only a condition of universal liberty and community of property corresponded to pure Natural Law, and that government and property first came into the world through the corruption of human nature and the breach with pure Natural Law which was thereby involved, are sometimes found declaring the State itself to be a creation of *jus gentium*: see e.g. Lessius, II, c. 5, *dub.* 1–3; Molina, II, d. 18, § 17 and d. 20; Gryphiander, *De civili soc.* §§ 60 sqq. But the *jus gentium* of which they spoke was for them identical with Natural Law, in the only form in which it could be applied to the real world. *The State as product of Jus gentium*

26. Melchior Kling (*Instit.* I, 2, folio 1 verso) remarks in general terms that philosophers, in contradistinction to jurists, generally identify *jus naturale* with *jus gentium*. This is correct; for while Oldendorp (op. cit. *tit.* 2–4) and Hemming both use the threefold division [of natural law, *jus gentium* and positive law], the later legal philosophers generally assume as their basis a simple distinction between natural and positive law. This is the case with Winkler (II, cc. 9–10), though he proceeds to divide *jus naturale* into (*a*) *jus naturale prius* (III, c. 1 sq.) and (*b*) *jus naturale posterius*, i.e. *gentium jus* (IV, c. 1 sq.), and to contrast both with *jus positivum seu civile* (V, c. 1 sq.). See also Beneckendorf, *Repetitio et explicatio de regulis juris*, Frankfort on the Oder, 1593, pp. 81 sqq. *Distinction of Natural and Positive Law, with jus gentium disappearing*

The ecclesiastical legal philosophers almost always start from the antithesis of *lex naturalis* and *lex positiva*. But along with the former, they postulate the existence of *lex aeterna* or *divina*, which they rank as superior to or coordinate with it; and in the same way [as they distinguish two 'ideal' laws] they proceed to divide *lex positiva* into *jus humanum* [positive secular law] and *jus divinum positivum* [positive revealed law]: cf. Soto, lib. I and II; Gregorius de Valentia, qu. 3–8; Bolognetus, cc. 3–7; Suarez, lib. II–IV. We find a similar view in Meiszner, lib. II–IV.

Among the jurists we may note Donellus, who (I, c. 6) recognises only two legislators—*natura seu naturalis ratio* (and God as immanent in it), and *potestas civilis*. He accordingly identifies *jus gentium* and *jus naturale*, inasmuch as all *jus gentium* is simply *natura constitutum* (§§ 4–5), and, conversely, all *jus naturale* referring to mankind manifests itself as *jus gentium* (§§ 6–9). In the same sense Vultejus remarks (*Comm. in Instit.* I, 2, pp. 12–41) that the threefold division is really only a twofold division into *jus naturale* and *jus civile*—*jus gentium* being only a species of the former. The same idea is expressed even more definitely by Althusius: cf. *Dicaeologia*, I, cc. 13–14 (and more particularly, as regards *jus gentium*, c. 13, nos. 18–20). Compare Salamonius, *In libr. Pand. jur. civil. Commentatio*, Basle, 1530, l. 1 D. 1, 1, fol. 6sqq.; Corasius on l. 1 D. 1, 1; Stryck, *Annotationes* to Lauterbach, *Coll.* I, 1, p. 15. Political writers almost always use the simple distinction of natural and positive law.

Tendency to neglect Jus gentium

27. This [i.e. neglect of *jus gentium*, even though it is allowed to be one of the forms of law] is what we find in Bodin: in Book I, c. 8, no. 107 he confines the absolute obligatory force of *jus gentium* to the cases in which it is in agreement with *jus naturale*. It also appears in Soto (who never touches on *jus gentium* until he reaches Book III, c. 1), Suarez (Book II), and other ecclesiastical legal philosophers. We find it even in the writers who seek to distinguish the natural-law from the positive-law elements in *jus gentium*, such as Molina (V, d. 69), Lessius (II, c. 2), and more especially Vasquez (cc. 27 and 51).

Grotius (I, c. 1, §§ 10–17) definitely assumes a simple bipartite division of law. Law is either *jus naturale*, resting on the *dictamen rectae rationis*, or *jus voluntarium*, depending on legislative will; and the latter is either *humanum* or *divinum*. As for *jus gentium*, it is a species of *jus humanum voluntarium*; it is the agreement of positive law as between all or a number of peoples; the Roman conception of *jus gentium naturale* has hardly any value (§ 11); natural law and positive law are confused in the Roman *jus gentium* (II, c. 8, § 26).

28. It is only in this sense that we find *jus gentium* occurring in Hobbes.

The State based on pure Natural Law

29. The ecclesiastical legal philosophers are particularly insistent in holding (1) on the one hand, that the union of men in a *vita socialis*, the institution of the original sovereignty of the community over individuals, and the devolution of authority on a secular government, are all derived from *jus naturale* and therefore from God, and cannot be changed even by the *consensus totius orbis*, and (2) on the other hand, that the various constitutional forms have their basis in *jus humanum*. Cf. Soto, IV, qu. 4, art. 1; F. Victoria, *Rel.* III, nos. 1–8; Bellarmine, *De laicis*, cc. 5–6; Rossaeus, c. 1, §§ 1–3; Molina, II, *disp.* 22, 23, 26–7; Suarez, III, cc. 1–5; Claudius de Carnin, I, cc. 6 and 9–10. The same view is expressed by Arnisaeus, *Polit.* c. 2, *De rep.* c. 1, §§ 1–4, *De autor. princ.* c. 3. The basis of the State and its authority in pure Natural Law is assumed as self-evident by most of the champions of popular sovereignty: cf. Buchanan, pp. 11–13; [Beza's] *De jure magistr.* p. 4, qu. 6, p. 75; Danaeus, I, cc. 3–4; Althusius, c. 1, §§ 32–9; Milton, the *Defensio* of 1651, cc. 2–3 and 5. The absolutists are, however, no less definite in *their* appeal to divine and Natural Law: cf. Graszwinkel, c. 1 sqq.; Salmasius, cc. 2–3 and 5–6. Further details are given in the author's work on Althusius, pp. 65–8, 72 n. 41, 93 n. 48.

30. See vol. III of the author's *Das deutsche Genossenschaftsrecht*, pp. 611 sqq. [translated in *The Political Theories of the Middle Age*, pp. 75 sqq.] and his work on Althusius, pp. 279 sqq. and 365.

Natural Rights

31. In particular, this idea [of a sacrosanct sphere of natural rights] served to decide questions such as the obligatory force of constitutional laws,

the right of resistance (passive or active), and the rights of a people against a ruler who transgressed the bounds of his authority: cf. the author's work on Althusius, pp. 305 sqq. 365 n. 95.

32. We find legal philosophers and political writers energetically developing and applying the old theories, (1) that Natural Law, as the *dictamen rectae rationis*, was unalterable by any human power and even by God Himself, (2) that all positive law was derived from it, and could only add to or take away from it when place and time might require, and (3) that an enactment contrary to Natural Law was entirely null and void, and, per contra, an enactment was the more perfect, the more nearly it approached the Law of Nature. Cf. e.g. Soto, I, qu. 4; Vasquez, c. 27; Gregorius de Valentia, II, d. 1, qu. 4; Bolognetus, c. 7; Molina, v, d. 68; Winkler, II, cc. 9–10, v, c. 1 sq.; [Beza's] *De jure magistr.* sect. 4, qu. 2–3; Beneckendorf, op. cit. pp. 81 sqq.; Vultejus, *Instit.* I, 2, pp. 37–44; Bodin, I, c. 8, no 107 and II, c. 2; Althusius, *Dicaeologia*, I, c. 13, no. 9 sqq. and c. 14, *Polit.* Praef. and c. 128 [? c. XXXVIII], §§ 128–9.

Natural Law as a political standard

Many writers (e.g. Hotoman, *Instit.* I, c. 2, pr.; Bachoven, *Instit.* I, 2, § 1; and Winkler, v, c. 1) divided *jus civile* into *mixtum* and *merum*, according as Natural Law was or was not included in it; but others contested even the bare possibility of a purely positive law: cf. Althusius, *Dicaeologia*, I, c. 14 (a law completely agreeing with Natural Law would not be *civile*, but a law with no element of Natural Law would not be *jus* at all); Ludwell, *Instit.* I, 2, § 1.

33. Vultejus (*Instit.* I, 2, § 11, p. 41 no. 6) expresses this idea in a particularly definite way: *jus naturale est in seipso in recta ratione firmum et immutabile... iterum est immutabile in totum, a quo interdum paulatim receditur, ut ad ipsum redeundi via sit commodior, ne, si directe ad ipsum eatur, ad ipsum non perveniatur.*

34. See the author's work on Althusius, pp. 63 sqq. and 338.

35. Bodin, I, c. 1, no. 1, gives the definition, *Respublica est familiarum rerumque inter ipsas communium summa potestate ac ratione moderata multitudo*. The definition of Gregorius (I, 1, § 6) is more detailed: *Respublica est rerum et vitae quaedam communitas unius societatis, quae efficit unum quoddam corpus civile ex pluribus diversis ut membris compositum, sub una potestate suprema veluti sub uno capite et uno spiritu, ad bene et commodius vivendum in hac mortali vita, utque facilis ad aeternam perveniatur.* Cf. also Althusius, *Polit.* c. 9; Hoenonius, I, § 3; Kirchner, I, § 3; Keckermann, *Praecogn.* p. 7; König, *Theatrum pol.* I, c. 1; Winkler, V, c. 4; Suarez, III, c. 1; Grotius, II, c. 9, § 3, cf. I, c. 3, §§ 4–6, II, c. 15, § 3, III, c. 20, §§ 2–4; Berckringer, I, c. 4; Boxhorn, I, c. 2, § 1.

Respublica and Civitas

Often a distinction is drawn between *Civitas* and *Respublica*, which are said to be related as *materia* and *forma*, or as *subjectum* and *finis*, or as body and soul. The *Civitas* thus becomes merely the group or community which is the basis of the State, while the *Respublica* is the constitution of that group; and on this basis the *Civitas* is defined as a body of persons, and the *Respublica* as an order of relations (an *ordo jubendi ac parendi*, or some such phrase)—the idea of *societas* being then connected with the former, and that of *summa potestas* with the latter. The distinction is particularly emphasised in Arnisaeus, *Polit.* cc. 6 and 7, *De rep.* I prooem. §§ 4 sqq., I, c. 5, s. 3, II, c. 1, s. 1; see also Besold, *Princ. et finis pol. doctr.* Diss. I, c. 5, §§ 1–3 and c. 8; Knipschildt, *De Civ. imp.* I, c. 1; Schönborner, I, c. 4; Werdenhagen, II, cc. 1 and 3; Berckringer, cc. 1 and 4.

36. Althusius expressly makes the chief task of politics consist in the

investigation of the nature and authority of *majestas*; cf. his prefaces (in the author's work on Althusius, pp. 18–20).

Sovereignty   37. On the history of the conception of sovereignty see the author's work on Althusius, Part II, c. v and pp. 351 sq., with the works there cited by Hancke, Weill, Dunning, Dock, Merriam, Rehm and Jellinek; and also Preuss, *Gemeinde, Staat, Reich als Gebietskörperschaften* (Berlin, 1889), pp. 106 sqq. [See also the exhaustive analysis of the conception in de la Bigne de Villeneuve, *Traité général de l'État*, vol. I.]

38. References for all these points may be found in the author's work on Althusius, pp. 151–8, 163–78 and 351 sqq. [Gierke also refers to the notes on pp. 213–15, 218–19 and 220–3 of the fourth volume of his *Genossenschaftsrecht*, in a section not here translated.]

39. See the author's work on Althusius, pp. 143 sqq.

Classification of States   40. The classification of forms of the State of course assumed a far greater importance when the Ruler was the 'Subject' or owner of Sovereignty than when he only *exercised* a sovereignty which always and everywhere belonged to the People; and indeed a strict interpretation of popular sovereignty reduced the classification of forms of the State into a mere classification of forms of government. Althusius was the first to express this consequence definitely; and he deals with classification only at the end of his *Politica* (c. 39), in expounding a theory of the *species summi magistratus*: see the author's work on Althusius, p. 35; and see also Buchanan, p. 20, and Milton, *The Tenure of Kings and Magistrates*.

The mixed Constitution: opponents and advocates   41. This explains why we find opponents of the conception of the *forma mixta* not only among (1) the advocates of the sovereignty of the Ruler, but also among (2) the devotees of popular sovereignty and (3) those of 'double sovereignty'. The opponents of the first kind are e.g. Bodin, II, c. 1, nos. 174–8, c. 7, no. 234; Gregorius, v, c. 1, §3; Barclay, v, c. 12; Bornitius, *Part.* pp. 46 sqq. and 102 sqq.; Reinkingk, I, cl. 2, c. 2, nos. 231 sqq. and cl. 5, c. 6; Graszwinkel, c. 6; Hobbes, *De cive*, c. 7, *Leviathan*, c. 19. The opponents of the second kind are Althusius, c. 39; Hoenonius, II, §42. Opponents of the third kind are Kirchner, III, §7, litt. e; Alsted, pp. 69 sqq.; Arumaeus, I, no. 1; Otto, *Diss. an mixtus detur reipublicae status*, in Arumaeus, II, no. 22; Brautlacht, III, c. 2, §10; Cubach; Beindorff; Hilliger; Konings; Schieferer. [Gierke also refers to a note on p. 219 of the fourth volume of the *Genossenschaftsrecht*, in a section not here translated.] Conversely, the mixed form receives the adhesion not only (1) of some of the advocates of popular sovereignty (such as Hotoman, *Francogallia*, c. 12, and Danaeus, I, c. 6), and (2) of advocates of 'double sovereignty' (e.g. Besold, *De statu reip. mixtae*, c. 2; Frantzken, *De statu reip. mixtae*, in Arumaeus, III, no. 27 and IV, no. 41, §§60 sqq.; Tulden, II, cc. 16–17; Berckringer, I, c. 12, §§15–21; Werdenhagen, II, c. 25; Liebenthal, d. VIII, qu. 1; Paurmeister; Limnaeus; Carpzov) [Gierke also refers to pp. 218 sqq. of the fourth volume of the *Genossenschaftsrecht*, in a section not here translated]; but also (3) of many of the advocates of the sovereignty of the Ruler. Examples of this last class are Molina, II, *disp.* 23; Suarez, III, c. 4, no. 5 and c. 19, no. 6, IV, c. 17, no. 4; Albergati, I, cc. 8 sqq., pp. 251 sqq.; Arnisaeus, *Polit.* c. 8, *De jure maj.* II, cc. 1 and 6, *De rep.* II, c. 6, s. 1 and s. 5 §§1–134, II, c. 1, §1, *De auct.* c. 1, §§4 sqq.; Busius, II, c. 6; Knipschildt, I, c. 8, nos. 61–3; Keckermann, II, cc. 4–6; Heider, pp. 982 sqq.; Schönborner, I, c. 16; Felwinger, *Diss.* pp. 147–84 [a reference is also added to other writers cited in a note on

p. 222 of the fourth volume of the *Genossenschaftsrecht*]. A similar view occurs in Grotius, I, c. 3, §§ 17–20, c. 4, § 13.

It should be added, however, that the conception of the mixed constitution has obviously a different significance, according as the right of the Ruler which is held to be divisible among a number of different 'Subjects' is regarded as (*a*) the one and only form of Sovereignty, or (*b*) merely a *majestas personalis*, or (*c*) a simple 'magistracy'.

42. Cf. Bodin, II, c. 1; F. Victoria, *Rel.* III, no. 10 (there is the same *potestas* and the same *libertas* in every form of State, whether *unus* or *plures* be the 'Subject' of sovereignty); Graszwinkel, c. 11 (whether the ruling authority be *persona unum* or *corpore unum*,* the same theory is applicable in regard to *imperium* and *obedientia*, and their *origo a Deo*); Arnisaeus, *Polit.* c. 11, *De jure maj.* I, c. 2, *De rep.* II, c. 7, s. 2; Claudius de Carnin, I, c. 10; Hobbes, *De cive*, c. 7, §§ 7 and 9, c. 10, *Leviathan*, cc. 18–19. *The absolutist view of democracy, as equally absolute with monarchy*

Those who maintained, in regard to monarchy, the principle that the king was superior not only to all the members of the community as individuals, but also to the community itself as a whole, were logically compelled to admit the corresponding principle in regard to democracy—that the governing community of the People was superior not only to individuals, but also to the whole body of the governed. In doing so, they allowed the conception of the sovereign Whole to transform itself into that of the majority [i.e. they regarded the majority, rather than the whole community of the people, as superior to the body of the governed]; but failure to analyse their conceptions adequately enabled them to avoid the paradoxical conclusion, which this involved, that the majority had a greater authority than all the members taken together. Thus we find Bodin saying of the *popularis status* (II, c. 7), *Cives universi, aut maxima pars civium*, caeteris omnibus *non tantum singulatim, sed etiam simul coacervatis et collectis, imperandi jus habent*. Other thinkers, in dealing with democracy, tacitly dropped the distinction between the sovereign community and the whole body of the governed [or, as Rousseau expressed it, between the people as *souverain* and the people as *état*], and simply spoke of the authority of the *populus universus* over *omnes ut singuli*. Bornitius (*Part*. p. 51) expressly remarks that in a democracy the sovereign *cives, collective uniti*, only govern *singuli*; for *cunctis non possunt* [*imperare*]. Hobbes was the first thinker who was able, without self-contradiction, to reject the view that in a democracy there was a personality of the people [as a governed body] which was distinct from the collective person of the people as Ruler; and he was able to do so because, in *every* form of State, he regarded the people as being, in relation to the Ruler, a mere sum of 'dissolute' individuals (cf. *De cive*, c. 6, §§ 13 and 17, c. 7, §§ 5–7, c. 12, § 8, *Leviathan*, c. 18).

43. Thus Besold (*De maj.* s. 1, c. 1, § 5) ascribes to the popular assembly in a democracy, acting by majority-vote, only a *majestas personalis*, while he assigns to the community of the citizens a *majestas realis*; and he consequently draws the conclusion that unanimity is required for constitutional changes and for any regulations which relate to the State itself. Diodorus of Tulden (I, cc. 11 and 12) takes the same line. The advocates of a 'double sovereignty', who distinguished between *majestas realis* and *personalis* even in treating of democracy, were theoretically bound to assume two different forms of the *The problem of the People as Ruler and the People as ruled*

---

* *Persona unum* = one in the sense of possessing a single legal personality (though several physical persons may unite to constitute that single personality): *corpore unum* = one in the sense of being a single physical person.

sovereign community of the People. Similarly, too, in the pure theory of popular sovereignty, the sovereign People [which is ultimately supreme in *all* forms of State] cannot be logically identified with the People which is instituted as the Ruling authority in a democracy. Even the advocates of the sovereignty of the Ruler, if they pushed the doctrine of a contract of submission [i.e. of a contract of government] to its logical conclusion, were bound to distinguish, as the two separate parties involved in this contract when a democracy was in question, (1) the originally sovereign People, and (2) the sovereign popular assembly deciding by majority-vote [to which the originally sovereign People had submitted itself by contract]: cf. Victoria, III, nos. 1, 6–8; Soto, IV, qu. 1, a. 1; Molina, II, d. 23, § 12; Fridenreich, c. 18.

It was impossible, however, to take these distinctions seriously without being involved in contradictions. Thinkers began by arguing, where other forms of State than democracy were concerned, that both the original rights of the People and those of its rights which still remained in action after the institution of the Ruler belonged to the same assembly—the assembly of all the members of the State—deciding as a *universitas* by majority-vote. Then, as soon as democracy was in question, they made a sudden *volte-face*, and required unanimity. [I.e. they claimed that the sovereign People, when exercising its original rights, must be unanimous, though they allowed that the popular assembly, when exercising the rights which it acquired by being instituted as Ruler, might decide by majority-vote.] This was an entirely arbitrary procedure; and yet without it the distinction of the two forms of the popular community remained without any practical significance. Many thinkers, accordingly, dropped any idea of a contract of submission [between the sovereign People and the popular assembly] in dealing with democracy, and substituted for it a special resolution of the sovereign People to retain its sovereignty: this is the line taken by Suarez, III, c. 4, nos. 1, 5–6, 11. Others, again, substituted [in lieu of a contract between the sovereign People and the popular assembly] a contract between the People and the governing body of the Republic, thereby abolishing any clear logical distinction between a Monarchy and a Republic. This is the line taken by Althusius (c. 39): while describing the People as itself the *summus magistratus* in a democracy, he nevertheless assumes a contractual relation between the People and its officials and ephors; cf. Rossaeus, c. 1, §2, and Milton, *Defensio* of 1651, c. 6. The majority of thinkers were altogether silent on this difficult question. Hobbes, however (loc. cit.), saw clearly this weak spot in the armour of the doctrine of popular rights; and he used the inherent self-contradiction of the view that in a democracy the People must be superior to the People in order to refute entirely the idea that a popular community, as distinct from its Ruler, could have any sovereignty at all, whether in the way of original rights or of rights that still remained in action after the Ruler's institution.

44. See the author's work on Althusius, pp. 143 sqq. and 356.

45. Op. cit. pp. 85, 91 and 341.

Monarchy and Republic as the two types

46. In this connection the three basic forms of government distinguished by Aristotle [the One, the Few and the Many] continued to be generally recognised; but there was an increasing tendency to unite with Aristotle's threefold division a logical distinction of governments into the *two* forms of Monarchy and the Republic—aristocracy and democracy being then taken together as forms of State with a collective government [i.e. government by

Notes to § 14

more than One]. Cf. Althusius, c. 39; Victoria, *Rel.* III, no. 10 (*unus vel plures*); Bornitius, *Part.* p. 45 (*majestas inest uni semper τῷ λόγῳ, interdum etiam persona, interdum multis**); Keckermann, *Polit.* II, c. 1; Arnisaeus, *De jure maj.* I, c. 2, *Polit.* c. 11 (the sovereign is *unum* either *natura,* or *conspiratione et analogia*); Grotius, I, c. 3, § 7 (*persona una pluresve*); Busius, I, c. 3, § 4 (*unus vel plures*); Berckringer, I, c. 4, § 10 (*unum numero vel analogia*); Graszwinkel, c. 11 (*persona unum* or *corpore unum*); Hobbes, *De cive,* c. 5, § 7 and c. 7, *Leviathan,* c. 17 (*unus homo vel coetus*). Althusius, Bornitius, Keckermann, Besold (*De Arist.* c. 1), Tulden (II, c. 12) and other writers use the technical expressions 'Monarchy' and 'Polyarchy'.

47. The believers in a mixed constitution regarded a division of the right of government as possible; and conversely the indivisibility of governing authority served their opponents as the chief ground for rejecting such a form of State. Both allowed that other 'Subjects' (and, more particularly, assemblies of the Estates in a monarchy) might participate to some degree in the exercise of the right of government. But believers in the mixed constitution—assuming that States in which the right of government was constitutionally limited could co-exist with absolute States—asserted the possibility of an *independent* right to participate in the exercise of State-authority; while their opponents—refusing to allow any binding force to a constitutional limitation of the Ruler—treated any modification of governing authority by the co-operation of other factors as only a variation *within* the mode of government (*ratio gubernandi* or *forma gubernandi*). *Mixed and limited constitutions*

Most of the advocates of the mixed form (cf. supra, n. 41) recognised in addition the merely 'limited' form of government (e.g. Molina, II, d. 23; Suarez, III, c. 4, no. 5, c. 9, no. 4, IV, c. 17, no. 4; Keckermann, I, c. 33, II, cc. 4–6; Heider, pp. 982 sqq.; Busius, II, cc. 6–7; Grotius, I, c. 3, §§ 16–18); but there were some of them who thought that while division of sovereignty was conceivable, limitation was not (Arnisaeus, *De jure maj.* I, c. 6, *De rep.* II, c. 2, s. 5). Even the opponents of the mixed constitution (supra. n. 41) —not only those who advocate popular sovereignty and 'double sovereignty', but also many of those who advocate the sovereignty of the Ruler—are willing to accept the idea of limited government, and to defend, in so many words, the inviolability of constitutional limitations on the right of the Ruler (Bornitius, *Part.* 43, *De maj.* c. 13; Fridenreich, cc. 18 and 29). On the other hand the thorough-going absolutists reject the limited form no less than the mixed (Bodin, I, c. 8, nos. 85–99; Gregorius, I, c. 1, § 9, XXIV, c. 7; Barclay; Graszwinkel, cc. 3, 4, 6, 11; Hobbes; Salmasius, c. 7).

48. Cf. the author's *Althusius,* pp. 80 sqq. and 341. The fact that Arnisaeus (op. cit. p. 81 n. 19) and Grotius (op. cit. n. 20) recognise other grounds [in addition to delegation by the people] for the acquisition of the rights of government, or again that Graszwinkel (c. 2) rejects the contract of government altogether, hardly weighs in the balance against the general trend of Contractarian theory.

49. Op. cit. p. 85, n. 30.
50. Op. cit. p. 85 n. 32.
51. The identity of the people as it now stands with the people as it originally existed was used to explain why a contract of government assigned to a primitive past was obligatory upon the present generation. In defence *The People identical through the generations of its life*

* "The 'Subject' of Sovereignty is always theoretically one; sometimes it may also actually be one person, but sometimes it may be composed of many."

of this identity we find an appeal expressly made to the principles of the [Roman-law] theory of Corporations in regard to the continuous existence of the *universitas* through all the changes of its members: cf. especially Junius Brutus [the author of the *Vindiciae contra Tyrannos*], qu. III, pp. 171 sqq.; but cf. also Althusius, c. 19, §§ 74 sqq., c. 9, § 16, c. 38, §§ 65 sqq., and Victoria, *Rel.* III, no. 11. Grotius uses the same idea (II, c. 5, § 31), extending it to cover cases of the forfeiture of *imperium* by delict or in war—*quia successio partium non impedit quominus unus sit populus*; cf. also III, c. 9, § 9.

The People as a Corporate Body

52. According to the *Vindiciae contra Tyrannos* the people, as a *universitas* which *unius personae vicem sustinet*, (1) acting in conjunction with the King, concludes a covenant with God (qu. II, p. 75), and (2) acting by itself, concludes a covenant with the King (qu. III, pp. 131 sqq. and 248 sqq.). Now since *universitas nunquam moritur*, and no prescription runs against it (qu. III, pp. 170–1), the people continues to possess inviolable rights and duties in virtue of both these covenants. (1) It is responsible to God, as *correus debendi* [or joint debtor] with the King, for the well-being of the Church, and it makes itself liable to divine punishment by tolerating godless magistrates; while according to the rule *quod universitas debet, singuli non debent*, the *primates* of the people *ex foedere cum Deo non tenentur* (qu. II, pp. 76, 84 sqq. and 115). (2) Again, in regard to the King, the people, as a *universitas*, has a higher authority, and in the event of his becoming a tyrant it has the right and duty of resistance and deposition (qu. III, pp. 143 sqq. and 292 sqq.); while *singuli privati* are in no way called upon to take such action (ibid. pp. 319 sqq.).

Althusius brings the popular community, as a *consociatio publica universalis*, entirely under the category of the *universitas* (*Polit.* c. 9 sq.). He ascribes to this *corpus consociatum*—the *totum corpus consociationis*, or *universitas populi*—inalienable sovereignty, the ownership of State-property, and the rights belonging to an employer in regard to all officers vested with public powers of administration; while, citing in justification the [Roman-law] theory of corporations, he excludes individuals from the enjoyment of all these rights (Praef. pp. 9, 17, 18, 19, 38). See also Buchanan, pp. 16 sqq. and 78; Hotoman, *Francogallia*, cc. 6–9 and 19; Rossaeus, c. 1, §§ 2–3; Mariana, I, c. 8; Marius Salamonius, *De princ.* I, pp. 19–20.

53. See, for example, Paurmeister, I, c. 17; Bortius, c. 6, § 2; Besold, *De maj.* sect. 1, c. 1, § 4 (*corpus*) and § 7 (*penes universitatem populi*); Limnaeus, *Cap. imp.* p. 352.

The use of the theory of Corporations in Grotius

54. Grotius employs the conception of the *universitas* and the principles of the [Roman-law] theory of corporations (1) in dealing with the contractual devolution or transference of supreme authority by the people (I, c. 3, § 13; II, c. 5, § 31, c. 14, §§ 2 and 10; III, c. 8); (2) in his account of delicts of the people and its responsibility for the delicts of its members (II, c. 21); (3) in regard to the question of the obligation of the people by the acts of the king (II, c. 14, § 10); (4) in justifying reprisals under international law (III, c. 2) and the taking of prizes (III, c. 6, § 8); and also in other respects.

And in ecclesiastical writers

55. See Victoria, III, no. 8; Vasquez, c. 47; Soto, IV, qu. 4, a. 1–2 (the people as *corpus*); Molina, II, *disp.* 23; Suarez, III, cc. 2–3 (the people as *communitas, corpus mysticum, corpus politicum*, originally possesses and transfers the supreme authority). See also Pruckmann, pp. 90 sqq. (contract with the *universitas* or *communitas*), p. 111, nos. 25 sqq.; Boxhorn, I, c. 2, § 1 (*corpus multorum*); Busius, I, c. 3, § 3 (*universitas cujuscunque totius legitimae civitatis uno imperio contentae*).

56. See Bodin, I, c. 8, nos. 85–99; Gregorius, I, 1, §§6–7 (*unum corpus civile* according to l. 30, D. 41, 3 and l. 1, §1, D. 3, 4); Knipschildt, V, c. 1, nos. 3–4.

57. The people united in a State is described as a *societas civilis*, naturally developed by the extension and perfection of the Family, in the following writers: Gregorius, I, c. 1, §6 and c. 2, §§1–6 (*societas, quae natura coaluit*), XIX, c. un.; Arnisaeus, *De rep.* I, c. 5, s. 4 and s. 5, *Polit.* c. 6 (the *civitas* is a *societas*, the *civis* is a *socius*); Besold, *Diss.* I, c. 3 (*societas civilis*, which *in utero naturae concepta, in ejus gremio nutrita est*); Kirchner, *Disp.* I, §3 (*societas populi, legitimo civilis potestatis imperio coalita*); Keckermann, pp. 12 sqq.; Fridenreich, c. 2 (growth from *consociationes domesticae*, like a many-branched tree from its roots) and c. 10; Schönborner, I, c. 4; Crüger, *Disp.* 1; Heider, pp. 25 sqq.; Werdenhagen, II, cc. 1–3 (the *populus* is a *societas civilis*); Tulden, I, c. 5 (*societas civilis*, which arose *ex naturae instructu*), and c. 6 (the *finis reipublicae* is *societatis civilis tutela atque cultura*); Conring (*societas civilis*, with *imperium*); Knipschildt, I, cc. 1 and 6; and many other writers.

A *societas civilis* founded by a union of men originally living in isolation is the basis adopted by Buchanan, pp. 11 sqq.; Mariana, I, c. 1; Rossaeus, c. 1, §1; Boucher, cc. 10 sqq.; Hoenonius, I, §§4 sqq.; Winkler, I, c. 10, II, cc. 9–10, V, c. 3 (*multitudo sese consociat*, and thus produces *societas civilis*); cf. the description of the State as *societas civilis et voluntaria* in Velstenius, dec. 2–5, and in Matthias, *Coll. disp.* 4–5 and *Syst.* pp. 20 sqq. The treatment of the community of the people as a contractually created 'society' is carried into greater detail by Salamonius, I, pp. 35 sqq. and 38–42, and by Paurmeister, I, c. 17, nos. 3 sqq. (the *societas* formed by *mutua conventio*), c. 3, no. 10 (*societas et libera conventio*), c. 30, nos. 1–3 (the ending of such *societas* by *contraria voluntas*).

Althusius, who is the first to develop a formal theory of the social contract as constituting the State, interprets the State throughout (like all other corporate bodies) as a *consociatio* or *societas* (*Polit.* cc. 1–9; *Dicaeolog.* I, cc. 8, 32, 78 and 81). Grotius constantly applies the conception of *consociatio* or *societas* to the political community (*Proleg.* cc. 15–16, I, c. 1, §14, II, c. 5, §§17, 23, 24, II, c. 6, §§24 sqq., III, c. 2, §6, c. 20, §§7–8).

58. Cf. the author's *Althusius*, p. 94 n. 51, p. 96 n. 59, p. 98 n. 63, p. 100 n. 68. Schönborner, I, c. 4, definitely says, *Essentia reipublicae est in personis vel imperantibus vel obtemperantibus, sibi invicem mutuis officiis obstrictis.*

59. Cf. the author's *Althusius*, pp. 96 sqq.

60. Thus, according to Molina (II, d. 22, §§8–9), *societas politica* arises from the union of originally independent individuals; but because the natural reason given by God impels them thereto, there results *eo ipso, quod homines ad integrandum unum corpus Reipublicae conveniunt, jure naturali, et sic a Deo immediate, potestas corporis totius Reipublicae in singulas partes, ad eas gubernandum, ad leges illis ferendum jusque illis dicendum, et ad eas puniendum*. The *homines convenientes*, because they are *partes*, are a *conditio sine qua non* of the authority thus resulting, but they are not its creators: otherwise it would be impossible to explain why the community has a right of life and death, while no individual has such a right over himself. Moreover, *longe diversa fit potestas, quae ex natura rei consurgit in Republica, a collectione particularium potestatum singulorum*; and a *Respublica* does not hold its power *auctoritate singulorum, sed immediate a Deo*.*

The People described as a societas

The theory of the Rights of the People in the theologians

---

* The theory of the theologians may be illustrated from the analogy of marriage. The agreement of husband and wife is necessary to the existence of marriage. But

Suarez (III, cc. 1-3) argues still more emphatically that, inasmuch as man is born free and subject to no human power, the *perfecta communitas* only arises in consequence of the *interventus humanae voluntatis*, and indeed *per voluntatem omnium qui in illa convenerunt*; but at the same time, man being by nature *subjicibilis*, this agreement of union corresponds in his case to the demands of natural reason. Moreover, although the community itself *coalescit medio consensu et voluntate singulorum*, the authority which it possesses is not acquired directly from the *singuli*, who did not previously possess any such power, and least of all any right of life and death; nor is such authority acquired directly from God; it is derived *ex vi rationis naturalis*, as a *proprietas consequens naturae* which God has willed; and therefore it follows that individuals, though they are creators of the *corpus politicum*, are not the source of the authority of that body over itself and its members.

See also Didacus Covarruvias, *Pract. qu.* I, cc. 1 and 4 (*societas civilis* is formed *lege naturali*, and by the same law it possesses all authority, which it proceeds to devolve upon a ruler): Soto, I, qu. 1, a. 3 and IV, qu. 4, a. 1-2 (God, *per legem naturalem*, gave individuals a right of self-preservation, and with it—because self-preservation is impossible in isolation—an instinct for society; and thus He gave the *congregata Respublica* authority over itself and its members); Victoria, III, nos. 4-8; Bellarmine, *De laicis*, cc. 5-6; Claudius de Carnin, I, c. 9.

Suarez on the origin of sovereignty

61. Suarez (III, c. 3, nos. 6-7) compares the sovereignty of the *corpus politicum et mysticum* with the liberty of the individual person. In both cases there is an authority over the self and its own members—an authority which is necessarily given with and by the fact of existence. Now as the child receives its existence from its father, but its liberty from God, in virtue of Natural Law, *ita haec potestas datur communitati hominum ab auctore naturae, non tamen sine interventu voluntatum et consensuum hominum, ex quibus talis communitas perfecta congregata est*. As the father can beget or not beget the child, but if he begets it can only beget it as a free being, so it only needs a human will directed to that end to bring the community into existence, but *ut illa communitas habeat potestatem praedictam, non est necessaria specialis voluntas hominum, sed ex natura rei consequitur et ex providentia auctoris naturae*. Just because they are not inherent in the nature of either, the sovereignty of the community and the liberty of the individual are both alike alienable and transferable. See the author's *Althusius*, p. 67.

The theologians really make the community an aggregate of individuals

62. Such a view is already implied in the argument, that sovereignty must originally belong to the community because there is no discoverable reason why it should belong to one person rather than another: cf. Victoria, op. cit. no. 7; Bellarmine, op. cit.; Molina, d. 22; Suarez, III, c. 2, nos. 1-4. But it appears more explicitly in the further conception, that the community is driven by the nature of things to transfer its original authority to a ruler because it cannot, as a *multitudo*, exercise that authority itself: cf. Victoria, op. cit. no. 8; Bellarmine, op. cit. (where it is definitely said that supreme authority *immediate tanquam in subjecto in tota multitudine est*, but is transferred by this *multitudo*). Soto argues in the same sense, IV, qu. 1, a. 1.

A similar line is adopted by Molina (II, c. 23). While describing the sove-

it does not explain, or create, the institution of marriage. The institution is an inherent part of the divine scheme; and the agreement of the parties is simply an agreement to fit themselves into that scheme, which exists *per se* apart from their agreement.

reignty of the people as the authority of a *body* over its members, he none the less takes the *totum corpus* to be the [mere] sum of all; and he depicts the transference of authority to a Ruler as a command of Natural Law, inasmuch as otherwise [i.e. if the transference were not made] all would be constantly obliged to act in unison and by unanimity.

Even Suarez, in spite of the emphasis which he attaches to the corporate nature of the unity of the people, cannot transcend the conception of that unity as a mere collection of all its members. He describes the *hominum collectio* (III, c. 2, no. 3), or the *tota communitas* (ibid. no. 4), as the original 'Subject' of supreme authority; and he contents himself with adding that *multitudo hominum dupliciter considerari potest* (1) *uno modo, ut est aggregatum quoddam sine ulló ordine vel unione physica vel morali...*, (2) *alio modo, quatenus speciali voluntate seu communi consensu in unum corpus politicum congregantur uno societatis vinculo et ut mutuo se juvent in ordine ad unum finem politicum, quo modo efficiunt unum corpus mysticum, quod moraliter dici potest per se unum.* He argues that it is only in this second mode or sense that the community is the 'Subject' of a *communis potestas, cui singuli de communitate parere tenentur*; in the first sense or mode it only possesses such authority, at the most, *radicaliter* (III, c. 2, no. 4; cf. II, c. 3, nos. 1 and 6—*rudis collectio sive aggregatum* as distinct from *corpus mysticum*).*

63. In Buchanan (pp. 11 sqq.), Mariana (I, c. 1), Rossaeus (c. 1, §1), Boucher (cc. 10 sqq.) and Paurmeister (I, c. 17, nos. 3 sqq.), the authority of the State is regarded as proceeding merely from the social union of free and equal individuals who originally lived in isolation. Althusius (*Polit.* cc. 1 sqq.) ascribes the rights of all associations to a *communicatio mutua* in things, services and rights which are useful and necessary for social life. Grotius (II, c. 5, §§ 17 sqq. and c. 20, III, c. 2, § 6) derives the rights of the State, including the power of punishment, entirely from the original rights of individuals. Milton (*The Tenure*, pp. 8–10) considers the authority of the State as the product of a contract of society formed among men who are naturally born free, 'this authority and power of self-defence and preservation being originally and naturally in every one of them, and unitedly in them all'. See the author's work on Althusius, pp. 105 sqq., 344 sqq. *The authority of the State as a sum of individual rights*

64. A typical example of this conception is the way in which Salamonius (pp. 33–42) attempts to prove that *populus ipse suis legibus ligatur*, although nobody can be *imperans* and *obediens* at the same time, and nobody can be *seipso potentior*. In reality, he argues, each law is a contract, and the people is a contractually united body of persons. The very beginning of the *civitas*, as a *civilis societas*, already implies binding contracts, and therefore laws. It is all a question, not of the obligation of the people to itself, but of mutual obligation between the individual members of the people—*societas non sibi obligatur, sed ipsi inter se socii*; and the Ruler, who occupies the position of *praepositus* or *institor* in the *societas*, is no less bound than the other members. Cf. Milton's phrase (op. cit. p. 8), 'a common league to bind each other from mutual injury'. *Salamonius on the State as a sum of contractual obligations*

---

* Here again (cf. the translator's note appended to note 60), the theory of the theologians seems really to be higher than Gierke allows. The consenting parties who are necessary to the existence of a political society (just as they are necessary to the institution of marriage) may be, as such, only an aggregate. But the *institution* which emerges from their act of agreement as a number of individuals is a part of the divine scheme, and is a true 'mystical body' in that scheme. The distinction is fundamental; and if we accept it the State is really a *corpus*.

244 Gierke's Notes

Althusius on the State as a partnership

65. Althusius identifies the body politic (*corpus symbioticum*) with the contractual community of the members of the people (*communio symbiotica universalis*): he bases all the rights of governing authority on the obligation, incurred in and by the contract of society, to participate in a *communicatio* of material and spiritual benefits and means of action; and he ascribes to the government only the position of 'administrator' of such matters as are the objects of this *communicatio*. Cf. *Polit.* cc. 9 sqq.; *Dicaeologia*, I, c. 81; and the author's work on Althusius, pp. 21 sqq.

The State in Grotius partly a Corporation partly a partnership

66. Cf. Grotius (II, c. 5, § 23): *consociatio, qua multi patresfamilias in unum populum ac civitatem coeunt, maximum dat jus corpori in partes, quia haec perfectissima est societas, neque ulla est actio hominis externa, quae non ad hanc societatem aut per se spectet aut ex circumstantiis spectare possit.* In § 24 he argues that the individual is entitled by Natural Law to terminate his membership [of the State]; but just as in the *societas privata* of Roman law a member cannot quit if his leaving affects the society, so here he can only quit on condition of paying in ready money his share of any debt with which the State may be burdened, or of providing an *idoneus* in lieu of himself if the State be engaged in war: moreover departure is often forbidden by positive law, and a *pactum sic initum* is vali. . In III, c. 20, §§ 7–8, he argues that it follows from the act of consent, implied in entry into civil society, that *res singulorum* may be sacrificed for the sake of *publica utilitas* in the event of the conclusion of a peace-treaty; but it equally follows, he adds, that individuals have a claim to compensation for war-losses from the means at the disposal of the community. The reason is that, though the infliction of injury and loss on an external enemy is lawful in war, *cives inter se sunt socii, et aequum est ut communia habeant damna quae societatis causa contingunt.* But positive law may ordain, none the less, *ut rei bello amissae nulla adversus civitatem actio sit, ut sua quisque arctius defendat.*

The People as a sum, or a Collection of units

67. For Althusius the sovereign People is identical with the *consociata multitudo*; with *homines conjuncti, consociati et cohaerentes*; with the *universa membra conjunctim*; with the *populus universus*; with the *consociatio universalis*; with the *totum corpus* (*Polit.* Praef., cc. 9 and 17; *Dicaeologia*, I, cc. 7–8.) Similarly the author of the *Vindiciae contra Tyrannos* identifies the sovereign with the *populus conjunctim non divisim*, the *universi*, or the *universa multitudo* (qu. II, pp. 75, 89 sqq., 91 sqq., 114; qu. III, pp. 149, 171 sqq., 297 sqq.). To Buchanan, the sovereign is the *universus populus* (pp. 16, 30, 48, 78–80, 87): to Hotoman, it is the *universus populus* or *universi* (*Francogallia*, cc. 6–9 and 19); to Danaeus, the *subditi* or *populus universus* (I, c. 4, pp. 36–44; III, c. 6, pp. 217 sqq.); to Boucher, the *multitudo jure coacta*, which must not be confused with the *incondita et confusa turba* (I, c. 9); to Mariana, the *universi* (I, c. 8); to Salamonius, the *multitudo hominum* or *universi* (I, pp. 20, 36); to Rossaeus, the *universi* (c. 2, § 11); to Hoenonius, the *universi*, or *populus universus*, or *populus tributim curiatim centuriatim vel viritim collectus* (II, §§ 46, 51; IX, § 5); to Milton, 'all as united together' (*The Tenure*, p. 9).

In the same way *majestas realis* is ascribed by Kirchner to the *societas populi coalita* (II, § 1); by Paurmeister, to the *populus universus* (I, c. 17); by Berckringer, to the *populus universus...collective*—but also, at the same time, to the *singuli* as members of this collective body (I, c. 4, §§ 6–8); by Alstedius, to the *subditi universi* (p. 18); by Werdenhagen, to the people as *collectivum quid*, possessed of quantitative and qualitative attributes (II, c. 6). Similarly, again, we find the 'Subject' of original sovereignty, and of the popular rights which persist after the alienation of that sovereignty, described in

Notes to § 14

Soto as the *multitudo collectim sumpta* or the *populus congregatus* (I, qu. 1, a. 3, qu. 7, a. 2; IV, qu. 4, a. 1–2); in Victoria, as the *multitudo* or *omnes simul* (III, nos. 8, 15); in Bellarmine, as the *tota multitudo* (cf. n. 62 supra); in Molina, as the sum of all (II, d. 22–3, 25; III, d. 6); in Suarez, as the *hominum collectio* or *multitudo* (cf. n. 62 supra). Grotius too regards the *universitas* as consisting only of *singuli quique congregati vel in summam reputati* (II, c. 21, §7); and Keckermann describes the people as *collectivum quid ordinatum* (*Praecogn.* p. 7).

68. The advocates of the theory of popular sovereignty, like those of the theory of 'double sovereignty', expressly emphasise the fact that the Ruler is superior to his subjects *ut singulis*, but inferior to them *ut universis*. Cf. the *Vind. contra Tyr.* qu. II, pp. 91 sqq., qu. III, pp. 391 sqq.; Buchanan, pp. 79–80 (the king is to *singuli*, as the people is to the king); Salamonius, I, p. 20 (the king is *major singulis, sed minor universis*, as being the *servus universitatis*, but not the *singulorum minister*) and p. 28; Rossaeus, c. 2, §11; Danaeus, III, c. 6, pp. 217 sqq.; Althusius, c. 9, §18 (*non singulis, sed conjunctim universis membris et toto corpori consociati regni competit*); Hoenonius, II, §46 (*universi*, not *singuli*, are the *Superior*); Alstedius, p. 18 (*superior singulis, inferior subditis universis*) and pp. 56 sqq.; Milton, *Defensio* of 1651, p. 70 (*Rex est Rex singulorum*, and also *universorum*, but only *si voluerint*).

Omnes ut singuli and ut universi

Conversely, the advocates of the sovereignty of the Ruler argue that the Ruler is superior not only to *singuli* but also to *universi*: cf. Soto, IV, qu. 4, a. 1; Molina, II, d. 23, §8; Bornitius, *Part.* p. 41, *De maj.* c. 4. Cf. also Bornitius, *De maj.* c. 6 (the end of the State is *salus seu beatitudo reipublicae sive populi universi primum, deinde singulorum*); Suarez, III, c. 2, no. 4 (supra, n. 62); Grotius, I, c. 3, §§7–9, 12, III, c. 8, §4.

69. Cf. Salamonius, I, p. 36 (although the *populus una interdum censetur persona*, it is only *ut ficte una*, and *vere populus non aliud est quam quaedam hominum multitudo*); Suarez, I, c. 6, no. 17 (*una persona ficta*), III, c. 2, no. 4 (*unum corpus mysticum, quod moraliter dici potest per se unum*); *Vind. c. Tyr.* qu. II, p. 75 (*universitas unius personae vicem sustinet*, as the *Lex mortuo** teaches); Limnaeus, *Capitul.* nos. 48 sqq. (*majestas realis* is the power *quae Reipublicae adhaeret, hoc est universitati, quae non nisi ficte personae nomen inducere potest, ex personis tamen constat*); Grotius, II, c. 21, §8; Werdenhagen, II, c. 6, §§22–4 (*persona* is used in political theory only for the *singulus*, but *in jure* it is also used for *populus*, for an office, for a *universitas*, and in all cases in which *plures personas unus sustinet*).

The unity of the People a 'Fiction'

70. When a decision of the whole people is required, thinkers often speak vaguely of a *consensus populi* or a *voluntas universorum*, without going into the question whether or no they mean a regular act of an assembly which must follow the forms that are necessary for the decisions of a corporation: cf. Buchanan, pp. 16 sqq., 30 sqq., 78; Rossaeus, c. 2, §4 (the *consensus populi* as the will of the *Respublica*); Salamonius, I, pp. 8 sqq., 11, 31 sqq.; Mariana, I, c. 9; Vasquez, c. 47; Molina, II, d. 25; Suarez, III, c. 4, nos. 1–2, c. 4, no. 5, c. 9, no. 4; Boxhorn, I, c. 3, §§15 sqq. (since rule is contrary to nature, it depends on the constant *consensus* of *imperans* and *subditi*); Grotius, I, c. 3, §§8 (*populi universim sumpti arbitrio*), 13 (*populi voluntate delata*), II, c. 6, §§3, 7, 13, III, c. 20, §5 (*populi totius consensu*); Salmasius, c. 6 (sovereignty belongs to the King either *vi* or *voluntate populi*).

The common will an agreement of many wills

---

* The reference actually given in the *Vind. c. Tyr.* is to *Lex mortui* 22 D, de fidei commissis.

But we often find the decision of the people definitely treated as equivalent to the tacit and cumulative acts of consent of so many individuals. This idea is applied to the conclusion of the original contract of government, or to some later act of approval of a limited government which is a substitute for that contract: cf. *Vind. c. Tyr.* qu. III, pp. 264sqq., 287sqq.; [Beza's] *De jure mag.* qu. 5, pp. 18–20 (where the condition is made that the *consensus* must not be forced); Danaeus, I, c. 4, p. 41; Hoenonius, IX, §§ 56–7; Suarez, III, c. 4, no. 4 (the *consensus* is 'tacit' when rule has been usurped, but it is *debitus* when subjection has been imposed by a just war), c. 10, no. 7 (*consensus tacitus*); Arnisaeus, *De auct.* c. 4, §§ 11–14, *De rep.* II, c. 2, s. 5, c. 3, ss. 7–8 (*consensus tacitus*, and until it is given there are no *subditi*); Knipschildt, VI, c. 4, nos. 12–13 (no right [of government] exists until *subditi paulatim consensuerunt*); Fridenreich, c. 10 (all Ruling authority rests upon *electio*, since it is the *consensus universorum* which has either devolved it upon the ruler originally, or legitimised it afterwards); Bornitius, *De maj.* c. 3, *Part.* pp. 47sqq. (*consensus spontaneus aut coactus, expressus vel tacitus, verus vel quasi*, is what constitutes the Ruler); Grotius, I, c. 4, §§ 5sqq., II, c. 6, § 18; and see the author's work on Althusius, pp. 305–7.

Similarly we often find writers who argue that the consent of 'the people' is required for laws contenting themselves with an informal *approbatio* (Molina, II, d. 23, §§ 6–7, v, d. 46, § 3) or an *acceptatio populi* (Suarez, IV, c. 19, and Claudius de Carnin, I, c. 3). In the same way *consensus tacitus* was held to suffice for certain alienations [of public property] (Grotius, II, c. 6, §§ 8, 10).

On the other hand, many thinkers demand a formal resolution by a regular assembly in certain cases. Most of them, though there are some exceptions, require it for the deposition of a lawful ruler who has become a tyrant 'in exercise'; cf. Soto, IV, qu. 4, a. 1; Molina, III, d. 6; *Vind. c. Tyr.* qu. III, pp. 292sqq.; Mariana, I, c. 6 (*conventus publicus*); Althusius, c. 38; cf. the author's work on Althusius, pp. 309–12. Some writers also require an act of a regular assembly for the appointment of the Ruler; cf. Soto, IV, qu. 4, a. 2 (*publicus conventus*); *Vind. c. Tyr.* qu. III, pp. 248sqq. It may also be required as a way of giving assent to certain alienations [of public property]; cf. Grotius, II, c. 6, § 9.

All must act if the People is to act

71. Molina, d. 23 (supra, n. 62). Althusius (c. 9, §§ 16 and 18) holds that only *universa membra de communi consensu* can dispose of the *jus majestatis*, because only *membra regni universa simul* can constitute that right; but he also believes (cf. his Preface: cf. also c. 9, § 19; c. 18, §§ 15, 84, 104, 123–4; and c. 38, §§ 125–9) that even the whole of the people, acting unanimously, cannot make any valid alienation or division of sovereignty. Hoenonius (II, § 39) regards *regnicolae* as competent to decide *jura regni* 'by common consent'; cf. also his phrase (§ 40) *ex communi placito…vita socialis inter membra reipublicae instituitur et regitur*.

When unanimity required

72. The assumption of unanimity was taken for granted in regard to the contract of society; cf. Althusius, c. 9, § 19; Suarez, III, c. 3 (*per voluntatem omnium qui in illa convenerunt*); Grotius, II, c. 5, § 23 (vide supra, nn. 59–62). The *consensus omnium* is required for any change in fundamental laws by Bortius (*De maj.* II, § 17–21); and, as we have already mentioned (supra, n. 43), Besold (*De maj.* s. 1, c. 1, § 5) and Tulden (I, c. 11) require the consent of *omnes singuli* in a democracy for any change of *ipsae leges democraticae*. According to Althusius (*Dicaeologia*, I, c. 87, nos. 37–43) a unanimous resolution

should also precede the imposition of new taxes. [Gierke adds a reference to a note in a previous section of his fourth volume (p. 241), which is not translated here.]

73. Cf. Althusius, c. 17, §58; Buchanan, p. 79 (*universus populus vel major pars* is legislator, creator of government, and judge of the King); Milton, *Defensio* of 1651, c. 5, pp. 63–4, c. 7, pp. 69–70 (*populi pars major et potior*, i.e. *plus quam dimidia pars populi*, is *Superior Rege*). Generally, a majority-decision was regarded as adequate both for the [original] choice of a form of State and appointment of a Ruler, and for any subsequent changes in the constitution; cf. Victoria, III, nos. 14–15 (in the appointment of a Ruler a majority is enough, *etiam aliis invitis*, since the consent of all cannot be attained; the whole of Christianity might give itself a Ruler by majority-decision; and in the same way a majority in a republic may, if it wishes, choose a monarch); Soto, qu. 4, a. 2; supra, n. 43. *[margin: When majority-decision allowed]*

74. In most writers we only find a reference to the general rules of the [Roman] law of corporations. Grotius is the first writer (II, c. 5, §17) to use the fiction that the majority-principle must have been introduced by an act of contract into all associations, both public and private (*quod in iis rebus, ob quas consociatio quaeque instituta est, universitas et ejus pars major nomine universitatis obligant singulos qui sunt in societate*). He argues (1) that in each contract of society we must assume a *voluntas in societatem coëuntium...ut ratio aliqua esset expediendi negotia*; (2) that this *ratio*, or way of transacting business, can only consist in the supremacy of the majority, because it is obviously improper *ut pars major sequatur minorem*; and therefore (3) that so far as special *pacta et leges* do not provide otherwise, *pars major habet jus integri*. Hobbes takes a similar view (*De cive*, c. 6, §§1–2). Only unanimity is valid in a *multitudo extra civitatem*; but it marks the beginning of the transformation of such a multitude into a State when its members agree *ut in iis rebus, quae a quopiam in coëtu proponentur, pro voluntate omnium habeatur id quod voluerit eorum major pars*. Otherwise no single will can be attained. If any person will not accept this agreement, the rest can constitute the State without him, and can exercise against him their original right—the *jus belli*: cf. ibid. §20. *[margin: The fiction that majority-decision is made equal to unanimous decision by a contract to that effect]*

75. See the author's work on Althusius, pp. 216–19, and §12, n. 129 of this volume [not here translated]. The author of the *Vind. c. Tyr.* invokes, as the organ for securing the observance of the rights and duties imposed by contract (whether it be the contract made with God, or that made with the king*), not the *universa multitudo*, but the *electi magistratus regni*—the *officiarii Regni non Regis*, or *consortes et ephori imperii*—inasmuch as these officers *a populo auctoritatem acceperunt*, and thus *universum populi coetum repraesentant*: qu. II, p. 89, qu. III, pp. 148 sqq. A similar view appears in the *De jure mag.* qu. 6–7 (*ordines sive status*); Buchanan, p. 30 (*ex omnibus ordinibus selecti*); Hotoman, cc. 13–14; Mariana, I, c. 8 (*proceres* or *deputati*). *[margin: Representation of the People by Estates or 'Ephors']*

Althusius includes both the 'Ephors' and the *summus magistratus* among the *administratores* of public authority, who are appointed and commissioned by the *consociata multitudo* because it cannot easily meet itself, and who, within the limits of their commission, *universum populum repraesentant* (c. 18, §§ 1–47): *Ephori sunt quibus, populi in corpus politicum consociati consensu, demandata est summa Reipublicae seu universalis consociationis, ut repraesentantes eandem potestate*

---

* The *Vind. c. Tyr.* supposes two contracts—that of people and king with God (the divine covenant), and that of people and king (the secular contract of government).

et jure illius utantur in summo magistratu constituendo, eoque ope [*et*] *consilio in negotiis corporis consociati juvando, necnon in ejusdem licentia coercenda et impedienda in causis iniquis et Reip. perniciosis, et eodem intra limites officii continendo, et denique in providendo et curando omnibus modis, ne Resp. quid detrimenti capiat privatis studiis, odiis, facto, omissione vel cessatione summi magistratus* (ibid. §48). These 'ephors' are appointed by popular election, but they may also be appointed, *ex populi concessione et beneficio*, by nomination or co-optation (§59): their commission may also be made hereditary *ex consensu consociationis universalis* (§107): they constitute a *collegium*, which acts *collegialiter* and by its *major pars* (§62): as such a college they discharge the *officium generale*, with which they are vested, of representative exercise of popular rights (§§63–89, c. 38, §§28 sqq.); but there is also, distinct from this 'general office' of the college, an *officium speciale* of individual 'ephors' (c. 18, §§90–1, c. 38, §§46–52).*

Hoenonius has a similar theory (II, §§46–51, IX, §§44–54): *ephori seu ordines regni* have to exercise the right of the sovereign people *ex jussu et consensu populi*: as *universi, quatenus universum populum repraesentant*, they are superior to the Ruler. Grotius argues (II, c. 6, §9): *populum autem consensisse intelligimus, sive totus cöiit...sive per legatos partium integrantium mandatu sufficiente instructos; nam facimus et quod per alium facimus;* cf. I, c. 3, §10, III, c. 20, §5. See also Fridenreich (c. 10), who holds that, in lieu of *universi*, smaller assemblies have often to elect the Ruler by virtue of 'delegation': Tulden (II, cc. 19–23), who regards the *optima forma* as a *monarchia temperata, optimatibus aut dilectis populi in partem regiminis admissis*): Milton (*Defensio* of 1651, c. 7, p. 70), who argues that the objection of Salmasius (that we regard *plebs sola* as *populus*) is incorrect; for we include *omnes ordinis cujuscunque cives* in the people, inasmuch as *unam tantummodo supremam curiam stabilivimus, in qua etiam proceres ut pars populi, non pro sese quidem solis, ut antea, sed pro iis municipiis, a quibus electi fuerint, suffragia ferendi legitimum jus habent*.

The People as superior to its representatives

76. The author of the *Vind. c. Tyr.* ascribes to the assembly of the 'ephors', as *Regni quasi Epitome*, equal rights with the people, and an equal superiority with the people over the king, inasmuch as any act of a majority of that assembly counts as the action of the people (qu. II, pp. 91, 94, 114; qu. III, pp. 148, 149, 248 sqq., 297 sqq., 326 sqq.); but he expressly insists that this assembly cannot, by any resolution or any omission on its part, forfeit the rights of the *populus constituens* (qu. III, p. 173). The same line is adopted in the *De jure mag.* (qu. 6–7): the ephors, in regard to the Ruler, are *defensores ac protectores jurium ipsius supremae potestatis* [i.e. they are the guardians of popular sovereignty], but they cannot actually prejudice the sovereign rights of the people itself. Buchanan (pp. 30 sqq.) only allows the assembly of Estates to produce a προβούλευμα in the sphere of legislation, vindicating the right of final decision for the *universus populus*.

Althusius safeguards the People as against its Ephors

77. Althusius expressly insists that though the Ephors, in their collective position as representatives of the sovereign People, are superior to the Ruler, and though, in their assembly, they exercise the rights of *majestas* in respect to him (c. 18, §§48–89, c. 33, c. 28, §§28–64, and also c. 17, §§55–61), they are merely commissioners of the people; *constituuntur, removentur, dejiciuntur aut*

---

* This whole theory of the 'ephorate' (which appears later in Fichte) is derived from Calvin's *Institutes* (IV, c. xx, §31) where he speaks of 'magistrates constituted for the defence of the people, to bridle kings, such as the Ephors in Sparta, the tribunes at Rome...and to-day, it may be, in each kingdom the Three Estates assembled'.

exauctorantur by the people; and they must recognise the people as their *Superior* (c. 9, §§ 22–3). Accordingly while he applies to the Ephors the principle that the action of corporate representatives counts as the action of the corporation itself (c. 18, §§ 11, 26, 53–8), he limits the application of this principle by the *limites* of their commission (ibid. §§ 41–6); and he expressly argues that the Ephors cannot transfer any right of the People to the Ruler, or forfeit any such right by omitting to exercise it, since, in that case, *penes Ephoros, non Rempublicam et Populum, summum Reip. jus esset* (ibid. § 124). Again, if there be any failure of the Ephors, he claims that all their functions revert to the community of the people, in virtue of its imprescriptible and inviolable right; and then these functions are to be exercised *consensu totius populi tributim, curiatim, centuriatim vel viritim rogati aut collecti* (ibid. § 123). Similar views appear in Hoenonius, II, §§ 46, 51, IX, § 50.

78. This is the view of Hotoman (cc. 13 sqq.), Boucher (I, c. 9; II, c. 20; III, c. 8), Danaeus (III, c. 2, p. 221), Mariana (I, c. 8), Milton (op. cit.): cf. Alstedius, pp. 56–61 (the *ordines* [or Estates] are a *Reip. compendium*), Fridenreich, c. 29, and Keckermann, c. 4, pp. 561 sqq. We also find German professors of public law (and especially Paurmeister, Besold and Limnaeus) generally ascribing to the people of the Reich the rights exercised by the Reichstag, and even the electoral right of the Electors, just as they also ascribe the rights of provincial Estates to the people of the province as the true 'Subject': cf. supra [in a part of vol. IV not here translated], p. 242 n. 129. Bortius (*De maj.* V, § 9), in speaking of *majestas realis*, remarks that its possessor is *tota Respublica, et secundario ordines et status regni*. *The People itself as the true 'Subject' of popular rights*

79. See the author's work on Althusius, pp. 90–91, 343.
80. Supra, n. 46.
81. Supra, n. 47.
82. The 'Subject' of Sovereignty in a Republic is *plures*, according to Victoria (III, no. 10), Bellarmine (*De laicis*, c. 6), Busius (I, c. 3, § 4), Keckermann (II, c. 2), and others; it is either *pauci* or *universi*, according to Bodin (II, c. 1) and Suarez (III, c. 4, nos. 1, 5–6, 11): it is *multi*, which may again be either *pauciores* or *universi*, according to Bornitius (*De maj.* c. 3, and Part. p. 45): it is *pauciores* or *tota civitas*, according to Winkler (V, c. 4). Similarly, in the view of Grotius (I, c. 3, § 7), *plures* are the *subjectum proprium* of *majestas* in a Republic; and *plures* or *universi* are the 'Subject' of *majestas personalis* in this form of State on the theory of the advocates of 'double sovereignty' (e.g. Alstedius, p. 14; Tulden, p. 12; Besold, *De maj.* sect. 1, cc. 2–7). The theorists of popular sovereignty also make a plurality of persons into the organ of government in Republics: cf. Mariana, I, c. 3; Danaeus, I, c. 6; and Althusius, c. 39, § 1 (*summus magistratus polyarchicus*). On the technical term 'Polyarchy' see n. 46 supra. *The plurality of the 'Subject' of Sovereignty in a Republic*

83. Cf. Bodin, II, c. 6 (the magnates, in a system of aristocracy, *collectim imperant*), and c. 7 (where the same is said to be true, in a *status popularis*, of the *cives universi*); Bornitius, *Part.* p. 51 (the *cives collectim uniti* are to be regarded as the Ruler); Keckermann, II, c. 2 (*plures ex aequo indivisim*); Althusius, c. 39, §§ 32 sqq. (when there is a *magistratus polyarchicus*, the ruler is *omnes conjunctim*), §§ 46 sqq. (when there is a [*magistratus*] *aristocraticus*, the exercise of majesty belongs *conjunctim et individue paucis optimatibus*), §§ 57 sqq. (when there is a [*magistratus*] *democraticus*, the *populus consociatus* is also the *summus magistratus*). Similar views occur in Hoenonius, IX, § 3, X, § 40; cf. also Gregorius, V, cc. 1–2; Molina, II, d. 23, §§ 1–14; Heider, pp. 976 sqq.; *The plurality a collective plurality*

Crüger, *Coll. pol. Disp.* I, III, IV; Arnisaeus, *De rep.* II, cc. 4–5; Knipschildt, I, c. 1, no. 50 (*plures ut universi*).

This collective plurality is a single, but artificial, Ruling 'person'

84. Arnisaeus (*De maj.* I, c. 2; *Polit.* c. 11) contrasts the republican Ruler, as *conspiratione vel analogia unus*, with the Ruler who is *unus natura*; Berckringer (I, c. 4, §10) opposes the *unus analogia* to the *unus numero*; Graszwinkel (cc. 3, 11) contrasts the *corpore unus* with the *persona unus*; Bornitius (*Part.* p. 45; *De maj.* c. 3) opposes the *unus τῷ λόγῳ* to the *persona unus*. Keckermann (*Polit.* I, c. 2) explains that the whole perfection of the *status polyarchicus* depends upon the *plures qui imperant* assimilating themselves by their unity to a monarch. According to Althusius (c. 39, §59) the essence of democracy lies in the fact that *populus ipse instar unius exercet jura majestatis et quasi unum repraesentat in imperando*. Hippolithus a Lapide (I, cc. 3, 4, 6, 14, 15) assigns the rule in an aristocracy to the privileged Estates as constituting *unum corpus, universitas vel collegium*, etc. Cf. also Suarez, III, c. 3, nos. 7–8.

Hobbes (*De cive*, c. 7, §§13–14, c. 12, §8, *Leviathan*, c. 18) insists most definitely that, as compared with the *natura unus* on which the will and action of the people is devolved in a monarchy, the democratic assembly or the aristocratic *curia* constitutes only an artificial unity. He draws the conclusion that, while a monarchical Ruler may contravene the Law of Nature, a republican Ruler cannot, on the ground that in the former case the natural and the artificial will are one and the same, but in the latter there is only an 'artificial will'. The pre-eminence of the monarchical form of State is constantly referred by most writers to the superiority of natural unity over unity, which is artificial; cf. e.g. Bodin, VI, c. 4, nos. 710 sqq.; Hobbes, *De cive*, c. 10, *Leviathan*, c. 19.

85. Cf. Bodin, II, cc. 6, 7; Bornitius, *Part.* 41, *De maj.* c. 3; Althusius, c. 39, §§32 sqq.; Hobbes, *Leviathan*, c. 18; Hippolithus a Lapide, c. 3, sect. 3, c. 6, sect. 3, c. 7. Mention has already been made (supra, nn. 42, 43) of the difficulties into which thinkers fell in this connection, when they sought to extend to democracy the distinction between the people as the 'Subject' of popular rights and the people as the duly constituted Ruler. Keckermann (II, c. 3) finds even in a democracy [no less than in an aristocracy] a system of reciprocal alternation of ruling and being ruled.

The community in a democracy identified with the majority

86. Bodin (II, cc. 1, 6–7) refers the whole distinction between aristocracy and democracy to the numerical relation of rulers and ruled, making the former a rule of the minority, and the latter a rule of the majority. But since, from this point of view, he ranks as a democracy a state of 20,000 citizens in which 11,000 participate in the popular assembly, and since, again, he allows a majority of the assembly so constituted to decide, it follows that the *universi vel major pars* who, on his definition, are the rulers in a democracy may in certain circumstances be represented by a minority of the community.

Grotius again and again enumerates together the king or the *major pars procerum* or the *major pars populi* as being the 'Subjects' of international rights, according to the form of the constitution: cf. e.g. III, c. 20, §§2–4. Hobbes (*De cive*, c. 5, §8) says bluntly: *voluntas autem concilii intelligitur esse, quae est voluntas majoris partis eorum hominum, ex quibus concilium consistit*; cf. c. 7, §5. See also Bornitius, *Part.* p. 45 (*universis aut majori parti*); Keckermann, II, c. 1; Besold, *Disc.* III, *De democratia*, c. 1, §1 (*populus vel major pars*).

87. Cf. Bodin, II, cc. 6–7; Althusius, c. 39, §§ 37 sqq. and 58 sqq.; Hobbes, *De cive*, c. 7, §§ 6 and 10 (in an aristocracy, he argues, just as in a democracy, the time and place of the meeting must be fixed, because otherwise there will be *non persona una, sed dissoluta multitudo sine imperio summo*. For this reason the *coetus* or *conventus* is often described as the Ruler; and Hobbes constantly avails himself of the formula that Sovereignty resides either in *unus homo* or in *unus coetus* or *unum concilium*). *The assembly in a Republic described as the Ruler*

88. See the antitheses in n. 84 supra.

89. Cf. Bodin, I, c. 8, nos. 105–6: *Princeps majorum pactis conventis aeque ac privatus obligatur, si regnum haereditario jure obvenerit, vel etiam testamento delatum sit*: otherwise [i.e. where he has not obtained the Crown by inheritance or by will], he is [only] obliged *quatenus Reipublicae commodo contractum est*. [Gierke seems to have telescoped the argument of Bodin, which is really to the effect (1) that a king succeeding by hereditary or testamentary right is bound as a private man by the *pacta conventa* of his predecessors in title, but (2) that such a king is only bound to respect such *pacta* to the extent to which his predecessors were themselves bound—i.e. to the extent to which they were made for the benefit of the State.] Cf. also Arnisaeus, *De jure maj.* I, c. 7. *How far is a Ruler obliged by the acts of his predecessors?*

Grotius (I, c. 7, §§ 11–37; II, c. 14, §§ 10–14; III, c. 20, § 6) also starts from the point of view of the law of inheritance. He distinguishes two cases. (1) When they are *omnium bonorum heredes*, the *successores* are absolutely obliged by the actions of their predecessors; (2) when *in jus regni dumtaxat succedunt*, they incur no personal obligation at all. In the latter case, however, there *is* still an obligation, which is produced and mediated *per interpositam civitatem*. There is a presumption that the devolution of supreme authority on a Ruler involves, as part of itself, the simultaneous devolution of the *jus se obligandi, per se aut per majorem sui partem*, which belongs to the people just as it belongs to any other group (II, c. 14, § 10). It thus follows that, in so far as the people itself is obliged in virtue of this *jus se obligandi*, the *successor* will also be obliged *ut caput* (ibid. § 12). Now an obligation of the people is to be assumed not merely in any case of *utiliter gestum* [where there has been an act done in the definite expectation of a benefit], but also in any case where *probabilis ratio* is present [where there is good ground for expecting a benefit from an act done]; and it is only in regard to contracts previously made by usurpers that the people—and with it, therefore, the *rex verus*—has merely a limited liability *de in rem verso* [for expenses actually incurred] (ibid. § 14).

90. Grotius, II, c. 14, §§ 1–2 and 6; III, c. 20, § 6. Controverting the thesis of Bodin, that the sovereign can dispense himself from his contracts, or recover his freedom of action (*in integrum se restituere*) in respect of such contracts, Grotius (II, c. 14, §§ 1–2) distinguishes *actus Regis qui regii sunt* and *actus regis privati*. The first sort of acts count *quasi communitas faceret: in tales autem actus, sicut leges ab ipsa communitate factae vim nullam haberent, quia communitas seipsa superior non est, ita nec leges regiae; quare adversus hos contractus restitutio locum non habet; venit enim illa ex jure civili*. At the same time Grotius maintains that the people can challenge such *regii actus* [though they count as acts done by itself] on the ground that they exceed either the special limits of the Ruler's right [in a given case] or the general limits of such right [in all cases]. The private acts of the king, on the other hand, count *non ut actus communitatis sed ut actus partis*; and in case of doubt they fall under the ordinary *Grotius distinguishes between the official and the personal acts of the King*

law, and are thus subject to *restitutio in integrum* and to the King's power of dispensing himself from *leges positivae*.*

In the same chapter (II, c. 14, §6) Grotius allows that contracts between the king and his subjects always give rise to a true and proper obligation; but he adds that it is only under Natural Law that this obligation can be asserted if the king has acted *qua rex*—though it may be also asserted at civil law if he has acted otherwise [i.e. *qua privatus*].

91. Grotius himself, in the passages just cited, has recourse to the right of the community of the people and the devolution of that right.

The analogy of the Body Politic

92. Cf. Guevara, *Horologium Principis*, I, c. 36 (based on John of Salisbury —see Gierke, *Political Theories of the Middle Age*, translated by F. W. Maitland, p. 24): cf. also Knichen, I, c. 6, thes. 11 (which is similar); Modrevius, *Of the betterment of the general welfare*, 1557, p. 162; Buchanan, pp. 13 sqq. (a comparison of *societas civilis* with the human body and its ordering, articulation, harmony and unity); Gregorius Tholosanus, I, c. 1, §§ 6–16, III, c. 1, § 1, X, c. 1, § 1, XVIII, c. 1, § 4, XXI, c. 1, §§ 4–10, and elsewhere (analogy of the *corpus civile* with the *corpus physicum*, in regard to head and members, soul and nerves, harmony and unity, and the different powers and functions of the different parts: see also his *Syntagma*, III, c. 2, §§ 1–2); Lessius, *Dedicatio* of 1605 to the Archduke Albert of Austria (comparison of the Prince with the *caput*, of the *respublica* with the *corpus*, of *civitates* with *membra*, of *cives* with *artus ex quibus membra et totum reipublicae corpus coalescit*); Besold, *Princ. et fin. polit. doctr. Dissertatio*, I, c. 5, § 4, c. 8, § 1, *Diss. de maj.* sect. 1, c. 1, § 4, sect. 3, c. 3, § 2, c. 7, § 3 (comparison of the State with a *corpus physicum* or *corpus humanum*, in respect of its head and members, and the different *functiones* of each); Berckringer, I, c. 4, § 10 (the Rulers are the head of a body, whose parts have also their functions); Werdenhagen, II, c. 24 (the essence of the State is *unio*—*summum illud venerandum vocabulum mysticum*—a union produced by *status et ordinatio harmonica*, just as in a physical body); cf. also Bodin, II, c. 7, no. 236 (*reip. partes ac veluti membra singula, quae principi reip. quasi capiti illigantur*). It still continued, in our period, to be a favourite habit of thinkers to pursue this analogy into a theory (1) of the growth, the successive ages, the maladies and the death of States, and (2) of the methods which were serviceable in preserving or restoring their health: cf. Buchanan, op. cit.; Gregorius, lib. XXI–XXIV; Besold, *Diss.* II, *de republica curanda*; Knipschildt, I, cc. 15–17. [On this analogy in general see Maitland, *Collected Papers*, III, pp. 285–303.]

Sovereignty as the Soul of the State

93. See Besold, *Diss.* I, c. 5, § 1; Arnisaeus, *Polit.* c. 6, *De rep.* I, 5, s. 3; Bornitius, *De maj.* c. 5, *Part.* p. 45 (the *finis principalis* of *majestas* is *animare imperio summo universali rempublicam*); Fridenreich, c. 10 (government is the *spiritus vitalis* of the body politic); Bortius, *De maj.* v, c. 8; Graszwinkel, c. 4 (*quod in universo Deus, in corpore anima, id in imperio majestas est*); Knipschildt, I, c. 1, nos. 50–51; Tulden, I, c. 9 (*urbs* = *corpus*, *civitas* = *anima*, *respublica* = *animus mens et ratio*). [With the dictum of Graszwinkel compare a dictum of the eighteenth century, quoted in Van Tyne, *Causes of the War of American Independence*, I, p. 218, to the effect that 'legislative sovereignty is as essential to the body politic as the Deity to religion'.]

* Grotius thus disagrees with Bodin so far as official acts of the king are concerned (the king cannot dispense himself from an official act of contract, or recover freedom of action in regard to such an act); but he agrees with him in regard to personal acts of the king.

Notes to §14

94. See Gregorius, I, c. 1, §§6–7 and XVIII, c. 1, §4 (*corpus civile, quod ex singularibus personis proprio corpore et animo compositis, tanquam membris, constat*); cf. also Besold, *De maj.* III, c. 7, §3.

95. See Victoria, III, no. 4; Soto, IV, qu. 4, art. 1; Molina, II, d. 22, §§8–9; Suarez, III, cc. 1–3 (supra, nn. 60–61). Vasquez, however, in c. 47, nos. 6–8, warns his readers against drawing conclusions from the analogy between the relation of *populus* and *cives* and that of *corpus* and *membra*. There are also, he contends, fundamental differences: the limb cannot change its position, and the citizen can; the foot or the hand cannot become head, but any citizen may; the death of the head causes death of the limbs, but the death of the head of the State produces no similar effect; in the body government remains always in the head, but in the State it may change its residence. *Vasquez on differences between the body and the Body Politic*

96. Althusius, Praef. and c. 9, §§18–19: 'majesty', like the *anima in corpore physico*, resides as an indivisible and inalienable unity in the *corpus symbioticum universale* considered as a whole: it is the basis of the rights of government which this whole exercises over its parts. Cf. also *Dicaeologia*, I, c. 7.

97. Grotius (II, c. 9, §3), referring erroneously to ancient writers,* ascribes ἕξιν μίαν or *spiritum unum* to the people, regarded as a *corpus ex distantibus* [sc. *compositum*]. He adds, *is autem spiritus sive ἕξις in populo est vitae civilis consociatio plena atque perfecta, cujus prima productio est summum imperium, vinculum per quod respublica cohaeret; plane autem haec corpora artificialia instar habent corporis naturalis*. Just as the latter [the natural body] *idem non esse desinit particulis paulatim mutatis*, so the former—the 'moral' body of the People—remains the same though its members change. But like the natural organism, the People may also succumb, and lose its rights; and it may do so (1) *interitu corporis*, that is to say, either by the simultaneous disappearance of all its members (§4) or by the disintegration of their unity (§5), or (2) *interitu spiritus*, that is to say, by losing any supreme authority (§6). On the other hand, the People still remains a 'Subject' of rights and duties, as much as ever, in spite of any alienation of territory (§7) or any alteration of the constitution (§8); and the union of two peoples to form one (§9), or the division of one people into several (§10), produces no loss of a people's rights, but only a *communicatio* or *divisio* of rights, as the case may be. See further I, c. 1, §6, c. 3, §7; II, c. 5, §23 (*maximum jus corporis in partes*), c. 6, §§4–5 (*imperium* in an undivided body politic is like the soul in the body), c. 16, §16 (the body politic remains the same even if the constitution be altered), c. 21, §7 (on *mors* of the body politic). *Grotius on the analogy of the Body Politic*

But Grotius, while he notes these analogies, also remarks (I, c. 3, §7) that in contrast with the 'natural body' the *corpus morale* may have one common head for a number of bodies [e.g. in the case of a federal State]. Going more into detail (II, c. 6, §§4–5), he argues that the 'moral body', being *voluntate contractum*, is different in kind from the 'natural body'. Owing to its contractual origin, the integral parts of a moral body are *non ita sub corpore ut sunt partes corporis naturalis, quae sine corporis vita vivere non possunt, et ideo in*

---

* Gierke here refers the reader back to vol. III of the *Genossenschaftsrecht*, p. 22, n. 47, and to the correction on p. viii of his preface to that volume. The point is that Grotius was doing violence to Stoic theory, and to Plutarch and the Roman lawyers who used that theory, when he ascribed to them his own idea that a single spirit pervades bodies composed of different parts. The Stoics and their followers, Gierke contends, held no such view.

usum corporis recte abscinduntur. The right of a moral body over its parts is *ex primaeva voluntate metiendum,* and the amputation of parts against their will is therefore unjustifiable; while, conversely, the part may secede from the body —not, it is true, without due reason, but the plea of necessity will serve as such a reason. Again 'the right of a part to protect itself' is greater than 'the right of the body over the part', *quia pars utitur jure quod ante societatem initam habuit, corpus non item.* Grotius also emphasises the point (in his note to II, c. 9, §3) that it is only ἀναλογικῶς that he speaks of the *corpus* and the ἕξις or *spiritus* of the People.

The double 'Subject' of sovereignty

98. Grotius, I, c. 3, §7: *ut visus subjectum commune est corpus, proprium oculus,* so the whole body politic and the Ruler are both simultaneously 'Subjects' of political authority [the one generally, and the other specifically].

99. Whereas Victoria (III, no. 4) still expressly insists that the *civitas* is no *inventum* or *artificium,* but *a natura profecta est,* and therefore properly comparable to the human body, Grotius already speaks of it as a *corpus artificiale,* and as *voluntate contractum* (cf. supra n. 97 and II, c. 9, §8).

Hobbes on the analogy of the Body Politic

100. Compare the introduction to the *Leviathan,* where *is qui summam potestatem habet* is described as *anima totum corpus vivificans et movens;* the authorities and officials are the artificial joints; rewards and punishments are the motor nerves; the wealth of all is the strength of the body; the safety of the people is its business or function; the counsellors are its memory; equity and the laws are its artificial reason; concord is its health, sedition its sickness, and civil war its death. Finally, *pacta quibus partes hujus corporis politici conglutinantur imitantur divinum illud verbum 'Fiat' sive 'Faciamus hominem' a Deo prolatum in principio cum crearet mundum.* Cf. *Leviathan,* c. 17; *De cive,* c. 5.

The organism of Hobbes is really a mechanism

101. Introd. to the *Leviathan*: just as *ars humana* imitates nature, which is the *ars divina,* and just as it creates (in the watch, or automaton, or machine with springs and wheels) an *artificiale animal* with a *vita artificialis,* so it also imitates that *nobilissimum animal* Man. *Magnus ille Leviathan, quae Civitas appellatur, opificium artis est et Homo artificialis, quamquam homine naturali, propter cujus protectionem et salutem excogitatus est, multo major*; and Man is here at one and the same time *materia* and *artifex.* Cf. *De cive,* c. 5 and c. 7, §§ 10 sqq., and *Leviathan,* c. 17, on the *voluntas artificiosa* of this body; *Leviathan,* c. 19, on *successio* as the way of continuation of its *vita artificialis;* ibid., c. 20 and following, on the mathematical rules for the construction of this artifice, and c. 21 [? c. 26] on laws as *vincula artificialia.*

People and State identified by Monarchomachi

102. Thus the *Vind. c. Tyr.,* qu. III, describes the king as *minister* or *servus Reipublicae* (p. 144), and the representatives of the People as *officiarii Regni non Regis* (p. 148), but otherwise always depicts the community of the People as the 'Subject' of supreme authority (pp. 143 sqq.; 248 sqq., 292 sqq.). In the same way Hotoman makes the immortal *Respublica* or the *Regnum* superior to the mortal king (*Francogallia,* c. 19); but he proceeds to identify this 'Subject' [of supreme authority] with *ipsa civium ac subjectorum universitas et quasi corpus reipublicae* and with the *populus* (ibid. c. 19; *Quaest. illust.* qu. 1), and he expressly declares that *summa potestas est populi* (*Francogallia,* c. 19). Boucher (I, c. 9) states in so many words that the sovereign People in its corporate unity is identical with the *Regnum* or *Respublica*: cf. II, c. 20, III, c. 8. Rossaeus (c. 2, §§ 1 and 11) ascribes to the king only a *potestas potestati Reipublicae subjecta,* and declares the *Respublica universa* to be *superior* [i.e. sovereign]. Mariana (I, cc. 8–9) sometimes describes the *Respublica,* and sometimes *universi,* as the 'Subject' of majesty. According to Hoenonius (II,

Notes to § 14

§§ 39, 41, 51, and IX, §§ 5, 44–50) it is the *Respublica*, the *Respublica seu membra ejus*, the *populus*, the *populus universus*, or the *totus populus*, which is the *verus dominus* of political authority, the source of all government, and *potior Monarchis*. In the treatise [of Beza] *De jure mag.* (qu. 6), *summum imperium* is ascribed to the People, but occasionally this *summum imperium* is itself personified: cf. pp. 26 sqq., where the *magistratus subalterni* are described as dependent not on the *summus magistratus*, but on *ipsa supremitas* or on *summa illa imperii seu regni δύναμις et authoritas*; cf. also pp. 37 sqq. and 74 sqq., where the Estates are regarded as *defensores ac protectores jurium ipsius supremae potestatis*, even as against the Monarch himself. In Buchanan (pp. 16 sqq., 48 sqq. and 78–90) and in Danaeus (I, c. 4; III, c. 6) it is the *populus universus* or *subditi* who appear as the 'Subject' of supreme authority.

103. The *Vind. c. Tyr.* (qu. II, pp. 89, 114 sqq.; qu. III, pp. 89, 114 sqq., 131 sqq., 144, 148, 192 sqq., 196, 292 sqq.)* deals in this way with the appointment of kings and representatives of the People, with the right of legislation, with the control of officials, and with the right of resistance or deposition in the event of disobedience to God or *felonia contra populum* [i.e. it sometimes ascribes all these rights to the *Populus*, and sometimes to the *Respublica*]. Hotoman (cc. 6–8) deals in the same way with the right of appointing, judging and deposing the king, and with the right of deciding about a disputed succession. Cp. Rossaeus, c. 2, §§ 8–9 (on the right of the *Respublica* in the matter of legislation and consent to taxation) with § 4: cf. also Boucher, I, cc. 10–19 and III, cc. 14–17. *Rights ascribed indifferently to People or State*

104. Cf. the *Vind. c. Tyr.* (qu. III, pp. 218 sqq. and 235 sqq.): the *patrimonium Regni* belongs to the People, and not to the king: the king has no right of property in the possessions of the Fisc, the demesne, etc., and he cannot therefore alienate any part of them: indeed, he is not even the *usufructuarius* (since he cannot so much as contract a mortgage), but only the *administrator*. Hotoman (c. 9) argues that the *nuda proprietas* in the demesne, regarded as the *dos Regni*, resides *penes universitatem populi sive Rempublicam*; cf. *Quaest. illustr.* qu. 1. According to Hoenonius (II, c. 39) *jura regni, ratione proprietatis et dominii, pertinent ad Rempublicam seu membra ejus, sed ratione usus et administrationis spectant ad magistratum, cui sunt commendata*; cf. also V, § 72, where a distinction is drawn between the *aerarium publicum*, which is *Reipublicae proprium*, and the *aerarium Principis*, which belongs to him as a private person. *So with public property*

105. Cf. *Vind. c. Tyr.* (qu. III, pp. 196 sqq.) on *Reipublicae consensus* in legislation. Rossaeus (c. 1, § 3) makes the *Respublica* choose the form of the State and determine *quibus velit imperandi et parendi conditionibus circumscribere*; and similarly (c. 2, § 11) he makes it able *potestatem Regis dilatare, restringere, commutare, penitus abrogare aliamque substituere*. According to Mariana (I, c. 9) the King cannot alter the *leges universae Reipublicae voluntate constitutas, nisi universitatis voluntate certaque sententia*. Cf. on this supra, n. 70. *So, too, with public decisions*

106. Althusius, in his Preface, begins by describing the *Respublica vel consociatio universalis* as the 'Subject' of the rights of majesty, which belong to this *corpus symbioticum* in the same sense as we may attribute to it *spiritum animam et cor…quibus sublatis corpus illud etiam pereat*. The *Princeps* is only an *administrator* [of the rights of this body]; and the true *proprietarius et usufructuarius* is the *populus universus in corpus unum symbioticum ex pluribus minoribus* *Similarly, Althusius identifies Respublica and Populus*

---

* Something has gone wrong with Gierke's references here, as he repeats the reference to p. 89 and pp. 114 sqq. twice over, for quaestio II and quaestio III.

256   *Gierke's Notes*

consociationibus consociatus. The *Respublica* cannot transfer or alienate these rights of majesty, even if it wishes, any more than an individual can share his life with another. At the same time, however—both in this context, and when he subsequently proceeds, in the body of his work, to justify these general principles in detail (cc. 9, 18, 19, 38) and to deal with the several rights of majesty (cc. 10–17)—he identifies this sovereign body which possesses the *regni proprietas* with the *populus*; and he identifies the *populus* in turn with the *universa membra consociata* or with *omnes simul*. Similarly he ascribes to the 'People' the property and usufruct in *res publicae et fiscales*, assigning to the *summus magistratus* [only] the power of administering them *instar tutoris*, with such rights as the 'People' has granted (c. 37, §§ 1–2); but in the same breath he describes the *Respublica* (ibid. §§ 117–18) or the *corpus consociatum* (c. 17, §§ 1 sqq.) as being the owner.

The persona Civitatis in Salamonius

107. Salamonius, *De principatu* (I, pp. 28–9), seeks to prove that *Princeps suis legibus ligatur* by the help of a distinction, based upon Cicero,* between the *Persona Civitatis* and the *Persona Principis*. Since it is the *Persona Civitatis* which is acting through the *Princeps* when he issues laws or does any other act of government, the Ruler who obeys his own law submits himself not to himself, but to *ea persona quam gerit*. It is true that he represents that 'person' [the *Persona Civitatis*]; but he only does so *ut gerens* [and he does not therefore absorb it into himself]. In reality, *both* 'persons' act at the same time; but they act in different ways—the *Civitas* acting *ut mandans*, and the *Princeps ut mandatarius*, with the result that the *mandans* acts *ut major*, and the *mandatarius ut minister*. It follows that it is *ipsa Civitas* which *vere agit et vere leges condit*.

It is really the same as the People

But Salamonius always identifies this *Civitas* [or *Persona Civitatis*] with the *universus populus* which creates the Ruler and remains his *Superior* (pp. 16–28); he treats the *leges ab universo populo scriptae* as being *pacta* between the People and the Ruler (pp. 8–16); and he interprets the People itself as a *societas*, and the Ruler as its *praepositus* or *institor* (supra, n. 69). See also his *Commentarioli*, folio 41 verso.

The Ruler confronts the Respublica or Populus as something external to it

108. It is true that the Ruler is often described as *Reipublicae pars*, and the principle that the whole is greater than the part is often applied in favour of the sovereignty of the People (e.g. in Salamonius, pp. 40–1, and in Mariana, I, c. 9). But as the 'Subject' of the rights of the Ruler this 'part' leaves the Whole, and is made to form an antithesis to a separately and independently existing personality of the People, of which it is depicted as being the servant, administrator, mandatory or agent; cf. supra n. 104 and n. 107. All the *Monarchomachi* accordingly insist that the People is *prior Rege* in time [as well as in importance], and that it only proceeds to erect a ruler, by its own free choice, *after* it has already constituted itself: cf. Buchanan, pp. 16 ff., p. 69; the *Vind. c. Tyr.*, qu. II, p. 148 (*Rex per populum, propter populum, non sine populo*); Rossaeus, c. 1, §§ 1–3; Boucher, I, cc. 10 sqq.; Danaeus, I, c. 4, pp. 36–44; Hoenonius, IX, §5 (*populus enim et prior et potior est Monarchis, quippe quos rectores et curatores Reipublicae is creat et constituit*). Althusius is particularly emphatic in explaining that the People (which is *tempore prior*, and which, as the constituent organ, continues to be *prior et superior* to the organs which it constitutes) first of all associates itself to form a 'body', and then—but only then—appoints *ministri et rectores* to avoid the difficulties of getting all its members to meet together. These 'ministers and

---

* Gierke here refers to vol. III of his *Genossenschaftsrecht*, p. 24 n. 52.

governors', it is true, *universum populum repraesentant, ejusque personam gerunt in iis quae Reipublicae nomine faciunt*; but they remain *famuli et ministri* of the 'associated multitude', and their right of action is derivative (c. 18, §§ 5–15, 26–31, 92–106; c. 19, §§ 2–3; c. 38, §§ 121–2). Even so, however, and even while he thus separates People and ruler as two parts, he also describes the constituent People at the same time (c. 18, § 18) by the style of *ipsa Respublica* [as if it were the Whole].

109. In the *Vind. c. Tyr.* the contrast is particularly marked between *Populus* and *Rex* as two separate 'persons', who first contract jointly with God, and then form a second contract with one another; on which it follows (1) that the king on his side has a right to take measures of correction against the People, in virtue of the contract made with God, inasmuch as he pledges himself for [the good behaviour of] the People by entering [jointly with it] into that contract (qu. II, pp. 84sqq.), and (2) that he also acquires rights as against the People, in virtue of the *contractus mutuo obligatorius* which he has made with it, if it becomes . *litiosus* by breach of such contract (qu. III, pp. 260sqq.). A similar view appears in Boucher, I, cc. 18sqq. Danaeus also, in dealing with the relation of the Ruler to the People, applies the idea of contract strictly [to both parties]: cf. I, c. 4, pp. 41 (where he speaks of a voluntary 'pact', the violation of which extinguishes rights on both sides), 43; III, c. 6, pp. 214sqq. (so long as the fundamental laws are observed by the Ruler, the People on its side cannot touch the constitution or, more particularly, the royal right of succession, inasmuch as *contractus populi cum Principe et ejus familia ab initio quidem fuit voluntatis, postea autem factus est necessitatis*; it is only in the event of the Ruler breaking the pact that the People also becomes free, or can proceed to the deposition of the Ruler and his family and an alteration of the constitution). Similar views are to be found in [Beza's] *De jure mag.* qu. 5 and 6 (where the idea of *mutua obligatio* appears throughout); Hotoman, *Francogallia*, cc. 13 and 25, *Quaest. illust.* qu. 1; Salamonius, I, p. 11; Rossaeus, I, c. 1, §4, c. 2, §6 (*obligatio reciproca*) and § 11 (resistance and deposition are only possible *ex justa causa*): Mariana, I, cc. 6 and 8; Hoenonius, II, §41 (*pactio reipublicae*) and IX, §§ 44–54.

The theory of contract involves a dualism of People and Ruler

In the same way Althusius, while he applies the category of *mandatum*, is not prevented thereby from treating the *commissio regni sive universalis imperii* to the supreme magistrate as a *contractus*, made by reciprocal oaths and entailing reciprocal obligations (cc. 19–20, esp. c. 19, §§ 6–7 and 29sqq.), which confers on the Ruler [as well as on the People] a right that is only forfeited by definite breach of contract (c. 38). He ascribes to the governing authorities full *administratio* and *repraesentatio* of the State-authority, within the limits of the constitution (c. 18, §§ 26sqq.); though he holds, it is true, that if they overstep their 'laws and limits' they cease to be 'ministers of God and the universal association', and are only '*privati...quibus obedientia in illis quibus suae potestatis limites excedunt non debetur*' (ibid. §§ 41–6 and 105). He treats the contract of government as a naturally imposed element in the constitution of a State (c. 1, §§ 32–9, c. 18, §§ 20–4), and he seeks to prove its presence in all forms of State (c. 39); but in dealing with democracy he substitutes [for the ordinary contract of ruler and ruled] a contract between the community of the people, which directly exercises the rights of majesty itself, and the bearers of authority who 'represent' it successively from time to time (c. 39, §§ 57–9). See the author's work on Althusius, pp. 144–9.

Approximations to Rousseau

110. Some degree of approximation [to Rousseau's theory] is to be found in Buchanan (pp. 16 sqq., 48 sqq., 78 sqq.), who is reproached even by Rossaeus (I, c. 1, §4) with contempt of the right of the Ruler; and still more in Milton, who goes to the length of allowing the deposition of the king by the People, in virtue of the right of self-determination of free-born men, even if there be no other occasion than the wish for a change of the constitution (*The Tenure*, pp. 14 sqq.). But there was no thinker before Rousseau who definitely and in principle denied that there was any contractual relation between the sovereign People and the Ruler; see the author's work on Althusius, pp. 91 sqq. [Locke's theory already makes the relation between them not a relation of Contract, but one of Trust: see below, n. 68 to §16.]

111. See Regner Sixtinus, I, c. 1, no. 23; Paurmeister, I, c. 3, no. 10, c. 18, nos. 6–10, c. 23, no. 13; Kirchner, II, §1; Boxhorn, I, c. 4, §§1–27; Alstedius, pp. 14 and 69 sqq.; Arumaeus, IV, no. 2; Otto, II, no. 14, §§17–19; Brautlacht, III, c. 2, §§5–9; Bortius, *De natura jur. maj.* c. 1, §2, c. 2, §16, c. 5, §9, c. 6, §§1–2; Besold, *De maj. s.* I, c. 1; Tulden, I, cc. 11–12; Werdenhagen, III, c. 2, §§7–9; Liebenthal, VII, §§3–13; Frantzken, *De pot. princ.* §§19–22 and 92–101; Carpzov, *Comm. in leg. reg.* c. 1, s. 14, c. 13, s. 1; Limnaeus, *Jus publ.* I, c. 10, no. 14, *Capitul.* p. 532, nos. 48–79; Berckringer, I, c. 4, §10: see also the author's *Genossenschaftsrecht*, IV, pp. 216 sqq. [not here translated] and his work on Althusius, pp. 165 sqq., nn. 124–9.

Idea of the State itself as the true Sovereign

112. We may trace such a feeling in Bortius (c. 5, §9), where he describes the *tota Respublica et secundario ordines et status Regni* as the *subjectum absolutum Majestatis*, and the King, in so far as *regimen translatum est*, as the *subjectum limitatum*. It may also be seen in Besold (*De maj. s.* I, c. 1, §4): *nunquam censendum est totam et universam Rempublicam per Principem repraesentari; caput est, non totum corpus; et quomodo in corpore humano etiam aliarum partium functiones sunt, ita et adhuc corporis publici et populi aliqua est Majestas.* (Berckringer says the same, almost word for word, I, c. 4, §10.) Compare also the attempt made by Fichlau (in Conring, *Opera*, III, pp. 976 sqq.) to interpret the doctrine of Althusius as if majesty were ascribed by him to the body of the whole association only *ratione fundamenti et radicaliter* [i.e. in theory, and not in practice].

'Real majesty' ascribed to the Respublica or Populus

113. In Paurmeister, for example, we often find the *summa potestas*, which in the passages quoted above in n. 111 he assigns to the *Respublica* or *Imperium*, also ascribed to the *populus* or *universus populus* (I, c. 17, nos. 1 sqq., c. 19, nos. 6 sqq.; II, c. 1, no. 11). Kirchner (II, §1) vindicates 'real majesty' for the *societas populi coalita*; Boxhorn (I, c. 5) attributes the majesty of the *Respublica* also to the *populus*; Alstedius (p. 18) ascribes sovereignty to the *populus* or *subditi universi*; and Bortius, while he generally vindicates it for the *Respublica*, gives it equally in cc. 2, 6 and 7 to the *populus*. Besold and Tulden also identify the *Respublica*, as the 'Subject' of 'real majesty', with the community of the people; indeed, they even identify the *Respublica* with *omnes singuli*, when they are distinguishing it [as the possessor of 'real majesty'] from the democratic authority possessing 'personal majesty' (n. 43 supra). Limnaeus, loc. cit., expressly describes the *Respublica*, which continues to remain in possession of 'real majesty' after the creation of a 'personal majesty', as being the *universitas* or *universus populus* (see supra, n. 69). Werdenhagen (I, c. 6) and Berckringer (I, c. 4, §§6–10) describe the 'Subject' of 'real majesty', which they sometimes call by the name of *Respublica* and sometimes by that of *Populus*, as *collectivum* (supra, n. 67).

Notes to § 14

114. Thus the *Respublica* or *Populus*, as the 'Subject' of real majesty, is generally held to possess (1) the right of originally appointing the Ruler, which comes into force again in the event of the extinction or forfeiture of the powers of the authorised Ruler; (2) the right of fixing and maintaining the conditions of the contract between ruler and ruled; and (3) the right of consenting to constitutional changes and alienations of territory. It is also, as a rule, held to possess (4) the right of resistance to, and deposition of, a Ruler who has broken the contract, and (5), in addition, all other rights which are reserved by special provision when 'personal majesty' is vested in the Ruler. See particularly Bortius, on the distinction between *jura regni* and *jura regia* (c. 1, §2); on the various *jura regni* which *ad ipsam Rempublicam*, or *ad populum, spectant* (c. 2); and on the several *jura regia sive regalia* in detail (c. 3). See also Paurmeister, I, cc. 19, 21, 22, 23 and 30; Besold, *De maj.* s. 1, c. 1, §§5–8, c. 6, §2, s. 3, cc. 2 and 7; Tulden, I, c. 11; Arumaeus, loc. cit.; Limnaeus, loc. cit.; Berckringer, I, c. 4, §8. *The particular rights involved in real majesty*

115. Cf. Besold, *De maj.* s. 1, c. 1, §7, where a distinction is drawn between the 'patrimony of the King' and the 'demesne of the Kingdom': as regards the latter, *nuda proprietas est penes Universitatem populi sive Rempublicam, usufructus autem penes Regem*, and therefore there can be no alienation without the consent of the People. See also Berckringer, I, c. 4, §8: the ownership of the demesne, as the *dos Regni*, is vested in the *universus populus*, but the usufruct belongs to the *imperans*. Cf. also Bortius, I, c. 2, §16. *State property belongs to the owner of real majesty*

116. This is particularly emphasised with regard to changes in fundamental law, or in the territory of the State (Besold, s. 1, c. 1, §§5 and 7; Tulden, I, c. 11; Bortius, c. 2, §§14–21); and in regard to the choice of a new ruler (Bortius, c. 2, §§3–13) and the deposition of a tyrannical ruler. For the right of deposition of the tyrannical ruler, see Boxhorn, II, c. 4, §§45 sqq. and *Disquis. polit.* c. 3; Hilliger in Arumaeus, II, no. 13, c. 9; Frantzken, ibid. IV, no. 42, §§92–101; Brautlacht, *Epit.* VIII, c. 5; Limnaeus, loc. cit.; Berckringer, I, c. 5; and Bortius, c. 7, who argues that *contrariatur majestati, si Princeps in perniciem et ruinam Reipublicae abutitur potestate; contra quod remedium est ut resistat populus et, si opus, deponat eundem;* for since the *Princeps eo ordine, vi et jure admissus est, ut salutem Reip. procuraret, dissolvitur obligatio...et hoc solo casu populus potior.* The same general theory [which is applied to the tyrannical ruler] is also applied by Bortius to the case of a breach of *pacta expressa*. *The owner of real majesty as controlling the owner of personal majesty*

117. The right of the Ruler to public power and public property was often conceived as a *dingliches Recht.** Cf. R. Sixtinus, I, c. 1, no. 38 (*quasi propria*); Paurmeister, I, c. 18, nos. 6–10 (*dominium verum et plenum* in all rights of government belongs to the People, but the *dominium utile*, the *usufructus* and the other *jura realia innominata* belong to the Ruler); Limnaeus, loc. cit. (*usufructus*). According to Berckringer (I, c. 4, §§6–7) the People abandons the 'exercise' of majesty *privative*, but retains the 'substance' *cumulative*, whether we regard it as retaining that substance *ratione juris et proprietatis*, or whether we apply the analogy of a case of 'letting' or *locatio* (there can be no question of 'selling' or *venditio*)†. In §8, however, Berckringer simply says that the *Personal majesty as a proprietary right*

---

* I.e. not as a right arising from the obligation to him of others, but as a proprietary right belonging to him *per se*, and therefore prior to obligation.

† I.e. the people as a whole retains the substance of majesty either in the simple sense of being owner, or in the sort of sense in which a person letting out property still retains a 'substance' though he has let out the control.

two 'majesties' are related to one another as *dominium* is to *usufructus*. Otto (§§ 18–19) regards the Ruler as only *administrator*.

118. On the varieties in the treatment of *majestas personalis* see the author's work on Althusius, pp. 168–71.

119. The statement of Berckringer (I, c. 4, §7) is obscure. He makes the people, by creating a 'personal majesty', cease to be a *persona actu*, but continue to remain a *persona potentia, immo actu, sed possibili*. It is equally difficult to detect any clear meaning in §20, where he deduces from the 'real majesty' of the *Respublica contrahens* the conclusion that the People, after erecting a Ruler, has still no Superior *realiter*, though it has one *personaliter*.

120. See the writer's work on Althusius, p. 171.

The People to Grotius merely an aggregate

121. This is the conception which Grotius applies in dealing with the acquisition of political authority by the voluntary or enforced subjection of a people (I, c. 3, §§ 8–13; II, c. 5, §31; III, c. 8); with the alienation of political authority, or some particular political right of government or property, whether by the Ruler or the People, or by both together (II, c. 6, §§ 3–14; III, c. 20, §5); with the loss of political authority (II, c. 9); with the right of resistance to that authority (II, c. 4); and with the obligation of the People in virtue of contracts concluded by the Ruler (II, c. 14; III, c. 20, §6). Cf. supra, notes 54, 66–7, 70, 89–90, 97.

Grotius limits popular sovereignty

122. Cf. I, c. 3, §§ 8–9: it is a mistaken theory that *suprema potestas* always belongs to the People; for the people can alienate or forfeit its original sovereignty just as much as an individual can alienate or forfeit his liberty. There is also error in the theory of those *qui mutuam quandam subjectionem sibi fingunt, ut populus universus regi recte imperanti parere debeat, rex autem male imperans populo subjiciatur*. See also II, c. 4, §§ 1–7, c. 5, §31; III, c. 8.

Grotius on the continuity of the State

123. II, c. 9, §8: the people is the same whether it is ruled *regio vel plurium vel multitudinis imperio*; nor does it change its identity if, having been before *sui juris*, it afterwards becomes subject *plenissimo jure. Nam imperium quod in rege est ut in capite, in populo manet ut in toto, cujus pars est caput; atque adeo rege, si electus est, aut regis familia extincta, jus imperandi ad populum redit*. Consequently, *non desinit debere pecuniam populus, rege sibi imposito, quam liber debebat; est enim idem populus, et dominium retinet eorum quae populi fuerant, immo et imperium in se retinet, quamquam jam non exercendum a corpore sed a capite*. For the same reason 'he who has received supreme power over a people previously free' must hold the same position in [international] conferences as that held before by the people itself: *sic, vicissim, qui regis fuerat locus eum populus liber implebit*. Cf. also II, c. 6, § 16: contracts made with a free people are always *pacta realia...quia subjectum est res permanens...immo etiamsi status civitatis in regnum mutetur, manebit foedus, quia manet idem corpus etsi mutato capite, et ut supra diximus imperium quod per regem exercetur non desinit esse imperium populi*.

124. He always speaks only of 'people' and 'king'; and, somewhat astonishingly, he never finds room for any technical employment of the expressions *subjectum commune et proprium*.

Grotius on Aristotle's view of the continuity of the State

The manner in which Grotius sets on one side the opposite views of Aristotle* is peculiar (II, c. 9, §8). Like other 'artificial things', he argues, the

---

* Gierke here refers to vol. III of his *Genossenschaftsrecht*, p. 21. For Aristotle's own views on the question, 'When is a State the same', see *Politics*, III, c. 3 (1276a 8–1276b 15). Actually the interpretation of these views by Grotius seems to be more accurate than Gierke's interpretation. Aristotle, as W. L. Newman says (vol. III of his edition, p. 149), 'decides that after *any* change of constitution the State is not

Notes to §14

State may be considered from different points of view: *civitatis species una est consociatio juris et imperii, altera relatio partium inter se earum quae regunt et quae reguntur; hanc spectat Politicus, illam Jurisconsultus*. Aristotle only spoke as a student of politics, and he therefore did not attempt to solve the question of the continuance of a public liability, because it belonged to *ars altera*. Grotius' mistaken conception of the argument of Aristotle (who clearly denies the existence of a public liability himself, and only leaves as an open question the appeal to legal opinion) is obvious. It is interesting, however, to notice that Grotius vindicates the 'social' [or partnership] conception of the State for jurisprudence, and the 'governmental' for political science, and that he places himself among the jurists.

125. Even in dealing with the question whether acts of the Ruler are binding on his successors, Grotius, although he speaks (cf. n. 89 supra) of an intervening obligation of the *civitas*, makes no use of his conception of the *subjectum commune*; he applies instead the different idea of the Ruler's having a collective authority [because he represents the collective people] which has the effect of obliging the community at large: cf. also n. 90 supra. *The commune subjectum never active*

126. In wars, agreements and treaties of peace it is not States as such which are involved, but their sovereigns—'those who have supreme power in the State' (I, c. 3, §4; II, c. 15, §3; III, c. 30, §2). Accordingly we often find *Rex* and *Populus liber* mentioned as alternatives (e.g. II, c. 6, §7, c. 9, §§8–9, c. 6, §16 and §31; III, c. 30, §§3–4); but we also find *Rex vel Civitas* mentioned as alternatives with the same meaning (e.g. II, c. 15, §16). *Externally*

127. See supra, n. 66. Grotius ascribes *dominium eminens* to the *Civitas*; cf. I, c. 3, §6—*dominium eminens, quod civitas habet in cives et res civium ad usum publicum*: cf. also II, c. 14, §7 and III, c. 20, §7—*res subditorum sub eminenti dominio esse Civitatis, ita ut Civitas, vel qui Civitatis vice fungitur, iis rebus uti easque etiam perdere et alienare possit*. But, here again, what he understands by *Civitas* is the community of the people; and he therefore holds that while the question of compensation concerns the relation of *Civitas et singuli*, the question of confiscation *ex justa causa* concerns only the relation of *Rex et subditi* (III, c. 20, §10). Cf. also II, c. 3, §19, on the possible reversion of land without an owner *ad universitatem aut ad dominum superiorem*. *Or internally*

128. Cf. I, c. 3, §§8 and 11, c. 4, §8; II, c. 9, §8. There may even be *reges sub populo*, but they are not true kings.

129. Cf. I, c. 3, §§11–15; II, c. 6, §3; III, c. 8, §1, c. 20, §5.

130. III, c. 8, §1. A conqueror may also institute at will intermediate stages between the two extremes of *subjectio mere civilis* and *subjectio mere herilis*. He can also abolish the conquered State entirely, and turn it either into a province or a *magna familia* (§2). Along with his right over the *universitas*, he also acquires the *res universitatis* and its *incorporalia jura*, inasmuch as *qui dominus est personarum, idem et rerum est et juris omnis quod personis competit*. It follows that, even when he leaves a conquered people in possession of the *jus civitatis*, he can take away from the *civitas*, or leave to it, as much of its property and its rights as he likes (§4). On the application of the *jus postliminii** to a people, see III, c. 9, §9; and on the moral limits to the right of conquest, see III, c. 15. *Grotius on rights of conquest*

the same, but that the question as to the fulfilment of contracts is a separate one'. In other words, Aristotle (just as Grotius says) only makes a pronouncement on the political question, and leaves the juridical question alone, as λόγος ἕτερος.

* The right of returning to a former status and resuming former privileges.

131. I, c. 3, §13: *at in regnis quae populi voluntate delata sunt, concedo non esse praesumendum eam fuisse populi voluntatem, ut alienatio imperii sui regi permitteretur.*

Grotius on the People as owner of political authority

132. I, c. 3, §11; II, c. 6, §3; III, c. 20, §5. In such a case, therefore, [i.e. where the King is king by contract,] it is the people only, and not the king, who can alienate right over the State or any part thereof. At the same time, the people can only do so *accedente consensu regis, quia is quoque jus aliquod habet, quale usufructuarius, quod invito auferri non debet* (II, c. 6, §3); and further the consent of the part of the people concerned is also necessary when it is a question of alienating a part of a State (ibid. §4). Even alienations which are necessary and advantageous do not form an exception [to the rule that popular consent is required]; but here we may take the mere fact of silence as consent (§8). The same is also true of the granting of enfeoffments and mortgages (§9). The Ruler cannot even alienate any of the lesser rights of government (*minores functiones civiles*), so that they become the inheritable rights of the recipient, unless the people expressly concurs, or tacitly gives authority by developing a customary rule to that effect (§10). The co-operation of the people is also necessary for regulations about a regency or the succession to the throne (I, c. 3, §15). If the Ruler seeks to carry into effect alienations which are invalid, the people has a right of resistance (I, c. 4, §10); and it also possesses this right in other cases in the last resort (ibid. §11).

133. II, c. 6, §7: *territorium et totum et ejus partes sunt communia populi pro indiviso*: a *liber populus*, or *Rex intercedente populi consensu*, can alienate without question uninhabited parts of the territory.

Grotius on the People as owner of State property

134. II, c. 6, §§11–13; III, c. 20, §5. The principle [of the people's ownership of State-property] carries the consequence that *patrimonium populi, cujus fructus destinati sunt ad sustentanda reipublicae aut regiae dignitatis onera, a regibus alienari nec in totum nec in partem potest. Res modicae* constitute no exception, except that here it is easier to argue from the people's knowledge and silence to its consent. On the other hand, the king may, as *fructuarius*, dispose of the income; and he may also mortgage effectively where, and in so far as, he has a right of imposing taxes by his own action [i.e. if the king can tax any property by his own action to get resources, he may also mortgage that property by his own action for the same purpose].

Grotius on the possible limitations of the Ruler

135. I, c. 3, §§8, 11, 16, 18, c. 4, §§12, 14; II, c. 14, §2. Grotius distinguishes two sorts of limitation [on the Ruler], according as it affects (1) only the *exercitium*, or (2) *ipsa facultas*, and according, therefore, as action contrary to the limitation (1) is simply illegal or (2) is null and void. Even limitations of the latter sort [i.e. limitations on *ipsa facultas*, which make any action exceeding the limits null and void] do not involve any diminution of the Ruler's sovereignty, because the annihilation of his 'faculty' proceeds *non ex vi superioris, sed ipso jure*. Nor is any division of sovereignty produced by a stipulation in favour of popular consent to laws, taxes, etc. Even the addition of a *lex commissoria*, by which the sovereignty devolved on the Ruler must in certain cases be counted as forfeit, and must therefore give way to the original sovereignty of the People, does not eliminate the exclusive sovereignty of the Ruler during his tenure.

136. The case is different, according to I, c. 3, §11, where rule is only vested in the Ruler as a *precarium* [i.e. as a thing of which the use only is granted, for a period determined by the will of the grantor].

137. I, c. 3, §§ 17–20. *Summum imperium*, although it is *unum ac per se indivisum*, is none the less divisible into *potentiales* and *subjectivae partes*; and there is an actual *divisio summitatis* between king and people if the people, in the fundamental contract, has reserved some of the rights of government, or has reserved a power of enforcement [of the conditions, or some of the conditions, of the contract]. Cf. I, c. 4, § 13: there is a *jus resistendi* if the king, in a case of divided *imperium*, encroaches on 'the part belonging to the people or senate'. *Grotius on division of Imperium*

138. Cf. vol. IV [of the *Genossenschaftsrecht*, not here translated], p. 217 n. 44, on Lampadius and Scharschmidt: cf. also the author's work on Althusius, p. 175 n. 157.

139. Cf. ibid. pp. 175–6.

140. F. Victoria (III, no. 7) ascribes original sovereignty to the *Respublica*. *Causa vero materialis, in qua hujusmodi potestas residet, jure naturali et divino est ipsa Respublica, cui de se competit gubernare seipsam et administrare et omnes potestates suas in commune bonum dirigere*. He argues that, even after the transference of this sovereignty, the Ruler is still bound by his own laws, because he is himself *pars Reipublicae*, and his laws are to be regarded 'as if they had been passed by the whole *Respublica*' (no. 23). But he expressly identifies this *Respublica* with the multitude, which is incapable of exercising political authority itself (no. 8); he places the king *super totam Rempublicam*, and thereby also *super omnes simul* (no. 15); and he thus makes the active 'person' of the State always resident in the Ruler (cf. also no. 11). *The views of Catholic writers on the natural rights of the People against the Ruler*

Vasquez ascribes to the *populus* both original sovereignty, and, in cases of doubt, a right of co-operation in legislation and alienations of territory, which arises from a reservation to be supposed in the act of transferring original sovereignty (cc. 42–3 and 47); but he describes *ipsa Respublica* as the 'Subject' of a right of resistance to a monarch who breaks his contract (c. 8).

According to Soto, the *Respublica* has the *jus seipsam regendi*, but 'by divine instruction' it transfers that right—retaining however (along with other rights) the right of deposing a monarch who has become tyrannical ['in exercise']. The *Respublica*, which is really nothing more nor less than the sum of *omnes*, is incapable by itself of exercising its sovereignty; and only by transferring sovereignty does it become a body which has also a head and is therefore capable of action. The result is that the Ruler *non solum singulis reipublicae membris superior est, verum et totius collectim corporis caput, totique adeo supereminens, ut totam etiam simul punire possit* (I, qu. 1, a. 3, qu. 7, a. 2; IV, qu. 4, a. 1–2). Cf. Covarruvias, I, c. 1, and Bellarmine, *De laicis*, c. 6 (*Respublica non potest per semetipsam exercere hanc potestatem*).

Molina definitely supposes two 'persons' in the State—the People and the Ruler. He reserves the name of *Respublica* for the community of the People, although he admits that the Ruler possesses sovereignty. The *Respublica*, he argues, originally has all authority (II, d. 22, § 9): it transfers it *secundum arbitrium* and on such conditions as it thinks fit (II, d. 23, §§ 1 sqq.); and it recovers it, by right of reversion, if the Rulership be vacated or forfeit (V, d. 3). It preserves, in cases of doubt, the right of approving laws (II, d. 23, §§ 6–7): it also preserves the right of property in the *bona Regni*, so that the Ruler cannot alienate any of them, just as he cannot divide the kingdom or surrender it to foreigners *non consentiente Republica ipsa*, or, again, alter the constitution or the succession to the throne (II, d. 25). The *Respublica* has a right of resistance to tyrants; it can, *quoad capita, convenire,* and depose or punish the tyrant 'by the express will of its whole body' (III, d. 6; V, d. 3, §2). None the less, *Rex est superior tota Republica* [within the terms of the authority granted to him]; and he is subject to no real *jus deponendi*, since (1) the *Respublica* can only proceed against him when he 'assumes a power not granted to him', and (2) when he does so, and thus acts outside the terms of the·'grant', neither he nor the people is *Superior* (II, d. 23, §§ 8–10).

Suarez regularly describes the *communitas, populus, totum corpus*, or *hominum collectio*, as the 'Subject' of original sovereignty, and also of the rights of transferring and recovering that sovereignty (III, cc. 2–4) and of the reserved rights of the people which are never transferred at all (III, c. 9, no. 4; IV, c. 19; V, c. 17); and he opposes this Group-person, as the *Regnum* or *Respublica*, to the Ruler. Accordingly he terms the contract of subjection a *pactum inter Regnum et Regem* (III, c. 4, no. 5); he speaks of a *consensus Regni* to laws (IV, c. 19, no. 6); and he vindicates for the *Regnum* or *tota Respublica* a right of insurrection against a king who has become a tyrant 'in exercise', arguing that, though the people has transferred to him a real ownership of political authority, it has added the condition *ut politice non tyrannice regnet*—so that, while in his essence *Rex superior est Regno*, a contingency may arise in which *tota Respublica superior est Rege* (III, c. 4, no. 6, c. 10, nos. 7–10; *Opus de triplici virtute*, pp. 1055–6).

See, in addition, nn. 62 and 67 supra, on the 'collective' conception of the personality of the people in the writers mentioned.

The Ruler limited by the contractual rights of the People

141. Cf. Waremund de Erenbergk, *De regni subsidiis*, c. 11, p. 150; Bornitius, *De maj.* c. 9 (*leges fundamentales et pacta cum populo*), c. 13 (where it is argued that the administration of parts of majesty may be devolved, so that an *imperium moderatum* takes the place of *summum imperium absolutum*), and *Part.* pp. 42–3 and 102 sqq.; Fridenreich, cc. 18 and 29 (on the possible limitation and restriction of the exercise of the supreme power by certain *pactiones*); Keckermann, I, c. 33, pp. 531–2 (on special pacts with subjects, which restrict but do not abolish monarchy); Busius, II, c. 7. See also Molina, II, d. 23, and Suarez, III, c. 4, no. 5, c. 9, no. 4, IV, c. 17 (the Ruler may be limited in the exercise of supreme power, in legislation, in taxation, etc., by a *translatio sub conditione*; for such a conditional transference is a *conventio inter communitatem et principem, et ideo potestas recepta non excedit modum donationis vel conventionis*).

Division of powers and the mixed constitution as affecting sovereignty

142. We find this dualism in Arnisaeus (*Polit.* c. 8, §§ 38 sqq.; *De rep.* II, c. 6, s. 1; *De jure maj.* II, c. 1, §1): 'majesty' is *unum individuum, non indivisibile…unum potentiale, non essentiale*: it contains 'parts', viz. the 'rights of majesty', and though it cannot, *simul sumta cum omnibus suis partibus*, belong to a number of persons, *nihil tamen prohibet quin partes in hoc toto unitae secerni, et divisim inter plures distribui, possint*.

The mixed constitution is interpreted by most of its adherents in the same sense of a *real* [and not merely conceptual] division of powers: cf. for example, Grotius in n. 137 supra; Heider, pp. 982 sqq.; Werdenhagen, II, c. 25; Limnaeus, *Jus publicum*, I, c. 10; Schönborner, I, c. 16; Keckermann, II, cc. 4–6; Liebenthal, VIII, qu. 1; Berckringer, I, c. 5, §7 and c. 12, §§ 15–21; Felwinger, *Diss.* pp. 417 sqq. But the 'person' of the Ruler still remains a divided 'person' when the essence of the mixed constitution is held to consist merely in a division of majesty into *ideal* [or conceptual] parts; cf. Paurmeister, II, c. 1 (cf. vol. IV of the *Genossenschaftsrecht* [not here translated], p. 218); Besold, *De statu reip. mixtae*, c. 1; Tulden, II, cc. 16–17; Carpzov,

Comment. in leg. reg. c. 13, s. 9, nos. 28–31. We find, however, in Besold, op. cit., and still more decidedly in Frantzken, *De statu reip. mixto*, an approximation to the view that the partners who share supreme power only constitute the person of the Ruler when they are taken *conjunctim*. Cf. also Suarez, III, c. 4, no. 5, IV, c. 17, no. 4 and c. 19, no. 6: where the king needs the *consensus Regni in publicis comitiis* for his laws, the 'supreme legislator' is not the king by himself, but *Rex cum Regno*. Other thinkers only speak vaguely of a common capacity for the rights of majesty: cf. Busius, II, c. 6, and also L. de Hartog, *A Dutch Writer on the State at the Beginning of the Seventeenth Century* (in an offprint from *Nieuwe bijdragen voor rechts-geleerdheid en wetgeving*, 1882), pp. 24 sqq. and 33.

143. Bodin, I, c. 8 and II, c. 1, and especially the argument (in nos. 85–99) that any constitutional limitation of the true Ruler by the rights of the *universitas populi* is unthinkable, because it at once makes the *universitas populi* itself the Ruler.

144. Bodin, VII, c. 2, nos. 640–1 (where there is a comparison of the *Respublica* to a minor). Cf. also vol. IV of the *Genossenschaftsrecht* [not here translated], p. 249 n. 156.

145. Gregorius, although he has a doctrine of the Sovereignty of the Ruler which makes it single, illimitable, indivisible, and irresponsible (I, c. 1, §9; V, c. 1, §3; VI, cc. 1–3; XXIV, c. 7; XXVI, c. 5, §§ 24–5 and c. 7), none the less makes a sharp division between *bona Reipublicae* and *bona patrimonialia Principis*; and he will only describe the former as being, at the very most, *quasi propria Principis* (III, cc. 2–3 and *Syntagma*, III, c. 2, §§ 8–10). He also allows the possibility of a limitation of supreme power *per legem electionis* (III, c. 7). *Even the absolutists suppose a personality of the People*

Bornitius, again, while he assigns the 'person of the State' decisively to the Ruler—by whom alone *Respublica statum adipiscitur et conservat* (*Part.* p. 45; *De maj.* c. 5), and who stands above the People, even when they are regarded as a community, in virtue of being the 'Subject' of a single and indivisible majesty (*Part.* pp. 47 sqq.; *De maj.* cc. 3 and 11)—at the same time refuses, like Gregorius, to recognise the Ruler's right of property in *bona Reipublicae* (*Part.* pp. 70 sqq.), and regards limitations of absolute power as possible (supra, n. 141).

Keckermann goes to the length of allowing the possibility of resistance and deposition even against the *absolute Imperans*, though he makes the exercise of these rights more difficult in that case than it is against the *Monarcha certis pactis et conditionibus assumptus* (I, c. 28, p. 431).

According to Claudius de Carnin, *Regia potestas* and *Reipublicae potestas* are identical (I, c. 10), inasmuch as by natural law the *Respublica* necessarily transfers, without any reservation, the whole of the power which rested originally in itself (I, c. 9); but the *acceptatio populi* continues to be necessary for legislation (I, c. 3).

Barclay [unlike these thinkers] recognises no rights of any description as belonging to the People. According to his argument every true monarchy is absolute; and its existence is incompatible with any limitations, or any division of power, imposed by fundamental law (II, IV, V, c. 12). All the rights of the People are transferred, and thereby cease to belong to the People (IV, c. 10; VI): *universa negotia Reipublicae demandantur Regi* (IV, c. 25); there is never any right of resistance or deposition (III, cc. 4–16; V, cc. 7–8). In Barclay, however, there is no question of any theoretical construction of a State-personality [i.e. he does not get beyond the conception of the personal king to a conception of the impersonal '*persona Civitatis*', which might have involved him in problems of the relations of the king to this *persona*].

Arnisaeus on the Ruler and the societas of the ruled

146. Cf. *Polit.* c. 6, *De rep.* I, prooem. §§ 4 sqq. and c. 5, s. 3-5. He thus assumes that, when the form of the State is changed, the *Respublica* disappears but the *Civitas* remains; and he states the question which Aristotle raised in connection with such changes* in the form, '*Quatenus acta Reipublicae obligent Civitatem?*' His conclusion is that 'contracts made by the *Respublica* only' do *not* bind 'the whole *Civitas*': on the other hand 'contracts made by the whole people', and 'agreements made and expenses incurred for the welfare of the *Civitas*' (in regard to which the 'tacit consent of the people' is to be assumed) continue to hold good 'if the *Respublica* disappears'. He also contrasts the personality of the People with that of the Ruler in other connections; and, more particularly, he refuses to include within the scope of the Ruler's 'majesty' the right of property in the territory and belongings of the State (*De jure maj.* III, c. 1). But he entirely excludes the People as such from all the rights of the *Respublica* (*De rep.* II, c. 2, s. 5, c. 3, s. 8; *Polit.* c. 14; *De auct. principum in populum*, cc. 2-3; *De jure maj.* I, cc. 3, 6); and he accordingly holds that where a monarch is limited by the constitutional rights of the People, there is no longer any question of a true monarchy, but only of a *forma mixta* (*De auct.* etc. c. 1, §§ 4 sqq.; *De jure maj.* I, c. 6). It follows that the *Respublica*, which includes and connotes the whole authority of the State (*De rep.* I, c. 5, s. 3), is identical with the Ruler; and the 'person' of the *Respublica* can therefore be also expressed by a personification of his *majestas* or *dignitas* (*De rep.* I, c. 5, s. 4; *De maj.* III, cc. 1 and 3). More especially, the immortality of his *dignitas* serves as a means of securing the continuity of the *Respublica* in the event of a change in the line of succession. 'So far as the rights of majesty and the *status imperii* are concerned', the successor to the throne is bound by the contracts (though not by the decrees) of his predecessors, where such contracts have been made *nomine dignitatis, et pro Republica*, in regard to matters appertaining to the dignity itself; but 'in matters appertaining to the fisc' [i.e. to his own private treasury, as distinct from the public funds], he is only responsible as heir (*De jure maj.* I, c. 7). Between the 'person' of the State or *Respublica*, as thus conceived, and that of the People, there may be an *obligatio inaequalis*; but there can be no really effective contractual relation (ibid. c. 6).

Hobbes' version of contract

147. *De cive*, c. 5; *Leviathan*, c. 14, c. 17: *tanquam si unicuique unusquisque diceret: Ego huic homini, vel huic coetui, auctoritatem et jus meum regendi me ipsum concedo, ea condicione, ut tu quoque tuam auctoritatem et jus tuum tui regendi in eundem transferas.* Cf. the author's work on Althusius, pp. 86 sqq., 101 sqq.; and for different conceptions see pp. 341 sqq.

Hobbes rejects the idea of the People as a 'person'

148. *De cive*, c. 6, § 1, c. 7; *Leviathan*, c. 19. In particular he argues that the assembled people, even when it wishes to retain supreme power, cannot continue to be a 'person' unless it immediately transforms itself into a *concilium* regularly meeting and deciding questions by a majority-vote, which involves a devolution by all and single of their whole personality, through a mutual contract, upon the democratic Ruler as *una persona* (*De cive*, c. 7, §§ 5-7). In an aristocracy, the constitution of a *curia optimatum* to rule as 'a single person' means that the people immediately 'ceases to exist as a single person' (ibid. §8), and is 'at that moment dissolved' (§ 9), 'being no more

* See supra, n. 124.

a single person, but a dissolute multitude' (§10). Similarly, if a monarch be chosen, *populus statim atque id factum est persona esse desinit* (§§12, 16).

149. *De cive*, c. 6, §20, c. 7, §§7, 9, 12, 14, 17; *Leviathan*, c. 19. The monarch in a monarchy, the Senate in an aristocracy, and the majority of the people in a democracy, are all *omni obligatione liberi*; they are not bound by any contracts made with individual subjects or with the whole body of subjects: they are not even pledged by any oath they may have taken. They cannot therefore do injustice to their subjects, either as individuals or as a whole. Any reservation of the rights of the People in a democracy, by means of a contract made at the time of the institution of the Ruler, is inconceivable, because the People was not a person before the establishment of the principle of majority-rule, and the only contract which was possible at that time was merely a contract between individuals and individuals. A similar reservation in an aristocracy, or a monarchy, would be null and void, because the people receiving the promise [that its reserved rights will be observed] disappears as a person with the institution of the aristocratic or monarchical Ruler, 'and when a person disappears, all obligation to that person disappears also'. A contract between the Ruler, *after* he has been instituted, and the People, is impossible, because all that then remains over against the sovereign is merely a 'dissolute multitude'. Nor can any legal nexus of any sort exist as between the Ruler and his individual subjects, because the will of individuals has been merged entirely in the sovereign will. *Hobbes refuses to admit a contract of Ruler and People*

150. *De cive*, c. 5, §11, c. 6, §§4–20, c. 7, c. 12, §§1–7, c. 13, c. 14, §§20–33; *Leviathan*, cc. 18, 19, 21, 23, 30.

151. *De cive*, c. 6, §§17–19, c. 7, §§4 and 15–17, c. 12, §5; *Leviathan*, cc. 18, 29.

152. See supra, nn. 84, 86, 87.

153. Hobbes' account of the similarity and difference between the monarchical and the republican sovereign illustrates particularly how much he identifies the 'personality' of the Ruler with the physical substance of a man or a body of men. The republican sovereign only really exists for him as long as it is actually in session: in the interval it sleeps; and this sleep becomes death if the right of meeting at its own discretion be lost. Cf. *De cive*, c. 7, §§6, 10, 13 and *Leviathan*, c. 19, and especially *De cive*, c. 7, §16, with the acute deductions in regard to temporary monarchies which are derived from this principle. *Sovereignty to Hobbes a physical fact*

154. *De cive*, c. 5, §§6–11; *Leviathan*, c. 17. This contract is more than a 'consent or concord': it is a real union of persons, *in personam unam vere omnium unio*. By it 'the wills of all are reduced to one'... *ut unus homo vel unus coetus Personam gerat uniuscujusque singularis, utque unusquisque auctorem se fateatur esse actionum omnium, quas egerit Persona illa, ejusque voluntati et judicio voluntatem suam submitteret*. *The Sovereign as plenary Representative*

155. *De cive*, c. 5, §§9–10, 11, c. 6, §1; *Leviathan*, cc. 16–18, 22. Hobbes declares absurd the opinion of those who say, 'of Kings bearing the Person of the State', *quod etsi singulis majores, universis tamen minores sunt; nam si per universos intelligunt Civitatis Personam, ipsum intelligunt Regem, itaque Rex seipso minor erit, quod est absurdum; sin per universos multitudinem intelligunt solutam, singulos intelligunt, itaque Rex, qui major singulis est, major quoque erit universis, quod iterum est absurdum.** Most thinkers are, however, in Hobbes' view, unable to see how *Civitas in Persona Regis continetur* (*Leviathan*, c. 18).

* See the statement of this argument in the English version of the *Leviathan*, c. 18, at the beginning of the third paragraph from the end of the chapter.

The People without a Ruler a mere multitude

156. Hobbes is never tired of drawing out the distinction between a community constituted as a person and 'a dissolute multitude to which no action or right can be assigned', or of describing the people without a Ruler as a mere 'multitude': cf. *De cive*, c. 6, §§ 1–3 and 20, c. 7, §§ 5, 10, 16, 18; *Leviathan*, cc. 16, 18, 19. He will not even allow the name of 'people' to be applied to such a body, and he remarks (*De cive*, c. 12, § 8) that it is a mark of revolutionary opinion *quod homines non satis distinguunt inter populum et multitudinem*. The 'people' is a unity with a single will and activity: the 'multitude' is not. The 'people' rules in every form of State, and even in a monarchy (for 'the people wills by the will of one man'): the 'multitude', in all forms, means the subjects. *In Democratia et Aristocratia cives sunt multitudo, sed curia est populus; et in Monarchia subditi sunt multitudo, et (quamquam paradoxum sit) Rex est populus*. If, following the vulgar use of language, we call the masses by the name of 'people'—if we speak of (what is totally impossible) a rebellion of the *civitas contra regem*, and describe the will of discontented subjects as 'the will of the people'—we are invoking, *sub praetextu populi, cives contra civitatem, hoc est multitudinem contra populum*.

The Ruler as soul of the body politic

157. *De cive*, c. 6, § 19: the usual comparison of the Ruler to the head is false; a comparison of him to the soul is the only proper comparison, because the soul is the instrument of the will, and it is through the instrumentality of him *qui summum habet imperium, et non aliter*, that 'the State has will', *et potest velle et nolle*. The chief council is a better analogy to the head; cf. *Leviathan*, Introduction and c. 19.

Hobbes on the personality of the State

158. Cf. supra, notes 100 and 101; *De cive*, c. 5, § 9, § 12, c. 6, § 1, c. 12, § 8; *Leviathan*, cc. 17–19. Hobbes' very definition of the State already includes the attribute of personality. In the *De cive*, c. 5, § 9 (after an account of the institution of a 'civil person' by means of a union of wills, and an explanation of how this 'person' differs from individuals, and even from *omnes simul, si excipiamus eum cujus voluntas sit pro voluntate omnium*) we get the definition: *Civitas ergo (ut eam definiamus) est persona una, cujus voluntas ex pactis plurium hominum pro voluntate habenda est ipsorum omnium, ut singulorum viribus et facultatibus uti possit ad pacem et defensionem omnium*. A similar definition also occurs in the *Leviathan*, c. 17. Here, after giving an account of the contract made at the time of the State's foundation, he continues, *quo facto multitudo illa una Persona est, et vocatur Civitas et Respublica; atque haec generatio est magni illius Leviathan vel—ut dignius loquar—mortalis Dei, cui pacem et protectionem sub Deo immortali debemus omnem*. Then follows the definition—'A State is one person, of whose actions a great number of men have made themselves authors by mutual agreements one with another, to the end that he should use the power of them all at his own will for peace and common defence'.

Contemporary views similar to those of Hobbes

159. About the same time as Hobbes (1642) Graszwinkel developed an absolutist theory of indivisible and illimitable 'majesty' (*potestas una, summa in se, et absoluta*) which held the same position in the State as God in the Universe or the soul in the body, and excluded any independent right in any other part of the State [cf. n. 93 supra]. But Graszwinkel failed to attain the conception of a single and homogeneous State-personality; and his failure was due not only to the theocratic basis from which he started (cc. 1–3), but also, and indeed primarily, to his dualistic conception of the nature of 'majesty'. He maintained the distinction between 'real' and 'personal' majesty; and all that he contended was that the one *might* [on occasion] exclude the other. E.g. 'real majesty' exists to the exclusion of 'personal

Notes to § 15

majesty' (*a*) in a Republic, (*b*) in a monarchy during an interregnum, (*c*) when it appears as a source of fundamental laws, and (*d*) where the monarch is *Rex sub conditione*. Conversely, the 'personal majesty' of a *true* king includes 'real majesty', which thus disappears as a separate entity (cc. 10–11).

Salmasius, in the *Defensio Regia* of 1651, is already obviously under the influence of Hobbes. Like Hobbes, he regards the *universus populus* or *universitas*, in a true monarchy, as a mere aggregate. He holds the original rights of the people to be entirely merged in the sovereignty of the king, arguing that these rights only belonged to *omnes collective sumpti*, i.e. to the people as a *concio*, and that the king has taken the place of such *concio* (*unus instar concionis*). He depicts the king as the one representative of the unity of the people (*unus instar totius populi*); and he holds that there is no community of the people confronting him which is capable of exercising any rights (cf. esp. c. 7). Salmasius, however, does not attempt to deduce any conception of the personality of the State from these ideas.

§15. THE NATURAL-LAW THEORY OF ASSOCIATIONS [*DIE ENGEREN VERBÄNDE*]

1. Bodin, who includes in his initial definition of the State the fact that it is composed of families (I, c. 1, no. 1), vigorously defends against Aristotle* the propriety of making the theory of the Family a part of Political Science, on the ground that the family is both a fundamental element in and an 'image' of the State (I, c. 2); and he proceeds at once (I, cc. 3–5) to treat in detail of the three powers which exist in the family [the power of the husband, that of the father, and that of the master]. Arnisaeus takes a similar line, *Polit.* cc. 2–5 and *De rep.* I, cc. 1–4: see also Danaeus, I, c. 3; Crüger, *disp.* II; Heider, pp. 32 sqq.; Velstenius, *dec.* II–III; Bornitius, *Part.* pp. 38 sqq.; Liebenthal, *disp.* II–IV; Olizarovius, lib. I. *The position of the Family in political theory*

On Besold's treatment of the three family societies and the general family-community which they compose, see vol. IV of the *Genossenschaftsrecht* [not here translated], p. 13. Gregorius does homage to a similar point of view (I, c. 2), but he does not discuss the Family in any detail. Conring also holds that it is only *societates domesticae* and the State which have their origin in Natural Law: cf. *Diss. de republica*, Op. III, pp. 763 sqq., and *De necessariis civitatis partibus*, ibid. pp. 748 sqq.

2. This is the line taken by Bodin, I, c. 6; Arnisaeus, *Polit.* c. 6, *De rep.* I, c. 5; Crüger, *disp.* III; Heider, pp. 25 sqq.; Velstenius, *dec.* IV–V; Bornitius, *Part.* p. 40; Liebenthal, *disp.* V; Olizarovius, lib. II–III.

3. Bodin first treats of corporations in his third book, under the head of

---

* Aristotle, in the beginning of the *Politics*, where he is controverting the *Politicus* of Plato, distinguishes the theory of the Family from that of the State. Later, however, in the course of Book I and the beginning of Book II, he deals largely with the theory of the Family as a part of the theory of the State.

The treatment of groups as institutions of administrative law

administrative law. Here he describes, as *Reipublicae partes ac veluti membra singula, quae principi Reipublicae quasi capiti illigantur*, first the Senate (c. 1), then the officials (c. 2) and the administrative boards (cc. 3–6), after that the corporations (c. 7), and finally the Estates (c. 8).

Gregorius similarly brings under the head of administrative law his account of the advantages and dangers of corporations (*De rep.* XIII, cc. 2–4). He regards corporations as being mere institutions of positive law after the State has once been formed—although, in the same context, he refers to the *natural* development of an ascending series of groups [while the State is being formed] (ibid. c. 2, §2).

Arnisaeus, in his comprehensive treatise on politics, only devotes a few scattered remarks to local communities and corporations at the end of his theory of the *subditi majestati* (c. 12, p. 133). Bornitius simply treats associations as subdivisions of Estates (*Part.* p. 72); and many other political theorists similarly consider local communities and corporations merely as political divisions of subjects—cf. Heider, pp. 268–71; Hoenonius, *disp.* 2, §§ 52–7; Velstenius, IV, qu. 8–9; Busius, I, c. 13 (in a context in which the family has also been previously treated in cc. 10–11, and the institution of clientship in c. 12); Kirchner, *disp.* XIV; Liebenthal, *disp.* V, §§ 1–78. We often find associations completely omitted by political theorists (e.g. Crüger), and still more often by the theorists of natural law (e.g. in the treatises cited above, § 14 n. 2).

4. This is particularly the case with the ecclesiastical theorists of Natural Law, and more especially with Molina and Suarez.

Bodin's classification of collegia

5. Bodin, distinguishing *collegia rerum divinarum ac publicae pietatis causa* from *collegia rerum humanarum*, divides the latter into those which have 'jurisdiction', and those which have not. In the former category of these secular 'colleges' he includes only 'magistrates and judges'; in the latter, 'colleges' for the *educatio juventutis*, and *medicorum, scholasticorum hominum, mercatorum, opificum, agricolarum sodalitia* [such colleges thus being either educational, or professional, or occupational]—see loc. cit. no. 330.

Later, in dealing with the 'powers of colleges', he gives pre-eminence to the 'colleges of magistrates and judges', as being *praecipua*, because they *non solum collegas singulos ac collegii totius minorem partem, sed caetera quoque religiosorum et opificum collegia, pro jure suae potestatis moderantur et coercent*. These corporate bodies of judges and magistrates are distinguished from other 'colleges', which are only concerned with their own particular *negotia communia*, by the fact (*a*) of their handling *tum sua tum aliena negotia*, and (*b*) of being constituted *potius aliorum quam sua causa*. But they too 'must rightly and duly administer law for their own members, individually as well as collectively', before they assign rights to others. Bodin adds one qualification. The right of a college to exercise jurisdiction itself over its members is a right which is only to be recommended in the case of the 'most prudent' colleges: for other colleges, the jurisdiction of superior colleges and of the Prince is preferable (nos. 332–3).

Bodin on the rights of private 'colleges'

6. Bodin argues that these other colleges [i.e. colleges other than those of magistrates and judges] *jurisdictione et imperio vacant*, and have only a 'right of coercion and moderate castigation' within the limits of their statutes: even Frederick II assigned no more power to Rectors of Academies and headmasters of schools. Where *collegia religionis causa constituta* are in question, the *judex ordinarius* has to decide how far a penalty or sentence of expulsion

imposed by a college is admissible. Any rule to the effect that disputes between members must only be brought before the college has no validity *in crimine et judicio publico*; and *in privatis judiciis* the decision of disputes by a college is only valid when it takes the form of an 'arbitral award'—and even so it must be passed by a unanimous resolution. The summoning of a meeting by the senior members or officers binds nobody to appear, unless the summoner *imperium habet*: failing that, recourse must be had to the government in order to issue a binding summons; but only moderate penalties can be imposed on those who absent themselves, even when such a summons has been issued. *Collegia* and *universitates* may issue edicts, *salvis legibus*; but they must not even discuss what is forbidden to them by law, or anything that is not included in the sphere of their corporate affairs (nos. 333–7).

7. Loc. cit. no. 331 (*victus communis* is no more necessary than an *aerarium commune*): see also no. 332 (a 'college' can only acquire a capacity of inheritance by a special privilege to that effect [cf. the modern French rule which requires administrative authorisation for the acceptance of a gift or legacy by an *établissement publique*]; the idea of a corporation does not necessarily require a capacity of inheritance, or even of acquisition). *Bodin on corporate property*

8. Although *universitas non potest peccare, immo ne consentire quidem*, Bodin holds that, in consequence of the identification of the majority with the whole body, penalties may be properly imposed on the corporate body (such as withdrawal of the right of meeting, cancellation of privileges, fines, and confiscation of property), if an offence has been committed after proper discussion and decision in due corporate forms. On the other hand, he would spare innocent individuals from incurring penalties which affect their body or life—or even their property, so far as it is possible to distinguish their property from that of the corporation. For the rest, basing himself on a full review of historical facts and on political considerations, he advises the following of a just mean between severity and excessive clemency (nos. 337–42). *Bodin on the offences of corporate bodies*

9. Gregorius, after speaking of the origin and the various species of ecclesiastical and secular corporations, and after limiting drastically the scope of *collegia licita* (*De rep.* XIII, c. 2), proceeds to discuss in his next chapter (c. 3), with an unusual wealth of detail, the offences of corporations (especially those of monopoly and heresy), and the three *remedia* which the sovereign can apply in dealing with such offences. They are (1) *reformatio institutionis* (by way of changes, prohibitions, visitations and penalties, §§ 2–15); (2) abolition (§§ 15–21); and (3) a rule to the effect that *non permittendae sunt facile novae religiones aut collegia* (c. 4). In the course of this argument there is no mention of any legal limits on the sovereign power. Cf. also XIII, c. 19 (on offences of fraternities and their suppression) and XXIII, cc. 3–4 (on 'factions and conspiracies, and their remedies'). On the juristic treatises of Gregorius, see above [vol. IV of the *Genossenschaftsrecht*, not here translated], p. 60 n. 2, p. 65 n. 17 and p. 91 n. 90. *Gregorius Tholosanus on the same theme*

10. Bornitius demands that 'for the preservation of the State', persons should be divided into three Estates (*Part.* pp. 68sqq.), and these Estates should be subdivided *in alias partes, quae collegia dicuntur, ut eo rectius et facilius sua munera expedire possint* (p. 72). Each of these colleges—including, in the spiritual Estate, those of priests, professors, doctors and the like; in the political, those of magistrates, judges and councillors; and in the private *Bornitius' theory of corporate bodies*

Estate, those of agriculturalists, merchants and artisans—is *auctoritate Principis factum et concessum*. The colleges, when formed, are then united to form a *corpus*, and a number of *corpora* are finally united to form a *universitas*.* For the most part they have *suam politiam in jure, legibus, privilegiis, pactis, suaque administrandi forma*; but the rights of *collegia in statu privato* [i.e. in the third or 'private' Estate] belong only to the sphere of private law as a *jus civium speciale* (p. 93), and such private colleges, like families, can only have a *politia privata* (p. 105). Cf. *De maj*. cc. 14–39 (where it is argued that a grant by the State is always necessary to justify collegiate self-government, *jurisdictio*, the choice of officers, *jus comitiorum*, the right of taxation, and the like).

Arnisaeus on corporate bodies

11. Arnisaeus (*Polit*. c. 12), at the end of his theory of the *subditi majestati*, speaks of their division into certain classes, *ut scilicet commode gubernari per jussa et imperia majestatis possint*. In this connection he discusses *collegia, corpora* and *universitates* on the basis of Bodin's scheme: he rejects entirely any toleration of associations without 'the consent and the confirmation of the State', but he allows to colleges a power of making rules *de rebus suis et in collegas*, and also, by authority of a special grant to that effect, a *jurisdictio in collegas*. Similarly, in his *de jure majestatis*, he interprets all corporate authority as the result of a 'concession' made by the State, except in so far as it is merely the exercise of a power to enter into contracts or of other rights at private law: cf. II, c. 2, §§ 8–9 and III, c. 7, § 10.

Busius on corporate bodies

12. This is the argument, essentially based on Bodin, which we find, e.g. in Velstenius, *Dec*. IV, qu. 8–10; Heider, pp. 268–71; and Liebenthal, *Disp*. V, §§ 1–78. Busius takes a more independent line: he starts by distinguishing the State, as the all-embracing *universitas*, from a *universitas* such as a local community or a *collegium* (I, c. 3, § 3); and he then proceeds to treat particularly of *collegia et corpora*, which he considers to be identical (I, c. 13). He defines a corporation as *universitas plurium civium, qui in certum aliquem finem contrahunt societatem ad similitudinem civitatis*: he refuses to tolerate any other associations than those which are authorised by the State: he recommends an extreme prudence, which will allow only useful corporations, will admit no discussion of public affairs, will only recognise 'statutes' [or by-laws] as 'private agreements', and will permit only private, but not public, associations. He also refuses to allow any liberty of meeting. Cf. Hartog [as cited in § 14 n. 142], pp. 15–16 and 20–1.

13. Cf. supra [vol. IV of the *Genossenschaftsrecht*, not here translated], pp. 11 sqq.

14. Cf. e.g. Oldendorp, *Isagoge*, I, p. 181; Winkler, V, c. 2 and c. 4, where a distinction is drawn between *respublica majestatis* and *respublica municipalis*. Winkler argues that 'majesty' has, 'of itself and in its own right', the whole of the authority of government; but he adds that *conceditur etiam magistratui provinciali aut municipali interdum, ut pro modo jurisdictionis sibi commissae legem ferat; sed haec omnia precario et indultu majestatis, non jure proprio*.

Ecclesiastical writers unfavourable to Groups

15. In this sense we find Covarruvias arguing (*Pract. qu*. I, c. 4) that the 'supreme jurisdiction of the king' (which he calls the '*Majoria*') excludes any independent right of nobles, or of *Civitates*, if the king himself takes action. It is only when the king fails to make provision, or is prevented from doing

---

* Does this mean that the colleges in any one Estate form a *corpus*, and these *corpora* in turn form the *universitas Regni*? Bodin has a somewhat similar view of the relations of *collegium, corpus* and *universitas*; but his *universitas* is only a local community (cf. pp. 64–65 supra).

Notes to § 15

so, that a *universitas* can appoint a *Rector* for itself. Molina (v, d. 3, §§ 3–5) ascribes all *jurisdictio* to the *tota Respublica*, and therefore to the king, with the result that magnates, towns, and the like, can only have a 'derivative jurisdiction': cf. II, d. 666, and Lessius, II, c. 33, dub. 2, on the right of taxation.

16. Suarez (I, c. 8) divides *potestas praeceptiva*, which can issue commands, into *potestas dominativa* (or *oeconomica*) and *potestas jurisdictionis* (or *politica*). The former may be found even in an 'imperfect community' [e.g. the Family]; for (*a*) the father has [naturally] a *potestas dominativa* over his child, and (*b*) such power may also arise from contract—either under natural law, through an agreement of marriage, or under positive law, through voluntary entrance into a relation of service. The *potestas jurisdictionis* is confined to the 'perfect community'. Only a 'supreme head' can have the legislative authority on which a *potestas jurisdictionis* follows; and an *inferior* can only exercise such authority within the limits in which it has been 'communicated to him by the head'. *Suarez regards all real authority as belonging to the State*

17. According to Suarez (III, cc. 2–3, 9) legislative authority, in the sphere of *leges civiles*, belongs only to sovereigns. This means that it belonged originally to the People, and has subsequently come to belong either to *Reges supremi* (and, in addition, other 'princes without a superior', and territorial princes subject to the emperor who have been duly enfeoffed as sovereigns), or to sovereign republics. *Per contra*, according to Book III, c. 9, nos. 16–21, the 'statutes' [or by-laws] of 'communities' have inherently nothing of the nature of *lex*. The 'statutes' of *civitates minores* [*civitas* being here understood to signify an Italian city of the medieval type], in the form in which they are recognised by Bartolus,* are either mere *pacta*, or *praecepta humana temporalia, sicut sunt praecepta patrisfamilias in domo sua*; and even the enactments of *civitates maximae* and *magnae* (species which ought not properly to be distinguished) are really either *pacta*, or (as Baldus holds) simply the expression and outcome of *jurisdictio*. The real question [when we are discussing the legislative powers of a municipality or *civitas*] is whether (1) the *civitas* is a 'free people', and, as such, *retineat in se aliquam potestatem supremae reipublicae et per illam se ipsam gubernet*, or (2) *illam* [sc. *potestatem*] *simpliciter transtulerit in aliquem principem, vel quolibet alio justo titulo* [*potestas illa*] *translata sit*. It is only of the former of these two alternatives that the *Lex 'omnes populi'* speaks. The instant a city is 'subject to some supreme Prince', it can no longer make laws *ex potestate propria*. At the most— and then only by virtue of a reservation made by itself at the time of 'transference', or as the result of a later 'concession' made by the sovereign—it is able *statuere de rebus ad suam peculiarem gubernationem et administrationem pertinentibus*. In other respects [i.e. apart from these particular matters] it needs the 'confirmation of the superior'. What is true of cities is similarly true of provinces, and particularly of *corpora mystica*. *Suarez on the rights of municipalities*

A similar view appears in I, c. 8, no. 5 and II, c. 1, nos. 8–10. Cf. also VI, c. 26, nos. 4–25: *magistratus civiles aut respublicae inferiores et civitates subjectae* can never establish any rule which runs contrary to the *jus commune* of the State; the *Superior*, on his side, can abrogate even the *statuta* which he has confirmed, but the *statuentes* themselves have no such power of abrogation

---

* On Bartolus, and his doctrine of the *civitas sibi princeps* (the Italian city-state as 'its own prince'), see C. N. S. Woolf's book on *Bartolus of Sassoferrato*, pp. 112 sqq.

if the confirmation he gave was *essentialis*, or if, even though it was only *accidentalis*, 'the Prince by confirming [a statute] made it his own law'—which is to be presumed the case.

Suarez on the validity of custom

18. Cf. VII, cc. 1–20. According to c. 3, nos. 8–9, c. 9, nos. 3–11 and c. 14, no. 4, a 'private person' or an 'imperfect community' (*una familia*) can pass neither a *lex expressa* nor even a *lex tacita*: they can only establish a *praeceptum*, or a *statutum, per modum pacti seu mutuae conventionis*—and the 'precept' or 'statute' must be clearly expressed. On the other hand, any 'perfect community' (*civitas, populus, congregatio ecclesiastica,* [*corpus*] *mercatorum*) may *consuetudinem introducere*, inasmuch as, passively regarded, it is *legis capax*, and, regarded actively, it can make laws *ut conjuncta principi vel facultatem ab eo habens*, although its inherent power extends only to the making of *statuta conventionalia*. None the less (according to cc. 13, 14, no. 5 and c. 18), the consent of the Prince is always necessary [to the validity of customary rules], whenever 'the people itself is not the supreme Prince'. In the case of communities with a power of making rules, this consent can be given by a general authorisation: in the case of other communities, the *de facto* toleration of a 'prescriptive custom' is adequate, but otherwise an act of personal assent is necessary—though that assent may be given tacitly, assuming always that the Prince is cognisant of the usage in question.

Suarez on taxation

19. Cf. v, c. 14: only the sovereign can *tributa imponere*: it is consequent on the nature of 'majesty' that any other person—though he may acquire a right to the exaction of traditional dues—can never acquire a right of taxation; and similarly, while the sovereign may grant to an inferior *ut nomine et auctoritate sua tributum imponat in particulari casu*, he cannot make a valid grant to an inferior of 'the general privilege of imposing a tax independently of his own approbation', since such a privilege would offend against the nature of the State and the *suprema potestas*.

Suarez on religious congregations

20. Thus the answers given by Suarez (IV, c. 6) to the question, *Q. ae communitates seu congregationes ecclesiasticae habeant potestatem leges condendi*, depend entirely on the fundamental principle that any autonomy belonging to ecclesiastical associations must either be the result of an 'ecclesiastical jurisdiction' granted by the Pope, or, if it takes the form of passing by-laws, then such by-laws can only be *regulae operandi positae ex conventione illorum qui sunt de communitate*: see especially nos. 12–13, 19 and 21.

The corporate body reduced to a mere partnership, like the Family

21. Thus in Gregorius (XIII, c. 2), Velstenius (*Decis.* IV) and Liebenthal (*Disp.* V), *collegia, corpora* and *universitates* are reckoned as *societates*: in Heider (pp. 268–71) they are contrasted, as *societates privatae*, with the *societas publica* of the State. Bodin (I, c. 2) compares families and corporations, without suggesting that there is any difference between the idea of family authority and that of the authority of the corporation: in his view families are already competent to make *statuta* (e.g. 'house-laws' [like that of the Habsburg family], or compacts of mutual inheritance); and he only refuses to allow the making of such *statuta* to *familiae obscurae* (no. 13). It has already been mentioned (supra, n. 10) that Bornitius assigns the rights of corporations proper [*collegia in statu privato*] to the sphere of private law. Arnisaeus (*Polit.* III, c. 12) also reduces the internal rights of associations to the level of the rights of 'societies' [or partnerships]: supra, n. 11, *ad finem*.

22. Busius (I, c. 13): their rights *continentur prope jure societatis*, but with some modifications, e.g. they are not dissolved by the death of their members, and they can act on the majority-principle; see n. 12 supra.

Notes to § 15

23. The traditional [Roman-law] theory of corporations is reproduced almost in its entirety in Gregorius (cf. also XIII, c. 2, §7 on *hospitalia* and *pia loca* regarded as *collegia*); in Besold [see vol. IV of the *Genossenschaftsrecht*, not here translated, pp. 11–16]; and in other writers. Some of the essential parts of that theory are also reproduced in Bodin; in Molina (cf. e.g. II, d. 3 on the property of corporations, d. 300 on loans to an *ecclesia* or *civitas*, and d. 536 on *hypotheca tacita* of the property of the administrators of a corporation); in Suarez; and elsewhere.

Continued use of the Roman law of corporations

24. This is the view adopted by Bodin (III, c. 7, nos. 334–6), when he draws a line of division between (1) affairs in which *omnes singuli* must agree, because there is a question of a right belonging to all the members *seorsum a communione*, and (2) affairs in which the majority decides, because *jus universorum* is concerned. Cf. Oldendorp, op. cit. I, p. 163, and Liebenthal, *Disp.* v, §§63–77. It is on the basis of this view that Bodin argues (loc. cit. no. 331) that it is compatible with the idea of a 'college' that there should be a *princeps collegii* who has *imperium in collegas* [i.e. over each distributively], but not that there should be a *princeps* with *imperium in universos* [i.e. over all collectively], as there is in a *consistorium*, a *gymnasium*, or a *familia*. Arnisaeus takes a similar line, op. cit. p. 133.

Bodin's distinction between 'distributive' and 'collective'

25. Thus Bodin (loc. cit. no. 332), in spite of his description of *jus collegii* as *jus universorum*, argues in favour of the continuance of this *jus collegii* until it is legally abolished, even when all the members [*collegae universi*] have disappeared—declaring that it is folly to identify the *collegium* with the *collegae*. [He thus assumes that a college is a fictitious individual, distinct from its individual members.] He also regards the capacity of owning property, and particularly that of inheriting it, as a special privilege granted to the *collegium* [as a fictitious individual].

But he also assumes a ficta persona

26. Bodin (loc. cit. nos. 334–6) deals in detail with the validity of the majority-principle, recognising that principle in so far as there is nothing to oppose it either in *jura singulorum* or in *leges ejus qui collegii creator est quasque princeps imperio suo valere jussit*. But majority-decisions, he argues, require a regular meeting, and the presence of two-thirds of the members; and then *plus possunt duae partes coactae quam omnes seorsum*. They bind the minority, and all individuals, but they do not bind the whole body itself or the majority. The majority can always abrogate its decisions, as the sovereign can abrogate a law, or the testator a will, or contractors a contract; and this is the case even with a unanimous decision, if the question concerned is one *de jure universorum*, though not if it be one *de jure singulorum seorsum*. Bodin mentions, in this connection, that he had himself prevented a decision of two of the *Ordines Francorum* which would have enured to the detriment of the Third Estate.

Bodin on the majority-principle

27. Cf. Busius, supra, n. 12; Arnisaeus, *De maj.* III, c. 7, §10 ('*vi conventionis*').

28. Cf. Bodin, loc. cit. nos. 337–42 (supra, n. 8), and Oldendorp, loc. cit. p. 39.

29. Thus Molina (II, *disp.* 3, §§7, 11, 12) draws a distinction between (1) *dominium universitatis*, which belongs to it *jure universitatis* and includes pastures and forests which are used by all and (2) *dominium particulare...quod... universitas seu communitas aliqua non secus habet ac si esset persona privata*. He holds that the taking of wood in the common forest (*disp.* 58), and the use of the common pasture (*disp.* 59), are dependent on the regulations made by the

The Catholic writers on village commons

local community as owner; but he argues that offences by members of a local community against such regulations—unlike encroachments on the pastures or forests of other communities—should be punished only by fines, and not by the exaction of compensation (unless it be a question of really considerable damage), because the common property still remains intact [after the offence has been committed). He refuses to admit that the lord of the manor court has any property in the common, and allows him only a joint right of user *suo ordine et gradu* (d. 3, §11, d. 59, §§3–5).

Similarly Lessius (II, c. 5, dub. 13–14) denies any obligation to pay compensation (unless 'great damage be held to have been done to the community') in cases where a community has prohibited the use of its pastures and public woods and a person has offended against such a prohibition *in loco publico communitatis cujus ipse est pars*.

Lugo (I, pp. 142 sqq., disp. 6, sect. 9) takes the same view [that no compensation is due], unless there is a question of considerable damage, or of use for profit by means of sale to others, or unless the common has been let to a third party. He argues that any offence [by a member of the community against its regulations], unlike encroachments on entirely strange woods and pastures, which belong to another community or to a private person, is only an offence against *oboedientia*, and not an offence against *justitia*. The relation between *universitas* and *singuli* is different, however, in a monastery [from what it is in the case of a secular body]. [In the latter case], *oppidani singuli retinent suum jus partiale ad illa bona*, and they have a right of controlling their shares, because full and free property remains with the community and its members, even if the administration thereof has been transferred to some manager on its behalf. [In a monastery], although the monks *in communi habeant eorum bonorum dominium, ita tamen tota administratio est penes communitatem vel praelatos, ut singuli neque ex parte possint condonare aliquid.*

Suarez on the various forms of community

30. Suarez distinguishes between (1) the 'natural community of mankind' and (2) the *communitas politica vel mystica*, which is 'only one in virtue of a specific act of union in a moral association'. The latter kind of community is either of divine foundation (the Church) or of human invention. The community which is of human invention is again either (1) 'a perfect community, which is capable of political government', or (2) 'an imperfect community', which does not form a *corpus* and is destitute of *vis coactiva*. 'Perfect communities' include not only the State but also local communities, and not only 'real' but also 'personal' groups (such as orders and fraternities)—provided that such local communities and 'personal' groups have *perfectum regimen et moralem unionem*, and so, while 'imperfect as parts in regard to the whole', are 'perfect as regarded in themselves'. Even so, they are 'not absolutely, but comparatively or relatively, perfect'. On the other hand the 'private household' under the paterfamilias is absolutely imperfect: cf. I, c. 6, nos. 18–20, and also supra, nn. 16 and 18.

31. According to I, c. 6, only a 'perfect community' is *passive legis capax* (nos. 1–16 and 21–22). But law need not always be imposed on the community qua community (*ut communitas est et corpus mysticum*). On the contrary, it generally affects the community not as being a community, but as being so many individuals (*non collective, sed distributive*, no. 17); and it may also refer to a part of the community only (nos. 23–4). Yet a law which only affects the community qua community—e.g. a law which commands or forbids some act which can only be done by the *corpus mysticum* itself—is still

a true law; for though such a law applies to *una individua communitas* and this community is called *una persona ficta* [i.e. though the law seems to be made for *one* 'person', which is contrary to the nature of law], yet the 'community' is a 'community' [i.e. a sum of persons], it possesses the necessary permanence, and it is directly intended to secure the common welfare of *all* its members. Moreover, the *singuli de illa communitate* are also indirectly obliged by such a law. See, in addition, I, c. 7, and (on the other hand) the passages on the contractual character of 'statutes' cited in nn. 17, 18 and 20 above.

32. Cf. the *Vind. c. Tyr.*, where it is argued that any part of the kingdom, and therefore any province or city—but not any individual, because the individual is not a 'part'—has the right and duty of resistance when the pact with God is broken (qu. II, pp. 94 sqq.). These parts too have severally promised for themselves [just as the whole kingdom has promised for itself] that they will be true and obedient to God in accordance with the stipulation He has made (pp. 99–100)—as is also the case, the author adds, with the Estates of the Empire in Germany, or with 'parts' of the Church, such as the *ecclesia Gallicana* [as a part of the Church Universal]. Therefore, *universi in regionibus et urbibus* may rise in revolt, *auctoribus magistratibus tanquam a Deo primum, dein a Principe constitutis* (p. 114); and cities and provinces which do not seek to avert an attack on God's church by force of arms are guilty of a grave sin (p. 228). [As *universi* in a province or city may resist, so, too, may the governors]: *qui alicujus partis regionisve tutelam susceperunt, tyrannidem tyrannumque ab ea regione urbeve arcere jure suo possunt* (qu. III, pp. 304 sqq. and 326 sqq.); and thus individual nobles [as having the *tutela* of a 'part'] may begin a revolt, though private persons can never assert the *jus gladii* against a tyrant. The treatise *De jure mag.* (qu. 6, pp. 26 sqq. and 74, qu. 7, p. 92) arrives at similar results. Danaeus (III, c. 6, p. 223) requires the consent of every province to any change of the constitution; and he adds that, when a province is not asked for its consent, 'some hold that it can choose for itself its own form of polity'—but this, he adds, is dangerous. *The Vindiciae on the rights of provinces and cities*

33. Cf. for what follows, the first eight chapters of Althusius' *Politica*, and also c. 9, §§ 1–7, c. 18, §§ 90–1, c. 38, §§ 76 and 110–14, c. 39, § 84: see also the connected account of the argument of these passages in the author's work on Althusius, pp. 21 sqq. Reference may also be made to his *Dicaeologia*, I, cc. 7–8, 25–33, 78–81.

34. Cf. vol. III of the author's *Genossenschaftsrecht*, pp. 544–5.

35. Althusius mentions (*Polit.* c. 4, § 25)—but without ascribing any great significance to it—the special category of the *corpus* (which is a broader association of a number of *collegia*), as assumed in Bodin and other writers. Like Bodin and others, he counts as 'colleges' not only (1) guilds and trade-corporations and (2) corporate Estates and ecclesiastical societies, but also (3) collegiate courts of justice, administrative Boards and ecclesiastical Boards (c. 4, § 30), and (4) assemblies of representatives (c. 5, §§ 54 and 60 sqq.), provincial diets (c. 8, §§ 49 and 56 sqq.), and general diets (c. 18, § 62 and c. 33). *Althusius' classification of collegia or 'Fellowships'*

36. In the first edition of the *Politica*, the category of 'political association' is lacking. In that edition Althusius begins his classification of associations by distinguishing the *consociatio particularis* from the *consociatio universalis* (i.e. the State); he then subdivides the *consociatio particularis* into the *consociatio naturalis necessaria* (i.e. the Family) and the *consociatio civilis spontanea*; and

finally he subdivides the 'voluntary civil association' into the *consociatio privata in collegio* and the *consociatio publica in universitate*.

37. On the political theory of Althusius see, in the previous section, nn. 36, 52, 57, 65, 67, 70–3, 75, 77, 82–5, 87, 96, 106, 108–9.

38. See supra [vol. IV of the *Genossenschaftsrecht*, not here translated], pp. 178 sqq.

The idea of of the Respublica Composita

39. This is the line followed by Casmannus (c. 66), who contrasts this *composita respublica* with *civitates confoederatae*. It is most marked in Hoenonius, who places the kingdom composed of a number of cities—under the name of *respublica composita* (d. 12)—half-way between the city-state, which he terms a *respublica simplex* (d. 11), and the 'confederation' proper. He vests the several parts of this 'composite State' with a large measure of autonomy, including even the right of secession (d. 9, §§ 44–54); but he regards *collegia et sodalitates* as merely useful divisions of the subjects of the State (d. 2, §§ 52–7).

German legal writers who largely follow the federal scheme of Althusius

40. See, for example, Matthias (*Coll. polit.* d. IV–V and *Syst. polit.* pp. 20–194). *Societas*, which is the primary conception, is either 'natural' or 'civil and voluntary'; 'natural society' includes the three 'domestic societies' [husband and wife, father and child, master and servant]: 'civil and voluntary society' shows itself first in its 'particular' form—in the *vicus, pagus, oppidum, collegium, corpus, universitas* and *civitas*—and then in its 'universal' form, the *respublica*.

Gneinzius treats successively of the Family (ex. II–VII), the provincial community (ex. VIII), *collegia* (ex. IX), and the *civitas* (ex. X): he declares 'Fellowships' to be useful (ex. IX, qu. 2), but regards them as permissible only *ex auctoritate superioris* (ibid. qu. 5).

Koenig begins his theory of the State by enumerating Families, *collegia, corpora* and *universitates* among the constituent elements of the *Respublica*; and he then sketches the process of development towards increasingly broader and higher forms of society (*Acies disp.* I, §§ 123–9; *Theatrum polit.* I, c. 1, §§ 376–91).

Werdenhagen starts his classification of *societas humana* (II, c. 13) from the distinction between 'particular' and 'universal' society. 'Particular' society he divides into the 'simple' society of the family community (cc. 14–17), and 'composite society', which may be either an extended family-group (c. 18) or a 'Fellowship' (c. 19). Under the head of 'universal society', which is also termed *universitas*, he counts the *vicus, pagus* and *civitas*; but he thinks it a misuse of language that institutions of higher education should be designated by this term (c. 20). He expressly insists that the 'principal cause' of every *collegium* is the agreement of its members, the 'grant of a superior' being the 'less principal' (though still an indispensable) cause (c. 19, § 5).

Berckringer (I, c. 17), in dealing with 'the conjunction of persons and things in the family, college, *corpus* and *universitas*', begins with the Family (§ 2); he then deals successively with the 'college', which is produced by the *consensus coëuntium et magistratus* (§§ 3–8), the *corpus* (§ 9), and the *universitas* (§§ 10–11)—including both the *universitas personarum* (§§ 12–17) and the *universitas rerum* (i.e. the territory, §§ 18–21)); finally, he treats of the union of both of these species of *universitas* in the *Respublica*, which, he holds, may be either 'simple' or 'compound' (§§ 22–8).

Kirchner, in treating of *sodalitia, collegia* and *corpora* (*disp.* XIV), regards all corporate bodies as having autonomy and judicial authority over their own members, with a certain power of coercion and punishment. In §1, litt. d, he speaks of a 'concession by the supreme power' as necessary; but in litt. e he states that corporations are advantageous to the State, and only a tyrant will ever suppress them entirely—though secret and nocturnal meetings are never to be tolerated (§3).

41. Cf. especially Keckermann (I, c. 15, pp. 255–75), *de speciali cura sub-* *Keckermann* *ditorum collectim consideratorum*. He distinguishes *subditorum communio ex natura* *on associations* (i.e. the Family) from *subditorum communio magis ex instituto civili*, though he admits that community of the latter sort is also based partly on natural law. Community by civil institution may be either (1) 'more particular', e.g. *collegium, coetus, conventus, synagoge* and *sodalitas*, or (2) 'more universal', as in any sort of *collectio plurium diversi status hominum in unum corpus et locum in quo simul habitant*. The latter species—the territorial corporation or *universitas*— may be either 'major' or 'minor'. The 'minor' sort is the local community, which appears as a *universitas rustica in vicis vel pagis*, and as a *universitas oppidana vel urbana* in the various sorts of towns. The 'major' sort of territorial corporation is an area composed of a number of rural and urban communities; and such an area may be either *angustior* (e.g. the 'district, prefecture, barony, county') or *latior* (e.g. the 'province, duchy, kingdom').

In spite of the structure which he thus builds, Keckermann rejects the principle of liberty of associations, as being incompatible with the monarchical principle. Where 'colleges have liberty of meeting', as the nobles have in Poland, it is a sure sign of the presence of aristocracy or democracy. The monarch cannot allow any association which has not received his consent, and he must punish secret unions severely; nor will he ever permit his subjects to erect a corporation *cui ipse non praesit sua auctoritate per personam aliquam a se delegatam*. He will also reserve the appointment, or at any rate the confirmation, of the officers of 'colleges', since the 'constitution and authority of the whole college' resides in these officers, and therefore the person appointing or confirming them 'has also control over the constitution and authority of the whole college'. Even in republics, he argues, this [right of appointing or confirming the officers of 'colleges'] is advisable (pp. 261–2). He treats the local community in the same way as the 'college', vesting the sovereign with the ordering of its constitution, the appointment of its officers, and a perpetual tutelary supervision (pp. 265 sqq.).

Schönborner adopts a similar view. He treats of the Family (I, c. 10), *collegia et corpora* (c. 11), *universitates* (c. 12) and the *civitas* (c. 13); but like Keckermann he allows the erection of corporations only 'by the authority of the sovereign', and he gives the same advice to the sovereign, word for word, in regard to [the appointment or confirmation of] officers. The same line is taken in the treatise *De statu politico seu civili libri sex*, I, disc. 35–42.

42. Keckermann (loc. cit.) adopts as his basis the conception of *communio*. *Prevalence* Matthias (loc. cit.) uses the idea of the *communicatio* produced by *societas*. *of idea of* Schönborner adopts Althusius' theory of *consociatio* and the *communicatio* *Partnership* *rerum, operarum, juris et benevolentiae* which it produces (I, c. 11); but he regards this *consociatio* and *communicatio* as creating a *corpus mysticum* which is like the natural body—*instar unius hominis est, ejusque personam repraesentat*— and he avails himself of this point of view to reproduce *in extenso* the whole of the Roman-law theory of corporations (I, c. 13).

Berckringer takes the same line as Schönborner. He uses the idea of a 'union of minds, services, persons, things and laws' (I, c. 17, §7); the fiction of the single personality, combined with the idea of the material identity of the *universitas* with its individual members (§10); the traditional theory of the *negotia juridica* and the delicts of corporations (§§12–17); and the customary distinction of the various species of public and common property (c. 16, §§15–33).

Grotius on associations

43. Afterwards, in his theory of contracts (II, c. 12), he treats of *societas negotiatoria* (§24) and *societas navalis* (§25), and devotes a whole chapter to *foedera* (c. 15).

44. Cf. I, c. 1, §3: a 'society without inequality' exists as between *fratres, cives, amici, foederati*: an 'unequal society' as between *pater et liberi, dominus et servi, rex et subditi, Deus et homines*. In the same way there are also two sorts of *justum—aequatorium* and *rectorium*.

45. II, c. 6, §§4–8; III, c. 20, §5: cf. the passages in nn. 97 and 132 to §14.

46. Cf. supra, nn. 57 and 66 to §14.

47. Cf. supra, n. 51 to §14 and pp. 51–2sqq., with nn. 97, 98, 99.

Grotius on the majority-principle

48. Cf. the decisive statement in II, c. 5, §17, quoted in n. 74 to §14. Grotius proceeds to discuss in detail a number of questions—the possibility of an equality of votes, in which case no decision can be attained [in matters of policy], but in criminal proceedings acquittal must follow (§19); the methods prescribed by Natural Law for arriving at a decision when there are more than two *sententiae* (§19); the rule of Natural Law by which *jus absentium accrescit interim praesentibus*, while positive law often requires the presence of two-thirds (§20); the 'natural order' among the *socii*, according to the ages of the members (§21); and the counting of a majority by the shares [belonging to the members] where a *res* (e.g. an inheritance or an estate) is the basis of the *societas* (§22).

Grotius on corporate liability for debt

49. III, c. 2, §1. It is true that the members are responsible for the sum involved in proportion to their shares, but they are responsible *non qua singuli, sed qua pars universorum*. As against this rule of Natural Law, the *jus gentium voluntarium* may introduce, and appears to have actually introduced, the rule that *pro eo, quod debet praestare civilis aliqua societas aut ejus caput*, 'there is a lien and obligation' (sometimes primary and sometimes secondary) 'on *all* the goods, corporeal and incorporeal, of the persons who are included in such a society or are subject to its head' (ibid. §2). There is a need for such a rule, since it is difficult to get at the *imperantes*; nor does it contradict Natural Law to such an extent as to be inadmissible.

Grotius on the delicts of corporate bodies

50. Cf. II, c. 21, §§2–7. A community is responsible, properly speaking, only for its own delicts; and thus it cannot be responsible for a *factum singulorum*, except as the result of its own *patientia* or *receptus* (i.e. harbouring the person or persons concerned). Conversely, *singuli* are responsible for the offences of the *universitas*, and *subditi* for the delicts of the *summa potestas*, only in cases where they have incurred a joint responsibility by giving assent thereto or by executing an unlawful command. The results [of a corporate delict] descend, it is true, from *universi* to *singuli*, because *ubi universi, ibi et singuli...universi non possunt nisi ex singulis quibusque constare, nam singuli quique congregati, vel in summam reputati, faciunt universos*. But the innocent minority must be treated gently in the matter of punishment, because, in spite of what has just been said, *distinctae sunt poenae singulorum et universitatis*. There is a distinction, for instance, between the death-penalty, as applied to individuals, and *mors civitatis, cum corpus civile dissolvitur*: similarly the enslave-

ment of individuals differs from the *servitus civilis* of the *universitas* or its transformation into a mere province. Similarly, again, the confiscation of corporate property is something different from the confiscation of private property. It is thus unjust that innocent individuals should lose their property through the delict of a *universitas* (cf. also §§ 11, 17, 18). On the other hand, a 'consequential loss' *may* affect innocent individuals; just as children suffer from a confiscation of property pronounced against their parent, so individuals suffer from the punishments inflicted on corporations—*sed ea in re, quae ad ipsos non pertinet nisi per universitatem.*

51. See the preceding note, and also nn. 67, 70, 89, 90, 121 and 127 to § 14.

52. In treating of the question raised in II, c. 21, §8—whether 'a penalty can be exacted in *every* case for the delict of a *universitas*'—Grotius argues that an affirmative answer appears to be inevitable, because *quamdiu universitas durat, idem corpus est.* The true answer, however, is in the negative. A distinction has to be drawn between attributes which are predicated *de universitate primo ac per se*, e.g. the possession of an *aerarium* or of *leges*, and those which only belong to it *de derivatione a singulis*, e.g. the attributes of learning, courage, or merit; for such attributes primarily appertain to individuals, *ut animum habentibus, quem universitas per se non habet.* In the latter case, therefore, the merit disappears *extinctis illis per quos ad universitatem meritum deducebatur*; and what is true of merit is also true of [the opposite of merit, i.e.] a delict which involves a penalty. The position is different, however, in regard to divine punishment, which often comes upon a later generation only. *Grotius tends to resolve corporations into individuals*

53. Hobbes' theory of associations, which is only indicated in the treatise *De cive*, is developed in the *Leviathan*, where the whole of c. 22 is devoted to it.

54. Cf. *Leviathan*, c. 22 and *De cive*, cc. 12–13. Hobbes compares *corpora legitima* to the muscles of the human body, and *illegitima* to its worms. [Hobbes remarks that in any event 'the great number of corporations' is 'like worms in the entrails of a natural man'.] *Hobbes on corporations*

55. Hobbes, in c. 22 of the *Leviathan*, also applies this idea to parliaments, which he regards as 'regular subordinate systems', with a personality of their own, which have been instituted for a limited time. They can only discuss proposals put before them by the Ruler, and they have no authority other than given by the terms of their summons; otherwise there would be two powers in the State. *Hobbes on Parliament*

56. This is the argument of the *Leviathan*, c. 22, but it already appears in the *De cive*, c. 5, § 10. In such a case [i.e. the case of a claim by a subordinate system against its members] the members may also occasionally protest with success against majority-decisions; but this is inadmissible in a sovereign assembly, where such a protest would bring in question the *suprema potestas* itself, and where, apart from that, *quicquid fit a summa potestate auctoribus fit civibus singulis et omnibus.*

57. In provinces and colonies he thinks a monarchical constitution preferable, as even democracies generally recognise. Trading companies, on the other hand, are best managed by a *coetus*, with a right of voting for all who contribute money: *Leviathan*, c. 22. *Hobbes on colonies and companies*

58. He states a different point of view in the *De cive*, c. 7, § 14. Dealing with the question whether the 'person' of the State can itself commit sin, he concludes that in a monarchy the Ruler himself commits a sin if he offends against Natural Law, *quia in ipso voluntas civilis eadem est cum naturali*; whereas *Hobbes on sins and delicts of groups*

in a democracy or aristocracy the sin is not that of the *persona civilis*, but of *cives illi quorum suffragiis decretum est—peccatum enim sequitur voluntatem naturalem et expressam, non politicam, quae est artificiosa*.

No question of a *delictum* [i.e. a legal offence, as distinct from sin or *peccatum*] can ever arise in this connection [i.e. in regard to the State], as it does in regard to *Systemata subordinata*. The point is simply that *peccatum*, i.e. sin as distinct from delict, cannot be attributed to a *persona civilis* [as such, and apart from the 'natural will' of its bearer].

Hobbes on the debts of groups

59. Hobbes would regulate responsibility for debts in *Systemata mercatorum* in a somewhat different way. In such 'systems' there should be an obligation 'of each member severally to pay the whole of the debt' to a third party, because that party knows nothing of an 'artificial person', *sed personas naturales eorum omnes obligari sibi supponit*. On the other hand a creditor who is also a 'member of the System'—being, in that capacity, a debtor himself [and so unable to take action against individuals which would also be action against himself]—can only take action against the system and its common funds. [In this latter case, therefore, the general rule enunciated in the text, that the system alone is liable, applies also to *systemata mercatorum*]. If the State, by virtue of its supreme power, demands money from such a system, the members must furnish the sum demanded by making proportionate contributions [i.e. contributions proportionate to their shares].

The Empire a mere name

60. Cf. e.g. Biermann's *Diss. de jure principatus*, I, p. 6, § 10; Michael, I, p. 188, §§ 9 sqq.; Cluten, II, p. 10, § 3 and pp. 35 sqq., §§ 9–15; Engelbrecht, II, p. 187, §§ 97 sqq.; Sinolt Schütz, I, ex. 1, th. 16–19. A different view appears in Wurmser, *Exerc.* III, qu. 2 and 22 (the Empire is now only a name): cf. also Limnaeus, VII, c. 1, no. 32 (Roman Empire and German monarchy have gradually merged to such an extent *quod nemo, nisi ille qui divum choros regit, dissolvere potens est*).

Suarez (III, c. 7, nos. 1–13 and c. 8) expressly denies the emperor's *imperium mundi*: even the Pope, according to III, c. 6, has no such *imperium*, because, apart from the States of the Church, he has no 'direct temporal power'. Cf. also Vasquez, cc. 8, 20, 21.

The idea of a societas gentium

61. Connanus (I, c. 5, nos. 1 and 4, and c. 6, nos. 2–3) holds that *jus gentium* is the product of a *societas humana*, in which the original unity of mankind has continued to be preserved even after its division into 'civil societies', and in which a relic of the old community of all men thus persists. For similar expressions cf. Omphalus, I, c. 38 and Winkler, I, c. 9.

Gregorius Thol. (I, c. 3, §§ 11 sqq.) regards *commune jus gentium* as the survival of a *civitas mundana*, with God for its king and all men for its citizens, which in all other respects has split into *coetus et civitates particulares*.

Gryphiander, in §§ 12 sqq. of his *De civili societate* (printed in Arumaeus, I, no. 6), speaks of a *universalis societas humana, cujus vinculum est jus naturale*. Cf. Johannes a Felde, I, c. 1, § 5.

Suarez (III, c. 2, no. 5, c. 4, no. 7, c. 19, no. 9) argues that in secular matters *aliqua unitas* still survives from the [original] unity of mankind, so that men continue to constitute a *societas et communicatio*; and although *unaquaeque civitas perfecta, respublica, aut regnum, sit in se communitas perfecta et suis membris constans, nihilominus quaelibet illarum est etiam membrum aliquo modo hujus universi*: this is the basis of international law.

Grotius speaks of [States as] *membra unius corporis* (II, c. 8, § 26, c. 15, §§ 5 and 12); of a *societas humana* (ibid. c. 20, cf. c. 21, § 3); and of *jus gentium* as securing property even to children and lunatics, *personam illorum interim quasi sustinente genere humano* (ibid. c. 3, §6).

62. Albericus Gentilis (in his *De jure belli* of 1588, pp. 11–13) refers the obligation of *jus gentium* to the fact that, although all peoples have never assembled [to enact it], *quod successive omnibus placere visum est, id totius orbis decretum fuisse existimatur*. He adds: *immo, ut rectio civitatis et legislatio est penes civitatis majorem partem, ita orbis rectio est penes congregationem majoris partis orbis.*

Ideas of a world Commonwealth

In the same way Victoria speaks of a human commonwealth, including all States as its members, in which majority-decisions are valid (*Rel.* III, nos. 12 and 15).

The *Vind. c. Tyr.* makes the unity of *humana societas* the source of a right and duty of neighbouring States to intervene for the protection of oppressed subjects against a tyrant (qu. IV, pp. 348–58)—just as (ibid. pp. 329–48) it makes the conception of a single Church the justification of intervention against religious oppression.

Boxhorn (I, c. 2, §§ 3–8) regards *jus gentium* as the outcome of the *universalis Respublica omnium hominum*.

63. The idea [of a natural community connecting States] is absent in Bodin and his school. In the view of Hobbes, as we should expect, the natural condition of States, like the primitive state of nature among individuals, is a condition of *bellum omnium contra omnes*; and a real international law is therefore absolutely impossible.

No internationalism in Hobbes

64. Suarez (loc. cit.) lays emphasis on the idea that it is only particular nations which are States with legislative power. There cannot, therefore, be any *leges civiles universales*; common adhesion to international law constitutes only a *societas quasi politica et moralis*; and it is only 'in a sense' (*aliquo modo*) that States are members of a larger whole. Connanus also (loc. cit.) terms the universal society only *quasi omnium urbs et civitas*, and international law only *quasi jus civile*.

Suarez on internatioual society

65. Cf. Bodin (II, c. 6, no. 224 and c. 7); Althusius (*Polit.* c. 17, §§ 25–53); Casmannus (c. 66); Hoenonius (dd. 12 and 13); Grotius (*Apologeticus*, Paris, 1622, c. 1). See also Brie, *Der Bundesstaat*, I, pp. 14 sqq. and G. J. Ebers' recent work on *Die Lehre vom Staatenbunde*, Breslau, 1910, pp. 10 sqq.

Federal ideas

66. See above [vol. IV of the *Genossenschaftsrecht*, not here translated], p. 274 no. 74. See also Werdenhagen (III, c. 25, § 16), on a federation as a *corpus foederatorum*, but not a *respublica*; Althusius (c. 33, §§ 122–36), on *comitia sociorum confoederatorum*; and Arnisaeus (*De rep.* II, c. 4, s. 2, §§ 22 sqq.), on *confoederationes arctiores* which have the appearance of a *Respublica*.

67. In I, c. 3, § 7 Grotius deals both with 'unions' (which he knows only in the form of personal unions), and with 'confederations' (*Staatenbunde*). In II, cc. 15–16, on the other hand, he deals only with *foedera* or treaties, which he divides into 'equal' and 'unequal'; and he remarks in an earlier passage (I, c. 3, § 21) that even an 'unequal treaty' does not extinguish sovereignty. Grotius was the first thinker to draw the contrast between unions and federations: cf. Juraschek, *Personal and Real Union*, p. 2, and Ebers, op. cit. pp. 17 sqq.

Grotius on unions and foedera

68. See Victoria, *Rel.* I, qu. 5, no. 8 and III; Vasquez, *Controv.* 8, 20, 21, 27; Soto, IV, qu. 4, a. 1–2, X, qu. 3, a. 1; Molina, II, d. 21; Lessius, II, c. 5 and III–IV; Suarez, I, c. 7, no. 5, c. 8, no. 9, III, c. 3, no. 8, cc. 6–8; Contzen, II, c. 16 and VI; Claudius de Carnin, I, cc. 13 and 15; Menochius, *Hiero-*

Catholic theory of the Church as superior

politica, I, c. 1 and II, cc. 1 sqq. Among the Monarchomachi, see Boucher, I, cc. 5–8 and 18, and II; Rossaeus, cc. 3–11; Mariana, I, cc. 8 and 10.

See also Pighius (†1542), *Hierarchiae ecclesiasticae assertio*, Cologne, 1551 (first printed 1538); Sanderus, *De visibili monarchia Ecclesiae, libri VIII*, Louvain, 1571; Schulting, *Hierarchiae anacrisis*, Cologne, 1604.

Theory of its potestas indirecta

69. See Bellarmine, *De membris ecclesiae militantis*, III, 6, *De Summo Pontifice lib. V*, and *De potestate summi Pontificis in rebus temporalibus adv. Barclaium*, Rome, 1610; Molina, II, d. 29; Suarez, III, c. 6; Barbosa on c. 6, x, 1, 33 [of the canon law]; Gonzalez Teller on c. 6, x, 1, 6, no. 34 and c. 6, x, 1, 33, nos. 14–19. A similar view is already to be found in Soto, IV, qu. 1, a. 1. Of course the theory which ascribed to the Pope a direct power over emperor and kings did not disappear: cf. e.g. Restaurus Caldus in *Tract. Utriusque Juris*, XVI, no. 30, qu. 50; Marta, *Tract. de jurisdictione*, Mainz, 1609 (esp. I, cc. 5, 8, 17–26 and IV); Laymann on c. 34, x, 1, 6 and c. 6, x, 1, 33.

Theory of its parity with the State

70. Cf. Gregorius Thol. VII, c. 2; Tulden, *De regimine civili*, I, cc. 17–18; P. de Marca, *De concordia sacerdotii et imperii seu de libertatibus ecclesiae Gallicanae libri VIII*, ed. J. H. Boehmer, Leipzig and Frankfort, 1708 (books I–IV first printed at Paris in 1641, and the whole work in Baluze's edition of 1603), esp. II, c. 1, where it is argued that while there are *potestates distinctae*, there is a *societas* between the two.* See also supra [vol. III of the *Genossenschaftsrecht*], pp. 813 sqq.

71. See supra, vol. III, pp. 799 sqq.

The Lutheran theory

72. A complete formulation of this expression is to be found in B. Carpzov, *Jurisprudentia ecclesiastica seu consistorialis*. In I, tit. 1, def. 2, he describes the 'double person' of the territorial prince, who exercises 'double power, ecclesiastical as well as political': in I, tit. 1, deff. 11–12, he treats of the consistories as his organs: in I, tit. 3, def. 27, he explains the ordered co-operation of the 'whole church' in the three Estates: see also *Decis.* 113. But a full elaboration of the theory of the episcopal system may already be found in M. Stephani, *De jurisdictione*, III, p. 1, cc. 1 and 15. In addition see Omphalus, I, c. 3 (there is a 'double polity', but the ecclesiastical commission of the territorial prince comes from God); E. Cothmann on *Cod.* 1, 2, qu. IV and *Cod.* 1, 2; Arnisaeus, *De jure maj.* II, c. 6, *De subjectione et exemptione clericorum*, etc. (published at Strassburg in 1635, but written in 1612); B. Meiszner, *De legibus*, IV, s. 2; Wurmser, *Exerc.* v, qu. 1–24; Cluten, in Biermann, II, pp. 18 sqq., §§ 5–8; Lampadius, p. 1, §§ 16–29; Schütz, II, exerc. 14, pp. 911–1000; Knipschildt, II, c. 3 and v, c. 8.

Zepper and others on the Calvinist polity

73. This view is worked out completely in e.g. Zepper, *De politia Ecclesiastica*, Herborn, 1595. He treats in Book I of the subject-matter of ecclesiastical administration; in Book II of ecclesiastical office; in Book III of church government. Church government is conducted by *conventus* in the four stages (cc. 1–7) of 'presbyteries', *conventus classici* [or 'classes'], provincial synods and general synods (subject to the general principle that *quae in inferioribus conventibus aut gradibus decidi possunt, ad superiores devolvi non debent*), and also by *visitationes* (cc. 8–11). But the secular authority has a power of co-operation, since *magistratus* and *ministerium* are two institutions of one and the same community, ordained for the Church by God (c. 12). Compare also the doctrine of the *Vind. c. Tyr.* (qu. II, pp. 74 sqq.) on the joint contract

---

* Cf., for this theory of 'alliance', the work of Warburton, Bishop of Gloucester, on *The Alliance between Church and State*, published in 1736. It was a work which had some vogue in England during the eighteenth century.

of people and king with God; the treatise *De jure mag.* (qu. 10); Hotoman, *Francogallia* (c. 22); and especially Althusius (c. 8, §§ 6–39, c. 9, §§ 31 sqq. and c. 28). Cf. also David Blondel, *De jure plebis in regimine ecclesiastico*, Paris, 1648, on the inalienable rights of the congregation, which are never transferred to the government.

None of this applies, of course, to the body of opinion which is based on the teaching of Zwingli. Zwingli rejected entirely the conception of a 'spiritual State' and a 'spiritual authority', and ascribed all power of ecclesiastical government, as being 'external' in its nature, to the Christian State: see his *Works*, I, pp. 197 and 346.

74. Cf. Stephen of Winchester, *Oratio de vera oboedientia* (1536), in Goldast [*Monarchia Sancti Romani Imperii*], I, pp. 716–33, where it is contended that *Reges, Principes et Magistratus Christiani unusquisque suae Ecclesiae supremum in terris caput sunt, et religionem cum primis procurare debent.* Cf. also Johannes Beckinsav, *De supremo et absoluto Regis Imperio liber unus*, with a dedication to Henry VIII, in Goldast, I, pp. 733–55; Waremund de Erenbergk, *De regni subsidiis* (cc. 1–2, pp. 12–43), who argues for a *jus majestatis, supremitatis, superioritatis absolutae potestatis...etiam in ecclesiasticis*); Alexander Irvine (Scotus), *De jure regni diascepsis*, Leyden, 1627; Keckermann, *Polit.* I, c. 32, who holds that *princeps habet jus majestatis ecclesiasticum, ideoque potestatem ordinandi ea quae ad cultum Dei et veram religionem tuendam pertinent*, p. 516; Fridenreich, *Polit.* c. 12; Hoenonius, *Polit.* I, § 43, V, §§ 3–55; Kirchner, *Disp.* VI; Graszwinkel, *De jure maj.* c. 5.

The territorial theory

See also Carolus Molinaeus, *Comm. ad Codicem*, on *Constit. Frid. Imp.* '*Cassa et irrita*', pp. 29–30; and Besold, *Diss. de maj.* sect. 2.

75. See above (vol. IV of the *Genossenschaftsrecht*, not here translated], p. 82, n. 65; and cf. Besold, *Diss. de maj.* sect. 2, *Diss. de jure coll.* c. 2, §§ 5–6, *Diss. de jure et divisione rerum*, c. 5.

76. See, on the one side, Hobbes, *De cive*, c. 17 and *Leviathan*, c. 39, and on the other, Milton, *Prose Works*, II, pp. 520 sqq.

Uniformity or toleration

Biermann (*Diss. de jure princ.* I, no. 16, §§ 21 sqq.) also combines the demand for freedom of conscience (§§ 26–8) with a general point of view which is 'territorial'.

77. Fourth edition, the Hague, 1661: first printed at Paris, 1648.

78. In this justification of the majority-principle (c. 4, §6) Grotius, it is curious to notice, deserts the individualistic point of view on which he strictly insists, in this very connection, in all the rest of his writings (cf. supra, n. 48).

Grotius' De Imperio

79. See c. 4, §§ 9–13. The *regimen constitutivum ex consensu*, which issues in e.g. the institution of the Sabbath and the appointment of deacons, belongs to the Church by Natural Law; *data enim universitate, hoc ipsum jus ex natura universitatis continuo sequitur*. Positive law may deprive the Church of particular rights; but it may also confer upon it an *imperium summum* or *inferius*.

80. Positive law may confer upon pastors an *imperium inferius*. But in that case such *imperium* is not the expression of the *sacra functio* they exercise—a function which is subject to the State only in the ordinary way. It is the outcome, and the expression, of political authority; and therefore pastors, in so far as they exercise such an *imperium, supremarum potestatum vicarii et delegati sunt*. Cf. c. 2 and c. 4, §§ 7–8, 11–12 and 14.

81. Cf. c. 1. Grotius proceeds to deal in detail with the action of sovereignty upon the different areas of ecclesiastical life, maintaining throughout

Grotius on the rights of the Sovereign over the Church

the principle that the indestructible rights of the sovereign continue still to exist, by virtue of Natural Law, even where certain rights are delegated, by virtue of positive law, to other ecclesiastical or secular 'Subjects'. It depends on the will of the sovereign whether he admits co-operation of the clergy (c. 6) or the participation of synods (c. 7, §§ 1–8) in the exercise of ecclesiastical authority, which includes the power of deciding on doctrine (c. 5). He can appoint the members of synods, or he can allow them to be elected with a reservation in favour of his own *jus imperii in electionem*; he has the power of summoning, adjourning and proroguing synods; and he possesses the right of confirming, changing or altering all the acts of synods (c. 7, §§ 9–17). Ecclesiastical legislation belongs to him, including the allowance and disallowance of confessions, and the ordering of all things which concern 'the public exercise of true religion'; the Church has no right of legislation at all in virtue of the law of God; and so far as it possesses such a right in virtue of positive law, it possesses it, at the most, only *cumulative et dependenter* (c. 8). The sovereign alone has *ecclesiastica jurisdictio*; all *jurisdictio* of the clergy, so far as it is not really simple *suasio et directio*, is based on delegation by the State, and is subject to *appellatio ab abusu* (c. 9). The sovereign has the confirming and dismissing of the holders of the necessary ecclesiastical offices (*presbyterium* and *diaconatus*); and while the original appointment of such persons belongs *naturaliter* (though at the same time *mutabiliter*) to the Church, the sovereign not only controls all appointments, but may also make them himself (c. 10). He car also institute ecclesiastical offices which are not 'necessary' (the offices of bishop and elder, c. 11): he retains supreme authority over all boards or corporations or persons in possession of ecclesiastical powers, since any *inferior potestas* exercising a *jus circa sacra* necessarily derives such right from him; moreover, the authority exercised by such inferior powers must be circumscribed, on grounds of expediency, within the narrowest possible limits (c. 12).

The only limit to *jus imperii circa sacra* admitted by Grotius, other than the impossibility of controlling *actus interni*, is the *jus divinum*; but even commands of the sovereign which are contrary to the word of God oblige the members of the State—not indeed to obey, but at any rate to abstain from active opposition (c. 3).

Antonius de Dominis

82. Views similar to those of Grotius are to be found in Marcus Antonius de Dominis, an archbishop of Spalato who went over to the Church of England (1560–1624): see his *De republica ecclesiastica libri X* (of which Part I appeared in London in 1618, Part II in London in 1620, and Part III in Hanover in 1622), more especially Book v, which assigns to the Church only a *potestas spiritualis*, and no *vera praefectura et jurisdictio*; cf. also Book VI, cc. 3–7.

Conring on Church and State

83. For Conring's views see the Corollaries to his treatise *De constitutione episcoporum Germaniae* (Exerc. VII in *Exerc. de rep. Germ. Imp.*), of May 26, 1647. According to the Third Corollary, *Ecclesia in hisce terris vere non est aliqua respublica, sed naturam potius habet collegii in republica constituti*. According to the Fourth, however, the 'authority and assent' of the *Respublica* are not needed *omni ex parte* for an 'ecclesiastical society', as they are for the institution of other 'colleges'; and according to the Fifth, the 'universal church', in virtue of natural law and the law of God, is 'one body' in exactly the same sense as the whole of mankind or *universitas omnium bonorum hominum*.

84. *Politia ecclesiastica* (Amsterdam, 1663 sqq.), vols. I–IV.

85. Ibid. Part I, Bk. I, tract. I, c. I. As distinct from the 'mystic and invisible Church', the 'external Church' is a 'visible collection', whose 'immediate foundation' is *consensus mutuus et arbitrium exserte declaratum eorum qui coëunt in ecclesiam*, though 'divine institution' is its 'ultimate foundation' (§4). The erection of the ministry also depends on consent. *The collegial theory of Voetius*

86. Ibid. §8. With strict logic, he rejects the theory of canon law in regard to the distinction of *ecclesia simplex* and *ecclesia collegiata*: all churches are 'collegiate', and none of them has any advantage over any other (ibid. I, I, tr. I, c. 6). He also pronounces against all separate ecclesiastical fellowships and fraternities (II, IV, tr. 4).

87. I, I, tr. 2, cc. 4–6. He describes the *populus seu corpus ecclesiasticum* as the 'Subject' or owner of ecclesiastical authority—not the 'people alone', nor the clergy alone, but the whole organised ecclesiastical people including its pastors.

88. In I, I, tr. I, c. I, §8 Voetius distinguishes four possibilities: (1) identity of the political with the ecclesiastical *corpus*, as in Israel, England, Switzerland and Geneva; (2) the recognition of the true religion as the only public religion, with toleration of different creeds and confessions, as in the Netherlands; (3) a heterodox political community, with toleration of the true Church, as in France; (4) a political community hostile to the true Church, as in most countries. *Four possible relations of Church and State*

89. I, I, tr. 2, cc. 4–5.

90. I, I, tr. 2, cc. 2, 5, 7–15; II, III, tr. I, cc. 3–5. He speaks accordingly of a separate *politia ecclesiastica, distincta a politia politica et oeconomica*, I, I, tr. 2, c. 7, §5.

91. I, IV, tr. 2, c. I, §§1–2. Property belongs to the 'visible church', because the 'mystical church' is not capable of holding property. It does not belong to *privati*, nor again to *collegia civica* or the *aerarium publicum*. We may describe what belongs to the Church as *bona Dei* or *patrimonium Christi*, because Christ is the Head of the 'mystical body' of which all believers are members.

92. Cf. Ludiomaeus Coluinus, *Papa Ultrajectinus, seu Mysterium iniquitatis reductum a clarissimo viro Gisberto Voetio, in opere Politicae ecclesiasticae*, London, 1668. This work seeks to prove that the theory of Voetius, if it shows more piety, also betrays more absurdity, than that of the papalists. Any theory which assumes two separate powers is unchristian.*

* The real author of this work was L. du Moulin (1606–80), who after studying medicine at Leyden and Cambridge was Professor of Ancient History at Oxford from 1648 to 1660, and afterwards lived at Westminster. He also wrote a work, in English, on *The Rights of Churches*.

§16. THE GENERAL THEORY OF THE GROUP (*VERBANDSTHEORIE*) IN NATURAL LAW

States as moral persons in a state of nature

1. See Spinoza, *Tract. pol.* c. 3, §§ 11–18; Pufendorf, *Elem.* §§ 24–6, *De jure nat. et gent.* II, c. 3, § 23; Thomasius, *Instit. jur. div.* I, c. 2, §§ 101 sqq.; Gundling, *Jus nat.* and *Disc.* c. 1, § 54; Hertius, *Comm.* II, 3, pp. 21 sqq.; Becmann, *Med.* c. 2; J. H. Boehmer, *P. gen.* c. 2, §§ 3 sqq., *P. spec.* I, c. 3, § 22 n. 6 (who speaks of 'a state of nature or liberty', involving a *species juris naturae*, as existing among free and equal 'moral persons'); Wolff, *Instit.* §§ 1088 sqq., *Jus nat.* IX; Heineccius, *Elem.* I, c. 1, §§ 21–2, II, c. 1, §§ 1 and 21; Daries, *P. spec.* §§ 790 sqq.; Nettelbladt, *Syst. nat.* §§ 1405 sqq. (*quaelibet gens, qua talis considerata, est persona moralis in statu naturali vivens, et plures gentes sunt plures istiusmodi personae*); Achenwall, II, §§ 210–88 (*jus naturale* exists among 'eternal societies', i.e. among *gentes* regarded as 'free moral persons'); Justi, *Natur und Wesen*, §§ 222–3; Locke, II, c. 12, §§ 145–6 [of the *Second Treatise on Government*].

2. See the author's work on Althusius, pp. 287 sqq. and 300 sqq.

3. On this point Spinoza (*Tract. theol.-pol.* c. 16 and *Tract. pol.* c. 2) agrees entirely with Hobbes.

4. This is the view not only of Hobbes (see supra, p. 85 and no. 63 to § 15), but also of Spinoza (*Tract. theol.-pol.* cc. 16, 17, 20 and *Tract. pol.* cc. 3, 4, 5).

5. This is the reason why the German writers on natural law, though following Hobbes closely in other respects, from the time of Pufendorf onwards, always attack his conception of the state of nature. Gundling comes nearest to Hobbes' conception (*Jus nat.* c. 3 and *Exerc.* 4, pp. 155 sqq.); but he arrives at totally different results.

Thomasius on the nature of Law

6. At first Thomasius regarded all law as the 'will' of a 'ruler'—treating *lex positiva* as the command of men, and *lex naturalis* as that of God; cf. *Instit. jur. div.* I, c. 1, §§ 28 sqq. and *Annot. ad Strauch diss.* I, pp. 2 sqq. In his later days he continued to believe in the imperative character of positive law; but instead of describing *lex naturalis* as a divine command with 'external obligation', he now defined it as merely a *consilium producens internam obligationem*, or a *dictamen rationis*, of which God was the ultimate author but not the legislator: cf. *Fund. jur. nat.* I, c. 5, §§ 28–81. [This later view involves him in some difficulties.] Making a general division of the *normae* which limit the action of human will into the ethical, the political and the legal (ibid. cc. 1–4), he proceeds to apply this triple division not only to positive rules, but also to the rules of nature (c. 5, §§ 58 sqq.); but he fails to make any real distinction between 'Natural Law' proper and 'natural ethics' or 'natural politics', because he cannot prove that Natural Law [regarded as a 'counsel' or 'dictate of reason'] possesses that attribute of being enforceable which he regards (c. 7) as essential [to law proper]. [We may compare with his change of front in regard to Natural Law a similar change in regard to customary law.] At first he regarded customary law as only existing in consequence of the sanction of a sovereign (*Inst. jur. div.* I, c. 2, § 109): afterwards, he allowed that it possessed the character of law even if it had no such sanction (e.g. in the case of customary law *inter gentes*); but he qualified this admission by adding that such customary law was a law without *obligatio*; cf. *Fund.* I, c. 5,

§ 78, *Addit. ad Huberi Praelect. Inst.* I, 2, nos. 7 and 12, and *Diss. de jure consuet. et observantia*.

8. This is the composite view which appears in Pufendorf; cf. *De off. hom. et civ.* I, c. 2 taken along with c. 3, and *J. n. et g.* II, c. 3 taken along with I, c. 6 (God may be regarded as 'Sovereign', and *lex naturalis* as His *voluntas*; but apart from *lex divina positiva* there is also a *lex divina per ipsam rerum naturam hominibus promulgata*). It was the original view of Thomasius (supra, n. 6); it appears in Alberti, c. 1; Cumberland, c. 5; Becker, §§ 2–6; Mueldener, *Pos.* I, § 1 (*jus naturae est decretum voluntatis divinae per rationem promulgatum*); H. de Cocceji, *Prodromus*; S. de Cocceji, *De princ. jur. nat. univ., Tract. jur. gent.* Parts I and II, *Novum systema*, I, §§ 56–60 ('a command of nature and its author, declared to mankind by reason'); Kestner, c. 1; J. H. Boehmer, *P. gen.* c. 1 (a 'norm' which proceeds from the 'will' of God, but 'is written in the hearts of men'); Schmier, I, c. 1, s. 1, § 3; Heineccius, I, c. 1, c. 3; Achenwall, *Prol.* and I, §§ 7 sqq. (a true law of God, in the juristic sense). *Natural Law and human Reason*

9. This is a view which appears in Horn; *sanctitas divina*, and not *voluntas divina*, is the source of natural law, and human reason (as a relic of man's being originally in the image of God) is the means of knowing what it is (II, c. 2). The same view appears in Huber; he holds that there can be law even without a *Superior* or force (I, 1, c. 1, §§ 2–5), and he regards natural law as a command of reason implanted in man by nature, and by God as the author of nature (ibid. c. 2). A similar view is also to be found in Gundling (c. 1, §§ 4–11), and in Leibniz, who derives natural law from the nature of God, and regards command and enforcement as unessential (*Op.* IV, 3, pp. 270 sqq., 275 sqq., 294 sqq.). Cf. also Wolff, *Instit.* §§ 39, 41, 67, and Montesquieu, *Esprit des Lois*, I, cc. 1–2 (*raison primitive...les lois de la nature dérivent uniquement de la constitution de notre être*). *Natural Law rationalised*

10. Cf. e.g. Gundling, c. 1, §§ 47–50; S. de Cocceji, I, § 56 (*idque metu poenae*); Achenwall, I, § 44 (*sub comminatione poenae*).

11. When, as in Grotius (*Proleg.* no. 11 and I, c. 1, § 10) and his precursors (on whom see the author's work on Althusius, p. 74), the assumption was made that there would be a Natural Law even if God did not exist, or if He were unjust, the logical consequence of that assumption was the abandoning of any idea that it was derived from the will or the nature of God; and this is what we find in Thomasius, *Fund.* I, c. 6 [cf. supra, n. 6]. After Locke in England, and Rousseau and his successors in France, had contented themselves with merely invoking 'the order of nature', the connection of Natural Law with the idea of God tended also to disappear among German thinkers; it is not present, e.g. in Justi, Scheidemantel, Schlözer, Hoffbauer or Fichte. Kant definitely holds that the notion that God is the author of the moral law is untenable; for God is Himself under that law, and He is obliged to act by its rules (*Works*, VII, pp. 8 sqq.). *Natural Law secularised*

12. Cf. Leibniz, *Nova methodus*, § 74, and introduction to the *Cod. jur. gent.* I, § 11; J. H. Boehmer, *P. gen.* c. 1; Schmier, *Jus publ. univ.* I, c. 1, s. 2, §§ 1–2; Achenwall, *Proleg.* §§ 98 sqq., I, §§ 34 sqq.; Fichte, *Works*, III, pp. 145 sqq.

Rights under Natural Law

13. In regard to international law, there was unanimity on this point. So far as the public law of the State was concerned, all the theorists who recognised a right of resistance to any breach of Natural Law by the sovereign sought to justify their view by assuming a return to the state of nature, and therefore to the right of self-help belonging to that state. Cf. the author's work on Althusius, pp. 314–5, and esp. Wolff, *Polit.* §§433sqq., *Jus nat.* VIII, §§1041sqq., *Instit.* §§1079sqq.; Daries, §§710sqq.; Achenwall, I, §2, II, §§200sqq.; Scheidemantel, III, pp. 364sqq.; and also Rousseau, III, c. 10.

Natural Law as obligatory

14. For this reason Natural Law was declared to be a 'perfect law' with 'coercive power': cf. Thomasius, *Instit. jur. div.* I, c. 1, §§103sqq.; Gundling, I, c. 1, §54; Achenwall, *Proleg.* §§98sqq. and I, §§34sqq.; Wolff, *Instit.* §§80sqq. [One exception was made]; in regard to the relation of the sovereign to his subjects, the opponents of any right of resistance held that Natural Law had only a 'directive power' [over the sovereign], and therefore only imposed an 'imperfect obligation'; but at the same time they did not abandon the idea that this imperfect obligation was a real legal obligation: cf. Pufendorf, *Elem.* I, d. 12, §6, *J. n. et g.* VII, c. 5, §8, VIII, c. 1; Thomasius, loc. cit. §§111–13; J. H. Boehmer, *P. spec.* I, c. 5, III, c. 1; Schmier, V, c. 1, s. 1 and c. 3, s. 1; Kreittmayr, §§32–5.

15. This idea is definitely formulated in e.g. Mevius, *Prodromus*, III, §13; cf. also Montesquieu, *Esprit des lois*, I, c. 2.

16. Cf. Pufendorf, *De off. hom. et civ.* I, c. 3, *J. n. et g.* II, c. 1; Thomasius, *Inst. jur. div.* I, c. 4, §§54–72; Becmann, *Med.* c. 2, *Consp.* p. 16; Hertius, *Comm.* I, 1, pp. 61sqq. (*de socialitate primo naturalis juris principio*), *Elem.* I, s. 1; J. H. Boehmer, *P. gen.* c. 1. See also Mevius, IV, §35, and Mueldener, *Pos.* II, §1; and (to some extent) Fénelon, c. III and Montesquieu, I, c. 2.

Socialitas and Societas

17. Thomasius (*Inst. jur. div.* I, c. 4) expressly warns his readers against confusing *socialitas* and *societas*. As against Hobbes and Spinoza, the advocates of *socialitas* contend that the state of nature was a state of peace; but they admit that this peace was unstable, and that it might at any moment (as still happens between States) pass into a state of war. Cf. Pufendorf, loc. cit.; Hertius, II, 3, pp. 21sqq.; Thomasius, *Inst. jur. div.* I, c. [3], §§51sqq. and c. 4, §§54sqq. (later, however, in *Fund.* I, c. 3, §55, he states the view that the state of nature was 'neither a state of war nor a state of peace, but a confused chaos', which was like war, yet not without a tendency towards peace); J. G. Boehmer, loc. cit. §38. The transition from mere *socialitas* to a definite 'society' is ascribed not to the operation of nature, but to reason and free choice; this is the view of Pufendorf, Hertius and Becmann (loc. cit.). These thinkers also assume that there is no *societas* among States; cf. Becmann, loc. cit., and Hertius, II, 3, pp. 21sqq. A different view, however, appears in Huber (I, 1, c. 5) and in Mevius (V, §§5–9, 18, 20); but they both regard *jus gentium* as being something more than mere natural law.

Positive law based on Natural Law

18. The theory appears in Pufendorf; Hertius, *Comm.* II, 3, pp. 21sqq.; Gundling, c. 1, §§77–9 and c. 3; J. G. Boehmer, c. 2, §§8sqq., and other writers. Cf. also the view of Huber (I, 1, c. 3) that anything opposed to civil society cannot be Natural Law, because the *desiderium societatis* is natural. Strauch (*Op.* no. 16, *de juris nat. et civ. convenientia*) goes still further [in the way of connecting natural and positive law].

'Pure' natural law and 'Social' natural law

19. Thus Mevius distinguishes between *jus naturale primaevum* and *jus naturale secundarium et voluntarium*. The latter is based on reason itself, and not on the mere fact of agreement; but its rules have to be determined by the

principle of 'social conjunction' (v, §§ 5–9). It is in this latter category that he places international law, assuming the existence of a *societas communis inter omnes populos* (ibid. §§ 18–20).

Heineccius admits that natural law, in the narrower sense, refers only to free and equal individuals (I, c. 1; II, c. 1, §§ 1–10); but he holds that *jus gentium* [as distinct from Natural Law in this narrower sense] is *ipsum jus naturale vitae hominum sociali negotiisque societatum atque integrarum gentium applicatum* (I, c. 1, §§ 21–22, II, c. 1, § 21).

To Daries, the 'moral state of man' is either 'natural' or 'adventitious'; and the 'natural moral state', in turn, is either 'absolute' or 'conditional'. Proceeding with his subdivisions, he next lays it down that the absolute state of nature, which is marked by 'liberty' and 'equality', may be either a state of 'solitude' or of 'society', and, in the same way, the conditional state of nature may be either 'non-social' or 'social'. Finally, he classifies the 'civil state' as belonging to the last of these categories [i.e. it is a conditional state of nature of the social type]; while he regards the state of the relations in which States stand to one another [i.e. the state of international relations] as a *status naturalis absolutus socialis* (cf. *Praecogn.* §§ 11–28, *P. spec.* §§ 790 sqq.).

Nettelbladt divides the whole body of 'natural jurisprudence' into that which is 'natural strictly so called' and that which is 'natural-social'. In his view, international law is a mixed body of law, composed both of *leges gentium stricte naturales* and of *leges sociales*—the reason being that the pure state of nature is here modified by the existence of a 'society constituted by nature' among all peoples (§§ 1419–24).

Achenwall distinguishes between the *jus mere naturale*, which is valid in a state of nature, and the *jus sociale naturale*, which is valid in a state of society, and includes the law of the Family, the law of the State and international law. At the same time, however, he holds that there is a sense in which pure natural law is itself social; for there is a *societas universalis* or *civitas maxima*—with God as its natural sovereign, and all men as its natural members—which lays down this *jus mere naturale*, and thus creates an obligation of sociability (cf. *Proleg.* §§ 82–97, I, § 1, §§ 43–4, II, § 1).

Hoffbauer has a complicated scheme. (1) He starts from the exalted idea of a 'pure natural law' which is valid for all forms of 'rational existence'—including even other forms than man, if such were known—and is partly 'absolute' (pp. 64 sqq.) and partly 'conditional' (pp. 70 sqq.). (2) Descending in the scale, he comes next to the 'applied Natural Law' of man (pp. 86 sqq.). (3) Here he distinguishes between an 'absolute' form (pp. 108 sqq.) and a 'conditional' (pp. 120 sqq.). (4) He then divides the conditional form of applied natural law into the 'universal' (pp. 122 sqq.) and the 'particular' (pp. 155 sqq.). (5) Finally, he subdivides the 'particular conditional form of applied natural law' into the 'extra-social' (pp. 156 sqq.) and the 'social' varieties (pp. 186 sqq.). Only when he reaches this fifth and last stage in his process of classification does society first appear in his scheme. A final reference may be made to Cumberland, c. 5.

20. Gundling, for example (c. 3, §§ 11–60), begins with a primitive state of perfect liberty and equality, and explains all forms of connection between human beings as having been instituted by conscious agreement, in consequence of the discoveries made under the pressure of necessity. He describes the *status civilis* accordingly as a work of art and a *status artificiosus*.

Society as an 'artifice'

Schmier (I, c. 1, s. 1, §§ 1–3) also assumes a state of nature in which free and equal individuals have no form of union; but he believes that the whole of mankind never lived, or could have lived, in a pure state of nature at one and the same time.

Locke's state of nature

21. Locke (*Second Treatise*, II, c. 2) regards the state of nature as the state which existed previously to the erection of civil society; but he also regards it as a state which still exists in the absence of civil society. From the latter point of view, he depicts the state of nature as a relation of man to man such as still occurs to-day, e.g. when a Swiss and a Red Indian meet in the backwoods of America (§ 14). He also speaks, it is true, of 'natural society'; but the only conclusion he draws from that idea is that men have a negative duty not to disturb or oppress one another (§§ 4–5). That he does not assume the existence of any real *community* is shown by his remarks about the substance of Natural Law, as something older and higher than all 'social laws' (ibid. §6; c. 2, §§ 6–13; c. 3, §§ 16–21; c. 5, §§ 25–51; c. 4, §§ 22–4). A similar view is to be found in Sidney, c. I, ss. 2 and 9, c. II, ss. 1 and 2.

Rousseau's state of nature

22. Rousseau has already attained these ideas in the *Discours* of 1753, and repeats them in the *Contrat Social* [of 1762], I, c. 1 sqq. He admits, indeed, that the Family is a natural *société*, but only until such time as the children are adults. Filangieri says much the same: in the state of nature there was no inequality other than physical, no law other than natural, no bonds other than those of friendship, necessity and the family: alas, that things could not remain as they were (I, c. 1). See also Sieyès, I, pp. 131 sqq. and 205 sqq.

Primitive liberty as conceived by German thinkers

23. Thus Justi (*Die Natur und das Wesen*, §§ 1–18) begins with an original state of nature which was marked by liberty and equality—a state in which men were half animals, and had no natural instinct for social life. Knowledge of the advantages of union first impelled them, after they had attained some degree of reason, to erect some form of society. At first, the existence of such a society imposed no limits on natural liberty; and even to-day that government is still the best which realises the purpose of the State with the fewest possible limitations upon natural liberty. Justi takes a similar line in his *Grundrisz* (§§ 5 ff.); and he interprets international law in a corresponding sense (ibid. §§ 222–3). Frederick the Great, writing in 1777, similarly assumes a pre-political condition, with no *société* (*Oeuvres*, IX, p. 195).

In the view of Kreittmayr (§§ 2 sqq.) the State is not based on *jus naturale absolutum*; it is based on history, as a *res mere facti*. Scheidemantel (I, pp. 44 sqq., 56 sqq., 68 sqq.) holds that the State is not a necessity of man's nature, and that the Law of Nature does not impose upon him any binding obligation to renounce his natural liberty. A. L. von Schlözer regards primitive man as *homo solitarius*, and treats all social institutions as artificial inventions (pp. 31 ff.). Cf. also C. von Schlözer, *De jure suff.* §3.

Fichte on the origin of Right or law

24. *Grundlage des Naturrechts* (1796–7), vol. I, Introduction and pp. 51 sqq. (*Works*, III, pp. 7 sqq. and 17–91), where Fichte argues that the rule of Right, or law,* is deduced without the aid of morality, and yet without any surrender of the unity of law and morality. That unity depends on the living self-consciousness of the Ego. The Ego is one, but in the form of subjective instinct [*Trieb*] it produces morality, while in the form of force (as a fact of

---

* *Recht* here is more than our English 'law' (1) because, on its 'objective' side, it has a connotation of something inherently 'right' and (2) because it implies, as its other or 'subjective' side, the right of the individual.

Notes to § 16

objective existence) it produces law. In all essentials, Fichte maintains his earlier theory of the origin of the rule of Right in his later *System der Rechtslehre* [lectures delivered in 1812], printed in his *Posthumous Works*, II, pp. 495 sqq.

25. *Works*, III, pp. 92 sqq.: cf. *Posthumous Works*, II, pp. 500 sqq.

26. *Works*, III, pp. 128 sqq.: the original rule of Right is 'the absolute right of the personality to be nothing but a cause in the world of thought', i.e. the right of the absolute will; but the original rights of different persons cancel one another, unless each person limits himself.

27. *Works*, III, pp. 92 sqq.: it is not an 'absolute', but a 'problematical' command.

28. *Works*, III, pp. 92 sqq., 140 sqq., 166 sqq. Subsequently, however, Fichte came to regard the existence of a legal community as an 'absolute law of the reason' and 'a necessity of thought'; and he accordingly made the rule of Right issue in an obligation to make and keep contracts. But he still continued to hold the firm conviction that 'a state of law is never produced by mere nature...without art and free will, or without a contract' (*Posthumous Works*, II, pp. 495–500). *Fichte's later view of law*

29. *Works*, III, pp. 137–49: *Posthumous Works*, II, p. 499. The Law of Nature is not law proper; inasmuch as the Ego is absolute, Natural Law has no sanctions other than loyalty and good faith, which lie outside the bounds of law: any right of compulsion which each can exert upon each is not enough [to constitute a genuine legal sanction]. On the other hand Right or law which is sanctioned by the force of the State is never Right unless it is based on reason. Both propositions are therefore true: (1) that 'all law is purely the law of reason' and (2) that 'all law is the law of the State'. *Natural and positive law in Fichte*

30. Cf. *Works*, VII, pp. 8 sqq.; and see also, on the relation of law to morality, pp. 11 sqq., 15 sqq., 26 sqq. and 182 sqq., in which a particularly strong emphasis is laid on external compulsion as the essential attribute of law. *Kant on law*

31. *Works*, VII, pp. 62 sqq., §§ 14–17, p. 131, § 45.

32. *Works*, VI, pp. 320, 415, VII, p. 54, § 8, p. 130, § 44, p. 107, § 41. Fichte also used this principle in order to deduce from it a duty of States still living in a state of nature (in their external relations to one another) to form some union; cf. VI, pp. 415 sqq., VII, p. 162, § 54, p. 168, § 61.

33. *Works*, VII, pp. 20, 133: the will of the rational individual is its own legislator; but when it proceeds to enact a law for itself, it should always adopt a maxim which is qualified to be a *universal* law.

34. *Works*, VI, pp. 329, 409, VII, p. 133, § 47.

35. On the position of Right or law before the State exists, see *Works*, VII, p. 130, § 44.

On the State's obligation to respect the law of Reason which is given *à priori*, see VI, pp. 338, 413, VII, pp. 34, 131, § 45, p. 136, § 49. On the inviolability of the principles of the liberty, equality, and independence of every individual, and on the illegality of institutions (such as slavery, and also hereditary nobility) which are contrary to these principles, see VI, pp. 322 sqq., 416 sqq., VII, pp. 34 sqq., 147 sqq. *Kant on the State and the law of Reason*

36. See Pufendorf, *De off. hom. et civ.* I, c. 12, §§ 2–3, *J. n. et g.* IV, c. 4, §§ 1–14, c. 5, §§ 2–10; Thomasius, *Inst. jur. div.* II, c. 9, §§ 58–95, *Fund.* II, c. 10, §§ 5–7; J. H. Boehmer, *P. spec.* II, c. 10; Heineccius, I, c. 9; Wolff, *Instit.* § 191: Nettelbladt, §§ 208 sqq.; Achenwall, I, §§ 106–8, 116 (*omnes res nullius*, *Kant on property*

usus omnium); Kant, VII, pp. 49, 57, 61, 66. (Kant accepts *communio fundi originaria*, as a principle involving an original common ownership of the surface of the earth; but he does not believe in a *communio primaeva*, in the sense of a community of property erected at a point of time and contractually established by the pooling of private possessions.)

Survivals of original community

37. See e.g. Pufendorf, *J. n. et g.* IV, cc. 4–6 and VIII, c. 5, §7, on the remnants of the original community of property which may still be traced in the right of the State to ownerless things and in its *dominium eminens*; Wolff, *Instit.* §§ 300–12, on the continuance of 'primitive community' in regard to *res usus inexhausti* and the sea, and again in the case of *jus necessitatis* and *jus innoxiae utilitatis*; and Nettelbladt, §§ 471 sqq.

38. Wolff (§§ 194 sqq.), though he has previously depicted the original community of property as *negativa*, sees no objection to making private property develop out of it by an act of division which is due to supervening needs, and is thus compatible with the law of nature.

Locke on property

39. According to Locke (II, c. 5, §§ 25–51) the individual may acquire property by a legitimate title in the state of nature. Though all things are common, he has a private right in his person; and he may thus acquire things [for himself by annexing them to his person, i.e.] by means of labour, which also includes occupation. No contract or law need precede such acquisition; but limits are set to the acquisition of private property in virtue of Natural Law (1) by the measure of the individual's own need, and (2) by the requirement that there shall be a supply of equal and equally good things for all. (Locke thinks that these conditions are satisfied so far as land is concerned.)

General view that property is pre-social

40. See Heineccius, I, c. 9; Schmier, I, c. 1, s. 2, §3; Nettelbladt, §§ 215 sqq.; Achenwall, I, §§ 110 sqq. (private property comes into existence by 'conditional Natural Law' [cf. n. 19 supra], first by way of occupation, and then in virtue of contracts).

The French physiocrats (Quesnay, Mercier de la Rivière, Dupont de Nemours and Turgot) are especially emphatic in proclaiming the origin of private property in the state of nature, and the duty of the State to recognise it in virtue of *les lois naturelles de l'ordre social*; cf. Roscher's *Wirthschafts-geschichte*, pp. 480 sqq., and Janet's *Histoire de la Science politique*, II, pp. 684 sqq.

Rousseau on property

41. Rousseau, *Contr. soc.* I, c. 9; but the theory already appears in the *Discours* [of 1753]. Rousseau, however, regards the establishment of private property by an act of appropriation in the state of nature as a usurpation, which is only legitimised when, in the act of concluding the social contract, all men surrender to the sovereign all their belongings as well as their powers, and receive them back again from the sovereign as legal possessions under the limits determined by the law of the community.

Möser on property as the basis of the State

42. Justus Möser always treats property in land as the basis of perfect liberty: he regards land-owners as the 'original contracting parties' of the State, and other owners as shareholders in the State-partnership (in which originally the shares were only shares in land, though later there came to be also shares in money); and he therefore considers them to be the only fully qualified citizens (cf. his *Patriot. Phant.* II, no. 1, III, no. 62, IV, no. 43).

Kant on primitive property

43. According to Kant (*Works*, VII, pp. 53 sqq. and 62 sqq.) there is already a real, if only provisional, *meum* and *tuum* in the state of nature, which first acquires a title of prescription [*peremptio*] and a guarantee in the civil state; cf. also pp. 56 sqq. and 64, on occupation as an original method of acquisi-

tion (but one which only exists in so far as the possession thus acquired can be actually defended).

44. Thus Mevius (*Prodromus*, v, §42) derives private property from an act of concession by a *societas civilis* (under reservation for cases in which the *societas* itself is in need). Horn (II, cc. 3–4 and 6) ascribes its origin to an act of distribution by the sovereign, who has received authority from God for that purpose [cf. Paley, *Principles of Moral and Political Philosophy*, Book III, c. IV], and who continues to enjoy a real 'eminent domain'. Bossuet (1, art. 3, prop. 4) finds its source in a creative act of the government; and Alberti (c. 7, §19) derives it from a direct declaration of will by the community, which at one and the same time establishes property and the limits of property. *Property as State-created*

45. Pufendorf (loc. cit.) requires a *pactum tacitum* to bring private property into existence; and Gundling (c. 3, §§27–31, 39–42, and c. 20) makes *dominium*, like *imperium*, originate in a 'pact'. Similarly A. L. von Schlözer argues (p. 46, §11) that rightful acquisition of property first becomes possible after its original community has been abolished by contract; for even occupation, and the appropriation of things by labour, were only admitted as proper titles after other persons had 'renounced their joint right therein' (p. 49). *Property as based on contract*

46. According to the theory originally developed by Fichte in his *Naturrecht* (*Works*, III, pp. 210 sqq.), but also maintained in his later period (*Posthumous Works*, pp. 528 sqq., 592 sqq., 594 sqq.), property arises from a contract of property, which is to be regarded as a part of the political contract; and thus it becomes possible only after the original right of each man to everything has been removed by an act of renunciation. Even so, however, 'absolute' property only exists in money and the value of money in exchange (in his *Rechtslehre* Fichte makes it also include house property); property in land still remains subject to obligations and limitations, and is only a 'relative' species of property. What is true of the right to own land is also true of the right to practise trade and industry; and the State has therefore to distribute rights of pursuing trades among its members, and to organise their industry, in order to satisfy the claim which all men have to subsistence. This constitutes the basis on which Fichte subsequently erected (in 1800) his theory of *Der geschlossene Handelsstaat* ('the close Trading-state'), with its economic omnipotence [cf. W. Wallace, *Lectures and Essays*, pp. 427 sqq.]. *Fichte on property*

47. In Germany Praschius is conspicuous for his advocacy of the fundamentally social character of Natural Law. The primary principle of that law, he holds, is love; and the greatest of the duties based on that principle is devotion to others and especially to the whole. Society is God's will: it is, even more than the individual, the mirror of the Trinity; and the aim of nature's plan is not the individual, but society; cf. §9, *add. triplex de vi et amplitudine juris socialis*, p. 47. The view of Placcius (Book I) is similar. Mevius (v, §4), Becker (§§5 and 12) and Alberti (c. 2, §9 and c. 10, §1) also assume the existence of an original community, of which traces continue still to exist in civil society. *Theories of Society as original and divine*

According to Kestner, the source of Natural Law and society is not *socialitas* or *consensus*, but the will of God (c. 1). Originally there existed a primitive *societas humana* which God had founded; the *imperium* in this society belonged to 'all mankind', and coercion was applied to misdoers by *caeteri collective sumpti* (c. 7, §2). After the disintegration of this unity the *imperium*, which 'hitherto belonged to all without distinction', passed to the separate 'societies' which were now established (c. 7, §3).

The two Cocceji (Henry and Samuel) similarly reject the principle of 'sociality', and base all social authority on the power over individuals originally bestowed by God on the whole body of mankind at large—a power which subsequently passed to separate peoples, when they arose, and from them in turn passed to their rulers. Later, however, Samuel Cocceji developed the view that political authority arises from the *imperium* over its own members originally bestowed by God on each family as a *corpus*—this *imperium* being afterwards transferred, with the aid of God's intervention, to the union of heads of families, and then in turn from this union to a Ruler (*Novum syst.* §§ 280, 612–13).

In France we find Bossuet regarding *société* as the *fait primitif*, and explaining the origin of *diverses nations*, as *sociétés civiles*, by the human passions which led to the disintegration of the primitive fraternal union of all mankind (1, art. 1–2).

In England, we find Filmer, in his *Patriarcha*, deriving all social authority from inheritance of the *patria potestas* bestowed by God upon Adam.

Individualism in eighteenth-century Germany

48. This individualism appears in Mevius (v, §§ 23, 25); Alberti (loc. cit.); Kestner (op. cit. §3); S. Cocceji (*Nov. syst.* III, §§ 199–207, where the theory of a contract is adopted). Thomasius, in spite of his assumption that there originally existed, *in statu integro*, a community between God and man and a community of all men with one another, and that this double community was the source of a social law of nature (1, c. 2, §§ 27–43 and 51–54), none the less applies the individualistic theory of contract in his *Institutes of Divine Law*; and in his later writings he drops his whole theory of the *status integer*, on the ground that such a state is beyond our knowledge.

Even in Leibniz and Wolff

49. Leibniz derives the existence of law from the community, and regards all communities as organic parts of the Kingdom of minds in the Universe at large, which constitutes a world-State under God's government (*Bruchstück vom Naturrecht*, in Guhrauer, 1, pp. 414 sqq., and Introduction to the *Cod. dipl. jur. gent.*, in Dutens' edition of his *Works*, IV, 3, pp. 287 sqq.). At the same time he defines the State as a contractual association (*Caesar.-Fürst.* c. 10); he makes the basis of punishment consist in the promise made by each individual to observe laws and legal decisions (*Nov. meth.* II, § 19); and he regards *conventio populi* as the source of the validity of all civil law (ibid. §71).

The idea of society as something naturally given still survives in the theory of Wolff; and it even leads him to think that peoples living in a state of nature form a natural society, which, as *civitas maxima*, possesses an *imperium universale* (*Instit.* § 1090). But his whole argument proceeds, none the less, on the assumption of equal, free, and independent individuals (*Instit.* §§ 70 and 77; *Jus nat.* 1, §§ 26 sqq.).

Individualism of Montesquieu

50. *Esprit des lois*, 1, cc. 1–3. Natural laws exist before man and before society: pure natural law is valid for *un Homme avant l'établissement des sociétés*, and it produces, first the desire for peace, then the satisfaction of the needs of sustenance, then the beginnings of connection, and finally a *désir de vivre en société*. In society, because the feeling of weakness and equality disappears, wars arise, both within and without; and these produce on the one hand international law, and on the other a civil law which varies considerably [from one State to another], according to circumstances.

Notes to § 16

51. See Möser's *Osnabrück History* and his *Patriotic Fantasies*: supra, n. 42. For his objection to the law of Reason see esp. *Patriot. Phant.* IV, no. 30, 'on the important distinction between actual and formal law'.

52. Vico starts from God and human nature: he believes that the primitive ideas of *bonum* and *aequum* continue to survive, even after the Fall, as ideas of justice and sociability; and he regards utility not as the source, but only the occasion, of law and society. *Vico and Ferguson*

Ferguson, rejecting the supposed state of nature and the original contracts, prefers to take men as he finds them, i.e. as living in society; and he regards social progress not as the opposite of nature, but as its consummation (*Essay*, I, c. 1). But he too is inconsistent; and having rejected contract and a state of nature, he proceeds to ascribe the historical beginning of society to the operation of two instincts—the instinct of affection which unites, and that of independence which divides (ibid. cc. 3–4).

53. Herder's *Ideen zur Geschichte der Menschheit*, IX, c. 4.

54. Cf. supra, p. 46 and nn. 60 and 61 to §14; Schmier, II, c. 1, s. 3, §§1–3; Heincke, I, c. 2, §§9–11.

55. Thus Bossuet (I, art. 3, prop. 1–6), in agreement with Hobbes, holds that the State first comes into existence through the complete and irrevocable subjection of all men to one sovereign, under the compulsion of nature; previously there had only been an anarchical sort of multitude, which possessed no sovereignty before this act of subjection, just as it possesses none afterwards. Unlike Hobbes, however, he ascribes the origin of sovereignty to the will of God, and not to a contractual act of surrender of rights. A similar view is to be found in Fénelon, chap. VI: cf. also Alberti, c. 14, §3. *Bossuet on the origin of the State*

56. Horn, II, c. 1: for further details see the author's work on Althusius, pp. 70–71.

57. Cf. supra, nn. 47–49 and 52–3 to this section.

58. Cf. supra, p. 60; Spinoza, *Tract. theol.-pol.* c. 16, *Tract. pol.* cc. 3–4; Gundling, *J.n.* c. 35 and *Disc.* c. 34.

59. Cf. supra, p. 46, and n. 63 to §14; Locke, II, c. 7, §§87–9 (the surrender by all of their natural right to self-help, and the surrender of power to the community, constitute civil society) and also c. 12; Sidney, I, s. 10, II, ss. 4, 5 and 20 (all society is constituted by the free association of individuals, who 'recede from their own right').

60. Cf. supra, p. 46, and n. 63 to §14; Huber, I, 2, c. 1; Pufendorf, *J. n. et g.* VII, cc. 2–3, *De off. hom. et civ.* II, c. 6; Thomasius, *Instit. jur. div.* III, c. 6; Hertius, *Comm.* I, 1, p. 286, §1 (*societas multorum hominum mutuis eorundem pactis conflata, et potestate instructa*); Becmann, cc. 5–6; J.G.Wachter, *Orig.* p. 34 (*civitas nihil aliud quam multitudo hominum majoris utilitatis et securitatis gratia potentias agendi suas naturales invicem jungentium ad producendam mutuam et communem felicitatem*); J. H. Boehmer, *P. spec.* I, c. 1; Heineccius, II, §§14, 109sqq.; Wolff, *Instit.* §836; Daries, *Praecogn.* §24, *P. spec.* §655 (*tum voluntates tum vires in unam transtulerunt personam vel physicam vel moralem*); Nettelbladt, *Syst. nat.* §115; Achenwall, II, §§2, 9, 11; Kreittmayr, §2. *The community as a mere aggregate*

61. *Contr. soc.* I, c. 6 (*l'aliénation totale de chaque associé avec tous droits à toute la communauté*), III, c. 18, IV, c. 2.

62. *Contr. soc.* II, c. 5. The individual, it is true, has no right to commit suicide; but he has a right *de risquer sa vie pour la conserver*. On this principle, we may say that the man who is willing to preserve his life at the cost of others must also risk losing it for the sake of others, if that be necessary. His *Rousseau on punishment*

life, after the conclusion of the contract, is no longer a simple *bienfait de la nature, mais un don constitutionnel de l'État*: the sovereign has now a share in deciding when it is to be sacrificed. Thus even capital punishment has a basis in consent, though it is also a sort of war against *un ennemi public*.

63. Beccaria, §2. 'In addition to the argument derived from the fact that suicide is wrong, Beccaria also presses into his service the assumption that the individual, in entering civil society, desired to incur the least possible sacrifice of his liberty.

State-power a pool of individual powers

64. Even Montesquieu himself had suggested no other way [of explaining social authority]; for according to the *Esprit des lois* (I, c. 3) *la réunion de toutes les* forces *particulières forme ce qu'on appelle l'État politique...les forces particulières ne peuvent pas se réunir sans que toutes les* volontés *se réunissent; la réunion de ces volontés est ce qu'on appelle l'État civil*.

Similarly Justi (*Natur und Wesen*, §§ 23-6) contends that the act of union in a moral body, which constitutes the moral basis of the State, depends on the union of many wills in a single will, and of all individual powers in a single power; this is the difference between the State and the state of nature, in which each will stands by itself.

A. L. von Schlözer (pp. 63 sqq. and 93, § 1) and C. von Schlözer (§ 11) both insist on the origin of the State in a *unio virium*, which produces society, and a *unio voluntatum*, which creates authority.

The State as a share-company

65. Cf. Justus Möser, *Patriot. Phant.* III, no. 62, on 'peasant properties considered as a form of share-holding'. All civil societies, he argues, are like share-companies: the citizen is one who is a shareholder. Originally there were only shares in land [cf. supra, n. 42]: subsequently, money-shares came into existence also; and nowadays all belongings, and even our bodies, are part of the capital. A slave [*Knecht*] is a man without a 'share' in the State, and therefore without losses or profits; but this contradicts religion no more than it does to be in the East India Company without holding a share. The basis of civil society is an express or tacit contract of society between the associated owners of land, who invest their properties as whole or half or quarter shares; and a body of directors is instituted for the purpose of keeping up and getting in the contributions: cf. II, no. 11.

Compare also Sieyès (1789), I, pp. 283 sqq. and 445 sqq. Individuals constitute a nation, as shareholders a company: the active citizens are 'the true shareholders in the great social undertaking', and the passive citizens (wives, children and foreigners) are only protected persons. Sieyès is never tired of repeating that political authority is 'constituted' by individuals, and only by individuals, and that the individual will forms the only element in the general will (cf. I, pp. 145, 167, 207, 211, II, pp. 374 sqq.).

Fichte's early individualism

66. In his *Beiträge* of 1793 ['Contribution to the judgment of public opinion on the French Revolution'], Fichte derives the State, as he also derives law, from the individual will, since 'no man can rightfully be bound except by himself' (*Works*, VI, pp. 80 sqq.; cf. also pp. 101, 103 sqq., 115 sqq.). In the same way he makes the beginning of the State, under the régime of Natural Law, depend on contracts, under which individuals agree to pool a part of their rights—renouncing the residue of their property in return for the guarantee of a fixed part, and pledging themselves to pay a fixed contribution to the protecting authority (*Works*, III, p. 207; cf. II, pp. 109 sqq. and III, pp. 269 sqq.).

In his *Grundzügen* of 1804-5 ['The Characteristics of the present Epoch'] we find a change: the State is not to be interpreted, 'as if it were based on this or that set of individuals, or as if it were based on individuals at all, or composed of them' (*Works*, VII, p. 146).

67. See Kant's *Rechtslehre*, §47 (*Works*, VII, p. 133), on 'the original contract by which all the members of a people (*omnes ut singuli*) surrender their external liberty, in order to receive it back again at once as members of a commonwealth, i.e. of the people regarded as a State (*universi*)'. [Kant adds that the individual, by this seeming surrender, 'has totally abandoned his wild lawless freedom in order to find his entire freedom again undiminished in a lawful dependence, that is, in a condition of right or law—undiminished, because this dependence springs from his own legislative will'.] *Kant bases the State on individuals*

68. This is the theory which appears in Huber, I, 2, cc. 1–2 (with a division of the contract of association into the three stages of a treaty of peace, a union of wills and the formation of a constitution, c. 1, §§ 1–13); Becmann, c. 12, §4; J. H. Boehmer, I, c. 1; Wolff, *Instit.* §§ 972 sqq., *Jus nat.* VIII, §§ 4 sqq.; S. Cocceji, *Nov. syst.* III, §§ 612 sqq. and 616 sqq.; Daries, *P. spec.* §659; Nettelbladt, §§ 1124 sqq.; Heincke, I, c. 2, §§ 1 sqq.; Scheidemantel, I, pp. 63 sqq. *The Two Contract theory*

According to A. L. von Schlözer, pp. 63 sqq. and 73 sqq., the civil society established by the *pactum unionis* lasts for centuries without any government, courts or coercion, until disturbances appear and the State is erected by a *pactum subjectionis*; cf. also pp. 95, 96 and 173 sqq.

The distinction between the two contracts finds an echo also in Justi, *Natur und Wesen*, §§ 23–7.

In Sidney (c. I, ss. 8, 10, 11, 16, 20; c. II, ss. 4, 5, 7, 20, 31; and c. III, ss. 18, 25, 31) and Locke (II, c. 7, §§ 87 sqq., c. 8) the contract of subjection recedes into the background in comparison with the contract of union, but it is by no means entirely abandoned. [More exactly, we may say that Locke uses the conception of Trust, and not that of Contract, to explain 'subjection'. The trust is a conception peculiar, on the whole, to English law. In private law [*Privatrecht*] the trust means that *A*, as trustor, vests rights in *B*, as trustee, for the benefit of *C*, as *cestui que trust* or beneficiary of the trust. In public law [*Staatsrecht*], to which Locke may be said to transfer the doctrine of trust, the People or 'Public' (which is both the trustor and the *cestui que trust*) acts in its capacity of trustor by way of conferring a 'fiduciary power' on the legislature (which thus becomes a trustee), for the benefit of itself, and all its members, in its other capacity of *cestui que trust* or beneficiary of the trust. This 'trust' conception pervades English political thought in the eighteenth century; not only is it applied internally, to the relations between the Public and the 'supreme legislature': it is also applied (for example by Burke) externally, to the relations between Great Britain and India, which is regarded as held in trust for the benefit of the people of India. *[Locke's theory of Trust]*

A trust is not a contract; and the trustee does not enter into relations of contract with the trustor—or with the beneficiary. Roughly, he may be said to consent to incur a unilateral obligation—an obligation to the beneficiary which, if it implies the trustee's possession and vindication of rights against other parties on behalf of that beneficiary, implies no rights for the trustee himself on his own behalf. If therefore political power be regarded as a trust, it follows that the Sovereign has not entered into a contract with the People, or the People with him—whether we regard the People as trustor or as beneficiary of the trust. The trust, in its application to politics, leaves no room for a 'contract of subjection'. We may say that Locke did not assign a contractual position to the sovereign because it would have given him rights of his own, derived from the contract; and he had no wish to vest the sovereign with *eigenes Recht*. Conversely we may say that Hobbes (who equally leaves no room for a 'contract of subjection') did not assign a contractual position to the People because it would have given *it* rights of its own; and he had no wish to vest the People with *eigenes Recht*.]

69. See Pufendorf, *De off. hom. et civ.* II, c. 6, *J. n. et g.* VII, cc. 2 and 5, §6. The same intercalation of constitution-making appears in Thomasius, *Inst. jur. div.* III, c. 6, §§ 29–31; Hertius, *Elem.* I, s. 3, *De modo const.* s. 1, §§ 2–3; Schmier, I, c. 2, s. 4, §3; Kestner, c. 7, §3; Heineccius, II, c. 6, §§ 109–12; Ickstatt, §§ 11–12.

70. This is the view of Achenwall, II, §§ 91–8, and of Hoffbauer, pp. 187–207.

71. See supra, p. 60 and n. 147 to § 14; cf. also Spinoza, *Tract. theol.-pol.* c. 16, *Tract. pol.* c. 5, §6, cc. 6, 7, §26, c. 11, §§ 1–4. The same view appears in Houtuynus, *Pol. gen.* § 99, no. 14; Titius, *Spec. jur. publ.* VII, c. 7, §§ 17 sqq. and note to Pufendorf, *De off. hom. et civ.* II, c. 6, §8; Gundling, *J. nat.* c. 35 and *Disc.* c. 34, §§ 1–17.

The One Contract theory

72. Cf. Rousseau, I, cc. 5–6 and III, cc. 1, 16–18 (with the author's work on Althusius, pp. 116–17 and p. 347 n. 50). Frederick the Great also believes in a constituent *pacte social* (*Oeuvres*, IX, pp. 195 sqq., 205); and the idea also appears in Filangieri, loc. cit., Möser, *Patriot. Phant.* II, nos. 1 and 62, and Sieyès, I, pp. 129 sqq. The contractual theory of Fichte also supposes only a single contract of all men with all men, the 'contract of state-citizenship'; but this single contract is composed of three fundamental contracts—that of 'property', that of 'protection', and that of 'association' (*Works*, III, pp. 1 sqq. and 191 sqq.; but in the *Posthumous Works*, II, pp. 499 sqq., his view is somewhat different). Kant always interprets the political contract as a single *pactum unionis civilis*; *Works*, VI, p. 320, VII, p. 133.

Psychological motive and legal act

73. This is the line of thought which appears in Huber, I, 2, c. 1, §§ 1 sqq. (man's innate idea of justice and his natural desire for society both impel him to the making of contracts, which remain, however, free acts of his will); Schmier, I, c. 2, s. 4, §2 (although the natural instinct for company which God has planted in man impels him towards society and the State, it is a matter of liberty for the individual whether *inter socios sese jungere et alienum imperium agnoscere velit*): S. Cocceji, op. cit. III, §200 (*natura mediate per pacta*); Heincke, I, c. 1, §§ 1 sqq. (*ipsa lex naturalis* is the *causa impulsiva*, and *pactum* the *modus constituendi*). The same is also true, to a certain extent, of Grotius, and of all the advocates of the theory of 'sociability', cf. supra, n. 16 to this section.

74. See Hobbes, *De cive*, c. 1 sqq., *Leviathan*, cc. 13–14; Gundling, *Jus nat.* c. 35, *Disc.* c. 34; Kestner, c. 7, §3; Daries, §657. Similar ideas are to be found in Thomasius, *Inst. jur. div.* III, c. 1, §§ 4–10 and III, c. 6, §§ 2–28 (it is not an *impulsus internus* which brings the State into being—for nature impels men, on the contrary, towards liberty and equality—but the *impulsus externus* of fear and necessity). Compare Scheidemantel, I, pp. 44–70 (the foundation of States is due in the first place to fear, and secondarily to other impulses leading men to renounce their natural liberty; but it is only achieved by free legal action).

J. H. Boehmer (*P. spec.* I, c. 1) thinks the primary cause of the founding of States to be *violentia improborum*, first producing bands of robbers, and then associations for mutual defence against these bands; and a similar view occurs in Heineccius, II, c. 6, §§ 100–4, and in Kreittmayr, § 3.

75. Thus Pufendorf regards *socialitas* as the primary and *metus* as the secondary cause of the founding of States, but he makes consent the constitutive factor; *J. n. et g.* II, cc. 1–2, VIII, c. 1, *De off. hom. et civ.* II, cc. 1, 5. Cf. also Locke, II, c. 7, §§ 87 sqq. and c. 9.

76. Kant, *Works*, VI, pp. 320, 415, VII, pp. 54, 62 sqq., 130, 162, 168.

77. Just as Althusius had already insisted (*Polit.* c. 1, §§ 28–9) that union in a civil society came about *ultro citroque*, so the voluntary character of the conclusion of a contract is strongly emphasised, on the one hand by [the absolutists] Hobbes, Spinoza, Gundling, etc., and on the other by [the radicals] Sidney, c. II, s. 5, and Locke, II, c. 8, §§ 95 and 99. Wolff (*Instit.* § 972) and Achenwall (II, § 93) also speak of the *liberum arbitrium* which is the decisive factor in the foundation of society. Pufendorf (*J. n. et g.* VII, c. 2, § 7 and *De off. hom. et civ.* II, c. 6, § 7), Schmier (see n. 73 to this section) and many other writers expressly reserve the right of every individual to stand aloof and remain in the state of nature. J. H. Boehmer denies the 'absolute necessity' of forming a State. Scheidemantel (I, pp. 68 sqq.) thinks that the State is not a necessity of human nature, and that the law of nature imposes no inevitable duty of surrendering liberty: it is only in certain circumstances that the State is necessary. Rousseau (*Contr. soc.* I, c. 6) insists even more upon liberty: he goes to the length of proclaiming (ibid. IV, c. 2) that *l'association civile est l'acte du monde le plus volontaire*: the man who opposes it cannot be compelled to join, but he is *étranger parmi les citoyens*. The same view recurs in Möser, A. L. von Schlözer and Sieyès; but Fichte goes furthest, holding that it is inconceivable that there should ever be any other legislator for an individual than his own will and his own deliberate and permanent purpose (*Works*, VI, pp. 80 sqq. and 101), and that the conclusion of the contract of State-citizenship is therefore purely a matter of free will (*Works*, III, p. 201). *General view that society is the resul of a free legal act*

78. According to Hobbes, Becmann, Gundling, etc., but equally also according to Rousseau (*Contr. soc.* I, c. 6), an understanding of the impossibility of the state of nature precedes the formation of the contract. In Spinoza (*Tract. theol.-pol.* c. 16, *Tract. pol.* cc. 3–4) reason takes a foremost place. In Sidney (II, s. 4), Locke (II, cc. 7, 9), Wolff (*Jus nat.* VIII, §§ 1 sqq.) and Achenwall (II, § 93), a process of deliberation and reflection, leading to a sense of the utility of social life, is supposed. A. L. von Schlözer speaks of the State as 'invented'. In Fichte and Kant reason rules in full sovereignty. *The act a calculated act of reason*

79. Cf. supra, p. 105.

80. Cf. supra, p. 106.

81. Cf. supra, pp. 106–107.

82. This is an admission which appears in Huber, I, 2, c. 1, §§ 33–5 ('on occasions'); Pufendorf, *J. n. et g.* VII, c. 2, § 20 and *De off. hom. et civ.* II, c. 6, § 13; Titius, *Spec. jur. publ.* IV, c. 10, §§ 2 sqq., VII, c. 7, §§ 17 sqq., and Notes to Pufendorf's *De off. hom. et civ.* II, c. 6, § 8; Schmier, I, c. 2, s. 4, § 3, no. 188; Locke, II, c. 8, §§ 101–12; Heincke, I, c. 2, §§ 2 sqq. ('as a rule'); Justi, *Natur und Wesen*, § 27 (contracts, resolutions and decrees are not essential: rules came into being afterwards, for the most part gradually and tacitly). *The idea of a tacit contract*

83. Cf. Huber, I, c. 1, §§ 14–26; Hertius, *De modo const.* s. 1, §§ 4–5, p. 289; Sidney, c. 3, s. 31 (until consent is there, the union only exists *de facto*); *Force and consent*

Locke, II, c. 8, c. 17 (until that time, there is only the appearance of a society); Achenwall, II, §98. Cf. also Rousseau, I, c. 3; Heineccius, II, c. 6, §§ 106 and 113; and A. L. von Schlözer, p. 95, §2.

Scheidemantel, on the other hand (I, pp. 65 sqq.) regards war, along with contract, as a rightful way of founding a State; cf. also Daries, §659, and Heincke, I, c. 2, §8.

The contract as 'an idea of reason'

84. Cf. Kant, *Works*, VI, pp. 329, 334, 416 sqq., VII, p. 133. A similar theory already appears in Becmann, *Consp.* p. 13, and in Kreittmayr, §3. Thomasius also suggests (in *Fund.* III, c. 6, §§ 2–6) that, whatever he has laid down previously, it is none the less dubious *an constitutio civitatis ita subito et uno quasi continuo actu facta fuerit.*

Since these lines were written there has been much discussion—arising from the contention, advanced by several writers, that the social contract was for Rousseau too [as well as for Kant] only an 'idea' [i.e. only a logical postulate, and not an actual fact in time]—with regard to the extent to which the social contract had been already interpreted in a purely 'ideal' sense before the days of Kant. See, on this matter, the *Addendum* to p. 121 of the author's work on Althusius (pp. 347–50 of the 2nd and 3rd editions).

85. Cf. supra, pp. 47 sqq., nn. 72–4 to §14; Pufendorf, *J. n. et g.* VII, c. 2, §§ 7 and 15, c. 5, §6, and *De off. hom. et civ.* II, c. 6, §§ 7, 12; Thomasius, *Inst. jur. div.* III, c. 6, §64; Locke, II, c. 8, §§ 97 sqq.; Rousseau, IV, c. 2; Hoffbauer, p. 240.

86. The question is raised most vigorously by Fichte, *Works*, III, pp. 16, 164, 178 sqq., 184 sqq.

Contract renewed by each generation

87. Pufendorf (*J. n. et g.* VII, c. 2, §20 and *De off. hom. et civ.* II, c. 6, §13) regards subjection as incumbent without any question on later generations; and it is only the subjection of fresh immigrants which he refers to a 'tacit pact' concluded at the time of their entry into the country. The same view occurs in Hertius, *De modo const.* s. 1, §§ 7–8, and in Titius, loc. cit.

Locke, on the other hand, rejects the idea that descendants are bound by the act of their ancestors, and he assumes a free act of agreement with the State, at the time of coming of age, which is evidenced by remaining in the country (II, c. 8, §§ 113–22). Similarly Rousseau writes (IV, c. 2), *quand l'État est institué, le consentement est dans la résidence.* Cf. Hoffbauer, pp. 189 and 242 sqq.

Freedom to renounce the contract

88. Pufendorf, Schmier, Locke, Rousseau and other writers, who expressly emphasise the right of individuals to keep aloof from contracts and to remain in the state of nature, none the less admit that when once accession has been expressly or tacitly declared, it is binding for life (supra, nn. 73, 77 and 78). Rousseau (III, c. 18) argues that it is only the sovereign community which can at any time annul the contract.

Fichte, however, argues that not only can a civil society itself alter its constitution at any time in spite of any provision in the contract to the opposite effect (*Works*, VI, pp. 103 sqq.), but each individual can also secede from the society at any time by virtue of his own free inalienable will, since it is the 'inalienable right of man to annul his contracts, even by unilateral act, as soon as he wills to do so' (pp. 115 sqq. and 159). In the same way a number of persons have the like right; and if they exercise it, their relations to the State are thenceforth only relations of natural law, so that they can conclude a new civic contract, and are thus able to erect a 'State within the

State' at will (ibid. pp. 148 sqq.; the famous example of such a procedure given by Fichte is the 'European State' of the Jews, but 'partial' examples which he cites are the army, the nobility and the hierarchy).

89. After Althusius had generalised the theory of a social contract [i.e. applied it to all forms of association], in a radical sense, and after Grotius had accepted this generalisation with some modifications, and Hobbes had incorporated it into his absolutist system (supra, §15, pp. 62–92), the thinkers who succeeded them—Pufendorf, Thomasius, J. H. Boehmer, Wolff, Daries, Nettelbladt, Achenwall, Hoffbauer, etc.—continued to follow this line of thought. We must admit one exception: Rousseau's conception of the political contract [as the one and only contract] leaves no room whatsoever for other forms of social contract [resulting in societies other than the State]. *Contract the basis of all associations*

90. See below. [Gierke's reference is perhaps to the intended section, which was never written, on *die Korporationstheorie im Kirchenrecht*. As his work stands, there is only a slight reference to the Church at the end of §18, p. 198.]

91. To meet the case of the Family, a category of 'necessary societies' was often added to the category of 'voluntary societies' in which the State and the Church were both included: cf. e.g. Daries, §549; Nettelbladt, §332; Achenwall, II, §9. Many thinkers also included the *societas gentium* among the necessary societies which were not dependent for their origin on an act of will: cf. Thomasius, *Inst. jur. div.* III, c. 1, §§4 sqq., and Daries, §549. But the difficulty of ascribing the origin of the Family-association, like that of other associations, to an act of contract, was often quietly evaded; and without further ado contract was declared to be the one and only source of all forms of social obligation—cf. Hoffbauer, p. 187; C. von Schlözer, §3; Fichte, *Works*, VI, pp. 80 sqq. Wolff takes this line (*Instit.* §836), but he prudently mentions quasi-contract in addition to contract proper. *The Family as based on contract*

92. Thomasius (*Inst. jur. div.* III, c. 1, §§4–10), Schmier (1, c. 2, ss. 1–3), Gundling (c. 3, §§49–55 and cc. 26 sqq.), and other writers still continue to treat *societas paterna* and *societas nuptialis* as being both equally non-contractual societies; while they regard *societas herilis* [the 'society' of master and servant —the third of the three sub-groups which together constitute the Family] as derived from contract. But Gundling adds that the authority of the father and that of the husband are not true forms of *imperium*. *Theories of the Family*

Locke (II, c. 6, §§52–76) regards only paternal authority—which he holds, however, to be a matter of duty rather than of right—as belonging to the state of nature. Rousseau (I, c. 2) pronounces the Family to be the oldest and the only natural society; but he argues that it continues to be natural only until the children have come of age, and that after that time it depends, like other societies, purely on contract. Most of the writers on natural law specifically include marriage among the *societates voluntariae*: cf. e.g. Daries, §549; Nettelbladt, §333; Achenwall, II, §§42–52. This view is expressed most vigorously by W. von Humboldt (p. 121), and he draws from it the conclusion that marriage should be freely dissoluble; the same conclusion appears in Hoffbauer, pp. 209–12.

93. Such theocratical assumptions are to be found in Praschius, Placcius, H. Cocceji and the earlier works of S. Cocceji; cf. supra, n. 47. They are also to be found in Filmer (who derives all authority from the paternal power *Theocratic views of the origin of the State*

bestowed directly by God upon Adam); in Bossuet (I, art. 3, prop. 4); and in Fénelon (c. v and conclus. 1). F. C. von Moser, in opposition to the 'dreams' of a social contract, also appeals to the idea of the divine origin of the State (*Neues patriot. Archiv*, vol. 1); for an attack on his view see A. L. von Schlözer, *Anhang*, pp. 173 sqq.

Horn's attack on the Social Contract

94. Horn attacks both the conceptions of contract. He attacks the conception of the contractual foundation of human society [the *Gesellschaftsvertrag*], on the ground that men had never lived in isolation and had never come together for the first time to make such a contract (I, c. 4, §§ 3–6); and he attacks the conception of the derivation of political authority from an act of contractual devolution [the *Herrschaftsvertrag*]—whether such devolution be regarded as made by the community (II, c. 1, §§ 17–18), or by individuals (ibid. § 19)—on the ground that there is no community distinct from the aggregation of individuals, and that individuals had never possessed a sovereignty to devolve. He declares not only the theories of Barclay, Salmasius and Grotius, but also that of Hobbes, to be revolutionary, and a danger to the State, since every *pactum* made by men can also be unmade. Just as he rejects the social contract as an explanation of the State's origin, so he rejects military force (ibid. c. 13), natural evolution (§ 14), the *jus naturale et gentium* (§ 15), and *necessitas et indigentia* (§ 16).

His view of authority as given by God

95. Horn admits that the *civitas* is constituted 'by nature' alone, but he holds that the *respublica*, which presupposes 'majesty', *non natura constituitur* (I, c. 4, §§ 3–6). God Himself is the 'sole and unique and direct cause of majesty', by communicating a part of His own authority to the monarch and thus appointing him 'vicar of God' (II, c. 1, §§ 4–12). Conquest, election, hereditary succession, and even actual appointment and investiture, are only *modi consequendi*, and they are destitute of constitutive or creative power (ibid. §§ 13–21).* In the same way the authority of the husband does not depend on any 'devolution' by the wife, *sed quamprimum nubit, maritus a Deo consequitur potestatem in uxorem* (ibid. § 19).

Yet he admits secular authority in Republics

96. Horn, III, c. un. §§ 1–5. True, genuine 'majesty' never exists in a republic, because such majesty can only be the 'work of Almighty God'. The subjection of individuals in a republican State is limited to the extent of their consent: there is no 'eminent domain'; and capital punishment is properly speaking excluded. But by 'pacts and conventions' formed in imitation of monarchy something like subjection is attained in a republic, *quoad efficaciam communis utilitatis*. A substitute is ultimately found even for 'eminent domain', as a result of the *societas omnium bonorum* into which the citizens of a republic enter;† and capital punishment itself is made possible by treatment of the criminal as an enemy and by the assumption of a previous act of consent to its infliction.

97. This revival of a philosophical theory of the natural origin of the State appears especially among political thinkers with an Aristotelian tend-

* I.e. they are ways of acquiring an authority already existing, because already constituted by God; but they do not cause such authority to exist, or constitute it as such.

† In a monarchy, the State's right of 'eminent domain', which enables it to expropriate land for a public purpose, is due to the fact that the King, as God's vicar, possesses God's final ownership. In a republic, the State may still expropriate land; but its right depends on the fact that the citizens have formed themselves into a company and made that company the final owner of the land.

ency: cf. the author's work on Althusius, p. 100 n. 68; Boecler, I, c. 1; Knichen, I, c. 1, th. 2, c. 8, th. 2; Rachelius, I, tit. 12, §2 and titt. 14–31.

98. Particularly by Vico and Ferguson (n. 52 supra).

99. This is the case with Leibniz (supra, n. 50) and Montesquieu (supra, n. 51). Even Herder (op. cit. pp. 210–22) does not eliminate contract altogether. It is only the 'first class, that of natural governments', which, in his view, depends upon the natural order of the family: the 'second class' is composed of communities based on 'contract or commission'; and the 'third class' consists 'of hereditary governments over men', which arise from war and force, but are legalised by a 'tacit contract'. *Even Herder uses the idea of Contract*

100. Such moderate opposition is to be found in Justi (supra, n. 82).

101. Hume (*Essays*, II, 6) argues that the duty of obedience to the State cannot be based on a foundation of contract, because the extinct promise of our ancestors no longer binds us to-day, and the assumption that all were born free, and only became members of the State by virtue of their own promise, is contradicted by experience. As a matter of fact, every man feels himself obliged without further question; and his remaining in the country does not depend on his free choice, and cannot therefore be interpreted as an act of consent. The real legal ground of the duty of obedience is the fact that we feel it to be a duty to obey, when once our primitive instincts of disobedience and ambition have been modified by a growing recognition that it is impossible for society to endure without obedience (pp. 269–303). *Hume on the Social Contract*

But Hume regards the making of an original contract, with a provision for resistance, as an actual fact. True we possess no documents to attest the fact, because the contract was made in the woods, before the discovery of writing, and it was not written on parchment or the bark of trees. But we may read it in the nature of man, since the surrender of our natural liberty in favour of our fellows could only come about by voluntary choice, and the beginnings of a government could not arise in the absence of consent (pp. 266–9). Cf. also *Essays*, II, 2.

102. This conception of the purpose of the State appears most definitely in Hobbes and the absolutists who adopted his views; cf. supra, nn. 74 and 78. It also appears in Rousseau, who (I, c. 6) regards the fundamental problem as being 'to find a form of association *qui défende et protège de toute la force commune la personne et les biens de chaque associé*, without abolishing the liberty and equality of all': see the author's work on Althusius, p. 345, n. 47, and see also p. 113 infra. *Rousseau's view of the purpose of the State*

103. This proposition [that the purpose of the State determines the extent of its authority] was never contested by the absolutists; it is the basis of the deductions of Spinoza (*Tract. theol.-pol.* cc. 16–17 and 20), and it is employed by Rousseau (I, c. 6, II, c. 4). It is expressly formulated by a number of writers—e.g. Hertius, *De modo const.* s. 1, §6 (the citizens are not absolutely bound, either to one another or to the Ruler, but only *quatenus ad finem societatis obtinendum expedit*, since it is not to be supposed that any further obligation has been intended); J. H. Boehmer, *P. spec.* I, c. 5, §§ 20–30; Wolff, *Instit.* §980, *Jus. nat.* VIII, §§35, 37, *Pol.* §215; Locke, II, c. 9, §131; Achenwall, II, §§10, 98; Daries, §§26 and 780–9 (in all States, certain 'natural limits' on political authority flow from the *scopus civitatis*: these are the only limits which exist in a *civitas necessaria*, but *limites pactitii* may also exist in addition in a *civitas voluntaria*); Beccaria, §2; Kreittmayr, §§1–2; Scheidemantel, III, pp. 330sqq. *The power of the State limited by its end*

Even the absolutists admit limits on the State

104. Cf. *Leviathan*, c. 21, on the matters which in their nature are not subject to the authority of the State; see also cc. 17–19, 21, 24, 26 and *De cive*, cc. 5–7, 14. Mevius (*Prodromus*, VI, §§ 1 sqq.) is like Hobbes in holding that men have submitted everything to the State—including even the rights which they hold by nature—and that no man, therefore, can invoke the law of nature against the State. But he recognises that the dictates of *jus naturale* and *jus divinum* in regard to the rights of the individual are objective limits on the exercise of authority by the State. A similar view, though it rests on a different basis, is to be found in Horn, II, c. 2, § 10 and c. 12, §§ 2–13; Bossuet, VI, a. 2 and VIII, a. 2; Fénelon, c. XI.

Spinoza on the State's limits

105. Spinoza regards each individual as having transferred all his power, and thereby *omne jus suum*, to the community, which thus possesses absolute power over all men: *Tract. theol.-pol.* c. 16, *Tract. pol.* cc. 3–4. But the authority of the State is limited, none the less, by the natural law of its own power. It cannot really issue *any* command, nor can the subject really transfer *everything*, inasmuch as he necessarily remains a man, and therefore a being who is spiritually and morally free. More especially, the individual reserves for himself the power of thinking what he likes, and of expressing his opinions orally and in writing. But where the power of the State ends, its right also ends; and reason, which always considers its own interest, impels the State accordingly to limit itself, in order that it may not suffer the loss of its power, and thus of its right, through resistance. In this way the State attains a recognition of the 'dictate of reason'—that its true object is not domination, but liberty: cf. *Tract. theol.-pol.* cc. 16–17 and 20, *Tract. pol.* c. 3, §§ 5–9, c. 4, § 4, c. 5, §§ 1–7. [It would thus seem to follow that Spinoza is not, after all, one of the 'absolutists', as has been suggested previously.]

The reader is referred, for an account of the views recently expressed by Menzel [*Wandlungen in der Staatslehre Spinoza's*, Stuttgart, 1898], which to some extent diverge from those stated here, to the Addenda to the author's work on Althusius [2nd edition], pp. 342 sqq., nn. 39–41, and p. 346 n. 49, and also to the Addenda to the 3rd edition, nn. 54–7. [The English reader may be also referred to Duff, *The Moral and Political Ideas of Spinoza*.]

106. *Contr. soc.* I, c. 6 (*l'aliénation totale de chaque associé avec tous droits à toute la communauté*); cf. also c. 7.

Rousseau on the rights of man

107. Ibid. II, c. 7. Although there can be no legal limits upon the sovereign power of the social body over its members, there are inherent limits arising from the very nature of the general will, of which all individual wills are part, and which can only will what is equal and just for all. Absolute as the sovereign may be, it can never really burden one subject more heavily than another, *parce qu'alors l'affaire devenant particulière son pouvoir n'est plus compétent*; and thus the individual, in the last resort, has not made any real alienation, but rather an advantageous exchange, receiving back for what he has given a greater security of his liberty, his equality and his life. This is not logic; and it is in vain that Rousseau tries to shelter himself, in a footnote, from a charge of illogicality. The reader is referred, for an account of the vigorous controversy which has arisen recently in regard to Rousseau's attitude to the theory of the rights of man, to the Addenda to the author's work on Althusius [2nd edition], p. 347 n. 50, and to the Addenda to the 3rd edition, n. 63.

108. Sieyès expressly says that societies only exist for the sake of individuals, and that the happiness of individuals is the only object of the social

state: *Works*, II, p. 32, I, pp. 417, 431. But the purpose of the State is also *Salus*
(if only implicitly) made to consist in the happiness of individuals, when it *publica as*
is defined by Hertius (s. 1, §1) as *tranquilla et beata vita*, or by Wachter *consisting*
(p. 34) as *mutua et communis felicitas*, or by Wolff (*Instit.* §972 and *Jus nat.* *in the*
VIII, §14) as *sufficientia vitae, tranquillitas et securitas*. *happiness of*
 There is less of an individualistic tinge in the formula of Justi (*Natur und* *individuals*
Wesen, §§30–44). He makes 'the common happiness of the whole State' the
object of commonwealths and their sovereign law (though he adds that, sovereign as it may be, it can never warrant any action that is unjust in itself): he
regards liberty, security and internal strength as the main elements of this
happiness; but otherwise he leaves each people free to determine the particular objects of its own life. But even Justi adds that the 'common happiness' consists pre-eminently in the happiness of the subjects, and secondarily
in that of the Ruler.

 A. L. von Schlözer (pp. 17ff.) distinguishes between (1) the *finis negativus*
of the State, which is limited to securing and protecting, as against fellow-
citizens, aliens and natural causes, the four kinds of property (in a man's
person, his possessions, his honour and his religion), and (2) the *fines positivi*,
which come to be added with the development of civilisation, and are
directed to the advancement of prosperity, population and enlightenment
(cf. p. 93, §1).

 109. The purpose of the State is defined by Kestner (c. 7, §4 and *Definitions*
§§17 sqq.) as *justitia colenda*; by S. de Cocceji (*Nov. syst.* §§280 and 613), as *of the State's*
defensio jurium singulorum; by Heineccius (§107), as *securitas civium*; by Daries *purpose*
(*Praecogn.* §24 and *P. spec.* §§656 and 664–6), as *securitas*; by Hoffbauer
(pp. 236 sqq.), as legal security; by Scheidemantel (I, p. 70), as 'the attainment of internal and external security by means of united resources'; by
Klein (II, pp. 55 sqq.), as 'protection of social life'. In Filangieri (I, cc. 1–12)
the purpose is *conservazione e tranquillità*: in Mercier de la Rivière, Turgot and
the other Physiocrats, it is *liberté et sûreté* of person and property: in Hume
(*Essays*, II, no. 3) it is simply justice, and King, Parliament, ministers and
the rest—including even the clergy—properly exist only in order to support
the twelve jurymen.

 110. Locke (II, c. 9, §§123–31), following this idea of 'insurance', denies *The State*
any other purpose to the State than that of guaranteeing natural rights, *as an*
particularly the rights of 'liberty and property'. *insurance*
 In the theory of W. von Humboldt the final object of human existence is *society*
the development of personality (pp. 9 sqq.). The State is only a means for
attaining that security of its citizens, and thereby that 'consciousness of legal
freedom', which are the indispensable conditions of such development
(pp. 16 sqq.). Security has to be attained both in regard to enemies without
(pp. 47 sqq.) and between the citizens themselves (pp. 53 sqq.); and therefore
the legitimate activities of the State are confined entirely to (1) the enacting
of administrative, civil and criminal law, (2) jurisdiction, (3) the care of
minors and lunatics, and (4) the provision of the means necessary for maintaining the structure of the State (pp. 100–77). Conversely, the making of any
provision for the common good (pp. 44 sqq.), and any attempt to influence
education, religion or moral improvement (pp. 61 sqq.), are injurious.

 Kant goes furthest of all in the limitations which he assigns to the purposes
of the State. It is confined to realising the idea of Right or law (*Works*,
VI, p. 322 and VII, p. 130); and that realisation must be attained without

reference to the consequences of good or bad which follow [i.e. the idea of impersonal Right must be carried into effect regardless of its effect on the Good of persons], cf. VI, pp. 338, 446, VII, p. 150. Kant expressly attacks the idea of the 'welfare-State'—i.e. the State directed to the well-being of its members—unless such well-being or happiness be understood only to mean a condition in which the constitution is in the greatest possible harmony with the principles of Right, or unless, again, a law which [immediately] aims at some form of happiness (e.g. opulence) is only intended to serve [ultimately] as a means of securing a system of Right, especially against external enemies; cf. VI, pp. 330 sqq., VII, p. 136.

111. Cf. e.g. Locke, II, c. 9, §131 and c. 11, §§134 sqq.; Wolff, *Instit.* §74; Sieyès, I, p. 417, II, pp. 3 sqq. and 374 sqq.; Kant, VI, p. 417, VII, p. 34.

Natural as opposed to civil rights

112. This theory [of a distinction between 'civil' and 'natural' rights] is already implied in advance by all the doctrines in which, from the Middle Ages onwards, the law of nature is exalted above the State; and it plays an important part in the thought of e.g. Althusius and Grotius. But it was only during the reaction against Hobbes' attempt to annihilate the idea of the natural rights of man that it was formulated as an explicit theory. Huber was particularly responsible for the development of a formal theory of the rights (of person, property, liberty of thought and freedom to follow the divine commands) which must be reserved in all forms of State for the individual, by means of the necessary articles in the contract [of government], and are thus removed from the control of the sovereign: cf. *De civ.* I, 2, cc. 3–5 and I, 3, c. 4. Pufendorf also reserves for the individual, as a man and as a citizen, natural rights which, though they are imperfectly protected as against the sovereign, are still indestructible: *Elem.* I, d. 12, §6, *J. n. et g.* I, c. 1, cc. 8–9, *De off. hom. et civ.* II, c. 5, c. 9, §4, c. 11. Hertius argues in the same sense, *De modo const.* s. 1, §6, and Schmier devotes a detailed exposition to the theory, III, c. 3 and V, c. 2, s. 1.

Thomasius on liberty of conscience

113. Cf. Thomasius, *Instit. jur. div.* I, c. 1, §§114 sqq. and *Fund.* I, c. 5, §11 sqq., where a clear distinction is first drawn [before he comes to the particular question of liberty of conscience] (1) between *jus connatum* and *jus acquisitum*, and (2) between the 'subjective' side of any body of law [law or 'Right' as expressed in the rights of 'Subjects' or persons] and its objective side [law or 'right' as expressed externally in a concrete body of rules]. See also J. H. Boehmer, *P. spec.* I, c. 5 and III, cc. 1–2, and Gundling, c. 1, §§51–62.

114. Locke, II, c. 11; cf. also Sidney, I, ss. 10 and 11 and II, ss. 4 and 20. The same view appears in the French physiocrats.

Wolff on natural rights

115. The main object of Wolff's enquiries into the extent to which the original law of nature is either over-ridden by the contracts which form the State, or still continues to preserve its validity, is simply to attain a basis for dividing the rights and duties of political man into those which are acquired and those which are innate. The conclusion which he attains is that the individual retains the sovereignty he enjoyed in the state of nature, in regard to all actions which the political authority is not warranted by its purpose in regulating; but he also vindicates the inviolability of those 'acquired' rights which are so much bound up with man's being that he cannot be deprived of them: *Instit.* §§68 sqq., 980; *Jus nat.* I, §§26 sqq. and VIII, §§35 and 47; *Pol.* §§215 and 433.

116. Cf. e.g. Daries, *P. spec.* §§ 710–46 (*jura naturalia absoluta*); Nettelbladt, §§ 143 sqq., 193 sqq., 1127, 1134–42 (there are *obligationes connatae* as well as *contractae*, and *jura connata* as well as *quaesita*); Achenwall, I, §§ 63–86, II, §§ 11 and 98–108; Kreittmayr, §§ 32 sqq.; Scheidemantel, III, pp. 172–343. See also Turgot, art. *Fondation*, § 6, p. 75: *les citoyens ont des droits et des devoirs sacrés pour le corps même de la société*. Compare also Blackstone, *Comm.* I, c. 1, pp. 124 sqq. [where Blackstone distinguishes 'absolute' rights from those which are 'social and relative'].

Vogue of theory of natural rights

Montesquieu, it is true, assigns to the State the object of realising as far as possible the spiritual and economic liberty of the individual (cf. e.g. XII, cc. 1–18, XIII, cc. 12 and 14, XX, c. 8, XXIII, XXV, cc. 9–13); but in attacking slavery he merely uses the idea of the inalienability of liberty (XV, cc. 1–18). [In other words, he speaks of liberty as achieved by the State, but at the same time regards it as independent of the State.]

Justi also (§ 18) pronounces that government to be the best which limits 'natural liberty' as little as possible and yet succeeds in achieving the purpose of the State.

117. This is especially true of Sieyès, whose *Reconnaissance et exposition des droits de l'homme et citoyen*, of July 1789 (I, pp. 427 sqq.), forms the basis of the public Declaration of the Rights of Man (I, pp. 413 sqq.). Along with freedom, which the citizens bring with them as their inalienable right into the social state (II, pp. 3 sqq.), he makes property, 'that God of all legislation' (II, p. 35), inviolable by the State: cf. also II, pp. 374 sqq.* In the present context, in which we are only concerned with the theoretical [and not with the historical] development, we need not reckon with the fact, on which Jellinek has remarked, that the American 'bills of rights' [e.g. the Virginia Bill of Rights, and the Pennsylvania 'Declaration of the Rights of the Inhabitants of the Commonwealth or State', of June and September, 1776] were anterior to the French Revolution of 1789 as constitutional assertions of the fundamental rights of individuals.

Droits de l' homme in 1789

In Kant also the innate and inalienable rights of the individual—in the three senses of the liberty of man, the equality of subjects and the independence of the citizen—form the limits and the canon of all political life: *Works*, VI, pp. 322 sqq. and 416 sqq. and VII, pp. 34 sqq., 147 sqq. A similar view is to be found in A. L. von Schlözer, pp. 51 sqq. Hoffbauer goes to the furthest length. He begins by developing a system of the absolute (or original), and the conditional (or acquired) rights, which belong to all rational existence (pp. 64 sqq.); he then proceeds to depict the absolute or original rights of man (pp. 111 sqq.); only after that does he arrive at man's conditional or acquired rights (pp. 120 sqq.). But even now he has first to discuss the 'universal', and then the 'particular', species of such rights, and afterwards, under the latter head, to treat of an 'extra-social' form, before he finally arrives at the 'social' form of the 'particular' species of 'conditional' rights [cf. n. 19 supra for this process of subdivision *in excelsis*].

Möser attacks the conception of the rights of man (*Misc. Writings*, I, pp. 306, 313, 335): but he definitely recognises in an earlier work (*Patriot. Phantas.* III, no. 62) the existence of free rights of the individual which are not forfeited in the social state.

---

* Reference may also be made to T. Paine's *Rights of Man*, Part I (of January, 1791).

The variations of Fichte's views

118. In this connection [i.e. as regards the passing of individualism into a system of social absolutism, and vice versa] the variations of opinion which Fichte could achieve without abandoning his theoretical basis are particularly significant. In 1793 he regards the purpose of the State as consisting only in 'the cultivation of liberty' (*Works*, VI, p. 101); in 1796, in speaking of 'the purpose of Right or law', he is already willing to think of an economic transformation of the State in conformity with the idea of Right; and in 1800 (III, pp. 387sqq.) he even derives his socialistic State, directed to the general welfare, from this idea [Gierke here is referring to Fichte's *Der geschlossene Handelsstaat*, on which see W. Wallace, *Lectures and Essays*, pp. 427sqq.]. By 1804 he is expanding the purpose of the State into 'the purpose of the human race', which leads him to interpret it as being the promotion of general culture (VII, pp. 144sqq.); and in 1807 he depicts the ideal of an educational State (VII, pp. 428sqq.). Later still, he attempts to reconcile this later purpose of education and moral development with the earlier purpose of 'the cultivation of liberty' (*Works*, IV, pp. 367sqq.; *Posthumous Works*, II, pp. 539–42).

Corresponding to the variations in his view of the State's function are the changes in his conception of the relation of the individual to society. At first he emphasises the inalienable rights of man which cannot be diminished by any form of contract (*Works*, VI, pp. 159–61). In his *Naturrecht* (1796–7) he argues vigorously, in opposition to Rousseau, that the individual is only merged into the organised whole in one part of his being and nature, but otherwise remains 'a completely free person, who is not woven into the whole of the body politic'(*Works*, III, pp. 204–6); and even in *Der geschlossene Handelsstaat* of 1800 he still maintains this point of view (III, pp. 387sqq.). In his *Grundzügen des gegenwartigen Zeitalters* (1804–5) he entirely alters his view: the individual is now completely merged in the perfect State which ought to be the goal of endeavour. He has nothing *per se*: he has everything in virtue of being a member of the State; he is entirely the instrument of the State, and he is only sovereign 'in regard to his necessary purpose as a member of the race' [i.e. he is only sovereign in so far as he is part of a general humanity which is itself sovereign in determining the purposes of its life]; cf. VII, pp. 147sqq., 153, 157sqq., 210. He takes the same line in the *Reden an die deutsche Nation* (1807–8); but later still he adopts more of a *via media*, emphasising the 'moral liberty of the will' which is still left to the 'instrument' of which he had previously spoken (II, pp. 537sqq.).

119. [Not only is individualism no bulwark against socialism and communism]: on the contrary, it rather appears as if the elevation of the individual into the *terminus a quo* and the *terminus ad quem* of social institutions were an inseparable element of socialistic and communistic systems.

Recognitions of the social whole in eighteenth-century thought

120. Leibniz approaches nearest to this way of thinking, in the introduction to his *Cod. jur. gent. dipl.* I, §§ 11–13. There are also statements in Ferguson (I, cc. 7–10) which make the social aim consist, not in the greatest possible amount of pleasure, but in the greatest possible amount of spiritual activity, and therefore in the free development of the powers both of the national community and of individuals: cf. also V, c. 3. Scheidemantel too rises to the view (I, pp. 75sqq.) that there are certain natural basic rules for the attainment of the aim of the State, of which the greatest is that the well-being of the whole and the private well-being of the parts are to be simultaneously and jointly pursued by every individual and every society,

Notes to § 16

but that, where there is any clash, the well-being of the whole must be preferred.

121. Horn accordingly makes a definite attack on theories of the original sovereignty of the people (II, c. 1, § 18), of the existence of a 'real majesty' [as distinct from 'personal'] (II, c. 10, §§ 11–15), and of the possibility of a *subjectum commune* of majesty (II, c. 11, § 1). But he equally impugns the possibility of the popular community possessing *any* right whatsoever as against the Ruler (II, c. 5, § 1).

122. Horn attempts to prove (III, c. un. § 2) that it is impossible for *plures conjunctim* to be the 'Subject' of majesty. When rule is ascribed to all *ut universi* in a democracy, it is *ipso facto* also attributed at the same time to all *ut singuli*; and the result is that, since *imperium et obsequium non inhabitant unam personam*, the existence of any 'Subject' at all is really denied. If, on the other hand, it be admitted that *singuli* are simply *subditi*, it follows that no other quality than that of being a body of *subditi* can be predicated of *singuli conjunctim*, i.e. of all when they are regarded as united in a *universitas*.* Moreover [apart from the logical difficulty] there is a further difficulty, which is involved in the recognition of the majority-principle. That recognition means either that *universi* are deposed [in favour of a mere majority] or that the rulers are, in part [i.e. as regards the minority], turned into being the ruled; but in any case a sovereign which changes with each vote would be a curious sort of sovereign. If we now turn from democracy to aristocracy, we find once more that there is no 'Subject' or owner of majesty. Here again, just as in democracy, a distinction has to be made between *universi* and *singuli*, though the two things thus distinguished are really one and indistinguishable. For if *singuli* have nothing, *universi* equally have nothing, and if *universi* have authority, *singuli* equally have a part of that authority; and the result [on the latter supposition] is that each member of the ruling class will have a *particula majestatis* which, like the whole of which it is a part, will be *summa*, and thus a number of *summa imperia* will arise. Horn then argues, in § 3, that it is no less impossible for *omnes* or *plures* to possess 'majesty' severally (*divisim*) than it is for them to possess it jointly (*conjunctim*).

Horn's attack on any form of plural sovereignty

123. Cf. III, c. un., and supra, n. 96 to this section.

124. Pufendorf (*J. n. et g.* VII, c. 5, § 5) delivers a vigorous attack on the 'sophistical' arguments of Horn, objecting to him that, at any rate *in moralibus*, the whole can possess attributes which no part possesses, and arguing accordingly that, *in corporibus moralibus compositis, aliquid tribui potest universis quod neque omnibus* (i.e. *singulis divisim sumtis*) *neque uni alicui ex illis singulis queat tribui; adeoque universitas revera est persona moralis a singulis distincta, cui peculiaris voluntas, actiones et jura tribui queant, quae in singulis non cadunt*. Compare also Schmier (I, c. 3, nos. 62–72), who seeks to prove, in opposition to Horn, both the philosophical and the legal justification of the distinction between a *totum compositum* and its *partes separatim acceptae*.

Critics of Horn's views

125. Spinoza agrees entirely with Hobbes in thinking that a social body controlled by a single mind (*ut omnium mentes et corpora unam quasi mentem unumque corpus componant*) can come into existence through the vesting of all power in the Ruler, in virtue of a transference of their power by all individuals, so that the Ruler, *qua Civitas*, henceforth represents the will of every individual. *Civitatis voluntas pro omnium voluntate habenda est: id quod*

The Ruler as representing the Group

---

* Cf. the argument of Hobbes, supra n. 155 to § 14.

Civitas justum et bonum esse decernit, tanquam ab unoquoque decretum esse censendum est: cf. *Eth.* IV, prop. 18 schol.; *Tract. pol.* c. 2, § 15, c. 3, §§ 1–5, c. 4, §§ 1–2.

Mevius (*Prodromus*, V, §§ 23–6) similarly holds that the *unio*, by virtue of which the State is *una velut persona* (*cui una mens, unus sensus, una voluntas, et anima inter multas velut una atque eadem*), is based on the submission of all wills to that of the Ruler, whence it follows that *imperantes totam multitudinem repraesentant et ejus vice sunt*—their action counting as the action of the 'whole community and of all severally', and the 'will and judgment of the Rulers being the will and judgment of the whole society or State'. See also Houtuynus, *Pol. gen.* § 99, no. 14; Micraelius, I, c. 10, §§ 14–17; Bossuet, I, a. 3, prop. 1–6, VI, a. 1, prop. 2–3.

126. Cf. *Tract. theol.-pol.* c. 16 (*coetus universus hominum, qui collegialiter summum jus ad omnia, quae potest, habet*); *Tract. pol.* cc. 3, 6 (*ut jus, quod unusquisque ex natura habet, collective haberent*); *Eth.* IV, prop. 18 schol.

127. E.g. the one conclusion that emerges in Bossuet (V, a. 1) is nothing more than the dictum, so often quoted since, that the monarch is *l'État même*.

128. Huber, *De jure civ.* I, 3, c. 4, §§ 8–83, II, 3, c. 1, § 35: see also, on the validity of the majority-principle, which is referred to an original act of agreement, I, 2, c. 3, §§ 27 sqq.; II, 3, c. 1, §§ 21–2 and c. 2, §§ 3–4.

129. Ibid. I, 3, c. 2, § 14, c. 6, § 26; I, 9, c. 5, §§ 51 and 65–72; II, 3, c. 6, § 2.

130. Ibid. II, 3, c. 6, §§ 1–10.

Pufendorf on corpora moralia as created by consent

131. Cf. *Elem.* I, def. 4, § 13, *J. n. et g.* I, c. 1, § 13: *persona moralis composita constituitur, quando plura individua humana ita inter se uniuntur, ut quae vi istius unionis volunt aut agunt pro una voluntate unaque actione, non pro pluribus censeantur*. Therefore, he argues, not only is a *pactum unionis* necessary in order to produce, first of all, the State (*J. n. et g.* VII, c. 2, § 6); a similar *pactum singulorum cum singulis*, to the effect that certain things shall be managed jointly and in the interest of *una persona moralis*, is also indispensable for families, corporations and local groups (*Elem.* II, d. 12, § 26). In another passage, where he distinguishes between *corpora naturalia, artificialia* and *moralia*, Pufendorf repeats his view that a *corpus morale*, which remains identical in spite of all the changes of its parts, may be produced by a simple *conjunctio hominum* (*J. n. et g.* VIII, c. 12, § 7). [In other words, a moral body may already exist in virtue of *conjunctio*, before any further step has been taken, such as the appointment of a representative organ to act on its behalf.]

Pufendorf on the conditions of real Group-personality

132. Cf. *Elem.* I, d. 4, § 3, *J. n. et g.* I, c. 1, § 13: *Idque tunc fieri intelligitur, quando singuli voluntatem suam voluntati unius hominis aut concilii ita subjiciunt, ut pro omnium voluntate et actione velint agnoscere et ab aliis haberi, quicquid iste decreverit aut gesserit circa illa, quae ad unionis ejus naturam ut talem spectant et fini ejusdem congruunt; unde est, quod cum alias, ubi plures quid voluerint aut egerint, tot voluntates et actiones extare intelliguntur, quot numero personae physicae seu individua humana ibi numerantur, in personam tamen compositam coalitis una voluntas tribuatur, et quae ab illis ut talibus proficiscitur actio, una censeatur, utut plura individua physica ad eandem concurrerint.* He adds that under these conditions [i.e. where there is a moral body acting corporately through a representative] corporate property comes into existence, which does not belong to *singuli*, and other similar developments follow. See also *J. n. et g.* VII, c. 2, § 5, *De off. hom. et civ.* II, c. 6, §§ 5–6: *uniri multorum hominum voluntates nulla alia ratione possunt, quam si unusquisque suam voluntatem voluntati unius hominis aut unius concilii subjiciat, ita ut deinceps pro voluntate omnium et singulorum sit habendum, quicquid de rebus ad securitatem communem necessariis ille voluerit*. Pufendorf argues, on this basis,

that a Group-person never arises from a simple contract of union; it must always be called into being by a number of contracts (*necessarium est, ut voluntates viresque suas univerint intervenientibus pactis*), which find their culmination in the contract of subjection; cf. *J. n. et g.* VII, c. 2, §6. It follows that a *Systema Civitatum* [i.e. a confederation], being a *nuda conventio*, and not having erected any *imperium*, is not a 'person' [since there is no man, or body of men, with authority to represent it], and cannot act by majority-decision: cf. *J. n. et g.* VII, c. 5, §20.

[In brief, the argument is that while simple *conjunctio* can produce a 'moral body' (see the end of the preceding note), and while such *conjunctio* may thus be the first step in constituting a 'moral person', there is something more needed before a real 'moral person' can emerge. That something more is the creation of a representative organ, and submission thereto; for only in the 'person' of the representative organ can the 'person' of the *corpus morale* really exist and function.]

133. The doctrine of *entia moralia* already occurs, in essence, in *Elem.* I, d. 1 sqq. [of the year 1660], but it is developed further in *J. n. et g.* I, cc. 1–2 [of the year 1672].

134. *J. n. et g.* I, c. 1, §3. They are mere *modi*, which do not come into existence, like *entia physica*, through 'creation', but through 'imposition': i.e. they are 'superadded' to something already in existence. They have no power of producing physical changes; and the only effect they produce is on the mind, by making men understand better the nature of their actions (§4). Just as they only come into existence by 'imposition', so they may be changed, or even abolished, by some alteration of such 'imposition' (whether by God or men); but the sort of change to which they are thus subject is one by which *ipsa personarum aut rerum substantia physica* is not affected (§23). *Pufendorf's theory of entia moralia*

135. Ibid. §§5–6. Pufendorf prefers the twofold classification of 'moral entities' under these categories [of substance and attribute] to the single classification which we should have to adopt if we confined ourselves to the idea that all *entia moralia*, being *modi*, are attributes of *homines, actiones* or *res*. *Some are substances: some only attributes*

136. Pufendorf begins by arguing that in the moral world *status*, as the basis of the existence of 'moral persons', corresponds to what *spatium* is in the physical world as the basis of the existence of physical persons in place and time.* He admits some difference: *spatium* can continue to exist after the disappearance of all natural objects; but *status* is inconceivable after the disappearance of the persons who exist in that medium (loc. cit. §§6–10). *Moral persons like substances*

Having drawn this analogy [between the basis of existence of moral and that of physical persons], Pufendorf proceeds to interpret 'moral persons' themselves in the light of the analogy of physical substances (§§12–15). [But while he thus interprets *persons* as being moral in a way analogous to that in which substances are physical], he thinks it unnecessary ever to interpret *objects* (*res*) as being 'moral' in this sort of way, since the attributes of objects (e.g. that they are 'sacred') can be referred on a deeper analysis to an *obligatio hominum* (§16).† Other *entia moralia* [i.e. moral entities other than

* Pufendorf's *spatium* is 'time-space': it is both temporal and spatial extent.

† We need not regard a thing, such as a sanctuary, as being an *ens morale*, on the ground that it has the attribute of being sacred, and that there must be an *ens* as the substance which carries that attribute. Really, the attribute of being sacred can be reduced, if we turn from the thing to the men behind the thing, to an obligation of men to regard the thing as sacred.

personae] are not *ad analogiam substantiarum concepta*: they are simply *modi*, or attributes, of a purely 'formal' character (§17). They exist, that is to say, either as 'qualities' (e.g. a 'title', or a 'power', or a 'right', or an 'obligation', are all qualities, §§18–21), or as 'quantities' (e.g. 'price', or 'credit', or the value of a business, are all quantities, §22).

Moral persons simple or compound

137. Loc. cit. §12: *Entia moralia, quae ad analogiam substantiarum concipiuntur, dicuntur personae morales, quae sunt homines singuli aut per vinculum morale in unum systema connexi, considerati cum statu suo aut munere, in quo in vita communi versantur. Sunt autem personae morales vel simplices vel compositae.*

Simple moral persons

138. Loc. cit. §12. The *persona moralis simplex* is therefore either *publica* (whether such 'person' be *principalis*, or *minus principalis*, or *repraesentativa*), or *privata* (according to profession, civic status, family standing, descent, sex and age). The *ens morale* can never be a *qualitas physica*: if a plebeian becomes a noble, or vice versa, no physical change is involved; and the Catholic doctrine of an 'indelible moral character' is therefore absurd (§23). [See n. 134 supra, on the 'imposition', and the consequent possibility of removal, of the *modus*—the attribute or character—which constitutes 'moral being'. It follows, on this argument, that 'imposition' makes the 'character', or *ens morale*, of a priest; and what has been 'imposed' can be removed. Holy orders, therefore, are not 'an indelible moral character'; to argue in that sense is to treat such orders as a 'physical quality' which cannot be altered.]

139. Loc. cit. §14 (the individual may 'bear' a number of 'persons' because he has a number of 'positions' (*status*) which do not conflict).

140. Loc. cit. §13: cf. supra, n. 132.

141. Loc. cit. §15: here we see that the *impositio* of an *ens morale* is not independent of every quality of the object: Caligula could make a fool into a senator, but not his horse.

Pufendorf also rejects the personification of inanimate objects which Hobbes achieves in c. 16 of the *Leviathan* [e.g. of a bridge on which there is a right of charging tolls] as an unnecessary fiction—*cum simplicissime dicatur, a civitate certis hominibus injunctam curam colligendi reditus istis rebus servandis destinatos, et quae eo nomine oriuntur actiones persequendi aut excipiendi.*

Nature of compound moral persons

142. Cf. *Elem.* I, d. 4, §3; *J. n. et g.* I, c. 1, §13, VII, c. 2, §6. It follows that *personae morales compositae* are not able *seipsas qua tales obligare*, any more than single persons are able to do so. Their decisions only bind *membra societatis qua singula, nequaquam autem societatem ipsam qua talem.* The contract for the foundation [of the society, as a 'compound moral person'] is not a case to the contrary: the society does not 'oblige itself' in any way even by that act; all that happens is that 'the members severally, as such, bind one another mutually, to the effect that they are willing to coalesce in a single body'. If an individual afterwards gives a vote, he too does not oblige himself directly thereby; it is only indirectly that he does so—i.e. in so far as he helps [by that vote] to form the will which under the *pactum fundamentale* is binding upon him. Cf. *Elem.* I, d. 12, §17.

143. Pufendorf himself often uses the expression *persona physica* instead of *persona moralis simplex*: cf. *J. n. et g.* I, c. 1, §13, VII, c. 2, §6 and c. 5, §8.

Such persons not natural, but created by agreement

144. Pufendorf expressly urges that 'naturally' a *confusio omnium voluntatum in unam* is impossible, and that a common will can only arise [by something more than a natural process, i.e.] by a *moralis translatio voluntatum*, whereby *illud quisque velle censetur, quod in alium contulit, [aeque ac] si ipse velit.* In the same way the union of the powers of individuals [as distinct from their

wills] does not come to pass naturally, but as a result of promises of obedience and the giving of guarantees for the fulfilment of those promises: cf. *J. n. et g.* VII, c. 2, §5 and *De off. hom. et civ.* II, c. 6, §§5–6; and see also, as regards the impossibility of *unio naturalis* and the nature of *unio moralis*, Otto's commentary on the latter passage. Pufendorf accordingly goes so far as to commend the comparison drawn by Hobbes between the State and an 'artificial man', *J. n. et g.* loc. cit. §13 and *De off. hom. et civ.* loc. cit. §10.

145. *Elem.* I, d. 12, §27; *J. n. et g.* VII, c. 2, §§15–19 and c. 5, §6; *De off. hom. et civ.* II, c. 6, §12. Such an agreement [establishing the validity of majority-decisions] is always to be presumed, in Pufendorf's view, because there is no better way than majority-decision of arriving at a united expression of will by an assembly. He admits that any individual, on entering a society, may reserve for himself a right of giving or withholding his assent [to a majority-decision] on any issue; but he argues that, even in that event, the mere *pertinacia* of such an individual does not affect the decision of the assembly adversely, for though the decision will not be binding upon him *ex suo consensu*, it will still be binding *ex generali lege ut caeteris sese commodum praebeat et ut pars se conformet ad bonum totius*. *Even their majority-decisions depend on a previous agreement*

146. *J. n. et g.* VII, c. 2, §§13–14; *De off. hom. et civ.* II, c. 6, §§10–11. The commentators—Titius, Otto, Trauer and Hertius—expressly censure Pufendorf for taking over from Hobbes, in these passages, the identification of the *Imperans* with the *Civitas*: cf. also Titius, *Observ.* 557.

147. Pufendorf accordingly describes the sovereign *Concilium* in a republic as a *persona moralis composita* or *conjuncta*: *Elem.* I, d. 12, §27; *J. n. et g.* VII, c. 2, §15, c. 5, §5; *De off. hom. et civ.* II, c. 8, §4.

148. Hert, for example, emphasises the fact that what is 'physically' impossible is sometimes 'morally' possible, and what is monstrous *in physicis* may be unexceptionable *in moralibus*: e.g. on a *consideratio physica* a plurality of men cannot be one, nor one man a plurality; but on a *consideratio moralis* a number of men may be taken together as a single person, or one man may be taken to be several persons. In the realm of nature a single head with a number of bodies, or a single body with a number of heads, is a *monstrum*; but this is by no means true of moral bodies. Cf. *Annot. ad Pufend. J. n. et g.* I, c. 1, §3 n. 4 and *Opusc.* I, 3, pp. 27sqq. and II, 3, pp 41sqq. *Hert modifies Pufendorf*

149. Thomasius defines a *persona* as *homo consideratus cum suo statu*. He distinguishes between the *persona simplex, sc. unicum individuum humanum*, and the *persona composita ex pluribus individuis certo statu unitis* (*Instit. jur. div.* I, c. 1, §§86–7); and he defines the State as a *persona moralis composita* (ibid. III, c. 6, §§62–3). Titius regards jurisprudence as almost exclusively concerned with *personae morales*, which are either *singulares* or *compositae* (*Observ.* 94, *Jus priv. Rom.-Germ.* VIII, c. 2). Cf. also Ickstatt (*Opusc.* II, op. 1, c. 1, §§14–15), who regards *persona moralis simplex* and *persona moralis composita* as distinct, exactly like Pufendorf. *Thomasius retains his theory*

150. Hert, *Opusc.* I, 1, pp. 286 and 288, II, 3, pp. 41 and 55; Gundling, *Jus nat.* c. 35, §34, c. 37, §§3–10, and *Exerc.* 16, §5 (*personae mysticae vulgo audiunt, ac morales compositaeque dicuntur*); Schmier, I, c. 3, nos. 62–72; and also Becmann, c. 12, §7.

151. Nettelbladt (*Syst. nat.* §83) can still remark incidentally that 'physical persons' are also called 'single' (*singulares*), and 'moral persons' also go by the name of 'composite' or 'mystical'; but he himself only uses the expression 'moral persons'. Cf. also Scheidemantel, III, p. 244.

152. Cf. e.g. J. H. Boehmer, *P. spec.* I, c. 2, §1, c. 3, §1 n. *o*; Heineccius, *Elem.* II, §20; Achenwall, *Proleg.* §§92–3, II, §§3 and 15; Hoffbauer, pp. 190, 244, 292, 310.

Leibniz adopts the terms *persona naturalis* and *persona civilis* in his terminology; but he also uses the adjectives *moralis* or *ficta* as synonymous with *civilis*: *Nova meth.* II, §16; Introd. to the *Cod. jur. gent.* I, §22; *Caesar.-Fürst.* c. 11; *Spec. demonstr. pol.* pr. 1 and 57.

Wolff also follows Pufendorf in part

153. In the theory of Wolff (*Instit.* §96) man is a *persona moralis* or *sittliche Person* in so far as he is regarded as the 'Subject' or owner of rights or obligations, and is thus in a *moralis status* or *sittliche Zustand*; cf. also §§850, 963, 1030.

Daries (*Praecogn.* §§9, 24) holds that by 'person in the juridical sense', or 'moral person', we mean man 'in so far as he has a certain moral status'—*ex quo manifestum est a personalitate ut ita dicam physica ad personalitatem moralem non valere consequentiam.*

Collective and representative unity

154. Thus Treuer, in a note to Pufendorf's *De off. hom. et civ.* II, c. 6, §5, holds that a 'union of wills' is possible by means of mere *societates et foedera*, without *imperium*—though a union by means of *imperium* is better.

Thomasius interprets the personality of the State in exactly the same way as Pufendorf (*Instit. jur. div.* III, c. 6, §§27, 31, 62–4, 157; *Fund.* III, c. 6, §7); but after including the State in the category of *societates mixtae*, which blend the principle of Fellowship with that of Rulership, he proceeds to add to these 'mixed societies' two other forms of society—the *societas inaequalis* of God and man, which rests on the pure principle of Rulership, and the *societas aequalis*, which rests on the pure principle of Fellowship (*Instit. jur. div.* I, c. 1, §§91–113, III, c. 1, §§57–74).

Titius ascribes the unity of the personality of the State entirely to the representation of all its members by the Ruler, who has thus a double personality, while the subject only possesses a single personality (*Spec. jur. publ.* I, c. 1, §§43sqq., VII, c. 7, §§19sqq.); but in dealing with the *universitas*, which he relegates altogether to the sphere of private law, he assumes the existence of a purely Collective *persona moralis composita* (*Observ.* 94, *Jus priv. Rom.-Germ.* VIII, c. 2).

155. *De modo const.* s. 1, §§2–3 (*Opusc.* I, 1, pp. 286–8); cf. also *Elem.*I,s. 3.

Hert's view that group-unity involves a Representative

156. Cf. *Opusc.* I, 1, p. 288 (*Quod enim de universitate dicitur, eam nec animam nec intellectum habere, non consentire nec dolo facere, hinc alienum est, quoniam universitas pars est tantum civitatis et quicquid juris spiritusve habet, accepit concessu vel expresso vel tacito compotum summae potestatis;** *atque hactenus persona est mystica, sive ex praescripto juris personae vicem sustinet; neque dubium est, quin hoc aspectu contrahere et delinquere possit*). Hert accordingly ascribes an absolute representative authority to the *Rector Civitatis* [the Head of the State], but he will only allow to the *Rector Universitatis* [the Head of a corporation] such representative authority as comes within the limits of the powers granted to him by the sovereign (note 3 to Pufend. *J. n. et g.* VII, c. 2, §§22; and *Opusc.* II, 3, p. 55).

157. *Opusc.* I, 3, pp. 27–44.
158. Ibid. II, 3, pp. 41–7.

His theory of one man with many 'persons'

159. In his treatment of the first set of cases [those in which one man sustains several persons], Hert begins by considering the possibility of the same

* 'By the concession of those who are in control (*compotes sunt*) of the supreme power.'

Notes to § 16

individual being reckoned, upon a *consideratio moralis*, as being several different persons in his different capacities (sect. 1, §§ 1–2). He proceeds to lay down some jejune general rules for such contingencies (sect. 1, §§ 3–7). He then discusses, as cases which come under these rules, (1) the union [in one man] of various rights of status which have their basis in the Family and the State (sect. 2), (2) the different capacities enjoyed simultaneously by the Emperor, and by the Estates, in the German Empire (sect. 4), and (3) the conjunction of a number of different powers [in the same individual] in the domain of private law (sect. 4).

160. In treating the second set of cases [those in which several men sustain one person], Hert begins by attempting to prove the possibility of several men uniting to form a single *persona moralis*. There are three sorts of *unum*— the *unum per se*, the *unum per accidens* and the *unum per aggregationem*—according as it is a 'natural', an 'artificial', or a 'moral' bond which unites the parts in question. A 'moral body' is brought into being by a 'moral bond', *quo per institutum humanum diversa individua ita colliguntur, ut unum esse intelligantur* (*Proleg.* §§ 1–2). He proceeds to suggest general rules for collective persons [of this moral order]. Either a *societas aequalis* or a *societas rectoria* may be the basis (§ 3): the Group-person may come to possess capacities and rights (e.g. of legislation, or the power of life and death) which belong to none of the single persons so grouped (§ 4); the associates continue to remain *certo aspectu singuli* (§ 5); the rights and duties of the collective person *non sunt singulorum nisi per consequentiam* (§ 6).

His theory of several men with one 'person'

Hert then distinguishes two 'sources' of this 'unity of persons' [in a moral body]. The one is '*Lex fingit*'; the other is '*Conventio hominum efficit*'. Under the first head—that of the feigned unity of persons (sect. 1)—he treats of *paterfamilias et filius* (§§ 1–7), of *defunctus et haeres* (§§ 8–16), of *defunctus et haereditas jacens* (§ 17), of *jus repraesentationis* (§ 18), and of *Christus et Ecclesia* (§ 19). Under the second head—that of contractual unity of persons (sect. II) —he deals with *matrimonium* (§§ 1–3), *civitas* (§§ 4–8), *universitas* (§§ 9–11), *correi debendi et credendi* (§§ 12–15), and *vasalli feudum individuum habentes* with feoffees (§ 16).

161. *Jus nat.* c. 3, § 52 (*in imperio civili imperantes soli mens civitatis sunt, etsi subjecti non carent mente, sed sapiunt ipsimet, immo aliquando imperantibus sapientiores sunt*); c. 35, § 30 (*magistratus voluntas est voluntas universorum et singulorum*); c. 37, §§ 2–3 and *Disc.* c. 34. The *persona moralis seu mystica* only appears, therefore, in Gundling's theory of the State when he is speaking of a republic: *Jus nat.* c. 35, § 34, c. 37, §§ 3–10.

Gundling holds that the State needs a representative

162. *Dissert. de universitate delinquente*, §§ 1–5. A *universitas* is only a 'multitude' united by 'consent': the object of such consent is *in unum coalescere, ut idem intelligere et velle censeantur*: from consent directed to that object *resultat unitas, cujus ratione personae mysticae vulgo audiunt, ac morales compositaeque dicuntur*.

He makes a corporation only a collective unit

163. Loc. cit. §§ 6–8. A *fictio juris* is in no way necessary to explain this Group-person. We can see for ourselves how a unity like that of an individual man comes into existence through the union of the wills of a number of men. It does not matter if it is only with the intellect, and not by sense-perception, that we realise the union of the Many in the One, and the distinction of the One from the Many. If it did matter [i.e. if sense-perception were a necessity], all *res incorporales* would be imaginary, and only what we see or hear or smell or feel or taste would be real; and that is absurd, for since there is

His rejection of the theory of fiction

no *demonstratio* without *mentis abstractio*, and no truth without demonstration, we should be driven to saying that truth itself is untrue.... Nor is a *fictio* necessary to explain the assumption of a *consensus universitatis*; for although a *consensus omnium* is not easy to attain, it none the less follows from the nature of a *universitas* (since it exists, but cannot continue to exist without motion, and must therefore necessarily choose *modus volendi aut nolendi possibilis* in order that it may set itself in motion) that 'the will of the major part should count as the will of the whole person constituted by a number of men'.

Gundling, however, admits that *universitates certo sensu artificiales sunt...quia pactis coaugmentantur quibus Hobbesius non male artificii nomen tribuit.* They are not created by nature, but by reflection and will.

His insistence on the collective principle

164. We must note, it is true, Gundling's contention (loc. cit. §§ 13-48) that a *universitas* may even be guilty of delict and suffer penalties accordingly. But it is also to be noted, first that such delict can only be committed (in his view) by the common action of all, and not by a majority or by the body of managers, and secondly that a *universitas* may also commit murder or similar crimes; while, as for the penalties of delict, it is only the guilty persons (either taken together or severally) who are affected by them, and the abolition of the corporation as such is not regarded as a possible penalty.

165. This distinction appears in Kestner, c. 7, § 3 (cf. also Hert, supra p. 122) and in Schmier, I, c. 3, II, c. 3, s. 1, §§ 1–3, V, c. 1, nos. 87sqq. and c. 2, nos. 52sqq.

Boehmer on equal and unequal societies

166. According to J. H. Boehmer, a *societas* means a *complexus plurium personarum unitarum inter se ad certum finem*: it constitutes a 'moral body', and the *spiritus* of that body is a union of the wills of all, in one will, such that *conjunctim considerati unam in moralibus repraesentent personam*. In an 'equal society', this 'union of wills' is based upon 'simple obligation'; but just for that reason it remains imperfect. In an 'unequal society'—though the ground or basis is still an 'association of equals'—the factors of *imperium* and *subjectio* are superimposed, by the 'submission of all wills to the single will of one man or of a whole council', with the result that *voluntas omnium in voluntate hujus ita concentratur, ut quod imperans summus in negotiis ad finem civitatis spectantibus vult, omnes velle moraliter censeantur.* (Cf. *Jus publ. univ. P. gen.* c. 2, § 4 n. *f*, *P. spec.* I, c. 2, §§ 1–18, c. 3, § 1 n. *o*, §§ 15–21.)

167. Cf. Heineccius, *Elem.* II, §§ 13, 115; Mullerus, I, c. 1; Wolff, *Instit.* § 839; Nettelbladt, *Syst. nat.* §§ 354–61; Achenwall, II, §§ 22–39; Daries, *Praecogn.* §§ 17–23, *P. spec.* 550sqq.; Hoffbauer, pp. 194, 199sqq., 205sqq.

The State as an unequal society

168. This view explains why the State, as a *societas perfectissima*, was regarded as beginning its existence with the substitution of an 'unequal society' for the original 'equal society' (which is sharply distinguished from 'democracy' (Boehmer, I, c. 2, §§ 6–12), and occasionally even described as 'anarchy' (Daries, §§ 651 sqq.)), when the imperfections of this equal society began to make themselves felt. It was often urged, too, in the strength of this view, that unity was more perfect in a monarchy than in a republic, where the Ruler in his nature reflected and represented an 'equal society'.

Corporations as equal societies

169. The family system of government was generally the only 'unequal society' which was recognised, other than the State; and all corporations, including the Church, were interpreted as being 'equal societies'; cf. § 18, infra [on the natural-law theory of corporations].

Difference of monarchy and republic

170. This is the reason why we often find the conception of the *persona moralis civitatis* treated as entirely irrelevant in regard to monarchy, and only

applied to republics: cf. Gundling, in n. 161 supra. Ickstatt expressly says that in a monarchy, where the king represents the whole State and all its members, *totius Reipublicae intellectus atque voluntas in intellectum et voluntatem personae moralis simplicis resolvitur*; whereas 'Polyarchy', or the government of Many, involves a *persona moralis composita*: *Opusc.* II, op. 1, c. 1, §§ 14–16 and 66.

171. Thus J. H. Boehmer applies the conception of the *persona moralis* of the State only in the sphere of international law: *P. gen.* c. 2, §§ 3–7, *P. spec.* I, c. 3, § 22.

172. We have already noticed, in n. 160 above, the lengths to which Hert was prepared to go in this direction.

173. Like Pufendorf and Hert (supra, n. 139 and nn. 157–60), Nettelbladt, in his *Syst. nat.* §§ 82 and 1194 and *Syst. pos.* § 16, and C. von Schlözer, in the *De jure suffragii*, § 11, both draw this parallel.

174. Heineccius allows that every 'society', including the State, is only the result of *consensus duorum pluriumve in eundem finem eademque media, quae ad finem illum obtinendum sunt necessaria*; but he also holds that—in view of the fact that 'one will and one mind' arise, either through *conspiratio in unum* or through *submissio omnium voluntatum* to the will of a Ruler—*omnis societas est una persona moralis*, and possesses, as such, like duties, rights, and even 'affections' (e.g. life, sickness and death) with the individual. Accordingly, he argues, every society confronts not only other societies and individuals, but also its own *socii*, as a distinct 'Subject' or owner of rights (*Elem.* II, §§ 13–25, 115). *Heineccius on the unity of a society*

175. Wolff's general theory of societies (*Instit.* §§ 836–53) is based throughout on the idea of a contract directed to the attainment of common ends by common means; and it is from this contract that he derives the whole system of law, and of rights and duties, which regulates the internal life of corporations—including the authority which 'all taken together' [*allen insgesammt*] exercise over 'individuals'. It is only in its external relations, he holds, that 'each society, because its members act with united forces, appears as a single person'; and it is particularly in this sphere (of their external relations to one another) that 'a number of different societies are to be viewed as if they were so many free individual persons'. Wolff thus finds no difficulty in describing a 'moral person' as the owner in any case of joint property where a number of persons are each deemed to have a share, since in such a case that 'number of persons, taken together, are treated as a single person, and what is true of an individual owner is true of them when taken together' (§ 196). [Not only does he thus recognise the simple 'moral person': he also recognises compound 'moral persons'.] He treats the Family as being a *societas composita*, because the members of which it is composed are not mere 'physical individuals', as they are in a 'simple society', but are 'whole societies which are treated as single moral persons', i.e. the society of husband and wife, the society of father and child, and the society of master and servant (§ 977). *Wolff's theory of Groups*

On the other hand [and while he thus recognises a variety of moral persons], Wolff regards even the moral personality of the State itself as nothing more than 'the whole community', in the sense of the sum total of all individuals, including the Ruler (§ 1030); and the result is, that while he thinks that international law can be based on the character of States as 'free persons living in a natural state' (§§ 977 and 1088), he never mentions the State as a person in dealing with its system of [internal] public law.

Daries'
scheme of
associations

176. Daries begins by constructing a comprehensive scheme of *jus sociale in genere* on the basis of a conception of *societas* which makes it a *status per quem personae in personam competit jus perfectum atque affirmativum*—or, in other words, a condition which involves a nexus of legal relations by which individuals are either connected with one another by equal rights and duties, or are set over against one another as rulers and ruled (§§ 517–61). On this basis he proceeds to interpret all societies, up to and including 'civil society' or the State (§§ 562 sqq.). In dealing with the State, he distinguishes the two sorts of nexus between its members—the nexus between the *imperans* and his subjects, and that of the subjects with one another (§§ 661)—but he makes the *imperans* the one and only 'Subject' of [political] rights (§§ 655 sqq.). He applies the conception of the 'moral person' only in regard to the external relations of a group [and not in regard to its inward unity]. Cf. *Praecogn.* § 24, *plures homines, quibus ad commune aliquid obtinendum concessa sunt jura, in uno eodemque statu morali vivunt atque ideo unam personam moralem constituunt.*

Nettelbladt's
theory of
associations

177. Nettelbladt lays the foundation [for his general view of associations] in his theory of *jurisprudentia naturalis generalis socialis* (as stated in his *Syst. nat.* §§ 362–414). In expounding this theory he starts from the definition of *societas* as a *conjunctio plurium hominum ad eundem finem conjunctis viribus obtinendum*, and then proceeds to develop in advance all the conceptions by the aid of which he afterwards explains the rights and duties of Family, Corporation, Church and State.

178. This is especially the case [i.e. Nettelbladt is forced to set the whole over against individuals] in regard to the 'equal society' which possesses *potestas*; for here authority over the individual *socii* is ascribed to the *societas ipsa*, and not, as in an 'unequal society', to an *imperans*, or, as in societies without *potestas*, to an *extraneus* (§§ 335–46 and 355–6). But Nettelbladt hastens to add that *societas* is to be understood, in such a case, as signifying only *omnes socii simul sumpti*.

179. Cf. *Syst. nat.* §§ 83–6, 329–30, 335, and *Syst. pos.* §§ 17 and 865. Nettelbladt does not seek to invoke the idea of a 'fiction' in this connection: he prefers to think that *tum...eorum intellectus, voluntates et vires sunt ut unus intellectus, una voluntas et una vis, sicque ab uno homine non nisi in corporum numero differunt, quae differentia hic non est attendenda* (§ 84). He also argues that while the conceptions of birth and death are not applicable to such a person, its origin may be compared to birth and its dissolution to death (§ 85). But he always identifies the 'moral person' with *plura individua humana simul sumpta* (§ 83); and thus he says of the State, *Cives alicujus Reipublicae simul sumti persona moralis sunt, quae est ipsa Respublica* (*Syst. nat.* § 1122; cf. §§ 1132–3, 1200, 1403 sqq.).

Achenwall's
theory of
associations

180. Cf. *Proleg.* §§ 92–3: a *societas*, as a body of men, *considerata generatim, abstrahendo nempe ab iis quae hoc vel illud singulum ejus membrum concernunt, spectari nequit nisi tanquam ens unum.* Since it is a whole of which the parts are men, it has the same natural rights and duties as each of its members, except in so far as the 'very nature of society' constitutes a difference. It is therefore a person, though it is called a 'moral' or a 'mystical person', or a 'moral' or a 'mystical body', to distinguish it from the individual, who is a 'single person'; and the whole system of the natural rights and duties of individuals is accordingly applicable to it, except in so far as *diversa hominis individui et societatis natura* makes modifications necessary. These modifications are then developed in II, §§ 16–21.

Notes to §16

181. Note, in this connection [i.e. as showing the individualistic basis of Achenwall's thought], the account which he gives, in developing his theory of *societas in genere* (II, §§ 2–40), of *jus sociale universum internum* (ibid. §§ 5–13). He always interprets this *jus* as consisting in the reciprocal rights and duties which belong to individuals as *socii*—i.e. the rights and duties which spring from their 'social juridical nexus', and are thus to be distinguished from their rights and duties as *homines*; though if more than two members are concerned [so that it is a case not of *A* versus *B*, but of *A* + *B* etc. versus *C*], he regards the sum of reciprocal rights and duties as involving a *jus sociale universorum in singulos singulique cujuslibet in universos*. On this basis, in an 'equal society' in which the 'right and obligation of all' are the same, there is no internal unity of the group transcending the aggregate of *universi*, and the *voluntas societatis qua unius personae* is thus identical with the *communis consensus sociorum* (II, §§ 22–31). In an 'unequal society', on the other hand, there is added to the collective unity [i.e. the unity of the aggregate of *universi*], which also exists in such a society [just as it does an 'equal society'], the further factor of representation of all, to a greater or less degree, by the *imperium* (II, §§ 32–9).

Achenwall's individualism

182. Already in his *Prolegomena* (§ 92) we find Achenwall contending that the conception of the 'moral person' can only be applied to any society *respectu non-sociorum*, and that it is therefore limited to 'particular societies'. (It cannot apply to the 'universal society of all men',* the existence of which is supposed in *Proleg.* §§ 82–90 and in I, §§ 43–4.) Accordingly, he only introduces the 'moral person' into his general theory of society when he is dealing with *externum jus sociale* (II, §§ 14–22); cf. the dictum in §15, *quum socii conjunctis viribus ad communem finem agant, atque ideo jura ac obligationes cum tali fine talique virium usu connexae ipsis communes sint, societas est persona moralis et ab exteris tanquam talis spectari debet et potest*. While holding this merely Collective conception, he finds no difficulty in regarding the Family—with its three relationships of husband and wife, parents and children, master and servant—as a 'compound society' whose members are 'mystical' and not 'individual' persons (*Proleg.* § 94, II, §§ 78 sqq.).

He reduces Groups to collective bodies

183. He says of the State (I, pp. 32 sqq.) that from the union of the powers and wills [of individuals] with the commands of its Head 'there arises a Whole, a composite being independent of other societies, which evinces itself in action determined by its own understanding and will, and is therefore capable of having rights and obligations—in other words, a civil society, a people'. In the same way he describes societies other than the State as 'composite persons' (III, pp. 244 sqq.). See also I, pp. 64 and 157 sqq., III, pp. 408 sqq., and n. 120 supra.

Scheidemantel has some idea of a Group-person

184. This had been the theory adopted—after Grotius had set the example (see n. 74 to § 14)—by Pufendorf (n. 145 to this section), Thomasius (*Instit. jur. div.* III, c. 6, § 64), Gundling (n. 163 to this section), Wolff (*Instit.* §§ 841–5, where it is argued that by the nature of society all must concur in an agreement that the will of the majority shall be regarded as being the will of all), and Nettelbladt (§ 388, where the majority-principle is said to exist by the very nature of the *persona moralis*, and by virtue of *jura societatis socialia*). The fullest argument in favour of this view is to be found in Ickstatt, *de jure majorum in conclusis civitatis communibus formandis* (*Opusc.* II, op. 1).

The basis of the rights of majorities on the old view

* It cannot apply to the 'universal society,' because that society, as its name indicates, includes all men, and there are therefore no *non-socii*.

He appeals, in the first place, to the nature of the 'moral person', as a unity possessed of reason and will, which must determine its decisions, in any case of *motiva disparia*, by the *motiva fortiora*—though it is only the external [or quantitative], and not the internal [or qualitative], weight of 'motives' that can settle the issue. He then adduces, as a further argument, the possibility of removing a dead-lock between the different elements of the group-will which is provided by the use of majority-decision; and he also appeals to practical exigencies. But he maintains, notwithstanding (c. 1, §§ 65-68), that the majority-principle is based on *pactum* [which is somewhat inconsistent with the idea that majority-decision proceeds from the nature of the moral person as a unity].

A peculiar view appears in Daries (§§ 750-62), who, in the spirit of primitive Teutonic law, demands unanimity, though he also assumes an *obligatio perfecta* of the minority to accede to the decision of the majority.

New demand for unanimity

185. In his treatment of what he calls this 'great controversy', Christian von Schlözer (*De jure suffragii*, §§ 9-14) cites Grotius, Locke, Pufendorf, Petroni, Cocceji and Schlettwein as supporters of the earlier '*communis opinio*' which regarded the validity of the majority-principle as derived from Natural Law. He describes the opinion of Wolff (unjustly) as doubtful. The main authorities he cites for his own view (which makes only unanimous decisions valid *per se*) are Hobbes—whose real doctrine, as stated in n. 74 to this section, is very different—and Rousseau. He also cites Achenwall (who does, as a matter of fact, identify the *voluntas societatis qua unius personae* with the *communis sensus sociorum*, II, §§ 24-8, and treats the validity of majority-decisions as a deviation—though a useful deviation—from the general rule of unanimity, secured by a special contract to that effect); and he cites in addition Wedekind, Höpfner, Köhler and Schmalz.

A. L. von Schlözer on the idea of the People

186. According to A. L. von Schlözer 'majesty' belongs originally to the people; but since the people is 'the whole of all the children of men', it can do as little with its sovereignty as a child can do with a fief which has fallen to it. Any real sovereignty of the people [as a whole] is altogether inconceivable, because the integrity of such sovereignty has already been destroyed [in any existing form of the so-called sovereignty of the people which we can actually observe] by the exclusion of women, minors and paupers, by the introduction of the majority-principle, and by the erection of a representative assembly: cf. p. 97, § 3 and pp. 157-61. [Since the people can thus do nothing with its original sovereignty], that sovereignty is devolved upon a Ruler, who may be either a number of persons or a single person; but if a number of persons be the Ruler, a '*Unum morale* must be pretended by that number' [i.e. they must feign themselves to be a single unit]: cf. pp. 73-8, 113, § 1. Schlözer proceeds to describe such a collective Ruler as a 'being composed of several individuals' or a '*corpus*'; but [though he thus seems to recognise group-existence,] he really remains a thorough-going individualist, even to the extent of holding that in a republic 'a new Ruler is created for each new decision of the government' [because a new majority composed of different individuals has to be created], and therefore a 'momentary Ruler' is all that can exist in such a State: cf. p. 113, § 2, p. 125, § 9, p. 131, § 13.

The common will a sum of wills

187. The 'common will', which (he remarks) thinkers from Rousseau onwards have irresponsibly identified with the 'common man',* is nothing

* Or, as we might express it, the 'general will' (which is the term that Rousseau really uses) is too readily identified with the 'general run' of people. Or again, to

but the 'sum of all individual wills'; and therefore it is only sovereign in pre-political society, where pure unanimity is the rule. In the organised State, even if it be an extreme democracy, it is always a number of particular persons, or a single person, which wills and decides for all. The people, which gives such persons or person their commission, is simply tricked, by means of frequent elections, into thinking that it wills and decides through its representatives; or it is dazzled with the illusory idea that 'law is the true sovereign'—the fact being that law, as an abstract thing, can only act through men [and therefore can only be sovereign through the person, or persons, who declare and enforce it]. Cf. pp. 76–7 [of A. L. von Schlözer's *Allgemeines Staatsrecht*, which Gierke is paraphrasing here, as in the previous note].

188. The social contract, according to A. L. von Schlözer, produces only a 'union of powers'; and a 'union of wills' first arises through a supplementary contract of government, by which each man promises that 'others shall will instead of him, and that he will acknowledge this will, external to himself, as his own will, and shall be compelled, if he break his word, to recognise that it is his will'. It is this fact (that 'the most part renounce their will, and transfer it to one man, or to a number of men, or to the majority') which is the basis of majority-decisions, representative assemblies and the rights of rulers; op. cit. pp. 76–9, 93, §1. The Ruler, being able to will and decide for all, is the 'depository of the common will'; pp. 95 and 100. *The will of the Ruler as representative*

189. C. von Schlözer, *De jure suff. in soc. aeq.* (of the year 1795), §11. In agreement with the theory of his father (A. L. von Schlözer), he adds that the *societas mere talis* is only a 'union of powers' to begin with; a new 'pact', by which each man surrenders his will, is necessary before a 'union of wills' can exist, and the comparison with a *persona* is only permissible when that pact has been concluded. He proceeds (§12) to attack the other arguments of the advocates of the majority-principle, on whom he significantly seeks to impose the burden of proof (§10). He frankly holds that any decision of any society requires an agreement of *all* its members, depending on their *pactum et consensus* (§9); and accordingly he will only recognise a decision by the *major pars* if it is based on special *pacta adjecta* to that effect (§15)—with the proviso that these *pacta adjecta* can never extend to the *pacta fundamentalia*, or the *jura singulorum*, or affect either (§18). He will not even allow that the absent are automatically bound by the vote of those present (§13): such a principle can only be introduced by *specialia pacta* (§19). *C. von Schlözer on the majority-principle*

190. Cf. p. 190: 'the conception of a moral person can thus be understood in the broad sense in which it includes every collective "Subject" or owner of rights and duties, whether such collective "Subject" be a society or no'. See also pp. 53, 66, 106, 206, 244, 292, 307 sqq., 310, 317 sqq. *Hoffbauer's theory of groups*

put the matter in another way, we may say that the *volonté générale* properly means a will that is general in respect of the quality of the object willed (which is the general good), but tends to be identified with a will that is general only in respect of the quantity of the subjects willing (or the general mass of the people). The confusion is inherent in Rousseau's thought; but it must be added, in fairness to Rousseau, that he did attempt to reconcile the two conceptions, feeling that the general mass, by the process of discussion of ideas which is the essence of the democratic system, was most likely to arrive at a general sense of what was really for the general good. In other words, the process of general thought, in the general body of a community, is the right way to the general good, which is the object of the general will and the sovereign standard of community-life.

324 Gierke's Notes

Hoffbauer's theory of Groups

191. Pp. 191 sqq. and 199 sqq.: originally, unanimity was alone valid, but the majority-principle may be introduced by means of a unanimous resolution, provided that it be understood that the majority-principle has no validity in regard to the constitution, or as against the rights of a member.

192. Pp. 205 sqq.: accordingly (Hoffbauer argues) it is the Ruler alone—or some 'society' which participates in Ruling authority—that appears in the area of internal public law as a 'moral person' (pp. 244, 246, 292, 307, 310); and the People itself appears as a person only in the area of [external, or] international law (pp. 317 sqq.).

193. W. von Humboldt's *Ideen*, p. 130; cf. §18 infra [on the natural-law theory of corporations].

194. See, more especially, II, c. 7, §89, c. 8, §§95–9, c. 12, §145.

195. II, c. 8, §96.

Locke on the majority-principle

196. II, c. 8, §§97–9: without a provision to that effect, the original contract would not achieve its aim of ending the state of nature; it would not produce at all, or would only produce for a brief space, a society with the qualities of a 'body incorporated': it would thus be without significance, and not a real contract at all.

Rousseau on the moi commun *of the body politic*

197. I, c. 6: *à l'instant, au lieu de la personne particulière de chaque contractant, cet acte d'association produit un corps moral et collectif composé d'autant de membres que l'assemblée a de voix, lequel reçoit de ce même action son unité, son moi commun, sa vie et sa volonté*. [The reader will readily note, in this passage as elsewhere in the *Contrat Social*, how much Rousseau is indebted to the writers of the School of Natural Law alike for his thought and his vocabulary. His *personne particulière* is the usual *persona singularis*: his *corps moral et collectif* is the *corpus morale collectivum*. We may almost say that the vogue of Rousseau depends on the fact that a great master of style gave to the world of letters, and the general reader, a system of thought which had hitherto been expressed mainly in Latin, and written by lawyers for lawyers.]

See in addition II, c. 2, on the indivisibility of sovereignty which issues from the unity of the *corps social*; II, c. 4, on the nature of sovereignty as an absolute power which the social body necessarily possesses over its members, just as the individual has *un pouvoir absolu sur ses membres*; and III, cc. 10–11, on the sickness, age and death to which *corps politiques* are subject in the same way as the physical bodies of men, and on the art of prolonging their existence (*le corps politique, aussi bien que le corps de l'homme, commence à mourir dès sa naissance, et porte en lui-même les causes de sa destruction*). [On the birth and death of 'moral bodies' cf. supra, nn. 174 and 179.]

Its personne morale *the 'Subject' of Sovereignty*

198. Cf. I, c. 6, where Rousseau explains that the *personne publique*, which is constituted by the union of all other persons, is called *République* or *corps politique*, but that it is also termed by its members (1) *État*, when it is passive, (2) *Souverain*, when it is active, and (3) *Puissance*, when it is compared with similar bodies outside. Cf. also I, c. 7, where he speaks of a *personne morale*, or *être de raison*, which in regard to foreign bodies is *un être simple, un individu*, and in regard to its subjects is *le Souverain*: II, c. 1, where he speaks of *un être collectif*; and II, c. 4, where a *personne morale* is made the 'Subject' of political authority.

Its volonté générale

199. II, c. 3: *Il y a souvent bien de la différence entre la volonté de tous et la volonté générale; celle-ci ne regarde qu'à l'intérêt commun, l'autre regarde à l'intérêt privé et n'est qu'une somme de volontés particulières: mais ôtez de ces mêmes volontés les plus et les moins qui s'entredétruisent, reste pour somme des différences la volonté*

Notes to § 16

générale. [It is interesting to compare Rousseau, on this fundamental matter, with Pufendorf: see nn. 131, 132, 136. There is of course a difference; but Pufendorf is the rock from which Rousseau hewed.]

200. IV, c. 2, where we also find an argument to prove that liberty is not destroyed by this agreement to respect majority-decisions. It is my own will that the *volonté générale* should be law: if I am out-voted, that shows that my view about the *volonté générale* was mistaken. I really willed what is now shown to be the *volonté générale*, and I did not really will what is now shown to be only my *volonté particulière*. Cf. also II, c. 2 n. *Rousseau on majority-decisions*

201. It is presumably always directed to what is right and beneficial: it is incorruptible, simple and clear, without subtleties, and attained with little if any debate. It will not, and cannot, decree anything contrary to equality and justice: no guarantees are needed against it; and all that is required is the prevention of any deception. Cf. I, c. 7; II, cc. 3–4; IV, c. 1. *On the quality of general will*

202. I, c. 6: *à l'égard des associés, ils prennent collectivement le nom du peuple, et s'appellent en particulier Citoyens, comme participans à l'autorité souveraine, et Sujets comme soumis aux lois de l'État.*

203. It follows that the size of the State diminishes liberty. With 10,000 citizens, each has one ten-thousandth part of sovereign power 'for his share': with 100,000, only one hundred-thousandth part; but in both cases each is *soumis tout entier*. Cf. III, c. 1.

204. I, c. 7; each pledges himself by the social contract *sous un double rapport: comme membre du Souverain envers les particuliers, et comme membre de l'État envers le Souverain*; a contract thus made *avec lui-même* is possible, because each contracts *envers un tout dont on fait partie*. Cf. II, c. 4.

205. I, c. 7; II, cc. 1–2; III, c. 16.

206. But the Sovereign can never incur such obligations towards a third party as contravene the act on which its own existence depends: I, c. 7.

207. The reason why the Sovereign can never bind itself as a whole to its members is this (I, c. 7): the body politic, being only able to view itself always under one and the same *rapport*, would by contracting with one of its own members be *dans le cas d'un particulier contractant avec soi-même* [i.e. since the sovereign is, and must always regard itself as being, identical with its members, it cannot contract with what is itself, any more than an individual can contract with himself. But the original contract of society is apparently an exception to this rule; cf. n. 204 supra.] *His Sovereign can never bind itself to its subjects*

208. III, c. 12–14. Any formal exclusion of a single citizen annuls the general will (II, c. 2 n.).

209. Cf. III, cc. 14, 18: cf. also the argument, in III, c. 11, that the sovereign will of yesterday does not bind that of to-day (*la loi d'hier n'oblige pas aujourd'hui*), and therefore the validity of [past] laws depends on the presumption that the sovereign is always confirming them tacitly by not revoking them.* *Yesterday's will not binding to-day*

210. III, c. 12: the sovereign can only act *quand le peuple est assemblé*.

211. Cf. II, c. 1: *le Souverain qui n'est qu'un être collectif ne peut être représenté que par lui-même*. Cf. also III, c. 15: sovereignty can no more be represented than it can be alienated, because though power can be transferred to others, *Rousseau on representation*

---

* Cf. Paine's *Rights of Man*, where the same idea is applied to each generation: 'Altho' laws made in one generation often continue in force through succeeding generations, yet...they continue to derive their force from the consent of the living ...and the non-repealing passes for consent'.

will cannot be: elected deputies of the people cannot be representatives, but only commissaries or delegates. What *le Peuple en personne* does not enact is not law; the people which is 'represented' is no longer free, and no longer a people.

The 'organic' metaphor in Rousseau

212. Although the legislative power is compared to the heart of the body politic, and the executive to its brain, and the importance of both for political life is measured by that comparison (III, c. 11), this solitary reference to the analogy of the organism remains without influence on Rousseau's general interpretation of Group-personality. [But cf. also note 197 supra.]

Rousseau's view of 'Government'

213. III, cc. 1–5, 16–17. The *gouvernement* is *un corps intermédiaire* between the Sovereign and the members of the State: it is *un tout subalterne dans le tout*; it is a new *personne morale dans la personne publique*. Since its province is simply the execution of the sovereign will, and since, in its capacity of *ministre du Souverain*, it holds a commission which can be limited at will and is always subject to recall, the 'government' has no will of its own, but has merely *une vie empruntée et subordonnée*. None the less it requires, if it is to fulfil its object, a unity of its own and its own special qualifications; and it therefore develops, in virtue of the authority with which it is vested, *une vie réelle, un moi particulier, une sensibilité commune à ses membres, une force et une volonté propre, qui tend à la conservation*. It is thus, in small, *ce que le corps politique qui le renferme est en grand*. There are different ways in which it may be constituted, but it is always a Whole with a definite totality of power, part of which it employs in order to keep its own members in co-operation, while it retains the rest for the purpose of acting upon the whole people. Three wills meet in this government—the individual wills of its component members; the common will of them all; and the general will of the whole State—but in a perfect condition of things the first of these would be non-existent, and the second would only be the expression of the third.

It is a collective person

214. In III, c. 1, Rousseau terms the 'person' of the government a *personne morale et collective, unie par la force des lois et dépositaire dans l'État de la puissance exécutive*. Its essential difference from the sovereign 'person', he holds, consists in the fact that it only exists in virtue of the Sovereign, and not, like the Sovereign, *per se*. As a whole, it is called the 'Prince'; and its members, who may be collective persons themselves in their turn,* are called 'magistrates'. In a monarchy, however, the government (according to III, c. 6) is identical with a '*personne naturelle*': *toute au contraire des autres administrations, où un être collectif représente un individu, dans celle-ci un individu représente un être collectif*.

215. Filangieri (I, cc. 1 and 11; VII, c. 53) follows Rousseau's theory entirely.

Sieyès generally follows Rousseau

216. Cf. Sieyès, I, pp. 50 sqq., 129, 144 ('a political society cannot be anything but the associated members of such society when taken together'), 167, 445 sqq.; II, pp. 195 sqq.

217. Cf. I, p. 129: the common will is a unity, but its essential elements are the wills of individuals; only they are no longer isolated. Cf. also I, p. 145, where it is said that 'the will of the individual is the only element in the social will'; and I, p. 167, where the will of the Nation is said to be 'the result of the will of the individual, because the nation is a sum of individuals', and where it is argued accordingly that this will can never be mediated or

* I.e. a 'college' of magistrates, which, as such, is a collective person, may be one of the parts of government.

expressed by estates or corporations, but only by heads [i.e. by direct individual suffrage], on the basis of a general unity and equality. Similarly Sieyès remarks (I, p. 207) that the common will of a social group 'must naturally be the general sum of the wills of all individuals'; cf. also pp. 431 sqq.

218. Cf. I, pp. 144–5, 167, 207–8: for the future, he argues, we must ascribe the quality of a general will to the will of a majority: this is based on the fact that each submits himself freely in advance, with a reservation of the right to emigrate [if he disagrees with the majority-will]: his staying in the country is a tacit confirmation of the obligation he originally assumed; and thus the common will always continues to be the sum of individual wills.

219. For Sieyès' views on representation see I, pp. 68 sqq., 129–30 (where he speaks of government conducted by proxy, and of the representative will of an assembly of deputies, in which the common will is, as it were, in commission); 134, 149 sqq., 195 sqq., 208 sqq. (where deputies are described as representatives, with a general mandate, which remains none the less at the free disposal of those who gave it, and is thus revocable as well as limited, so that the decision of the representatives is 'the product of the generality of the wills of all individuals'); 375 sqq., 385 sqq., II, pp. 275 sqq. and 372–4 (where it is argued that everything in the social state is a matter of representation, and that men increase their liberty when they allow themselves to be represented in as many ways as possible, just as they diminish it when they accumulate a number of different representative capacities in one person). *But Sieyès admits representation*

220. Cf. II, pp. 371 sqq.: there is, essentially, only one political authority, but there are different forms of representation based on different mandates.

221. This is the case with Scheidemantel, the Schlözers (father and son), and Hoffbauer; cf. pp. 126–7 supra, and nn. 183 and 186–90 to this section.

222. Cf. Fichte's *Naturrecht*, II, pp. 19–21 (*Works*, III, pp. 204–6): it is only 'hypothetically' that the individual is also a subject, for he only becomes such *if* he fails to fulfil his duties. Cf. also *Works*, VII, pp. 153 sqq. *Fichte and Rousseau*

223. See, for all this, the *Naturrecht*, II, pp. 15–18 (*Works*, III, pp. 202–4): cf. also II, pp. 23–4 (*Works*, III, pp. 207–8).

224. *Naturrecht*, II, pp. 17, 19, 23–4, 34 sqq. (*Works*, III, pp. 203, 204, 207–8, 215 sqq.). In the later *Rechtslehre* (*Posthumous Works*, II, pp. 495 and 632) he still holds that the whole is only the 'totality of the members', and that there can be nothing in the whole which does not exist in a part.

225. Thus he remarks that 'physical, or mystical, persons' may either of them exercise public authority, but he proceeds to explain a 'mystical person' as being the majority at any given time, and therefore as 'frequently also a variable person'; *Naturrecht*, I, pp. 191 and 195 (*Works*, III, pp. 159 and 161). Again, arguing that marriage is a natural and moral society, he counts husband and wife as 'one person', and he draws the conclusion that, within the household, there is complete community of property, though externally the one 'juridical person' is represented by the husband alone, who can act for his wife along with himself: similarly a married couple, as one juridical person, has only one vote, which is given by the man, though his wife may also give it on his behalf in the popular assembly if he be prevented from doing so; but unmarried and independent women have their own right to vote (*Naturrecht*, II, pp. 158 sqq. and 213 sqq. = *Works*, III, pp. 304 sqq. and 343 sqq.). Cf. also II, p. 1 = *Works*, III, p. 191. *Fichte on moral persons*

226. *Naturrecht*, II, p. 250 = *Works*, III, p. 371: *Rechtslehre*, p. 638.

227. *Naturrecht*, I, pp. 122 sqq. and 180 sqq. = *Works*, III, pp. 102 sqq. and 150 sqq.: *Rechtslehre*, pp. 507 sqq. and 627 sqq. No account can be given here of the subtle chain of deduction by which Fichte attempts, in his *Naturrecht*, to solve 'by a strict method' the problem 'of finding a will such that it is simply impossible for it to be other than the common will, or, in other words, a will in which private will and common will are synthetically united'; nor can we attempt to describe the modifications in the solution of this problem which are introduced in the *Rechtslehre*.

Fichte on the majority-principle

228. *Naturrecht*, Introduction, III, and vol. I, pp. 198, 217 sqq., 225 sqq. = *Works*, III, pp. 16, 164, 178 sqq., 184 sqq. Absolute unanimity is needed not only for the political contract, but also for every alteration of a 'constitution based on Right and Reason' (though *any* person may take in hand the transformation of a constitution which is not based on Right into one which is): relative unanimity is sufficient for the election of individual magistrates, and also for decisions of the people in regard to a magistracy or Ephorate which has offended against Right, i.e. a very considerable majority (say seven-eighths) may exclude dissentients from [participating in the action of] the State on such issues.

229. *Naturrecht*, I, pp. 179 sqq., 196, 201 sqq., 206, 210–16, 222 sqq. = *Works*, III, pp. 150 sqq., 163, 166 sqq., 170, 173–7, 182 sqq.; see also *Works*, IV, pp. 238 sqq. For the exercise of its sovereignty the People must assemble as the 'community', though in great States it need not assemble in one place, but may gather 'here and there in really considerable bodies'.

Fichte on representation and on 'Ephors'

230. *Naturrecht*, I, pp. 179 sqq. and 192 sqq. = *Works*, III, pp. 150 sqq. and 160 sqq. In order that the common will, which shows itself primarily in the unanimous will of all, may always remain a really common will, the exercise of public authority must be transferred to one or more persons (the Executive), and this transference involves in its turn the appointment of representatives of the people to watch the Executive (the Ephorate, or body of 'overseers'). The reason which Fichte gives is significant: since both the law-breakers and the injured persons, who represent private wills, are simultaneously also members of the community, it follows that the community [if *it* attempted to deal with the conflict, instead of leaving it to its representatives] would be both judge and party to the suit in the case at issue between the two sides. [We may note that Fichte's 'Ephorate' has an ancestry: it goes back through Althusius to Calvin, cf. supra p. 248.]

The People always finally Sovereign

231. *Naturrecht*, I, pp. 192, 204–9, 224 = *Works*, III, pp. 160, 169–73, 183: thus he speaks of the responsibility not only of the government, but also of the ephorate; of the final decision of the community; of the right of revolution in the last resort; and of the total cancellation, by the community's immediate declaration of its will, of any assumption seeming to suggest the *expression* of that will by those who are really its *executors*.

232. *Naturrecht*, I, pp. 213–15 = *Works*, III, pp. 175–7.

233. Such an organic conception appears in the *Grundzüge des gegenwärtigen Zeitalters* (*Works*, VII, pp. 144 sqq.), the *Reden an die deutschen Nation* (ibid. pp. 380 sqq.), and the *Staatslehre* (ibid. IV, pp. 409 sqq. and 419 sqq.).

234. In particular, he never attains any conception of the State's personality.

235. See Kant's *Metaphysik der Sitten*, *Works*, VII, pp. 1 and 20.

236. *Works*, VII, pp. 120–3 and 142–6.

237. *Works*, VII, pp. 161 and 165, and the essay *Zum ewigen Frieden*, VI, pp. 405 sqq. Kant derives the whole of international law from the axiom that States stand to one another in the position of 'moral persons' in the state of nature—subject, however, to an obligation of Right that they should enter into a system of legal relations. Arguing that it is wrong to abolish the existence of the State as a moral person, and to turn it instead into a mere 'thing', he deduces from that argument the illegality of arrangements by which one State can acquire another, as if it were a thing, through inheritance, purchase, exchange or donation, or by which 'States can marry one another', as has hitherto been the usage in Europe [cf. *tu, felix Austria, nube*]. *Kant's view of States as moral persons*

238. The three powers are 'the united common will expressed in three persons' (*Works*, VII, p. 131): they are 'co-ordinated' with one another 'as so many moral persons'; but at the same time they are also 'subordinated', under a system by which each of them, 'while commanding in the capacity of a separate person, issues its commands under the limits imposed by the will of a person who is superior' (ibid. VII, p. 134). The supreme Head of the State can be either 'a physical or a moral person' (ibid. VI, p. 323; VII, p. 134): the high court of justice is 'a moral person' (ibid. VII, pp. 25 and 97): People and Sovereign, 'legally considered, are...always two separate moral persons' (VII, p. 138). *Authorities in the State moral persons in Kant's view*

239. Kant often opposes the 'State', in the sense of the Ruler, to the 'people' (e.g. VI, pp. 418 and 421); but, conversely, he often defines the 'State' as 'a union of a multitude of men under rules of law' (VII, p. 131), and he thus identifies it with the 'People' (VII, p. 133). *Kant on State and People*

240. *Works*, VI, pp. 327 sqq., VII, pp. 131 and 133. The people becomes a State when *omnes ut singuli* surrender their external freedom, in order to receive it back again at once *ut universi*, 'as parts of a common existence, i.e. of the people regarded as a State'; all now decide about all, and therefore each about himself; and since no man can do wrong to himself, this is the origin, and the only origin, of binding law.

241. *Works*, VI, pp. 327–8 and 416–20, VII, pp. 54, 62–3, 66–7, 106, 131–2. Kant always speaks of the 'will of the whole people', 'the agreement of all', 'the united will of a whole people', 'a collectively general (or common) will vested with power', 'the united will of all', 'the consentient and united wills of all', etc. In doing so, however, he limits the right to join in expressing this will to those who have the right to vote—a class which does not include those who work for wages—though he admits the principle of equal voting by heads within this class (VI, pp. 327–8). *Kant on the will of the People*

242. *Works*, VI, pp. 328–9; cf. pp. 331 and 336, where the Supreme Head of the State appears as the 'representative' or 'agent' of the sovereign power, and where it is argued accordingly that 'his will gives commands to his subjects, as citizens, only because he represents the general will'.

243. Cf. VII, pp. 36–7, where Kant, arguing that the theory of law, like that of morals, is a theory of duties, contends that man can and must be considered, from the standpoint of such theory, 'in the light of his attribute of possessing capacity for freedom—a capacity which is wholly supra-sensual —and therefore in the light of his pure human character, as a personality independent of physical determination, in contradistinction to himself in his other character of a being affected by such determination, i.e. a member of the human species (*homo phaenomenon*).' See also p. 153, n. E, where Kant *Kant on 'phenomenal' and 'noumenal' Man*

explains that a subject who is undergoing a penalty is, as such, a different person from the 'co-legislator' who enacts the penal law. 'When I pass a penal law against myself as a law-breaker, what happens is that the pure law-giving Reason in me (the *homo noumenon*) subjects me to that law as one capable of breaking it, and therefore as another person (the *homo phaenomenon*), at the same time that it subjects all the other members of the civic association'. Cp. the consequences derived from this distinction [of noumenal and phenomenal man] in the *Tugendlehre* (pp. 195 sqq., 222, 241 sqq., 244 sqq.), where they are made to include (1) the possibility of a duty which one must enforce upon oneself, (2) the absolute value of persons, as ends in themselves, and never means to ends outside themselves, and (3) the possibility of being one's own court of law.

244. Cf. *Works*, VI, pp. 329 sqq., VII, pp. 158–9 and especially p. 173.

The survival of the 'organic' metaphor

245. We find such analogies with the organism drawn by a number of writers. Spinoza (cf. *Tract. pol.* c. 2, § 15, c. 3, §§ 1, 2, 5, and *Eth.* IV, prop. 18 schol.) generally describes the *civitas* as *unum corpus* with *una mens*. Pufendorf (*J. n. et g.* VIII, c. 12, § 7) expounds a theory of the 'three species of bodies' (natural, artificial and moral); and ascribing to the moral species a unity which is produced by a *vinculum morale*, and remains constant through all the changes in its composition, he concludes that the State, as an example of the moral species, *est res quaedam unica et continens, animalis instar*. Hertius, in the *De modo const.* sect. 1, §§ 2–3, speaks of *una quasi persona, seu unum corpus*, which remains identical through all changes and preserves permanent attributes, and of an *anima in corpore*, existing in virtue of an *imperium*; cf. his *Annotationes* to Pufendorf's *Jus nat. et gent.* I, c. 1, § 3 n. 4—*quamquam negari queat entium moralium et naturalium magnam interdum esse similitudinem, e.g. corporis humani et civitatis, quae etiam corpus vocatur et animam sive vitam habere dicitur* (see also p. 122 supra). Analogies with the organism are also drawn by Gundling, *De univ. delinq.* §§ 6–8; Schmier, I, c. 3, no. 66; J. H. Boehmer, *P. spec.* I, c. 2, §§ 1–2 (*corpus morale*, and *unus spiritus*); Achenwall, n. 180 to this section. Note also the elaboration of the analogy with the various limbs and organs of the natural body by Knichen (*Opus. pol.* I, c. 6, th. 11, where head, eyes, tongue, ears, hair, arms, feet, joints, heart and neck are found for the *corpus mysticum ad corporis viri verique modum concinnatum*, and reference is made to the similar, if in some respects different, *jeux d'esprit* of Guevara, Facius and Hobbes).

246. Cf. supra, nn. 195, 197 and 224 to this section.

The idea of the mechanism

247. This idea [of an artificial imitation of the living organism] appears in Spinoza, loc. cit. We also find it in Pufendorf, who expressly commends the analogy with *homo artificialis* (n. 144 to this section), and argues (*J. n. et g.* VIII, c. 12, § 7) in favour of the permanent unity of the 'moral body' from the axiom laid down by Hobbes in his *Philosophia prima*, c. 2, § 7, that *si rei alicui propter formam talem, quae sit principium motus, nomen inditum sit, manente eo principio idem est individuum*. The idea also appears in Hertius (supra, n. 148 and n. 160 to this section), in Gundling (n. 163 to this section), and other writers; cf. also Horn, supra p. 115.

248. Cf. supra, pp. 128–130 and 131–4. Rousseau even describes the governing body, in so many words, as a *corps artificiel* which is created by another *corps artificiel*, III, c. 1.

249. We thus find the analogy of the organism entirely absent from the writings of Thomasius, Wolff, Daries, Nettelbladt, the Schlözers (father and

son), Hoffbauer, W. von Humboldt and Kant. Mercier de la Rivière explicitly says that a nation is not a *corps unique*, and that it has no single will: *ce qu'on appelle une nation en corps n'est donc jamais qu'une nation rassemblée dans un même lieu, où chacun apporte ses opinions personnelles, ses prétentions arbitraires et la ferme résolution de les faire prévaloir*. A majority is never more than a 'collection of interests' and a variable 'result of egoisms'; and unanimity is impossible (c. 18).

250. A. L. von Schlözer says (p. 3) that 'the most instructive way of dealing with the theory of the State is to treat the State as an artificial machine, entirely composed of assembled parts, which has to operate for a definite end'; cf. pp. 99, 157. Kant similarly speaks of the 'mechanism' or the 'machine-like character' of the constitution of the State, and describes the State as 'the mechanical product of the union of the people by coercive laws' (*Works*, VII, pp. 157–8). Sieyès, though he does not wholly succeed in avoiding the comparison with a body (I, pp. 283 sqq. and 445 sqq.), bases the State entirely on 'the mechanics of social art' which reason provides (I, pp. 128, 195 sqq., 217 sqq.; II, p. 370). [Tom Paine, would-be engineer and bridge-builder, similarly uses mechanical analogies in his *Common Sense* of 1776: e.g. 'as the greater weight will always carry up the less, and as all the wheels of a machine are put in motion by one, it only remains to know which power in the constitution has the most weight; for that will govern'.] *The State a machine*

251. We find this [failure to face the problem of Group-personality] in Praschius, Placcius, Alberti, Filmer and other anti-individualist thinkers. It is also to be found in Justi. It is true that he emphasises strongly the organic nature of the 'moral body', arguing that the commonwealth is 'a single indivisible body, which has the closest connection in all its parts', and seeking to prove, by this argument, the necessity of a single group-authority controlled by a rational will, the existence of a system of mutual interaction by which all the parts affect one another and the whole, and the pernicious results of any superfluous part which contributes nothing to the general system. But he has nothing whatever to say about the personality of the State or the people (cf. his *Natur und Wesen*, §§ 23–6, 28, 45–50, and his *Grundrisz*, §§ 15, 17, 23 sqq., 29 sqq.). *Failure to face the problem of Group-personality*

252. Mevius for example, though he makes it the object of political association *ut una velut persona sit, cui una mens, unus sensus, una voluntas et anima inter multos velut una atque eadem*, makes the unity of this person depend for its existence entirely on the submission of all other wills to the will of a representative Ruler (see n. 125 to this section). In the same way S. de Cocceji will only recognise a representative and collective unity of [group-]persons,* notwithstanding the fact that he extends the conception of the social body, with authority over its members, until it is made to embrace the State, the Corporation, the [College of] Magistrates and the Family. The result is that all these bodies remain for him *corpora artificialia seu mystica*, except that the Family is *magis naturale* than the rest. Cf. his *Nov. Syst.* §§ 199, 205, 280–1.

253. Leibniz argues (*Nova methodus*, § 16) that the legal 'Subject' (the *subjectum* of a 'moral quality' which may be either a right or an obligation) can be either a *persona* or a *res*. Defining the former as a *substantia rationalis*, he then distinguishes between *personae naturales* (*Deus, angelus, homo*) and *Leibniz's theory of associations*

* I.e. they are 'one' in virtue of being 'represented' by a single agent, or 'one' in the sense of being a collective aggregate of wills, but not 'one' inherently and in themselves.

persona civilis (collegium, quod quia habet unam voluntatem certo signo dignoscibilem— e.g. ex pluralitate votorum, sorte, etc.—ideo obligare et obligari potest). He regards a *res* as the 'Subject' of rights and duties when e.g. property is left to an *officium*, or an *officium* is made responsible for some act, and generally in any case of *jus reale*.

He describes a *persona civilis seu moralis*, in so many words, as a *persona ficta*, brought into existence *ad instar naturalis* by an artificial union of wills, and to be regarded, in the last resort, as an aggregate or collection of rights. *In jure reipublicae persona ejus civilis seu moralis continetur*; *nam omnes personae civiles seu fictae corporum, collegiorum, universitatum in aggregatione jurium consistunt (Spec. dem. pol.* prop. 1, p. 525): *persona civilis omnium jurium collectio est* (ibid. prop. 57, p. 585); cf. also the Introduction to *Cod. gent. dipl.* I, § 22, p. 306, and *Caesar.-Fürst.* c. 11. He regards the person of the State as identical with that of the Ruler; and he makes it accordingly a *persona naturalis* in a monarchy, but a *persona civilis* in a republic (Introduction to *Cod. gent. dipl.* loc. cit.; *Caesar.-Fürst.*, loc. cit.; *Spec. dem. pol.* prop. 1, 12, 57). In international law, therefore, both 'natural' and 'civil' persons are in his view 'Subjects' of rights (Introduction to *Cod. gent. dipl.* loc. cit.); but he argues that if friendship is nowadays rare *inter principes* (*Spec. dem. pol.* prop. 41, p. 560), neither friendship nor enmity is possible *inter Respublicas*. Such feelings arise *ex animo*, and *animus non nisi personarum naturalium est, civilium nullus*; and [while the 'civil person' of a republic thus cannot have friendship or enmity with another State, because it has no *animus*, neither can the 'natural persons', or individuals, who constitute such a corporate person, because these] natural persons and their *animi* are in a state of perpetual flux (ibid. prop. 42, p. 561).

For a critique of the view recently advanced by C. Ruck (*Die Leibnizsche Staatslehre*, Tübingen, 1909)—that Leibniz understood the personality of the State in our modern sense, and created the legal notion of 'organ' to express the relation of the Ruler to that personality—see the author's review in the *Deutsche Literaturzeitung* of 1910, pp. 566–8.

No real idea of Group-personality in the eighteenth century

254. Any such legal conception of Group-personality is not to be found in Montesquieu, Vico or Ferguson. Frederick the Great has some elements of the conception: on the one hand, he represents the State as an animate body with limbs and organs, and explains its birth, its maladies, its death, and the peculiarities of its nature, by means of a comparison with the individual man (*Antimach.* cc. 3, 9, 12, 20; *Considérations*, in his *Works*, VIII, 24; *Essai sur les formes*, ibid. IX, 197 sqq.): on the other hand, he regards the Ruler as only [an 'organ', or] *le premier serviteur et premier magistrat de l'État* (*Antimach.* c. 1; *Mémoires*, in his *Works*, I, 123; last Testament, ibid. VI, 215; *Essay*, ibid. IX, 197); but in spite of these two complementary ideas he never attains to any clear expression of State-personality.

Justus Möser knows nothing of any 'person' of the State (*Patriot. Phant.* I, no. 62): he even disputes the right of a nation to give itself freely a new constitution, on the ground that it is 'not a single being in itself', but is composed of two classes which, if either is united internally, are only connected together in their relations with one another as separate parties to a contract (*Misc. Writings*, I, pp. 335 sqq.).

Herder again—however vigorously he may champion the idea of development; however resolutely he may insist on regarding the life of a people as the common life of an organism; however frequently he may speak of a national spirit and a national character—none the less fails to transcend a mechanical conception of monarchical institutions when he seeks to analyse actual States (*Ideen*, IX, c. 4, XIX, c. 6). While he traces 'the first breath of a common existence' in the constitutions of towns, guilds and universities, he never carries his account of the 'body politic' to the point where he reaches the conception of an immanent Group-personality (ibid. xx, c. 5).

§17. THE NATURAL-LAW THEORY OF THE STATE

1. Cf. Huber, I, c. 1, §§ 12–23; Hert, I, 1, pp. 1 sqq.; J. H. Boehmer, *P. gen.* c. 3, §§ 11 sqq.; Schmier, *Jus publ. univ.*, *Diss. praeambula*; Daries, *P. spec.* §§ 654 sqq.; Achenwall, II, §§ 85–7; Heincke, *Proleg.* c. 1, § 10. By all these writers *jus publicum universale* is identified with *jus publicum naturale*, or with a part of *jus sociale naturale*; and the distinction drawn between public law and political theory is explained as consisting in the fact that the State is considered in the former *ratione justi*, and in the latter *ratione utilis*. J. H. Boehmer was the first to compose a separate compendium of *jus publicum universale* [or, as French writers express it to-day, '*droit constitutionnel comparé*'] under that title.

Universal public law

2. At first we find no distinction drawn, by those who are engaged in attacking the older doctrines, between the pure theory of the sovereignty of the people and the theory [of the co-existence] of *majestas realis* and *personalis*: cf. Micraelius, I, c. 10, §§ 12 sqq. and qu. 7, pp. 112 sqq.; Cellarius, c. 9, §§ 18–25; Felwinger, *De maj.* §§ 22 and 41; Huber, I, 2, c. 3, § 24, I, 3, c. 1, §§ 11–20; Pufendorf, *J. n. et g.* VII, c. 2, § 14, c. 6, § 4, and *De off. hom. et civ.* II, c. 9; Thomasius, *Instit. jur. div.* III, c. 6, § 121; J. H. Boehmer, *P. spec.* I, c. 4, § 22 n. *i* and III, c. 2, § 5, n. *x*; Schmier, II, c. 1, s. 2, § 1, nos. 48 sqq.

Attacks on the theory of 'double majesty'

Gradually, however, both of these theories [that of popular sovereignty and that of 'double majesty'] were lumped together, and any conception of *majestas realis* was stigmatized as a product of 'monarchomachism'. Horn [who wrote about 1660] is already condemning 'real majesty' as a *monstrum* and *fabulosus foetus*: indeed he even declares the theory of 'real majesty' a criminal theory, and expresses a pious wish for the execution of its advocates, adding that, if they live in a neighbouring 'plebeian' State, a request addressed to that State for their execution would be warranted by international law (II, c. 10, §§ 11–15). See in addition Ziegler, I, c. 1, §§ 44 sqq.; Boecler, II, c. 1, pp. 93–8 (where the theory of real majesty is said to be a theory of *regicidae*); Becmann, c. 12, § 11; Hert, *Opusc.* I, 1, pp. 307–19; Kestner, c. 7, § 9; Stryck, *Diss.* XIV, no. 7, c. 2, no. 54; Gundling, *Jus nat.* c. 38, § 22 (such theories are *inventa otiosi ingenii*); Alberti, c. 14, § 3; Heineccius, *Praelec.* I, c. 3, §§ 8–9 and *Elem. jur. nat.* II, §§ 130 sqq.; Rachelius, I, tit. 32, § 2 (the theory is *summa pernicies*); Heincke, I, c. 2, § 15, c. 3, § 4; Kreittmayr, § 5; Scheidemantel, I, pp. 111 sqq. (where even the theory of Rousseau is described as a theory which makes 'real' majesty exist by the side of 'personal', and is controverted accordingly).

Fortunes of Grotius' theory of the subjectum commune

3. Thus Becmann writes (c. 12, §7): *subjectum majestatis est tum Respublica seu persona moralis quam Respublica induit, tum personae singulares quae moralem istam repraesentant.* But what he understands by *Respublica* is no more than *universi* or *omnes simul*; and he proceeds to assume a system under which this collective body is represented by the *Imperans* so perfectly that neither is superior or subordinate to the other, but the one stands to the other in the same relation as an object does to its reflection in the mirror. Cf. also Treuer, on Pufendorf, *De off. hom. et civ.* II, c. 7, §9 (*respublica perpetuum majestatis subjectum manet*); Rachelius, I, tit. 32, §2; Mullerus, I, c. 7, §65.

4. Schmier, for example, holds that it is possible to follow Grotius in assuming both a *subjectum commune* and a *subjectum proprium*, provided that the distinction be interpreted as it is by Boecler and van der Mühlen in their notes to Grotius—i.e. provided that it be understood to refer merely to the inseparable connection of majesty with the *corpus reipublicae rite formatum* and the possible reversion of that majesty to the people (II, c. 3, s. 1, §1). Kulpis (in his *Exerc. ad Grotium*, II, §6 n.) and Hert (p. 298, §12) take a similar line. Ickstatt interprets the *subjectum commune* of Grotius as signifying merely the original sovereignty of the people, and he therefore prefers to substitute the terms *subjectum constitutivum* and *activum* [for *subjectum commune* and *proprium*]; cf. *Opusc.* II, no. 1, c. 1, §12.

5. Cf. Horn, II, c. 11, §1; Pufendorf, *J. n. et g.* VII, c. 6, §4, *De off. hom. et civ.* II, c. 9; Kestner, c. 7, §9; Boecler, *Instit.* II, c. 1; Alberti, c. 14, §3; Stryck, *Diss.* XIV, no. 7, c. 2, no. 55; Heincke, I, c. 2, §15, c. 3, §4.

6. Cf. supra, pp. 111 and 115-6; see also, for answers to Horn's theory, Huber (I, 3, c. 2, §§7-9) and Pufendorf (*J. n. et g.* VII, c. 5, §5, *De off. hom. et civ.* II, c. 8, §4).

7. See Spinoza, *Tract. theol.-pol.* c. 16, *Tract. pol.* c. 6sqq.; Micraelius, I, cc. 10, 13-15; Huber, I, 3, c. 2, 1, 7, c. 1; Pufendorf, *J. n. et g.* VII, c. 5, *De off. hom. et civ.* II, c. 8; Leibniz, *Spec. pol. dem.* prop. 16-18; Hert, *Opusc.* I, 1, pp. 319sqq.; Titius, VII, c. 7, §§17-28; Bossuet, II, art. 1; J. H. Boehmer, *P. spec.* I, c. 3, §13, c. 4, §§29-34; Schmier, I, c. 3; Heineccius, II, §§116sqq.; Wolff, *Instit.* §§990sqq., *Jus nat.* VIII, §§131sqq.; Daries, §§747sqq.; Nettelbladt, §§1133, 1153sqq.; Achenwall, II, §§149sqq.; Scheidemantel, I, pp. 39-40; Hoffbauer, pp. 206 and 295sqq.; A. L. von Schlözer, pp. 75sqq. and 95, §2. The last of these writers states: 'the Ruler is the Ruler, the depository of the common will, be he one, or some, or many: crown, sceptre and throne are *essentialia* in Schaffhausen and in Stamboul'. This principle 'overturns once and for all the insolence of the single ruler, and awakens the democrat from his dreams of liberty' [i.e. it shows to the one that he is but a depository, who has received his authority as a *depositum*—'a thing for custody, to be redelivered on demand'—as it shows to the other that even in the democracy of his dreams there cannot be absolute liberty, without any sceptre or throne, since while there is a society with a common will man cannot be, as Shelley dreamed,

Sovereignty the same in all forms of State

> Sceptreless, free, uncircumscribed, the king
> Over himself].

On the other hand we find Gundling contending (*Jus nat.* c. 37, §§3-10 and *Disc.* c. 36) that, while there is rule by *una persona* even in a republic, this 'person' is only *moraliter una*, and the process of deliberation which must necessarily precede its decisions makes the *suprema potestas* weaker.

8. Cf. Huber, I, 2, c. 3, and his *Opera minora*, I, no. 2, c. 7; Pufendorf, *J. n. et g.* VII, c. 2, §14, c. 6, §§4sqq.; Alberti, c. 14, §3; Hert, *Opusc.* I, I, pp. 311sqq.; Gundling, c. 37; J. H. Boehmer, *P. spec.* I, c. 4, III, c. 2; Titius, VII, c. 7, §§20–6; H. Cocceji, *Prodromus*; S. Cocceji, §§617–18; Schmier, II, c. 4, s. 2, §2, no. 109sqq.; Heineccius, II, §138; Ickstatt, *Opusc.* II, op. I, c. I, §§14–15; Kreittmayr, §5.

9. In developing these ideas, the thinkers of this age were no more successful in eluding the contradictions which they inevitably entailed than those of a previous age had been (cf. supra, p. 43 and n. 43 to §14). Most of them assumed that there must have been, even in a democracy, a formal *translatio imperii*, which had taken the form of a contract of subjection made with a permanent popular assembly or a majority thereof. (See Micraelius, c. 10, §§9sqq.; Huber, I, 2, c. 3, §§25sqq., c. 4, §§1sqq.; Pufendorf, *J. n. et g.* VII, c. 5, §§6–7, *De off. hom. et civ.* II, c. 6, §9; Becmann, c. 12, §§4sqq.; Hert, *Opusc.* I, I, pp. 286sqq. and 317sqq.; Kestner, I, c. 7, §3; Heineccius, II, §§129sqq.; Daries, *Praecogn.* §24 and *Jus nat.* §§658–60; Ickstatt, §§8sqq.) Those who made this assumption were forced to suppose that the other party to the contract [i.e. the party other than the permanent popular assembly or a majority thereof] was either (1) the sum of all individuals, or even (2) a minority of those individuals;* and they were thus compelled to make democracy an exception from the general scheme which they applied to all other forms of State. [Strictly speaking, we may argue that on the first hypothesis, i.e. the hypothesis that the sum of all individuals contracts with the popular assembly, there will be no exception from the general scheme, which makes *all* individuals contract with a Ruler; but there will be the difficulty, or the absurdity, that the two parties to the contract are the same, and *A* is merely contracting with *A*. On the second hypothesis, i.e. the hypothesis that a minority of individuals contracts with the majority of the popular assembly, this difficulty or absurdity disappears, because the parties are different; but there is now an exception from the general scheme, because it is only a minority (and not, as in the general scheme, *all*) which is the other party to the contract with the Ruling authority.]

The problem of interpreting democracy in terms of contract

Other thinkers dropped the idea of a contract of subjection altogether in treating of democracy, and only spoke of a separate agreement or decision (following on the primary contract of society) to retain sovereignty instead of transferring it. This idea, which agrees with the doctrine of Suarez, appears particularly in Schmier, II, c. I, s. 3, §3 and c. 4, s. 2, §3; and he is led by its logic to argue that the reversion of original sovereignty to the people [in a case where that sovereignty has not been retained, but transferred] does not *ipso facto* produce a democracy, but only the possibility of instituting either that or another form of State [according as the people, now in possession of the reversion of its sovereignty, decides either to retain it or to transfer it]. The idea may also be traced in Wolff, *Instit.* §982 and *Jus nat.* VII, §§37 ff.; Nettelbladt, §1132; and Achenwall, II, §§96–98 and 174–179. But the thinkers who propounded this idea failed to explain how the nature of social authority could be changed [i.e. how vague popular sovereignty could pass into a definite democratic authority] when the 'Subject' of such authority underwent no change.

10. Spinoza, *Tract. theol.-pol.* c. 16, *Tract. pol.* cc. 6–11. It is true that

---

* The other party which contracts with a majority of the popular assembly may naturally be supposed to be the minority.

Spinoza on monarchy

Spinoza regards an *omnino absolutum imperium* as desirable only in a democracy, which he considers the most natural and perfect of all forms of State—or, to a less extent, in an aristocracy. But just for this reason [i.e. just because he confines absolutism to democracy or aristocracy], he rejects monarchy, as being a form of government which is necessarily absolute by its very idea, and he substitutes for it a mixed constitution. [Strictly speaking, Spinoza does not 'reject' monarchy. He argues that, *potentia* being *jus*, the form of State which has most *potentia* will have most *jus*; and he criticises monarchy accordingly, *not* because it is absolute, but because it cannot be absolute—in other words because one man cannot, however much he may try, possess as much *potentia* (by which Spinoza means mainly power of intellect) as a number will possess, and cannot therefore possess as much *jus*. Having criticised monarchy as defective in power, and therefore in right, Spinoza proceeds to fortify it, in the seventh chapter of the *Tractatus politicus*, by a great council, which will bring intellect to its service, and by a number of other devices. We may call this a mixed constitution, and it is, in effect, a mixed constitution; but Spinoza was thinking of a fortification of monarchy, and not of a mixture of different political elements. On his own theory monarchy remains, in its fortified condition, as a possible form of State—not rejected, but not preferred, even in its fortified condition, to other forms.]

11. Filmer, who rejects in his *Patriarcha* all forms of State except monarchy, regards monarchy as necessarily absolute.

French theories of monarchy

12. Bossuet (II, art. 1; III, art. 2–3; IV, art. 1; V, art. 1; VI, art. 1–2; VIII, art. 2; X, art. 6) argues that the people cannot be conceived apart from the Monarch, because he is *l'État même*; and while *lois fondamentales* may secure liberty and property, they only bind the monarch [internally,] in virtue of the authority which they derive from God and reason, and never oblige him externally. A similar view appears afterwards in the Physiocrat absolutists, who simply eliminate the theocratic elements in the older theory: cf. Mercier de la Rivière, c. 14, p. 102, c. 17, p. 129, cc. 19, 23–4 (the only rational form of State is a legal despotism, an absolute hereditary monarchy, where, the private interest of the monarch coinciding with the interests of his subjects, the mathematically evident and inevitable principles of the *ordre social* reign undisturbed).

German writers on monarchy

13. Cf. Cellarius, c. 9 ('he who is limited by fundamental laws is no longer sovereign'); Pelzhoeffer, II, c. 3; Becmann, c. 12, §§ 4–7; Boecler, II, c. 1. Mevius also (*Prodromus*, V, §§ 23 sqq.) regards all the rights of the *universitas* as absorbed in its single, plenary and exclusive 'representation' by the will of the Ruler, and holds that by the law of nature the *potestas imperantium* is necessarily *una, summa, absoluta, soluta legibus et rationibus non obnoxia*. On the other hand the supreme authority must do nothing whereby *societas pereat vel infirmetur*: it must not, therefore, bring the State under a foreign yoke, alienate land, alter the fundamental laws or exercise tyranny (§ 30); and it must use *bona publica* only for *usus publici*, and impose taxes only in case of necessity. Cf., in the same sense, Alberti, c. 14, §§ 3–10.

Horn's view of monarchy

14. Horn, *De civ.* II, c. 10, §§ 1–15. In a limited monarchy, *summa potestas* resides exclusively in the monarch, and it is only its 'exercise' which is limited: the monarch can therefore, in case of need, break even the rules of the constitution, which can never be anything more than a contract to which he has freely assented. The obligation imposed on him by an oath to the

constitution is only a religious obligation; and he can never be deposed, because he has no *Superior*.

15. Pufendorf attacks Hobbes for making the two conceptions [that of 'supreme' power, and that of 'unlimited' power] interchangeable: cf. *J. n. et g.* VII, c. 6, §13.

16. *J. n. et g.* VII, c. 2, §14; *De off hom. et civ.* II, c. 6, §11; cf. n. 132 to §16.

17. *J. n. et g.* VII, c. 2, §14. If *populus* is understood to signify a 'Subject' or owner of rights (*unum aliquid unam habens voluntatem et cui una actio tribui potest*), it becomes identical with *civitas* and its will becomes identical with that of the Ruler; and thus the paradox holds good in a monarchy that *Rex est populus*. But if *populus* is understood to mean the *multitudo subditorum*, as contrasted with the *homo vel concilium habens imperium*, it ceases entirely to be a unit to which any ownership of rights can be ascribed; and the theory of the 'right' of resistance, which confuses *multitudo* with *populus* and proceeds, on the basis of that confusion, to the impossible conception of a rebellion of the *civitas* against the *Rex*, is as absurd as it is seditious. On the other hand individual subjects of the State continue to be the possessors of separate wills, although they are merged in a *corpus morale* with *una voluntas* (*J. n. et g.* VII, c. 4, §2; *De off. hom. et civ.* II, c. 7, §2); and as possessors of separate wills, they continue to be 'natural' Subjects or owners of rights, to whom the Ruler owes obligations and to whom he may do an injustice (*J. n. et g.* VII, cc. 8–9, VIII, c. 1; *De off. hom. et civ.* II, cc. 9, 11). But individuals cannot appeal to any coercive sanction in support of their natural rights: they must endure the misuse of the State's authority as men endure storms and bad weather: they must go into exile themselves rather than expel their ruler; but they may be competent to resist if the worst comes to the worst and the fundamental contract itself is broken (*J. n. et g.* VII, c. 8; *De off. hom. et civ.* II, c. 9, §4). *Pufendorf's view of popular rights*

As compared with this exposition, Pufendorf's attempt to prove the possibility of an obligation existing between *optimates* and *cives* in an aristocracy is both obscure and involved in self-contradiction. In dealing with this possibility, he not only invokes the argument that, although *populus ut persona moralis expiravit*, the *personae physicae* are still there: he is even willing to contend that the people does not become a *multitudo dissoluta* (though it ceases to be a *persona perfecta*) after the transference of its sovereignty; and he alleges in favour of this contention the argument that 'at any rate when there is a Senate, to serve, as it were, as its head, the people forms a person' (*quia utique jam cum senatu tanquam capite suo personam constituit*; cf. *J. n. et g.* VII, c. 5, §8). [Pufendorf's view appears to be that while a people with a king as its head is not a person, a people with a Senate as its head *is*; and his reason may perhaps be that while there is some similarity between the people and a Senate, and while the two may both somehow be 'persons', there is a great difference between the people and a King, who is so distinct from his people that he is a unique 'person', and they in comparison are only a *dissoluta multitudo*. But whatever his reason may have been, he certainly falls into self-contradiction; for after proclaiming (in the preceding paragraph) that there is only *one* 'State-person', he allows *two* to enter in an aristocracy: (1) the 'person' of the *concilium habens imperium*, and (2) the 'person' of the people, with this council serving as its head.]

18. *J. n. et g.* VII, c. 6, §§13–17. In dealing with *bona publica* Pufendorf follows a similar line [to that which he follows in dealing with political *Normal monarchy and State-property*

authority]: he assigns ownership of such *bona* to the *civitas qua talis*, and he ascribes to the king only the position of a 'tutor', debarring him from alienating *bona publica* except by consent of the people: *J. n. et g.* VIII, c. 5, §8; *De off. hom. et civ.* II, c. 15, §5. At the same time he regards a monarch appointed for a fixed time as something inconceivable.

19. *J. n. et g.* VII, c. 6, §§7–12; *De off. hom. et civ.* II, c. 9.

Thomasius on monarchy

20. *Instit. jur. div.* III, c. 6, §63 (definition of the State as a *persona moralis composita*, which can will and act as a unit through the Ruler); §§115–26 (on the nature and attributes of majesty); §§127–31 (on the difference between an *imperium absolutum* and an *imperium limitatum* with fundamental laws); §§132–41 (on the possible varieties in the *modus habendi*). But Thomasius prefers to call 'non-patrimonial monarchies' by the name of *fidei commissaria* rather than by that of *usufructuaria* (§135);* he does not consider a *monarcha temporarius* to be absolutely inconceivable (§§122–6); and he does not allow that there can ever be a right of resistance to the sovereign (§§119–20).

21. *Spec. jur. publ.* VII, c. 7, §§17–28 and 30. In a *civitas* which is *una, vera et perfecta*, constitutional limitations do not affect the *suprema potestas*, but only the *modus exercendi*.

Gundling on monarchy

22. To some extent, indeed, Gundling may be said to be nearer to the theory of Hobbes: he follows him, for example, in the interpretation he places on the original contract (cf. supra, pp. 60 and 108); in his conception of the Ruler as the soul of the State (cf. n. 161 to §16 above); and in the description he gives of the authority of the State (*Jus nat.* c. 36 and *Disc.* c. 35). But he recognises contracts made with subjects as binding (*Jus nat.* c. 12, §§43–6 and *Disc.* c. 11, §§43–6); and he limits the principle that in a normal State the people has no right of resisting the Ruler who breaks his contract, by remarking that, all the same, no injustice is done to a tyrant when he is expelled (*Jus nat.* c. 38, §§19–23 and *Disc.* c. 37, §§19–23).

23. The commentators on Pufendorf similarly adopt his views (e.g. Otto, Treuer, etc.), although with some reservations.

24. H. Cocceji, *Prodromus*; S. Cocceji, *Novum syst.* §§617–18, 633 (there can be no alienation of territory without the consent of the people, except in *regna patrimonialia*), and §638 (there is no right of resistance).

25. *Diss.* XIV, no. 7, *De absoluta principis potestate*, c. 3; and *Diss.* IV, no. 1, *De statibus provincialibus*, c. 1, nos. 22 sqq. and c. 4.

26. *Opusc.* II, op. 1, c. 1, §§13–15 (see n. 170 to §16 above) and §66.

27. *Grundrisz*, §§5, 11, 32, 34, 35.

28. *Systema*, I, c. 3, §§5, 13, 26; III, c. 1 (there is never a *jus resistendi*).

29. The same homage to Pufendorf's authority is also, and especially, to be seen in the treatises which describe the positive public law of the German territorial principalities.

J. H. Boehmer on sovereignty and its limits

30. Boehmer, like other thinkers of his time, regards the personality of the State as residing entirely in the *Imperans* (whether a person or a body of persons); and he makes the will and act of this *Imperans* count, externally and internally, as the will and act of all for every purpose falling within the area of the State's function (*P. spec.* I, c. 2, §18, c. 3, §§1, 15–21). This representative 'Subject' or person necessarily possesses, as its *jus proprium et independens*, a 'majesty' which vests it with two sorts of consequential rights—the rights of free action appertaining to the state of nature (so far as external

* See nn. 30 and 35 infra, on the difference.

relations are concerned); and the *jus summi imperii* (including all the particular powers required by the State's function), so far as internal regulation is concerned (ibid. I, c. 4).* But though this 'majesty' is indivisible, equal at all points, all-embracing, permanent, and subject to no positive law, the sovereign who possesses it still remains bound by the *lex naturalis* (*P. gen.* c. 1, §§ 14–22). He has therefore duties as well as rights in regard to his subjects; and these duties are derived partly from the nature of civil society [as based upon natural law] and partly on specific contracts [which rest upon the same basis]. On the other hand the obligation thus arising, if it is *perfecta* for his subjects, is only *imperfecta* for him; and therefore there is never any right of coercion or resistance as against him (*P. spec.* I, c. 2, §§ 18–21 and III, c. 2, §§ 9–25). Further, it is only individual *subditi* who confront the sovereign as 'Subjects' or owners of rights: the community of the people, as such, has no personality (ibid. III, c. 2, §§ 4–6).

Boehmer admits that there are various forms of State, 'according as the nexus constituted by pacts is stricter or looser'. On the one hand, there are *regna herilia*, where *imperium* has been extended, by means of contracts to that effect, beyond the limits required by the State's function: on the other, there are *regna limitata*, where the Ruler is subject to limitations imposed by contract; and there are also hereditary and elective monarchies (or *imperia patrimonialia et non patrimonialia*), though the latter must not be called by the name of *usufructuaria*† (ibid. I, c. 3, §§ 30–6; II, c. 3, § 15; III, c. 4, § 15). But the people never has any share, *stante imperio*, in the exercise of political authority; and it has therefore no legislative or judicial capacity, and no right of resistance or deposition (I, c. 3, §§ 25–6; II, c. 3, § 14; III, c. 2, §§ 4–16 and c. 4, §§ 32–3). If, therefore, the sovereign is bound by *leges fundamentales, qua pacta*, he alone can interpret such laws or pacts, and he cannot be forced to observe them (III, c. 2, § 13 and c. 4, § 16). Should he break the rules of the constitution, the people is bound to obey; and even if the *clausula nullitatis* be added to any rule—e.g. if the performance of an act of government without consultation of the representatives of the people be expressly declared to be null and invalid—the nullity of an act done in contravention of that proviso can only be established by the next successor, and not by the people itself (I, c. 4, § 1). The position is different, Boehmer allows, *vacante imperio*, since sovereignty reverts to the people in the event of such vacancy. Even here he adds a qualification (III, c. 4, pp. 9–11). Vacancy, he argues, can occur in a non-patrimonial monarchy without the consent of the people coming into play, as the result of an *alienatio regni* [in which case there will be no reversion to the people, and no consent of the people]. [See also n. 33 infra.]

31. Kestner, for example, though he follows Pufendorf in other respects

---

* Boehmer's argument may be illustrated by a pedigree:

The fundamental right of *majestas* (*jus proprium et independens*)

| *jura libertatis naturalis* | *jus summi imperii* |
| (*quantum ad externa*) | (*quantum ad interna*) |

jura particularia imperii

† Cf. supra, n. 20, where Thomasius is quoted as rejecting this name in favour of *fidei commissaria*. For the difference between the two, see n. 35 infra, and Huber's explanation there given.

(c. 7, §§ 3 sqq.), allows the people a *jus resistendi* where there is evident tyranny (§ 19).

32. We find this view in Ludewig, I, 1, op. 8, c. 1; Kestner, c. 7, §§ 11–12; Heineccius, II, §§ 147–9. On the other hand the conception of the patrimonial State is retained not only by Thomasius, Cocceji and Boehmer (see nn. 20, 24 and 30 supra), but also by Huber (I, 3, c. 2, §§ 16 sqq.), Schmier (II, c. 2, s. 2, § 3), Wolff (*Instit.* § 986), Nettelbladt (§ 1198), Achenwall (II, §§ 158–73), and others.

Vacancy of the throne and the rights of the People

33. J. H. Boehmer, for example, expressly treats *de juribus subditorum vacante imperio* (*P. spec.* III, c. 4). He distinguishes two cases of vacancy: (1) *totalis interitus reipublicae*, which dissolves the 'body civil' and leaves the ground clear for a fresh act of association (§§ 2–3); and (2) simple disappearance of *imperium*, which transforms any State in which it occurs into a democracy, and thus makes the people capable of a fresh *translatio imperii* (§§ 4 sqq.). A testamentary disposition by a deceased Ruler does not bind the people in the latter of these cases, even if he were competent to alienate his kingdom (§§ 7–8).* Vacancy of *imperium* may arise through an alienation made *ultra vires* (§§ 9–11); or through death (§§ 12–16), if there are no rights of succession to prevent the vacancy (§§ 17–27); or through abdication (§§ 28–31); but not through deposition (§§ 32–3). [We may remember the vote of the Convention Parliament of 1689—that James II 'has abdicated the government' (or *imperium*) and 'the throne is thereby vacant'. On the other hand we may also remember that 'abdication' here was a euphemism for deposition.]

Cf. Thomasius, *Instit.* III, c. 6, §§ 67–114, *Fund.* III, c. 6, §§ 9–10, and Boecler, II, c. 1.

Absolutist views of popular rights

34. Filmer and Bossuet reject simultaneously both an original and a reversionary sovereignty of the people. In a similar way we find Horn deriving the succession to the throne from the expressed or presumed will of the previous Ruler (II, c. 9, §§ 7–18), and refusing to allow any eventual reversion of *majestas* to the people, though he concedes the reversion of an original *jus eligendi*, II, c. 11, § 1 [provided there be no expressed or presumed will of the previous Ruler?]. He regards the people without a Ruler as a *corpus sine anima*, and therefore a *cadaver* [but how, we may ask, can a *cadaver* exercise a *jus eligendi*?]

Huber on monarchy

35. Huber, *De jure civ.* I, 2, c. 1, §§ 16, 20, c. 3, § 24, cc. 5–7; I, 3, cc. 1–2. Even in *imperia herilia* or *despotica*, he argues, all that is added is simply an increase of the *efficacia* of majesty (I, 3, c. 2, §§ 10–15). Conversely, if we turn [from these absolute forms to the less absolute, i.e.] to *imperia patrimonialia* and *non patrimonialia* (and the latter of these, Huber remarks, is not a case of a mere right of usufruct, but of a limited right of property, properly to be regarded as a quasi-usufruct, and analogous to a *fidei commissum* or the property of a man in his wife's dowry),† we merely find a difference in the

---

* *Ergo*, the will of the King of Spain in 1700, leaving his possessions to the grandson of Louis XIV, did not bind the people of Spain.

† These subtleties are fascinating. A King who rules a non-hereditary monarchy (e.g. a King of Poland in the seventeenth and eighteenth centuries) has neither a mere usufruct in an *imperium* which is the property of another, nor the full ownership of an *imperium* which is his own property. He is in a half-way house, which, however, is nearer to ownership than to usufruct. He is like a man who is the holder of what we may roughly call a trust-property (the *fidei commissarius* of Roman Law),

modus habendi of majesty [but not in 'majesty' itself], ibid. §§ 16–31. It is a matter of indifference, Huber adds, whether the *summa potestas* is acquired *volente* or *invito populo*, by election or by inheritance, in perpetuity or for a period (§§ 32–50); and the size and style (i.e. form) of the State are matters of no significance (§§ 51–6). See also his *Instit. Reip.* I, cc. 3–5.

36. *De jure civ.* I, 2, c. 3. We must neither follow Hobbes in exaggerating sovereignty to a point at which the people becomes a mere flock of sheep (§§ 3–8), nor the author of the *Vind. c. Tyr.* and Althusius and other writers in minimising it until Rulers become nothing more than *ministri populorum* (§ 9). The truth is that a contract between king and people is the basis of their relations (§§ 17–20); and in interpreting this contract we must start neither from Hobbes' view that the people necessarily devolved the whole of its rights, nor from the view of Althusius that the people could not in any way alienate its supreme authority, but rather from the assumption that there is at one and the same time a real alienation of majesty and a reservation of popular rights which limit its exercise (§§ 21–51). Cf. 1, 2, cc. 4–7, 1, 3, cc. 1, 4–5; *Opera minora*, I, no. 2, cc. 1–7. *He admits limits on the monarch*

37. *De jure civ.* I, 3, c. 5. Fundamental laws are binding in virtue of natural [and not of positive] law: they are not to be confused with 'privileges' or *pacta cum singulis*.

38. Rights of the people [as a whole, and as against the government] exist even in a democracy, where they arise from the limits imposed on majority-government (I, 2, c. 3, §§ 39–51): they also exist, to the same extent, in an aristocracy and a monarchy when the case is one of *translatio simplex* (ibid. c. 5). Cf. 1, 3, c. 4. *He allows rights of the People*

39. *De jure civ.* I, 3, cc. 4–5.

40. Huber (in I, 3, c. 5, §§ 23 sqq.) investigates these limits [limits imposed on the ruler by 'express fundamental laws'] in some detail. If we start from a theory which makes all limitation of the *summa potestas* purely 'constitutional' in character [i.e. dependent on express constitutional rules], we are not precluded by our basis from believing in a provision which makes the assent of the people, or an *approbatio in senatu*, a necessary condition of the validity of certain of the Ruler's acts (I, 3, c. 2, § 57); nor are we, again, precluded from believing in a voluntary submission of the Ruler to private law and the civil courts (I, 9, c. 5, §§ 7–25). What we *are* precluded from holding, on that basis, is that the Ruler can really be bound by ordinary positive law, or subject to any coercion whatever; for we cannot suppose [as we should have to suppose if we tried to hold such a view] either (1) that the Ruler possesses a power of command and coercion over himself, or (2) that the people can be legally secured in the possession of such a power over him—except, indeed, at the price of a simultaneous cession by him of part of the *imperium* (I, 3, c. 1, §§ 10, 24–38; I, 9, c. 5, §§ 26–49). But the people possesses a right of resistance in defence of its rights against a Ruler who breaks his contract, since the question then raised is one of natural, and not of positive law (I, 9, c. 3); and the people may even punish a tyrant *His theory of express fundamental laws*

or he is like a husband who has a sort of property in his wife's dowry. Just as the former's trust-property is subject to the request (or 'precative disposition') of the testator, and as the latter's property in the *dos* is subject to certain limits in favour of his wife, so the king in a non-hereditary monarchy has a property subject to the 'request' of his people, or to certain limits in favour of his people. And the people itself is a testator, or a wife, or anything else, but not a living or masculine proprietor.

when once he has proceeded to forfeit his *imperium*, either by violating the *lex commissoria*, or by manifestly going beyond his rights (I, 9, c. 4).

Huber identifies the State and the Ruler

41. For this identification of the person of the State with that of the Ruler, cf. the following dicta in Huber's *De jure civili*: *civitates per eos qui habent summam potestatem personae fiunt* (I, 3, c. 6, §26); *summa potestas est ipsa civitas* (I, 9, c. 5, §51); *voluntas imperantium est voluntas civitatis* (I, 3, c. 2, §14 and c. 6, §26); again, because the *civitas jus personae habet*, the Ruler (who *is* the *civitas*) can bind by legislation his individual subjects, who are *diversae personae*, but he cannot bind himself (I, 3, c. I, §32) [since that would be a case of the same 'person' binding and being bound at the same time]. See also I, 9, c. 5, §§65–72. It follows from Huber's argument that if the Ruler submits himself voluntarily to the courts in private-law cases, he is prosecuted and sentenced *nomine suo in semet ipsum*.

Yet he recognises the People as a universitas

42. Huber argues, with particular reference to the opposite opinion of Hobbes, that the people, when transferring sovereignty, *unum quod est*; it retains the *jus personae* [after that transference], and remains a *universitas, quamvis nec congregatus sit neque sciat tempus futuri conventus*; and therefore it can have rights against the Ruler, and, in particular, can effectively reserve such rights [at the time of transference], or acquire them by virtue of subsequent contracts (I, 3, c. 4, §§8–83 and c. 5, §§58–9).

He would limit all governments by popular rights

43. Starting from democracy as the form of State which approaches nearest to the state of nature, Huber begins by enumerating the reservations which are implicitly made [in favour of the whole people] under a democratic constitution, when the will of the majority is made the Ruling Will (I, 2, c. 3, §§25–51 and c. 4); and he then argues for the existence of the same reservations [in favour of the whole people] in *all* forms of State, on the ground that the Ruler in any form of State has merely taken the place of the majority (ibid. c. 5). But he goes further; and he argues with some warmth in favour of express constitutional limitations on 'majesty', such as are common in monarchies, but are seldom to be found in democracies, and only infrequently in aristocracies, where they are particularly necessary (I, 3, c. 4; I, 7, c. 1; I, 8, cc. 2–4). In our century of oppression by princes [the seventeenth], he says, it is particularly necessary to champion the cause of liberty; but if it is particularly necessary in monarchies, it is also necessary in Republics (I, 2, c. 8).

44. [There is a contradiction involved in Huber's attempt to limit democracy by the rights of the people, because] in dealing with democracy he tries to assign to a minority the popular rights which he vindicates elsewhere for the community. He assumes the existence of two pacts (one between *singuli* and *singuli*, and the other between *minor pars* and *major pars*), and vindicates a *facultas resistendi* for the minority in the event of a breach of the latter of these pacts [by the majority]; cf. I, 2, c. 4, §§1–25.

45. Cf. e.g. Micraelius, I, c. 10, §§9–16 and qu. 1–5, pp. 108sqq. (where there is also an argument for the right of resistance in case of necessity); Felwinger, *De maj.* §§27sqq.; von Seckendorf, *Fürstenstaat*, II, c. 4, c. 7, §12, III, c. 3, no. 8; Möser, *Patriot. Phant.* IV, no. 51. The same tendency appears in many of the exponents of positive constitutional law.

46. Seckendorf, for example, qualifies the idea of sovereignty (though he describes it as a 'supreme and final power of command for the preservation and maintenance of the common advantage and existence') in two ways—by insisting strongly on the responsibility which attaches to sovereignty in

virtue of its being an office (*Fürstenstaat*, II, c. 1; *Christenstaat*, II, cc. 6–7), and by rejecting entirely the notion that the sovereign is exempt from positive law (*Fürstenstaat*, II, c. 4, §2).

Fénelon, too, though he believes in the necessity of an *autorité souveraine*, which creates the body politic by giving it unity, and brings about a pooling of powers (*multiplication des forces*) in that body, and though he adds that this authority must necessarily be 'absolute' (c. V), none the less protests against any identification of such a final and supreme authority of the last instance with mere arbitrary and unlimited power (c. XI); and he therefore attacks *despotisme des Souverains* as well as that *de la populace*, while he eulogises a monarchy qualified and moderated by the rights of the people (c. XV)— notwithstanding the fact that he refuses to recognise any original sovereignty of the people or any right of resistance (cc. VI and X). [For the view of sovereignty as an 'authority of the last instance' cf. Loyseau, *Traité des Seigneuries*, II, §6: *la Souveraineté est le comble et la période de la puissance où il faut que l'Estat s'arreste et establisse*. Loyseau, writing about 1610, was a natural authority for Fénelon, writing towards the end of the seventeenth century. We may also note (1) that Loyseau made a distinction between sovereignty *in abstracto*, which was a *property* inherent in and attached to the State and sovereignty *in concreto*, which was the *exercise* or enjoyment of that property by a person or body of persons (though he proceeds to confuse this distinction by arguing that a king 'may acquire by prescription a property in sovereign power, and thus add property in it to exercise of it', *Traité des Offices*, II, c. 2, §§25–6); and (2) that it was a tradition of the French lawyers, from Bodin onwards, that even if 'majesty' were a 'supreme power...exempt from laws', this only meant exemption from positive laws of the ordinary sort, and majesty was none the less subject (*a*) to 'fundamental laws' such as the Salic Law ('which are connected with majesty itself', Bodin, *De rep.* I, 88), and (*b*) to the *lex divina*, the *lex naturae* and the *lex omnium gentium communis* (ibid. 84).]

Fénelon's qualification of sovereignty

[*Compare Loyseau's views*]

47. Cf. supra, p. 137.

48. Cf. Leibniz (*Caesar.-Fürst.*, *Praef.* pp. 329sqq., cc. 10–12 and 26–33) on the degrees of *majestas*, *supremitas* and *superioritas*; on the possible discrepancy between the internal and the external position of the sovereign; and on the possibility of division and distribution of political authority. We may note especially (c. 11, p. 360) the defence of these views against Hobbes and other writers: they are very ready, Leibniz writes, to produce a *monstrum*, but their conception of sovereignty is only in place in *ea Republica cujus Rex Deus est* [i.e. in a State where omnipotence really exists]; it does not apply to any civilised State, or even to Turkey, and it contradicts human nature. We may therefore say that Leibniz believes that the *supremitas* of the Prince is not destroyed by the existence of a contract guaranteeing rights to the people or the Estates, or even by the presence of a *lex commissoria* [which delegates *imperium* to be exercised as a fiduciary power derived from the community]; cf. c. 33.

Leibniz's theory of sovereignty as relative

49. Thus we find Titius, Treuer and Hert censuring Pufendorf for adopting Hobbes' identification of the *Imperans* and the *Civitas*; and similarly we find the first two of these, along with Otto, blaming him for not introducing 'fundamental laws' as limits upon the representation of the State's will by the will of the Ruler (*Comm.* on II, c. 6, §§10–11 of the *De off. hom. et civ.*; Titius, *Observ.* 159, 557).

People and Ruler as both personae

50. Hert, it is true, makes 'the person of the State' reside entirely in the *summus imperans*; but he holds none the less that a *persona et corpus* may be attributed to the people, *quatenus primo pacto continetur* [i.e. so far as it is constituted a 'person' and a 'body' by the original contract]. As a collective person, which comes into existence by virtue of the original contract of society, the people has *nihil commune cum imperio* [i.e. it is not a 'Subject' or owner of rights in anything like the same way as the Ruler]; but it may acquire rights afterwards by contract or by prescription. Again the *populus conjunctus pacto primo* continues to survive even when the *pactum secundum* [i.e. the contract of government or subjection] is dissolved, and it has in that case to re-constitute the *pactum secundum* afresh: cf. *Opusc.* I, 1, pp. 288, 291, 295–8.

Schmier regards the *summa potestas* as the soul of the State, and he makes the 'Subject' or owner of this power 'the person of the State' (II, c. 1, s. 1, §§ 1–3). But he also holds that the *populus collective sumptus* continues to possess a status of its own as against the Ruler. It was the original 'Subject' of sovereignty (II, c. 1, s. 3); sovereignty reverts to it *vacante imperio* (II, c. 3, s. 1, §1, c. 4, s. 2, §3; V, c. 2, nos. 65–9); it is at all times a *universitas* capable of possessing rights (V, c. 2, s. 1, s. 2, §3, c. 3, s. 2, §§ 2–3). [He proceeds to classify those rights.] (1) Like individual *subditi*, the community in general enjoys everywhere certain *reserved* rights (II, c. 4, s. 1, §1; V, c. 2, s. 1): more especially, no change of the succession, and no alienation or mortgage of any of the rights of sovereignty, can have any validity in a 'non-patrimonial' State without the consent of the people (II, c. 2, s. 1, §§ 2–3 and s. 2, §3). (2) The people may also *acquire* extensive rights in virtue of contracts or *leges fundamentales* (II, c. 4, s. 1, §2; V, c. 2, s. 1, nos. 6 and 8)—such as, for example, the right of giving its assent to laws (III, c. 2, nos. 28–30); and it may similarly acquire rights by prescription (II, c. 2, s. 3, §2, nos. 174–200). The *summa potestas* may thus be either 'absolute' or 'limited' [according to the degree of these popular rights]. Yet even where it is limited, it still remains *intacta*, although there may be certain acts of the Sovereign which have no validity without the consent of the People or the Estates, and even although a *lex commissoria* may be imposed upon him (II, c. 1, s. 2, §2). The community has no right—at any rate in cases where it is not the real and true sovereign itself—to resist or depose the Ruler who has broken his contract, unless it be by way of self-defence against a Ruler who has become *hostis apertus* (II, c. 4, s. 2, §2; V, c. 2, s. 1 and c. 3, s. 1). [The rights assigned to the people in the first part of this argument would thus appear to be denied in the second part.]

Heineccius, while emphasising the exclusive representation of the State by the Ruler, and insisting on the unity and indivisibility of sovereignty, yet recognises the people as possessing the collective personality of a *societas aequalis*; and he also admits that, besides the popular rights which are everywhere established, in all forms of State, there may also exist additional popular rights in virtue of special constitutional provisions to that effect (*Elem.* II, §§ 129–149; *Prael. academ.* I, c. 3, §8: cf. note 32 supra).

51. *Instit.* §§ 979–89: *Jus nat.* VIII, §§ 29–36.

52. *Instit.* §989; *Jus nat.* VIII, §§ 37 sqq. Even the representation of the people by the Ruler in the sphere of external relations, Wolff adds, is merely a matter of presumption; but when any different arrangement has been established by fundamental laws, that arrangement is effective only if, and so far as, it is known to other peoples (*Instit.* §994).

Notes to § 17

53. On Wolff's distinction between *imperium absolutum* and *limitatum*, see his *Jus nat.* VIII, §§ 66 sqq. and *Instit.* § 983; and on the application of this distinction to various forms of the State, *Jus nat.* loc. cit. §§ 131 sqq. and *Instit.* §§ 990 sqq. In dealing with the nature of *leges fundamentales* Wolff views them as contracts, which it is beyond the legislative competence of the Ruler to modify, but which may be altered by the people, provided that they are not entirely based on an act of voluntary self-limitation by an otherwise unlimited Ruler, and provided also that such alteration does not affect adversely the acquired rights of the Ruler or his successors (*Jus. nat.* loc. cit. §§ 77 sqq., and *Instit.* §§ 984, 989, 1007, 1043). The people, in his view, has a duty of unconditional obedience, even where there is abuse of the *summum imperium*; and he regards as inadmissible any proviso which makes the duty of obedience cease in a case of bad government. On the other hand, he constantly insists on the right of passive resistance, whenever any order is issued which contravenes the commands or the prohibitions of Natural Law, or whenever, in a constitutional State, the limits of the fundamental laws are violated. He even regards the people as a whole, or the injured part thereof, as entitled to offer active resistance whenever an attack is made on the rights reserved to the people—on the ground that in such a case there is a reversion to the state of nature, and each must therefore protect his rights for himself (*Jus nat.* loc. cit. §§ 1041–7; *Instit.* §§ 985, 1079; *Polit.* § 433). *Wolff's view of popular rights*

54. *Syst. nat.* § 1132: *potestas civilis est originaliter penes omnes cives simul sumptos, a quorum arbitrio dependet an, quomodo, et in quem eam transferre velint*: it is only where the foundation of the State has proceeded from some third party [distinct from both people and government] that the position is different.

55. Loc. cit. §§ 1133 sqq., 1153 sqq. There is indeed (Nettelbladt argues) a presumption against any limitation of the Ruler by the recognition of *jura popularia* to share in the exercise of *potestas civilis*, and [still more] against any limitation of his rights by the admission of the people to the status of joint-holders of supreme authority; but there is equally a presumption in favour of a view of monarchy as merely 'usufructuary', under a system in which *jura potestatis* are vested entirely in the *princeps*, but the *jura circa potestatem* reside as entirely in the people (§§ 1198–9). In all forms of State the civil power is subject, by the nature of the case, to *limites* and *officia*; and the *Respublica* therefore confronts the *Superior* as a 'Subject' or owner of rights (§§ 1127, 1134). In the event of an open transgression of *limites*, the people has the right of revolt (§ 1270).... The conception of sovereignty is so much attenuated in the theory of Nettelbladt that he makes mere *potestas civilis* (*die Hoheit im Staat*) the criterion of the State, and even holds that the *summa potestas* (*la souveraineté*) may be *subordinata* thereto (§§ 1125–9). [If *summa potestas* can thus be 'subordinate' to *civilis potestas*, the sovereignty which is indicated by it cannot be more than the 'courtesy' title of sovereign, as when we speak of 'our sovereign Lord the King'. It is not a true *summa potestas* in the legal sense—the authority of the last instance, which finally decides.] *Nettelbladt on popular rights*

56. Loc. cit. § 1200: the *princeps*, as a 'public person', is a person in the state of nature, who is one with his people (*una persona cum populo*) in the sphere of external relations.

57. In a monarchy the *populus* is always a *persona moralis* distinct from the king; but in its character of a moral person the people varies—sometimes *Nettelbladt on the People as a moral person*

being altogether *subditus*; sometimes retaining reserved powers, and therefore [and to that extent] remaining *in statu naturali*; sometimes possessing political authority jointly with the prince, and therefore living, along with him, in the state of nature (§ 1201). The same position also exists in an aristocracy, as between the *populus* and the *collegium optimatum* (§ 1217). In a democracy, on the other hand, the Senate is a *persona moralis subdita populo, non in statu naturali vivens* (§ 1220), as also are all the magistrates (§§ 1226 sqq.).

On the Estates as a moral person

58. Loc. cit. §§ 1210–12. The Estates exercise the rights of the people 'in their name' (whether these rights be merely the general rights *circa potestatem*, or particular rights of exercising authority [apart from the prince], or rights of sovereignty* shared with the prince); and therefore they 'represent the people, and have its rights'. We have thus three separate 'Subjects' or owners of rights [the Ruler, the People, and the assembly of the Estates] who may all live in a state of nature; for the 'body of the Estates', in so far as it exercises rights of sovereignty in the name of the people, is also free from subjection [and therefore in a state of nature].

59. *Naturrecht*, pp. 240, 244, 246, 292 sqq., 308 sqq., 317.

60. Loc. cit. p. 310.

Daries on sovereignty and its limits

61. Daries holds that the essence of the State requires an *imperium summum* and an *imperans* (§§ 655 sqq.). The content of majesty is always the same (§§ 667 sqq.): the 'Subject' of majesty may be either a collective person or an *individuum* (§§ 747 sqq.). But there are *limites majestatis*—both the natural, which are to be found in all forms of State, and the *pactitii*, which are found in constitutional States in addition to the natural (§§ 780 sqq.). Limited monarchy, where the people has only given a *consensus conditionatus*, and where the Ruler is bound by *leges fundamentales vel capitulationes*, is none the less monarchy; and the erection of *ordines imperii* with powers of supervision, or even the presence of a *pactum commissorium* [a *Wahlkapitulation*, pledging the monarch at the time of his election?], does not turn it into a mixed form of State (§§ 786–9).

Achenwall on constitutional types of State

62. Achenwall regards all *civitates ordinatae* as based on *pacta fundamentalia*, which cannot be altered by unilateral action (II, § 109). By the principles of 'universal absolute public law', the contract of government issues in an *imperium summum plenum et illimitatum*, either of the 'people', or of a 'physical person', or of a 'moral person' (§§ 112 sqq.); but by 'universal conditional public law'† the *imperium* may be limited by 'fundamental laws', and we thus find, by the side of absolute monarchy, *monarchia minus plena* and *monarchia limitata*—the monarch, in the latter of these two varieties, being obliged to act by the consent of the people, and the people possessing either a *corregimen de facto* or a formal *co-imperium* (§§ 148 sqq.).

Scheidemantel on the limits of majesty

63. Scheidemantel holds that every State requires 'a common Head', who represents the 'majesty' of the State, and is either the whole society, or some of its members, or one (I, pp. 38 sqq.). Majesty, as 'the highest form of existence in the State', is not subject to any laws, but may be bound by divine commands and by the fundamental laws which it has accepted for itself by contract (I, p. 116).

* Strictly speaking, the word *Hoheit* (which is here translated as sovereignty) means something different from sovereignty in Nettelbladt, being identified with *civilis potestas* and distinguished from *la souveraineté* (n. 55 supra, *ad finem*). But it is difficult to render the word otherwise.

† For these elaborate classifications of *jus*, see p. 291.

Notes to § 17

64. A. L. von Schlözer treats the relation of the Ruler and the People as *Schlözer's* entirely a contractual relation (pp. 95 sqq.), which should ideally be defined *constitutiona-* in a fundamental contract made under oath (p. 102, §6); but he allows the *list theory* Ruler the right to denounce the contract at any time, and he gives the People the right of denouncing it under given conditions (p. 108, §10). Though he rejects the theory that 'law should be the one and only Ruler', and though he emphasises strongly the necessity of a 'Sovereign' or 'Ruler' who constitutes the common will, and represents the State, either as an '*individuum*' or as '*unum morale* feigned by a majority' (pp. 77–9, 95, 100), he none the less imposes fixed limits upon the power of this sovereign in the course of his argument (cf. p. 94, §1)—contending that he is bound by positive as well as by natural law (p. 96, §2, p. 101, §6), and that he is subject to the fundamental contract (p. 102).

65. Daries, e.g., regards the withholding of justice as causing a return to *Theories of* the state of nature (§733). Achenwall allows individuals only the right to *resistance* emigrate, when the fundamental contract is broken; but he allows a *universitas*, or an *insignis pars populi*, the right to resist by force of arms and expel the tyrant, if the danger threatened by acquiescence in wrong is greater than the disadvantages of rebellion, §§200–7 [cf. Bentham's *Fragment of Government*, where resistance is held to be 'allowable to, if not incumbent on, every man...when...the probable mischiefs of resistance (speaking with respect to the community in general) appear less to him than the probable mischiefs of submission' (c. IV, §XXI); cf. also Paley's *Moral and Political Philosophy* (Book VI, c. III)—'the justice of...resistance is reduced to a computation of the quantity of the danger and grievance on the one side, and of the probability and expense of redressing it on the other'].

Scheidemantel thinks the nation entitled, if there be real tyranny, to rise in forcible resistance, on the ground that the bond between the prince and the nation is broken by abuse of the power of the State and transgression of the limits of that power, and that the nation thus returns to the liberty and equality of the state of nature (III, pp. 364–75).

Schlözer allows a *droit de résistance* if there be evident tyranny, along with a power of enforcing that right by coercion, deposition or punishment, 'all being in accordance with the notion of a contract in general'. But he does not think the individual justified in exercising, or the masses capable of using, this right: 'woe, therefore, to the State where there are no representatives; and happy Germany—the only land in the world where a man can take action against his ruler, without prejudice to his dignity, by due process of law, and before an external tribunal' (pp. 105–7). [Schlözer, writing in 1793, is thinking of the *Reichskammergericht* at Wetzlar, dissolved, along with the *Reich* itself, in 1806.]

The reader is also referred to the author's work on Althusius, p. 315 n. 128.

66. *Discourses*, III, sect. 44. The power of parliament is 'essentially and *Sidney on* radically in the people, from whom their delegates and representatives have *parliaments* all that they have'. In England, however, unlike Switzerland and the Netherlands, the several counties and towns are not separate sovereign bodies, but only 'members of that great body which comprehends the whole nation'; and therefore the representatives do not serve the bodies by which they are elected, but the whole nation. If these representatives could assemble of themselves [i.e. without a royal summons—a summons which, at the time when Sidney was writing (1680–3), Charles II steadily refused to

issue], they would be responsible to the nation, and the nation only: when it is impossible for them to assemble, they have only a responsibility to their consciences and to public opinion. But this great power of the representatives, instead of diminishing liberty, really maintains it. It is identical, at bottom, with the power of the electorate. The people still remains sovereign, because only the possessor of an unlimited right can give an unlimited power of representation. The reason for the people giving such power, instead of imposing 'instructions' or mandates, is simply a prudent self-restraint. [Sidney's argument, in favour of true 'national' representation and against 'instructions', is a harbinger of Burke's famous speech to the Bristol electors in 1774 (*Works*, in Bohn's edition, vol. I, p. 447; cf. a similar passage in his *Reflections*, vol. II, p. 457). Mr Norton, a member of one of Elizabeth's parliaments, had already argued in 1571 that in parliamentary representation 'the whole body of the realm, and the service of the same, was rather to be respected than any private regard of place or person' (Hallam, *Con. Hist.* I, c. v, p. 267).]

67. *Discourses*, II, sects. 7, 32 (on solemn, sworn and binding contracts between the magistrates and the nation).

Sidney on the People

68. The People, Sidney argues, is the source of all authority (I, s. 20); it creates authority (II, s. 6), and it determines its limits (II, ss. 7, 30–33); it necessarily retains legislative power, even in a monarchy (III, ss. 13–14, 45–6); and it continues to be a judge above all the magistrates (III, s. 41). The ruler is an officer appointed by and responsible to the people (II, s. 3; III, ss. 1 sqq.): no obedience is due to his commands if they are unjust (III, ss. 11, 20): resistance is permissible, if he abuses his office (III, ss. 4 sqq.), and he may even be deposed (III, s. 41, cf. s. 36—'the general revolt of a nation cannot be called a rebellion'); the people too [as well as parliament] thus retains the right of free assembly (III, ss. 31, 38).

Locke on the rights of the People

69. Cf. Locke's *Second Treatise*, II, c. 10, §132, cc. 13–14. The people (or 'the community') continues to be the fountain of all powers, and retains a right of reversion therein (II, c. 11, §141, c. 19, §§220 and 243); but its 'supreme power' only expresses itself in the event of the dissolution or forfeiture of authority (II, c. 13, §149), and the legislative power is sovereign 'whilst the government subsists' (II, c. 13, §150). [Locke goes further than Gierke allows in his view of the rights of the People. In c. 10, §132, anticipating Rousseau, he argues that 'the majority, having...the whole power of the community naturally in them, may employ all that power in making laws for the community from time to time, and executing those laws by officers of their own appointing, and then the form of government is a perfect democracy'. Normally, we must admit, Locke regards the people as delegating its power to a 'legislative', rather than as making laws itself. Even so, as we have already had reason to notice (supra, n. 68 to § 16), he does not speak of a contract between people and legislative, but of a unilateral act of the people vesting a trustee or 'fiduciary' power in the legislative. It follows upon this view that, while this fiduciary legislative may be called 'supreme', or even 'the one supreme power', the people is always a super-sovereign, having another and higher 'supreme power to remove or alter the legislative when they find the legislative act contrary to the trust reposed in them'. Thus the people comes into action, *not* in the presumably rare event of a breach of contract, but in the presumably more frequent event of 'action contrary to the trust'. For such an event, to judge from the analogy of the

Notes to § 17

treatment of the trustee in English *Privatrecht*, may be confidently expected by the trustor who is also the beneficiary of the trust—all the more as he is in addition (in Locke's theory of the political trust) the judge of its execution.]

70. The people is the sovereign judge which decides whether the powers appointed by it, including the legislative power, observe their limits. If a formal organisation of its rights is lacking, it can appeal to Heaven: if it has once removed the powers which have forfeited their authority, it can either content itself by simply placing authority in fresh hands, or erect an entirely new constitution. [Locke actually says, in c. 10, §132, where he is speaking of legislative power which has been given for lives, or for any limited time, that upon reversion 'the community may dispose of it again anew into what hands they please, *and so* (not '*or*') constitute a new form of government'. (The references which Gierke gives are to c. 19, esp. §§212, 220, 242–3, and to c. 18, §§199–210; but they do not support his account of Locke's views.) Nor does Gierke's phrase about the people 'appealing to Heaven if a formal organisation of its rights is lacking' correspond to what Locke actually says (c. 19, §242). There is nothing in Locke about absence of formal organisation of rights: for him the community is 'presently incorporate' by the original contract of society, continues to remain in that condition, and is thus formally organised for vindicating its rights. Again, the 'appeal to Heaven' means something more definite, and more legal, than Gierke's brief quotation suggests. Locke is arguing that if a controversy arises between the prince and some of the people on a matter on which law is silent or doubtful, the proper umpire is the body of the people, who have given him his power as a trust and can therefore decide upon his use or abuse of that power. If the prince, however, declines that way of determination, 'the appeal then lies nowhere but to Heaven'—i.e. the case is carried in the last resort to the divine ordeal of battle in civil war.]

Locke on the People as sovereign judge

71. Cf. supra, p. 108.

72. *Contr. soc.* II, cc. 1–2, 7; III, cc. 15–16; cf. supra, p. 112.

73. On sovereignty as inalienable, see *Contr. Soc.* II, c. 1. Sovereignty, being nothing but the exercise of the general will, is inalienable. A contract of subjection [*pacte de gouvernement*] would mean the dissolution of the people —*il perd sa qualité de peuple*. Will simply cannot be 'transferred': the sovereign may say, 'I do will what such and such a person wills', but not, 'I shall will whatever such and such a person may will to-morrow'.

Rousseau on sovereignty

On the indivisibility of sovereignty, see II, cc. 6–7. The people is the only legislator: it needs to be instructed by an enlightened law-giver, because it is not always able to see the good which it always wills; but the law-giver has only the office of proposing and drafting—*le peuple même ne peut, quand il le voudrait, se dépouiller de ce droit incommunicable*.

On sovereignty as illimitable, cf. III, c. 16. A contract between people and king is inconceivable: sovereignty is illimitable as well as inalienable: *la limiter c'est la détruire: il n'y a qu'un contrat dans l'état, c'est celui d'association, et celui-ci seul exclut tout autre; on ne saurait imaginer aucun contrat public, qui ne fût une violation du premier*.

On the impossibility of representation, see III, c. 15.

74. Government is a commission...*un emploi dans lequel, simples officiers du Souverain, ils exercent dans son nom le pouvoir dont il les a faits dépositaires, et qu'il peut limiter, modifier ou reprendre quand il lui plaît, l'aliénation d'un tel droit étant incompatible avec la nature du corps social et contraire au bout de l'association* (III, c. 1).

On Government

The 'institution of the government' is not a contract, but a twofold act—the passing of a law in regard to the future form of administration, and the putting of this law into effect. The fact that the political body can thus achieve an administrative act [i.e. the act of putting the law into effect] before the existence of an administration is explained by this body's astonishing conjunction of apparently contradictory properties [or, as Rousseau puts it, 'by one of those astonishing properties... by which it is able to unite operations which seem to be contradictory']: it executes its own law *par une conversion subite de Souveraineté en Démocratie*—that is to say, by simply instituting *une nouvelle relation de tous à tous* [in which, for the nonce, the citizens become magistrates], as when the English House of Commons turns itself into a committee of the whole House (III, c. 17).

75. *Contr. soc.* III, cc. 11–14, 18; cf. supra, n. 209 to §16.

On the provisional character of the constitution

76. Ibid. III, c. 14: *à l'instant que le Peuple est légitimement assemblé en Corps Souverain, toute juridiction du Gouvernement cesse, la puissance exécutive est suspendue et la personne du dernier Citoyen est aussi sacrée et inviolable que celle du premier Magistrat, parce qu'où se trouve le Représenté, il n'y a plus du Représentant.* Cf. also III, c. 18: every constitution is only provisional, and all offices are revocable: regular assemblies are required, each of which must open with the putting of two questions: (1) *s'il plaît au Souverain de conserver la présente forme du Gouvernement?* (2) *s'il plaît au Peuple d'en laisser l'administration à ceux qui en sont actuellement chargés?*

77. *Contr. soc.* I, cc. 6–7, II, cc. 2, 4.

The dualism implicit in Rousseau's theory

78. Ibid. III, cc. 1–6, 16–17; supra, nn. 213 and 214 to §16. Rousseau, of course, is not blind to the contradiction between his own theory and the actual facts of contemporary constitutional law; but he treats all existing conditions as illegal, and without any binding force. According to his theory the moment at which this second moral person [that of the *Gouvernement*] assumes the independent ruling authority which it is capable of exercising, and tends to exercise, marks the violation of the *traité social*, the dissolution of *le grand État*, and the constitution of a new State, composed of the governors only, and excluding the citizens, who thus revert to the liberty of the state of nature, and are not obliged, though they may perhaps be compelled, to render obedience (III, c. 10).

Sieyès' modification of Rousseau's views

79. In the theory of Sieyès, for example, the person of the State is simply the community of associated individuals (cf. n. 117 to §16), and this community, in virtue of its inalienable and illimitable sovereignty, cannot be bound either by a fundamental constitution or by law: on the contrary, it can abolish all positive law whenever it wishes, in the strength of the community-will which is the final source and supreme controller of such law, and it can create new law by the simple expression of such will (I, pp. 131–6, 143, 202 sqq.). But this omnipotence of the collective sovereign only appears in action when the nation uses its supreme right in a controversy about the basic constitution, and proceeds to form a constituent assembly by appointing extraordinary and plenipotentiary representatives (I, pp. 138–42). On the other hand, even in ordinary times, when there is no such assembly in session, the law which the nation itself has enacted controls the *corps constitués*, including the legislative no less than the executive, as a universally binding constitutional norm (I, pp. 127–37, II, pp. 363 sqq.; cf. also nn. 118 and 119 to §16, supra). Cf. also Filangieri, I, cc. 1, 11, VII, c. 53.

Notes to §17

80. Fichte lays considerable emphasis on the rule of law. In order to secure it, he postulates a government which, though it is responsible to the sovereign people, has its own independent basis; and he rejects as 'illegal' forms both democracy proper, in which the community is judge and plaintiff at the same time, and despotisms in which the government is irresponsible (*Works*, III, pp. 12sqq., 150sqq.). *— Fichte on the rule of law*

81. *Works*, III, pp. 150sqq., 160–3, 286sqq.

82. Ibid. III, pp. 15sqq., 163, 166sqq.

83. Ibid. III, p. 169. So long as the appointed ruling authority lasts, its will is the common will, and any other will is a private will.

84. Ibid. III, p. 170.

85. Ibid. III, pp. 171sqq.

86. Ibid. III, p. 173. Fichte is not thinking here of a single large popular assembly, but of assemblies in different places, which must, however, be 'really great masses'. Such 'great masses' are necessary, in order that the force of the people may be unquestionably superior to that of executive officers (p. 177). *— Fichte on meetings of the community*

87. Ibid. III, pp. 182sqq. The people is never a rebel; for what is greater than the people? Only God. The leaders of popular movements are presumptively rebels; but the presumption is cancelled as soon as the people follows them, and thus declares them to be in agreement with the real general will. See, to the same effect, Fichte's *Sittenlehre* (of 1798), in *Works*, IV, pp. 238sqq. *— On popular resistance*

88. Fichte speaks expressly of a 'contract of devolution', arguing that in the making of that contract the magistrates negotiate with the people as a 'party' to it, and are excluded from membership of the people in perpetuity by accepting its terms. Once they have accepted these terms, and made themselves responsible, they can neither resign their office, nor be deprived of it, except by the common consent of both parties; and they must be given a free sphere of action in promoting the general good (*Works*, III, pp. 163–5, 175–7). *— On the contract of devolution*

89. *Works*, III, p. 176.

90. Once the assembled people re-enters upon its sovereignty, as 'the Community', the magistrates become merely a 'party': the ephors appear as accusers, and the executive officers as defendants: condemnation involves the penalties of high treason and perpetual banishment, but acquittal restores the person or persons acquitted to the position of 'magistrate' (*Works*, III, pp. 174sqq.). *— On the magistrates and the community*

91. In his lectures on *Die Grundzüge des gegenwärtigen Zeitalters* (1804–5), Fichte detaches the State from its individual members (cf. n. 66 to §16). It is now described as 'a notion invisible in its essence': it is 'not individuals, but their continuous relation towards one another—a relation of which the living and moving author is the activity of individuals, as they exist in space': again it is 'the result' which emerges from the union of the leadership of the governors with the strength of the governed when they follow that leadership (*Works*, VII, pp. 146–8). In his *Rechtslehre* also [1812] he adopts throughout an impersonal view of the State, ascribing sovereignty to 'the emergent will for law and right' which is manifested in the Ruler (*Posthumous Works*, II, p. 629, cf. *Works*, VIII, p. 157). A similar view appears in the *Staatslehre* [1813], where supreme authority is vindicated 'for the highest human reason of a given age and nation' (*Works*, IV, pp. 444sqq.). *— Fichte's later philosophy*

92. *Esprit des lois*, XI, c. 6: legislative power inherently belongs to *le Peuple en corps...comme dans un État libre tout homme qui est censé avoir une âme libre doit être gouverné par lui-même*.

Montesquieu avoids the problem of sovereignty

93. In dealing with the theory of separation of powers (XI, c. 6), Montesquieu avoids entirely any treatment of the problem of sovereignty. In dealing with the classification of States, he speaks of the *souveraine puissance* of the *Peuple en corps* in democracies (II, c. 2); but so far as other forms of State are concerned he only speaks of 'government' by a minority or a single person (II, cc. 3–5)—though he occasionally describes a king as *Souverain* (e.g. VI, c. 5). He never makes any reference whatever to the personality of the State: the issue to which his attention is always directed is whether the three *sortes de Pouvoir* should be united in a single man or body of men, or divided between several.

Frederick the Great and the People

94. Frederick the Great indubitably comes very near to a theoretical recognition of the sovereignty of the people. Not only does he refer the origin of all ruling authority to a contractual act of devolution by the people: he also identifies 'People' and 'State', in contradistinction to the Ruler appointed in virtue of that contractual act; and his famous saying that the Prince is *le premier serviteur de l'État* also reappears in his writings in the form that he is *le premier domestique des peuples qui sont sous sa domination* (*Antimach.* c. I, *Oeuvres*, I, p. 123, VIII, pp. 25 sqq., IX, pp. 196–7). [Gierke naturally seeks to cite the great authority of Frederick the Great. But it is not clear that Frederick was doing anything except to repeat, in a literary exercise, the current maxims of the Age of Enlightenment; nor is it certain whether, in identifying People and State, he meant (1) that the State is only the People, or (2) that the People is only the State—two seemingly identical propositions which are none the less very different.] The reader is also referred to the expressions of the constitutionalist theory in Voltaire, de Mably, Blackstone, de Lolme, etc.; cf. the author's work on Althusius, p. 187 n. 186.

Justi on popular rights

95. Justi regards the State as a single moral body, with a joint force and a single will (*Natur und Wesen*, §28). In this body, it is 'the basic authority of the people' which is the source of all other authority and is constantly appearing in action itself—determining the fundamental laws of the State, and limiting and binding the ruling authority which it confers (§46). Only the 'use' of the common possessions and powers is devolved upon the Ruler: the *dominium eminens* (*Obereigentum*) in respect of them all remains with 'the People', or 'the whole State', of which the Ruler is the 'Representative' (§49). The bearer of ruling authority cannot, therefore, use his authority for purposes repugnant to its final cause, or damage its substance (§50); and if he attempts to do so, the people may revoke the commission which it gave (§47). If the Ruler cannot fulfil his commission, or if he violates the fundamental contract, his rights disappear (§§141–2, 146, 161). He must always 'have in view the united will of the people' (§§149–50): the basic authority of the people affords a presumption in favour of 'a limited ruling authority' (§57); but even where the Ruler is unlimited this basic authority of the people still remains in force (§§67, 74). See also Justi's *Grundrisz*, §§9, 11, 15, 17, 23 sqq., 29 sqq.

Dualism of People and Ruler in his theory

96. The 'supreme active authority', once it has been appointed, is independent, and not subject to the judicial cognisance of the people, because the people is *paciscens* [i.e. a party to a contract in which it has stipulated certain conditions in its own favour] and cannot be judge in its own case

Notes to §17

(*Natur und Wesen*, §67). While the supreme authority observes the limits of the fundamental laws, it has the use of the whole power of the body politic, and thereby also of the powers and possessions of its individual members (§§45, 48): the Ruler and the People are the two main parts of this body, connected together by the closest of ties, which can only be broken by a definite breach of contract (§§128, 130–42).

97. *Natur und Wesen*, §§93 sqq., 130–42.

98. The people is the source of all authority; and moreover, in the rational and only lawful and definitive State (which Kant calls the *Republik*), it is also the 'Sovereign', inasmuch as true sovereignty or ruling authority belongs to the legislative, and the agreed will of the people should be the legislative (*Works*, VI, pp. 227 sqq., VII, pp. 131 sqq., §§45–6). The associated people itself thus emerges, by virtue of the political contract by which it is constituted, as 'the universal Head' (VII, p. 133, §47). The *Regent* (*rex* or *princeps*), as being the moral or physical person entrusted with executive authority, is to be regarded as the 'agent' of the people, or 'the organ of the Ruler' [i.e. of the true Ruler—the people itself]. He is 'subject to the rule of law, and bound thereby, and therefore he is bound by another than himself, that is to say, by the Sovereign', who can 'take away his authority, depose him, or reform his administration' (VII, pp. 134–5, §49, p. 137; VI, pp. 332, 336). Similarly the people is the fountain of justice—though it has to exercise the right of judicial decision indirectly, through representatives chosen from and by itself (the Jury),* and, further, to leave execution to the courts of justice (VII, p. 135). Being 'the most personal of all forms of Right', the sovereignty of the People is inalienable: any contract, by which the people pledges itself to return the sovereignty it has once attained [by concluding the original political contract, which *ipso facto* constituted the political body so created sovereign over itself], is 'inherently null and void'; and if any man exercises the power of sovereignty as a legislator, 'he can only have control over the people through the common will of the people, but he cannot have control over the common will itself' (VII, p. 159, §54). *Kant's theory of popular rights*

99. Cf. *Works*, VI, pp. 329–30: 'an idea of the reason—that is to say, an idea such as to oblige every ruler, in enacting law, to enact it *as though* it could have proceeded from the will of the whole people, and, again, to oblige every subject, so far forth as he wishes to be a real citizen, to regard the law *as though* he had concurred in the will enacting it in the manner aforesaid... this is the touchstone of the rightfulness of all public law': cf. also VII, p. 158. [We may almost say that Kant's philosophy is a philosophy of the *as though* (*als ob*), in the sense that when a thing is done 'as though' it were another thing (e.g. when law is enacted by somebody other than the people 'as though' it were enacted by the people), it becomes that other thing. The real difficulty which Kant is facing is whether a law for the general good can be enacted otherwise than by the general will. He answers that it can be— *Kant's theory of the as though*

---

* Kant's view appears to go beyond English practice, where the jury finds the facts on which the judicial decision is based. His distinction between the *Rechtsprechung* of the jury and the *Ausführung* by the *Gerichtshof* corresponds to old Teutonic ideas and practices, in which the people assembled in a folk-moot judge, and a judicial officer (such as the sheriff) executes the judgment; but it does not correspond to the relations between judge and jury in England, where the jury is in no way analogous to a folk-moot, but is derived from a royal prerogatival method of 'inquisition' into the facts, through 'sworn' representatives of local knowledge and opinion picked by royal officials, leading to a decision given by a royal judge.

provided that the enactor enacts 'as though' he were the general will. We might rejoin that no man or body of men other than the general will can act as the general will acts—i.e. can have gone through the dialectical process of social discussion, and taken the broad general social view, which a whole society can go through and take.]

Kant not a democrat in practice

100. The people cannot 'ratiocinate effectively' about the origin of the supreme authority to which it is subject, and it must 'obey the *de facto* legislative authority, be its origin what it may'. It 'cannot, and must not, judge otherwise than as the Head of the State for the time being (*summus imperans*) may will'. The Head of the State alone is exempt from all coercive law: he is 'not a member, but the author and sustainer of the commonwealth', the one and only 'gracious sovereign Lord' in the State; and although there are norms or standards which the Ruler should observe in enacting laws, any and every law is binding on his subjects. It follows that the people can never enjoy a right of resisting the powers that be (it cannot even plead that right in case of necessity), or possess any authority to coerce or punish the Head of the State; nor can any constitutional provision be conceived, or admitted, by which a 'publicly constituted opposition' can be invoked to protect the rights of the people against the Head of the State in the event of his violation of the constitution, since any such authority would itself be the Head of the State, or would postulate the existence of a third Head of the State [to judge between it and the *summus imperans*]. True, there are 'indestructible rights of the people as against the Head of the State', but the only protection of such rights is 'liberty of the pen, the one palladium of popular rights'. See *Works*, VI, pp. 323, 326 and 330–7, 449–50, VII, pp. 136–41, 158 sqq.

On this basis Kant also rejects the possibility of any alteration of the constitution by the people, and contents himself by appealing to 'the powers that be' to observe the law of Reason, which requires that they should realise a constitutional system of government and thus create the only rightful and abiding constitution; *Works*, VII, pp. 157 sqq.

101. It is true that Kant believes that the 'associated people', in a constitutional State of this pattern, should not only represent the Sovereign [in the sense of representing the final and sovereign law of Reason], but should actually be sovereign itself, in the sense of exercising legislative authority through the deputies whom it elects; but since it cannot, in its capacity of legislative, enjoy any executive powers, or pronounce any judicial decision, the people is left completely impotent as against the other powers; *Works*, VI, pp. 416–20, VII, pp. 131–6, 159–60.

102. Cf. *Works*, VII, pp. 158–9, §52: 'this is the only permanent constitution of the State, in which law is self-governing and depends on no special person'. Cf. also pp. 156 and 173.

103. Cf. nn. 41 and 47 to §14.

'Mixed' and 'limited' States

104. Thus Horn argues that there cannot be a *mixta Respublica*, because *majestas* is no more divisible or communicable than *intellectus Petri cani communicari potest*. Any division of the rights of supreme authority means a complete confusion and destruction of *majestas*: even in Poland (as was also the case in Scotland at an earlier date) the King is still the Sovereign, although his *modus habendi majestatem* is *limitatus* by the pact which obliges him to consult the *proceres*. *De civ.* III, c. un. §3, and II, c. 2, §8, c. 10, §5; cf. Becmann, c. 24, §6.

Notes to § 17

105. Cf. Micraelius, I, c. 13, §§ 3 sqq.: there is a *forma mixta*, but it only exists in the sense of a *forma temperata*, and this designation is preferable. Similarly Knichen, after giving an exhaustive account of the position of the controversy, arrives at the view that it is best to avoid the conception of a *forma mixta*, because the question is really one of *limitata* (rather than of *mixta*) *summa potestas* (*Opus. pol.* I, c. 8, th. 8, pp. 318–22).

Fénelon also, while he rejects equally *despotisme des Souverains et de la Populace*, regards a *forma mixta* as impracticable, because it involves *partage de la Souveraineté* (c. XII); and he describes, with an obvious prepossession in its favour, a system of *monarchie modérée par l'aristocratie*, in which the King needs the consent of an aristocratic chamber for legislation, and that of the people itself for the imposition of new taxes (c. XV).

106. If this line was taken [i.e. if it was argued that limited sovereignty was inconceivable, and that States with constitutional limitations upon the rights of the Ruler were only 'mixed', and not pure, forms], the result, on the basis adopted by Bodin and Hobbes and other advocates of absolutism, was simply to demonstrate the non-existence of such States; for on their view the real sovereign must always be either one man, or a single aristocratic council, or the people itself as a single unit, and no constitutional limits were legally binding upon that sovereign.

Arnisaeus, on the other hand, though he regards any limitation of sovereignty as inconceivable, admits the possibility of its division (cf. n. 47 to § 14). Spinoza too sketches the ideal of a limited monarchy, although he considers absolute monarchy alone to be real monarchy (cf. *Tract. pol.* cc. 6–7, and supra, n. 10 to § 17).

107. Pufendorf, *Jus nat. et gent.* VII, cc. 4, 5, §§ 12–15, c. 6, § 13; *De off. hom. et civ.* cc. 7, 8, § 12.

108. Thomasius, *Instit. jur. div.* III, c. 6, §§ 32–3, 38–56, 59–61, 156–60.

109. J. H. Boehmer, *Jus publ. univ.* I, c. 3, §§ 25–6: the *mixtus status*, when it occurs, is in any case a *monstrum Reipublicae*, because it depends on a division of powers, and such division disturbs *unio*.

110. Hert, *Elem.* I, 11, § 8.

111. Schmier, *Jus publ. univ.* I, c. 4, nos. 30–55: a genuine *forma mixta*, when it occurs, is necessarily *informis*, because *majestas* is indivisible [and to divide it therefore destroys the *forma Reipublicae* and makes it *informis*]. All that is compatible with the essence of the State is (1) 'limitation' of majesty in regard to its *modus habendi* and (2) the participation of others in its *administratio*.

112. Gundling, *Jus nat.* c. 37, §§ 21–36, *Disc.* c. 36. Any *respublica* is 'irregular', when the 'Subject' of majesty is several different persons, and not *una persona physica vel moralis*, and when majesty is therefore divided, and the State is without unity and a soul or spirit. There is nothing, therefore, in a *respublica mixta*, and Sidney's view is a mere chimaera; but people may all the same live happily in such a State, *per accidens*, as they do in England, Germany and Poland. Cf. *Jus nat.* c. 38, §§ 19–23, where Gundling argues that the people may draw the sword in a 'limited and irregular form of State', in which *tuetur...unusquisque jus suum ex pactis quaesitum*; but it is otherwise, he adds, in a regular form of State.

Gundling on the mixed State

113. Heineccius, *Elementa*, II, § 138.

114. Heincke, *Syst.* I, c. 3, §§ 24–5 (note the sharp distinction, in § 26, between the mixed constitution and the *forma temperata*).

'Irregular' States

115. We find Hert, for example (loc. cit.), already developing [in his *Elementa* of 1689] a formal scheme of *respublicae irregulares* which includes five subdivisions—Despotisms, Patrimonial States, Vassal States, and Unions or Confederations, in addition to Mixed States. Schmier (I, c. 4, ss. 1–3 of his *Jus publ. univ.* of 1722) distinguishes three kinds of irregular *civitates—ex defectu finis, ex defectu formae, ex defectu nexus*. Cf. also Gundling [in 1714], n. 112 of this section.

116. Otto's *Commentaries* on Pufendorf, § 12 on *De off. hom. et civ.* II, c. 8.

117. Titius, *Spec. jur. publ.* VII, c. 7, §§ 31–3 and 53–63. In the *civitas laxa*, we have to ascribe *majestas pluribus simplici saltem obligatione connexis divisim vel indivisim*; but even in such a case the State is one, and the 'Subject' of political authority is *unum, sed non satis unitum*.

Theories of partnership in sovereignty

118. See Besold, *Diss. de statu Reip. mixto*, c. 1 (where the phrase *communicata majestatica potestas* occurs); cf. also the author's work on Althusius, pp. 169 n. 138, 181 n. 170, 355 nn. 77 and 78. In using the argument that the Emperor and the Estates of Germany were only *conjunctim* [and not severally or separately] the 'Subject' of a single and indivisible sovereignty, thinkers were especially concerned to rebut the attacks of Hippolithus a Lapide and Pufendorf on the prevalent theory, and to vindicate the constitution of the Empire from any taint of irregularity.

119. Huber, *De jure civ.* I, 3, c. 1, §§ 21–3, c. 5, §§ 24 sqq., 79 sqq., I, 8, c. 6. Such communities [in which sovereignty is shared] may arise in consequence of the rights of majesty being either alienated or prescriptively acquired by one of the three parties concerned—prince, nobles and people; I, 3, c. 89. While there is no possibility of applying legal coercion to a Sovereign, the application of such coercion to the *Imperans* is a conceivable thing when the people *in societatem imperii, saltem pro parte, receptus est*; I, 9, c. 5, § 49.

120. For attempts to defend the mixed form of State by the doctrine of partnership in sovereignty see e.g. Cellarius, c. 9, § 35 (*conjunctim sumpti*); Kestner, c. 7, §§ 5 and 8 (*in solidum*); Alberti, c. 14, § 11; H. de Cocceji, *Prodromus* (a different view appears in S. de Cocceji, § 624); Heineccius, II, § 126; and especially Scheidemantel (I, pp. 156–62). Scheidemantel—agreeing with Pufendorf, Real, Mercier and Rousseau, as against Grotius, Arnisaeus, Piccartus, Montesquieu, Mably and Justi—attacks any division of the rights of majesty as an offence against the unity of the State, describing the appearance of such division as 'a disease'; but he admits the possibility of a partnership in majesty, i.e. a participation of several 'Subjects' in the exercise of its rights.

121. Thinkers, as a rule, were shy of treating in any detail this problem of the nature of the shares [possessed by the different 'Subjects' of majesty], contenting themselves with such phrases as were suitable for describing the legal position of ownership by *gesamte Hand* in German law [cf. supra, p. 185, n. *]. There were some who assumed, in respect of systems of joint majesty, a *condominium plurium in solidum* analogous to the *condominium* of private-law groups; cf. Kestner, loc. cit., and especially Vitriarius (I, 7, §§ 4–6), who speaks of a single Right with 'Subjects' who are 'diverse and mixed', parallel to the obligation of *correi debendi* [where there are multiple debtors, but a single 'Object' owed by them all; cf. supra, p. 123, n. *]. There were others who spoke of 'ideal' shares: cf. Besold, loc. cit., and Frantzken, *Diss. de statu Reip. mixtae* (in Arumaeus, III, no. 27).

122. Thus we find Hulderic ab Eyben arguing—in his *De sede Majestatis Romano-Germanicae* (*Scripta*, III, no. 5), c. 1, §§ 31 sqq.—that in a mixed form of State several 'Subjects' together form the 'common Subject' (*miscetur non majestas, sed subjectum*); but he proceeds to add that the *exercise* of supreme authority [i.e. the actual use of majesty, as distinct from majesty 'in itself' when regarded as an abstract power] may be either (1) divided among several users, or (2) managed on a joint system in some respects, but divided in others (§ 37)—the latter being the case in Germany, in so far as the authority of the territorial princes is really a case of the distribution of imperial sovereignty among different persons for separate use (c. 3) [i.e. in Germany imperial sovereignty is in some respects managed on a joint system, in which the Emperor and the Estates are associated, but in other respects it is divided among territorial princes]. *The 'shares' in the partnership*

123. Achenwall, II, §§ 186–7.

124. Like Arnisaeus, Grotius, Limnaeus, and other thinkers of previous centuries, we find Clasen (II, c. 9), Felwinger (*Diss. de Rep. mixta*, pp. 417 sqq.), and Boecler (II, c. 2; III, cc. 1, 8), still maintaining the conception of a *forma mixta* with a real *divisio majestatis*.

125. Thus Treuer, in commenting on Pufendorf, *De off. hom. et civ.* II, c. 7, § 9, contends that *majestatis divisio* is generally possible and advantageous, and does not produce a *monstrum*, because *respublica perpetuum majestatis subjectum manet*.

126. Leibniz (*Spec. demonstr. polit.* prop. 16, p. 537) argues that in dealing with the *jus majestatis*, as in dealing with any *jus*, we have to draw a distinction between *ipsa vis et potestas* and *exercitium*. On this basis we can explain *mixturae formarum*: Poland is a democracy if we look at the *vis*, but a monarchy if we look at the *exercitium summae potestatis*. *Leibniz on the mixed State*

127. On the beginnings of the theory that the three 'powers' should necessarily be divided—a theory which may already be traced in Buchanan and Hooker and Sidney—see the author's work on Althusius, pp. 157 n. 102, 163 n. 119, 355 n. 79. Sidney regards a 'mixed or popular government', combining all the three forms of State, as the best (c. II, ss. 8–29); but he does not definitely bring the idea of division of powers into connection with this doctrine. Locke also does not examine the relation of the system of division of *powers*, which he postulates in II, cc. 12–14 and 19, to the mixture of the different *forms* of which he speaks in II, c. 10, § 132. [Gierke is here reading too much into Locke. The passages cited (II, cc. 12–14 and 19) do not warrant the view that Locke postulates a system of division of powers—at any rate so far as their exercise is concerned. He simply seeks to distinguish, *in thought*, between the different functions of political authority. He is dealing with the logical analysis of functions, rather than with the practical question of separation (or union) of the organs which exercise functions. Distinguishing three functions, he only remarks (1) that in practice 'the legislative and executive powers come often to be separated', because the former is not always in session, while the latter is always in action, and (2) that the executive and federative powers are 'really distinct in themselves' (the one dealing with internal administration, and the other with treaty-making and foreign policy), but 'are almost always united' in exercise (II, c. 12, §§ 144, 147). This implies a distinction between a legislative organ which is not always in session, and a joint executive-federative organ which is always in action; but it is a distinction merely based on continuity or dis- *Division of powers* [*Locke's theory of the three powers*]

continuity of operation, and Locke's theory of the 'supreme power' of the legislative (subject always to the over-sovereignty of the community itself) is a theory which does not square with the idea of a separation of powers as necessary to liberty. On the whole, Locke believes in a united or single sovereignty, which is immediately vested in the legislative, and ultimately in the community—though he admits that where 'the executive is vested in a single person who has also a share in the legislative, there that single person, in a very tolerable sense, may also be called supreme'. But this is a guarded phrase, extorted by English conditions, and immediately qualified and modified (II, c. 13, §151); and Locke also hastens to add that 'the executive power placed anywhere but in a person that has also a share in the legislative is visibly subordinate and accountable to it' (§152).]

128. *Esprit des lois*, XI, cc. 2, 4, 6, VI, cc. 5–6.

129. Ibid. XI, cc. 4, 6. But Montesquieu is in favour of as much division of powers as possible even in simple forms of State, and he deals with the way in which it may be achieved under different constitutions, XI, cc. 7–30.

Montesquieu on division of powers

130. Montesquieu goes to the length of declaring that a constitution, in which *le peuple en corps* can draw all the powers into its own hands, is the greatest menace to liberty: XI, cc. 5, 6. In a proper State not only the judicial, but also the executive power is independent of the popular assembly or the assembly of popular representatives: *le pouvoir arrête le pouvoir*, and the three powers can impede one another in moving, *mais comme par le mouvement nécessaire des choses elles seront contraintes d'aller, elles seront forcées d'aller de concert*, XI, cc. 4, 6.

131. *Contr. soc.* III, c. 2.

Rousseau's attitude to mixed constitutions

132. Ibid. III, cc. 4, 7. It depends on circumstances whether the *gouvernement mixte* is to be preferred to the *gouvernement simple*: strictly speaking, there is hardly such a thing as a *gouvernement simple*.

133. Ibid. II, c. 2. Whether we look at the 'Subject' owning, or the 'Object' owned, Sovereignty is indivisible: political theorists behave like Japanese jugglers, who cut a child into pieces, throw the pieces up into the air, and make a living child come down; *tels sont à peu près le tours de gobelet de nos politiques; après avoir démembré le corps social, par un prestige digne de la foire ils rassemblent les pièces on ne sait comment*.

134. Ibid. III, c. 1: just as all voluntary action has two causes which must both be operative, *volonté* and *puissance*, so, in the body politic, there must necessarily be a distinction between *volonté* and *force*, or in other words between *puissance législative* and *puissance exécutive*; and while the former of these must belong to the sovereign body, it need not necessarily possess the latter.

135. See n. 74 to this section; cf. also *Contr. soc.* II, c. 6 and III, c. 1, where the argument is pressed that legislation, being the only possible expression of the general will on general objects, is the only possible activity of the Sovereign when acting as such; while political activity of any other kind, being *action particulière*, is merely an *action de magistrature*, even when the Sovereign itself undertakes that activity. [See n. 74 supra, on the sovereign community turning itself into a democracy, and the citizens making themselves magistrates, for purposes of executive action.]

136. Cf. supra, n. 78 to this section.

Sieyès on division of powers

137. Such an approach to the principle of division of powers appears in Sieyès, I, pp. 283 sqq., 445 sqq., II, pp. 363 sqq., 371 sqq. and 376 sqq. Here

division of powers is justified by the argument that though there is only one political authority—that of the social body itself—there are different organs of that authority, based on different commissions given by the society. Sieyès also attempts to argue for a system of *concours* of powers, instead of a balance or equilibrium.

See also Fichte's *Naturrecht*, I, pp. 193 sqq. (*Works*, III, pp. 161 sqq.). Fichte, however, subsequently rejected the idea of division of powers in his *Rechtslehre* (*Posthumous Works*, II, p. 632).

138. This combination of the mixed constitution and division of powers appears in Blackstone, *Commentaries* (1765), I, c. 2 sqq.; in de Lolme, *The Constitution of England* (1775, first published in French in 1771); in the Abbé de Mably, *Doutes proposés aux philosophes économistes sur l'ordre naturel et essentiel des sociétés politiques* (1768), Lettre x, and *De la législation ou des Principes des lois* (1776), III, c. 3; and in other writers. [Among other writers who combine the mixed constitution and division of powers may be mentioned Paley, who in his *Principles of Moral and Political Philosophy* (1785), Book VI, c. 7, argues (1) that the British constitution is formed by 'a combination of the three regular species of government', and (2) that the security of the constitution depends on a 'balance of the constitution', or 'political equilibrium', securing each part of the legislative—King, Lords and Commons—'from the encroachments of the other parts in the exercise of the powers assigned to it'. The balance, Paley argues, is double: it is both a balance of power, and a balance of interest. Paley differs from the general continental usage in speaking of a balance or equilibrium, not of the three powers (legislative, judicature and executive), but of the three parts of the legislative. This was natural in England, where the legislative, or King in Parliament, was regarded as everything, so that any parts or divisions must necessarily be parts of it. It is this point of view which enables Paley to identify the mixed constitution with division or balance of powers; for if King, Lords and Commons are the powers divided or balanced, then—since they represent respectively monarchy, aristocracy and democracy—the constitution is a mixed constitution uniting all these three forms. It may be added that Paley's view is the general English view of his time. It is expounded by Burke in the *Thoughts on the Cause of the Present Discontents* (*Works*, in Bohn's edition, I, p. 333), and also in the *Reflections*, where the constitution is described as 'the engagement and pact of society' by which 'the constituent parts of a State are obliged to hold their public faith with each other' (*Works*, II, p. 294). This general idea is criticised by Paine, both in his *Common Sense* of 1776 (where he assumes that 'the component parts of the English constitution' are 'the base remains of two ancient tyrannies', monarchy and aristocracy, 'compounded with some new republican materials in the presence of the commons', and then argues that 'to say that the constitution of England is a union of three powers, reciprocally checking each other, is farcical'), and in the *Rights of Man* of 1791–2 (where in Part I, Conclusion, he criticises 'mixed government, or, as it is sometimes ludicrously stiled, a government of *this that and t'other*', as a cause of corruption (because the hereditary part tries to buy up the elective) and of irresponsibility (because each part tries to shuffle off blame on the others)....It seems curious, by the way, that the English thought of the eighteenth century does not regard the judicature as a 'part' of the Constitution, in any way parallel to the other 'parts' of which we have spoken. But the reason is simple. Concentration on the King in Parliament eliminates

Division of powers and the mixed constitution

[Paley, Burke and Paine]

the judges, who are not, as a body, a 'part' of that organisation. At the same time we must notice that Paley, when he comes to the administration of Justice (VI, c. 8), is quite clear that it is 'the first maxim of a free State' that 'the legislative and judicial characters be kept separate', and that there should be a 'division of the legislative and judicial functions'. Similarly Burke, though he regards the King and the two Houses as the constituent parts of the State, and as jointly sovereign, also says in his *Reflections* (*Works*, II, 476) that 'whatever is supreme in a State ought to have as much as possible its judicial authority so constituted, as not only not to depend upon it, but in some sort to balance it'.... On the general theory of the parts of the constitution and separation of powers see the Report of the Committee on Ministers' Powers (Cmd. 4060), pp. 8 ff.]

The theory of the mixed constitution in Germany

139. See, e.g., Wolff, *Instit.* §§ 993, 1004; Daries, § 767 (but he argues, in §§ 786-7, that limited monarchy is not a *forma mixta*); Nettelbladt, §§ 1142, 1155-7, 1197 (who suggests, in dealing with the mixed constitution, that sovereignty can belong to several 'Subjects' at the same time in any one of three ways—(1) in *partes divisae*, or (2) *indivisa*, on a basis of joint ownership, or (3) partly divided and partly joint—and that none of these ways is absurd); and Ickstatt, *Opusc.* II, op. 1, c. 1, §§ 18–21 (who takes the same line).

Hoffbauer (*Naturrecht*, pp. 307-14) treats mixed constitutions with special fullness. He divides them into three kinds—'limited', 'the mixed in the proper sense of the word', and 'partly limited and partly mixed'. He is the only writer who attempts, after distinguishing the different 'Subjects' of sovereignty involved, to re-unite them again in 'a moral person in the wider sense' (pp. 206, 292); but he does so by extending the conception of the moral person to a point at which it ceases even to imply the existence of a partnership among the different juxtaposed 'Subjects' (p. 190; cf. n. 190 to § 16).

140. Frederick the Great himself (*Antimach.* c. 19) had already declared that the English Constitution was more worthy to be adopted as a model than the French.

141. Justi ranks as the best constitution the form which is a 'mixture' of the three simple forms, with a 'division' and 'equilibrium' of the different 'powers'; and this is the basis of his sketch of an ideally good constitution for all times and places (*Grundrisz*, §§ 135-69; *Natur und Wesen*, §§ 51-61, 93-7, 142).

142. A. L. von Schlözer holds that all *Principes simplices* are a menace, and only a *Princeps compositus* is endurable. We must therefore mix forms of State, as a physician mixes his drugs; and a mixture of the three forms, with a division of sovereignty, is 'the best attempt of poor humanity, which anyhow must have a State'. This ideal form has been attained in England; 'but it has not been discovered by Philosophy, or Romulus, or the Earl of Leicester:* it is due to accident, guided by *bon Sens*, and favoured by circumstances'; pp. 144-55, §§ 23-8; p. 115, § 3.

Kant on the logic of the mixed constitution

143. Kant achieves this result by his famous comparison of the legislative, executive and judicial powers to the three terms (major premise, minor premise, and conclusion) in a practical syllogism; *Works*, VI, pp. 418-20, VII, pp. 131-6, 159-60. The three powers are co-ordinate with one another as 'independent moral persons'; but at the same time, inasmuch as none of

* Simon de Montfort?

Notes to § 17

the three can usurp any of the functions of the other two, each is also subordinated to the others; ibid. VII, p. 134. Cf. also p. 153 supra.

144. See Pufendorf, *J. n. et g.* VIII, c. 12, §§ 1–4 (it follows, he argues, that responsibility for past debts continues, ranks and orders still remain the same, etc.); Alberti, c. 15, §§ 5–9; Schmier, II, c. 4, s. 2, § 1; Locke, II, c. 19, §§ 211 sqq.; Hertius, *Opusc.* I, 1, p. 296, §§ 11–12, II, 3, p. 54, §§ 7–8; Gundling, c. 38, §§ 11 sqq.; Scheidemantel, III, pp. 409 sqq. *Continuity of public rights and duties*

145. Pufendorf, loc. cit. §§ 5–6, argues that when a State is divided into a number of States, its debts must also be divided *pro rata*. An independent colony is not, however, responsible for the debts of the mother-country, since this is a case not of alteration but of procreation. When several States unite to form an entirely new State, rights and liabilities are transferred to this new State; and when a previously independent State is made a province, the State annexing it must similarly take over its liabilities, along with its rights, as *in ipso corpore haerentia*. Cf. also Schmier, loc. cit., who holds that *divisio* or *unio* does not mean the destruction of the existing political authority, but partition of it or participation in it; Hertius (*Opusc.* I, 1, pp. 293 sqq., §§ 9–10), who distinguishes the four cases of merger, annexation, simple adhesion, and personal union; Gundling, c. 38; Scheidemantel, III, pp. 408–26.

On complete disintegration of the State, either through the total disappearance of its physical basis or the total dissolution of its nexus, cf. Pufendorf, loc. cit. § 8; Schmier, V, c. 4, s. 2, § 3; Alberti, c. 15, § 10; Hert, loc. cit. p. 295, § 10; Locke, II, c. 19, § 211; Rousseau, III, c. 11.

146. Cf. nn. 126, 129, 147, 161, 168, 170, 186, 213–14, and 238 to § 16; and also n. 7 to § 17.

The most detailed treatment of the question [i.e. the question of the nature of the 'person of the State' when the Ruler is a collective body of persons] is to be found in Ickstatt, *Opusc.* II, op. 1, *de jure majorum in conclusis civitatis communibus formandis*. He starts from the principle that a decision of the State is a *voluntas totius reipublicae determinata de medio quodam saluti publicae effectum dandi*; that this determination of the will belongs to the 'active Subject' of 'supreme power'; and that it is therefore achieved by the will of a 'single moral person' in a monarchy, and by the decision of a 'composite moral person', based on previous deliberation and argument, in 'polyarchical' forms of State. He proceeds, on the basis of this principle, to deal with majority-decisions both under *jus publicum universale* (c. 1) and under the public law of Germany (c. 2). See also Heincke, I, c. 3, §§ 16–23. *Rules for the action of a collective Ruler*

147. This was regarded as one of the cases in which *unus homo plures personas sustinet*; cf. nn. 139, 159 and 173 to § 16. See also Huber, I, 3, §§ 24–38, and Nettelbladt, § 1194.

148. Titius refuses to distinguish public and private law by the different purposes to which they are directed, 'as is generally done'; he prefers to distinguish them by the different 'Subjects' of rights to which they relate. Public law relates to *Subditi constituendi*, and to *Imperantes constituendi et constituti qua tales*; private law relates to *Subditi constituti*, and to *Imperantes juxta conditionem privatam*. Accordingly, while *Subditi constituti* in a formed and operative State [as contrasted with *Subditi* who have still 'to be constituted' when the State is in process of formation] no longer possess a *persona publica*, and have only a private personality, the Ruler always possesses a *persona duplex*, and we must always distinguish his public and his *Public and private law* private personality. There are, however, mixed situations (such as that presented by the private law peculiar to princely families);* and the 'private person' of the *Princeps* is not necessarily *subdita* (*Spec. jur. publ.* I, c. 1, §§ 43–52).

149. Cf. e.g. Huber, I, 9, c. 5, § 72; Hert, *Comment. et Op.* I, 3, p. 52, §§ 4–5; Wolff, *Instit.* § 1012 (where a distinction is drawn between *actus regii et privati*).

The Ruler and his officials

150. Mevius, for example (*Prodromus*, v, § 29), and Hert (loc. cit. p. 53, § 6) argue that the Ruler, and therefore the State itself, acts when the *ministri summae potestatis* act, provided that the latter are acting within the limits of their office. Schmier, on the other hand, argues altogether in terms of private law (III, c. 5, nos. 48–64, *de obligatione summae potestatis ex facto et non facto officialium*). See also Stryck, *Diss.* IV, no. 15, *de obligatione Principis ex facto ministri*.

The inheritance of obligations by a Ruler

151. Huber, I, 9, c. 5, §§ 53–72: *obligationes, quae propter rempublicam initae sunt, tenent omnino successorem, non ut haeredem, sed ut caput civitatis, immo ut ipsam Civitatem*: where such obligations are concerned, there is no question of *probabilis ratio*, *versio*† and the like; the only question is whether the *Imperans, qui personam Civitatis constituit*, has acted within 'the limits of his power'. Pufendorf, *J. n. et g.* VIII, c. 10, § 8: *ipsa civitas obligata*, but its obligation exists only when there is *probabilis ratio*, and does not extend *in infinitum*. Schmier, II, c. 4, s. 1, § 3: the question is whether the *corpus Universitatis* is bound; and this is the case when a contract has been made, *nomine populi et ad salutem communem*, within the sphere of the Ruler's office.

All these three writers, it should be added, seek to apply the usual rules of simple inheritance in dealing with 'patrimonial' States; it is only when they are dealing with *regna voluntaria* or *usufructuaria* that they distinguish between inheritance of private property and succession to the Crown. Titius (IV, c. 5) opposes this point of view. He argues that when a Ruler has duly acted in the name of the *Respublica*, and thus the *Respublica 'per caput suum voluit'*, his successor incurs responsibility in all cases alike [whether the monarchy be patrimonial or non-patrimonial] for one and the selfsame reason—viz. that '*respublica velut persona immortalis adhuc durat...et nunc etiam adhuc vult*'. It is true that in non-patrimonial monarchies the successor does not take over his legal position from the *defunctus*; but he takes over his position, none the less, from the *civitas ipsa*. The analogy of the limited responsibility of a tenant succeeding to a fief does not hold good [in regard to a non-patrimonial monarchy]: the new tenant of the fief succeeds to a *homo singularis*, while the new holder of the Crown succeeds to the *caput corporis liberi et adhuc durantis*; in the one case it is the *factum defuncti* which is in question, while in the other it is the *factum personae viventis*. The same rule, therefore, applies to elective [or non-patrimonial] monarchies as to other forms; and exceptions [from this general rule of the successor's responsibility] can only be recognised when there has been an act of the predecessor contravening the fundamental laws—for then it can be said that *respublica non egit*—or when there has been a case of *inconsulta prodigalitas* or some other special circumstance. [Roughly expressed,

---

* The *Hausrecht* or dynastic rules regulating e.g. marriage.

† *Versio = versio in rem* = an application of money or other proceeds by the previous ruler to the *res* to which the new ruler succeeds, so that the new ruler benefits by such application, and may therefore be held to incur a correlative obligation. Cf. n. 89 to § 14.

the difference between Titius and his three predecessors is that they were ready to allow that the *hereditary* king of a patrimonial monarchy inherited all the rights and obligations of his predecessor in title, but held that a *non-hereditary* king was in a different position; Titius, on the contrary, contends that there is no difference between the two, because in either case the rights and obligations are really those of the immortal State, and their continuity is not affected in any way by the hereditary or elective character of the Ruler. Perhaps we shall understand the theory of the predecessors of Titius better if we assume that in their view a 'patrimonial' monarchy is not simply an hereditary monarchy: it is a monarchy in which, as Loyseau says, 'the king by title of prescription possesses or owns sovereignty', and therefore (if sovereignty be regarded as the essence of the State) owns, or *is*, the State (*l'État c'est moi*). On this basis the king in such a monarchy of course takes over everything alike from his predecessor—public rights equally with private, and public obligations equally with private—because there is no distinction between public and private, all public status having become the possession or property of the king. When we get to non-patrimonial monarchies, we shall have to distinguish 'private' and 'public'; but if we hold the view of patrimonial monarchies just described, it will only be when we get to monarchies other than patrimonial that we shall begin to make this distinction. Titius, we may add, is really challenging the idea at the bottom of the 'patrimonial theory', at any rate by implication.]

J. P. von Ludewig (*Op.* 1, 1, op. 8, pp. 539–646, *De obligatione successoris in principatus*) puts the conception of patrimonial monarchies completely aside, and thus rejects the usual distinctions drawn by other writers. He uses, as the thread to guide him through the labyrinth, the dictum of Baldus, that the successor is responsible if, and to the extent that, there has been action *nomine et auctoritate Reipublicae inter tot mortes principum suorum immortalis* (c. 1, §8). He accordingly denies that the successor is bound in any case where the 'limits of the office and dignity' have been overstepped by his predecessor; and he therefore decides the question of the extent of the successor's responsibility, in any particular case, by the *formula imperii* [which fixes 'the limits of the office and dignity'], c. 4. But even Ludewig, in the issue, falls back into a private-law point of view, cc. 5–7 [i.e. he lets drop the thread of the public-law rights and duties of the immortal *Respublica*, and goes back to terms of the private-law rights and duties of the personal ruler].

152. J. H. Boehmer (*P. spec.* 1, c. 3, §35, 11, c. 3, §16) goes to the length of making *all* responsibility [incumbent upon a successor] depend simply and solely upon hereditary succession to the *universitas juris*; and he accordingly considers *successores titulo singulari* (e.g. rulers by right of election or by virtue of contract) as not intrinsically obliged, because they rule *ex novo plane jure*. But he adds that it is proper for such rulers to recognise any act of a predecessor which has been done *intuitu officii* or has brought advantage to the State.

153. See the author's work on Althusius, pp. 305–6. The only dispute turned on the question, what was necessary to constitute legitimation [of an irregular ruler]. At first, thinkers were generally content to answer, 'The express or tacit assent of the people'. Later, we find the advocates of popular sovereignty insisting exclusively on the necessity of an absolutely free assent of the people (e.g. Sidney, III, s. 31, and Locke, II, c. 16,

When the usurper becomes legitimate

§§ 175–96, c. 17, §§ 197–8), while the advocates of the sovereignty of the Ruler require, in addition, an act of renunciation by the legitimate ruler (e.g. Kestner, c. 7, §§ 20–1; H. Cocceji, *De regimine usurpationis rege ejecto*, Frankfort, 1705; Schmier, II, c. 2, s. 2, § 1, nos. 82–98; Nettelbladt, §§ 1267–8; and Achenwall, II, § 98). Often, however, the mere fact of possession was allowed to confer a prescriptive title to ruling authority.

From an opposite point of view [i.e. from a point of view which does not seek to safeguard the rights of the legitimate ruler] we find Hobbes (*Leviathan*, c. 21), Conring and J. H. Boehmer (*P. spec.* III, c. 12, § 17) declaring that the people is quit of all responsibility to the legitimate ruler as soon as he is no longer in a position to protect them; while Horn (II, c. 9, §§ 4, 21), though rejecting prescription as a title to rule, allows majesty to be extinguished by the *de facto* acquisition of majesty by a new ruler. The theory of the *fait accompli* then gains ground gradually, even among the disciples of Natural Law.

Different views of the usurper's position

154. The stricter school of thinkers continued to maintain the old theory —that any representation of the State by a usurper was impossible; that all his acts of government were void, and imposed no obligation; that refusal of obedience to him was the right and duty of every individual; and even that private persons were free to attack him as a public enemy and put him to death. We find this view not only in Althusius and the other *monarchomachi*, in Suarez and the rest of the Catholic writers on Natural Law, and in Bodin, Arnisaeus and their successors, but also in Huber (I, 9, c. 1, c. 5, § 51), Schmier (loc. cit.), Fénelon (who holds, c. VIII, that *le Roi de Fait* and *le Roi de Droit* must be distinguished, and that the theory of obedience being due even to the *de facto* king, as *Roi de Providence*, is erroneous), H. Cocceji (loc. cit.), Nettelbladt (§ 1267) and others.

On the other hand, we find Grotius—on the ground that *some* sort of government is necessary—already contending that the people is obliged to obey the actual holder of political authority, in things necessary, even before there has been any legitimation by *longum tempus* or by *pactum* (I, c. 4, § 15); and he therefore limits the right of resistance to any actual ruler (ibid. §§ 16–20), just as he also holds (II, c. 14, § 14) that contracts made by a ruler during an interregnum involve the people and the subsequent legitimate ruler, at the very least, in responsibility *de in rem verso* [i.e. for expenditure incurred, as we might say, 'in connection with the estate'; cf. n. 151 supra]. Pufendorf has a different theory: the usurper genuinely represents the State in its external relations, and he thus binds it in that respect by his donations etc.; but internally his acts—his laws as well as the donations or alienations he makes—can be rescinded by the legitimate authority; *J. n. et g.* VIII, c. 12, § 4. On the theory of the *fait accompli*, the usurper represents the authority of the State at all points, even in regard to his subjects [i.e. internally no less than externally], as soon as the expulsion of the rightful owner of political authority has been achieved. Cf. Boehmer, loc. cit., and also Kant, *Works*, VII, p. 139.

155. Horn, refusing to recognise any personality of the State, naturally ascribes the ownership of all public property to the *Princeps* alone; *De civ.* II, c. 3, §§ 5–9.

The Ruler in relation to State property

156. Cf. especially Mevius (*Prodromus*, v, § 32); Huber (who speaks of public property as being *in patrimonio civitatis*, since the *civitas* has *jus personae*, II, 4, c. 1, §§ 24 sqq.); Pufendorf (who regards public property as owned by the *civitas qua talis*, and considers the king as having only the rights of a

tutor therein, so that he has no right to alienate it apart from the people, *J. n. et g.* VIII, c. 5, §8, *De off. hom. et civ.* II, c. 15, §5); Titius (III, c. 7, §§2sqq.); Wolff (who distinguishes *bona regis regia et publica* from *bona privata seu propria, Instit.* § 1012); Daries (*bona publica sunt in dominio totius civitatis, bona privata in dominio civium*, the latter partly belonging to the Prince and partly to his subjects, §§687sqq.); Nettelbladt (§§ 1347sqq.); Achenwall (II, § 123); Scheidemantel (who speaks of 'the property of the whole nation', assigns 'its supreme administration' to the sovereign, but assumes a right of the whole nation to consent to its alienation, pp. 320sqq., 333sqq.).

157. Theorists began by distinguishing *res publicae* from *patrimonium reipublicae*, according as public property was destined for common use by all individuals (*ad usus singulorum*) or for the immediate purposes of the State itself (*ad usus universorum*): cf. Huber, II, 4, c. 4, §§2sqq.; Titius, III, c. 7, §§5sqq.; Daries, §687; Scheidemantel, pp. 330sqq. *Classification of State property*

In regard to the first of these categories (*res publicae*) there was a difference of opinion. Were *res nullius* to be included without further question in the category of State-property (this was the view of Horn, loc. cit. §§5-9, and Titius, loc. cit. §§11sqq.); or at any rate (if that were not allowed) could they be brought into this category by a declaration made by the State, in virtue of its right of majesty (the view of Gundling, c. 36, §§217-20, and of Scheidemantel, loc. cit.)? Or did *res nullius* come to be the property of the State only in virtue of its actually exercising a right of occupation, such as it was intrinsically free to exercise, though the right might be to some extent limited by other rights of exclusive appropriation which had their basis in positive law (this is the view of Huber, II, 4, c. 1, §§30sqq., c. 2, §§12-25, and of Nettelbladt, §§ 1345-6)?

State-property in the strict sense (i.e. *patrimonium reipublicae*) was generally divided into property belonging to the *aerarium* and property belonging to the *fiscus* (cf. Pufendorf, loc. cit.; Gundling, c. 36, §§211-2; Wolff, §§ 1038-9); but Gundling remarks that there is fundamentally no difference between the two. [Some remarks may be added in elucidation. (1) The conception of *res nullius* is fully discussed by Pound, *Introduction to the Philosophy of Law*, pp. 197sqq. (2) On occupation as a basis of State-property, and on the possible limitation of the State's right of occupation by positive-law rights, cf. Mommsen, *History of Rome* (Eng. trans.), III, p. 96, where (in connection with the legislation of the Gracchi) the problem is discussed how far the State's right to its 'occupied domains' could be modified by private rights, based on positive-law titles of long prescription or recent acquisition. (3) Finally, as regards the distinction between *aerarium* and *fiscus*, we may note that this really belongs to the system of dyarchy instituted by Augustus, under which the senate and the *princeps* seemed to rule conjointly, and while the former had the *aerarium*, the latter had the *fiscus* as a separate treasury—both, be it noted, being public and official treasuries.]

158. Huber distinguishes four species of property in a monarchy—*res privatae principis, res dominicae, res fiscales* and *res aerarii*—but he admits that the second and the third are often difficult to distinguish (II, 4, c. 4, §§35-50). Gundling (loc. cit. §§213-16) and Wolff (§ 1040) both rank demesne as a third species of public property, by the side of that of the *aerarium* and that of the *fiscus*; and they hold that the prince possesses a limited right of ownership in the demesne, being unable to alienate it freely on account of its connection with territorial sovereignty. *The Ruler's demesne*

Demesne included in State property

159. This is the view of Daries, §§ 691–4. He simply distinguishes *bona fisci* and *bona aerarii*, including under the former what is intended immediately for the personal support of the territorial prince [this, of course, differs from the old Roman use of the term], and under the latter all that is directly designed for the maintenance of the State itself; and, on this basis, he allows the prince *administratio* only of the latter, but gives him both *administratio* and *jus utendi* of the former.* A similar line is taken by Achenwall (II, § 124), and more especially by Nettelbladt (§§ 1347–9), who distinguishes from the demesne [which is the property of the State] not only the *patrimonium principis*, but also the *bona familiae ejus qui princeps est (Haus- und Stammgüter)*.

Ownership of the State's territory

160. Cf. Wolff, *Instit.* § 1125; Nettelbladt, §§ 1144–51. Only as regards patrimonial States was the conception of 'property', amounting to a full right of ownership, extended to include the whole country; but many thinkers rejected the whole idea as untenable for that very reason [i.e. they rejected the whole idea of the patrimonial State, because it involved as a consequence the King's ownership of his territory as his own property]. Cf. p. 144, supra.

Dominium eminens in Horn and other writers

161. Horn (II, c. 4) is the strongest advocate of the view that *dominium eminens* is not only *imperium*, but a *verum dominium*, a real legal property which the State has reserved for itself in distributing private property, and which signifies the whole body of the limits to which private property is subject. But see also Huber (I, 3, c. 6, §§ 30–53), Pufendorf (*Elem.* I, def. 5, § 5), J. H. Boehmer (I, c. 4, §§ 25–7), Stryck (*Diss.* XIV, no. 7) and Wolff (*Instit.* § 1065).

Other views in regard to this question

162. Titius, for example, distinguishes sharply between *dominium publicum*, which only differs from *dominium privatum* in that the 'Subject' or owner is different, and *dominium eminens*, which is really *pars imperii*, and only nominally 'property' or *dominium* (III, c. 5, § 51, c. 7, § 2). Gundling argues that the basis of expropriation is not *dominium eminens*, which only belongs to the prince in a *civitas herilis* [i.e. in a patrimonial State], but *imperium eminens* (c. 36, §§ 226–9). Daries also rejects the conception of *dominium eminens* as a basis for the rights of taxation and of expropriation of *bona privata* (§§ 695–701). Cf. also Achenwall, who writes of a *jus eminens* which takes the two forms of *dominium eminens* over things and *potestas eminens* over persons (II, §§ 145–7), and Scheidemantel, who holds that the rights of 'majesty' in regard to private possessions are not derived from any property vested in it, but from its superior authority, though many writers call this 'a superior property' or eminent domain (pp. 360–4).

* The translator, in this clause, has inverted the statement in Gierke's text, which apparently makes Daries assign to the prince only *administratio* of *bona fisci*, but both *administratio* and *jus utendi* of *bona aerarii*.

§18. THE NATURAL-LAW THEORY OF CORPORATIONS

1. Cf. e.g. Cellarius, *Pol.* cc. 2–8; Johannes a Felde, *Elem.* I, c. 1; Boecler, I, cc. 2–6; Clasen, I, cc. 2–6; Mullerus, *Instit.* I, cc. 2–7; Horn, *De civ.* I, cc. 1–4; Alberti, cc. 10–14. See also Pufendorf (*J. n. et g.* VI–VII and *De off. hom. et civ.* II, cc. 2–5), who, however, refuses to admit the Family as a separate and independent stage in the development of associations (which would set it on the same level as the three *personae morales compositae* constituted by the domestic groups of husband and wife, parent and child, and master and servant), and accordingly designates 'the most perfect society' of the State as *societas quarta*. Thomasius takes the same line [i.e. he recognises only the three domestic groups and the State as societies] in *Instit. jur. div.* III, cc. 1–7 (cf. also c. 1, §§ 13–14, where he argues that the Family, regarded as a union of the three *societates simplices*, has no specific purpose of its own); and so does Schmier (I, c. 2, ss. 1–4). Cf. also Praschius, §§ 6–11; Placcius, Bk. 1; Rachelius, I, titt. 15–31.

The position of the Family

Even Wolff, although he begins with a detailed theory 'of authority and society (*Herrschaft und Gesellschaft*) in general' (*Instit.* §§ 833–52), is like other thinkers [i.e. in omitting fellowships and local communities]; he only admits as natural-law groups (*a*) the societies constituted under the family-system (though he allows four of these—the 'marital', the 'parental', the 'magisterial' and the Family—§§ 854–971), and (*b*) the State (§§ 972 sqq.). Achenwall takes exactly the same line (*Proleg.* §§ 91 sqq. and Part II, §§ 1 sqq., where he treats of *societas in genere*, of the four *societates domesticae*, and of the State).

2. Thomasius (loc. cit. c. 1, §§ 15–32) explicitly justifies a direct transition from the Family to the State, without any consideration of intervening groups, on the grounds (1) that a local community has no specific purpose, and (2) that a State might possibly be composed only of a single territorial community, which proves that *vici et provinciae non tam a civitate differunt specie ac finibus, quam ut partes a suo toto*, § 30 [i.e. local communities differ from a State, not as being a different species with their own specific purpose, but only in the way in which parts differ from the whole which they jointly constitute—that is to say, in the way of quantity. Thomasius implicitly assumes that a 'part' is the same, in kind and purpose, as the 'whole' to which it belongs]. Schmier takes the same line, I, c. 2, s. 4, no. 127.

Thomasius on local communities as only 'parts'

3. Thomasius, *Instit. jur. div.* I, c. 1, § 98.

4. Cf. Schmier, V, c. 1, who speaks of *subditi conjunctim aut collegialiter spectati*. See also Pufendorf, *J. n. et g.* VII, c. 2, §§ 21–2; Hertius, *Elem.* II, 2, § 41; J. H. Boehmer, *P. spec.* II, cc. 4–5; Scheidemantel, III, pp. 244 sqq.

5. See [as examples of a theory which admits a variety of societies, over and above the Family and the State] Mevius, who enumerates in his list *societas domestica*, with its three species, the *corpus, pagi, urbes, terrae seu regna, foedera* (*Prodromus*, V, § 19); Micraelius, who reckons *societas domestica* (I, cc. 2–6), the *vicus* and *pagus* (c. 7, §§ 1–24), the *tribus, collegium, corpus et universitas* (ibid. §§ 25–32), *oppida, regiones* and *civitas* (c. 8); Knichen, who includes the four 'domestic societies', *collegia, territoria*, and the *civitas* (I, cc. 4–6); and Becmann, who makes two divisions—the one including the Family, *corpora*,

Theories favourable to intervening groups

collegia, systemata and the *respublica*; the other embracing *vici, pagi* and *urbes*, which, however, are only *partes integrantes reipublicae* (*Med.* cc. 7–11).

Leibniz on groups

6. Leibniz, *Deutsche Schriften*, I, pp. 414–20. Leibniz starts, it is true, by enumerating only six sorts of 'natural society'—the four societies of the family-system (those of husband and wife, parent and child, and master and servant, with the addition of the household composed of these three and intended to provide for temporal needs); the civic community (the town or rural area, intended to promote temporal well-being); and the Church of God (for the purpose of eternal felicity). But when he comes to the 'classification of societies', he distinguishes equal and unequal, limited and unlimited, and simple and compound; and he adds that 'limited' societies require federation, as they cannot all attain their purpose of promoting well-being by themselves. The final result is thus a system of many societies, including households, social groups (guilds or castes), villages, monasteries, orders, towns, rural areas, and finally the whole human species, which is 'also a community' when regarded as the Church of God.

The State and other groups regarded as alike

7. S. Cocceji, for example, in his *Novum systema*, after giving an account of the Family (III, c. 4) and the State (c. 5), expressly declares that 'the like' (*par ratio*) is true of all *corpora et universitates* (§ 205); and later on, when he is dealing with the conception of the *corpus artificiale*, he treats the State as only a 'conspicuous example' of that type, along with the *collegium*, the *judicium* and the *familia* (IV, §§ 280–1). Wolff, Heineccius, Achenwall and other writers also treat corporations as the products of a like process to that which has brought the State into existence.

8. See the section on *jurisprudentia naturalis generalis socialis* in Nettelbladt's *Systema naturale* (§§ 326–414), and the section on *jurisprudentia positiva generalis socialis* in his *Systema jurispr. pos.* (§§ 846–912).

9. Cf. e.g. Daries, *Instit. jurispr. univ.*, *Pars spec.*, sect. 3–5; Heincke, *Prol.* c. 1, §§ 4–6; Hoffbauer, *Naturrecht*, pp. 186sqq.

Theories of 'concession'

10. Cf. Perezius, *Jus publ.* pp. 318–19; M. Schookius, *De seditionibus*, Groningen, 1664, III, c. 8, pp. 835sqq.; Felwinger, *Diss. de coll. et sodal.* pp. 308sqq., §§ 18sqq.; Mastrilio, *De magistratibus*, Venice, 1667, III, c. 4, §441; Becmann, *Med.* c. 10, § 8; Knichen, *Opus. pol.* I, c. 5, th. 4.

State control of meetings

11. Cf. Horn, *De civ.* II, c. 2, §14: *majestas* only can assemble people together in *comitia, concilia et conventus; qui sine superioris praescitu aut jussu multitudinem congregare fuerit ausus, jus majestatis praecipuum nefarie inviolat.* See also Schookius, loc. cit. pp. 832sqq., 837, 839; Felwinger, loc. cit. §§ 51–3; Mastrilio, loc. cit. §§ 444–6.

State control of group-life

12. Cf. Schookius, loc. cit. pp. 835sqq. (there can be no elections and no assembly of any kind without governmental supervision and co-operation); Felwinger, §§ 44–7; Mastrilio, III, c. 3, §§ 47sqq. and c. 4, §§ 444–6 (the *Princeps* must confirm *venditiones, impositiones, alienationes, expensiones, electiones officialium et alia acta universitatum*: the utmost that is possible without the assent of the prince is the raising of a levy in an emergency, when there is danger in delay); Knichen, I, c. 5, th. 8–9; Becmann, c. 10, § 8; Andler, *Jurispr.* pp. 102sqq. (all *statuta* of corporations require confirmation).

Myler ab Ehrenbach contends (c. 5, pp. 198sqq.) that territorial towns [i.e. towns in one of the territorial principalities of Germany] and all other territorial corporations can never appoint magistrates *proprio jure*, but must always appoint them *auctoritate principis territorialis*: such magistrates, therefore, are subject to confirmation and supervision by the prince, and derive all their jurisdiction from the 'ocean' of his plenitude of power within his territory; the territorial prince retains a co-ordinate jurisdiction, his *delegatus* has precedence, and his personal appearance causes the lapse of all corporate authority.

Von Seckendorf, too, has nothing to say about local communities or corporations as exercising rights of their own in a principality: he only mentions them as the objects of the prince's care and supervision (II, c. 8, §9, c. 14; III, c. 2, §5, and c. 3 to c. 6, §7).

13. Schookius, p. 838; Felwinger, §§54sqq.; Knichen, I, c. 5, th. 15 (a corporation may be abolished not only for delict or misuse of its powers, but also *utilitatis publicae causa*); von Seckendorf, add. 42 to II, c. 8, §9 (where he argues for freedom of trade and the abolition of guilds).

14. Spinoza would abolish all *collegia* or guilds in an aristocracy, when an aristocratic State is composed of a single city (*Tract. pol.* c. 8, §5); but in an aristocratic State composed of a number of cities he would allow the several cities considerable independence, even though they ought to constitute *unum imperium* and not a mere confederation (c. 9). In a monarchy he suggests mechanical subdivisions, which he calls *familiae*, as the basis of the royal council (cc. 6–7). *Attitude of Spinoza and Hume to groups*

Hume, in sketching the constitution of an ideal State (in which he refuses to follow the fantasies of Plato and More, but allows some merit to Harrington's *Oceana*), divides the country into 100 counties, and each county into 100 parishes. Each parish chooses one representative, and the 100 representatives of each county choose 10 county-magistrates and a senator. The 100 senators of the whole country exercise executive power: the county representatives, meeting in their particular counties, 'possess the whole legislative power of the commonwealth—the greater number of counties deciding the questions, and where they are equal, let the senate have the casting vote'.* In this way the advantages of a large and those of a small commonwealth may be combined (Essays, Part II, Essay XVI, *Idea of a Perfect Commonwealth*).

15. In the article *Fondation*, in vol. VII, p. 75, §6 of the *Encyclopédie*, Turgot vindicates for the State the right of reforming or completely suppressing all foundations. The public good is the supreme law, and the State must not be deterred from pursuing it either by a superstitious regard for the intentions of the founder or by fear of the pretended rights of certain bodies: *ni par la crainte de blesser les droits prétendus de certains corps, comme si les corps particuliers avoient quelques droits vis-à-vis l'état; les citoyens ont des droits, et des droits sacrés pour le corps même de la société; ils existent indépendamment d'elle, ils en sont les élémens nécessaires et ils n'y entrent que pour se mettre avec tous leurs droits sous la protection de ces mêmes lois, auxquelles ils sacrifient leur liberté; mais les corps particuliers n'existent point par eux-mêmes, ni pour eux, ils ont été formés pour la société et ils doivent cesser d'être au moment qu'ils cessent d'être utiles.* *Turgot on 'particular bodies'*

16. *Contr. Soc.* II, c. 3: *Quand il se fait des brigues, des associations partielles aux dépens de la grande, la volonté de chacune de ces associations devient générale par rapport à ses membres et particulière par rapport à l'État; on peut dire alors qu'il n'y a plus autant de votans que d'hommes, mais seulement autant que d'associations. Les différences deviennent moins nombreuses et donnent un résultat moins général.* If *Rousseau's dislike of associations*

---

* The translator has cited Hume's own words instead of Gierke's paraphrase, which is not quite accurate.

one of these associations gains preponderance, there is no *volonté générale* at all.

17. Ibid.: *il importe donc, pour avoir bien l'énoncé de la volonté générale, qu'il n'y ait pas de société partielle dans l'État*. If there are such societies, they must be made as numerous and as equal as possible: cf. IV, c. 1.

Churches and church-property

18. The most important of the opinions expressed in the Assembly, with regard to the theoretical legal basis of secularisation, are collected in Hübler's work on *Der Eigentümer des Kirchenguts* (Leipzig 1868) and in P. Janet's article on *La propriété pendant la Révolution Française* (*Revue des deux Mondes*, XXIII (1877), pp. 334–49). [See E. de Pressensé, *L'Église et la Révolution Française*, 1890.] These opinions, as a rule, start from a general view of the relation of all corporations to the State, since there was almost universal agreement about the nature of church-property as corporation-property. [Burke has a striking passage in the *Reflections* (*Works*, Bohn's edition, II, 378) on the revolutionary view of church-property as corporation-property. 'They say', he writes, 'that ecclesiastics are fictitious persons, creatures of the State, whom at pleasure they may destroy, and of course limit and modify in every particular: that the goods they possess are not properly theirs, but belong to the State which created the fiction.' He does not seek to refute this conception of the *persona ficta*; he simply dismisses it as a 'miserable destruction of persons'; and he contents himself with arguing that church-property is 'identified with the mass of private property, and that its owners have the same title of accumulated prescription as other owners'. Mackintosh, in his reply to Burke (*Vind. Gall.* sect. 1, ad finem), makes a distinction between the Church and other corporations. Other corporations are 'voluntary associations of men for their own benefit', and their property *is* part of the mass of private property, so that 'corporate property is here as sacred as individual'. But the Church is a peculiar corporation—'the priesthood is a corporation endowed by the country, and destined for the benefit of other men', so that it may properly be limited or modified if its possessions and powers are not used for that benefit.]

Views on the ownership of church-property in the Assembly

19. The Abbé Maury, for example, argued, on October 13, 1789, that church-property was the property of the clerical corporation, and the property of a *corps* was as truly property as that of *individus*. It was sophistry to distinguish between the legal basis of the one sort of property and that of the other: in both cases the right of property was not prior to the law, but was created by the law; and *détruire un corps est un homicide*, because it is to take away its *vie morale*. The Abbé de Montesquieu argued to the same effect on October 31....We also find isolated attempts to defend the theory of the property-rights of *institutions* [i.e. to argue that even foundations or *Stiftungen*, as distinct from the *corps* or corporation, may acquire property rights]: this was the line taken by Montlosier on October 13. Another speaker, the Abbé Grégoire, in a speech of October 23, ascribes church-property to founders and their families, or to parishes and provinces. [The debate about the question, 'Who owns church-property', is as old as the investiture-contest in the time of Gregory VII—when one side, representing the lay tradition of the *Eigentumskirche* (or 'proprietary church'), answered, 'The laity (kings and magnates) who built the church and own the land on which it stands', and the other, representing the ideas of canon law, replied, 'The saint to whom the church is dedicated, and, by extension, the institution which represents the saint'. The old issue may be said to be repeated in the

French Revolution, with the nation adopting the lay tradition of the *Eigentumskirche*, and challenging the canonical idea of church-property as *Anstaltsgut*.]

20. This is the view which underlies the speeches of the radical orators who argued that church-property was simply the property of the State. Mirabeau in particular, in his speeches of October 31 and November 2, arrives at the conclusion that the real ownership is vested in the nation, although —or rather, because—church-property is owned by corporate bodies. For corporations do not exist, as individuals do, before the creation of civil society, and they are not, as individuals are, *élémens de l'ordre social*: they owe their existence entirely to the State, and they are only its shadows (*aggrégations qui ne sont que son ombre*). It is the State which, at its discretion, grants or denies them the capacity of owning property; and it can also abolish them and take their property for itself. But if the possessions of a corporation are thus 'only uncertain, momentary and conditional', and even its mere continuance is altogether precarious, we must *supposer pour ces biens un maître plus réel, plus durable et plus absolu*. We find such a 'master' in the nation: *celui seul, qui doit jouir des biens du corps lorsque ce corps est détruit, est censé en être le maître absolu et incommutable, même dans le temps que le corps existe*. Barnave, Malouet, Dupont and Le Chapelier argued in the same sense: Garat, speaking on October 24, added an historical corroboration of this view; Treilhard and Chasset were even more radical, denying altogether the existence of corporate bodies.

Mirabeau on church-property

21. It was in this sense that Thouret sought, on October 23 and 30, to develop the ideas of Turgot. *Les individus et les corps diffèrent par leurs droits;... les individus existent avant la loi, ils ont des droits qu'ils tiennent de la nature, des droits imprescriptibles; tel est le droit de propriété: tout corps, au contraire, n'existe que par la loi, et leurs droits dépendent de la loi*. The State can thus modify or abolish corporations at will: it can withdraw their capacity for holding property, just as it gave it. *La destruction d'un corps n'est pas un homicide*: indeed, its destruction is a duty; what society needs is real owners, and we cannot consider as real owners these *propriétaires factices qui, toujours mineurs, ne peuvent toucher qu'à l'usufruit. Les corps n'existent pas par eux, mais par la loi; et la loi doit mesurer l'étendue dans laquelle elle leur donnera la communication des droits des individus:... tous les corps ne sont que des instruments fabriqués par la loi pour faire le plus grand bien possible; que fait l'ouvrier, lorsque son instrument ne lui convient plus? Il le brise ou le modifie*.

The argument of Thouret

Dupont argued in a similar sense on October 24, and Pétion on October 31: Talleyrand had already done so, on the proposal for secularisation, on October 10. The terms of the decree of November 2 corresponded to this line of argument: it did not directly assign church-property to the State: it declared, *Tous les biens ecclésiastiques sont à la disposition de la Nation* [which could then use them to endow those 'real owners' (the individual peasant or bourgeois) who, on Thouret's argument, are 'what society needs'].

22. In his pamphlet on the *Tiers État*, Sieyès argues that all corporations destroy the unity of the nation, which includes only individuals, and only what is equal and common in all individuals. If public officials let themselves be compelled to form *corps*, they must lose electoral rights during the term of their office; while as for ordinary citizens, it is a requirement of social order that they should not unite in corporations. It is the very acme of perversity if the legislator should himself create corporations, or should

Sieyès on Corporations

acknowledge and confirm them when they create themselves, or should declare the most privileged and greatest of corporations, the Estates, to be parts of the National Assembly: cf. *Political Writings*, I, pp. 167–72. [Cf. also Mackintosh, *Vind. Gall.* sect. 1: 'Laws cannot inspire unmixed patriotism. But ought they for that reason to foment that *corporation spirit* which is its most fatal enemy?']

His defence of corporate property

23. In his *Observations sommaires sur les biens ecclésiastiques* (1789), Sieyès gives vigorous expression to the idea that, while the existence of every *corps moral* (clergy, town, hospital, college, and the like) depends on the national will, and while the abolition of a corporation must carry with it the confiscation of its property, it is none the less true that a moral body, so long as it remains such, has rights of property which are no less sacred, and no less inviolable, than those of individuals, or indeed of the nation itself—for the nation, after all, is only a moral body. The State, therefore, may kill corporations, and it may become their heir by doing so; but it cannot legally declare that their property belongs to itself [during such time as they remain corporations], *Pol. Writings*, I, pp. 461–84. In his pamphlet on Tithes (1789), and in his Proposal for a provisional decree relative to the clergy (1790), Sieyès argues in the same way; ibid. I, pp. 485–98, II, pp. 29–70.

24. *Pol. Writings*, I, pp. 292 sqq. (esp. p. 295), 380 sqq., 509 sqq., 561 sqq.

His attitude to local communities

25. Thus he says (in his pamphlet *On the means*, etc., I, p. 208) that the division into *départements* is not like that into estates, fraternities and guilds: it is as different as day is from night. But he defends himself from the accusation of wishing to turn France into a federation (preface to part I, p. xii), and from that of having dissolved it into an aggregate of petty republics (II, pp. 225 sqq., 235 sqq.). He always insists that the *départements* and *communes* continue to remain parts of one whole, even though they are recognised as separate wholes for affairs within their own sphere (I, pp. 382–5, 561).

26. He mentions only the Church as a corporative element, and he depicts it in terms of unrelieved 'territorialism', *Natur und Wesen*, §§ 197, 213–220. [On 'territorialism', cf. n. * to p. 89.]

Scheidemantel on associations

27. Cf. I, p. 253. 'We should above all things direct our attention', Scheidemantel writes, 'to the societies in our territorial principalities; for any group in the State, which has been formed by specific agreement, or by mere chance, for the pursuit of a definite object, has an influence on the government, even if it be only in an indirect way. A prudent constitution will allow no secret assemblies, and it will recognise no societies as legal save those which have received the express or tacit assent of majesty.' If this is not done, there will be parties and cabals. Every group should be dissolved and punished. Liberty in England is the mother of mischief, and the Roman laws were wise. No subject can or should institute societies of his own motion (III, pp. 291 sqq.). Cf. also I, pp. 295 sqq., III, pp. 244, 246. [Even in England we find Paley, who was not illiberal, following a line of argument which is not dissimilar (*Moral and Political Philosophy*, VI, c. III ad finem). 'As ignorance of union, and want of communication, appear amongst the principal preservatives of civil authority, it behoves every State to keep its subjects in this want and ignorance, not only by vigilance in guarding against actual confederations and combinations, but by a timely care to prevent great collections of men...from being assembled in the same vicinity....Leagues thus formed and strengthened may overawe or overset

[The views of Paley]

Notes to § 18

the power of any State.' But Paley, writing in 1785, was probably thinking of the Gordon riots of 1780 and of 'combinations' of workers; and he would have been the last to deprecate the existence of the Tory or, for that matter, of the Whig party.]

28. Cf. I, p. 255: even permitted societies should be kept under careful supervision; they must be made to produce their rules and regulations from time to time, to render accounts, and to submit to visitation. This should particularly be the case with professedly religious societies; but it should also hold good of 'free societies', such as the East India Companies, which are never free in any but a relative sense, and must always be subject to a presumption against their being left independent. Cf. III, pp. 245–6. *He insists on State control*

29. A capacity for rights and duties is only allowed to a corporation as a means to the public benefit; and it is a condition of the exercise of that capacity that a corporation should act in that sense (III, pp. 292–4).

30. Cf. III, pp. 293–4, where Scheidemantel requires confirmation of the by-laws of societies, regulation of the subscriptions of their members, the due rendering of accounts, and confirmation of their appointments of officers of their own; cf. also II, pp. 204 sqq., on the necessary limitations and the proper police supervision of guilds, and III, p. 248, on the constitution, structure and government of local communities (which are instituted 'by command of the Sovereign', and must exercise their rights of legal coercion in his name).

Scheidemantel totally rejects any idea of autonomy [as belonging to societies]: law is the declared will of majesty: the rules of a privileged society are merely a matter of contract between its members, and they only acquire civil obligation 'when majesty arms them with obligation' (I, pp. 164–6). Customary law, he thinks, is often really a matter of wilful disobedience: it generally arises through 'culpable heedlessness or malice'; in any case it has no validity if it contravenes reason, or the purpose of the State, or law (I, p. 225).

31. 'No good prince, however, will take it for himself except in case of necessity' (III, p. 293).

32. Thus Scheidemantel includes together, under the head of public societies, not only 'colleges' [of magistrates] which have been instituted for the purpose of exercising powers of government, but also churches, academies, privileged trading companies and local communities which the government has recognised as public; and in the same way he lumps together, under the head of private societies, the privileged as well as the unprivileged, and the simple (i.e. the relations of husband and wife, parent and child, and master and servant) as well as the compound (households, fraternities, guilds), III, pp. 244–50. Elsewhere he treats schools and universities (II, pp. 183 sqq.), academies and learned societies (ibid. pp. 194 sqq.), and guilds (ibid. pp. 204 sqq.), purely from the point of view of their being 'police' institutions of the State [i.e. institutions which enable the State to supervise the behaviour of its members]. He even makes 'domestic societies' subject to the general rights of majesty under which all societies have to live and move, III, pp. 249, 294–7. *Scheidemantel treats associations as State institutions*

33. In his *Staatslehre* (*Works*, IV, p. 403) Fichte remarks that the low view of the State which is commonly held may be seen, *inter alia*, 'in the zeal for liberty, i.e. in lawlessness of acquisition; in the contention that churches, schools, trade-guilds and fraternities—indeed, almost everything that cannot *Fichte's similar view*

be expressly referred to civil legislation—are not State-institutions, but institutions proceeding from private persons', with which the State is only concerned in connection with its duty of protection. Fichte is especially concerned to make the guild a definite State-institution (with a fixed membership determined by the Government, and with tests of skill imposed by it, etc.); cf. his *Naturrecht*, II, p. 58 (*Works*, III, p. 233), and his *Rechtslehre*, II, p. 555.

Kant on foundations

34. Thus we find Kant—especially in the appendix to the second edition of his *Rechtslehre*, I, no. 8 (*Works*, VII, pp. 120–3), 'on the rights of the State in the way of inspecting perpetual foundations on behalf of its subjects'—placing a definition of the *Stiftung* in the forefront of his argument. It is 'a voluntary beneficent institution, confirmed by the State, which has been erected for the benefit of certain of its members who succeed to one another's rights until the time of its final extinction'. But [though he thus admits their continuous life,] he proceeds to explain that these 'corporations', in spite of rights of succession, and in spite of the constitution which they enjoy as *corpora mystica*, may be abolished at any time without any violation of right. When he comes to details, he applies this theory to benevolent institutions for the poor, invalids and the sick; to the Church as a 'spiritual State'; to schools; to the nobility as a 'temporary guild-fellowship authorised by the State'; to orders; and to foundations based on primogeniture [i.e. to what we should call entails or family settlements].

In another passage of the *Rechtslehre* (II, note B, loc. cit. p. 142) he starts from the idea that 'there cannot be any corporation in the State, or Estate, or order, which can transmit land as owner, according to certain rules, for the exclusive use of succeeding generations, *ad infinitum*'. He proceeds to give as examples the 'order of knights' and the 'order of clergy, called the Church', but he also adds, as another and parallel example, 'pious foundations'.

35. Loc. cit. pp. 120–3, 142–3.

Kant's dislike of voluntary associations

36. It is the secularisation of 'commanderies' [the relics of the old Teutonic Order in East Prussia?], and of ecclesiastical endowments, which Kant more particularly justifies—and indeed not only justifies, but demands. Though he supports his demand by an appeal to the change in 'public opinion' which has been produced by 'popular enlightenment', it is significant that he thinks it a sufficient warrant for secularisation if the support previously given to endowments by 'popular opinion' has been withdrawn 'merely by the leaders who are entitled to speak on its behalf' (loc. cit. pp. 121–2, 142–3).

But Kant desires equally to eliminate the system of Estates, and more especially the hereditary Estate of the nobility, loc. cit. p. 123. He even denounces any separate institution or pious foundation for charity or poor-relief, arguing that the only proper system is one of State-provision, by means of regular contributions made by each generation for itself, in the form of legal and compulsory payments; loc. cit. pp. 120–1, 144. [Kant's argument —that each generation should meet its own problems, without the aid of the pious benefactions of the past—is characteristic of an age which was shaking off the yoke of a past which it supposed to be outworn, and proclaiming the right and duty of each generation *fare da se*; cf. Paine's repeated phrase that 'each generation is competent for its own purposes', and compare also his scheme for the complete transference of all poor-relief to the State (*Rights of*

Man, Part II, c. 5) with Kant's similar proposal. Hegel, in his *Philosophy of Law*, §§242–5, speaks of the fortuitousness of alms-giving and charitable institutions, and praises, in comparison, a system of obligatory general regulations and orders. He is particularly critical of the boundless charitable foundations in England.]

37. *J. n. et g.* VII, c. 2, §§21–3. After dealing with these 'peculiar subordinate bodies', Pufendorf proceeds to treat of appointments to public offices [thus connecting associations with the working of the State]. *Pufendorf on associations*

38. Pufendorf makes an exception in favour of 'colleges' which *probari debent*, such as the Christian communities in ancient Rome. Apart from this exception, he treats as *corpora illegitima* not only bodies which are formed for inadmissible objects, but also those which have arisen *absque consensu summorum imperantium*.

Like Hobbes, he divides all *corpora* (including both the legitimate and the illegitimate) into the two species of 'regular' and 'irregular', according as there is a proper *unio voluntatum,* or some other bond of union (e.g. *conspiratio* produced by *affectus, spes, ira* or the like).

39. Accordingly, in a State which has grown from the union of a number of bodies, these bodies must surrender to it whatever is necessary for it: a State which allows bodies to enjoy independent rights in public matters is a State which renounces part of its *imperium* and becomes *irregularis et biceps*.

40. While the State is entirely and absolutely represented by its Sovereign, it is otherwise with 'bodies'; here acts done by the *rector* (or *coetus*) who is entrusted with the *regimen corporis* can be deemed to be the *actio totius corporis* only when they fall within the corporate sphere, as duly delimited in accordance with the constitution and the laws. Outside that sphere, the agents are personally liable....Pufendorf also regards a 'protestation' against the decisions of an assembly [i.e. the defiance of a 'body' by some of its members] as permissible; and he holds that in a dispute between a corporation and its members *non corpus judex erit, sed civitas, cui corpus subest*.

41. *J. n. et g.* VI, c. 1, §1: *Quemadmodum corpus humanum ex diversis membris componitur, quae et ipsa, in se considerata, corporum instar prae se ferunt—ita et civitates ex minoribus civitatibus constant.*

42. Thomasius, however, confines the idea of *societas inaequalis* to the communion between God and man; and he divides merely human societies into *mixtae* and *aequales*. He does not, therefore, use the distinction of 'equal' and 'unequal' societies in determining the relations between the corporation and the State; cf. *Instit. jur. div.* I, c. 1, §§93–113. In a similar way we find Mullerus (*Instit.* I, c. 1), Praschius (§§6–11) and other writers, employing this distinction only in order to point out differences of *internal* structure in the two sorts of society [and not in order to explain their *external* relations to the State].

43. Cf. n. 156 to §16, *supra*: see also Pufendorf, *Elem.* II, 6, §20 (where he applies the argument against guilds).

44. *Introd. in jus publ. univ.*, P. spec. II, c. 4.

45. Loc. cit. §7 n. *p*. If the Ruler tolerates *collegia injusta et improba*, these bodies have *effectus civiles*; but if he disapproves of them, even the justest of such 'colleges' (e.g. the early Christian communities) are instantly destitute of all rights. *J. H. Boehmer on corporate bodies*

Their property

46. Loc. cit. §9 n. *r*. More especially, these 'public colleges' must render accounts to the sovereign; and they cannot dispose of their property without his consent. This is the case with *bona civitatum, communitatum, academiarum, immo et ecclesiarum—quid enim aliud sunt quam coetus publici?*

Their power of legislation

47. Cf. II, c. 3, §§ 16–28 and c. 4, § 12. Boehmer ascribes legislative activity exclusively to the Sovereign; and he explains the legal validity of customary law, of foreign law [in cases of private international law?] and of 'statutes' [i.e. by-laws of corporations], by his having given them his approbation. He regards municipal self-government in general not as a right belonging to municipalities (*städtisches Recht*), but as a form of legislative authority delegated to *magistratus inferiores*. The by-laws of *collegia et corpora* [i.e. corporate bodies other than municipalities], in regard to their own affairs, are in his view merely *pacta* among the members, requiring, as such, subsequent confirmation by the sovereign. But the sovereign may go further: he may make even these by-laws [though they are only internal *pacta*] dependent on his previous sanction; and he is acting rightly if he does so. In any case, he has the two rights of *inspectio* and *directio*: he can cancel by-laws which are an abuse; and he can, in general, prescribe the procedure to be followed in any respect.

Their power of jurisdiction

48. Cf. II, c. 3, § 26; c. 4, § 12 n. *u*; c. 7, § 24; c. 8, § 13. *Jurisdictio* and the power of punishment belong only to the Sovereign or his delegates: *collegia* and *societates aequales* have no *jurisdictio* or *jus puniendi*. They may appoint *arbitri* for themselves, but they can never appoint *judices* without being guilty of *majestas laesa*. They may determine by pact that there shall be certain 'conventional' punishments; but they must leave to the *Superior* the carrying of them into effect.

Their power of imposing dues on their members

49. Boehmer argues (II, c. 9) that, while all 'societies and colleges' need a 'common chest', an *administrator* [or treasurer], and subscriptions from their members, there is a difference in this respect between the equal and the unequal society: *in aequali societate obligantur membra ex pacto; in inaequali ex imperio*. The Sovereign alone has a right of taxation. Any person other than the Sovereign who imposes a contribution must act either *ex imperantis indultu expresso vel tacito*, or *ex consensu subditorum*: he can never act *suo jure*. In case of necessity, however, the consent of a majority is sufficient [i.e. it counts as the *consensus subditorum*]; and Boehmer even allows that, *tempore extremae necessitatis*, a community [which would otherwise need the permission of the Sovereign] may act on its own authority—though he adds that this should rather be explained as proceeding *ex praesumta voluntate imperantis*. See n. 46 supra.

Their officers

50. According to II, c. 6, there can be no public office *nisi ab Imperante*. In order, therefore, to appoint 'magistrates' for themselves [i.e. to appoint the officers of any society to which they belong], subjects require the permission of their Ruler. If they choose *consules*, for example, they are acting *non suo, sed Imperantis nomine*: they are therefore responsible to him; and he may deprive them of their right of appointing, and make his own nomination, if they abuse their right of choice. Indeed, the Sovereign cannot allow a right of free election without disturbing his 'majesty'; and for that reason he generally requires that his sanction shall be necessary for all elections (§ 6 n. *m*). We may notice especially how Boehmer, in dealing with the duty of municipal magistrates to render accounts—a duty which, he holds, cannot be effectively abolished by any prescription or privilege to the

contrary—bases it upon the fact that the municipal magistrates really conduct their administration as public officials, *nomine Imperantis* (§§ 7–8 nn. *n* and *o*). He also holds that an officer of a corporation can never be legally prevented from appealing to the Sovereign (c. 6, §9).

51. Cf. II, c. 3, §§ 56 sqq., and esp. §64 n. *b*. Privileges which run counter to the public good—such as a *privilegium senatui datum de non reddendis rationibus de bonis civitatum*, or again a monopoly—are absolutely void. Privileges which may become prejudicial in altered circumstances, as so many of the *privilegia collegiorum* readily may, are subject to recall. *Their privileges*

52. Cf. n. 46 supra, and see also II, c. 10 (esp. §§ 7 and 17–18) on the *jus Imperantis circa* ἀδέσποτα [i.e. in regard to *res nullius*]. But he defends himself against the reproach that he is depriving towns of the ownership of their property by his arguments (c. 6, §8 n. *o*, III, c. 3, §5 n. *c*).

53. *Introd. in jus publ. univ.* c. 2, §§ 9–10. In the following section (11) he argues acutely that on this basis international law is neither *jus publicum* nor *jus privatum*, inasmuch as *actiones gentium* fall into neither of the two categories [i.e. that of 'public' and that of 'private' actions] which are required by the conception of the State, but are simply *liberae*. [On Boehmer's argument the actions of States when regarded as powers or *gentes* in the international system (or want of system) are neither private actions, done by private citizens or private bodies or the prince in his private capacity, nor public actions, done by citizens in their public capacity or the prince in his capacity of a public person. They are *liberae*, or indeterminate.... So Boehmer seems to argue; but it is difficult to see why the *actio* of a *gens*, if the act is really that of the *gens* (and not, for example, that of a casual pirate in the West Indies, of English nationality, who happens to plunder a French ship), should not be regarded as an act of the *Princeps qua talis*, or of citizens *qua membra Reipublicae*. We can hardly say that the *gens* is not the State. But the use of the separate word *gens* in international law (like the use of the word 'power') has led to a divorce between the theory of international and that of internal relations, which is only slowly being abolished.] *Boehmer on public and private law*

54. He deals (II, cc. 4 and 5) with (1) the *jus imperantium circa collegia et universitates* and (2) their *jus circa sacra*. In dealing with the former subject, he refuses to allow that 'public colleges' have anything more than the status of 'private colleges' when regarded in their nature as *universitates* and compared with the Sovereign (e.g. they have not *jura reipublicae*, as he has, but only *jura collegiorum*: they have not a *jus fisci*, as he has; and so forth). They are only *suo modo publica* ['public—in a way of their own'] in virtue of the Ruler having greater rights over them and their property than he has over individuals and their property. [In other words, they are public in the sense of being under public control, but not in the sense of having a public position.] Cf. III, c. 3, §5 n. *c*. *On 'public colleges'*

55. *Jus publicum*, as Titius uses the term, includes only the relations of the *Imperans*, as such, to his subjects.

56. Cf. e.g. Daries, §§ 661–3.

57. In the second book of his *De jure civitatis*, which is devoted to the rights of the subject, Huber proceeds—after dealing first with persons in general (s. 1, c. 1), then with the family (s. 1, cc. 2–6), and then with citizens (*Bürger*) and the differences among them (s. 2)—to treat, in sect. 3, *De jure universitatum*. Under this head he discusses the *universitas in genere* (c. 1); guilds and trading companies (c. 2); universities (c. 3); religious societies (c. 4); local *Huber's classification of universitates*

communities (c. 5); the responsibility of *singuli ex facto universitatis* (c. 6); and the hierarchy of the Roman Catholic church (c. 7). He follows a similar order in *Instit. Reip.* sect. II.

58. *De jure civ.* II, 3, c. 1, §§ 3 and 19. He remarks, however, that the name of *societas* is often given to bodies *quae maxime sunt universitates*, and he cites the East India Companies in Holland as examples.

Their definition and their powers

59. *De jure civ.* II, 3, c. 1, §§ 10–14, 24. Huber's full definition of the *universitas* is: *coetus sive corpus subditorum alicujus civitatis, sub certo regimine, permissu summae potestatis, ad utilitatem communem sociatus.* The *regimen* of a *universitas* may be conceded (as it is in the State itself) to one or more persons, or to the majority of the members (§ 20); but the concession must always be limited [as regards 'universities' other than the State] to the narrowest scope of action that necessity will permit, in order that the power of the State may be weakened as little as possible (§ 34). *Universitates prohibitae*, even when they are actually tolerated, exist only *de facto*, and not *de jure*; but a period of toleration has the effect of tacit approbation (§§ 26–30). Associations which are not for the real benefit of the *socii* or the State are to be suppressed (§§ 31–3).

Their authority derived from the State

60. Huber, *De jure civ.* II, 3, c. 6, §§ 9 and 19–20: *potestas rectorum universitatum pendet a tenore mandati quod habent a summa potestate, a qua jus suum habet universitas.* The rectors do not 'represent' the *universitas*: they have no *praefectura* other than what is derived from the Sovereign: *quod agunt, non ad mandatum populi, sed Principis, exigendum est.*

He uses similar language in *Prael. Dig.* III, 4, no. 4: *universitates reipublicae subordinatae* cannot appoint permanent representatives, because they are unable *modum et finem potestatis concedere suis rectoribus; sed...quidquid habent juris id accipiunt ab eo penes quem est summa potestas; proinde qui id genus universitatis praesunt, non repraesentant populum universitatis, sed potestatem summam cui parent.* Corporations may therefore give an authorisation in a particular matter of legal action, which has a binding effect on those who consent; but they cannot vest their officers with a general power of binding the whole corporation (which explains, *inter alia*, the *lex 'Civitas'*), cf. *De jure civ.* II, 3, c. 6, §§ 3 sqq. and *Prael.* III, 4, no. 4. Nor can corporations devolve on their officers a *jus contribuendi* (*De jure civ.* II, 3, c. 6, § 18), or a *jurisdictio* (ibid. § 21); for any jurisdiction that they have is derived from the State (ibid. III, 1, c. 6, § 8). Finally, they can only make by-laws if they are authorised to that effect, and subject to the sovereign's right of giving his sanction (ibid. I, 3, c. 6, §§ 59 sqq.; II, 3, c. 2, §§ 25 sqq.; III, 1, c. 2, §§ 14–17).

Schmier's theory of corporations

61. Schmier, *Jurisp. publ. univ.* V, c. 1, nos. 87–114, where, after an account of the *universitas* in general, there is a discussion of local communities, universities, guilds and trading companies. Schmier expressly bases the requirement of State-concession on the ground that *regimen, imperium seu jurisdictio ad universitatem constituendam necessaria nequit ex alio fonte quam summae potestatis largitate in inferiores derivari* (no. 92). When he comes to details, he makes a grant by the State the source of the corporation's right of choosing officers, administering property, imposing taxes, exercising jurisdiction, and generally enjoying autonomy and self-government; cf. V, c. 2, nos. 53–64, and also c. 3, nos. 69–79.

62. Ibid. III, c. 3, no. 20.

Similar theories

63. Cf. e.g. Kreittmayr, *Grundrisz*, § 19. Subjects may form 'particular societies'; but such societies enjoy *jura communitatis* only in virtue of the assent

of the State, and they are thus subject to a *jus supremae inspectionis et directionis* on the part of the territorial prince. We may also note that even Pufendorf's ideas, and still more those of Hert, are partially in agreement with this trend in the natural-law theory of society.

64. See n. 6, supra.

65. *Instit.* §§838–9. Wolff adds, in §849, that it is only societies whose objects are inadmissible which give rise to no rights and duties.

66. *Instit.* §846. The laws of a society are prescriptions relating to matters 'which must always be done in one way, and that only, if the purpose of the society is to be secured'. 'All societies, therefore, must have laws, and enjoy the right to make laws': they have also the right of threatening punishment and of actually punishing offenders. Each new member promises, expressly or tacitly, that he will observe the laws; but since the laws of a society retain their authority by virtue of the consent of its members, the society has the power of abrogating or amending its laws, or of making new laws. Cf. §853. *Wolff on the inherent rights of societies*

67. Wolff finds a justification for requiring the Ruler's assent to the alienation of the property of a local community in the fact that it is incumbent upon him to see to the common interest, and, again, that he has a *dominium eminens* over such property—as indeed he has over all kinds of property (*Instit.* §1129).

68. S. Cocceji, *Nov. syst.* IV, §280: *constituitur tale corpus consensu*: cf. §205, on the principle of *par ratio* as between all *corpora et universitates* and the State [i.e. what is true of the State is equally true, or no less likely to be true, of corporations]. *Similar views in other German writers*

69. Heineccius, *Elem. jur. nat.* II, §§13–25. The basis of the State's authority over corporations is the natural-law principle that, while in every society 'the well-being of the society is the supreme law of its members', the 'utility' of the 'greater society' must take precedence, in a 'compound society', over that of the 'lesser societies' contained in it.

70. Daries, *Instit. jurispr. univ. Praec.* §§17–23, *P. spec.* §§550–6, 674–8. He derives the existence of associations from the contract [by which they are formed]; but he bases the authority [of the State] over corporations on the principle that in a 'compound society' the relation of the *subordinata* to the *subordinans societas* is like that of the *socius* to the *societas*, and therefore the interest of the 'greater society' takes precedence in the event of a clash of interests (§§554sqq.). He therefore includes among the *jura majestatis* the *jus efficiendi ne societates partiales fini utilitatique civitatis sint impedimento*, and (consequent upon that right) the further right of legitimising as 'just' such societies as are compatible with the purpose of the State, and of abolishing others as 'unjust' (§§674sqq.).

71. *Syst. nat.* §§327–47. A similar view reappears in the *Jurispr. pos.* §899; but in §853 a distinction is drawn between (1) *jura universitatis*, whether *originaria* or *contracta*, and (2) rights which belong to *magistratus constituti in universitate ex concessione Superioris*, and are therefore exercised by them in the name of the State, and not in virtue of their representing the *universitas*. *Nettelbladt's theory of associations*

72. In his *Syst. nat.* Nettelbladt first classifies societies by their purposes (§348), and then proceeds to arrange them, by a variety of criteria, into *naturales et non naturales* (§349), *simplices et compositae* (§§350–1), *perpetuae et temporariae* (§352), *licitae et illicitae* (§353), and *aequales et inaequales* (§§354–61). *Their classification*

<table>
<tr><td>'Equal societies' possessing authority</td><td>73. To the category of *societates* which are *aequales* and also (if only in cases of doubt) *cum potestate*, there belong both (1) *collegia*, or *societates simplices plurium quam duorum membrorum*, and (2) *corpora*, or *societates compositae*, the members of which are themselves 'colleges' (§ 354). In these *collegia* and *corpora* there are present certain peculiarities—which do not, however, prevent their being included in the category of *societas aequalis*—such as a *directorium societatis* (§ 357), a *peculiare collegium repraesentativum* (§ 358), and *deputationes collegii* for particular issues (§ 359).
74. *Syst. nat.* § 361.</td></tr>
<tr><td>The inherent rights of associations</td><td>75. The *jura socialia societatis* which appear in Nettelbladt's theory are the admission and exclusion of members (§§ 364 sqq. and 407); the appointment of *imperantes, directores* and *officiales* (§ 367); the power of disposition in regard to their own assets (§ 407); the right of meeting and making decisions (§§ 374 sqq.); autonomy (§§ 398–9); a *potestas judicandi* in regard to the affairs of the society (§ 413); self-government, including the right of self-taxation (§ 407); and finally the right of disposing of the property of the society—though the property itself is [not an inherent right, as the right of disposing of it is, but] a *jus societatis contractum* (§ 396). Only as regards equal societies possessing *potestas* does Nettelbladt assign all these *jura socialia societatis* to the society itself. In the case of equal societies without *potestas*, they belong to a third party: in the case of unequal societies, they belong to the *imperans* or *superior*. On the other hand, he regards the ownership of the property of the society as belonging in case of doubt—even in the two latter sorts of society [the equal society without power, and the unequal society]—to the community itself, and not to the person who wields authority (§ 396).</td></tr>
<tr><td>The compound society</td><td>76. In an earlier passage of his *Systema naturale*, where he is seeking to determine the nature of the *societas composita*, Nettelbladt deals with the inclusion of 'moral persons' in a higher unity as its 'members'; but he draws attention to the facts (1) that it is not *all* the societies within a society which are members of it, and (2) that not *every* society whose members belong to other societies is a 'compound society' (§§ 350–1). He proceeds, in the same context, to distinguish between (1) the position of a *corpus* composed of *collegia* which have social objects of their own, and (2) the position of a *collegium* divided into mere 'deputations' or sections (§ 359). In a later passage, where he is dealing with the theory of *membra civitatis*, he treats in some detail of the position of 'moral persons' as members of the State (§§ 1588 and 1226–50).</td></tr>
<tr><td>Public societies in the large sense</td><td>77. *Syst. nat.* §§ 1227–30, where he includes among the 'public societies which are eminently such' *collegia seu corpora ordinum* and *collegia optimatum*, but *not* the *collegia senatoria* in a democracy.</td></tr>
<tr><td>Colleges of magistrates</td><td>78. Ibid. §§ 1231–4. On the other hand, these 'societies which are magistracies' [i.e. administrative or judicial Boards] may possess the *jus magistratus* itself [not as of right derived from the sovereign, but] either *jure proprio* or *jure administratorio*; and they may in addition acquire special privileges.</td></tr>
<tr><td>Public societies in the strict sense</td><td>79. Ibid. §§ 1235–7. In this case [i.e. as regards 'public societies strictly so called'] the place of the *jus magistratus* is taken by a *jus ad certas functiones, regimen reipublicae concernentes, obeundas absque corrigendi potestate*.</td></tr>
<tr><td>Local communities</td><td>80. Ibid. §§ 1238–40. These *universitates personarum* [such as territorial communities] may be either *ordinatae* or *inordinatae*: they may, or may not,</td></tr>
</table>

Notes to § 18

have magistrates of their own; and they may be governed either by a *collegium* or a *persona*. *Circuli* [the German *Kreise*, roughly analogous to our English counties] belong to this category; but 'circles' which are the member-States of a federation are themselves *systemata Rerumpublicarum*.

81. Ibid. §§ 1241–2, 1247, 1250. In any case of doubt, we can only regard the society itself as the 'Subject' or owner of this authority; but an individual, or a part of the society, may also be such a 'Subject' (§ 1245). — *Private societies*

82. Ibid. §§ 1243, 1247, 1249–50. Nettelbladt does not go into any further details about the extent of State-control over corporations when he is dealing with Natural Law. It is from positive law, and from such law only, that he seeks e.g. to derive the limits upon the rights of local communities, churches and families to alienate property; *Jurispr. pos.* § 903. — *State-control of corporations*

83. Ibid. §§ 1243–4.

84. Ibid. §§ 1245, 1248. It goes without saying that this argument refers primarily to the position of the evangelical church in Germany.

85. Achenwall, *Jus Nat., Proleg.* §§ 82, 91–7, and II, §§ 2 sqq. On this basis Achenwall too makes every contract between more than two persons for the formation of a society produce a *jus sociale universorum in singulos* (II, § 8); and he regards a *societas aequalis* as one in which this *jus*, or social authority, remains with the whole community, and nothing more than a *praerogativa*, or a *praecipua obligatio* (in any case nothing in the nature of an *imperium*), is vested in a single person or body of persons (II, §§ 22–31). — *Achenwall on the social authority of associations*

86. Hoffbauer, *Naturrecht*, pp. 190 sqq., where a distinction is drawn between 'essential' (*immanentia*) and 'incidental' (*transeuntia*) rights of societies, and where 'social laws' and 'social authority' (in its three species of directorial, executive and inspectorial) are treated as being essentially involved in any contract for the formation of a society. Hoffbauer also speaks of societies as having officials of their own—but not, he adds, independently of the Ruler; and he differentiates 'equal societies' in which all the members must concur from 'unequal societies' in which there is not such general concurrence. — *The views of Hoffbauer*

87. Ibid. p. 288. But Hoffbauer adds that these 'private societies' cannot employ any coercive authority to vindicate their rights against their members.

88. A. L. von Schlözer, *Allg. Staatsrecht*, p. 70, § 19, VIII. Schlözer cites as examples 'musical clubs' and 'the Church'!

89. W. von Humboldt, *Ideen*, pp. 41 sqq., 83, 113 sqq., 115.

90. It is sufficient to refer to the way in which Mevius (*Prodromus*, V, § 19) eulogises 'subordinate societies' as the foundation and mainstay of the State. The most important task of politics, he urges, is concerned with *bona familiarum* and with *corporum, collegiorum, urbium formatio*; the prosperity of civil society and that of its contained groups are mutually dependent on one another; and there must be a happy mean between the independence of corporate bodies and their subjugation to the political Whole. On the basis of these ideas he will not refuse liberty of meeting and association *simpliciter*, but only when there are *causae publicae, curae imperantium concreditae* (V, § 26). We may also remember the views of Leibniz [cf. supra, note 6]. — *Mevius in praise of groups*

91. Montesquieu, it is true, regards the monarch as the source of all authority; but he also believes that constitutional government, and therefore true monarchy, is impossible unless authority is diffused through *canaux moyens*, and thus made, as it were, to flow into a Delta of *pouvoirs intermédiaires*

Montesquieu on the need of intervening powers between the State and its subjects

subordonnés et dépendants. There is therefore need for the prerogatives *des Seigneurs, du Clergé, de la Noblesse et des Villes*, as well as for political bodies (i.e. *parlements*) to declare and preserve the laws (*dépôt des loix*). Any destruction of these intervening powers must produce, if not a Republic, at any rate a despotism, as was shown, for example, in the case of Law's operations in France [1716–20] and in the conduct of Ferdinand of Arragon. See the *Esprit des lois*, II, c. 4; cf. also III, c. 7, V, cc. 9–11 (where Richelieu is criticised), VI, c. 1 and VIII, c. 6; and cf. the argument, in v, cc. 14–16, that despotism, as distinguished from monarchy, is based on uniformity, equality, centralisation and the lack of all qualifying and moderating elements.

Möser's eulogy of the old Germanic Groups

92. We need only refer to the account which Möser gives in his *Patriotische Phantasien* of the struggle of towns and guilds and leagues for liberty (I, nos. 43, 53, 54), and to his glorification of the Hansa (I, no. 45; III, no. 49). In the course of this glorification he hazards the remark that if 'the towns and guilds and leagues' had won the day in their struggle with the territorial principality, there would be sitting to-day at Ratisbon, 'side by side with an insignificant Upper House...a united body of associated towns and communities for dealing with the laws' which their forefathers once imposed on all the world; and then 'it would not be Lord Clive, but a counsellor of Hamburg, who would be issuing his commands on the Ganges' (I, no. 43).

We may also note Möser's historical accounts of the glory and the decline of fraternities and guilds (I, nos. 2, 4, 7, 32, 48, 49; II, nos. 32–5), and, more especially, his disapproval of the attack made upon them by the Recess of the Imperial Diet of 1731 (particularly in regard to the obligations of honour* imposed by craft-guilds, I, no. 49). We may equally note his general derivation of the constitution of the [German] territory, or *Land*, from a union of the 'Fellowship' type between free proprietors of estates, followed by an analogous process of Fellowship-formation among manumitted serfs and freemen who were not proprietors. (In this last connection there are several passages in Möser which deserve notice; e.g. in III, no. 54, he refers to the institution, by lords of manors, of 'a mutual protection society and articles of fraternity' among the peasantry, who then institute 'articles as between themselves' for their own domestic concerns.† Again, in III, no. 66, he treats of 'the origin and advantage of what are called *Hyen, Echten* and *Hoden*' among free men who have not a plot of land of their own: cf. p. 353, where he remarks that 'such a *Hode* was something in the nature of a guild chartered by the State, which could freely pass a rule about itself, and by such means maintain the rights of free men'; cf. also IV, nos. 63–4.)

Finally, we may also refer to Möser's account of the origin of territorial Estates from leagues and confederations, and of their development into a body which represented the whole territory as a *Landschaft* [or local Diet], IV, no. 51.

Möser on liberty of association

93. Ibid. II, no. 2 and III, no. 20: 'every civil society, great or small', should 'properly be a legislature for itself', and should not form itself on a

* The German is *Handwerksehre*. The guilds imposed standards of decent work. Hegel in his *Philosophy of Law* (§§ 249–54) speaks of society as assuming a moral character in corporations, and of the individual as having his 'honour' in and through his corporation.

† This may remind us of the 'frith-guilds' and the later 'frank-pledge' in our own country.

Notes to § 18

general plan or on philosophical theories. Cf. also IV, no. 41 ('each *Gau* and *Hof*' [or, as we might say, each hundred and manor] had of old 'its own autonomy'), and III, nos. 54, 66.

94. For Möser's views in regard to towns, cf. I, nos. 43, 53, III, no. 20 (every small town ought to have its own particular political constitution); and I, no. 39 (where he opposes the exemption of the servants of country-landowners from civic taxes). For his views about guilds, cf. I, nos. 2, 4, 48–9, II, nos. 32–5; and as regards rural communities, cf. II, no. 1 (on the sovereign right of each peasant community to exclude strangers and sojourners) and II, no. 41, III, nos. 43, 52–3. *On towns, guilds and rural groups*

95. Cf. e.g. the proposals for the founding of a company for world-trade by the united towns of Germany (I, no. 43); the founding of a separate college of advocates [like our Inns of Court] with an exclusive corporate constitution (I, no. 50); the founding of a 'circle-association' for putting a stop to distilling in the event of a shortage in corn (I, no. 64); the starting of a company for conducting trade in corn on the Weser (I, no. 52); etc. *Proposals for new associations*

96. Loc. cit. III, no. 20, p. 71.

97. *J. n. et g.* VII, c. 2, §§ 21–2; cf. nn. 37–40, supra.

98. Pufendorf deals with corporate property in *Elem. jurispr. univ.* I, def. 5, §§ 5–6. *Propria sunt non solum quae ad personas singulares pertinent, sed et quae ad personas morales conjunctas seu societates qua tales.* Neither third parties, nor the members themselves when they are not 'conceived as the whole society', own any right in such common property. But in addition to common property of this description, which is in the *plenum dominium* of the society, a society may also possess property of another description, where the 'use' belongs to 'individual members' (*singuli*)—and indeed (Pufendorf adds) there are many cases of such property where the use is open also to *extranei*. *Pufendorf on the rights and duties of corporations*

Pufendorf also deals (*Elem.* II, def. 12, § 28; *J. n. et g.* VII, c. 2, § 22 and VIII, c. 6, § 13) with obligations incurred by a *corpus* in consequence of the legal transactions of its *rector* or *coetus*. He assumes, like Hobbes, that in such cases the corporate property is liable for the satisfaction of the claims of its members; but where the claims of third parties are concerned, he holds that the individual members are responsible, each of them *pro rata*—though if there be refusal to discharge a claim, each can be made responsible for the whole amount.

Finally, he deals with *delicta universitatum* (*J. n. et g.* VIII, c. 3, §§ 28–9; *De off. hom. et civ.* II, c. 13, § 19). He expounds the usual theory, but he suggests that innocent individuals should not be included in any punishment, and that all punishment should cease with the disappearance of the persons who were concerned in any given delict. He justifies the latter suggestion on the ground that, though there are certain attributes, such as possessions or rights, which belong to the *universitas per se*, there are others, such as learning or moderation or courage, which cannot be ascribed to a *universitas, nisi ex derivatione a singulis*. To be deserving of punishment is an attribute of the second kind; for a *universitas*, 'as such', has no *animus merens poenam* ['no intention deserving of punishment']. [Cf. Grotius, supra, n. 52 to § 15.]

99. This is the view we find in Thomasius, Treuer and Titius; cf. n. 131 to § 16.

100. Cf. pp. 121–3 supra. Gundling's *dissertatio de universitate delinquente* (cited by him in his *Jus nat.* c. 36, §§ 23 and 26, in order to prove the impropriety of the punishment inflicted by Poland on the city of Thorn) belongs

to the literature of criminal law, and can only be discussed in connection with it.

Gundling's confusion of corporation and partnership

101. Cf. nn. 160 and 163 to §16. Gundling, in dealing with the *contractus societatis*, or, as he calls it, 'mascopey', and in treating of *communio incidens* [i.e. 'quasi-society', as Wolff terms it, n. 163 infra], uses Roman law as the basis of his argument (*Jus nat.* c. 23, §§61–3). But (1) he treats a society as being a single 'Subject' or owner of rights, and (2) he regards as contrary to Natural Law the positive-law rules which make it improper for a society to agree to exclude suits for the division of its common property, or which treat the death of its members as producing its dissolution (c. 25, §23).

102. Cf. nn. 58 and 59 to this section: cf. also Huber's *Prael. Instit.* II, 1, no. 7 (*civilis hominum societas, quae nec familia sit nec libera Respublica*), and *Dig.* III, 4, no. 1.

103. *Dig.* III, 4, no. 1, XVII, 2, no. 2; *De jure civ.* II, 3, c. 2, §2.

Huber's use of the term universitas

104. Thus a university *is* a *Universitas*, but gymnasia and elementary schools are not, because they have no *regimen certum*; *De jure civ.* II, 3, c. 3, *Dig.* III, 4, no. 2. In dealing with groups of the type of the local community (*universitates familiarum*), Huber treats *vici* which have no magistrates of their own as not being *universitates*, even though they have common property; and he takes the same view of provinces, when they have no separate constitution, with provincial Estates of their own, but are directly administered by a prefect (*De jure civ.* II, 3, c. 5, nos. 4, 18–22; *Dig.* III, 4, no. 2).

105. *Collegia magistratuum* are not *universitates*, for they do not possess a *scopus et usus a summa republica diversus et coëuntibus peculiaris* (*De jure civ.* II, 3, c. 5, §23).

His Collective view of corporations

106. This idea of a purely 'collective' (or 'bracket') Group-personality appears in Huber's theory of the *res universitatis* (*Prael. Instit.* II, 1, nos. 4, 8), and of other forms of corporate property (*De jure civ.* II, 3, c. 1, §35). It also appears in his theory of the legal transactions of corporations, and more especially in his view of the obligations which a *universitas* can incur. Here, in the usual manner of his time, he refuses to recognise that a *universitas* can be bound by contract, except when *omnes et singuli* have given a formal assent, or when its representatives have been acting within the terms of a specific mandate: otherwise, he confines the liability of a *universitas* to cases where it has profited by some transaction [i.e. where there has been a *lucrum emergens*]; and he takes the general view that an *obligatio universitatis* entails a proportionate or 'limited' liability of all its members (as being the *partes ex quibus totum componitur*)—cf. *De jure civ.* II, 3, c. 6, §§1–18; *Dig.* III, 4, no. 4.

We find the same idea of a merely 'collective' Group-personality in Huber's theory of the delicts of a *universitas* (*De jure civ.* II, 3, c. 1, §§39–43, c. 6, §13; *Dig.* III, 4, no. 5), and of its capacity for being represented in a suit at law (*Dig.* III, 4, nos. 4, 6). A similar trend appears in his treatment of the validity of majority-decisions. While he derives it from the 'social' or partnership element in a *universitas*, on the ground that the principle may have been agreed upon beforehand [by each individual partner] in the society, he also limits its application strictly, and that on the very same ground—e.g. he holds that it is only the [individual] *consentientes* and their heirs who ought to incur liability in virtue of an obligation [arising from a majority-decision] (*De jure civ.* II, 3, c. 6, §§23–4).

Huber emphasises, again and again, the identification of the 'collective person' with the sum of the members. *Ipsa universitas est persona* (ibid. c. 1, §36): *ipsum corpus sociatorum est universitas, non forma conjunctionis, ut aliqui argutantur (Instit.* II, 1, no. 7).

107. See n. 60 to this section. Huber accordingly refuses to recognise any real autonomy of a society *(Instit.* I, 2, §§5, 12). It is not, of course, inconsistent with this that he should regard it as possible for a *universitas* (like any individual subject of a State) to possess not only *dominium*, but also *imperium*, *outside the State*. He concludes, however, that [though this is possible] it is not really the case with the *Societas Indica* [the Dutch East India Company], for the Company only exercises an *imperium* belonging to the United Provinces: *De jure civ.* II, 3, c. 2, §§ 14–21; cf. also §29. *His view of the authority of corporate bodies*

108. The only distinction which Huber draws between *societates* and *collegia*—bodies which he regards as in other respects very similar to one another—is that the majority-principle is the rule in the latter, and the exception in the former. If, therefore, the rule of the majority is introduced into it by an agreement among its members to that effect, a *societas* is thereby transformed into a corporation. It is thus that *societates* are often raised to the position of *universitates (jure universitatis donantur)*: this is what happened to the Roman companies of tax-collectors, as it has also happened to modern colonial and trading companies, *quae, quum primo fuerint Societates, deinceps in formam Collegiorum reductae sunt, nec aliter administrari possunt (De jure civ.* II, 3, c. 2, §§ 2–13; *Dig.* XVII, 2, no. 2). *His view of the relation of partnerships and corporations*

109. Vide supra, n. 60 to this section.

110. A view like that of Huber appears in Schmier: see n. 61 supra, and compare what he has to say about the *jura universitatis (Jurispr. publ. univ.* v, c. 2, nos. 52–64) and the *delicta universitatum* (ibid. III, c. 2, nos. 95–104) with his argument about the rights and duties of a *universitas* in regard to its members (ibid. v, c. 3, nos. 69–86). In dealing with this last topic, he speaks of the members as being in a position of dependence which obliges them to render obedience and loyalty, but as having a corresponding claim on the society to promote their prosperity and to protect them; and he explains both the position and the claim by the fact that the authorities of the corporation *summam Potestatem repraesentant, atque in illius virtute et participatione mandata et judicia imponunt*. *Schmier on the universitas and its members*

We may also note the fusion of a natural-law theory of *societas* with a Roman-law theory of corporations in Micraelius (I, c. 7), Felwinger (pp. 908–24), Knichen *(Opus. pol.* I, c. 5, th. 1–15), and Kreittmayr *(Grundrisz*, §§ 11, 19).

111. This result is already to be seen plainly in Huber. He expressly says that *jus quo universitates utuntur est idem quod habent privati (Dig.* III, 4, no. 3); and he uses very plain language in enunciating the view that the inherent rights which a *universitas* can claim for itself are limited to matters connected with its possessions *(causae patrimoniales)* (cf. *De jure civ.* II, 3, c. 1, §38). When he deals with the public-law rights of a corporate body, he makes them belong not to the *universitas* itself, but to its officers as representing the public authority. *The results of Huber's views*

112. J. H. Boehmer, for example, uses the conception of the *societas aequalis* in order to justify the status of the *collegium seu universitas* as *una persona moralis*, and to prove the identity of this collective person through all the changes in its membership. He goes on to make this conception the basis of his theory of the possessions, the debts, and the legal transactions and *Boehmer bases the corporation on the societas aequalis*

delicts of the *universitas*: indeed he makes it the basis of a general distinction between *omnes conjunctim sumpti* and *singuli*, which he uses again and again in connection with all these points (*Introd. in jus publ. univ.*, *P. spec.* II, c. 4, § 1 n. *i*, § 3 n. *l*, c. 10, § 5 n. *pp*).

113. See pp. 171–3, supra.

114. See, as representing this whole line of thought, Nettelbladt, *Syst. nat.* §§ 1238–40 and Hoffbauer, p. 288.

115. Montesquieu, on the other hand, while he takes an 'institutional' view of corporations, champions their cause; cf. n. 91 to this section.

The corporation confused with the foundation

116. This is the case with Turgot (n. 15 to this section); and the same failure to distinguish between corporations and foundations appears in the debates of the National Assembly (see nn. 20–3 to this section). We may also trace an unconscious transition from the idea of a society as being an association to the idea of it as being a State-institution or foundation in the theory of Scheidemantel—and this notwithstanding the fact that he interprets all groups as 'associations' (without seeking to distinguish between *societas* and corporation), and that he bases all the rights and duties of groups on a contract between their members: cf. III, pp. 244 sqq.

117. See above, pp. 168–9.

118. This is particularly the case with W. von Humboldt, *Ideen*, p. 129.

Huber recognises bodies which are not universitates as moral persons

119. See n. 128 to § 16. In particular, we find Huber expressly arguing that *vici* without magistrates of their own cannot be *universitates*, even when they have *res communes, et earum nomine agere et convenire possunt ut personae*; for these rights, he contends, may be exercised wherever there is simple co-ownership [i.e. the co-owners may act and meet in respect of what they own], whether or no there is also a *societas* (*De jure civ.* II, 3, c. 5, § 4). [Just as he allows some rights of acting and meeting to a village which is not a *universitas*, so] Huber would also allow merely tolerated societies (e.g. Anabaptists and Arminians) to enjoy the rights which are necessary for their continued existence, although they are not *universitates*: e.g. they should have the right of entering into contracts, though not that of receiving legacies (ibid. III, cc. 8–9; *Dig.* III, 4, no. 3).

120. See nn. 154, 162 and 165 to § 16.

121. See nn. 155, 166 and 167 to § 16.

Extension of the connotation of the moral person

122. On the extension of the conception of the 'collective person' in Hert and Gundling, see nn. 160 and 163 to § 16. It is also instructive to notice the line taken by Huber, when he is seeking to find the differentia of *societas*, as contrasted with *universitas*. (This is a task which he essays in the course of an exposition of the *contractus societatis*—an exposition which is made to include a theory of the partnership in property between husband and wife, under the name of *societas conjugans*.) He entirely avoids the pit-fall of making the differentia consist in the absence of moral personality. See *Dig.* 17, 2, nos. 2–13; and see also nn. 108 and 119 to § 16.

Boehmer, too, [makes no sharp distinction between *universitas* and *societas*; he] distinguishes a *universitas* from a *societas negotiatoria* only by the fact that it is not instituted *ad commune lucrum et quaestum*; cf. *P. spec.* II, c. 4, § 1 n. *i*. Scheidemantel, in much the same way, applies the conception of the 'composite' person to families and partnerships also [as well as to corporations proper]; III, pp. 244 sqq.

123. The fundamental ideas [of this Fellowship theory] were expressed in England by Locke, II, c. 8, §§ 95–9.

Notes to § 18

124. The fact that he even manages to establish a relation of this order between 'natural' and 'positive' feudal law shows how far Nettelbladt could go in this direction.

125. Cf. supra, pp. 124–6sqq., and nn. 170sqq. to §16. Nettelbladt accordingly makes the distinction between the *status internus* of a society and its *status externus* (§334) the fundamental basis of his theory of corporations. Achenwall goes even further in drawing a hard and fast distinction between the *internum jus* of a society (II, §§6–13) and its *externum jus* (ibid. §§14–22): in the one case [i.e. as regards *internum jus*], he only employs the idea of a *nexus juridicus socialis*: in the other, he uses that of a *persona moralis*. *Distinction of the internal and the external position of groups*

126. See nn. 65–70 to this section, and also nn. 75, 81 and 85–6.

127. Wolff, *Instit.* §§841, 846; Heineccius, §14; Cocceji, §280; Daries, §762; Nettelbladt, §§336sqq.; Achenwall, II, §§24sqq.; C. von Schlözer, *De jure suff.* §3; Hoffbauer, pp. 187, 192.

128. Cf. nn. 175, 178, 181 to §16.

129. Wolff, *Instit.* §§979sqq.; Nettelbladt, §§338–9; Achenwall, II, §§32–9; Hoffbauer, pp. 192–3 and 205sqq.

130. The argument of Achenwall deserves special notice in this connection (II, §§24–8). All the members of a *societas aequalis* have identically the same *jus ac obligatio*: therefore the 'common consent of the members' must determine the means which are necessary for achieving the end of this society; and where this common consent has not been given and declared in the original pact itself, it has to be expressed in *conclusa* formulated subsequently to the pact. Inasmuch, however, as all the members cannot always assemble and give their consent to these later *conclusa*, an agreement (*lex societatis pactitia*) is made at the time of the initial institution of the society, determining the proper procedure to be followed in the future: the *modus consentiendi validus* thus comes to be fixed in advance; the rules of precedence which may have to be followed, and the method of counting a majority of votes, are agreed upon, etc. A similar argument appears in Wolff, *Instit.* §§841 sqq. (on the methods of 'common consent'); Nettelbladt, §§374sqq.; Hoffbauer, pp. 199sqq. *Achenwall on the basis of majority-decisions*

131. Nettelbladt, §§363–6. The reception of new members is an act whereby the *societas*, in virtue of the *jus societatis sociale*, declares that an *extraneus* who desires to be a member is thenceforth to count as such. It is an act which alters *status* [i.e. the existing system of relations in the society], and therefore modifies rights and duties [for all the old members], to an extent determined by the purpose of the society [e.g. the higher the purpose, the greater will be the change which an increase of the number of members makes in the existing system of relations and the existing rights and duties of members]. No particular rules can be laid down in regard to the quality and quantity proper to the members of a society; all that is needed is *voluntas recipiendi* and *voluntas societatis recipientis*; the contract [by which a new member is received] is a valid contract even when, as is the case among the freemasons, the candidate does not know the exact object of the society, but knows that it is a permissible object. Cf. Wolff, *Instit.* §§836–7 and 846; and cf. also the views of S. Cocceji (III, §105) on the *status collegii* [the system of relations existing in an association] which regulates participation in corporate rights, and on the *actio praejudicialis* which members have given them for the protection of such rights. *The reception of new members into a society*

388   *Gierke's Notes*

Expulsion or resignation from a society

132. Logically enough, Nettelbladt refuses to recognise either a right of the member to quit a society freely, or a right of the society to expel a member by its own exclusive action; and he will only allow exceptions to be made in either respect *vi juris necessitatis ob collisionem officiorum* ['under duresse of the law of necessity, in cases where there is a conflict of duties'], cf. §§ 368–70 and *Jurispr. pos.* § 855. Hoffbauer takes the same line, pp. 198–9.

Wolff, on the other hand, is willing to allow a member to quit a society if there is no agreement to the contrary, provided that it is not to the detriment of the society; indeed, he is even willing to allow it—provided that an *idoneus* is substituted—in cases where there is an express agreement that a member shall not quit a society without its assent. Conversely, he holds that a society has always the right to expel a negligent or hostile member (§§ 852–3). Heineccius holds that any *societas* lasts only as long as there is *consensus*, and a member is therefore always free to quit (II, § 14). According to Achenwall (II, §§ 12–13), a *universitas* has the right and duty to coerce or expel a member who offends against the agreement on which it is based; and, conversely, members have a right of coercion or resignation as against a *universitas* which adversely affects their rights.

133. Nettelbladt, §§ 362, 367, 371. See also his *Jurispr. pos.* (§§ 856–9 and 876) on the rights and duties of the officials of an association in positive law; on the responsibility which officials incur in consequence of their *administratio*; and, more particularly, on the position of the *syndicus* of an association.

134. Nettelbladt, §§ 83 and 372, and *Jurispr. pos.* §§ 846 and 865. Heineccius takes the same view, II, §§ 20–1; and so does Achenwall (*Proleg.* § 93)—with a reservation, however, in favour of those exceptions to the general rule [that corporations have the same rights as individuals] which arise from the *diversa hominis individui et societatis natura*.

Analysis of Nettelbladt's method of dealing with associations

135. Under the head of *jurisprudentia naturalis generalis socialis*, Nettelbladt treats first of the *generalissima de societatibus principia*—of the general conception of associations, and their origin, end, status, authority, kinds and members (§§ 326–71). He then deals with the application to *societates* of the rules of Natural Law which relate to *singuli*, discussing such application in detail with reference to *actiones, res, leges, negotia, jura, obligationes, possessio vel quasi*, and *remedia juris* (§§ 372–414).

Under the head of *jurisprudentia positiva generalis* (*Jurispr. pos.* Book II), he begins by remarking (§ 846) that the rules which have been previously stated with regard to *singuli* (Book I, §§ 5–845) are also applicable to *societates personarum*. He then proceeds to treat of *universitates personarum* in general (sect. 1)—dealing with their different species (tit. 1); with their *potestas, directorium* and *officia*, and, more especially, their *munera* (tit. 2); and with their membership (tit. 3). Next, he treats (in a somewhat different order from that followed in his treatise on Natural Law) of the application to *universitates* of the positive-law rules relating to *singuli*. Here he deals first (sect. 2) with the theory of persons (tit. 1), things (tit. 2) and actions (tit. 3); he then deals (sect. 3) with *leges et actus juridici*; he proceeds (sect. 4) to *obligatio* (tit. 1), *jura* (tit. 2) and *possessio* (tit. 3); and he finally deals (in sect. 5) with *remedia juris*.

Achenwall (II, §§ 16–21) also draws a parallel between Natural Law in regard to 'societies' and Natural Law relating to individuals, distinguishing, in both cases, between three sorts of rights and duties—the absolute, the hypothetical, and those which arise from *laesio*.

136. *Syst. nat.* §373; *Jurispr. pos.* §866. A similar argument appears in Achenwall (II, §24) and Hoffbauer, pp. 192 sqq.

137. *Syst. nat.* §§374–92. Nettelbladt discusses under this head (1) meetings, which may be either 'stated' or specially summoned, and either direct or representative; (2) *jura directorialia* (e.g. the summoning of meetings, the making of proposals, the collecting of votes and the formulating of resolutions); (3) votes and their different species (e.g. voting by heads and voting by *curiae*); (4) the right of voting, which belongs to all equally in any case of doubt, but lapses for the time being when a member abstains from voting or is absent in spite of having been duly summoned, and does not exist at all when the issue in question affects a member personally; (5) the order of voting, and the right to alter a vote given before a decision is finally taken; (6) the counting or weighing of votes; (7) the method of counting; (8) the formulation of decisions; (9) unanimity of votes, majority of votes, and equality of votes (in the last event, he remarks, *nihil conclusum est*, but the use of the lot eventually decides the issue); (10) the majority-principle (which is satisfied by a relative majority), and the exceptions to that principle; (11) *itio in partes* [or the taking of a division], and, more especially, the decision of the question whether an issue is really present which is suitable for settlement by that method; and (12) the cancelling of a decision. He expressly remarks that all the rules suggested are equally valid for the decisions of a representative body or for those of a collegiate body of officials. *Nettelbladt's account of the deliberations and decisions of corporate bodies*

138. *Jurispr. pos.* §869. Nettelbladt also mentions the requirement that all should be summoned, and at least two-thirds should be present; the greater weight which is sometimes recognised as due to *sanioritas* [i.e. to the *sanior*, as distinct from the *major, pars*]; the *calculus Minervae*, §867 [what we should call the 'casting vote']; the continuance of the right to vote in spite of *non usus*, and the validity of a vote in one's own favour (a principle to be assumed in Germany on the analogy of canon law), §868. He also treats in detail of corporate seals (§870) and the proper proofs of *voluntas et consensus* (§871). *His account of the rules of positive law in these matters*

139. Cf. Wolff (§§841–5), who even deduces from Natural Law the principle that where the contributions or benefits of the members are unequal, their voting power should be unequal, and proportionate to what they give or receive. See also Daries, §763, along with §§750–62; Achenwall, II, §§26–8 (where, however, the reader is referred to *leges conventae* [i.e. positive law] for most of the particular questions raised); and Hoffbauer, pp. 199–204. Christian von Schlözer (*De jure suffr.* §§8–23) also seeks to derive the rules of corporate action from Natural Law, but he holds that Natural Law does not warrant either the principle of majority-decision, or the binding of those who are absent by the vote of those who are present. He thinks that, if the idea of the *societas aequalis* is to be preserved, an agreement must be attained by means of *pacta adjecta* [i.e. positive rules super-added to Natural Law] before there can be any validity attached to the act of a majority, whether the majority be the ordinary form of majority (which in any case of doubt must be absolute, and not relative) or some specially qualified form. The same is true in regard to casting votes; in regard to the obligation incurred by absent members (here there should also be further rules both about the competence of those present to take a decision and about the giving of votes by letter or by proxy); in regard to voting, for reasons of equity, by *curiae* or classes; and, finally, in regard to *jus eundi in partes* and *unio suffragiorum sibi* *Other writers on the rules of voting* *invicem adversantium* [i.e. the right of claiming a division, and the general methods of getting some sort of unity out of a number of conflicting views on an issue].

140. Cf. n. 184 to § 16, and the following notes.

The rights and limits of a majority

141. See Nettelbladt, §§ 388–9 (where it is argued that there can be no majority-vote *in causis jura singulorum concernentibus*), and § 392 (where it is contended that decisions from which *jura quaesita* have subsequently arisen cannot be abrogated). Similarly Hoffbauer holds (p. 204) that a majority has no power to touch the rights which a member enjoys in the society (and therefore no power to touch the constitution), or even to touch any rights of a member derived from any other source. C. von Schlözer contends that where pure natural law is followed—and where, accordingly, there is neither any majority-vote nor any obligation of the absent by the vote of those present—no question arises of [the majority modifying] the *jura singulorum* or the *leges fundamentales* (loc. cit. § 13); and even where the validity of the majority-principle has been agreed upon by additional contracts [supplementary to the original contract constituting the society], the *pacta fundamentalia* and the *jura singulorum* are exempt from the operation of these contracts, and can only be altered by a *novum pactum* [in substitution for the original contract constituting the society].

142. *Syst. nat.* §§ 393–6; cf. Wolff, §§ 197 and 1128–9 (where it is further suggested, in regard to the possessions of a community, that they belong to 'the descendants' also),* and Achenwall, II, § 19.

143. *Jurispr. pos.* §§ 872–7 (where he deals specially with the legal questions of *salarium*, the 'year of grace' [i.e. a year's revenue granted to the family of an official at his death], family-property, and the *administratio bonorum*).

The by-laws of an association

144. *Syst. nat.* § 398. The same line is taken by Wolff, § 846 (see n. 66 to this section), and by Achenwall. The latter argues in II, §§ 29–30, that all the *leges* of the 'equal society' are *leges conventionales*, to which new members tacitly submit; but it is only *ut singuli* that the members are bound by these laws, and *ut universi* they are *supra leges*, and can alter them at pleasure. In the same way he also argues (loc. cit. § 34) that in the 'unequal society' the *imperans* promulgates laws by which he is not himself bound, and which he can alter at will. But even in the 'unequal society' the *leges fundamentales* [as distinct from ordinary laws] are always to be regarded as *pacta* [and are therefore unalterable except by the consent of both parties to the pact]; cf. Nettelbladt, § 399, and Achenwall, § 35.

145. *Jurispr.* §§ 884–91 (where he also treats of conflict of by-laws, their relation to common law, and their interpretation and application).

146. *Syst. nat.* §§ 400–2. He pays particular attention to the contracts into which the *Superior* can legitimately enter *societatis nomine, limites suae potestatis non transgrediendo*; but he holds that in 'equal societies' which possess *potestas* it is only a decision of the society itself which can authorise such contracts.

The obligations of associations

147. *Syst. nat.* §§ 404–5, where Nettelbladt argues that the 'obligations of individuals' are the duty of obedience and the duty of accepting office in the society, and that 'obligations of the society' [as distinct from those of individuals] arise from undertakings given by representatives, from *versio in rem ipsius societatis*,† from the acts of a *mandatarius legitimus* acting within the

---

* I.e. Wolff recognises not only (1) the present society and (2) the present *singula membra*, but also (3) 'the descendants', as having rights in the possessions of a community. † See n. 151 to § 17 supra.

Notes to § 18

limits of his powers, and from *actio societatis*. A similar argument appears in his *Jurispr. pos.* §§893–4. In §898 he also deals with the non-admissibility [as regards societies] (*a*) of the principle of compensation as between *stationes fisci* [the different 'accounts' in the common fund?] and (*b*) of the principle of *restitutio in integrum* [the rescinding of an act by an official, in order to prevent the legal consequences which ordinarily attend such an act from taking effect].*

148. *Jurispr. pos.* §§895–7. He adds that a member is never responsible for another member; nor is a *successor in universitate*, unless he has an obligation as heir.

149. Ibid. §877. He also remarks, in the preceding section, that a *universitas*, as a 'moral person', cannot administer its own property itself.

150. Achenwall (II, §21) holds that a *societas*, as such, is capable of all obligations—both the 'absolute' and the 'hypothetical', and both the hypothetical arising from permissible and the hypothetical arising from non-permissible actions. Scheidemantel only remarks (I, p. 220) that 'penalties attached to whole communities should only affect the benefits which arise from the particular nexus of the given society'.

151. *Syst. nat.* §§406–7. He enumerates as *jura societatis* (in contradistinction to *jura singulorum*) the following: (1) the admission of members; (2) the expulsion of members; (3) the disposition of the *res societatis*; (4) the making of provision for the *negotia societatis*; (5) the imposing of contributions for the attainment of the society's objects, including contributions from the *res et facta singulorum*; (6) *dispositio de ipsis juris societatibus* [*ipsis juribus societatis*?], even if such disposition be to the advantage or disadvantage of individual members and even if it takes the form of self-limitation or renunciation (e.g. that of renouncing a *jus prohibendi*). *Nettelbladt on jura societatis*

152. *Jurispr. pos.* §§899–903. Such peculiarities in the rights and duties of societies include privileges or charters; acquisition by *pollicitatio*; the loss [of property] after the lapse of 100 years, or by destruction; and limitations on the power of alienation.

153. *Syst. nat.* §§408–9, and also §§293 sqq.

154. *Jurispr. pos.* §§904 and 906 (which treat of interdicts [or, as we might say, 'injunctions'] and the peculiarities of fiscal law in regard to 'societies'). *On possession by societies*

155. Loc. cit. §905. As regards *jura affirmativa*, possession of such rights is acquired [by other parties, as against a *universitas*] through toleration by the *universitas* itself, and not through toleration by individual members; while, conversely, the acquisition of possession by a *universitas* [as against other parties] can only be defeated by a stoppage of the proceedings of the *universitas ipsa*. As regards *jura negativa*, possession of such rights is acquired [again by other parties, as against a *universitas*] through prohibition addressed to the *universitas* and the acquiescence of the *universitas ipsa*; while, conversely, the acquisition of possession by a *universitas* can only be defeated, once more, by a stoppage of the proceedings of the *tota universitas* and the acquiescence of all its members therein.

156. *Syst. nat.* §§410–12 and *Jurispr. pos.* §§908–9 (reprisals, Nettelbladt argues, are not only permissible between States: they are also permissible, in a peculiar way, between Churches; but other *universitates* have no more right in this respect than belongs to individual subjects). *On legal remedies of societies*

* The argument appears to be that ordinary societies do not enjoy the benefit of these principles, while the 'great society' of the State does.

157. *Syst. nat.* §413: the jurisdiction of a society is no proper jurisdiction, such as that which universally appertains to States: it is rather a *conventionalis potestas judicandi*.

158. *Syst. nat.* §414 (which deals with the processes of *actio, exceptio* and *provocatio*). In his *Jurispr. pos.* §§878–82, Nettelbladt deals more fully with the modes of legal action open to *universitates*. He draws a distinction between cases in which the *causa universitatis qua talis* is 'divisible', and those in which it is 'indivisible'. In cases of the first sort, the members (*singuli*) are in a position to make an effective disclaimer, though they are open to doubt as witnesses; but in cases of the second sort also they are not altogether free from suspicion as witnesses, and the distinction is thus really slight....A *universitas* should take an oath by means of three or four of its members....Nettelbladt also discusses the documentary evidence proper in such processes, and the proper proofs of descent in family-disputes.

In §911 he deals with the prior rights of a *universitas* in cases of *concursus* [i.e. of a conflict of claims]; and in §912 he treats of the conflict of claims arising when a *universitas* itself is involved in debt. In the latter case he holds that, inasmuch as the substance of the property is inalienable, there can only be a *concursus anomalus*, with a sequestration and division among the claimants of the *income* arising from the property.

159. *Jurispr. pos.* §846; cf. also Achenwall, II, §8.

160. Cf. especially Wolff, §977, and Achenwall, *Proleg.* §94 and II, §§41–84 (with nn. 175 and 182 to §16 above): see also Cocceji, §281; Daries, §§606sqq.; and Nettelbladt, *Syst. nat.* §§666sqq. (where he classifies six sorts of family 'society'—*paterna, adoptiva, tutelaris, herilis, domus, conjugalis*), along with *Jurispr. pos.* §851.

On the other hand Hoffbauer, who treats marriage as an equal society which can be freely dissolved (pp. 209sqq.), considers that the relation of parents to children and servants is not a 'society' (pp. 214sqq.), and that the family is not a 'compound society' (p. 221).

Nettelbladt treats aristocratic Houses as corporations

161. In his *Positive Jurisprudence* Nettelbladt reckons as *universitates* the German Empire, the Catholic and Evangelical Churches, local communities, *corpora et collegia*, and families (including *gens, familia* and *domus*), §§848–51. He treats the divisions of the family as *membra universitatis*, arguing that it is only special rules in regard to the acquisition or loss of members which distinguish such divisions from one another (§§860–62). He brings family-property (or *bona stemmatica*) which is *in dominio vel quasi dominio familiae* under the general head of *res universitatis* (§875); and he applies to its alienation (apart from a requirement that all the members of the family should give their consent) the general rules of Roman law in l. 3 C. *de vend. reb. civ.* (§903). He speaks of families as parties in civil suits (§882); and he refers to *statuta familiarum* [family by-laws or 'rules of the house'], which may be either *pacta*, or *dispositiones capitis familiae*, or *normae Superioris* (§886).

In his *Syst. nat.* he draws a distinction between (1) the rights of ruling families to the property of the 'House' or 'line', (2) the property-rights of the Fisc, and (3) the *patrimonium Principis* (§1349); and he also speaks of the *autonomia familiarum illustrium* (§1510).

162. See especially Nettelbladt, *Syst. nat.* §§358–9, on the application of the general rules relating to 'societies' to any *peculiare collegium repraesentativum* and to *deputationes collegii*; see also his *Positive Jurisprudence*, §850, on the division

of *corpora et collegia* into (1) *separata* and (2) those which are only *pars alterius universitatis*.

163. See, more especially, Wolff. He distinguishes, in his theory of common property, between three forms of *communio*: (1) the *communio negativa* of the state of nature; (2) *communio positiva*, with such and such shares for each participant; and (3) *communio mixta*, in which the property itself belongs to a *universitas*, and the individual has only a right of common user (*Instit.* §§191–7). He interprets, however, the second of these forms—that of positive co-ownership—as being 'like ownership by a single person'; and all that he assigns to the individual participant, other than the right of disposition in regard to his share, is a right of annulling the unity of ownership 'if the common right be not enjoyed conformably to the condition that it must remain common' (§196 and §§330–1). We may compare with this his remarks on collective credits and debts (§424); on common citizenship of towns (§573); on *societas negotiatoria* (§§639–48, and especially §642, 'on the share of each member in the property of the society'); on *communio incidens* or 'quasi-society' (§692); and, finally, on the 'mining contract' in regard to shares in mines (§683), which he surprisingly brings under the head of lottery-contracts (*Glücksverträge*). *Mere systems of co-ownership regarded as 'moral persons'*

Nettelbladt not only assumes the existence of a single personality of many individuals when such individuals play the part of a 'moral person' *conjunctim*: he also assumes its existence when they *disjunctim unam personam sustinent*, e.g. where it is a case of *correi* [i.e. persons severally responsible for the same debt], or of representatives and the persons they represent (*Jurispr. pos.* §§17–18). In his theory of *communio positiva* (*Syst. nat.* §§203–4), of *condominium* (§§222–5), and, more especially, of general and particular community of property (§§226–7), the [Teutonic] idea of 'the joint hand' makes its appearance—particularly in the fact that, while he ascribes the common property to all the members of a group taken as a whole, he also ascribes to each individual a quasi-private property in his share. In this last connection it is to be noted that he confines *dominium* proper to *res corporales*; but he regards a *quasi-dominium* in *res incorporales* as co-existing with *dominium* proper (§215). [Hence the share of an individual, being an 'ideal' or incorporeal thing, can only be the object of quasi-private property; but this quasi-private property coexists with the *dominium* proper of the whole group.]

164. It has already been remarked that the parallel between the division of one individual into several 'persons' and the union of several individuals in one 'person' helped to turn into an abstraction the idea of a person composed of a number of individuals; cf. n. 173 to §16 supra.

165. Thus, for example, the whole of the theory regarding the authority of a community over its members is inapplicable to a society composed of two persons only, though such a society is none the less expressly recognised as a 'moral person'; and the consequence is that the greater part of the general theory of societies is inapplicable in such a case. Cf. Achenwall, II, §8 (who remarks that, provided there are more than two members, the sum of the reciprocal rights and duties thus involved gives rise to a *jus sociale universorum in singulos singulique cujuslibet in universos*): cf. also Heineccius, II, §14, and Nettelbladt, *Syst. nat.* §§84 and 333. Similarly we find thinkers compelled [by this general point of view which led them to make concessions to the rights of individuals] to accept as causes of the dissolution of a *societas* *The group as merely so many individuals*

the fact of the death of its members, or the disappearance of a member, or resignation, etc.: Nettelbladt, §333.

Yet it exists apart from individuals

166. We may notice especially, for the light which it throws on this tendency, the way in which Nettelbladt (loc. cit. §86) seeks to justify his assumption that the 'moral personality' of a *societas* can persist in a single member, or even without any member, if there be ground for expecting its reconstruction: *essentia enim personae moralis consistit in individuorum consociatione, et si adhuc superest unum individuum, id repraesentat reliqua; si vero nullum actu adest, quae in spe sunt individua pluralitatem individuorum constituunt.* We may also note the interpretation of community-property in Wolff; cf. n. 142 to this section.

167. Cf. nn. 114 and 130 to this section, and also nn. 176 and 181 to §16.
168. Cf. supra, pp. 179–180.
169. Cf. especially the views of A. L. and C. von Schlözer, and of Hoffbauer, as stated in nn. 186–92 to §16.
170. Humboldt's *Ideen*, pp. 121, 123 sqq., 125, 129. 'The less a man is enabled to act otherwise than as his will desires or his force allows him, the more favourable is his position in the State.'
171. Ibid. pp. 129–32.

Denial of any international society

172. Cf. Pufendorf, *Elem.* §§24–6 and *J. n. et g.* II, c. 3, §23; Gundling, c. 1, §54; Hertius, II, 3, pp. 21 sqq.; Huber, I, 1, c. 5; J. H. Boehmer, *Jus pub. univ.*, P. gen. c. 2, §§3–7, P. spec. I, c. 3, §22 n. *l.* Justi also argues (§§222–3) that international law does not depend on the existence of a social union of States or a joint federal State. It is rather that a state of nature exists between different nations, and that they live in that state, like individuals, by their own will, without any association, in perfect liberty and equality. But they live on the same globe; they are therefore subject to the fundamental rule that they must do as they would be done by; and there thus exist among them duties of good-fellowship—though there is no society. Cf. also Spinoza, *Tract. pol.* c. 3, §§11–18, and Horn, *De civ.* c. 2, §§4–9.

Admission of such a society

173. Mevius, *Prodromus*, §§5–9 and 18–20: the *societas communis inter omnes populos* is the source of international law, and the authority of that law depends, not on any agreement, but on the rational order which holds good for this *socialis populorum conjunctio.* Cf. also Johannes a Felde, I, c. 1, p. 5; Praschius, §3; Placcius, Bk. III; Leibniz, Introduction to *Cod. Gent. dipl.* I, §13, *Fragment on Natural Law*, p. 420, and *Caesar.-Fürst.* cc. 31–2; Bossuet, I, art. 5.

Thomasius on the societas gentium

174. Thomasius, *Instit. jur. div.* I, c. 2, §§101–4, III, c. 1, §§38–56. He censures the Aristotelians for neglecting the *societas gentium*: he proves its existence (*quia universum genus humanum natura est unitum ad certum finem*); and he describes it as a *societas maxime naturalis*, which produces a *juris communio.* But international law proper is in his view only a part of the *lex divina naturalis* discoverable by human reason; it is not a *jus humanum*, or system of positive law. For (1) there is no *Superior*; (2) contracts only oblige men *lege intercedente*, just as custom only binds them by virtue of a *tacita approbatio principis*; and (3) the assumption of an express or tacit *pactum universale* is a mere fiction.

The views of Wolff and his successors

175. Wolff, *Instit.* §§1090–2; Daries, §544 (where the *societas universalis omnium hominum* is treated as a *societas necessaria*); Nettelbladt, *Syst. nat.* §§1420 sqq. (there is a *societas natura constituta* 'for the preservation of the human race'); Achenwall, *Proleg.* §§82–90, I, §§43–4, II, §§210–88 (on the *societas universalis*). In all these writers there is a general recognition that

Notes to § 18

there is also such a thing as positive international law: Wolff, for example, speaks of a *jus gentium voluntarium, pactitium*, and, to some extent, *consuetudinarium*; and Nettelbladt admits *leges [gentium] sociales seu systematicae* as well as *leges gentium stricte naturales*.

176. Thomasius argues that the *societas gentium* is not a *respublica universalis*, but a *societas aequalis* with no *imperium*, and that, far from perfecting the State, it is *imperfectior civitate* (*Instit. jur. div.* III, c. 1, §§ 52–3; *Fund.* III, c. 6, § 5). The same line of thought appears in J. a Felde, I, c. 1, p. 5; and Nettelbladt also remarks (§ 1420) that the society of peoples is a *systema gentium* rather than a *civitas maxima*.

177. Wolff, § 1090. Achenwall also uses this term (*Proleg.* §§ 82 sqq.); cf. Vico (p. 156), *omnes orbis terrarum respublicae una civitas magna cujus Deus hominesque habent communionem*.

Kant finds the ideal goal of human progress in a World-State (*Völkerstaat* or 'World-Republic') with a definite cosmopolitan constitution and a single Head; but he holds that the only goal which can be attained under present conditions is the institution of a 'League' ('Federation' or 'Fellowship') for the prevention of war (*Works*, VI, pp. 340–6, 415–20; VII, pp. 162 and 168 sqq.). *Kant and Fichte on a league of nations*

Fichte, who differs from all other writers on Natural Law in deriving international law not from the relations of States to one another, but from those of the individual citizens of different States, desires a voluntary 'League', which is not to be a *Völkerstaat*, but is to possess judicial and executive authority for producing a state of peace (*Naturrecht*, II, pp. 261 sqq.; *Works*, III, pp. 379 sqq.; *Posthumous Works*, II, pp. 644 sqq.).

178. Pufendorf, *De systematibus civitatum*, § 8, *J. n. et g.* VII, c. 5, § 16, *De off. hom. et civ.* II, c. 8, § 13; Horn, *De civ.* II, c. 2, § 14; Becmann, *Med.* c. 22; Huber, *De civ.* I, 2, c. 2, §§ 20 and 28, I, 3, c. 3; Thomasius, *Instit. jur. div.* III, c. 6, §§ 57–8; Schmier, I, c. 4, no. 67; Hertius, *Elem.* I, s. 12, §§ 7–8 and II, s. 18; Gundling, c. 37 (36), §§ 37–47; Titius, *Spec. jur. publ.* VII, c. 7, § 37; J. H. Boehmer, *P. spec.* I, c. 3, §§ 27–9; Daries, §§ 808–11; Achenwall, II, §§ 189–90; Heincke, I, c. 3, §§ 27–31; A. L. von Schlözer, p. 117, § 6.

179. Pufendorf, *J. n. et g.* VIII, c. 9, *De off. hom. et civ.* II, c. 17; Huber, III, 4, c. 3; Gundling, c. 12 (11), §§ 34–42 and also c. 24 (23), §§ 16–19 on 'Mascopeyen' [or 'contracts of society'] among nations, and on *societates bellicae* and common governments; Daries, §§ 802–5; Achenwall, II, §§ 240–2.

Thomasius (*Instit. jur. div.* III, c. 1, §§ 35–7 and c. 8, §§ 1–27) adopts a peculiar line of argument. He regards any federal association between a number of States, when it represents only a *social* form of *unio voluntatum* and is constituted for a limited period, as being a *societas perfectior civitate*, on the ground that it supplements in certain directions the power of a single State which is inadequate by itself. Such an association, he thinks, is indeed an 'arbitrary' community; but it marks an approach to *societas naturalis*. He draws, however, a sharp distinction between a *societas inter plures respublicas confoederatas* and a *systema civitatum*: the former he regards as constituted only for a definite object (*certae utilitatis gratia*), but the latter as a *perpetua unio...indefinitae gratiae causa*. *Thomasius on federations*

180. Pufendorf, *De syst.* §§ 9–15 and *J. n. et g.* VII, c. 5, § 17; Huber, I, 2, c. 2, §§ 24–7; Daries, §§ 806–7.

181. Hert, for example, writing in 1689 (*Elem.* I, 12, § 5 and II, 17, §§ 1–5), already notes that unions under a single king are possible not only where

The theory of a 'real union' of States

there is no other bond of connection, but also when there is a considerable amount of community between the countries so united. Titius, writing in 1703, in his commentary on Pufendorf's *De off. hom. et civ.* II, c. 5, § 14, draws a sharp distinction between a mere personal union, *sub uno capite*, and a real union, in which there is also a common exercise *nonnullarum imperii partium*; and he holds that a *systema* exists in the latter case only, and not in the former. Treuer takes the same line, in his commentary on the same passage; cf. also Schmier, I, c. 4, nos. 68–76. The same view also appears in Heineccius (1737), *Elem.* II, § 119 (but he was not, as Juraschek assumes (p. 13), the first to take this view). See also Nettelbladt, § 1172, who adds the idea of [the union of] a predominant State with subsidiary States. Apart from these writers, we generally find the idea of *unio per incorporationem* expounded.

The theory of the corpus confoederatorum

182. Pufendorf, *De syst.* §§ 16sqq., *J. n. et g.* VII, c. 5, §§ 18sqq., *De off. hom. et civ.* II, c. 8, §§ 13sqq.: there is *unum corpus*, but no *civitas*, for *singulae civitates summum in sese imperium retinent*, and they have only bound themselves contractually *circa exercendum communi consensu unam aut alteram partem summi imperii*: we cannot, therefore, ascribe to this category [of *corpora confoederatorum*] a State composed *ex pluribus corporibus subordinatis*, or, again, a State which leaves some degree of independence to conquered provinces. Cf. Huber, I, 2, c. 2, §§ 20–3: the federal assembly *non est omnium caput, sed plura capita repraesentat...non vere imperat, sed imperata singulorum communiter exequitur*; the sovereignty of the members of the federation remains intact (I, 3, c. 3). See also Thomasius, *Instit. jur. div.* III, c. 6, §§ 57–8, where, however, the term *compositae respublicae* is used; Hertius, *Elem.* I, s. 12, §§ 7–8 and II, s. 18; and Gundling, c. 37 (36), §§ 37sqq. Schmier remarks that it is only an appearance of *una respublica* that is ever present: *revera sunt et manent inter se distinctae et diversae, utpote voluntates res bonaque sua seorsim et separatim habentes* (I, c. 4, nos. 77–88). Titius (*Diss.* § 76 and *Jus publ.* VII, c. 7, §§ 34–5) speaks of *corpus civile ex pluribus civitatibus ita compositum, ut unaquaeque civitas summum ac plerumque etiam plenum imperium habeat, sed ita limitatum, ut quaedam ejus partes conjunctim ab omnibus sint exercendae*. See also J. H. Boehmer, *P. spec.* I, c. 3, §§ 27–9; Daries, §§ 808–11; Achenwall, II, § 190; Heincke, I, c. 3, §§ 27–31 (a *systema civitatum*, he holds, is a *corpus morale* which wears the appearance of a single State owing to the common exercise of the rights of sovereignty; it is a *societas juris naturalis*); Kreittmayr, § 4; A. L. von Schlözer, pp. 117–18 (what is in question, he thinks, is a 'civil society' or 'community' of States, but not a State).

Such a body cannot act by majority-decision

183. Pufendorf, *De syst.* §§ 17–21 and *J. n. et g.* VII, c. 5, §§ 19–21: it is necessary that there should be some meetings, and it is possible that there should be a permanent federal council, but the deputies attending the former continue to be *ministri sociorum*, while the latter (the *concilium deputatorum*) has only a 'delegated power', and its *vis et auctoritas provenit a sociis*: the majority-principle is inapplicable, since it means the presence of an *imperium*, and here every member has the right of secession. Horn takes a similar view, holding that everything has to be done *ratione pacti et sociorum liberrimo consensu* (II, c. 2, § 14); and A. L. von Schlözer also considers that the use of a majority-vote is not possible in a federal Diet, and that, for this very reason, such a political system has no final judge and is devoid of responsibility (pp. 118–19).

Views to the contrary

184. Huber allows a certain amount of validity to majority-decisions (I, 3, c. 3): the same view is taken by Hert, in his notes to Pufendorf's *J. n. et g.*

VII, c. 5, § 20, and by Schmier, loc. cit. no. 88. J. H. Boehmer (I, c. 2, § 4), Achenwall (II, § 190), and Kreittmayr (§ 4) regard the rules of *societates aequales* as applicable to federations. Daries takes the same view (§§ 808–11); but he considers that a *directorium*, with a *jurisdictio conventionalis* between the members of the federation, is also possible.

185. Pufendorf, *De rep. irreg.*, *J. n. et g.* VII, c. 5, §§ 12–15 and 20, *De off. hom. et civ.* II, c. 8, § 12: he regards any federal body in which the validity of the majority-principle is agreed upon as being a *corpus irregulare*. Gundling (loc. cit.) clings to the view that any such political system should be termed a *monstrum*. J. H. Boehmer (I, c. 3, § 29), while he introduces the idea of the two possible origins of a federal system (it may be due to the negative fact of disintegration or devolution, as well as to the positive fact of *foedus* or integration), describes the 'irregular system' as pitiable.   *Irregular or monstrous forms of federation*

186. Cf. Otto's commentary on Pufendorf's *De off. hom. et civ.* II, c. 8, § 12: Hertius, I, s. 12, §§ 6–9 and II, s. 19, where formations intermediate between a federation and a State with provinces, such as the German Empire, are merely treated as being *respublicae irregulares*, in just the same way as ordinary unions and federations; Schmier, I, c. 4, s. 3, §§ 1–3; and Titius, VII, c. 7, §§ 36–54. Titius, we may also note, applies to federal forms of the State the general distinction which he draws between States which are *adstrictae* and those which are *laxae* (cf. n. 167 to § 17 above, and p. 155); and he accordingly includes the 'systems' (or *civitates compositae*) which have been constituted by a *foedus adstrictum* under the head of *adstrictae*, and those which are due to the disintegration of a unitary State under that of *laxae*. See also Huber (I, 3, c. 3, §§ 17–20), who admits that there are deviations from the general norm in the German Empire; and see also Kreittmayr (§ 4), who tries to meet the difficulty by suggesting that side by side with the *systema civitatum foederatarum aequale*, such as is to be found in Switzerland and Holland, there may also exist an unequal system of federated States, like the political structure of Germany. A. L. von Schlözer also holds (p. 118) that 'scattered in a number of fragments, the 300 members of the giant body of Germany' only constitute a mere society [and not a State].   *The problem of the Holy Roman Empire*

187. *Caesarinus-Fürstenerius*, c. 11, and *Demonstr. pol. prop.* 57. Leibniz, it is true, does not base himself upon Natural Law in defending the cause of federalism. On the one hand, comparing the difference between a *confoederatio* and a *unio* with that between a *societas* and a *collegium* or *corpus*, he will only admit the emergence of a new *persona civilis* when there is a corporate group [and therefore he will not admit that there is such a *persona* in a *confoederatio*, which is only a *societas*, and not a corporate group]; on the other hand, he abandons the idea of sovereignty, holding that a real political authority of the Group-person, exercised over the member-persons, is compatible with the *libertas et suprematus* of these member-persons. [It follows that Leibniz (1) from the first point of view, cannot apply the natural-law idea of the 'moral' or 'civil' personality of Groups to federations, and (2) from the second point of view, cannot apply the natural-law idea of the sovereignty of the State to federations, or indeed to any other form of State, since he has abandoned that idea *in toto*; cf. supra, n. 48 to § 17, and cf. also n. 253 to § 16. In dealing with federations, Leibniz is thus outside the ground of Natural Law, because he is unable to use either its idea of Group-personality or its idea of State-sovereignty.]   *Leibniz on federalism*

188. *Esprit des Lois*, IX, cc. 1–3. In treating of the *république fédérative*,

Montesquieu on federations which he sometimes describes as *état plus grand* and sometimes as a *société des sociétés*, Montesquieu makes no definite distinction between the different forms which it may assume (cf. Brie, *Der Bundesstaat*, I, p. 31); but at any rate he leaves room, under this heading, for a real federal State. He regards the German Empire (which he describes in another passage—Bk·x, c. 6—as a *république fédérative mixte*, with a Head who is *en quelque façon le Magistrat de l'union et en quelque façon le Monarque*) as being a more imperfect form than the federations in Switzerland and Holland, on the ground that monarchy is not so suitable for a federal constitution.

189. *Syst. nat.* §§ 1160, 1172–7, 1183, 1221–5, 1406–9. Hoffbauer is in agreement with him, pp. 314–15.

Nettelbladt on the respublica composita 190. *Syst. nat.* §§ 1160, 1172, 1174, 1408. A *respublica composita* is present when *diversae respublicae unam rempublicam, cujus potestati civili subjectae sunt, constituunt*; but the member-States are not sovereign, and therefore they are not, in external relations (though they are *in relatione ad Rempublicam majorem*), independent *gentes* (i.e. 'persons' in international law).

191. A composite State may be a monarchy or a republic: so may also its *respublicae minores* (§ 1175). In such a State there is a *duplex potestas civilis*—the *summa* and the *subordinata*; and the latter of these powers may, in turn, be exercised doubly—both by the member-States to the exclusion of the *summa potestas* [i.e. the federal authority] and by the member-States concurrently therewith (§ 1176). Similarly there is a *duplex subjectio* (§ 1177). Such a State may come into existence either by integration of States or by way of disintegration (§ 1183). Again, in such a State, we have a new distinction between different kinds of members added to the other distinctions which we generally find in States—the distinction between *membra immediata* and *membra mediata* (§§ 1122–3). If we regard the *membra rerumpublicarum minorum*, we find that the Heads of these lesser or contained States are *superiores* on what we may call a 'downward' view, but *subdita* on an 'upward' view, while the other members of such States [i.e. the members other than the Head] are *in duplici subjectione*, with the lower *superior* taking precedence in case of conflict; §§ 1224–5. [Gierke adds that he intended to treat the theory of the federal State, as it appears in the literature of positive German public law, in a subsequent section; but this section was never published.]

192. A later section (§ 20) was to have been devoted to this theme; but the section has not been written.

VI
LIST OF AUTHORS CITED
    A. 1500 to 1650
    B. 1650 to 1800

A. LIST OF AUTHORS CITED: 1500–1650

ALBERGATI, F., a native of Bologna, who published at Bologna, in 1599, a work entitled *Il Cardinale*, and at Rome, in 1583, a *Trattato del modo di ridurre a pace l' inimicitie private*. Gierke refers to his *Discorsi politici* as an attack upon Bodin which is based on Aristotle (Rome, 1602).

ALSTED, J. H. A., 1588–1638, professor of philosophy at Herborn (in Nassau), and teacher both of philosophy and theology; an encyclopaedic writer on both of these and on a number of other subjects. Gierke refers to his *De Statu Rerumpublicarum*, Herborn, 1612.

ALTHUSIUS, J., 1557–1638, professor of law at Herborn, 1590, and syndic of the town of Emden, 1601. Gierke first drew the attention of scholars to his writings by the monograph which he devoted to them in 1880. The two of his writings which he repeatedly quotes in this section are: *Politica methodice digesta*, 1st edition, Herborn, 1603; 3rd, 1614 (the 3rd edition has lately been reprinted, with some few omissions, and edited with an introduction, by C. J. Friedrich, Harvard University Press, 1932); *Dicaeologia*, Herborn, 1617, a work in two books, *totum et universum jus quo utimur complectentes*.

ARNISAEUS, H., a student and teacher of medicine, philosophy and politics, who, after first professing ethics at Frankfort on the Oder, and then medicine at Helmstedt, became physician to the King of Denmark, and died at Copenhagen in 1636. In his political doctrines he was an opponent of Althusius. He published two volumes of 'collected political writings' (Leipzig, 1633: later edition, Strassburg, 1648). Gierke refers to five of his political writings: *Doctrina politica in genuinam methodum quae est Aristotelis reducta*, first published in 1606, and suggesting by its very title an attack on Althusius' *Politica methodice digesta* of 1603; *De jure majestatis libri tres*, first published in 1610; *De auctoritate principum in populum semper inviolabili*, first published in 1611; *De Republica, seu reflectionis politicae libri duo*, first published in 1615; *De subjectione et executione clericorum*, published in 1612. J. Maxwell, sometime bishop of Ross, published *Lex, Rex: the Law and the Prince*, in 1644, 'with a confutation of the ruinous grounds of H. Arnisaeus' (and of William Barclay, *q.v.*).

ARUMAEUS, D., 1579–1673, a jurist, professor of law at Jena, and said to be founder of the study of public law in Germany. He published in 1617–23 five volumes of *Discursus academici de jure publico*, written by himself and by other scholars.* Gierke refers to various contributions which appear in this collection.

AYALA, B., born at Antwerp about 1548, a jurisconsult, who held at one time a financial post in the army of Philip II of Spain, and wrote a work *De jure et officiis bellicis et disciplina militari*, published at Douai, 1582, and republished at Antwerp in 1597.

BARCLAY, W., 1543–1605, a Scotsman from Aberdeen, who studied law at Bourges under Cujas, and himself became professor of civil law at Angers. In addition to commentaries on Roman law, he wrote: *De Regno et regali*

---

* Such *discursus* are often disputations held before—or, as we should nowadays say, theses supervised by—the professor who edits the collection.

potestate, adversus Buchananum, Brutum [i.e. the author of the *Vind. contra Tyrannos*], *Boucherium et reliquos Monarchomachos*, Paris, 1600 (Gierke cites the Hanover edition of 1612). Locke refers to this work at the end of the *Second Treatise*. Barclay also wrote a work on the Papacy, which was published posthumously, in 1609, under the title of *De Potestate papae, an quatenus in principes saeculares jus et imperium habeat*, representing the Gallican point of view.

BEKINSAV (Becconsall), W., 1496–1559, fellow of New College, Oxford, and author of *De supremo et absoluto Regis imperio*, a work dedicated to Henry VIII, and published in 1546 (Gierke cites the reprint in Goldast's *Monarchia Sacri Romani Imperii* of 1611).

BELLARMINE, R., 1542–1621, cardinal-archbishop of Capua, member of the Jesuit order, and one of the chief writers of the Counter-Reformation. Gierke refers to his *De potestate summi pontificis in rebus temporalibus adversus Barclaium* (first published in 1610, but cited according to the Cologne edition of 1611). This work, as being Ultramontane, and as attacking the more Gallican attitude of Barclay's work on the Papacy, was at once condemned by the Parlement of Paris in the year of its publication. Gierke also refers to other writings of Bellarmine, more particularly his *De Laicis*, in the Cologne edition of his *Opera omnia*, 1620.

BENECKENDORF . Author of *Repetitio et explicatio de regulis juris*; Frankfort on the Oder, 1593.

BERCKRINGER, D., sometime tutor to the children of the Elector Palatine; became professor at Utrecht in 1640, and died in 1667. Gierke refers to his *Institutiones politicae sive de Republica*, published at Utrecht in 1662. He is also said to have written, in answer to Hobbes, an *Examen elementorum philosophicorum de bono cive*, which was never published.

BESOLD, C. B., 1577–1638, a jurist, who became professor of law at Tübingen in 1610; but crossing over to the Catholic side during the Thirty Years' War (in 1630), he became professor of civil and public law at Ingolstadt, in Bavaria, in 1635. He was a voluminous writer, both on legal and (after his conversion) on ecclesiastical subjects. Gierke refers to his *Opus politicum* (or, as it was called in an earlier form, which first appeared in 1618, *Politicorum libri duo*), and cites it according to the Strassburg edition of 1626. It is a collection of 'Discourses', which are sometimes cited separately by Gierke (e.g. *Discursus III de Democratia*, and the 'Discourses' *De statu Reipublicae mixtae* and *De jure Universitatum*).

BEZA, T., 1519–1605, the great Calvinist teacher in the age succeeding Calvin himself. To him we may ascribe, for reasons given by A. Elkan, *Die Publizisten der Bartholomäusnacht*, the authorship of the anonymously printed *De jure magistratuum in subditos et officio subditorum erga magistratus*, which professes to have been printed at Magdeburg in 1578. The work deals with the problem of resistance, as it had been raised in the minds of the French Calvinists after the massacre of 1572, and seeks to re-define the Calvinistic attitude to that problem. There is a French version (of 1574), entitled *Du droit des Magistrats*, which was printed before the Latin original.

BIERMANN . Author of *Dissertatio de jure Principatus*.

BLONDEL, D., 1591–1655, Huguenot preacher and writer: successor to Vossius in the chair of history at Amsterdam in 1650. *De jure plebis in regimine ecclesiastico*, Paris, 1648.

BODIN, J., 1530–96, French jurist and man of affairs. *Six livres de la République*,

1577. In Latin, under the title of *De Republica*, 1584. Cited by Gierke in the second Latin edition, Frankfort, dated 1591. A full account of Bodin is given in J. W. Allen's *Political Thought in the Sixteenth Century*.

BOLOGNETUS, 1539–85, ecclesiastical writer on jurisprudence. *De lege, jure et aequitate*.

BORNITIUS, J., a German jurist of the first half of the seventeenth century. Four works, including one on sovereignty (*De majestate politica*, Leipzig, 1610), are cited by Gierke in note 16 to §14. The dates range from 1607 to 1625.

BORTIUS, M. *De natura jurium majestatis et regalium*, printed in Arumaeus (*q.v.*), I, no. 2 (1616).

BOUCHER, J., 1550?–1644, Catholic teacher at Reims and afterwards at Paris, where he was a champion of the League; afterwards canon of Tournai. He wrote *De justa Henrici III abdicatione e Francorum regno*, Paris, 1589. Barclay (*q.v.*) attacks him as a Catholic *monarchomachus*, along with the Protestants Buchanan and Languet.

BOXHORN, M. Z., 1602 (or 1612)–53, professor in the University of Leyden; classical scholar, historian and writer on politics. Gierke cites *Institutionum politicorum libri duo*, 2nd edition, Leipzig, 1665.

BRUTUS, STEPHANUS JUNIUS, probably the pseudonym of Hubert Languet, 1518–81; see *Cambridge Historical Journal*, 1931. *Vindiciae contra Tyrannos*, Edinburgh (really Basle), 1579. (Walker's translation, of the seventeenth century, has been reprinted with an introduction by H. J Laski.)

BUCHANAN, G., 1506–82, classical scholar, historian and tutor of James VI of Scotland. *De jure regni apud Scotos*, 1579 (cited in the 2nd edition of 1580).

BUSIUS, P., ?–1617, professor of law in the University of Franeker, in the United Provinces. *De Republica libri III*, Franeker, 1613. The British Museum Catalogue also mentions a *Tractatus de vi et potestate legum humanarum in tres partes dissectus*, Douai, 1608.

CARNIN, CLAUDIUS DE. *Malleus tripartitus*, Antwerp, 1620.

CARPZOV, B. C., 1595–1666, jurist. *Commentarius in Legem Regiam Germanorum, sive capitulationem Imperatoriam*, 1623. *Jurisprudentia ecclesiastica seu consistoralis*, 1649. The first of these works, dealing with the conditions to which the Emperor agreed at his election, is a treatise on the public law of Germany at the time: the second deals with Protestant Church law in Germany.

CASMANNUS, O., ?–1607, theologian and philosopher, who taught at Stade (in Hanover). He published a work on *Psychologia anthropologica* in 1594. Gierke refers to his *Doctrinae et vitae politicae methodicum et breve systema*, Frankfort, 1603.

CLAPMARUS, A. C., 1574–1604, publicist. *De arcanis rerumpublicarum libri VI*, first published posthumously, 1605.

COLLIBUS, HIPPOLYTUS A, 1561–1612, a jurist, of Italian origin, born in Zurich, who served the Elector Palatine from 1593 onwards. He wrote works on the *Nobilis* (1588), the *Princeps* (1593), the *Palatinus sive Aulicus* (1600) and the *Consiliarius* (1596). The third of these appeared in the *Speculum aulicarum atque politicarum observationum* printed at Strassburg in 1600, along with a reprint of the fourth.

CONNANUS (Connan, F. de), 1508–51, a French jurist. *Commentarii juris civilis*, Paris, 1538 (cited in the Basle edition of 1557).

CONRING, H., 1606–81, professor at Helmstedt, first of medicine and afterwards also of law: one of the great polymaths of his day, who wrote on theology as well as on medicine, law and politics. Gierke refers to the *Dissertationes* (e.g. *de Republica* and *de necessariis partibus civitatis*) in vol. III of his *Opera*, as published at Brunswick in 1730.

CONTZEN, A., 1573–1635, Jesuit confessor and controversialist. *Politicorum libri X*, Mainz, 1621.

CORASIUS, J. (Jean de Coras), 1513–72, French teacher of law at Toulouse; a Huguenot, who perished in the massacre of St Bartholomew. Gierke refers to his *Commentarii* on some titles of the Digest, and his *Enarrationes* on certain *responsa*, published at Lyons, 1560.

COTHMANN, E., 1557–1624, jurist and professor of law at Rostock. Gierke refers to his Commentary on Justinian's *Institutes* and *Code*, 1614, 1616.

COVARRUVIAS Y LEYVA, DIEGO (Didacus), 1512–77, professor of canon law at Oviedo, and bishop of Ciudad Rodrigo and Segovia; president of the Council of Castille; one of the chief jurists of his time. Gierke refers to his *Practicae Quaestiones* (in the *Opera omnia*, printed at Frankfort, 1583).

CRÜGER, J., *Collegium Politicum*, Giessen, 1609.

CUJACIUS (Cujas), J., 1520–90, professor at Bourges, the greatest jurist of his time. Gierke refers to his *Paratitla* to the *Digest* and the *Code*, and his notes on the *Institutes*.

DANAEUS (Daneau), L., 1530–96, French Calvinist minister. *Politices Christianae libri VII*, 1596 (cited in the Paris edition of 1606).

DOMINIS, M. A. DE, 1566–1624, a Dalmatian, who, after being professor at Padua and Brescia, became Archbishop of Spalatro. He wrote a work *De Republica Ecclesiastica*, and being anxious to publish it, he took counsel with Sir Henry Wotton at Venice, and proceeded to England, where he received preferment, and published in 1617 the first part of his work. Another part was printed in England in 1620, and a third part in Germany in the same year. The whole work includes ten books and fills three folio volumes.

ERENBERGK, W. DE, Eberhard von Weyhe, a German jurist and statesman, 1553–1633 *circiter*, who used the Latin pseudonym Waremundus de Erenbergk in some of his writings. His *Aulicus politicus* (Hanover, 1596), to which Gierke refers in note 6 to §14, was printed under the pseudonym of Durus de Pascolo. (It is included in the *Speculum*, etc., mentioned above under Collibus, H. a.) He used the other pseudonym, however, for a treatise *de regni subsidiis* (Frankfort, 1606), which Gierke also quotes.

FELDE, J. A, see Bibliography B.

FELWINGER, see Bibliography B.

FRANTZKE, G., 1594–1659, German jurist and administrator. He wrote Commentaries on the *Institutes* (Strassburg, 1658), as well as on the *Digest* (Strassburg, 1644).

FRANTZKEN   . Gierke cites under this name a disquisition *de statu reipublicae mixtae* (or *mixto*), printed in Arumaeus (*q.v.*), and another *de potestate principis*. (Should they properly be cited under the name of Frantzke?)

FRIDENREICH, Z. *Politicorum liber*, Strassburg, 1609.

GENTILIS, A., 1551–1611, professor of civil law at Oxford, 1587–1611. Gierke refers to his *De jure belli* (1588–9), which preceded by many years the work of Grotius.

GNEINZIUS, C., *Exercitationes politicae*, Wittenberg, 1617–18.

GRASZWINKEL, DIRK, 1600–66, a Dutch jurist, who worked with Grotius and was associated with John de Witt. He wrote on behalf of the Venetian State, as well as against Selden's *Mare clausum*. Gierke refers to his *De jure majestatis*, the Hague, 1642.

GREGORIUS, P., 1540?–96?, teacher of law first at Toulouse (hence called Tholosanus) and afterwards at Pont-à-Mousson. *De Republica libri XXVI*, 1586, cited in the Frankfort (? Lyons) edition of 1609.

GREGORIUS DE VALENTIA—see Valentia.

GROTIUS, HUGO, 1585–1645. *De jure belli et pacis*, Paris, 1625, cited in the Amsterdam edition of 1702. *De imperio summarum potestatum circa sacra*, Paris, 1646, cited in the 4th edition, the Hague, 1661.

GRYPHIANDER . *De Civili Societate* (in Arumaeus, *q.v.*).

HEIDER, W., 1558–1626, professor of ethics and politics at Jena, and a follower of Aristotle. *Systema philosophiae politicae*, 1610 (cited in the Jena edition of 1628).

HEMMING, N., 1513–1600, professor at Copenhagen; a follower of Melanchthon. *De lege naturae apodeictica methodus*, 1577, cited in the Wittenberg edition of 1652.

HOBBES, T., 1588–1679, *Elementa philosophiae de Cive*, originally published at Paris in 1642 with the title *de Cive*: published under the fuller title in the Amsterdam edition of 1647, which Gierke has used. *Leviathan*, 1651; a Latin version was made by Hobbes for the Amsterdam edition of his works in 1668, and Gierke has used this version.

HOENONIUS, P. H., 1576–1640, teacher of law at Herborn; in the service of various German princes. *Disputationum politicarum liber*, 3rd edition, Herborn, 1615 (a work of the nature of a system of public law).

HOTOMAN, F., 1524–90, French jurisconsult and Huguenot: lived, after the massacre of St Bartholomew, in Geneva and Basle. *Francogallia*, Geneva, 1573, cited in the Frankfort edition of 1665. (Translated into English in 1711 by Viscount Molesworth, with a famous preface on the nature of Whig principles.) Gierke also refers to his *Quaestiones illustres*.

KECKERMANN, B., 1571–1609, professor at Heidelberg, and a follower of Aristotle. *Systema disciplinae politicae*, Hanover, 1607.

KIRCHNER, H., published a number of works at Marburg, including one entitled *Legatus* (the rights, dignity and office of the Ambassador, 1614). Gierke cites his *Respublica*, Marburg, 1608. Coryat's *Crudities* includes his oration 'in praise of the travell of Germany in particular'.

KLING, MELCHIOR, 1504–71, jurist and lecturer at Wittenberg. *Enarrationes in libros IV Institutionum*, 1542.

KNICHEN, A., see Bibliography B.

KNIPSCHILDT, P., 1596–1657; publicist and syndic at Esslingen, an imperial Free Town. *Tractatus politico-juridicus de juribus et privilegiis civitatum imperialium*, Ulm, 1657.

KÖNIG . *Acies disputationum politicarum*, Jena, 1619. *Theatrum politicum* (n.d.).

LAMPADIUS, J., 1593–1649, jurist and minister in the duchy of Brunswick. *De jurisdictione imperii Romano-Germanici 1620 circiter*. Conring (*q.v.*), and later Kulpis (see Bibliography B), were concerned in the later editions of the work, published under the title of *De republica Romano-Germanica*.

LAPIDE, HIPPOLYTUS A (the pseudonym of B. Chemnitz), writer and publicist, 1605–78; *De ratione status in imperio nostro Romano-Germanico*, 1640. (*Ratio status* here is not *raison d'état*, but 'general principles of government'.)

LAUTERBACH, W. A., 1618–78, jurist and professor at Tübingen. *Dissertationes academicae*, 1694. *Compendium juris*, 1679. Both of these works appeared posthumously.

LESSIUS, L., 1554–1623, Jesuit, professor of philosophy at Douai, and afterwards of theology at Louvain. *De justitia et jure*, 1606 (cited in the edition published at Antwerp in 1612).

LIEBENTHAL, C., 1586–1647, professor of 'practical philosophy and rhetoric' at Giessen. *Collegium politicum*, 1619, cited in the Marburg edition of 1644.

LIMNAEUS, J. L., 1592–1665, jurist, chancellor in the duchy of Brunswick. Gierke refers to *Jus publicum Imperii Rom.-Germ.* 1629–45. He also wrote a commentary on the *Wahlkapitulationen* (*Capitulationes imperatorum*), from Charles V onwards, published in 1651 at Strassburg.

LIPSIUS, J., 1547–1606, professor at Leyden (with Scaliger), and afterwards at Louvain. *Politicorum libri VI*, Antwerp, 1589 (cited in the edition of 1604). (Lipsius advocated a system of one exclusive religion, and his policy for dissidents was *ure et seca*.)

LUGO, J. DE, 1583–1660, Spanish Jesuit, professor of theology in Rome; made cardinal in 1643. (Quinine, first distributed in his palace by the Jesuits, who had received it from South America, was called *poudre de Lugo*.) *De justitia et jure*, cited in the Lyons edition of 1670.

MACHIAVELLI, N., 1469–1527. *Il Principe*, published posthumously, 1532.

MARCA, P. DE, 1594–1662, French canonist and bishop. *De concordia sacerdotii et imperii, seu de libertatibus ecclesiae Gallicanae*, 1641 first part, 1663 as a whole.

MARIANA, J., 1537–1624, Spanish Jesuit, who from 1574 to his death lived and wrote at the house of his order in Toledo. *De rege et regis institutione*, Toledo, 1599, cited in the Frankfort edition of 1611.

MATTHIAS, C. (member of a Brandenburg family?). *Collegium politicum*, Giessen, 1611. *Systema politicum*, Giessen, 1618.

MEISSNER, B., 1587–1626, professor of theology at Wittenberg. *De legibus*, Wittenberg, 1616.

MENOCHIUS, J. S., 1576–1655, teacher in the Jesuit College at Milan. *Hieropolitica*, cited in the 2nd edition, Cologne, 1626.

MILTON, JOHN, 1608–74. *The tenure of kings and magistrates*, 1648–9. *Eiconoclastes* (an answer to *Eikon Basilike*), 1649. *Defensio pro populo Anglicano* (an answer to the *Defensio regia* of Salmasius, *q.v.*), 1650–1. Gierke cites these in the 1848 edition (London) of Milton's *Prose Works*.

MOLINA, L., 1535–1601, a Spanish Jesuit, who taught for many years at the Portuguese University of Evora. *De justitia et jure*, cited in the Mainz edition of 1614.

MOLINAEUS (Dumoulin), C., 1500–66, a famous French teacher of law and legal writer, who was for some time a refugee in Germany, at Tübingen. *Commentarii ad Codicem* (Tübingen lectures), printed 1604.

OBRECHT, G., 1547–1612, professor of law at Strassburg. *De justitia et jure*, no. 1 in *Selectissimae disputationes*, Strassburg, 1599. *Secreta politica*, 1617, cited in the Strassburg edition of 1644.

OLDENDORP, J., 1480–1561, a jurist who was for some time syndic at Lübeck and then professor at Cologne; afterwards settled at Marburg. *Juris naturalis, gentium et civilis isagoge*, Cologne, 1539. Gierke also mentions a work in German, 'Counsels how one may maintain good policy and order in towns and territories', Rostock, 1579. Oldendorp was syndic at Rostock before he went to Lübeck, and this treatise on practical politics, published at Rostock, may have been written originally before he left Rostock in 1534.

OLIZAROVIUS, A. A. *De Politica hominum societate*, Danzig, 1651. The name suggests a Polish origin (Olizarowski).

OMPHALUS (Omphalius), J., 1500–67, German jurist. *De civili politia libri III*, Cologne, 1565.

OSSE, M. VON, 1506?–57, jurist and administrator in the Saxon electorate. *Testamentum* (treating of the duties of a sovereign), addressed to the Saxon Elector. Parts were printed in 1607 and 1622, but the first complete edition was that of Thomasius, 1717. The 'testament' was a regular genre in the sixteenth and seventeenth centuries.

OTTO, D., 1600?–60?, German jurist. *Dissertatio* (in Arumaeus, *q.v.*) *an mixtus detur reipublicae status. Tractatus politicus de majestate imperii et imperantis* (Strassburg, 1623?). *De jure publico Romani imperii*, Jena, 1616 (the first compendium of German public law).

PAURMEISTER (Baurmeister), T. VON, 1555–1616, jurist and administrator, and a critic of Bodin. *Commentarius rerum politicarum et juridicarum. De jurisdictione imp. Rom. libri II*, 1616.

REINKING, D., 1590–1664, jurist and administrator. *Tractatus de regimine saeculari et ecclesiastico*, Giessen, 1619.

ROSSAEUS (Rose, Guillaume), 1542?–1602, preacher and almoner to Henri III; bishop of Senlis; a violent partisan of the League and opponent of Henri IV. *Liber de justa reipublicae christianae in reges impios et haereticos auctoritate*, Paris, 1590. Rossaeus, like Boucher (*q.v.*), is a Catholic *monarchomachus*.

SALAMONIUS, J. MARIUS. *De Principatu libri VII*, Rome, 1544, cited in the Paris edition of 1578. This is a work which, in the profundity of its thought, deserves to be counted among the classics of the sixteenth century. Gierke also cites his Commentary on the *Digest*, Basle, 1530.

SALMASIUS (Claude de Saumaise), 1588–1653, French classical scholar; at one time professor at Leyden: invited by Prince Charles to write a defence of his father Charles I. *Defensio regia pro Carolo I*, November, 1649, cited in the Paris edition of 1651. Milton, on the instruction of the Council of State, replied in his *Defensio pro populo Anglicano*.

SCHÖNBORNER, G., 1579–1637, German jurist, and administrator in Silesia. *Politicorum libri VII*, 1614, cited in the 4th edition, printed at Frankfort, 1628.

SELDEN, JOHN, 1584–1654. *De jure naturali et gentium, juxta disciplinam Ebraeorum*, London, 1640. *Mare Clausum*, London, 1635.

SOTO, D., 1494–1560, Dominican, teacher at the University of Salamanca. *De justitia et jure*, 1556 (cited in the Venice edition of 1602).

STRYK, S., see Bibliography B.

SUAREZ, F., 1548–1617, Jesuit, professor of philosophy in Spain, one of the greatest thinkers of his order. *Tractatus de legibus ac Deo legislatore*, 1611 (cited in the Antwerp edition of 1613).

TULDEN, T. VON, *obiit* 1645, professor at Bois le Duc. *De Regimine civili*, cited in the Louvain edition of his works, 1702.

VALENTIA, GREGORIUS DE, 1551–1603, Spanish Jesuit, professor of theology at Ingolstadt. *Commentarii theologici*, Ingolstadt, 1592.

VASQUEZ, F., 1509–66, ecclesiastical writer on natural law. *Controversiarum illustrium aliarumque frequentium libri III*, Frankfort, 1572.

VICTORIA, F., *obiit* 1546, Dominican. *Relectiones tredecim*, Ingolstadt, 1580. An earlier edition, *Relectiones undecim* (*de Potestate Ecclesiae*, etc.) had appeared in 1565.

VOETIUS, G., 1593–1680, Dutch minister, and afterwards professor at Utrecht. *Politica ecclesiastica*, Amsterdam, 1663–76, vols. I–IV.

VULTEJUS, H., 1565–1634, jurist and classical scholar, professor of jurisprudence at Marburg. *Jurisprudentiae Romanae a Justiniano compositae libri II*, Marburg, 1590. Gierke also refers to his Commentaries on the *Institutes*.

WERDENHAGEN, J. A., 1581–1652, a German scholar, theologian and professor, from Helmstedt, who lived at Leyden about 1627–33, and wrote there some of his main works; occupied afterwards in affairs at Bremen and Magdeburg, and in the duchy of Brunswick. *Politica generalis, seu introductio universalis in omnes Respublicas*, Amsterdam, 1632.

WINKLER, B., 1579–1648, taught at Leipzig and Basle; afterwards syndic at Lübeck; one of the early writers on natural law. *Principiorum juris libri V*, Leipzig, 1615.

WINTONENSIS, STEPHANUS (Stephen Gardiner), 1483?–1555, Master of Trinity Hall, Cambridge, 1525–49, and again in 1553; bishop of Winchester, 1531; doctor of civil and of canon law. *Oratio de vera oboedientia*, London, 1535 (cited by Gierke from Goldast's *Monarchia* of 1611, I, pp. 716–33).

WURMSER . *Exercitationes*.

ZEPPER, W. Z., 1550–1607, the first systematic writer on the problems of the constitution of the Protestant churches; professor at Herborn, at the same time as Althusius. *De politia ecclesiastica*, Herborn, 1595.

ZWINGLI, U. Z., 1484–1531. Gierke refers to his Works, as edited by Schuler and Schulthess. See A. Farner's monograph on *Die Lehre von Kirche und Staat bei Zwingli*, 1930.

B. LIST OF AUTHORS CITED: 1650-1800

ACHENWALL, G. A. (1719–72) [professor of law in the University of Göttingen, and a student of contemporary comparative politics, who travelled in England and Holland, and was honoured by George III. He published, in 1749, an outline of contemporary politics in the greater European monarchies and republics. Gierke refers to one of his legal works], *Jus Naturae*, as printed in 1781, when the 7th edition appeared. This contains (*a*) *Prolegomena*, 5th edition (first printed in 1758); (*b*) *Pars prior*, 7th edition (first printed in 1750); and (*c*) *Pars posterior*, 8th edition (first printed in 1750).

ALBERTI, V. (1635–97) [Lutheran theologian, and professor at Leipzig], *Compendium juris naturae orthodoxae theologiae conformatum*, Leipzig, 1678. [The work has been described as 'an attempt to interpret natural law as the order prevailing in the original sinless condition of man'.]

ANDLER, F. F. VON (1617–1703) [lecturer in law at Würzburg], *Jurisprudentia qua publica, qua privata*, etc., 1670.

BECCARIA, C. B. (1738–94) [an Italian publicist, of noble family, who became a professor of law and economics in Milan], *Dei delitti e delle pene*, Monaco, 1764.

BECKER, O. H. [sometime *Regierungsrath* in the principality of Waldeck], *Jus mundi seu vindiciae juris naturae*, cited in the 2nd edition, 1698 (first printed in 1690).

BECMANN, J. C. (1641–1717) [professor at Frankfort on the Oder, who wrote a *Historia orbis terrarum geographica et civilis*, and also historical works about the principality of Anhalt. The works to which Gierke refers are his] *Meditationes politicae*, Frankfort, 1679, and his *Conspectus doctrinae politicae*, Frankfort, 1691.

BLACKSTONE, Sir W. (1723–80), *Commentaries on the Laws of England*, 1765–69.

BOECLER, J. H. B. (1611–72) [professor of history at Strassburg; an elegant Latinist, and a classical scholar as well as an historian and writer on politics. The work to which Gierke refers is his] *Institutiones politicae*, Strassburg, 1674.

BOEHMER, J. H., 1674–1749 [professor in the University of Halle, and one of the foremost scholars and jurists of his day, especially in civil and ecclesiastical law. His works on *Jus ecclesiasticum protestantinum* and on *Jus parochiale* exercised a great influence. Gierke cites his] *Introductio in jus publicum universale*, in the Prague edition of 1743 (first printed in 1709). [The newly founded University of Halle had a flourishing school of law in the first half of the eighteenth century: see Gundling, Heineccius, Nettelbladt, Thomasius and Wolff *infra*.]

BOSSUET, J. B., 1627–1704 [bishop of Meaux]. *Politique tirée des propres paroles de l'écriture Sainte*, Paris, 1709 (cited from his *Œuvres complètes*, Tome XVII, Paris, 1826).

CELLARIUS, B. [1614–89, preacher and professor of theology at Helmstedt. Besides a theological work, on the controversies between the churches of the Augsburg Confession and the Roman, he wrote *Tabulae ethicae politicae et physicae*. The work to which Gierke refers is] *Politica succincta*, Jena, 1658 (cited in the 11th edition, of 1711).

CLASEN, D., *Politicae compendium succinctum*, Helmstedt, 1675. [Clasen also wrote a work *De religione politica*, Magdeburg, 1655. He also wrote on the 'theology' and 'oracles' of the 'Gentiles'—i.e. of the ancient world.]

COCCEJI, H. DE, 1644–1719 [a jurist who succeeded to Pufendorf's chair at Heidelberg, but left Heidelberg in 1688, and became professor at Frankfort on the Oder in 1690. He exercised an influence on the study both of natural law and of public law. Gierke refers to his] *Prodromus juris gentium*, Frankfort, 1719, and *Hypomnemata juris ad seriem Institutionum Justin.*, Frankfort, 1698.

COCCEJI, S. DE, 1679–1755 [third son of H. de Cocceji; at first, like his father, a professor at Frankfort on the Oder; but afterwards busily occupied in judicial activities and reforms in Prussia under Frederick William I and Frederick II. Gierke refers to three of his writings]: *Disputatio de principio juris naturalis unico, vero et adaequato*, Frankfort, 1699 [a 'disputation' for the doctorate, in which he expounded his father's ideas on natural law, as based on the will of God. As his father had never published his views, except in lectures, this *Disputatio* first gave them prominence]; *Tractatus juris gentium*, Frankfort, 1702; *Novum systema justitiae naturalis et Romanae*, 1740. [The 1740 edition is actually called *Elementa justitiae, etc.*: the title *Novum systema* is first used in a later reprint of 1744.]

CUMBERLAND, R., 1632–1709 [really 1631–1718. Cumberland was a member of Pepys' college, Magdalene, and a friend of Pepys: he became bishop of Peterborough in 1691. He published in 1672 his *De legibus naturae disquisitio philosophica*, dedicated to another of his Magdalene friends, one of the great lawyers of the reign of Charles II, Sir Orlando Bridgeman. The work is an answer to Hobbes, on utilitarian lines. Gierke cites it as] *De legibus naturae*, 2nd edition, printed at Lübeck and Frankfort, 1683. [The book was translated from the Latin by Barbeyrac (for whom see under Pufendorf, *infra*), with notes, 1774.]

DARIES, J. G., 1714–91. [He became professor of moral and political philosophy at Jena in 1744. From Jena he moved to Frankfort on the Oder in 1763, where he held the chair of law till his death. He was a voluminous writer, who published works on metaphysics and ethics as well as on law and politics. Gierke refers to his] *Institutiones jurisprudentiae universalis*, cited in the 7th edition, Jena, 1776 (first published in 1746).

EHRENBACH, J. N. MYLER AB, 1610–77 [a man of affairs, as well as a student of politics, who played a considerable part in his time. He was deeply versed in the public law of the Empire. In 1656 he had published an *Outline of the main rights of the Princes and States of the Empire*, which attained great vogue. Later, he planned a larger work, in a number of parts, under the title of *Opus de jure publico imperii Romano-Germanici*. The work to which Gierke refers is the 7th part of this *opus*, dealing with officials, magistrates and their assistants, under the title of] *Hyparchologia*, Stuttgart, 1678.

FELDE, JOHANNES A [a critic of Grotius, and also the writer of a *tractatus de peste*], *Elementa juris universi et in specie juris publici Justinianei*, Frankfort and Leipzig, 1664.

FELWINGER, J. P. [? professor at Altdorf c. 1650–75: acted as *praeses* at disputations on politics, in the fashion of the day], *Dissertationes politicae*, Altdorf, 1666.

FÉNELON, F. DE SALIGNAC DE LAMOTTE, 1651–1715 [tutor to the Dauphin under Louis XIV, and afterwards archbishop of Cambrai. Gierke refers to an] *Essai sur le gouvernement civil, selon les principes de Fénelon*, 3rd edition, by

A. M. Ramsay, London, 1723. [Fénelon's own writings are the *Télémaque* o 1699, and the *Dialogues des morts, composés pour l'éducation d'un prince*, first published in 1712, and republished in an enlarged edition by Ramsay in 1718.]

FERGUSON, ADAM, 1723–1816 [professor, first of natural philosophy, and afterwards of moral philosophy, at Edinburgh]: *Essay on Civil Society*, 1766; *Principles of Moral and Political Science*, ['being chiefly a retrospect of lectures delivered in the College of Edinburgh'], 1792.

FICHTE, J. G., 1762–1814 [professor of philosophy at Jena, 1794–1799; dismissed for his views; after its foundation in 1810, Rector in 1811–12 of the University of Berlin]. Gierke refers to

I. Fichte's *Collected Works*, in the Berlin edition of 1845–6, and therein to the following works:
   (a) *Contributions to the justification of the opinion of the Public on the French Revolution*, 1793 (*Works*, VI, pp. 103 sqq.);
   (b) *Foundations of Natural Law according to the principles of Scientific Theory*, published in 1796–7, at Jena and Leipzig (*Works*, III, pp. 1 sq.);
   (c) *A System of Ethical Theory according to the Principles of Scientific Theory*, 1798 (*Works*, IV, pp. 1 sqq.);
   (d) *The Self-contained Commercial State* [*Der geschlossene Handelstaat*], published in 1800 at Tübingen (*Works*, III, pp. 387 sqq.);
   (e) *The Foundations of the Present Age*, lectures delivered in 1804–5, published at Berlin in 1808 (*Works*, VII, pp. 257 sqq.);
   (f) *The Theory of the State, or the Relation of the Primitive State to the Law of Reason*, lectures delivered in 1813, first published at Berlin in 1820 (*Works*, VII, pp. 367 sqq.).

II. *Posthumous Works*, published in Berlin, 1834; especially the work entitled *A System of Jurisprudence*, lectures delivered in 1812 (in II, pp. 493 sqq.).

FILANGIERI, G., 1762–86 [an Italian publicist, of noble Neapolitan family, who continued the work of the school of legal and political philosophy at Naples inspired by Vico]. *La scienzia della legislazione*, Naples, 1780.

FILMER, Sir R. [*circ*. 1588–1653; a Kentish Royalist who published in 1648 *The Anarchy of a Limited or Mixed Monarchy*, attacking the theory of Philip Hunton's *Treatise of Monarchy* of 1643, along with the writings of Grotius, Hobbes and Milton. It is curious, in this connection, to notice (1) that Locke seems to owe some of his theory to Hunton, and (2) that Locke, very naturally, seeks to prepare the way for his own theory, in the *Second Treatise*, by attacking Filmer in the *First*. Gierke refers to the work by which Filmer is best known], *Patriarcha*, published posthumously in 1680.

FREDERICK II [King of Prussia], 1712–86. [Gierke refers to three of his writings:]
   (a) *Considérations sur l'état présent du corps politique de l'Europe*, 1738 (*Œuvres* VIII, pp. 1 sqq.);
   (b) *Antimachiavelli*, 1739; edited by Voltaire 1740 (*Ibid*. VIII, pp. 59 sqq.);
   (c) *Essai sur les formes du gouvernement et sur les devoirs des Souverains*, 1777 (*Ibid*. IX, pp. 195 sqq.).

GUNDLING, N. H., 1671–1729 [the son of a clergyman, trained for the Church, who turned to law under the influence of Thomasius, and became ultimately professor of natural and international law at Halle. He wrote a great number of dissertations and compendia—partly, it is said, to escape from the distractions of an unhappy marriage. Gierke refers to]:

(a) *Jus naturae et gentium*, as printed in the 2nd edition (Halle and Magdeburg, 1728: the 1st edition had appeared in 1714);

(b) A *Discursus* on natural and international law [published posthumously, as many of his *Discursus* were], Frankfort, 1734;

(c) *Exercitationes academicae*, more especially:

(1) *Exerc.* IV, pp. 155 sqq. (entitled *Status naturalis Hobbesii in corpore juris civilis defensus et defendendus*, and belonging to the year 1706);

(2) *Exerc.* XVI, pp. 829 sqq. (*De universitate delinquente ejusque poenis*, 1724).

HEINCKE, F. J., *Systema juris publici universalis*, 1765. [This is the only information which Gierke gives. The *Allgemeine Deutsche Biographie* gives an account of F. J. Heinke (1726–1803), a Silesian who studied at Prague, where he became director and President of the Law Faculty—eventually entering the service of the government in Vienna in 1767. But the *Biographie* does not mention any *Systema juris* as having been published by him.]

HEINECCIUS, J. G., 1681–1741 [professor of law at Halle, and elsewhere, and one of the greatest of the German jurists of the eighteenth century. Gierke refers to three of his works]:

(1) *Elementa juris naturae et gentium*, first published in 1737 (printed in vol. 3 of *Opera omnia*, Geneva, 1741 onwards);

(2) *Praelectiones academicae in Hugonis Grotii de jure belli et pacis libros*, published in 1744 (*Opera omnia*, VIII, 1);

(3) *Praelectiones academicae in S. Pufendorfii de officio hominis et civis libros*, 2nd edition, 1748.

HERDER, J. G., 1744–1803 [German critic, man of letters, and collector of *Volkslieder*: Gierke refers to his] *Ideen zur Geschichte der Menschheit*, 1784–5 (in his *Collected Works in Philosophy and History*, vols. IV–VII).

HERTIUS, J. N., 1652–1710 [one of the leading jurists of Germany in the seventeenth century, and professor of law at Giessen. Gierke refers to]:

(a) *Elementa prudentiae civilis*, 1689 (cited in the 2nd edition, Frankfort on the Main, 1702);

(b) *Commentationum atque opusculorum vol. II*, as published in 1737, at Frankfort on the Main (the items had been first published in 1700 and 1716).

HOFFBAUER, J. C. [1766–1827; professor of philosophy at Halle], *Naturrecht aus dem Begriffe des Rechts entwickelt*, 1793 (cited in the 3rd edition, Halle, 1803).

HORNIUS, J. F., 1620–70? [not mentioned in the German or Dutch National Biographies. Gierke refers to two works]: *De subjecto juris naturalis*, Utrecht, 1663; *Politicorum pars architectonica*, Utrecht, 1664 [reprinted as *Architectonica de Civitate*, with notes by S. Kuchenbecher, Leyden, 1699].

HUBER, U., 1636–94 [a Dutch jurist of eminence, professor at Franeker in Friesland]:

(1) *De jure civitatis*, 1674 (cited in the Franeker edition of 1713);

(2) *Praelectionum juris civilis tomi III*, 1666 (cited in the Leipzig edition of 1735);

(3) *Institutiones juris publici*, in *Opera minora*, I, 1 (the Utrecht edition of 1746).

HUMBOLDT, W. VON, 1767–1835 [thinker and statesman; Prussian minister of education, 1809–10]:

(1) *Ideas for an essay on the limits of the activity of the State*, 1792.

Parts printed in *Thalia* [Schiller's Leipzig magazine], 1792, and in the *Berlin Monthly*, 1792; published complete, Breslau, 1851.

List of Authors Cited: 1650–1800

HUME, D., 1711–76 [*Essays Moral and Political*, 1741–2. Gierke refers to the edition of the] *Political Essays*, translated into German by C. J. Kraus, Königsberg, 1813.

ICKSTATT, S. A., 1702–76 [a jurist in the Bavarian service; for some time professor, at Ingolstadt, of public and international law and the law of nature, under the style of *jus oeconomicocamerale*], *Opuscula juridica varii argumenti*; vol. I, Ingolstadt and Augsburg, 1747; vol. II, Munich and Ingolstadt, 1759.

JENA, G. VON, 1620–1703 [a jurist in the service of the Great Elector and his successor; for some time professor at Frankfort on the Oder], *Collegium juris publici*, Frankfort on the Main, 1658 (it also appeared as *Fragmenta de ratione status*, 1657). [A series of dissertations.]

JUSTI, J. H. G. VON, 1720–71 [professor at Vienna of 'applied politics'; afterwards in the Prussian service]:
  (1) The *Foundations of a good government*, in five books, Frankfort and Leipzig, 1759;
  (2) The *Nature and Being of States*, Berlin, Stettin and Leipzig, 1760.
  [The work on applied politics for which Justi was best known was entitled, *The Bases of the power and prosperity of States, or a detailed account of the whole science of policy (Polizeiwissenschaft)*, of which vol. I appeared in 1760, and vol. II in 1761. But this was only one of a considerable number of political writings—among them the two which Gierke cites. Justi had a varied and wandering career, which led him incidentally into the management of mines; but he found time to write a great number of books, and his friends called him the Buffon of Germany.]

KANT, I., 1724–1804 [professor of logic at Königsberg]. *Collected Works*, in chronological order, edited by G. Hartenstein, Leipzig, and especially:
  (1) *On the saying, 'That may be right in theory, but it has no value in practice'*, 1793 (*Works*, VI, pp. 303 sqq.);
  (2) *Perpetual Peace*, 1795 (*Ibid*. VI, pp. 405 sqq.);
  (3) *Metaphysic of Morality* (*Ibid*. VII, pp. 1 sqq.), containing the 'Metaphysical Elements of Jurisprudence', and the 'Metaphysical Elements of Ethics', which appeared separately in 1797 and were put together in one volume in 1798.
  [In English, see T. K. Abbott, *Kant's Critique of Practical Reason, and other works on the theory of Ethics*.]

KESTNER, H. E., 1671–1723 [professor of law at Rinteln, near Minden]:
  (1) *Jus naturae et gentium, ex ipsis fontibus ad ductum Grotii Pufendorfii et Cocceji derivatum*, Rinteln, 1705;
  (2) *Compendium juris universi*, Rinteln, 1707.

KLEIN, E. F., 1744–1816 [a jurist who took a considerable part in the development of Prussian law towards 1800, and also lectured at the University of Halle, 1791–1801], *Short Essays*, Halle, 1797 (the Essay 'On the nature of civil Society' is in II, pp. 55 sqq.).

KNICHEN, R. G. [died in 1682; was the son of A. Knichen, who had been a professor of law, and had defended the cause of the territorial princes against the towns. He wrote] *Opus politicum*, Frankfort on the Main, 1682.

KREITTMAYR, W. X. A. VON, 1705–90 [Bavarian State-Chancellor, and codifier of the law of Bavaria], *Outline of general and of German public law*, Munich, 1770.

KULPIS, J. G., 1652–98 [professor of public institutions and public law at Strassburg, 1683–6; afterwards in government service in Würtemberg], *Dissertationes academicae*, Strassburg, 1705.

LEIBNIZ, G. W., 1646–1716.
  A. *Opera omnia*, ed. Dutens, Geneva, 1763—the various essays on law and politics, in IV, 3, pp. 159 sqq., including:
    (1) *Nova methodus discendae docendaeque jurisprudentiae*, 1667;
    (2) *Observationes de principio juris*, 1670;
    (3) *Monita quaedam ad S. Pufendorfii principia*;
    (4) *De suo codice gentium diplomatico monita*;
    (5) *Caesarini-Fürstenerii tractatus de jure suprematus ac legationum Principum Germaniae*, 2nd edition, 1678;
    (6) *Specimen demonstrationum politicarum pro eligendo Rege Polonorum*.
  B. *German Writings*, edited by Guhrauer, 1838–40—the 'Fragment on the Law of Nature' in I, pp. 414 sqq.

LOCKE, JOHN, 1632–1704:
  (1) *Two treatises on Government*, London, 1690;
  (2) *Letter on Toleration* [first published in Latin in 1689, and then in an English Translation in the same year; other letters added, 1690, 1692 and 1705]. Cited from the *Works*, as published in London, 1801, vol. V, pp. 207 sqq. and vol. VI.

DE LOLME, J. L., 1740–1806 [a Swiss political writer, mainly on English politics], *La Constitution d'Angleterre*, 1771, translated into English, 1775.

LUDWIG, J. P. VON, 1668–1743 [professor of philosophy, and afterwards of history and public law, at Halle], *Opuscula minora*, Halle, 1720.

MABLY, ABBÉ DE, 1709–85 [French publicist]:
  (1) *Doutes proposés aux philosophes économistes sur l'ordre naturel et essentiel des sociétés politiques*, The Hague [a work directed against Mercier de la Rivière, *q.v.*];
  (2) *De la législation, ou des principes de loi*, Amsterdam, 1776.

MEVIUS, D., 1609–70 [jurist; professor at Greifswald, where his father and grandfather had both been professors before him; sometime syndic of Stralsund, and also in the service of Sweden and Mecklenburg], *Prodromus jurisprudentiae gentium communis*, Stralsund, 1671.

MICRAELIUS, J., 1597–1658 [professor at Stettin; historian of Pomerania], *Regia Politices Scientia*, Stettin, 1654. [In 1647 there had already been published, at Stettin, *J. Micraelii aphorismi de regia politici scientia.*]

MONTESQUIEU, C. DE SECONDAT, Baron de la Brède et de Montesquieu, 1689–1755 [president of the court at Bordeaux], *Esprit des lois*, 1748 (cited in the Amsterdam edition of 1749).

MOSER, F. K. VON, 1723–98 [publicist and statesman, engaged in government service in South Germany, and for some time also in Austria]: *Master and Servant* [i.e. the sovereign and his minister], *described with patriotic freedom*, Frankfort, 1759 (written in 1758); *On the German national spirit*, 1765; *On Governments, Governing and Ministers: material* [literally 'rubbish'] *for improving the way of the coming century*, Frankfort, 1784.

MÖSER, JUSTUS, 1720–94 [lawyer and statesman in the bishopric of Osnabrück, where he was *advocatus patriae* and secretary to the order of Knights; a popular author, compared by Goethe to Benjamin Franklin]: *History of Osnabrück*, Osnabrück, 1768; *Patriotic Phantasies*, edited by his daughter, Berlin, 1778–86; *Miscellaneous Writings*, edited by Nicolai, Berlin, 1797–8.

List of Authors Cited: 1650–1800

MUELDENER, J. C., the elder. *Positiones Inaugurales*, 2nd edition, Halle-Magdeburg, 1698 (first printed in 1692).
MULLERUS, J. J. [? Professor Utriusque Juris at Copenhagen], *Institutiones Politicae*, Jena, 1692.
NATIONAL ASSEMBLY—Proceedings of the French N.A. in regard to the confiscation of ecclesiastical property, October 10 to November 2, 1789; *Gazette Nationale ou le Moniteur universel* (par l'an IV de la République, pp. 291 sqq.). Cf. Hübler, *Der Eigentümer des Kirchenguts*, pp. 46 sqq., 56 sqq. Paul Janet, *Revue des deux Mondes*, Tome 23 (1877), pp. 334–49. [Gierke's reference to the *Gazette Nationale* is puzzling. When he adds the reference to l'an IV, is he thinking of an edition, such as appeared at Milan, 1802–5, which contained in 74 vols. the Gazette from May 5, 1789, to the 28th of Nivôse, year IV?].
NETTELBLADT, D., 1719–91 [professor of law at Halle, and one of the greatest teachers of law in later eighteenth-century Germany]: *Systema elementare universae jurisprudentiae naturalis*, cited in the 5th edition, Halle, 1785 (first printed in 1748: the present arrangement was first adopted in the 3rd edition of 1776); *Systema elementare jurisprudentiae positivae Germanorum generalis*, Halle, 1781. [Nettelbladt was a pupil of Wolff at Marburg, and followed him to Halle.]
PEREZIUS, A., 1583–1672 [a Spanish jurist, settled in the Netherlands, who was professor at Louvain from 1614 onwards], *Jus publicum, quo arcana et jura Principis exponuntur*, Amsterdam, 1657.
PLACCIUS, V. P., 1642–99 [a German scholar from Hamburg, who studied in German universities and Italy, and afterwards practised and taught law in his native city. He was a man of means, who corresponded with various scholars of his day, and wrote on a variety of subjects], *Accessiones juris naturalis, privati et publici*, Hamburg, 1695.
PRASCHIUS, J. L., 1637–90 [a citizen of Ratisbon, where he held high office and was deep in all civic affairs: philologist, writer of verse, and dramatist, as well as a writer on laws and politics], *Designatio juris naturalis ex disciplina Christianorum*, Ratisbon, 1688.
PUFENDORF, S., 1632–94 [publicist, jurist, and historian: taught at the university of Heidelberg, 1661–8: professor in Lund, on the invitation of Charles XI of Sweden, 1670 onwards: historiographer at Stockholm in 1677, and at Berlin in 1688: one of the greatest scholars of his century, and one of the greatest figures in the history of natural law]:
(1) *Elementorum jurisprudentiae universalis libri II*, 1660 (cited in the Frankfort and Jena edition of 1680);
(2) Severinus de Monzambano [pseudonym* adopted by Pufendorf to cover his exposition and critique of the political position of Germany], *De statu Imperii Germanici*, Geneva [really the Hague], 1667 (cited in the edition published at 'Utopia', 1668). There is a new and critical edition by F. Salomon, Weimar, 1910, in *Quellen und Studien zur Verfassungsgeschichte des Deutschen Reichs*, III, 4;
(3) *De jure naturae et gentium libri VIII*, 1672 (cited in the Frankfort and Leipzig edition of 1744, with notes by Hert and Barbeyrac);
(4) *De officio hominis et civis secundum legem naturalem libri II*, Leyden, 1673 (cited in the Leyden edition of 1769, with 'observations' by Titius, Carmichael, Treuer and Barbeyrac);
(5) *Dissertationes academicae selectiores*, Upsala, 1677.

  * Cf. Caesarinus-Fürstenerius above, under Leibniz.

[Barbeyrac (1674–1729), a Huguenot who taught in Berlin, Lausanne and Groningen, translated into French, and annotated, not only (3) and (4) above, but also Grotius *De jure belli et pacis*.]

[Pufendorf's *De habitu religionis Christianae ad vitam civilem liber singularis*, 1687, may also be mentioned, as dealing with the relations of Church and State and the problem of toleration at a time when the Revocation of the Edict of Nantes had disturbed men's minds. It is almost contemporary with Locke's *Letter on Toleration*, which deals with the same problems in the same atmosphere.]

RACHELIUS, S., 1628–91 [jurist and politician: professor of natural and international law at Kiel after 1665], *Institutionum jurisprudentiae libri IV*, Kiel and Frankfort, 1681.

DE LA RIVIÈRE, P. F. J. H. LE MERCIER, 1720–94 [a disciple of Quesnay, and one of the Physiocrats], *L'ordre naturel et essentiel des sociétés politiques*, Paris, 1767.

ROUSSEAU, J. J., 1712–78:
(1) *Discours sur l'origine et les fondements de l'inégalité parmi les hommes*, Paris, 1753;
(2) *Du contrat social, ou principes du droit politique*, Amsterdam, 1762;
(3) *Lettres écrites de la Montagne*, Amsterdam, 1764.

[Cf. C. E. Vaughan, *The Political Writings of Rousseau*, Cambridge, 1915.]

SCHEIDEMANTEL, H. G. [1739–88, professor of law at Jena and Stuttgart], *Public Law, treated according to reason and the customs of the leading nations*, Jena, 1770–73.

SCHLÖZER, A. L. VON, 1735–1809 [travelled in Sweden and Russia: professor at Göttingen: publicist, historian and educationalist, who, *inter alia*, continued the work of Achenwall on contemporary politics and institutions in his *Theorie der Statistik* of 1804. Gierke refers to his] *General Public Law and the Theory of Constitutions*, Göttingen, 1793.

SCHLÖZER, C. VON [1774–1831: eldest son of the foregoing; professor of the political sciences at Moscow, *circ.* 1790–1827; lecturer at Bonn, 1828–31], *Kleine Schriften*, Göttingen, 1807, especially:
(1) *De jure suffragii in societate aequali*, Göttingen, 1795, pp. 11 sqq.;
(2) *Primae lineae scientiarum politicarum*, pp. 81 sqq. [Moscow, 1802.]

[His chief importance perhaps lies in the field of political economy. He published at Riga in 1805 and 1807 two volumes on *The Principles of Political Economy or the Theory of National Wealth*.]

SCHMIER, F., 1680–1728 [canonist: professor and rector of the University of Salzburg: prior of Feldkirch]: *Jurisprudentia publica universalis*, Salzburg, 1722; *Jurisprudentia publica imperii Romano-Germanici*, Salzburg, 1731.

SCHOENAU, F. A. Pelzhoeffer de, Baron, *Arcanorum status libri X*, Frankfort, 1710.

SECKENDORF, V. L. VON, 1626–92 [historian and ducal librarian in the duchy of Gotha; afterwards chancellor in one of the Saxon duchies; a disciple of Boecler (*q.v.*) at Strassburg]: *The German Principality*, 1656 (cited in the 5th edition, 1678); *The Christian State*, 1685; *German Addresses*, 1686.

SIDNEY, ALGERNON, 1622–82, *Discourses concerning government* [an answer to Filmer's *Patriarcha*, written shortly after its publication in 1680; first printed in 1698], cited in the Edinburgh edition of 1750.

SIEYÈS, E., Abbé, 1748–1836. [His writings, including his *Qu'est-ce que le Tiers État* and his *Observations sommaires sur les biens écclesiastiques* of 1789, are cited

List of Authors Cited: 1650–1800

by Gierke in a German translation.] *Political Writings*, a complete collection by the German translator, 2 volumes, 1796.

SPINOZA, B., 1632–77. *Tractatus Theologico-politicus*, cited in the Hamburg edition of 1670; *Tractatus Politicus*, in the *Opera Posthuma* of 1677, pp. 267 sqq.; *Ethica*, *ibid.*, pp. 1 sqq. [The best modern edition is that of van Vloten and Land, 1895.]

[STRYK, S., 1640–1710, professor at Frankfort on the Oder and afterwards, from 1692 to his death, at Halle, where he was also dean of the Faculty of Law and Rector of the University. His chief work was his *Usus modernus Pandectarum*. Gierke refers *passim* to his *Dissertationes*.]

THOMASIUS, C., 1655–1728 [professor at Leipzig and afterwards at Halle: a philosopher and a man of general culture as well as a famous jurist, who advocated the use of German instead of Latin, and attacked Aristotle and scholasticism. His name is connected with the beginnings of the University of Halle, and with its legal fame]:
  (1) *Institutiones jurisprudentiae divinae*, written in 1687 (cited in the Frankfort and Leipzig edition of 1709);
  (2) *Fundamenta juris naturae et gentium ex sensu communi deducta*, Halle and Leipzig, 1705;
  (3) *Dissertationes*, 4 volumes, Halle, 1723.

TITIUS, G. G., 1661–1714 [lectured at Leipzig on law from 1688, but did not become Professor until 1710: a pupil of Thomasius]:
  (1) *Specimen juris publici Romano-Germanici*, 1698 (cited in the 2nd edition, Leipzig, 1705);
  (2) *Dissertationes juridicae*, Leipzig, 1729.

TURGOT, A. R. J., baron de l'Aulne, 1727–81. Article on *Fondation* in the *Encyclopédie*, vol. VII, 1757; *Lettres sur la tolérance* [? 1753], in *Œuvres*, Paris, 1844, II, pp. 675 sqq.

VICO, J. B., 1668–1744 [philosopher, historian and jurist; professor at Naples, where he inspired a school of legal and political philosophy. Gierke refers to] *De universi juris uno principio et fine uno*, Naples, 1720; *Principi di una scienza nuova intorno alla commune natura delle nazioni*, Naples, 1725 (cited in the Milan edition of his *Opere*, 1836, vols. III–IV).

WACHLER, J. G., *Origines juris naturalis, sive de jure naturae humanae demonstrationes mathematicae*, Berlin, 1704.

WOLFF, C., 1679–1754 [philosopher, mathematician and jurist: professor of Mathematics and Natural Philosophy at Halle, 1706–23; after troubles there, professor at Marburg, but restored to Halle by the action of Frederick the Great in 1740 as professor of *jus naturae et gentium*; a friend of Leibniz, and one of the great figures in the history of German philosophy. Gierke refers to his]
  (1) *Jus naturae methodo scientifica pertractatum*, Frankfort and Leipzig, 1740–50;
  (2) *Institutiones juris naturae et gentium*, Halle, 1750. (In German, under the title of *Grundsätze des Natur- und Völkerrechts*, 1754);
  (3) *Rational Thoughts on the social life of mankind, and particularly on the Commonwealth* [von dem gemeinen Wesen], Halle, 1721.

VII

INDEX TO GIERKE'S TEXT AND NOTES

References to the notes are in *italic* figures

Absolutist theory of politics (see also Ruler): 41, 44, 45, 139, 141–8, 166: *231–2, 265–6, 336, 340*
Achenwall: 126, 148, 157, 178: *291, 320, 321, 322, 346, 347, 381, 387, 388, 390, 391*
Acts of corporate bodies: 187–8: *271, 389–90*
Althusius: 37, 45, 46, 48, 51, 53, 64, 70–7, 106, 164: *232, 240, 241, 243, 244, 246, 247–9, 255–6, 256–7, 277–8, 341*
Aristocracy: 49: *311, 337, 342, 346*
Aristotle: 36, 46, 155, 163: *260–1, 266, 269, 304*
Arnisaeus: 36, 60, 67: *230, 266, 270, 272, 355*
Associations (natural-law theory of): 62–92; cf. also 162–98: *279, 320, 331–2, 367 ff., 372–3, 375, 379–81*. See also Classification
Auctoritas (Hobbes's theory of): 82

Barclay: *231, 265–6*
Beccaria: 106: *298*
Bellarmine: 87: *284*
Besold: 37, 67, 86, 155
Beza (*de jure magistratuum*): *231, 248, 255*
Bill of Rights: 143: *309*
Blackstone: 144
Bodin: 37, 40, 59, 64–7: *231, 250, 251, 265, 269–71, 272, 274, 275*
Boehmer: 123, 144, 155, 171–2, 173, 174, 183, 185: *318, 338–9, 340, 363, 375–7, 385, 386, 397*
Bornitius: 67: *265, 271–2*
Bossuet: 105: *295, 296, 297, 336, 340*
Burke: 107: *348, 359–60, 370*
Busius: 68: *272, 274*
By-laws (*statuta*) of associations: 189: *273, 376, 378, 379, 390*

Calvinism: 70, 88–9, 92, 151: *284–5*
Capital Punishment: 106: *297–8, 304*
Centralist theory of associations: 62–9, 163–4, 165–9, 180–4
Churches: Bodin on, 65: Suarez on, 68: Church and State, 87–92, 198: *283–7*: Church based on contract, 110: property of Churches, 90, 92, 167: *287, 370–1, 374*

City-State: 63, 76
Civilians: 37–8 (see also Corporation, Roman-law theory of)
Civitas: 53, 56, 60, 115, 123: *235*
Classification: of States, *236*: of *collegia*, *270, 277–8*: of associations generally, *279, 367 ff., 377–8, 379–81*
Cocceji, H. and S. de, 144, 175: *296, 331, 368*
Collective theory of Group-personality: 45–7, 49, 56, 69, 116–17, 118, 120, 121, 123, 124, 126–7, 128, 130–1, 134, 135–7, 139, 181, 182, 184, 193–4: *242–3, 244–5, 249–50, 260, 274, 281, 297, 312–3, 316, 317, 318, 326, 384–5, 393*
Collegialism: 90–2: *287*
Collegiate magistrates: 66–7, 177, 182: *270, 380*
Collegium: 64–7, 72, 171–2, 177: *270–2, 274, 277, 279, 375, 377, 380, 385*
Commons (village): 69: *275–6*
Communio (of property): 103, 192: *294, 393*
Communitas (Suarez's theory of): 64: *274, 276–7*
Community (*Gemeinde*): Fichte on, 151–2: *351*
Concession (groups created by): 66, 166, 174: *368, 378*
Confederations: 86, 197: *283, 296*
Conquest (rights of): *261*
Conring: 36, 92: *230, 286*
Constitutionalism: 139, 140, 141–8, 151–3: *346–7* (see also Limited Sovereignty)
Continuity: of the People: *239*
of the State, 50, 56, 160, 161: *260–1, 266, 325, 361*
of the original contract, 110: *239*
Contract, general theory of: 46, 48, 51, 53, 56, 59, 60–1, 62, 63, 70, 71, 73–4, 75, 76, 77, 78, 79, 90, 92, 95, 102, 104, 106–7, 107–11, 113, 128–30, 131–2, 134, 135, 145, 148, 149, 164, 169, 185, 186: *243, 247, 257, 264, 266, 267, 299–300, 301–5, 312, 314–15, 317, 319, 323, 325, 335, 341, 351, 384*
Contract of government (*Herrschaftsvertrag*): 48, 60, 107–8, 122, 145, 151, 171: *267, 304, 335, 347, 351*
Contract of property: 104: *295*

Index

Contract of society (*Gesellschaftsvertrag*): 48, 60, 107–8, 149, 166: *301, 304*
Corporate bodies: natural-law theory of, 162–98: *367–98*; cf. also 62–92 (and *269–72, 280–1*)
Corporation (Roman-law theory of: see also *universitas*): 45, 62, 67, 68, 75, 84, 135, 162, 173, 174, 182: *240, 275*
Corporative articulation (of the State): 64, 65, 164, 165, 166 (see Intermediate Groups)
Corpus: 64–7, 80: *272, 277*
Corpus confoederatorum: 86, 197: *283*
Customary Law: 68, 189: *274, 288–9, 373*

Daries: 121, 125, 148, 175: *291, 316, 320, 322, 346, 347, 366, 379*
Debts of corporate bodies: 79, 84: *280, 282*
Delicts of corporate bodies: 67, 69, 79, 83–4, 118, 181, 189–90: *271, 280–1, 281–2, 318, 383*
Demesne (of Ruler): *365–6*
Democracy, 49, 58, 117, 141, 146: *237, 238, 250, 257, 311, 335, 342, 346, 354*
Divine right (see also Theocratic): 87–8
Dominicans: 36, 87
Dominium eminens: 103, 162: *261, 304, 352, 366, 379*
Double majesty (theory of): 43, 44, 45, 48, 54–5, 140: *258 ff., 383*
Double Subject of sovereignty (Grotius's theory of): 55–8, 140: *261, 334*
Dualism (of theory of Group-personality): 121 (see also Collective and Representative)
Dualism (of theory of State-personality): 53, 54–5, 58, 59, 60, 145, 150, 156–7: *256–7, 352–3*

Ecclesiastical Theorists (Catholic): 36, 45, 46, 51, 59, 67, 69, 87–8, 105: *229, 233, 234, 240, 241–3, 263–4, 270, 272–3, 275–6, 283–4* (see also Theocratic)
End of the State: 41, 112, 113: *305–7, 310*
Ends of Society and social groups: 111–14
England: 101, 128, 142, 144, 157: *347–8, 359, 360, 375*
Entia moralia (Pufendorf's theory of): 118–19: *312–3*
Ephorate (idea of): 151–2: *247–9, 328, 351*
Episcopal system: 88, 89
Estates (the three): 48, 50, 65, 75, 88, 143, 144, 146, 148, 165, 177: *247, 249, 271–2, 346, 356, 357, 374, 382*

Family (theory of): 63, 65, 71, 72, 80, 83, 105, 111, 163, 170: *269, 274, 303, 318, 319, 321, 367, 368, 392*
Federalist theory of associations: 70–9, 164–5, 169–80, 184–95
Federations: 71, 86, 196–8: *283, 395–8*
Fellowship: theory of, in Althusius, 71–6; in Grotius, 78: in Nettelbladt, 184–95: general references, 69, 116, 117, 118, 123, 124, 135, 163, 164, 165, 172, 175, 177, 180, 181, 183: *277, 382*
Fénelon: 105: *343, 355, 364*
Ferguson: 105: *297, 310*
Fichte: 101–2, 104, 107, 131–4, 136, 151–2, 164, 168: *292–3, 295, 298, 300, 301, 302, 310, 327–8, 351, 373–4, 395*
Fiction (*ficta persona*): 47, 56, 69, 119, 123, 135–6, 137, 191: *245, 247, 250, 275, 317–18, 320, 332, 370*
Filmer: *296, 303, 336, 340*
Foundation (*Stiftung*): 134, 168, 184: *369–70, 374, 386*
France: 65, 66, 128, 130, 142, 166, 183
Frederick the Great: *292, 300, 332, 352, 360*
Freedom of Conscience: 90, 113: *285, 308*
French Revolution: 95, 114, 130, 166–7: *370–1*
Fundamental laws: *341–2, 343, 344, 345, 346, 353*

General Will (*volonté générale*): 47, 127, 129, 131, 133, 134, 166: *322–3, 324–5, 327, 329*
Gentilis: *283*
Germany: 65, 70, 73, 86, 95, 101, 124–5, 131, 142, 146, 154, 155, 156, 159, 164, 167, 179, 185, 194, 198: *249, 347, 355, 356, 357, 360, 368, 382–3, 397, 398*
Gesamte Hand: 185, 192, 194: *356, 393*
Government (Rousseau's theory of): 130, 150, 158–9: *326, 349–50*
Graszwinkel: *268–9*
Gregorius (of Toulouse): 36, 51, 59, 67: *230, 240, 265, 270, 271, 282*
Grotius: 36, 45, 46, 50, 51, 55–8, 77–9, 86, 90–2, 100, 106, 140: *229, 234, 241, 244, 247, 250, 251–2, 253–4, 260–3, 279–80, 282, 283, 285–6, 334, 364*
Groups: natural-law theory of, to 1650, 62–92: after 1650, 95–6, 105–37, 162–98: reception and exclusion of members, *387–8* (see also Associations)
Group-authority: 81, 105–7, 112, 176–8, 183: *273, 380, 381, 385*
Group-personality: 76, 81–2, 84, 114–37, 139, 193: *312–13, 331, 332*

Guilds: 66, 172, 180: *374, 382–3*
Gundling: 121, 123, 144, 155, 182: *291, 317–8, 334, 338, 355, 383–4*

Hanseatic League: 86: *382*
Heincke: 144, 155
Heineccius: 147, 155, 175: *291, 319, 344, 379, 388*
Herder: 105: *305, 332–3*
Hert: 121, 122–3, 147, 155, 170–1, 182, 185; *315, 316–7, 330, 344, 356, 395–6, 397*
Historical theory (of Law and the State): 104, 111, 223–6
Hobbes: 37, 41, 44, 51, 60–1, 79–84, 97, 101, 106, 108, 112, 115, 116, 118, 136, 138, 139, 141, 143, 164, 169, 170, 181: *232, 247, 250, 251, 254, 266–9, 281–2, 283, 288, 306, 330, 341*
Hoffbauer: 127, 148, 178–9: *291, 309, 323, 324, 360, 381, 390, 392*
Holy Roman Empire: 85, 86, 196, 197: *282, 397*
Horn: 105–6, 111, 115–6, 141, 142: *289, 295, 304, 311, 333, 336–7, 340, 354, 366*
Hotoman: *231, 254, 255*
Huber: 106, 117, 145–6, 155–6, 173–4, 182–3, 184: *289, 300, 308, 340–2, 356, 362, 377–8, 384–5, 386*
Hugo: 86
Humboldt (W. von): 127, 179, 194–5: *303, 307*
Hume: 111: *305, 307, 369*

Ickstatt: 144: *315, 318, 321–2, 334, 361*
Individual (and Group): 68–9, 78–9, 96–105, 106, 114, 129, 130, 135–6, 193–4: *242, 243, 281*
Individualism (see also Collective): 52, 55, 61, 71, 76–7, 84, 96, 101, 102, 110, 112, 113, 120, 121, 126, 129, 131, 134, 136, 139, 159, 193–7: *296–7, 298–9, 306–7, 310*
Institutions (Groups regarded as): see Foundation and State-institutions
Insurance Society (State as): 113, 131: *307–8*
Intermediate groups: 72, 163, 164, 166, 167: *367–8, 381–2*
International law: 97, 99, 133, 134, 195–6: *319, 329, 332, 377, 394–5*
International society: 85–6, 96–7, 195–6: *282–3, 394–5*
'Irregular' States: *356, 397*

Jesuits: 36, 87 (see also Molina and Suarez)
Jury: *353*
Jus divinum (i.e. revealed Law): 98
Jus gentium: 38–9, 85: *233, 234*
Justi: 153, 159, 164, 168: *292, 298, 307, 309, 331, 352–3, 360, 394*

Kant: 102–3, 104, 107, 108–9, 109–10, 134–5, 153, 159, 164, 168, 184: *293–4, 299, 302, 307–8, 309, 329–30, 331, 353–4, 360, 374–5, 395*
Keckermann: *265, 279*
Kreittmayr: 144

Law: divisions of, 38–9: *233:* law, and state of nature, 96 ff.: law, and community, 100: law, and morality, 98, 100, 102; Gierke's conception of, 223–6: the view of Thomasius, *288–9, 308:* of Fichte and Kant, *293* (see also Public Law and International Law)
Leibniz: 104, 137, 146, 157, 164, 175, 196, 197: *296, 316, 331–2, 343, 357, 368, 397*
Liberty of association: 72, 78, 80, 168, 169, 171, 172, 179, 180, 194: *279*
Liberty and equality: 101, 103, 112, 196: *292* (see also Natural rights)
Limited sovereignty (see also Constitutionalism): 43, 44, 45, 48, 57, 59, 141–8, 154: *239, 262, 264, 339, 341–3, 344, 346, 347, 354–5*
Limits of the State: *305–6* (see also End of the State)
Local communities (*Gemeinde*): 62–3, 67, 69, 71, 73, 74, 78, 163, 164, 175, 177, 180, 183: *279, 367, 368–9, 372, 380–1, 382–3, 384* (see Municipalities)
Locke: 101, 103, 106, 113, 128, 136, 149, 157: *292, 294, 299–300, 302, 303, 307, 324, 348–9, 357–8*
Loyseau: 49: *343, 363*
Ludewig: *363*
Lugo: *276*
Lutheranism: 88: *284*

Machine (Group regarded as a): 52, 61, 136: *254, 330, 331*
Mackintosh: *370, 372*
Majestas (see Sovereignty, Double majesty, Real majesty, Personal majesty)
Majority decision: 47, 69, 78, 82, 83, 110, 117, 120, 127, 128, 129, 131, 133, 134, 186, 188, 197: *247, 275, 280, 281, 311, 315, 318, 321–2, 323, 324, 325, 327, 328, 361, 384, 385, 387, 389–90, 396–7*
Mandatum: 125, 135, 161
Marriage: 77, 92, 123, 194: *241, 303, 327, 392*
Meeting (right of): 80, 166, 168: *271, 368*
Merchant companies: 80: *281, 282, 383*

Mercier de la Rivière: *331, 336*
Mevius: 196: *290–1, 295, 306, 312, 331, 336, 381, 394*
Middle Ages: 35, 38, 40, 50, 52, 59, 71, 103, 154, 165, 196: *308*
Milton: *243, 248*
Mirabeau: *371*
Mixed Constitution: 41, 42–3, 44, 48, 58, 59, 60, 138, 148, 153, 154–9, 197: *236–7, 239, 264–5, 354–61*
Molina: 45, 51, 59, 105, 107: *241, 242–3, 263, 273, 275–6*
Monarchomachi: 45, 53, 106: *231, 254–5, 256*
Monarchy (see also Patrimonial monarchy and Ruler): 43, 49, 116, 141–8: *237, 238, 318, 336–7, 338, 340–2, 362–3*
Montesquieu: 104, 152–3, 157, 159, 179, 197: *296, 298, 309, 352, 358, 381–2, 386, 397–8*
Moral persons (*personae morales*): 97, 118–22, 124–7, 129, 130–1, 133, 134, 135–7, 142, 160, 166, 168, 169, 175, 181, 184, 185, 186, 187, 192–4, 195, 196: *288, 312–4, 315, 317, 318–9, 320, 321, 324, 326, 327, 329, 345–6, 380, 386, 393, 394*
Möser: 104, 107, 179–80, 194: *294, 298, 309, 332, 382–3*
Municipalities (rights of,): *273, 277, 368–9, 376, 382, 383*

Natural Law: general view, 35–40, 95–6, 97–103: *233–4, 235, 288–9, 289–91, 293*
Natural origin of Society: 46, 51, 63, 108, 111: *300*
Natural rights: of Man, 61, 112, 113–4, 138: *234–5, 290, 306, 308–9*
of Societies, 176, 178: *379, 380, 391*
Netherlands: 70, 86: *347, 397, 398*
Nettelbladt: 126, 148, 164, 165, 175–8, 185–91, 197–8: *291, 315, 320, 345–6, 360, 379–81, 387, 388–93, 394, 395, 398*

Obligation: of groups, 130, 189: *383, 384, 390–1*
of international law, 85–6, 196
of Natural Law, 97–100: *289, 290*
of Ruler by acts of predecessors: 161: *251, 261, 266, 362–4*
Omnes ut singuli and *ut universi:* 47, 49, 79: *245, 275, 311, 329*
Organic conception of Society: 50–2, 114, 132–3
Organic metaphor (body politic): 51, 132, 136: *252–4, 268, 319, 320, 324, 326, 330–1, 332*
Organs (of State): 51, 130, 133, 139: *332*
Otto: 159

Paine: *325, 331, 359, 374–5*
Paley: 90: *359–60, 372–3*
Papacy: 87, 92: *282, 284*
Parliaments: 80, 83, 149: *281, 347–8* (see also Estates and Representation)
Partnership: see *Societas*: partnership in sovereignty, 155–6, *356–7*: the State as a partnership, 107: *298*
Patrimonial monarchy: 57, 58, 143, 144: *259–60, 339, 340, 362–3, 366*
People: as a *societas, 241, 244–5, 266*: as a *universitas: 240, 244, 342, 344, 345–6*
as a personality, 45–8: *265–6*; sovereignty of, see Popular sovereignty: rights of, see Popular rights: will of, *245–6, 329*
people and Church, 89: *287*
people and State, 53–4, 61: *254–5, 255–6, 329, 353*
Grotius's view, 54–8; Hobbes's view, 60–1: *268*; Althusius's view, 74; Rousseau's view, 127–30
position of, in absolutist theory, before 1650, 58 ff.; after 1650, 141 ff.
Person (*persona*): 56, 82, 122 (see also Group-personality, Moral persons and Personality)
Personal majesty: 54–5: *237, 258, 259, 260, 333*
Personality: individual, 134–5
of groups (see Group-personality)
of People and Ruler, 44–50: *265–6*
of the State, 50–61, 116–7, 129, 133, 139, 146, 152: *256, 258, 266, 268, 319, 332, 361*
Physiocrats: 113: *294, 307, 336*
Poland: 156: *279, 340, 354, 357, 383*
Politics (as distinct from public or constitutional law): 36, 137: treatises on, *229–30, 230–1, 232*
Popular rights: 57, 58, 141 ff., 145, 146: *241–2, 249, 255, 258, 259, 262, 263–4, 337, 339, 340, 341–2, 344, 345, 352, 353–4*
Popular sovereignty: 43, 44, 48, 52, 56, 106, 128–30, 131, 134, 140, 147, 149–53, 158: *238, 245, 248–9, 258–9, 260, 262, 322, 328, 335, 347–9, 350, 352, 353–4*
Positive Law: in relation to Natural Law, 38, 100, 102, 103, 185: *233–5, 288–9, 290, 293*
Potestates: of Church and State, 87 ff.: *284*
Powers: separation of, 134, 152–3, 154–6: *263, 264–5, 329, 352, 354, 356, 357–60*
Primary Assembly: in Rousseau, 130, 131, 133, 150: in Fichte, 133, 151–2
Procuratorial power: 47 (see also Representation)

Property: origin of, 103–4: *293–5* (see also Contract)
  property of associations, 168, 171, 172, 188–9, 191, 192–3: *271, 370–2, 376, 383, 391, 392*
  Church-property, 90, 92, 167: *287, 370–1, 374*
  State-property, 53, 54, 57, 59, 161–2: *255, 259, 262, 337–8, 352, 364–6*
Protestantism: its theory of the Church, 88–92: *284–7*
Provinces: rights of, 65, 70, 71, 72, 73, 74, 75: *277, 384*
Public Law: 36, 37, 38, 39, 97, 137, 172–3: *333, 361–2, 377*
Pufendorf: 103, 106, 107, 118–21, 142–4, 146, 147, 154–5, 169–70, 181, 184, 196–7: *289, 294, 295, 301, 302, 308, 311, 312–16, 330, 337, 343, 361, 362, 364, 367, 375, 383, 396, 397*

Raison d'état: 36: *230*
Real majesty: 54–5: *237, 244, 258, 259, 333*
Reason: as basis of Natural Law, 98–9: *289, 293*: as basis of Contract, 109: *301–2*
Rechtsstaat: 138: Kant's view of, *307–8*
Regimen: Grotius's theory of, 91: *285–6*
Representation: theory of, 47, 61, 79, 81–5, 116, 130, 131, 133, 134, 150, 160–1: *247–8, 325–6, 327, 328, 347–8, 350* (see also Estates and Parliaments)
Representative theory of Group-personality: 61, 82–4, 116–7, 118, 120, 121–2, 123, 128, 130, 135–7, 139, 173, 181, 184, 194: *267, 312–3, 316, 317, 323*
Republics: 49, 116: *238, 249, 251, 304, 318*
Resistance: theory of, 70, 72, 75, 152: *290, 337, 341–2, 344, 345, 347, 349, 351, 354, 364*
Respublica: 53, 60, 65, 115: *235, 254–5, 255–6, 257, 258, 266, 334*; Respublica composita, 198: *278, 398*
Right (*Recht*): definition of, 39: Fichte on, 102: *293*: Kant on, *293, 307–8*
Rights of Man (see Natural rights)
Rousseau: 41, 48, 54, 97, 101, 104, 106, 108, 112, 128–31, 133, 136, 149–50, 158–9, 164, 166, 167: *258, 292, 294, 297–8, 301, 302, 303, 305, 306, 322–3, 324–5, 326, 327, 330, 333, 349–50, 358, 369–70*
Ruler: personality of, 48–50, 123: *256, 344*: two capacities of, 161: *251–2, 361–2*

  sovereignty of, 43, 48, 54–8, 58–60, 140, 141–8: *238, 245, 268, 322, 323, 338–9, 341–2, 353, 354*
Ruler and Natural Law, 97–8
Ruler and Mixed Constitution, 154 ff.

Salamonius: 53: *231, 243, 256*
Scheidemantel: 126, 148, 168: *310, 321, 346, 347, 356, 372–3, 386*
Schlözer, A. L.: 127, 148, 159, 179: *295, 298, 299, 307, 322–3, 331, 334, 347, 360, 381, 396, 397*
Schlözer, C.: 127: *322, 323, 389–90*
Schmier: 121, 147, 155, 174: *292, 300, 334, 335, 344, 355, 362, 378, 385*
Secession, right of: 70, 110: *302*
Sidney: 106, 149: *299, 347–8, 357*
Sieyès: 107, 131, 169: *298, 307, 309, 326–7, 331, 350, 358–9, 371–2*
Sociability, theory of: 100–1: *290, 301*
Social Natural Law: 101, 196: *290–1*
Societas, conception of: 40, 45, 46, 51, 60–1, 63, 68, 75–7, 77–8, 95, 100, 107, 115, 118, 123–7, 135, 137, 138, 163, 169, 173–4, 175, 180–1, 182, 183, 184, 185: *241, 244, 274, 278, 279, 290, 319–21, 379, 380, 385*
Societas gentium: 85: *282–3, 303, 394–5* (see also International society)
Societates: classification of, by Bodin, 64–7: *270*; by Althusius, 71–3: *277–9*; by Nettelbladt, 177–8: *379–80*; by other writers, *367–8*
Societates aequales and *inaequales*: 123–4, 127, 128, 170, 171, 172, 173, 174, 175, 176–7, 183, 185, 186, 187, 189, 196, 197: *280, 316, 318, 320, 321, 375, 380, 385–6, 387, 390*
Society: general theory of, 62, 75–6, 78 (see also Associations and Groups)
Soto: 45: *263*
Sovereignty: problem of, 37: *236*; natural law theory of, down to 1650, 40–4, 71, 74: *242, 249, 263, 267*
  residence of, 44–61: *258*; sovereignty and groups, 62, 64 (see State-control of Groups); sovereignty and international law, 85
  sovereignty in federations, 85, 197; sovereignty and churches, 87 ff.: *285–6*; natural-law theory of, from 1650 to 1800, 137 ff.: *311, 334, 338–9, 342–3, 345, 346, 352*
  Rousseau's view of, 129–30: *324, 349, 358*
  (See also Limited sovereignty: Personal majesty; Popular sovereignty; Real majesty; Ruler)

Spinoza: 97, 106, 108, 112, 117, 142, 164: *306, 311, 336, 355, 369*
State of nature: 85, 96–105, 195, 196: *288, 290, 291–2, 394*
State-control of Groups: 66–7: *270, 368 ff., 373, 378–9, 381*
State-institutions (*Anstalten*): associations regarded as, 66, 67, 168, 180–4, 185, 194: *269–70, 370–2, 373–4*; Church regarded as, 90: *285, 370–1*
Stryck: 144
Suarez: 36, 45, 46, 51, 59, 64, 68, 69, 105: *229, 242, 243, 264, 273–4, 276–7, 282, 283*
Subject (or owner) of rights: the Subject of Sovereignty, 42 ff.; Grotius's theory of the double Subject, 55–8; Hobbes on the Subject of Sovereignty, 60–1, 139: Rousseau, 129
Switzerland: 65, 70, 86: *347, 397, 398*
Systems: Hobbes on, 79–84; federal systems, 86, 196, 197: *396*

Taxation: 68, 162: *274, 276*
Territorial theory of the Church: 89 ff.: *285*
Teutonic ideas: of Fellowship (q.v.), 135, 191; of kingship, 135; of the Law-State (see *Rechtsstaat*), 138
Theocratic ideas: 40, 87, 104, 105, 111: *295–6, 303–4* (see also Ecclesiastical)
Thomasius: 98, 100, 113, 121, 144, 155, 196: *288–9, 296, 300, 308, 315, 316, 338, 367, 375, 394, 395*
Titius: 121, 144, 155, 173: *315, 316, 356, 361–2, 362–3, 396, 397*
Trust: Locke's conception of, *299–300, 348–9*

Turgot: 166: *309, 369*

Unanimity (as opposed to majority decision): 47, 110, 127, 133, 186, 188, 195: *246–7, 322, 324, 328*
Unions of States (personal and real): 86, 197: *283, 395–6*
Universitas: 45, 56, 61, 64 ff., 73, 79, 91, 116, 117, 123, 146, 171, 173–4, 177, 181, 182–3, 184, 186, 187, 189, 191, 192: *240, 271, 272, 274, 281, 316, 317, 318, 378, 383, 384–5, 386, 392*
Usurper: position of, *363–4*
Utopias: 166: *369*

Vacancy: of throne, *339–40*
Vasquez: *253, 263*
Vattel: 40
Venice: 156
Vico: 105: *297*
Victoria: *263, 283*
Vindiciae contra Tyrannos: 45, 70: *231, 240, 247, 248, 254, 255, 257, 277, 283*
Voetius: 92: *287*

Will of All: 129, 131: *245–6, 322–3, 326, 328, 329* (see General Will)
Wolff: 113, 121, 125, 147–8, 175, 185, 196: *294, 296, 308, 316, 319, 344, 345, 367, 379, 388, 389, 390, 393, 395*
World-State: 85, 196: *283, 395*

Zepper: *284–5*
Zwingli: *285*